solanin

VIZ Signature Edition

STORY & ART BY INIO ASANO

solanin
CONTENTS

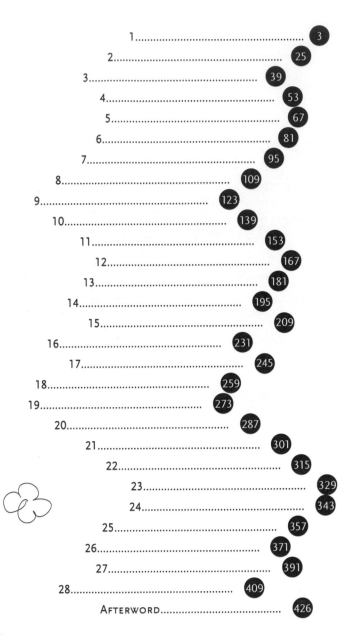

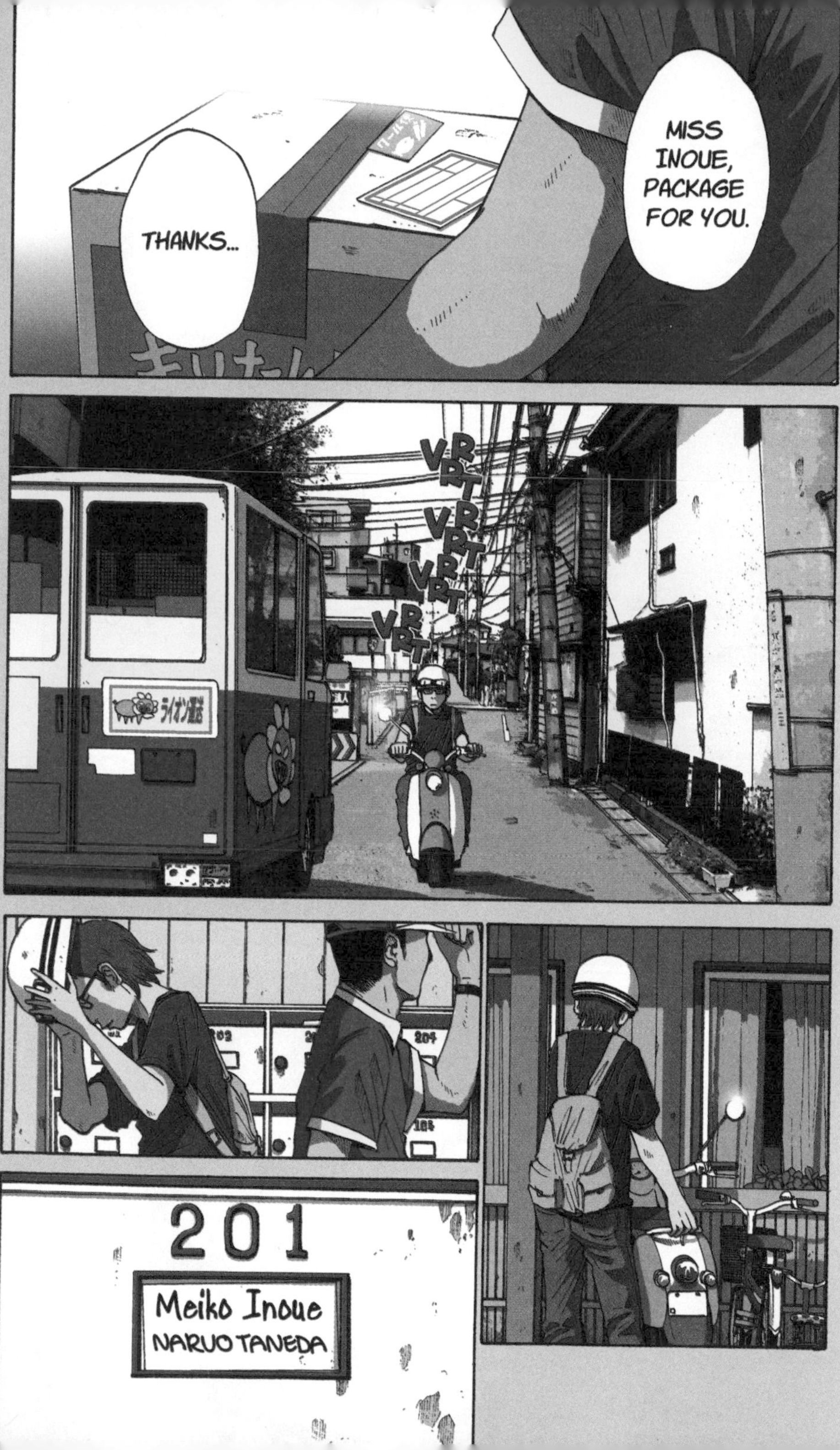
MISS INOUE, PACKAGE FOR YOU.
THANKS...
VRT VRT VRT VRT
201
Meiko Inoue
NARUO TANEDA

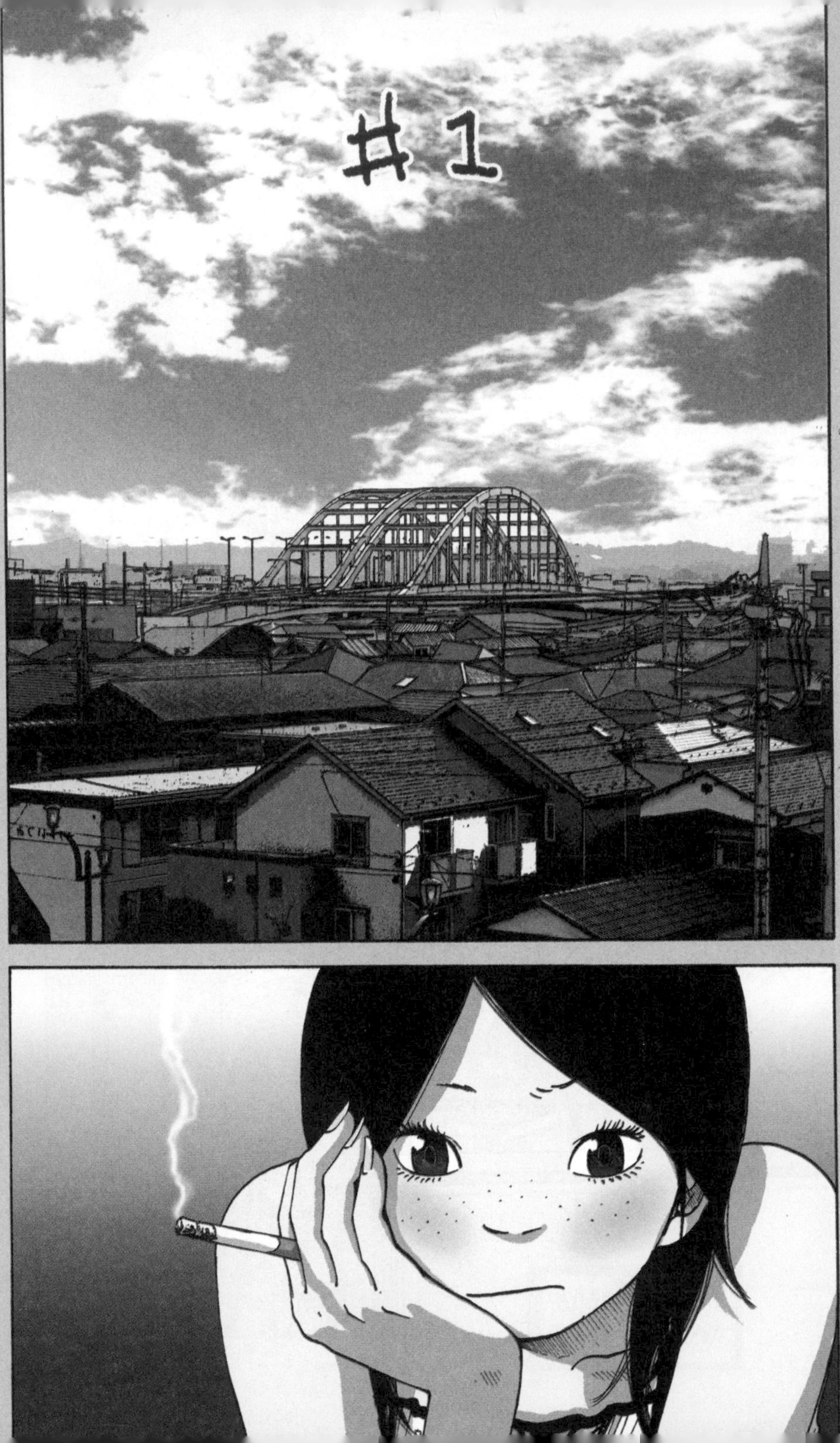
♯1

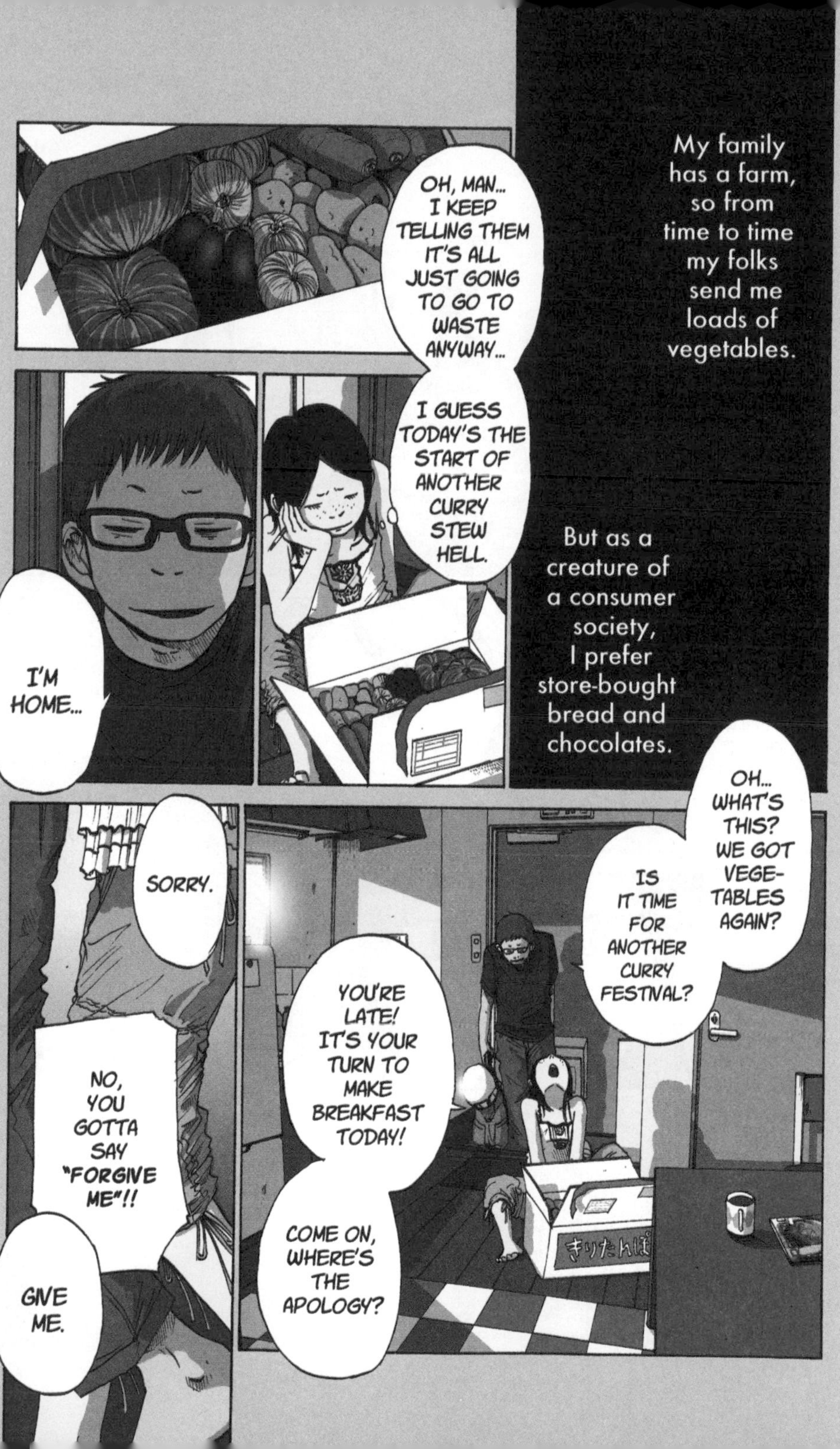
My family has a farm, so from time to time my folks send me loads of vegetables.
But as a creature of a consumer society, I prefer store-bought bread and chocolates.
OH, MAN... I KEEP TELLING THEM IT'S ALL JUST GOING TO GO TO WASTE ANYWAY...
I GUESS TODAY'S THE START OF ANOTHER CURRY STEW HELL.
I'M HOME...
OH... WHAT'S THIS? WE GOT VEGE-TABLES AGAIN?
IS IT TIME FOR ANOTHER CURRY FESTIVAL?
YOU'RE LATE! IT'S YOUR TURN TO MAKE BREAKFAST TODAY!
COME ON, WHERE'S THE APOLOGY?
きりたんぽ
SORRY.
NO, YOU GOTTA SAY "FORGIVE ME"!!
GIVE ME.

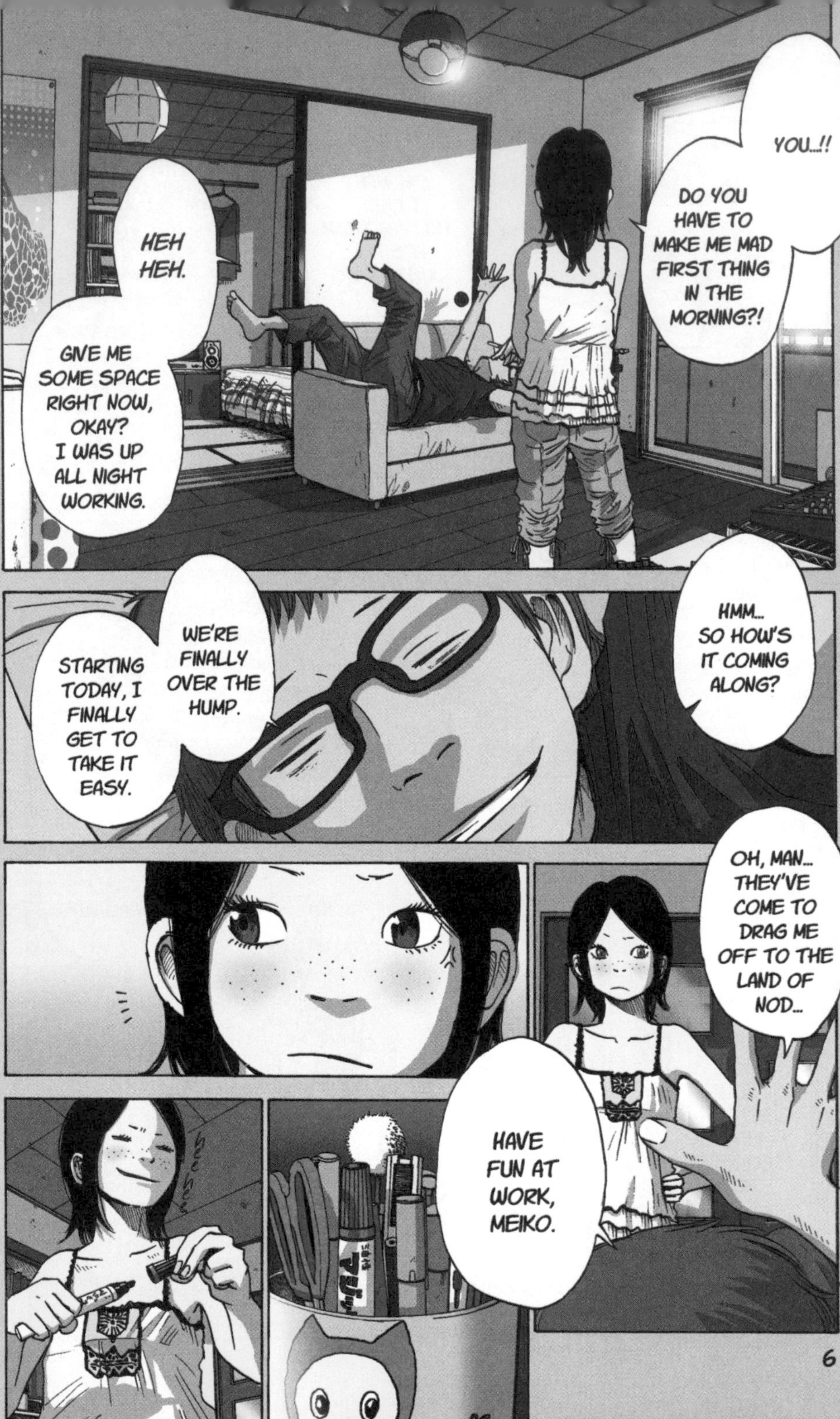
YOU...!!
DO YOU HAVE TO MAKE ME MAD FIRST THING IN THE MORNING?!
HEH HEH.
GIVE ME SOME SPACE RIGHT NOW, OKAY? I WAS UP ALL NIGHT WORKING.
HMM... SO HOW'S IT COMING ALONG?
WE'RE FINALLY OVER THE HUMP.
STARTING TODAY, I FINALLY GET TO TAKE IT EASY.
OH, MAN... THEY'VE COME TO DRAG ME OFF TO THE LAND OF NOD...
HAVE FUN AT WORK, MEIKO.
hee hee

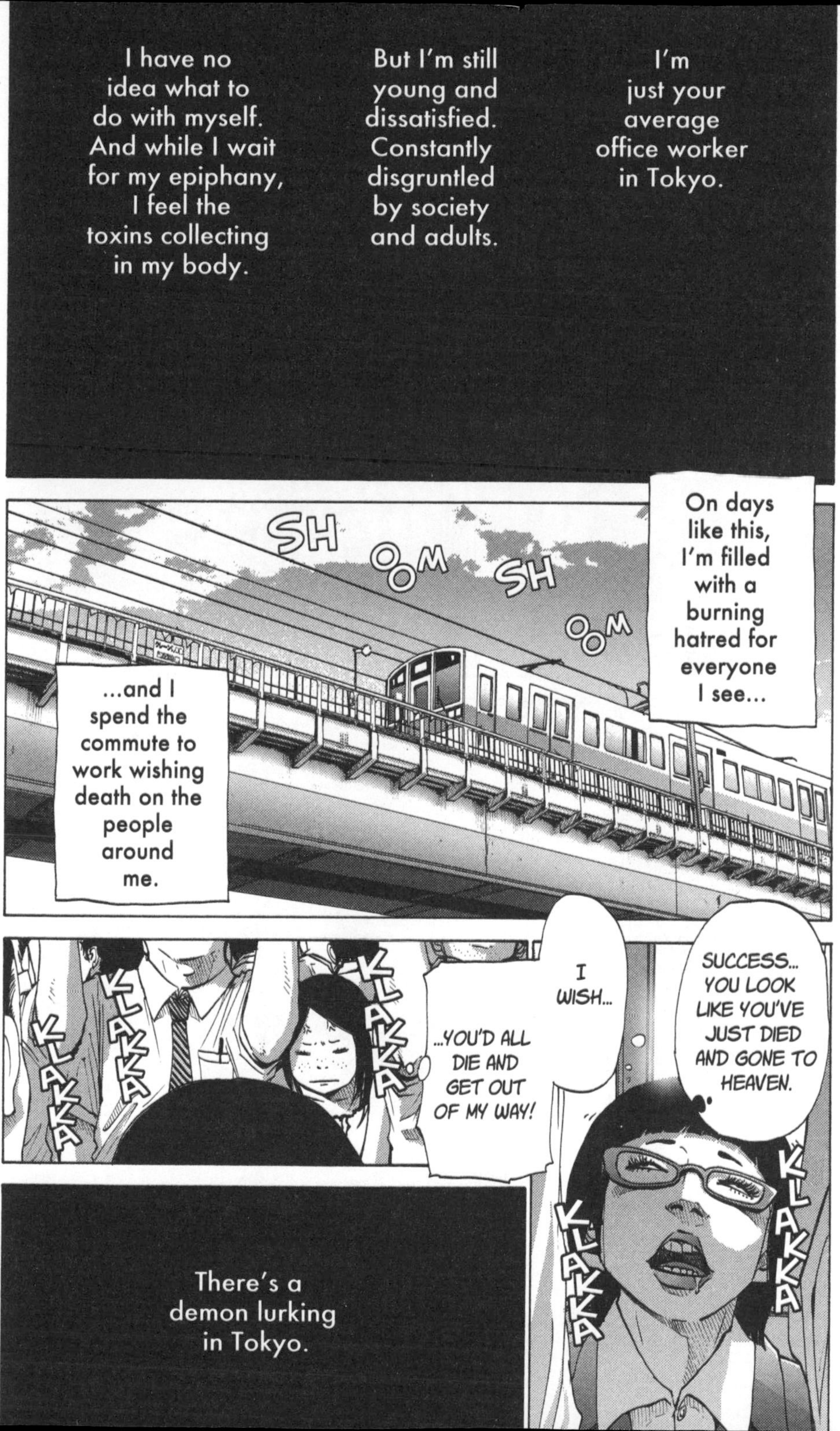

I'm just your average office worker in Tokyo.
But I'm still young and dissatisfied. Constantly disgruntled by society and adults.
I have no idea what to do with myself. And while I wait for my epiphany, I feel the toxins collecting in my body.
On days like this, I'm filled with a burning hatred for everyone I see...
SHOOM
SHOOM
...and I spend the commute to work wishing death on the people around me.
SUCCESS... YOU LOOK LIKE YOU'VE JUST DIED AND GONE TO HEAVEN.
KLAKAKA
KLAKAKA
I WISH...
...YOU'D ALL DIE AND GET OUT OF MY WAY!
KLAKAKA
KLAKAKA
There's a demon lurking in Tokyo.

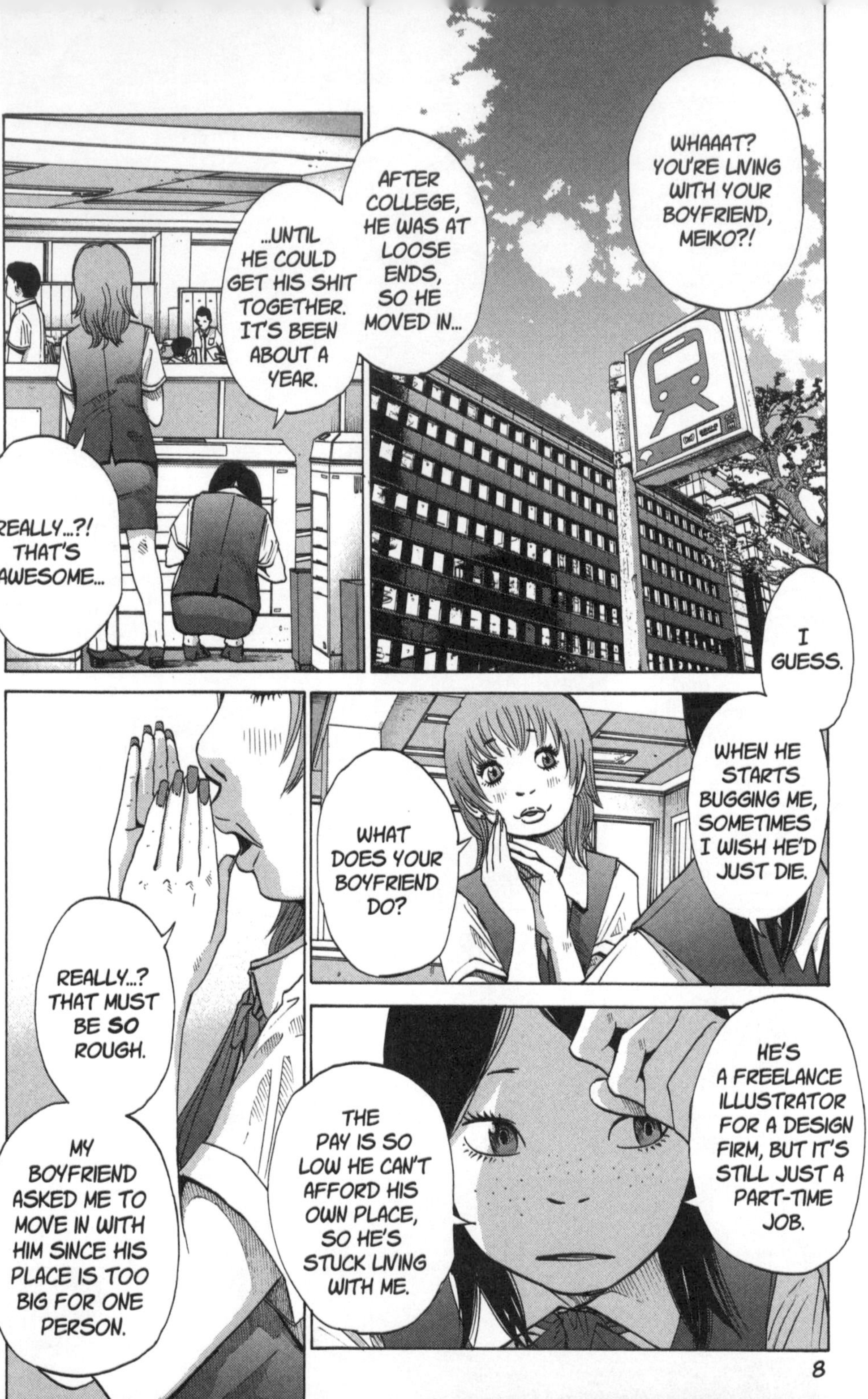
WHAAAT? YOU'RE LIVING WITH YOUR BOYFRIEND, MEIKO?!
I GUESS.
AFTER COLLEGE, HE WAS AT LOOSE ENDS, SO HE MOVED IN...
...UNTIL HE COULD GET HIS SHIT TOGETHER. IT'S BEEN ABOUT A YEAR.
REALLY...?! THAT'S AWESOME...
WHEN HE STARTS BUGGING ME, SOMETIMES I WISH HE'D JUST DIE.
WHAT DOES YOUR BOYFRIEND DO?
HE'S A FREELANCE ILLUSTRATOR FOR A DESIGN FIRM, BUT IT'S STILL JUST A PART-TIME JOB.
THE PAY IS SO LOW HE CAN'T AFFORD HIS OWN PLACE, SO HE'S STUCK LIVING WITH ME.
REALLY...? THAT MUST BE SO ROUGH.
MY BOYFRIEND ASKED ME TO MOVE IN WITH HIM SINCE HIS PLACE IS TOO BIG FOR ONE PERSON.

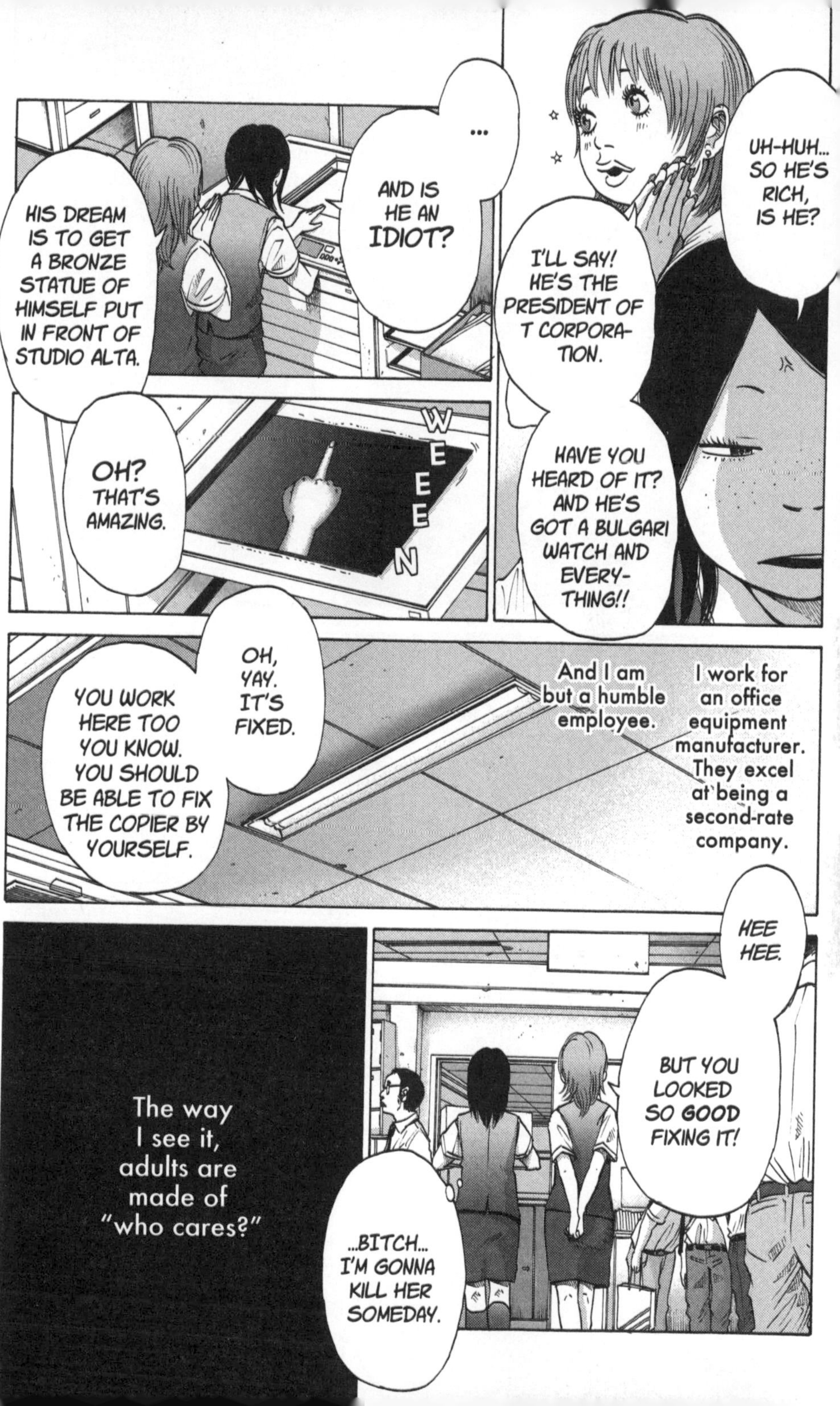

UH-HUH... SO HE'S RICH, IS HE?
I'LL SAY! HE'S THE PRESIDENT OF T CORPORATION.
HAVE YOU HEARD OF IT? AND HE'S GOT A BULGARI WATCH AND EVERYTHING!!
...
AND IS HE AN IDIOT?
HIS DREAM IS TO GET A BRONZE STATUE OF HIMSELF PUT IN FRONT OF STUDIO ALTA.
WEEEN
OH? THAT'S AMAZING.
I work for an office equipment manufacturer. They excel at being a second-rate company.
And I am but a humble employee.
OH, YAY. IT'S FIXED.
YOU WORK HERE TOO YOU KNOW. YOU SHOULD BE ABLE TO FIX THE COPIER BY YOURSELF.
HEE HEE.
BUT YOU LOOKED SO GOOD FIXING IT!
...BITCH... I'M GONNA KILL HER SOMEDAY.
The way I see it, adults are made of "who cares?"

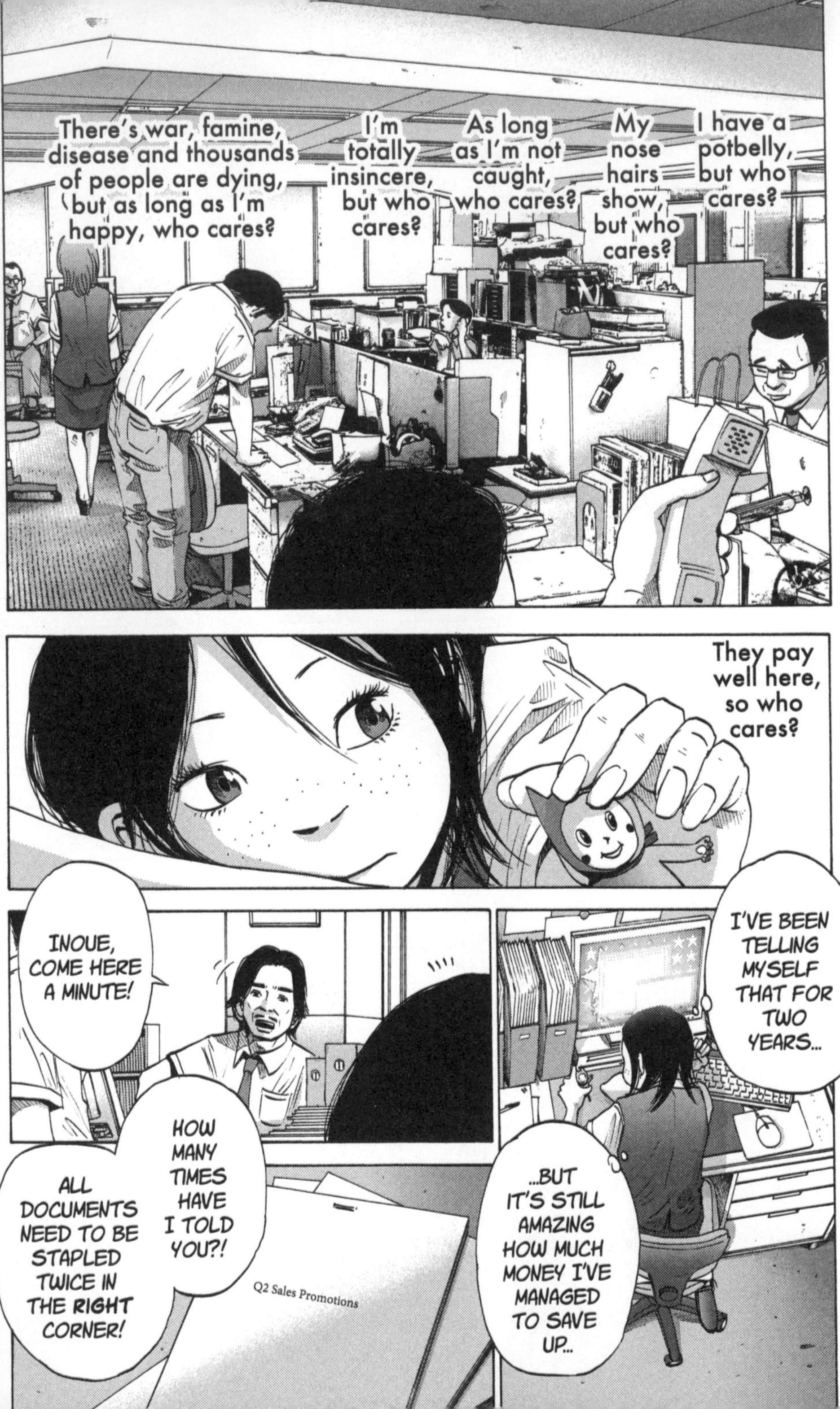
I have a potbelly, but who cares?
My nose hairs show, but who cares?
As long as I'm not caught, who cares?
I'm totally insincere, but who cares?
There's war, famine, disease and thousands of people are dying, but as long as I'm happy, who cares?
They pay well here, so who cares?
I'VE BEEN TELLING MYSELF THAT FOR TWO YEARS...
...BUT IT'S STILL AMAZING HOW MUCH MONEY I'VE MANAGED TO SAVE UP...
INOUE, COME HERE A MINUTE!
HOW MANY TIMES HAVE I TOLD YOU?!
ALL DOCUMENTS NEED TO BE STAPLED TWICE IN THE RIGHT CORNER!
Q2 Sales Promotions

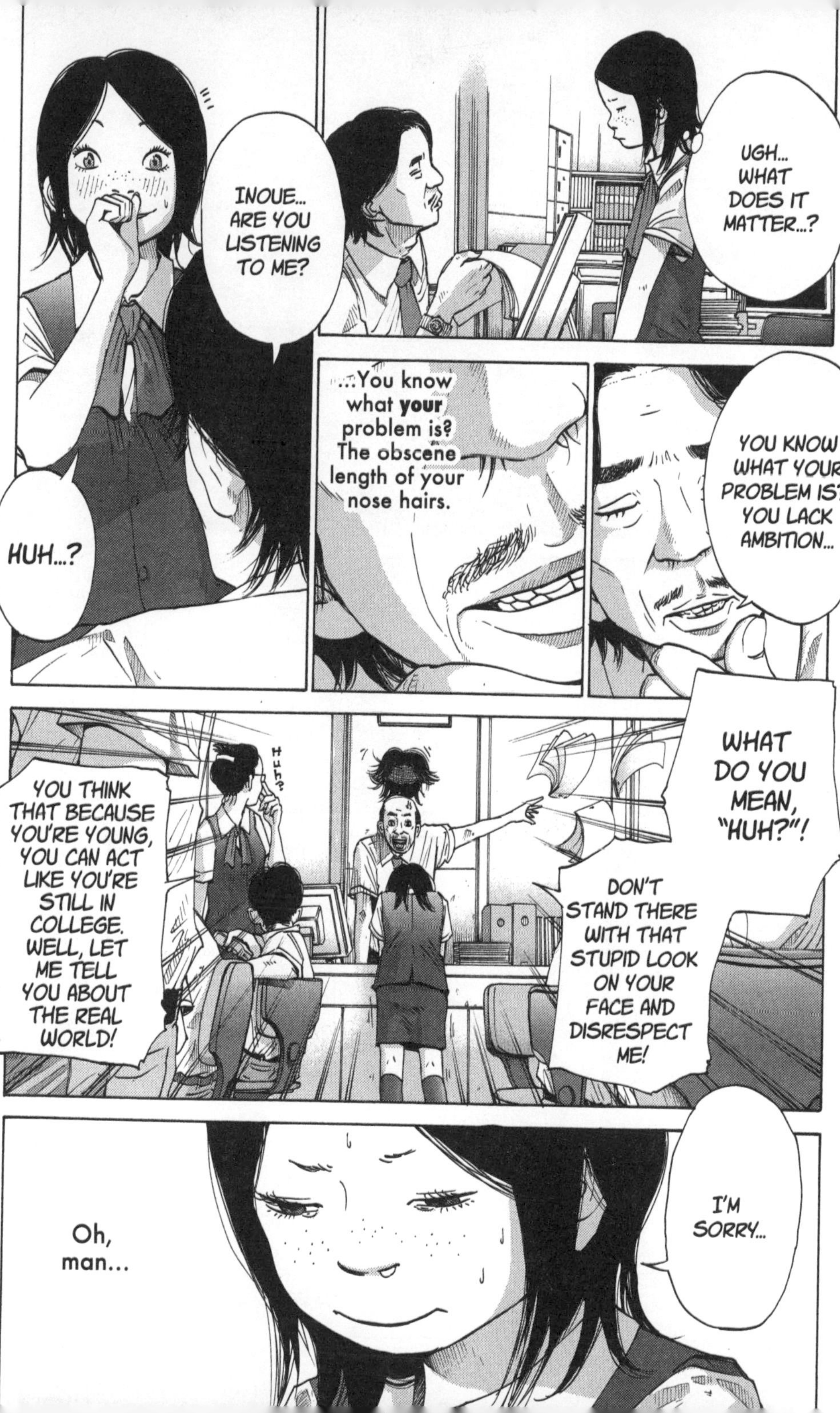
UGH... WHAT DOES IT MATTER...?
YOU KNOW WHAT YOUR PROBLEM IS? YOU LACK AMBITION...
...You know what **your** problem is? The obscene length of your nose hairs.
INOUE... ARE YOU LISTENING TO ME?
HUH...?
WHAT DO YOU MEAN, "HUH?"!
DON'T STAND THERE WITH THAT STUPID LOOK ON YOUR FACE AND DISRESPECT ME!
Huh?
YOU THINK THAT BECAUSE YOU'RE YOUNG, YOU CAN ACT LIKE YOU'RE STILL IN COLLEGE. WELL, LET ME TELL YOU ABOUT THE REAL WORLD!
I'M SORRY...
Oh, man...

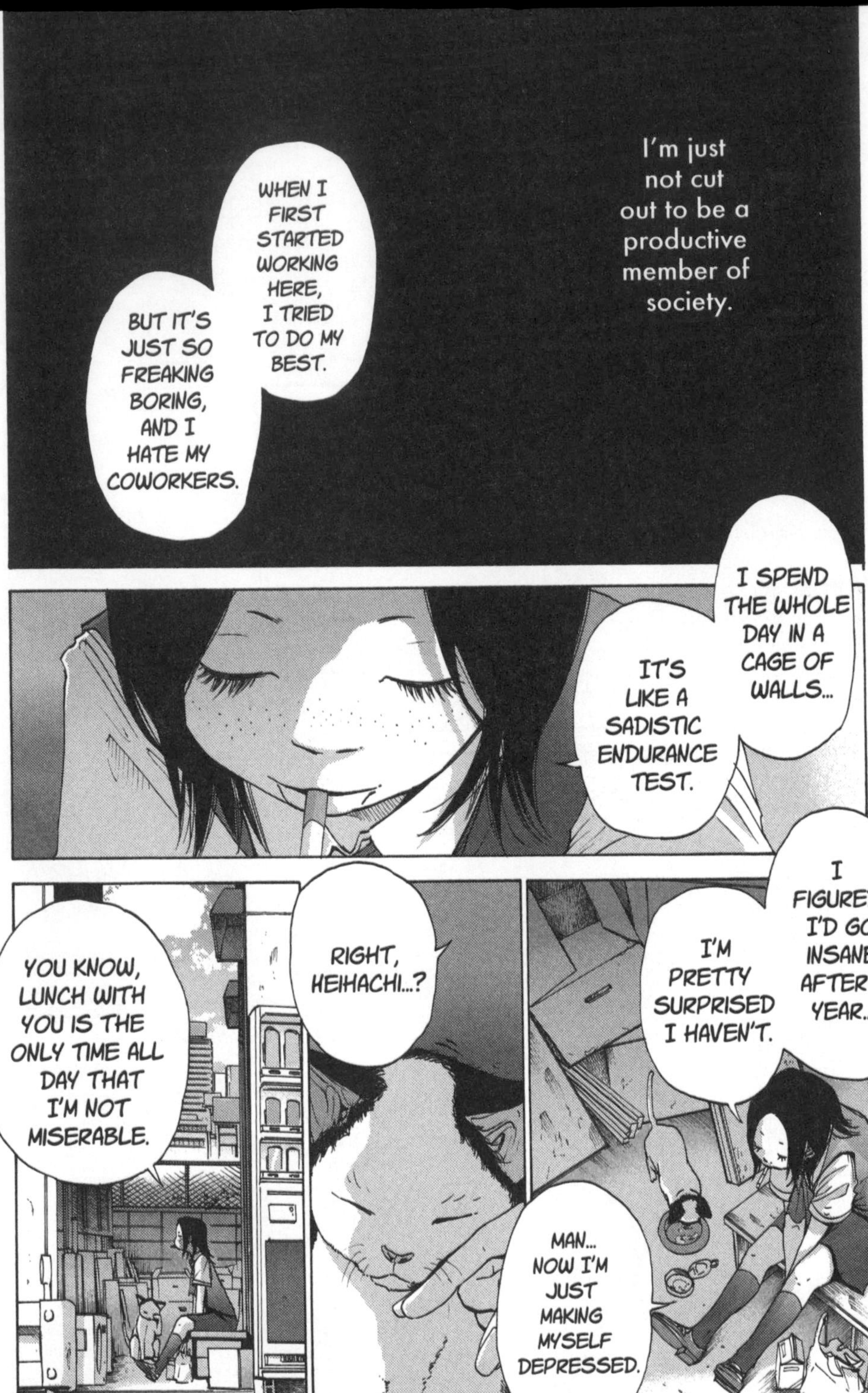
I'm just not cut out to be a productive member of society.
WHEN I FIRST STARTED WORKING HERE, I TRIED TO DO MY BEST.
BUT IT'S JUST SO FREAKING BORING, AND I HATE MY COWORKERS.
I SPEND THE WHOLE DAY IN A CAGE OF WALLS...
IT'S LIKE A SADISTIC ENDURANCE TEST.
I FIGURED I'D GO INSANE AFTER A YEAR...
I'M PRETTY SURPRISED I HAVEN'T.
RIGHT, HEIHACHI...?
YOU KNOW, LUNCH WITH YOU IS THE ONLY TIME ALL DAY THAT I'M NOT MISERABLE.
MAN... NOW I'M JUST MAKING MYSELF DEPRESSED.

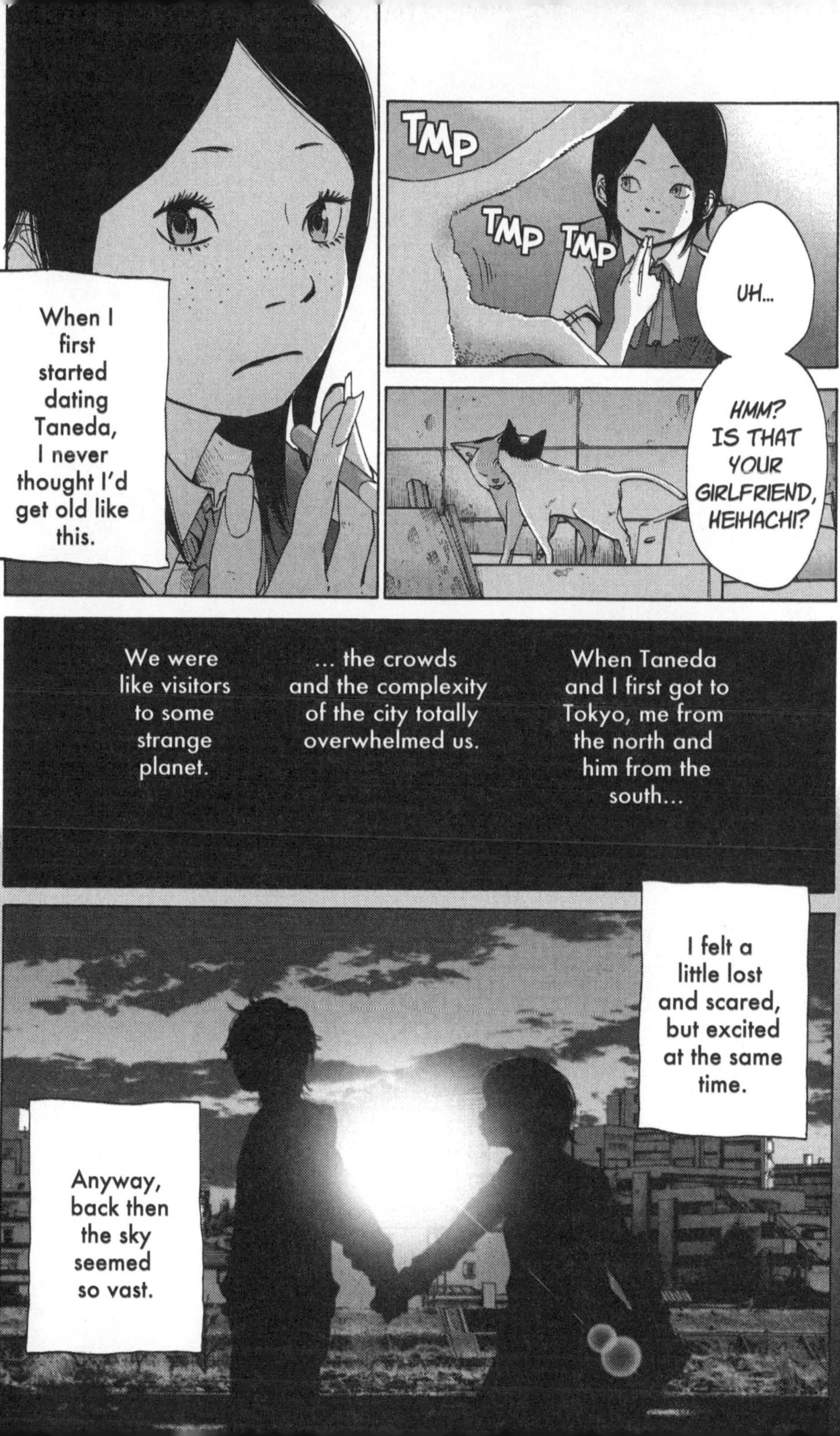
TMP
TMP TMP
UH...
HMM? IS THAT YOUR GIRLFRIEND, HEIHACHI?
When I first started dating Taneda, I never thought I'd get old like this.
When Taneda and I first got to Tokyo, me from the north and him from the south...
... the crowds and the complexity of the city totally overwhelmed us.
We were like visitors to some strange planet.
I felt a little lost and scared, but excited at the same time.
Anyway, back then the sky seemed so vast.

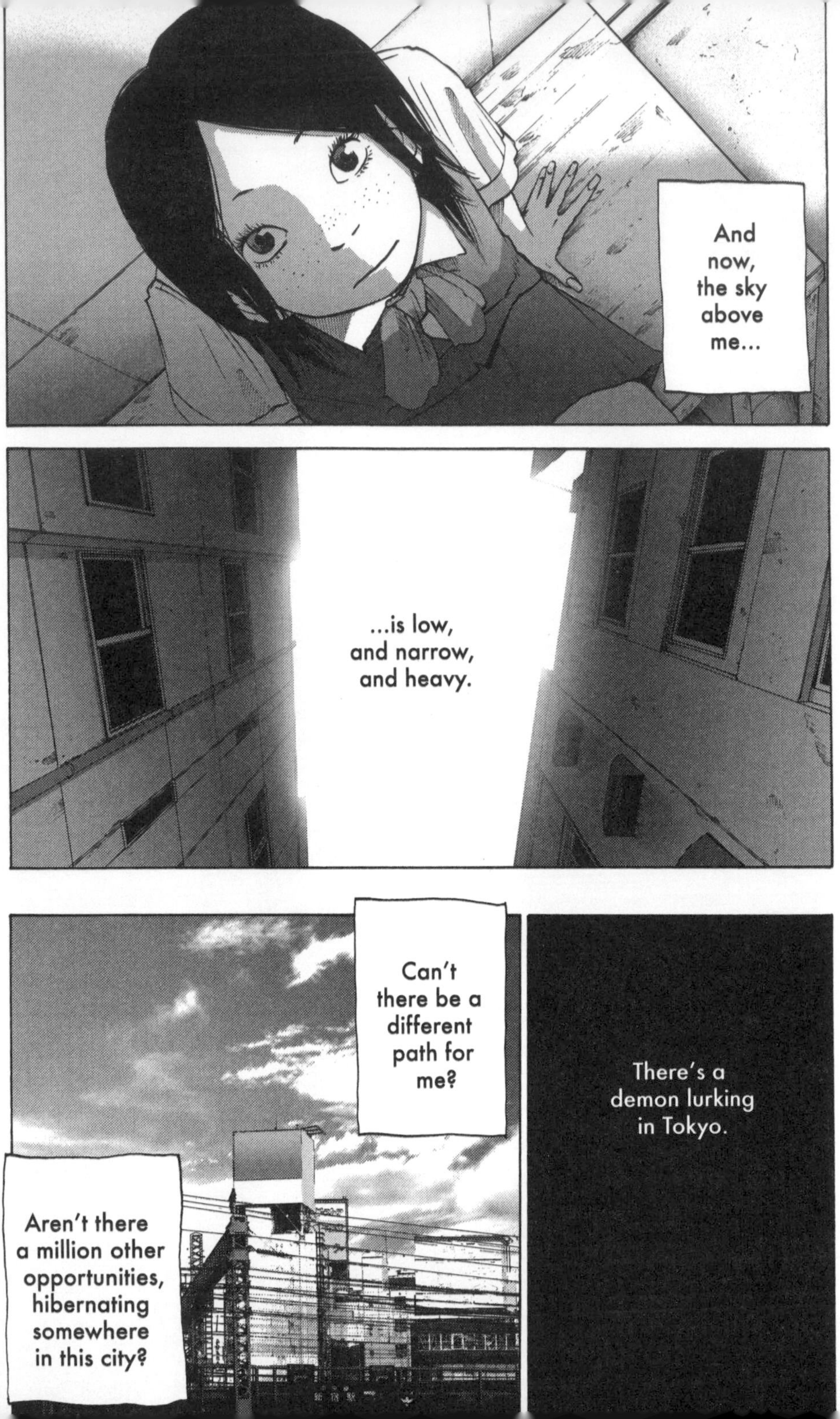
And now, the sky above me...
...is low, and narrow, and heavy.
There's a demon lurking in Tokyo.
Can't there be a different path for me?
Aren't there a million other opportunities, hibernating somewhere in this city?

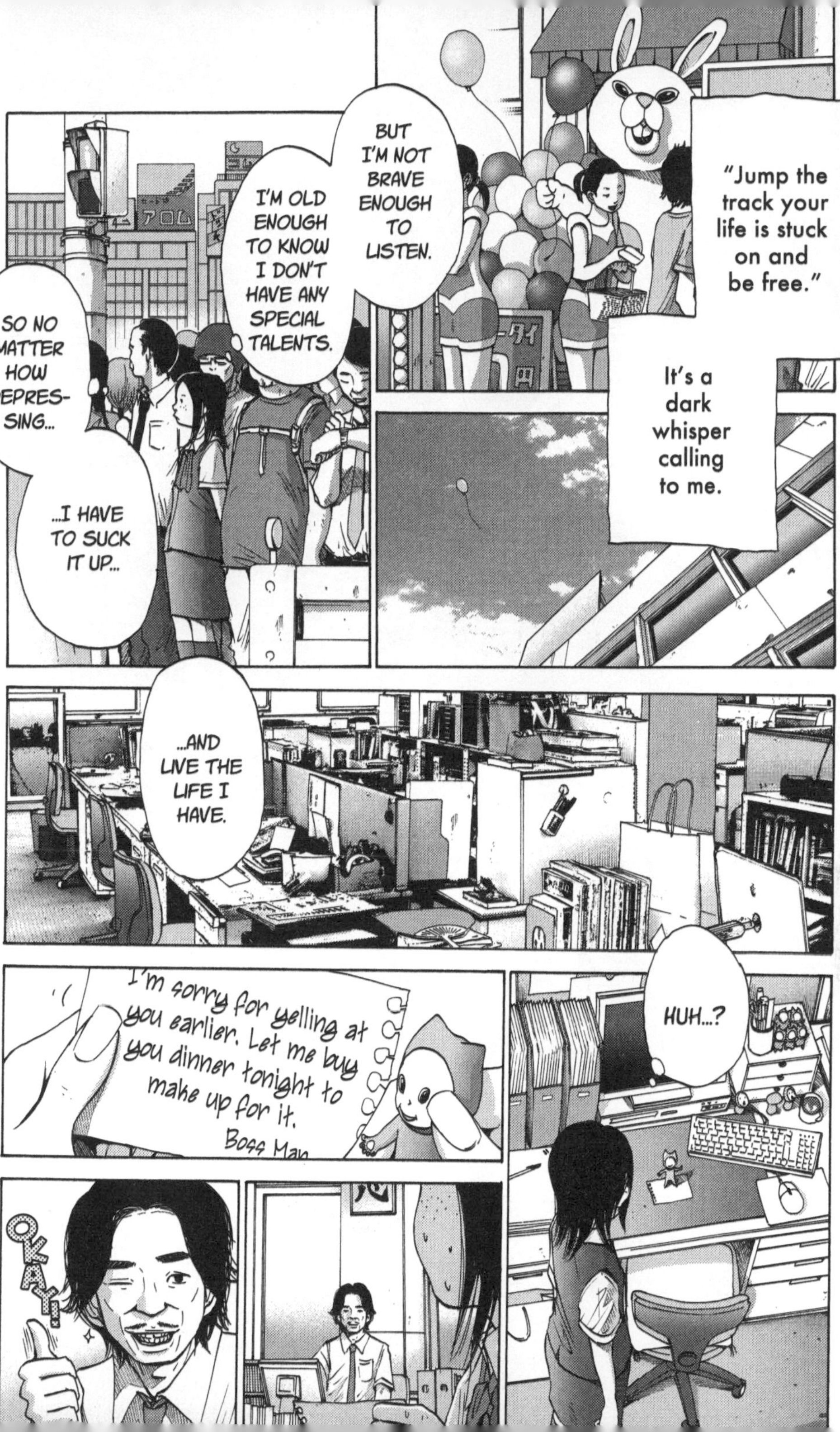
"Jump the track your life is stuck on and be free."
It's a dark whisper calling to me.
BUT I'M NOT BRAVE ENOUGH TO LISTEN.
I'M OLD ENOUGH TO KNOW I DON'T HAVE ANY SPECIAL TALENTS.
SO NO MATTER HOW DEPRES-SING...
...I HAVE TO SUCK IT UP...
...AND LIVE THE LIFE I HAVE.
HUH...?
I'm sorry for yelling at you earlier. Let me buy you dinner tonight to make up for it.
Boss Man
OKAY!

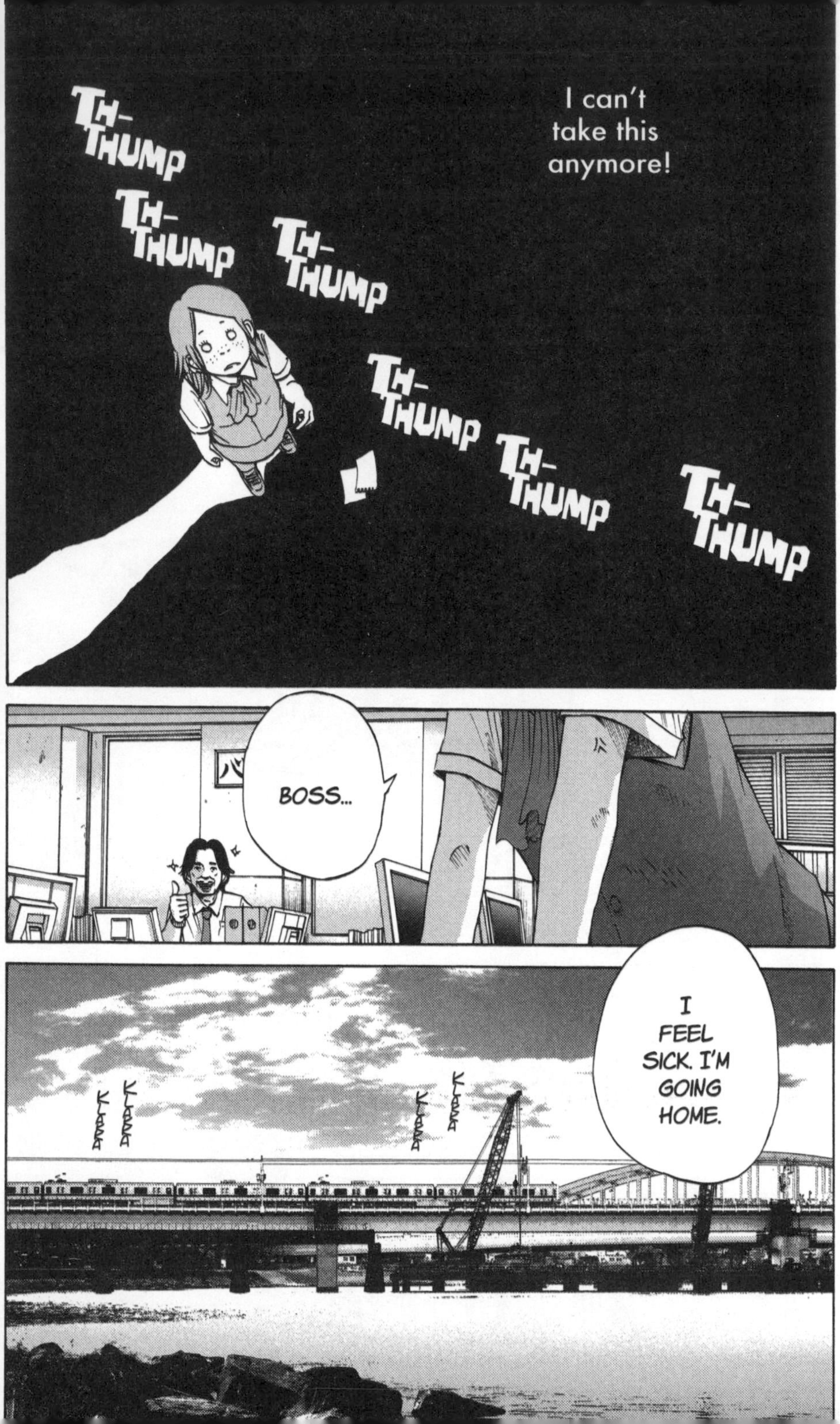
I can't take this anymore!
TH-THUMP
TH-THUMP
TH-THUMP
TH-THUMP
TH-THUMP
TH-THUMP
BOSS...
I FEEL SICK. I'M GOING HOME.

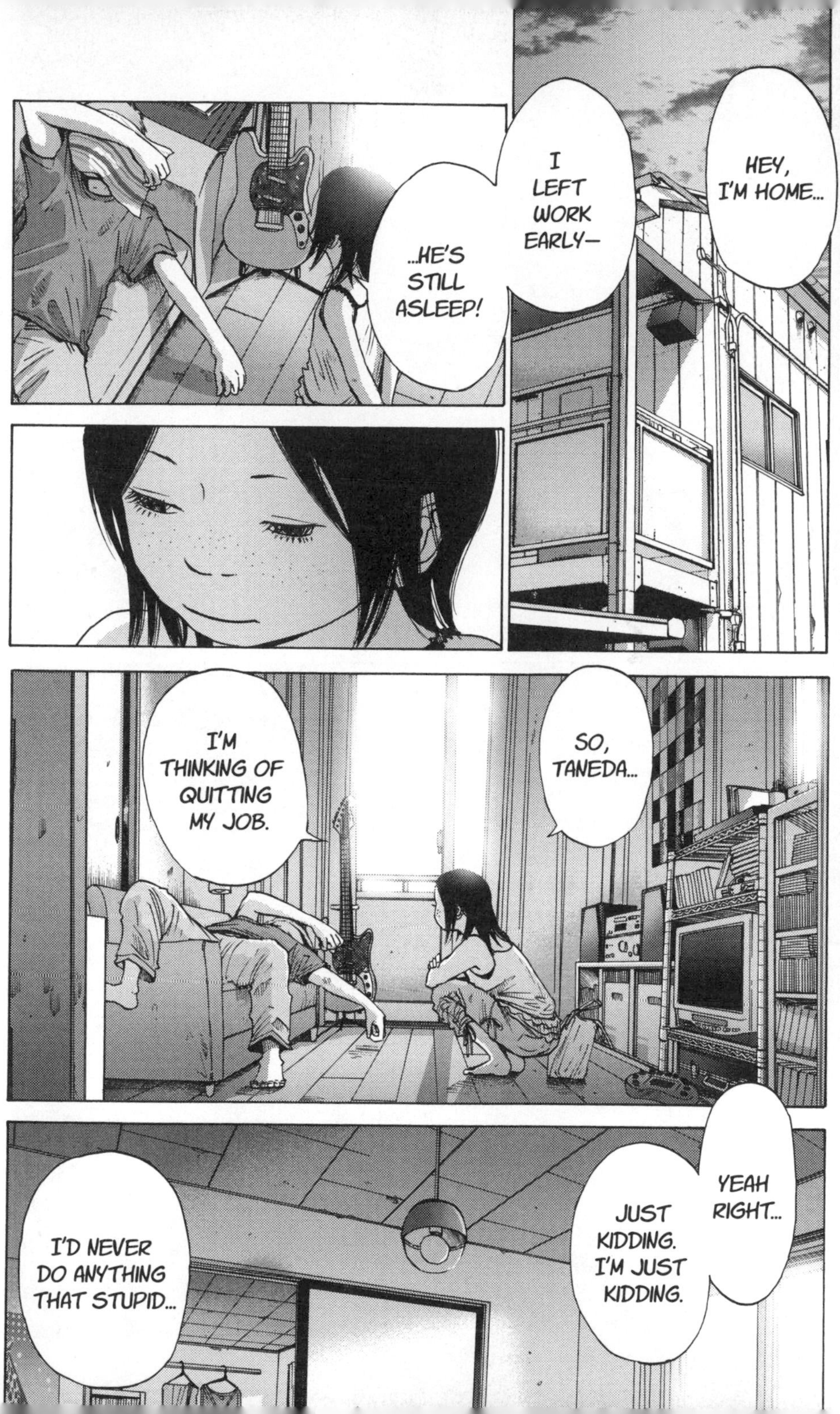
HEY, I'M HOME...
I LEFT WORK EARLY—
...HE'S STILL ASLEEP!
SO, TANEDA...
I'M THINKING OF QUITTING MY JOB.
YEAH RIGHT...
JUST KIDDING. I'M JUST KIDDING.
I'D NEVER DO ANYTHING THAT STUPID...

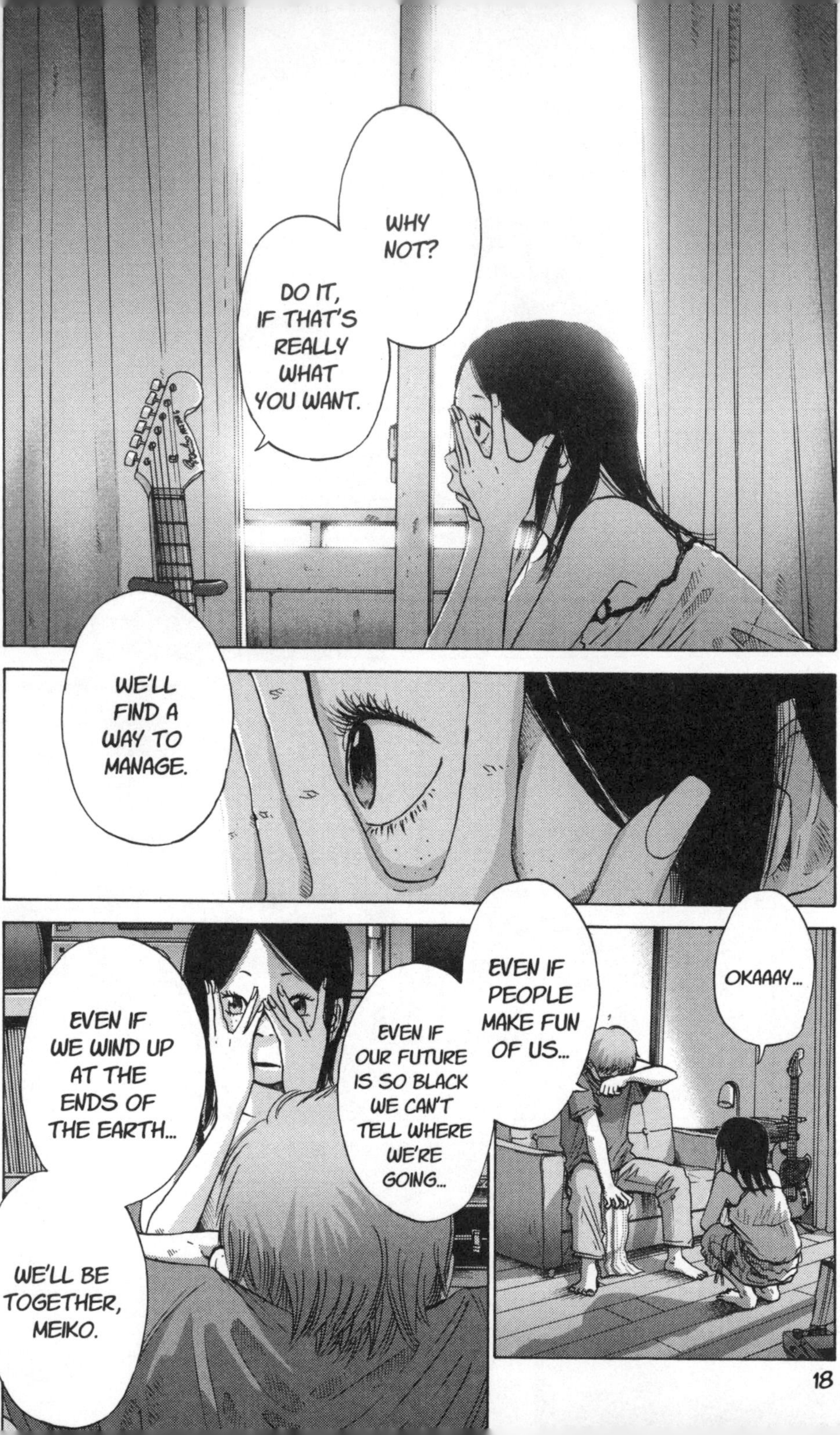

WHY NOT?
DO IT, IF THAT'S REALLY WHAT YOU WANT.
WE'LL FIND A WAY TO MANAGE.
OKAAAY...
EVEN IF PEOPLE MAKE FUN OF US...
EVEN IF OUR FUTURE IS SO BLACK WE CAN'T TELL WHERE WE'RE GOING...
EVEN IF WE WIND UP AT THE ENDS OF THE EARTH...
WE'LL BE TOGETHER, MEIKO.

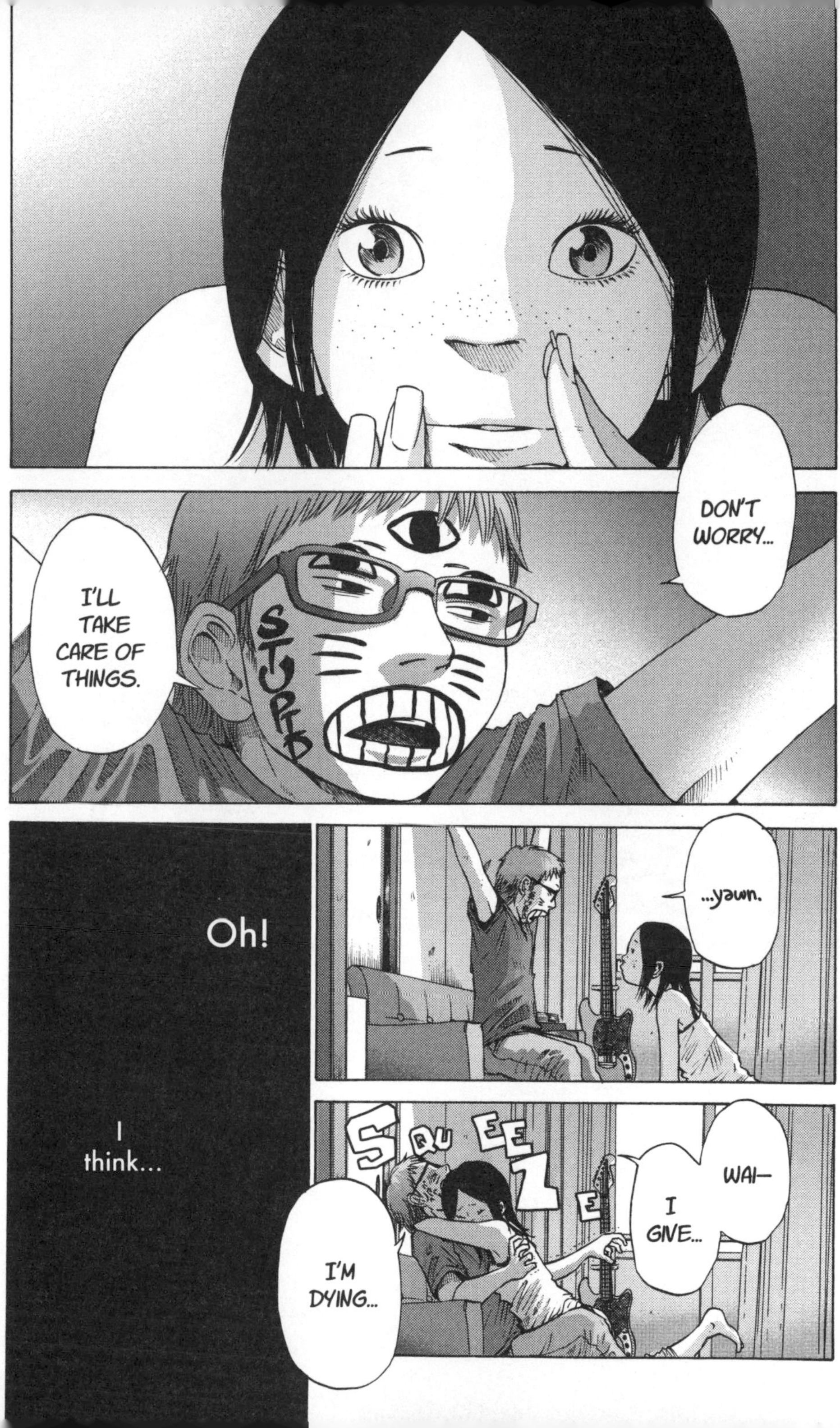
DON'T WORRY...
I'LL TAKE CARE OF THINGS.
STUPID
...yawn.
WAI— I GIVE...
SQUEEZE
I'M DYING...
Oh!
I think...

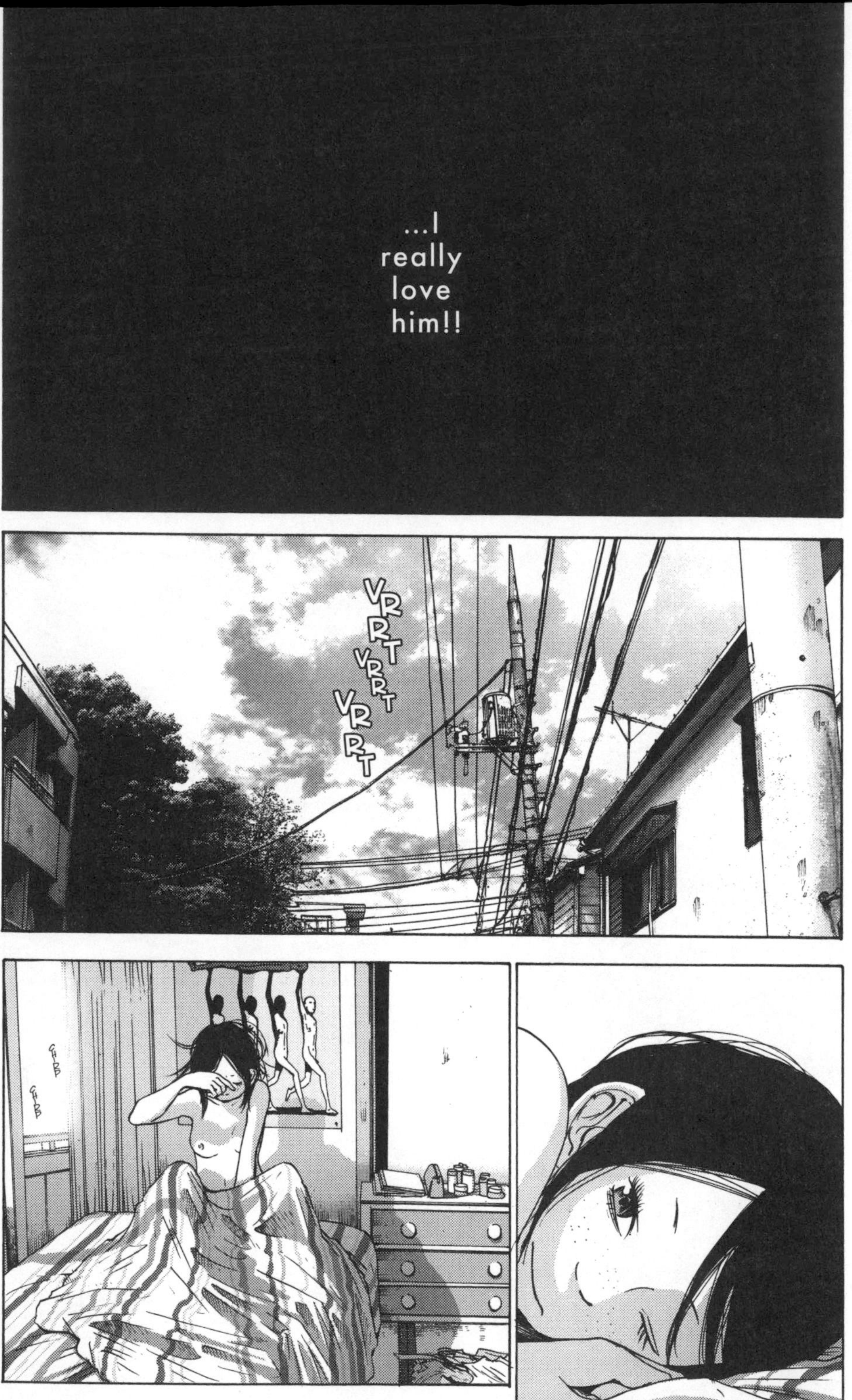
...I really love him!!
VRRT VRRT VRRT
CHIRP
CHIRP

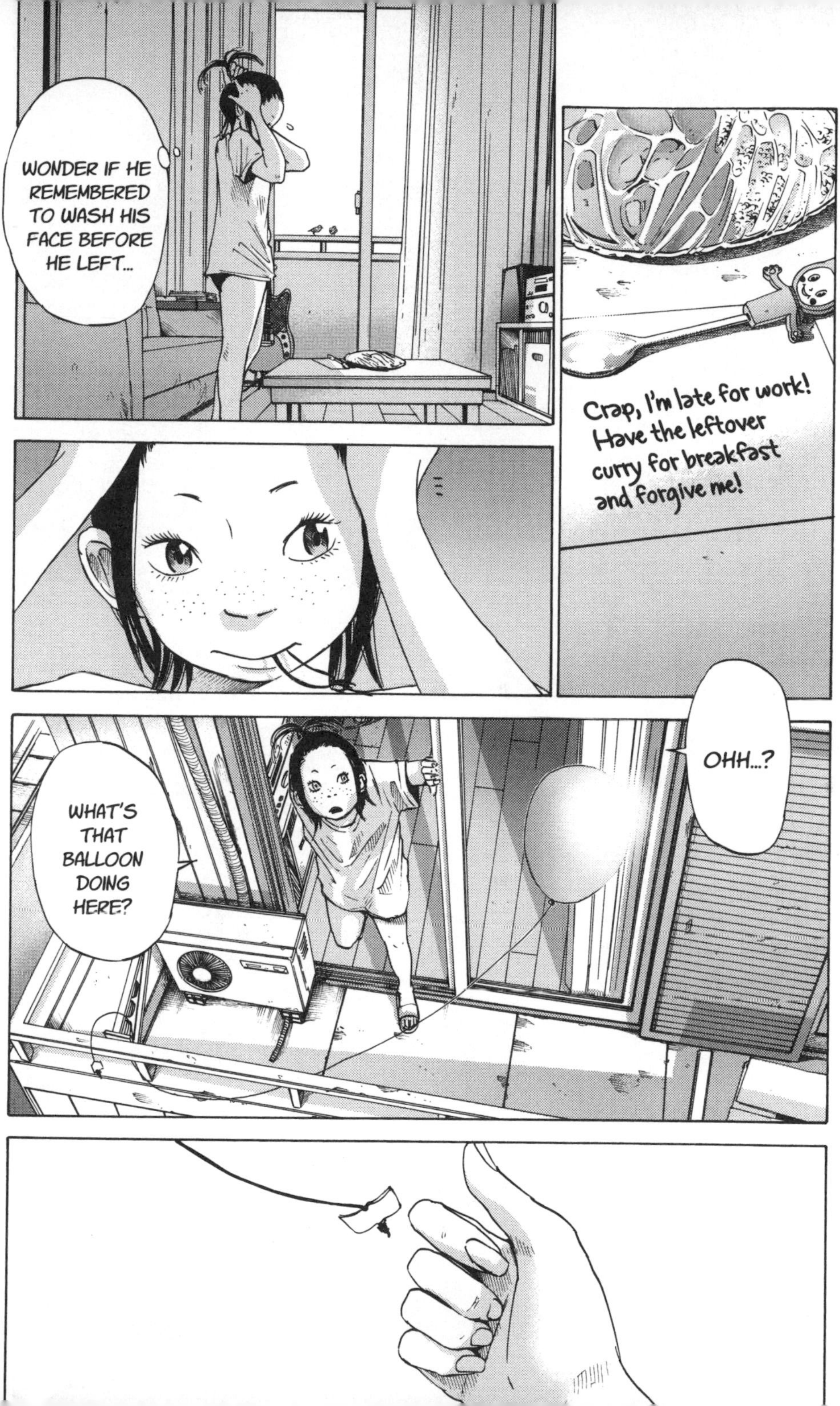
Crap, I'm late for work! Have the leftover curry for breakfast and forgive me!
WONDER IF HE REMEMBERED TO WASH HIS FACE BEFORE HE LEFT...
OHH...?
WHAT'S THAT BALLOON DOING HERE?

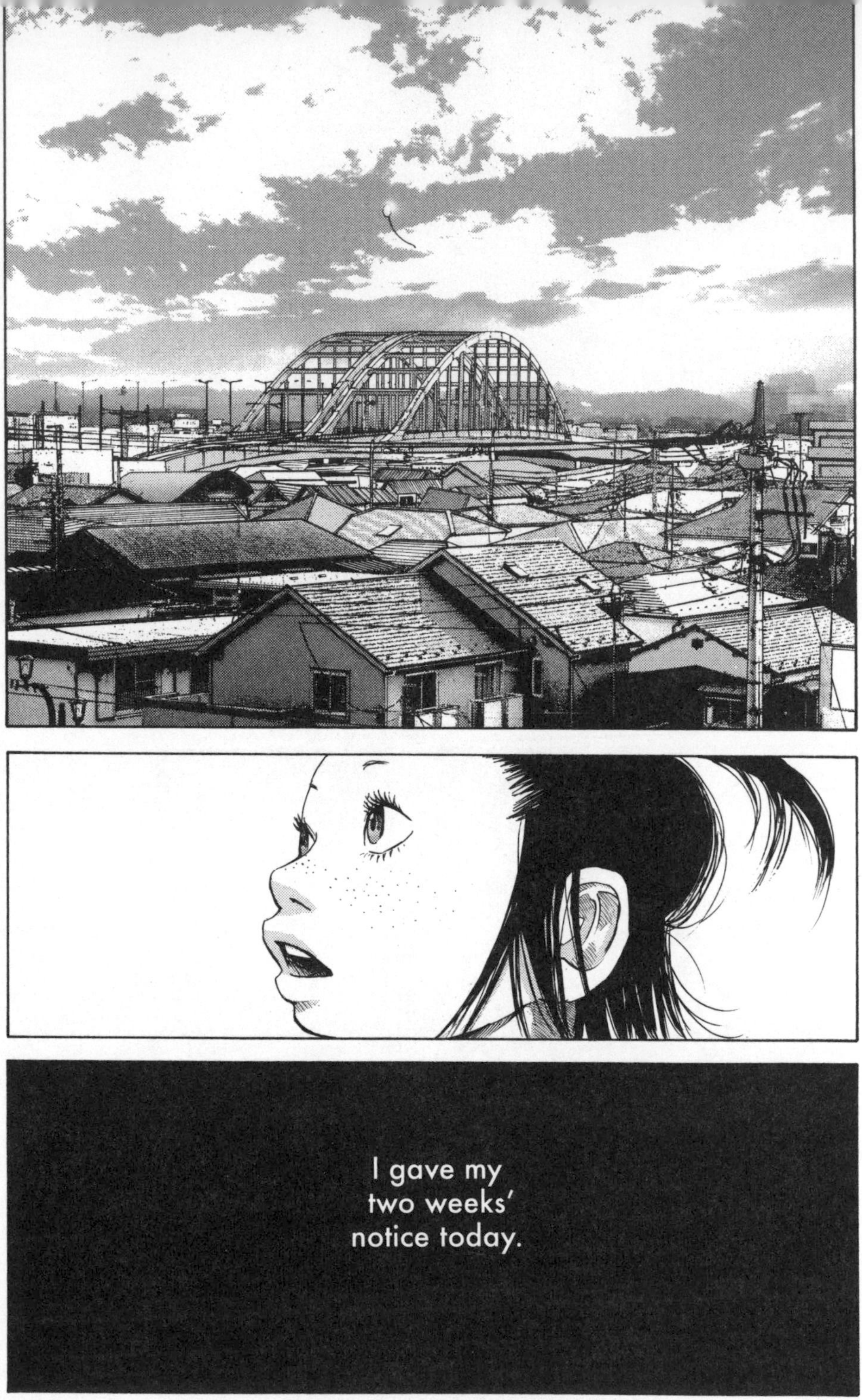
I gave my two weeks' notice today.

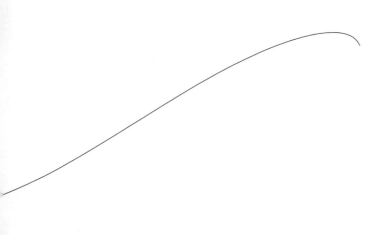

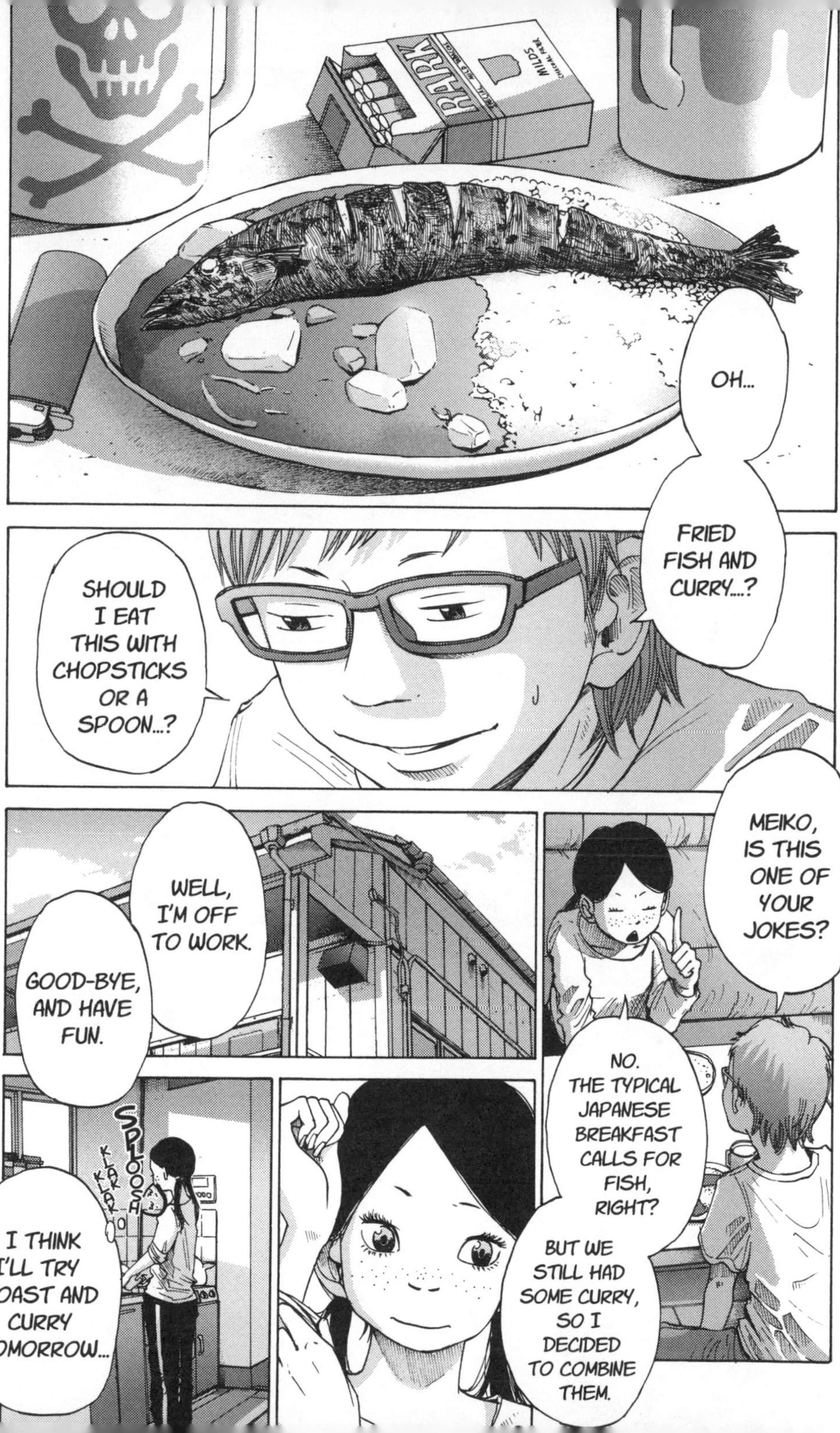
RARK
OH...
FRIED FISH AND CURRY...?
SHOULD I EAT THIS WITH CHOPSTICKS OR A SPOON...?
MEIKO, IS THIS ONE OF YOUR JOKES?
NO. THE TYPICAL JAPANESE BREAKFAST CALLS FOR FISH, RIGHT?
BUT WE STILL HAD SOME CURRY, SO I DECIDED TO COMBINE THEM.
WELL, I'M OFF TO WORK.
GOOD-BYE, AND HAVE FUN.
SPLOOSH
KLAK KLAK
I THINK I'LL TRY TOAST AND CURRY TOMORROW...

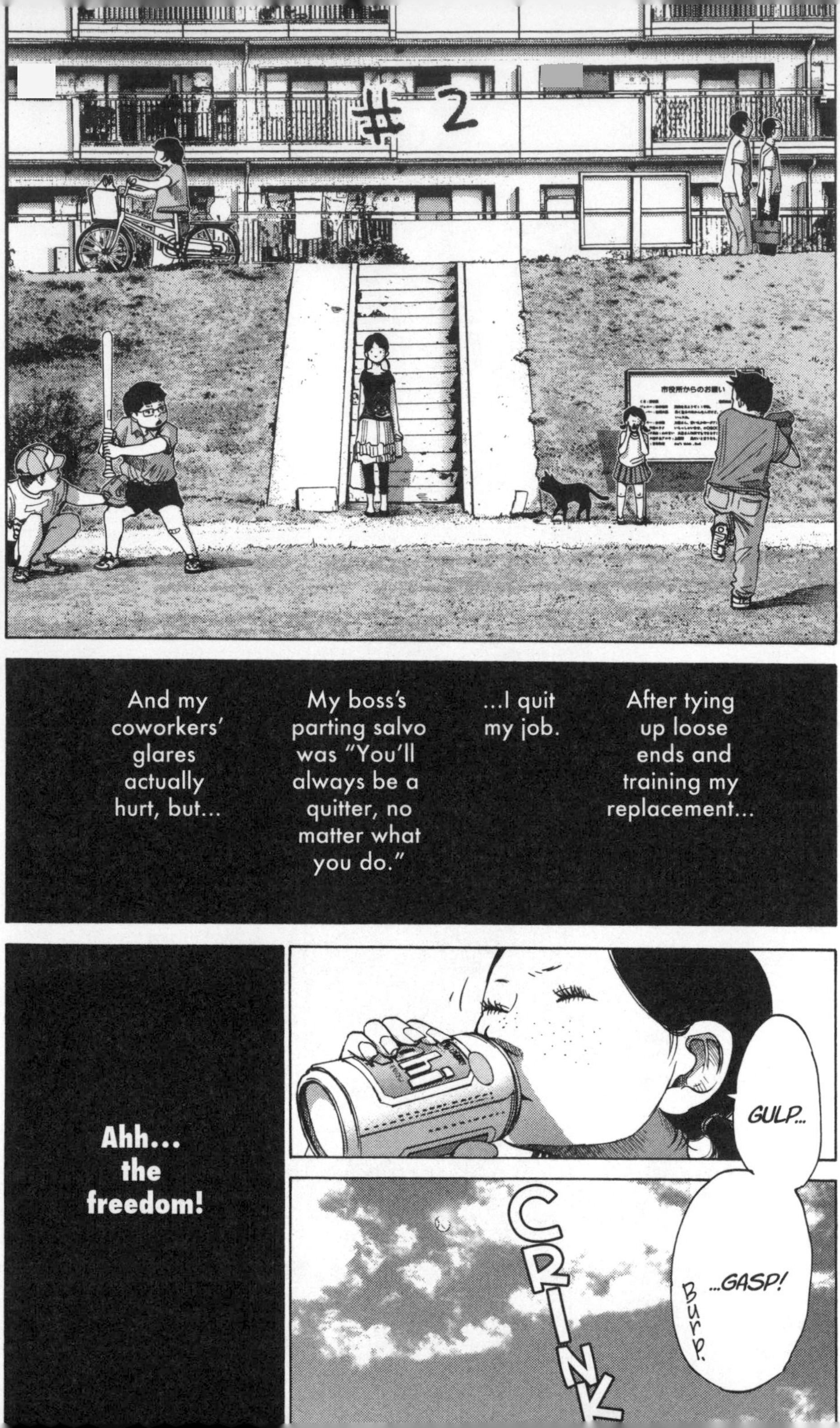

2
市役所からのお願い
After tying up loose ends and training my replacement...
...I quit my job.
My boss's parting salvo was "You'll always be a quitter, no matter what you do."
And my coworkers' glares actually hurt, but...
GULP...
...GASP!
CRINK
Burp.
Ahh... the freedom!

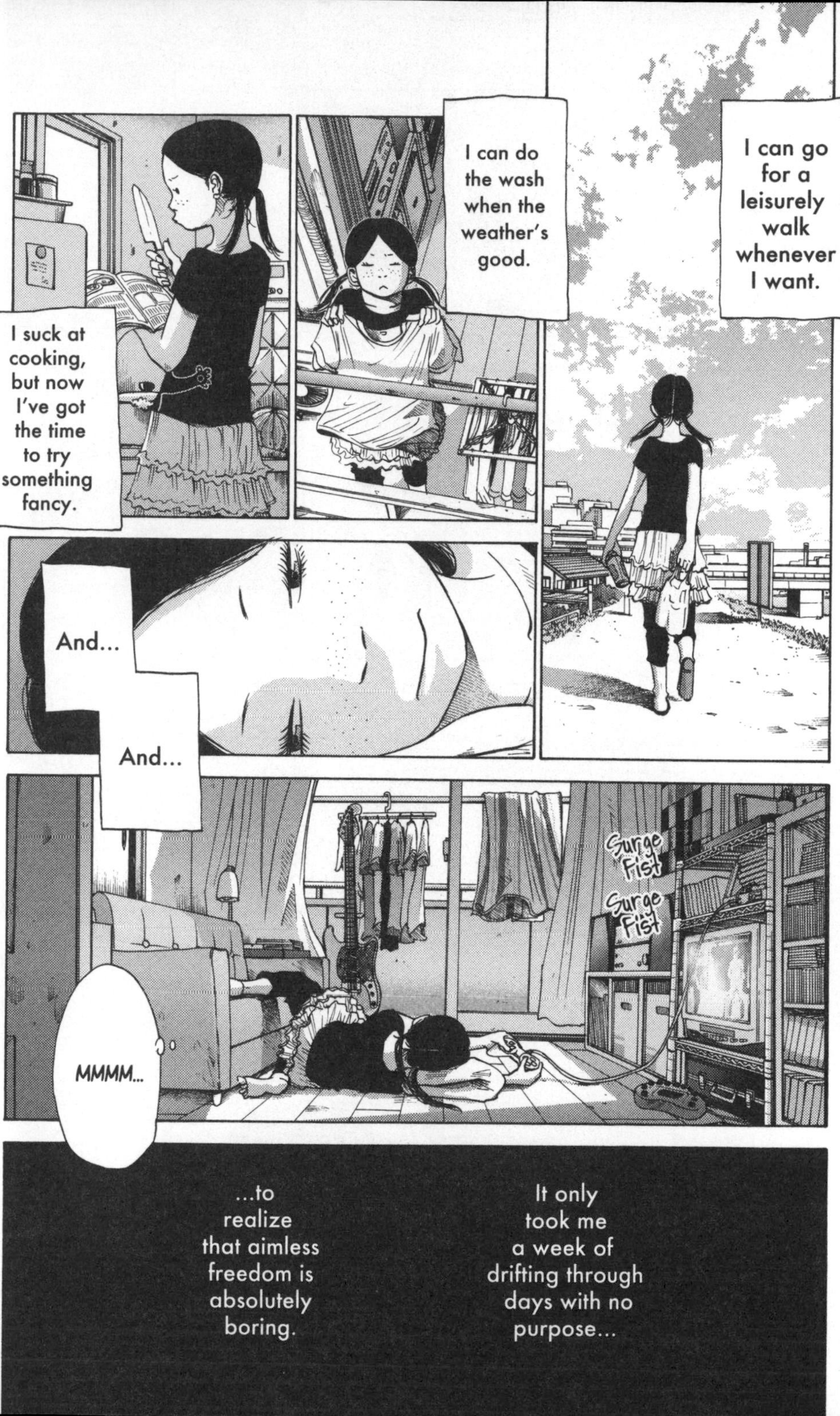
I can go for a leisurely walk whenever I want.
I can do the wash when the weather's good.
I suck at cooking, but now I've got the time to try something fancy.
And...
And...
Surge Fist
Surge Fist
MMMM...
It only took me a week of drifting through days with no purpose...
...to realize that aimless freedom is absolutely boring.

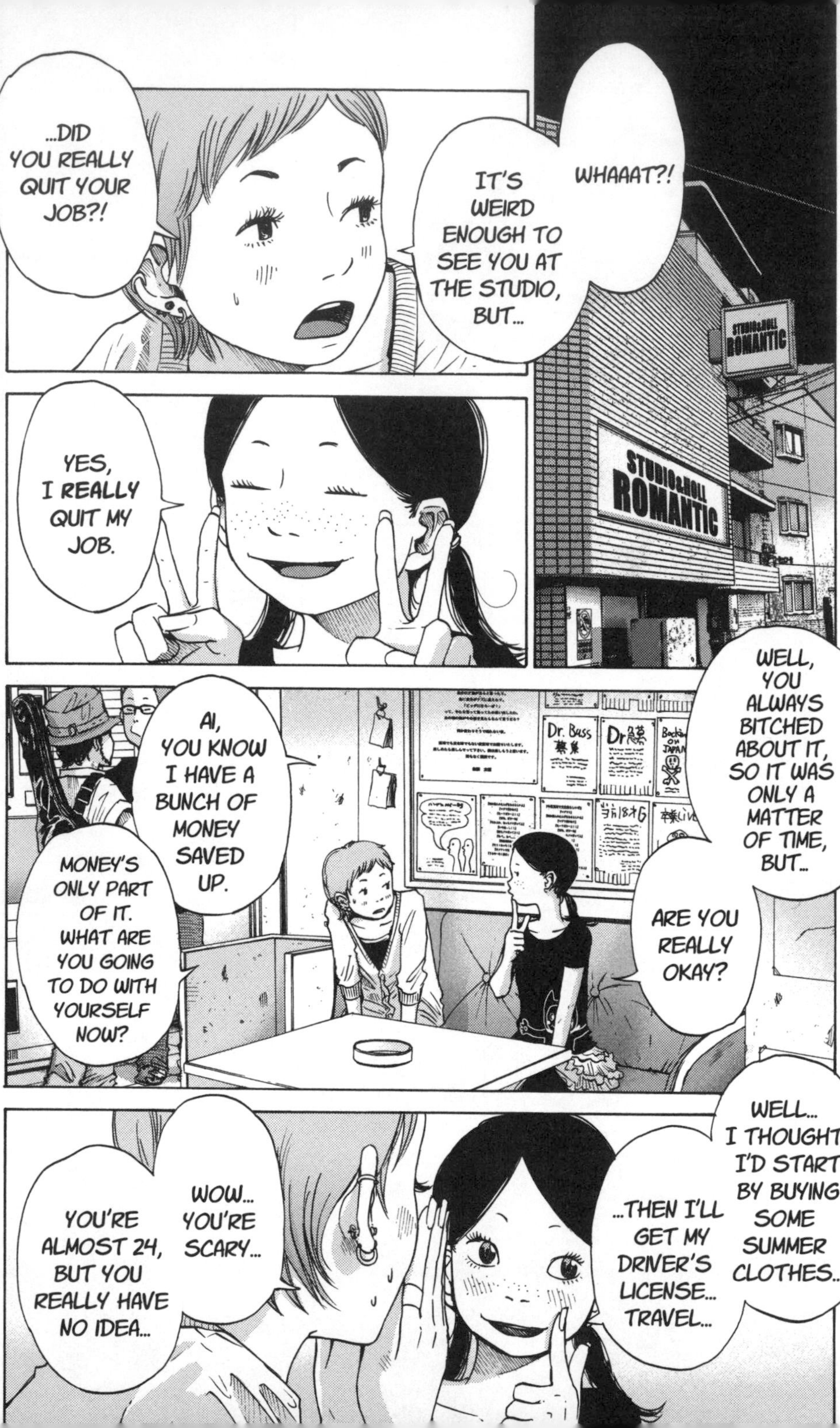
WHAAAT?!
IT'S WEIRD ENOUGH TO SEE YOU AT THE STUDIO, BUT...
...DID YOU REALLY QUIT YOUR JOB?!
STUDIO&HOLL ROMANTIC
STUDIO&HOLL ROMANTIC
YES, I REALLY QUIT MY JOB.
WELL, YOU ALWAYS BITCHED ABOUT IT, SO IT WAS ONLY A MATTER OF TIME, BUT...
ARE YOU REALLY OKAY?
AI, YOU KNOW I HAVE A BUNCH OF MONEY SAVED UP.
MONEY'S ONLY PART OF IT. WHAT ARE YOU GOING TO DO WITH YOURSELF NOW?
WELL... I THOUGHT I'D START BY BUYING SOME SUMMER CLOTHES...
...THEN I'LL GET MY DRIVER'S LICENSE... TRAVEL...
WOW... YOU'RE SCARY...
YOU'RE ALMOST 24, BUT YOU REALLY HAVE NO IDEA...

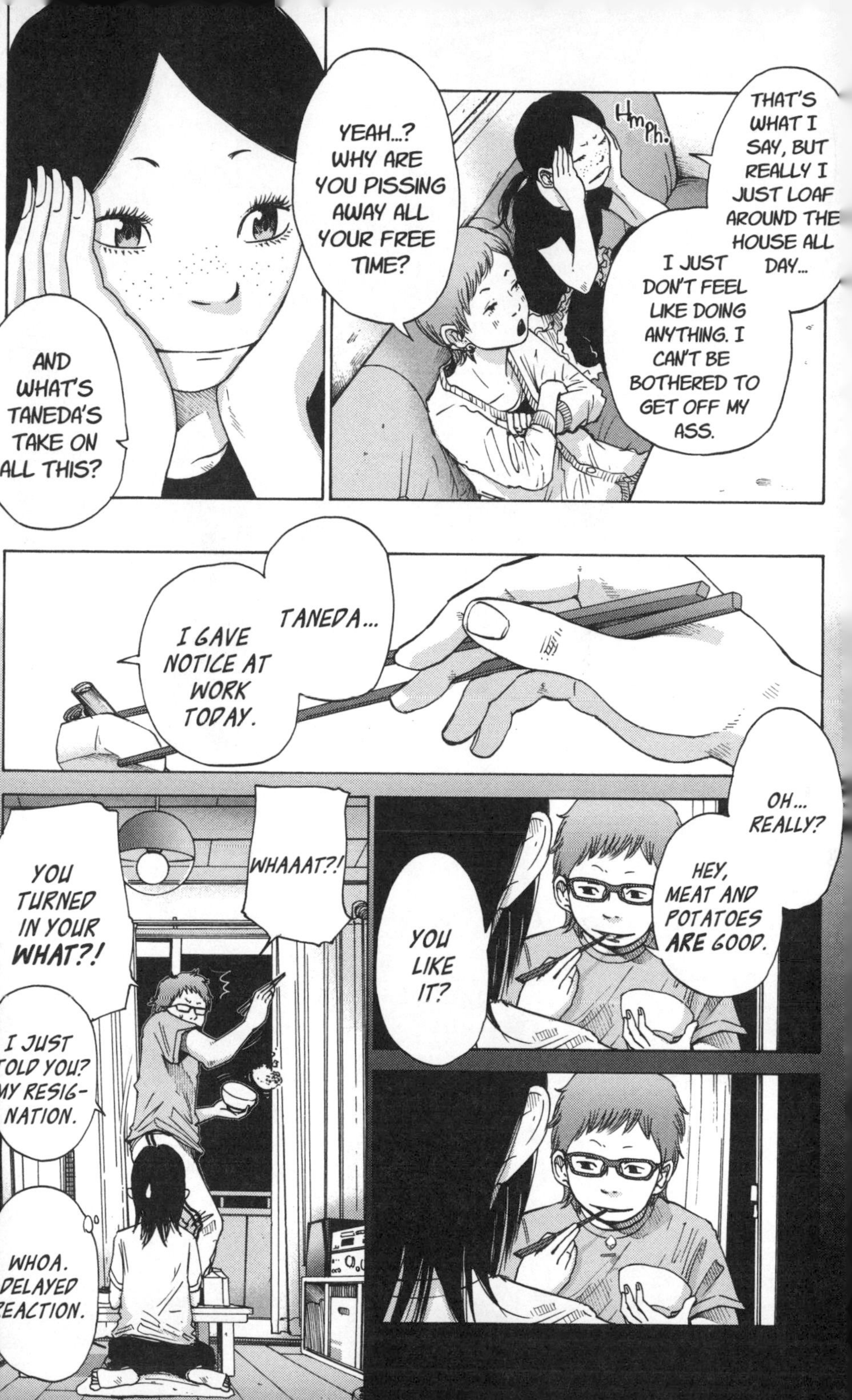

THAT'S WHAT I SAY, BUT REALLY I JUST LOAF AROUND THE HOUSE ALL DAY...
Hmph.
I JUST DON'T FEEL LIKE DOING ANYTHING. I CAN'T BE BOTHERED TO GET OFF MY ASS.
YEAH...? WHY ARE YOU PISSING AWAY ALL YOUR FREE TIME?
AND WHAT'S TANEDA'S TAKE ON ALL THIS?
TANEDA...
I GAVE NOTICE AT WORK TODAY.
OH... REALLY?
HEY, MEAT AND POTATOES ARE GOOD.
YOU LIKE IT?
WHAAAT?!
YOU TURNED IN YOUR WHAT?!
I JUST TOLD YOU? MY RESIGNATION.
WHOA. DELAYED REACTION.

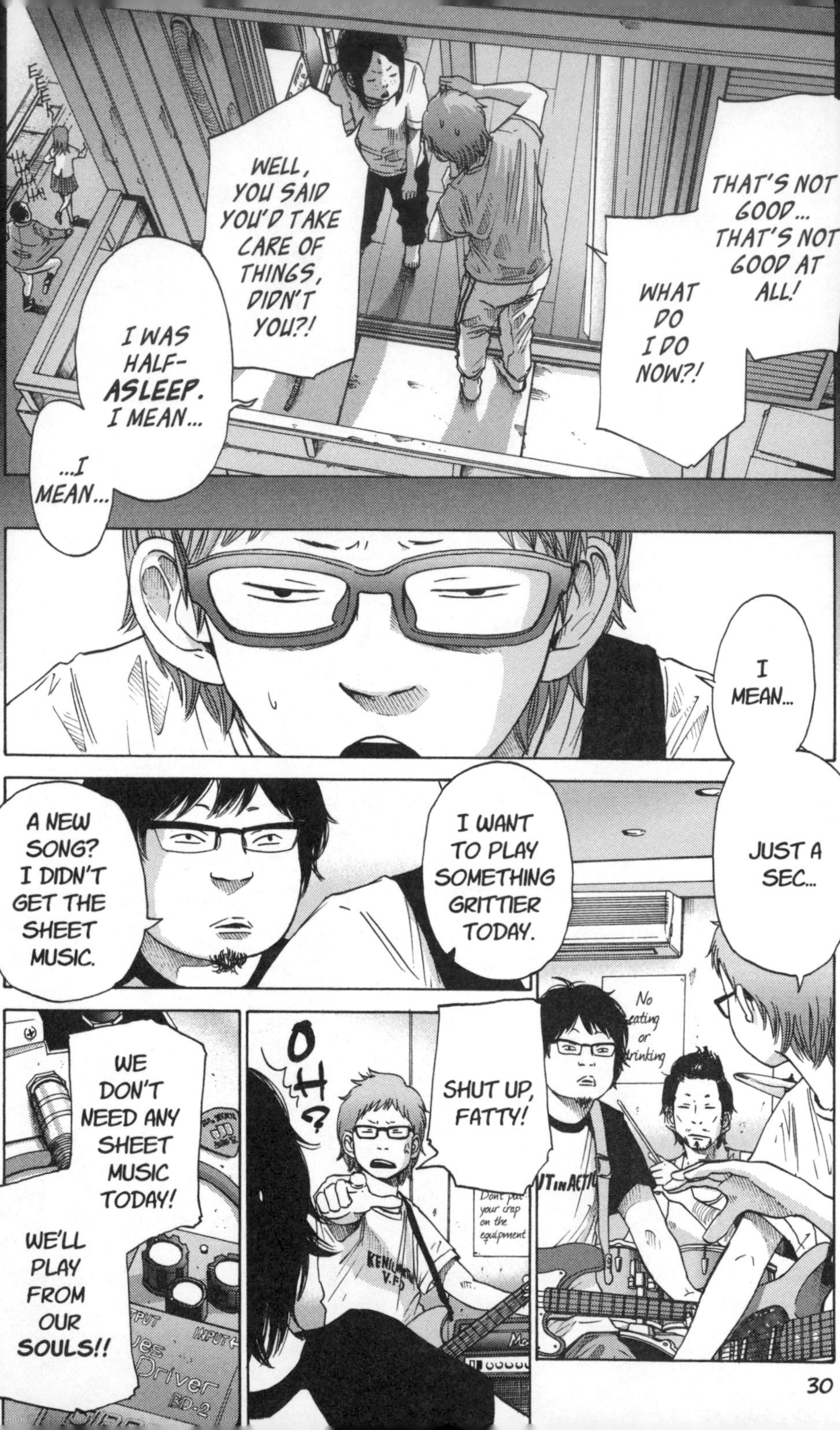
THAT'S NOT GOOD... THAT'S NOT GOOD AT ALL!
WHAT DO I DO NOW?!
WELL, YOU SAID YOU'D TAKE CARE OF THINGS, DIDN'T YOU?!
I WAS HALF-ASLEEP. I MEAN...
...I MEAN...
I MEAN...
JUST A SEC...
I WANT TO PLAY SOMETHING GRITTIER TODAY.
A NEW SONG? I DIDN'T GET THE SHEET MUSIC.
No eating or drinking
SHUT UP, FATTY!
OH?
Don't put your crap on the equipment
WE DON'T NEED ANY SHEET MUSIC TODAY!
WE'LL PLAY FROM OUR SOULS!!

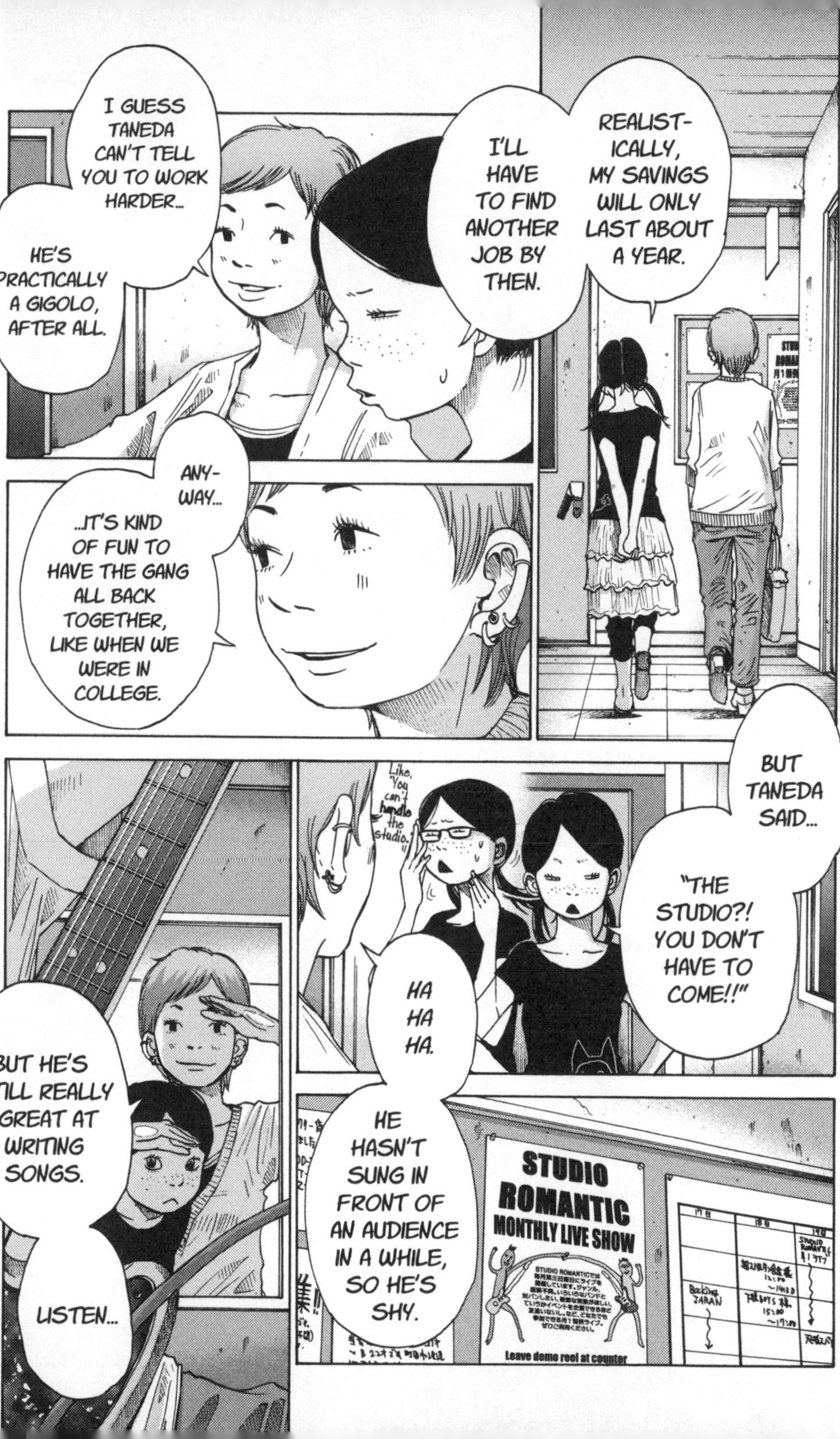
REALISTICALLY, MY SAVINGS WILL ONLY LAST ABOUT A YEAR.
I'LL HAVE TO FIND ANOTHER JOB BY THEN.
I GUESS TANEDA CAN'T TELL YOU TO WORK HARDER...
HE'S PRACTICALLY A GIGOLO, AFTER ALL.
ANYWAY...
...IT'S KIND OF FUN TO HAVE THE GANG ALL BACK TOGETHER, LIKE WHEN WE WERE IN COLLEGE.
BUT TANEDA SAID...
"THE STUDIO?! YOU DON'T HAVE TO COME!!"
Like, "You can't handle the studio."
HA HA HA.
HE HASN'T SUNG IN FRONT OF AN AUDIENCE IN A WHILE, SO HE'S SHY.
STUDIO ROMANTIC
MONTHLY LIVE SHOW
Leave demo reel at counter
BUT HE'S STILL REALLY GREAT AT WRITING SONGS.
LISTEN...

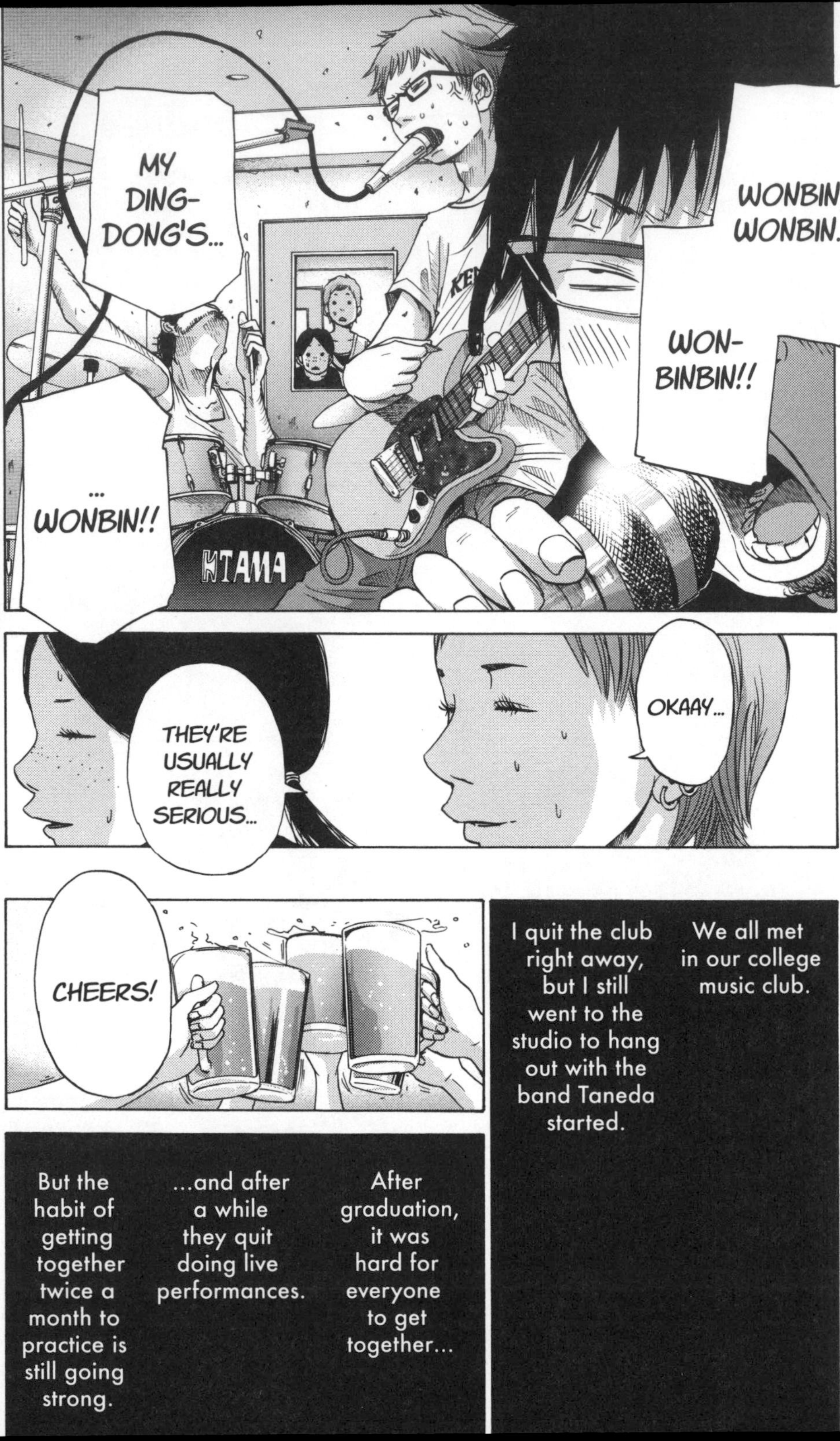
WONBIN, WONBIN...
MY DING-DONG'S...
WON-BINBIN!!
...WONBIN!!
TAMA
OKAAY...
THEY'RE USUALLY REALLY SERIOUS...
We all met in our college music club.
I quit the club right away, but I still went to the studio to hang out with the band Taneda started.
CHEERS!
After graduation, it was hard for everyone to get together...
...and after a while they quit doing live performances.
But the habit of getting together twice a month to practice is still going strong.

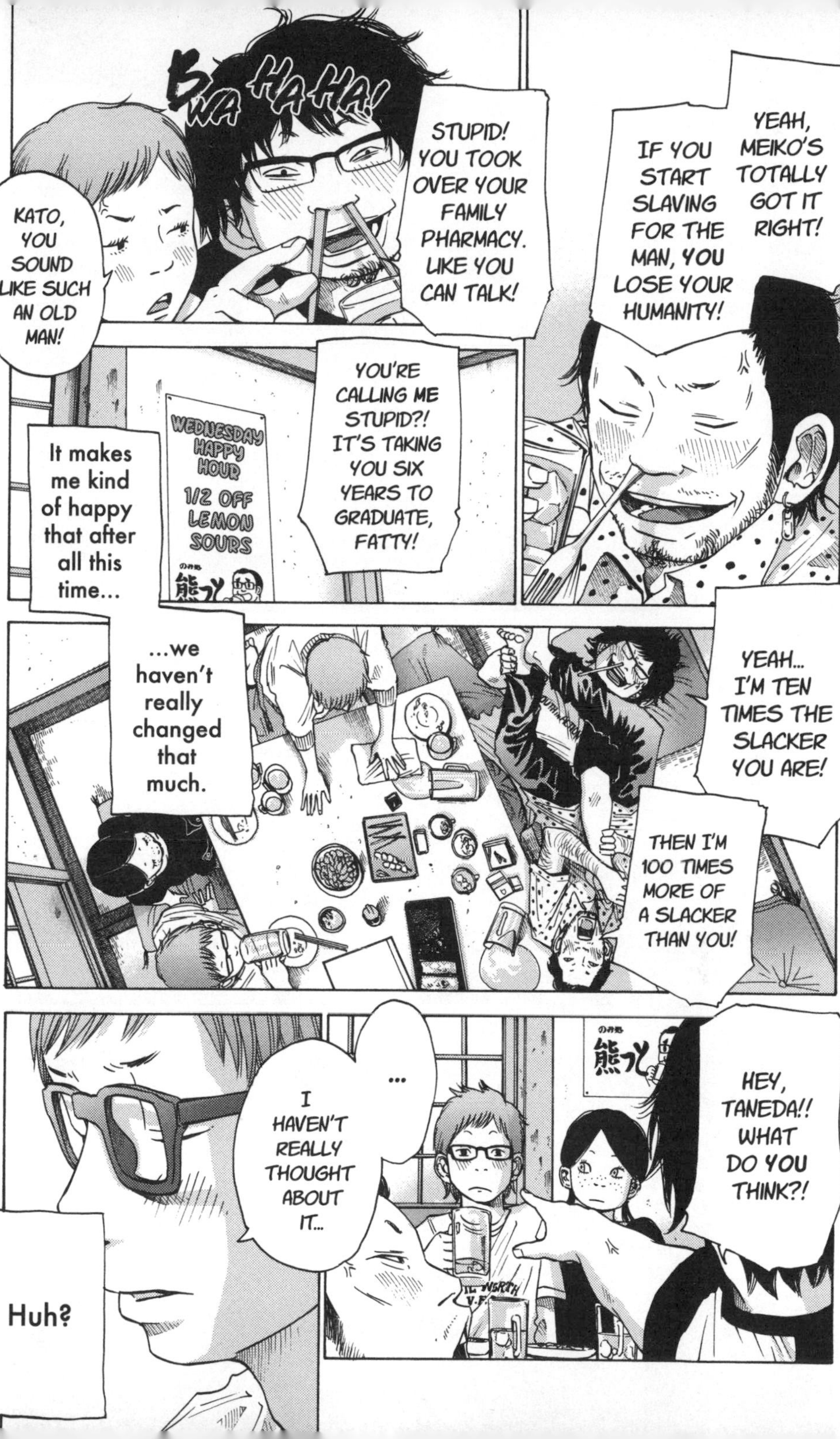

YEAH, MEIKO'S TOTALLY GOT IT RIGHT!
IF YOU START SLAVING FOR THE MAN, YOU LOSE YOUR HUMANITY!
STUPID! YOU TOOK OVER YOUR FAMILY PHARMACY. LIKE YOU CAN TALK!
BWA HA HA!
KATO, YOU SOUND LIKE SUCH AN OLD MAN!
YOU'RE CALLING ME STUPID?! IT'S TAKING YOU SIX YEARS TO GRADUATE, FATTY!
WEDNESDAY HAPPY HOUR
1/2 OFF LEMON SOURS
It makes me kind of happy that after all this time...
YEAH... I'M TEN TIMES THE SLACKER YOU ARE!
THEN I'M 100 TIMES MORE OF A SLACKER THAN YOU!
...we haven't really changed that much.
HEY, TANEDA!! WHAT DO YOU THINK?!
...
I HAVEN'T REALLY THOUGHT ABOUT IT...
Huh?

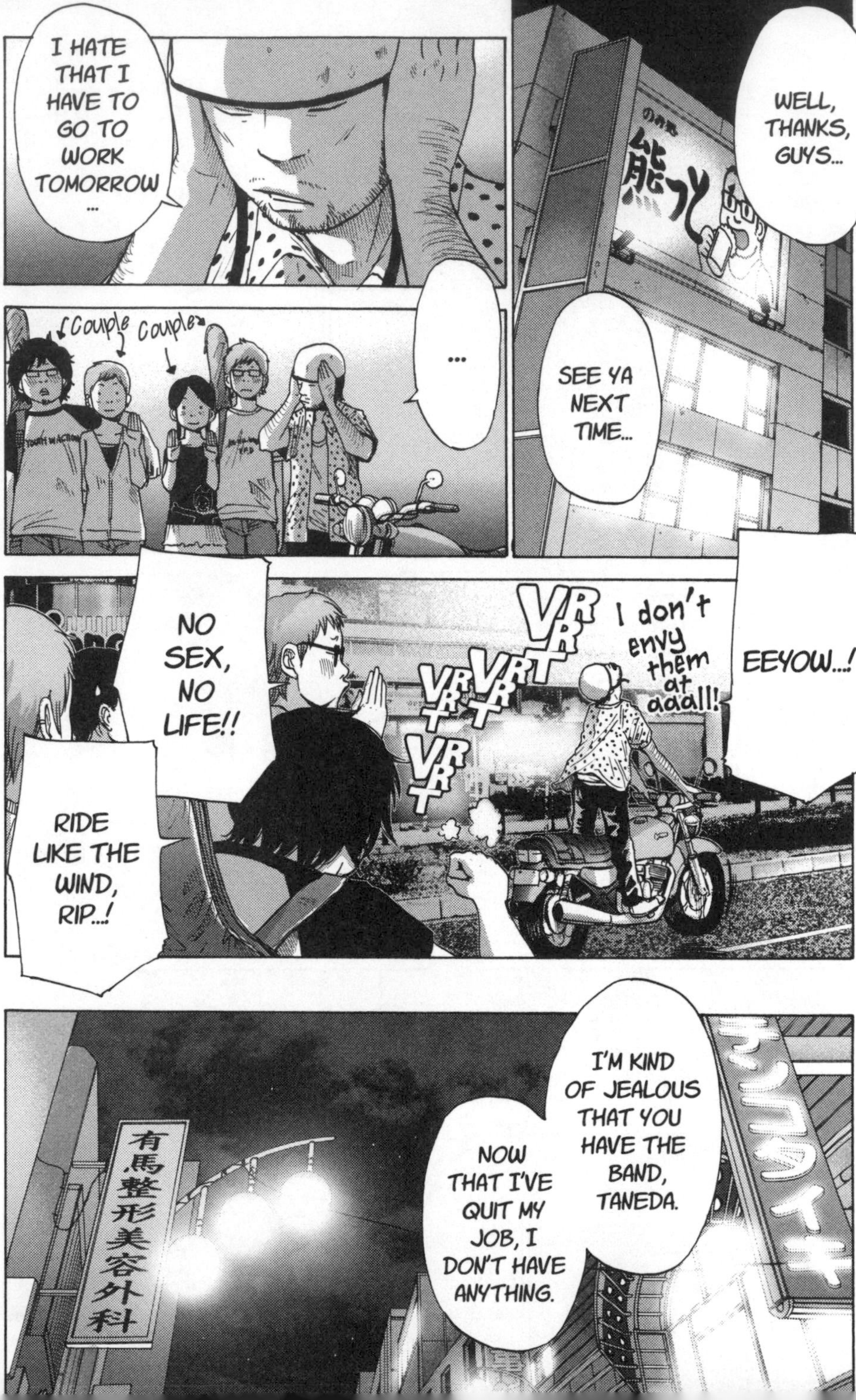
WELL, THANKS, GUYS...
I HATE THAT I HAVE TO GO TO WORK TOMORROW ...
SEE YA NEXT TIME...
...
Couple
Couple
EEYOW...!
I don't envy them at aaall!!
VRT
VRT
VRT
VRT
NO SEX, NO LIFE!!
RIDE LIKE THE WIND, RIP...!
I'M KIND OF JEALOUS THAT YOU HAVE THE BAND, TANEDA.
NOW THAT I'VE QUIT MY JOB, I DON'T HAVE ANYTHING.
有馬整形美容外科

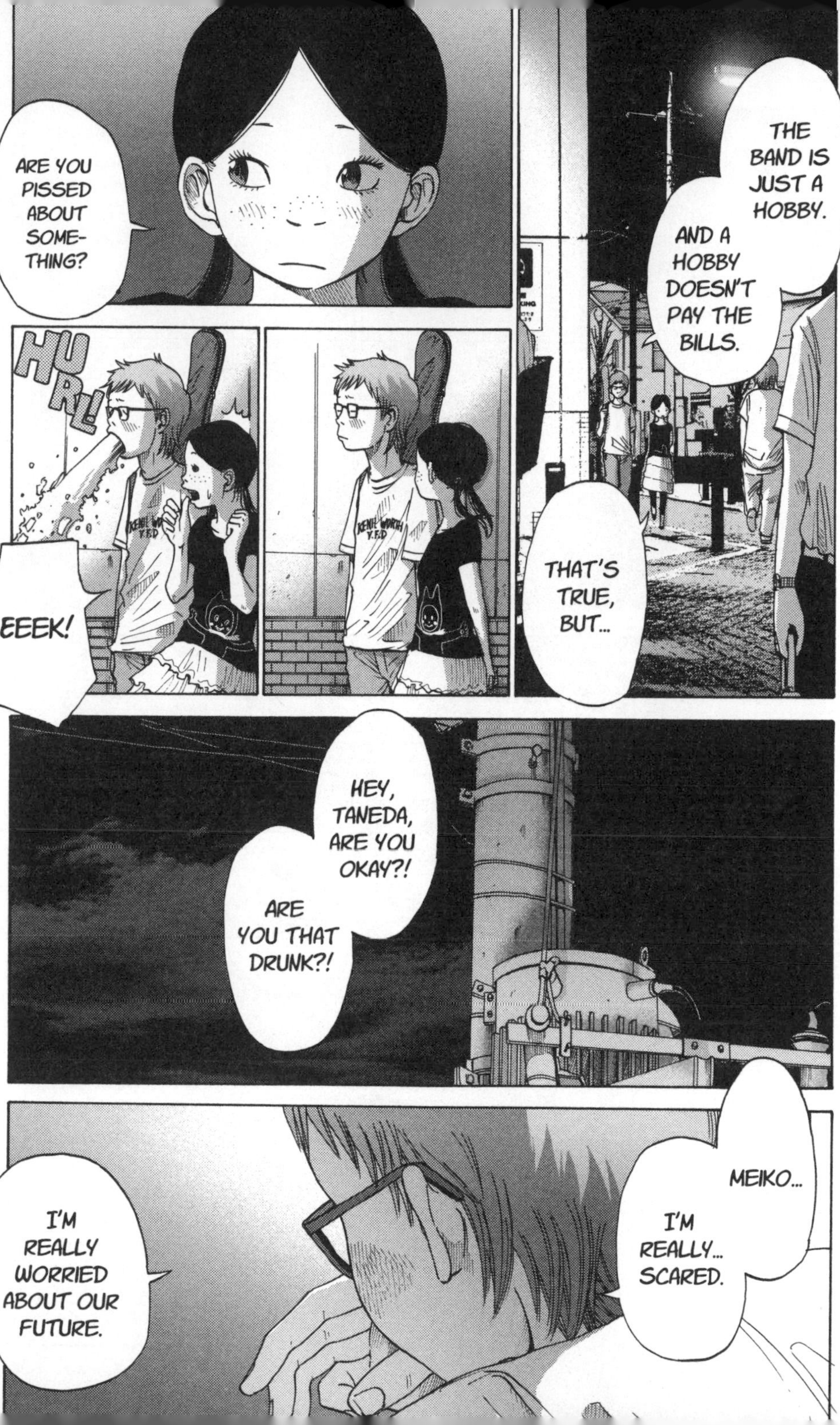
THE BAND IS JUST A HOBBY.
AND A HOBBY DOESN'T PAY THE BILLS.
THAT'S TRUE, BUT...
ARE YOU PISSED ABOUT SOME-THING?
HURL!
EEEK!
HEY, TANEDA, ARE YOU OKAY?!
ARE YOU THAT DRUNK?!
MEIKO...
I'M REALLY... SCARED.
I'M REALLY WORRIED ABOUT OUR FUTURE.

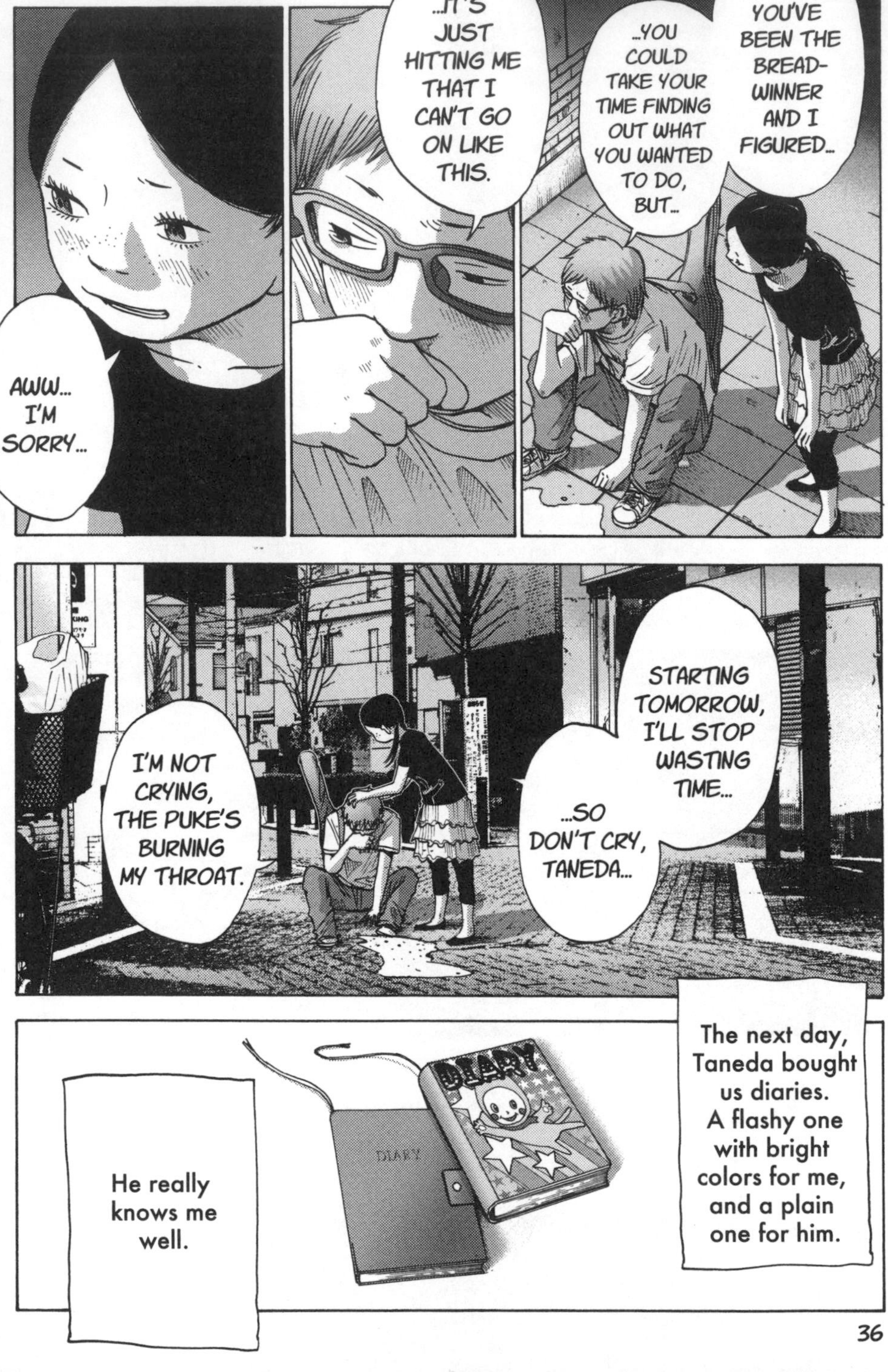
YOU'VE BEEN THE BREAD-WINNER AND I FIGURED...
...YOU COULD TAKE YOUR TIME FINDING OUT WHAT YOU WANTED TO DO, BUT...
...IT'S JUST HITTING ME THAT I CAN'T GO ON LIKE THIS.
AWW... I'M SORRY...
STARTING TOMORROW, I'LL STOP WASTING TIME...
...SO DON'T CRY, TANEDA...
I'M NOT CRYING, THE PUKE'S BURNING MY THROAT.
The next day, Taneda bought us diaries. A flashy one with bright colors for me, and a plain one for him.
DIARY
He really knows me well.

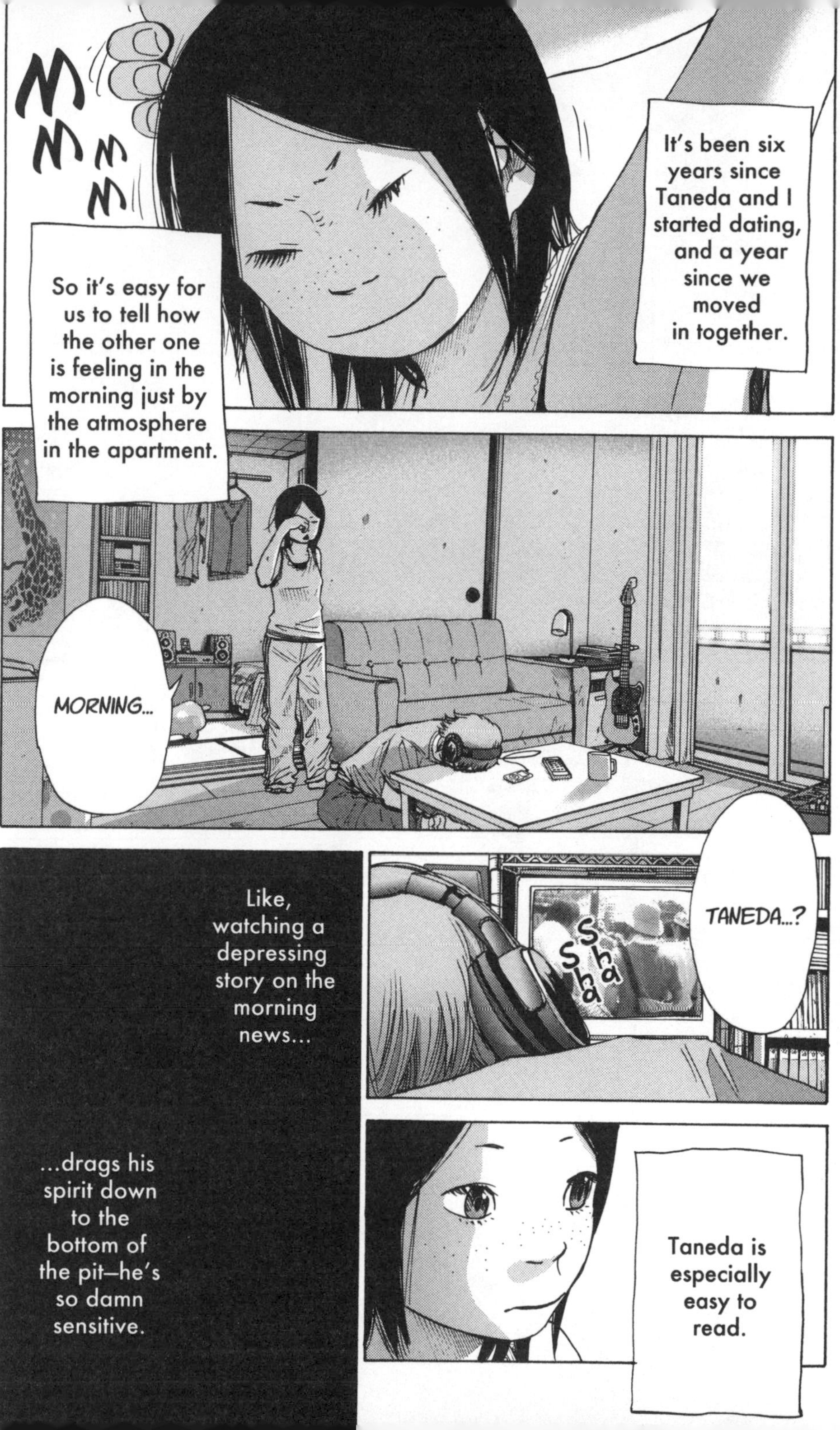

It's been six years since Taneda and I started dating, and a year since we moved in together.
So it's easy for us to tell how the other one is feeling in the morning just by the atmosphere in the apartment.
MORNING...
TANEDA...?
Sha Sha
Taneda is especially easy to read.
Like, watching a depressing story on the morning news...
...drags his spirit down to the bottom of the pit—he's so damn sensitive.

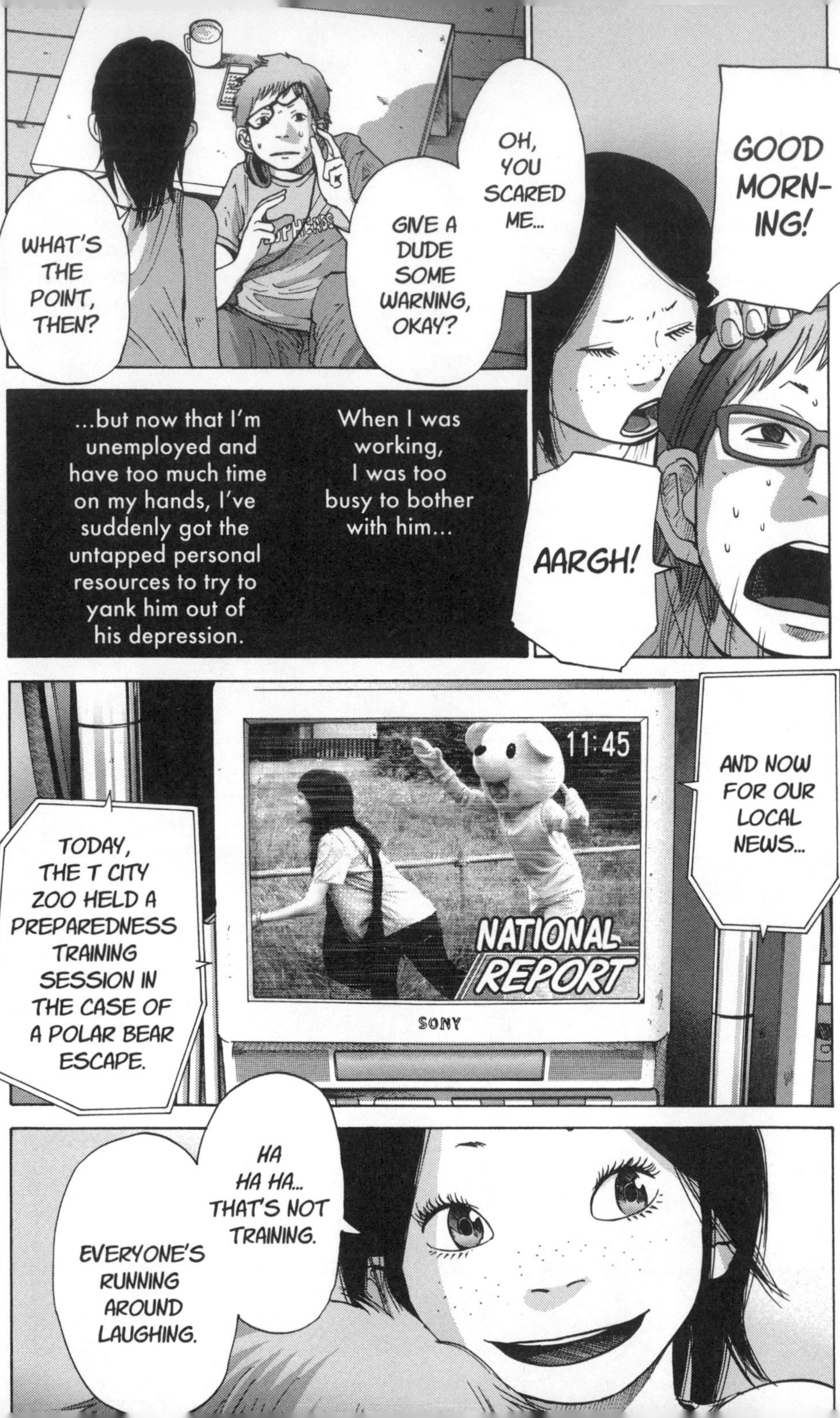
GOOD MORNING!
AARGH!
OH, YOU SCARED ME...
GIVE A DUDE SOME WARNING, OKAY?
WHAT'S THE POINT, THEN?
When I was working, I was too busy to bother with him...
...but now that I'm unemployed and have too much time on my hands, I've suddenly got the untapped personal resources to try to yank him out of his depression.
AND NOW FOR OUR LOCAL NEWS...
11:45
NATIONAL REPORT
SONY
TODAY, THE T CITY ZOO HELD A PREPAREDNESS TRAINING SESSION IN THE CASE OF A POLAR BEAR ESCAPE.
HA HA HA... THAT'S NOT TRAINING.
EVERYONE'S RUNNING AROUND LAUGHING.

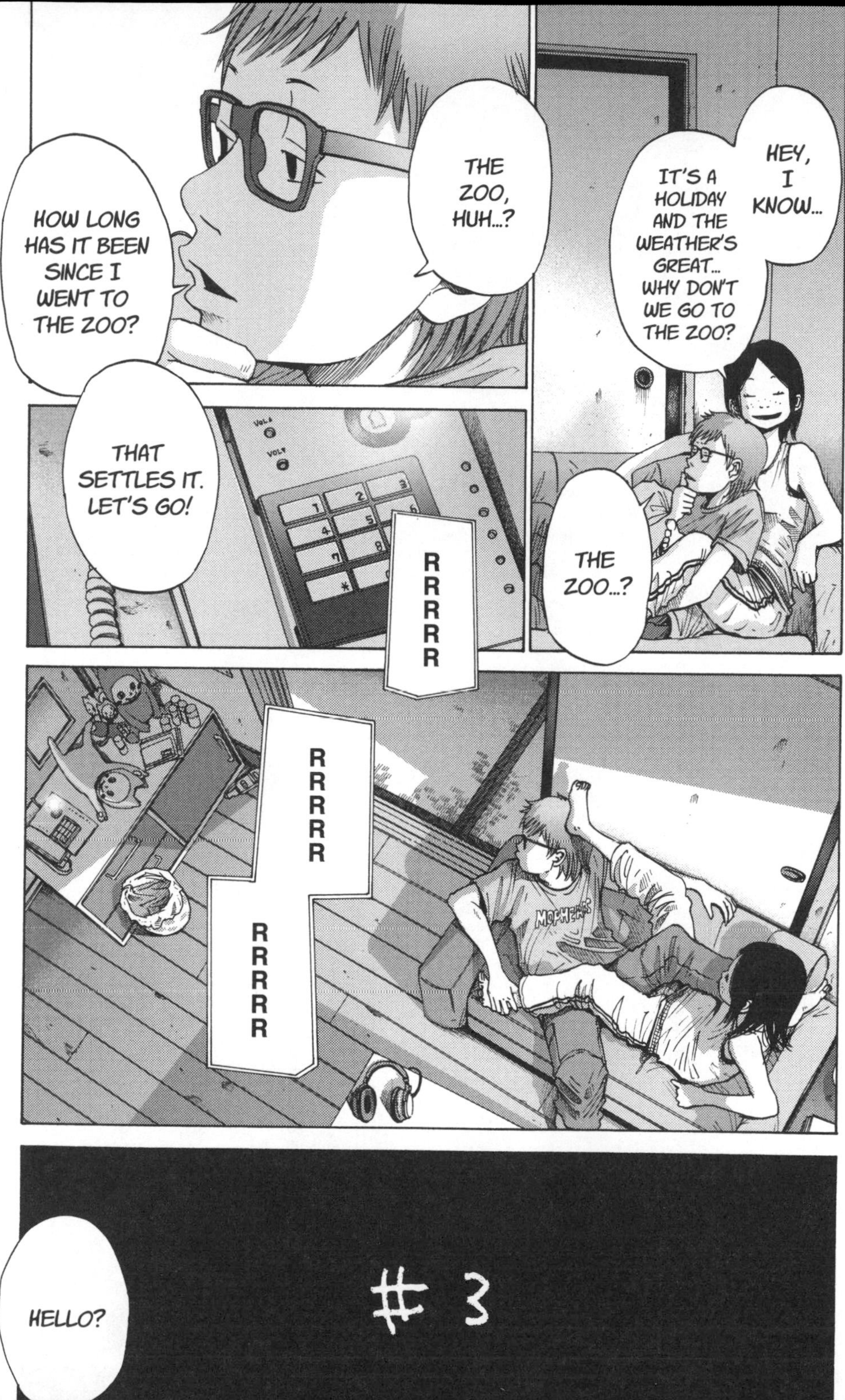
HEY, I KNOW...
IT'S A HOLIDAY AND THE WEATHER'S GREAT... WHY DON'T WE GO TO THE ZOO?
THE ZOO...?
THE ZOO, HUH...?
HOW LONG HAS IT BEEN SINCE I WENT TO THE ZOO?
THAT SETTLES IT. LET'S GO!
RRRRR
RRRRR
RRRRR
#3
HELLO?

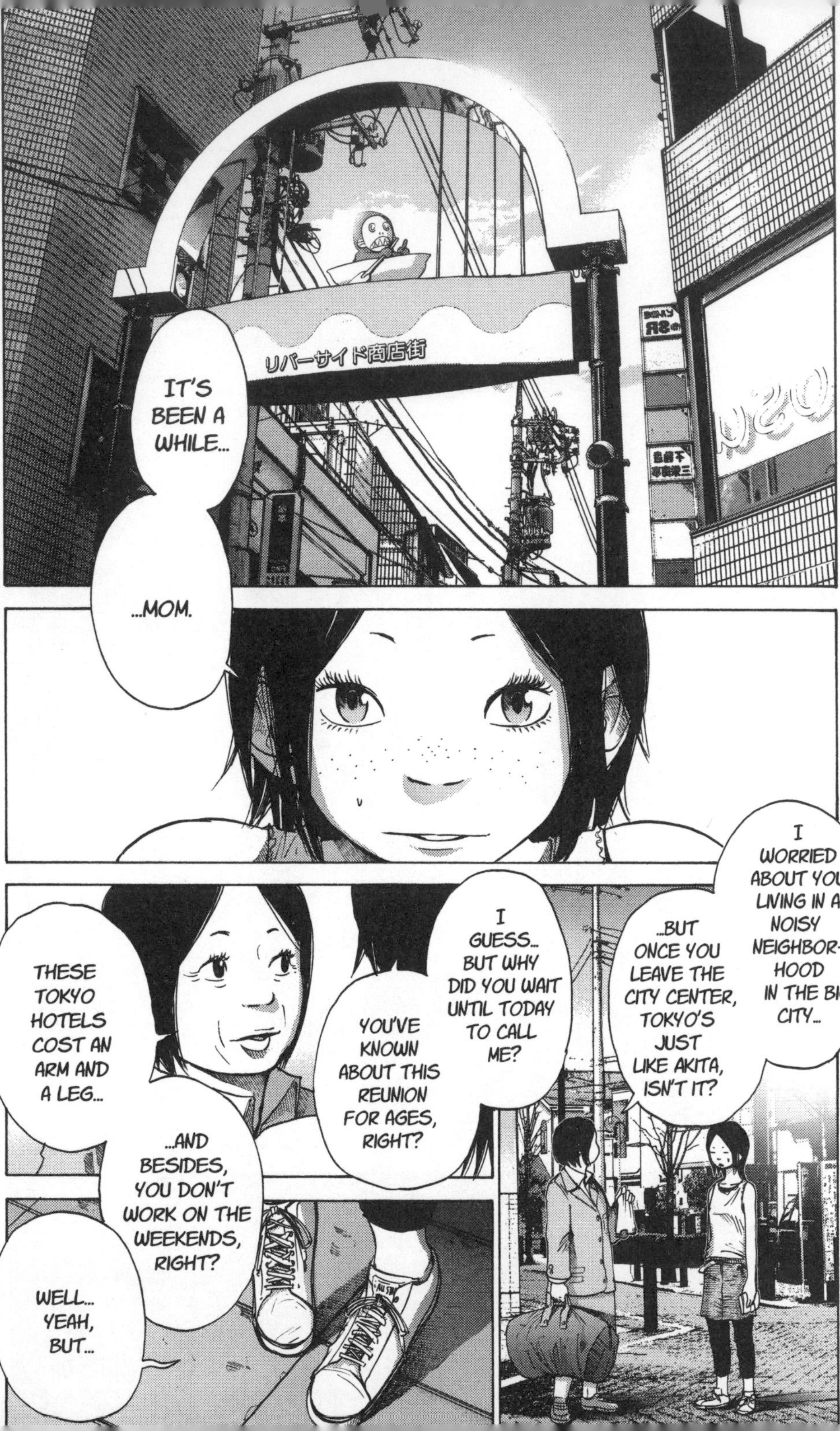
リバーサイド商店街
IT'S BEEN A WHILE...
...MOM.
I WORRIED ABOUT YOU LIVING IN A NOISY NEIGHBOR-HOOD IN THE BIG CITY...
...BUT ONCE YOU LEAVE THE CITY CENTER, TOKYO'S JUST LIKE AKITA, ISN'T IT?
I GUESS... BUT WHY DID YOU WAIT UNTIL TODAY TO CALL ME?
YOU'VE KNOWN ABOUT THIS REUNION FOR AGES, RIGHT?
THESE TOKYO HOTELS COST AN ARM AND A LEG...
...AND BESIDES, YOU DON'T WORK ON THE WEEKENDS, RIGHT?
WELL... YEAH, BUT...

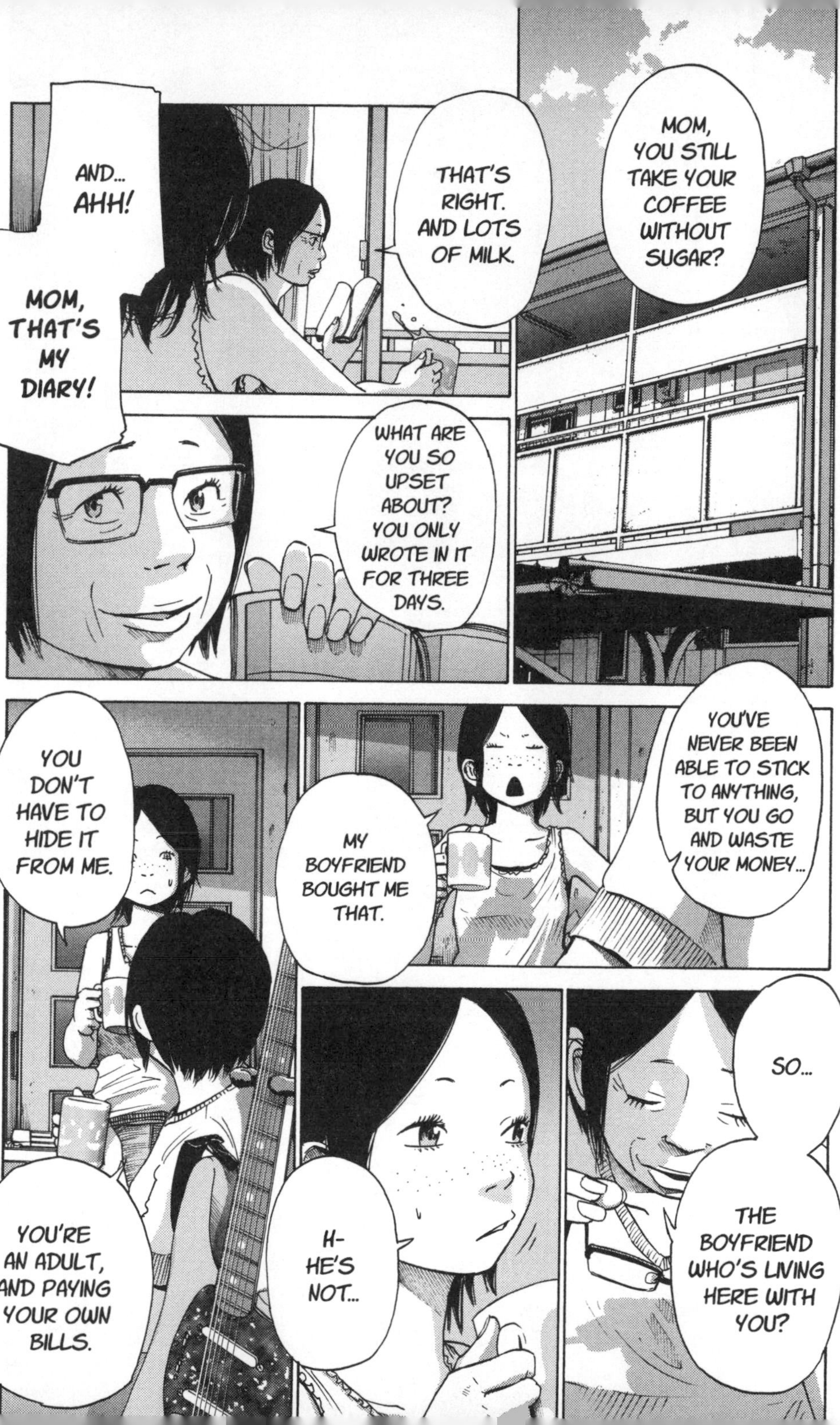
MOM, YOU STILL TAKE YOUR COFFEE WITHOUT SUGAR?
THAT'S RIGHT. AND LOTS OF MILK.
AND... AHH!
MOM, THAT'S MY DIARY!
WHAT ARE YOU SO UPSET ABOUT? YOU ONLY WROTE IN IT FOR THREE DAYS.
YOU'VE NEVER BEEN ABLE TO STICK TO ANYTHING, BUT YOU GO AND WASTE YOUR MONEY...
MY BOYFRIEND BOUGHT ME THAT.
SO...
THE BOYFRIEND WHO'S LIVING HERE WITH YOU?
H-HE'S NOT...
YOU DON'T HAVE TO HIDE IT FROM ME.
YOU'RE AN ADULT, AND PAYING YOUR OWN BILLS.

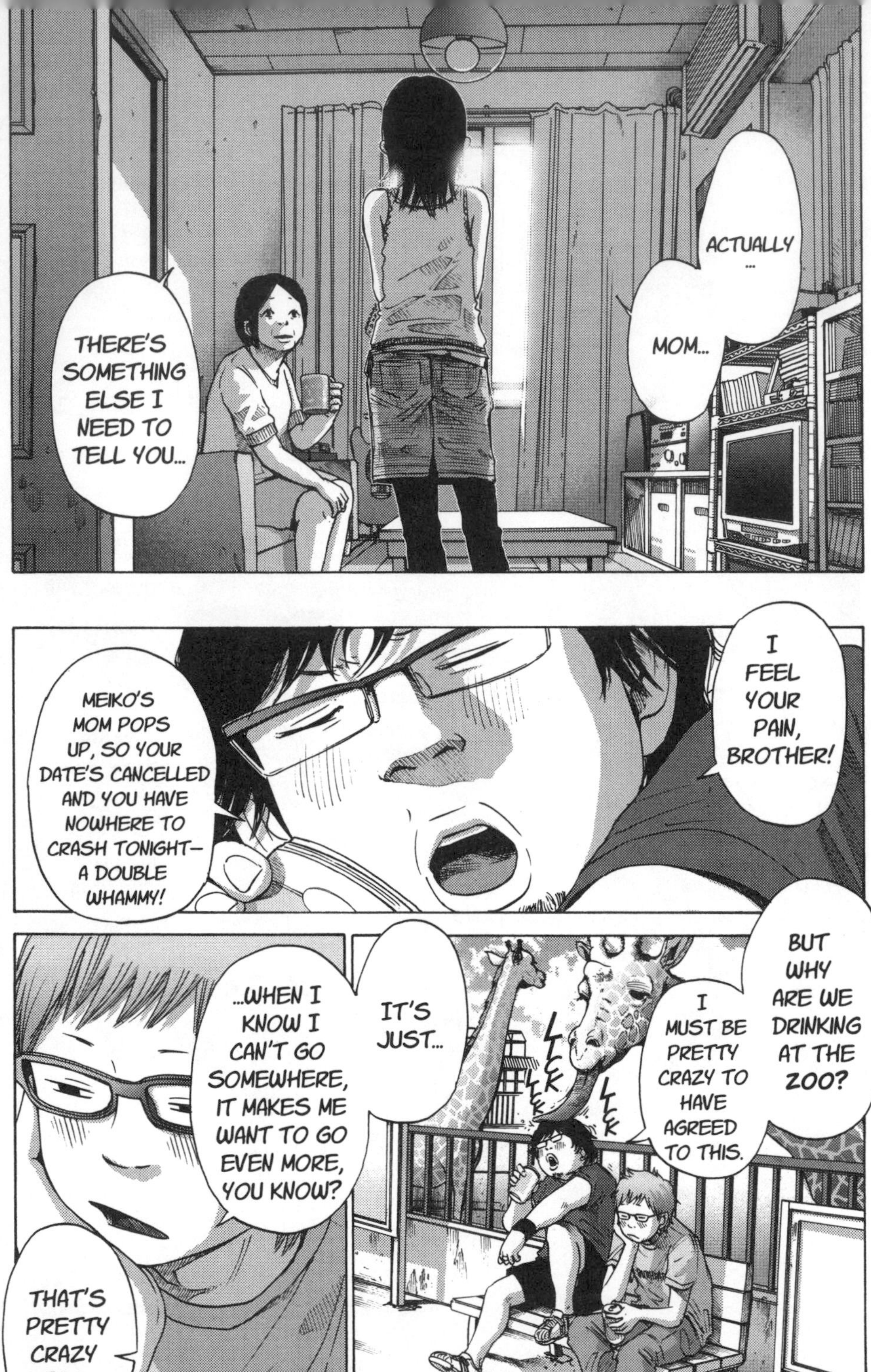
ACTUALLY ...
MOM...
THERE'S SOMETHING ELSE I NEED TO TELL YOU...
I FEEL YOUR PAIN, BROTHER!
MEIKO'S MOM POPS UP, SO YOUR DATE'S CANCELLED AND YOU HAVE NOWHERE TO CRASH TONIGHT— A DOUBLE WHAMMY!
BUT WHY ARE WE DRINKING AT THE ZOO?
I MUST BE PRETTY CRAZY TO HAVE AGREED TO THIS.
LICK
LICK
LICK
IT'S JUST...
...WHEN I KNOW I CAN'T GO SOMEWHERE, IT MAKES ME WANT TO GO EVEN MORE, YOU KNOW?
THAT'S PRETTY CRAZY TOO.

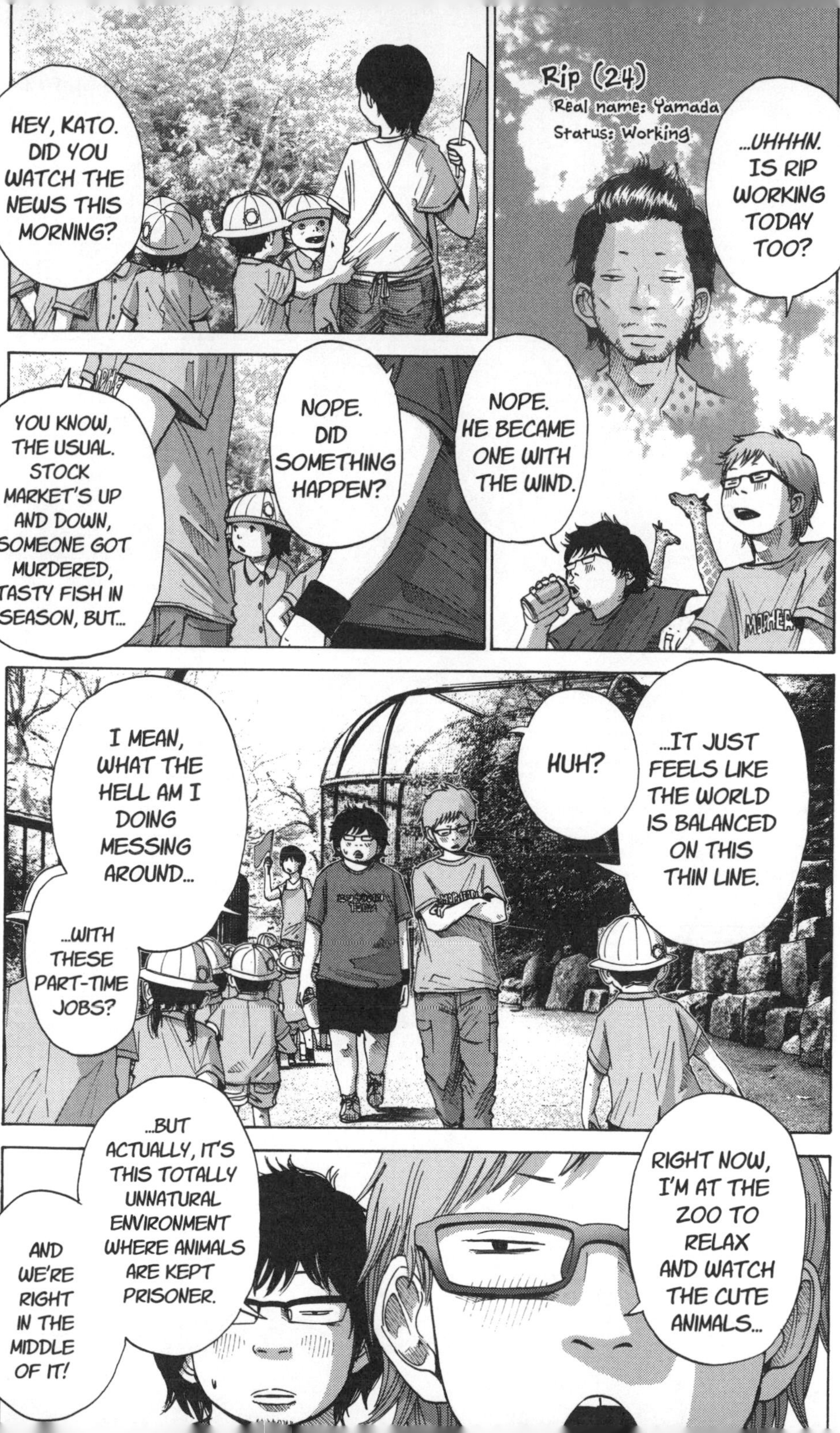
Rip (24)
Real name: Yamada
Status: Working
...UHHHN. IS RIP WORKING TODAY TOO?
NOPE. HE BECAME ONE WITH THE WIND.
HEY, KATO. DID YOU WATCH THE NEWS THIS MORNING?
NOPE. DID SOMETHING HAPPEN?
YOU KNOW, THE USUAL. STOCK MARKET'S UP AND DOWN, SOMEONE GOT MURDERED, TASTY FISH IN SEASON, BUT...
...IT JUST FEELS LIKE THE WORLD IS BALANCED ON THIS THIN LINE.
HUH?
I MEAN, WHAT THE HELL AM I DOING MESSING AROUND...
...WITH THESE PART-TIME JOBS?
RIGHT NOW, I'M AT THE ZOO TO RELAX AND WATCH THE CUTE ANIMALS...
...BUT ACTUALLY, IT'S THIS TOTALLY UNNATURAL ENVIRONMENT WHERE ANIMALS ARE KEPT PRISONER.
AND WE'RE RIGHT IN THE MIDDLE OF IT!

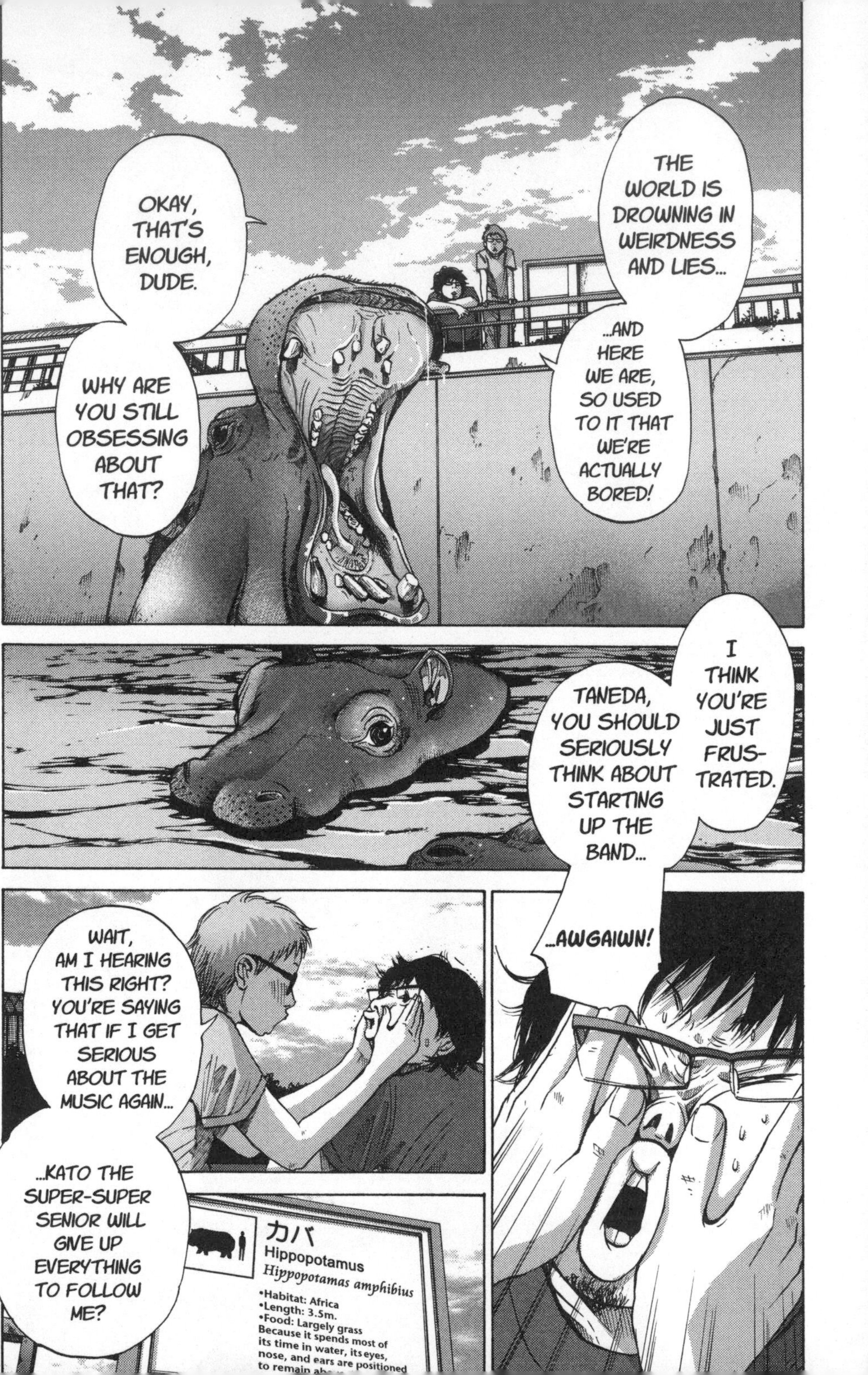
THE WORLD IS DROWNING IN WEIRDNESS AND LIES...
...AND HERE WE ARE, SO USED TO IT THAT WE'RE ACTUALLY BORED!
OKAY, THAT'S ENOUGH, DUDE.
WHY ARE YOU STILL OBSESSING ABOUT THAT?
I THINK YOU'RE JUST FRUS-TRATED.
TANEDA, YOU SHOULD SERIOUSLY THINK ABOUT STARTING UP THE BAND...
...AWGAIWN!
WAIT, AM I HEARING THIS RIGHT? YOU'RE SAYING THAT IF I GET SERIOUS ABOUT THE MUSIC AGAIN...
...KATO THE SUPER-SUPER SENIOR WILL GIVE UP EVERYTHING TO FOLLOW ME?
カバ
Hippopotamus
Hippopotamas amphibius
•Habitat: Africa
•Length: 3.5m.
•Food: Largely grass
Because it spends most of its time in water, its eyes, nose, and ears are positioned

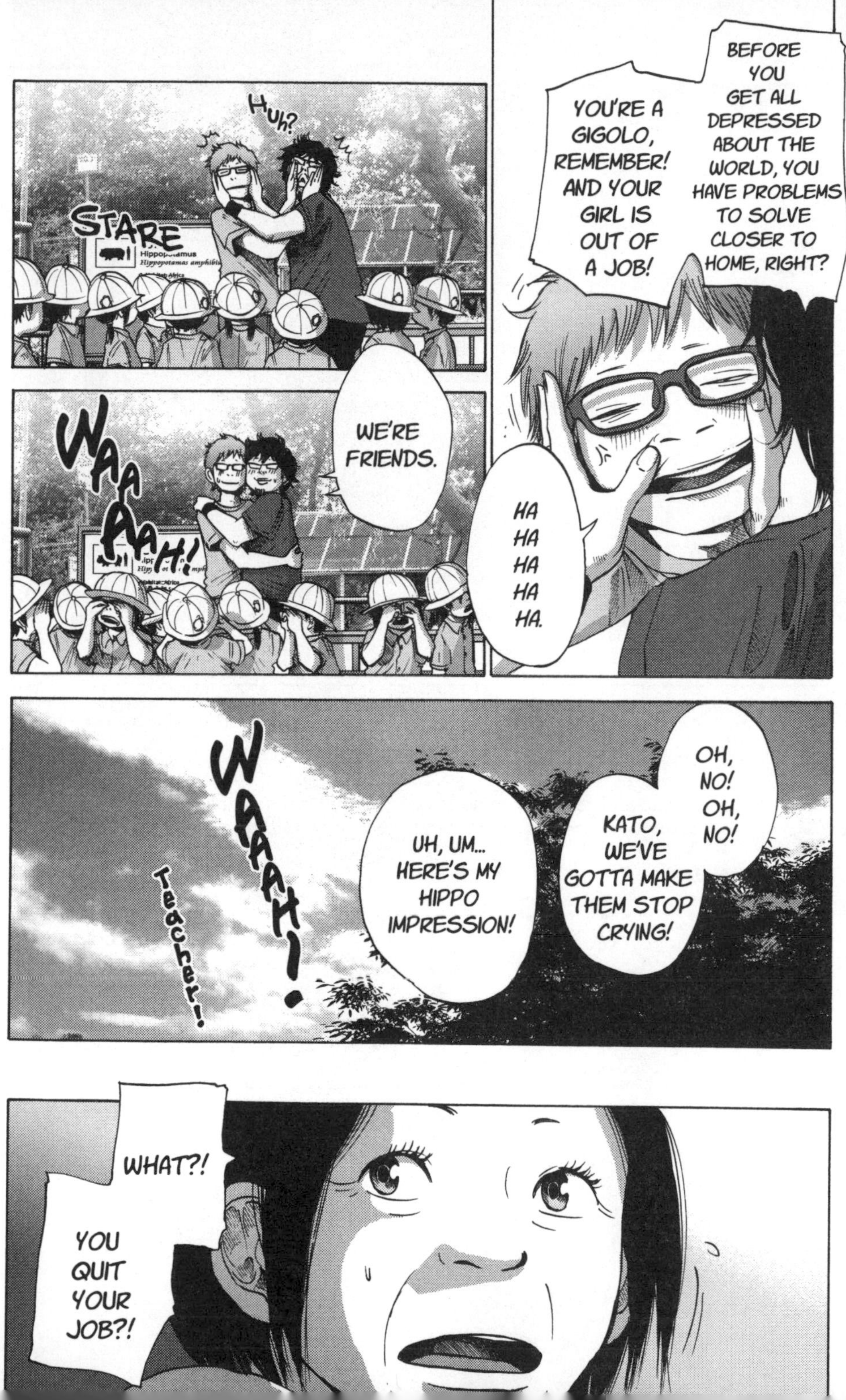

BEFORE YOU GET ALL DEPRESSED ABOUT THE WORLD, YOU HAVE PROBLEMS TO SOLVE CLOSER TO HOME, RIGHT?
YOU'RE A GIGOLO, REMEMBER! AND YOUR GIRL IS OUT OF A JOB!
HA HA HA HA HA.
Huh?
STARE
WE'RE FRIENDS.
WAAAAAH!
OH, NO! OH, NO!
KATO, WE'VE GOTTA MAKE THEM STOP CRYING!
UH, UM... HERE'S MY HIPPO IMPRESSION!
WAAAAH!
Teacher!
WHAT?!
YOU QUIT YOUR JOB?!

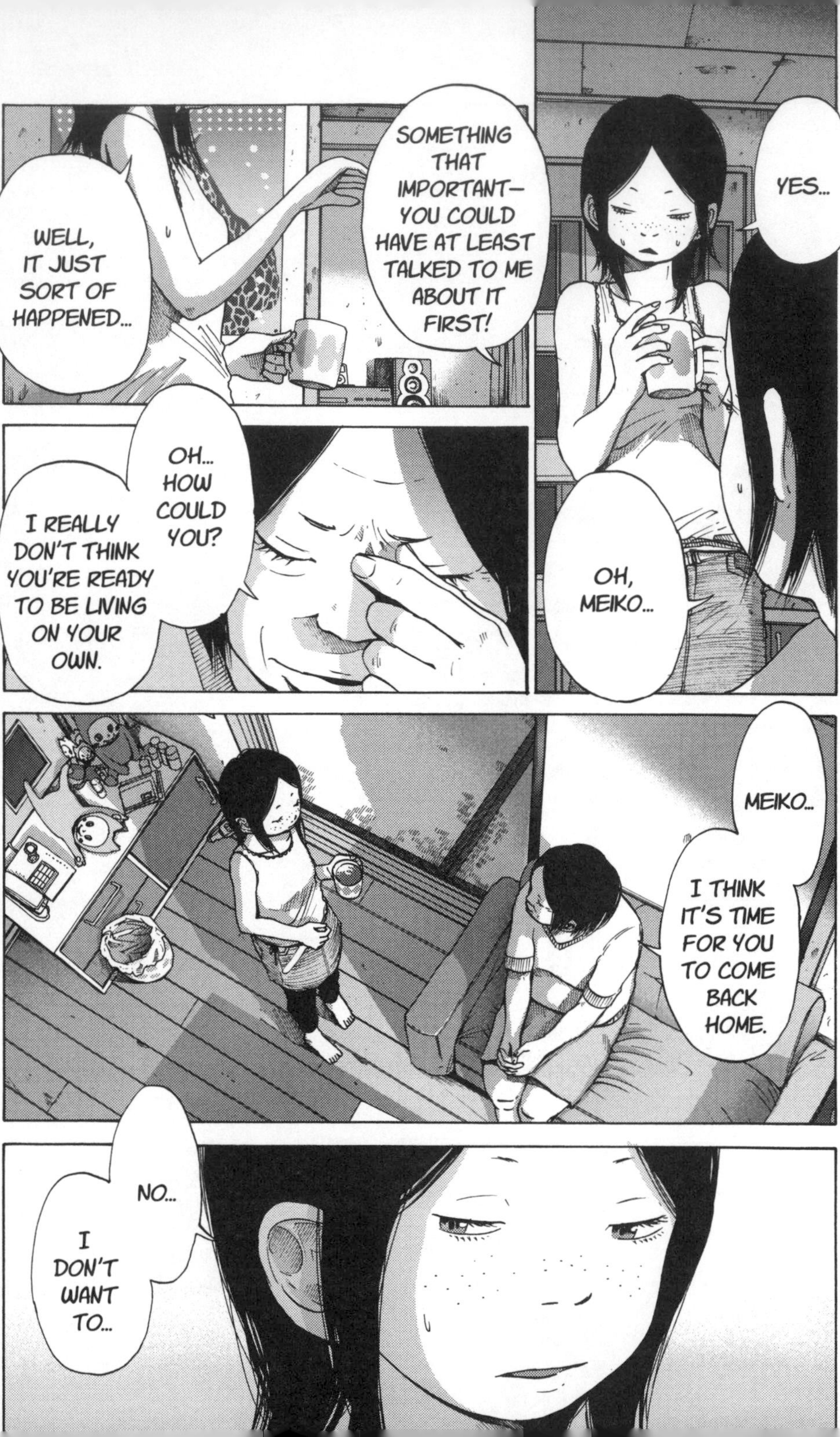
YES...
OH, MEIKO...
SOMETHING THAT IMPORTANT— YOU COULD HAVE AT LEAST TALKED TO ME ABOUT IT FIRST!
WELL, IT JUST SORT OF HAPPENED...
OH... HOW COULD YOU?
I REALLY DON'T THINK YOU'RE READY TO BE LIVING ON YOUR OWN.
MEIKO...
I THINK IT'S TIME FOR YOU TO COME BACK HOME.
NO...
I DON'T WANT TO...

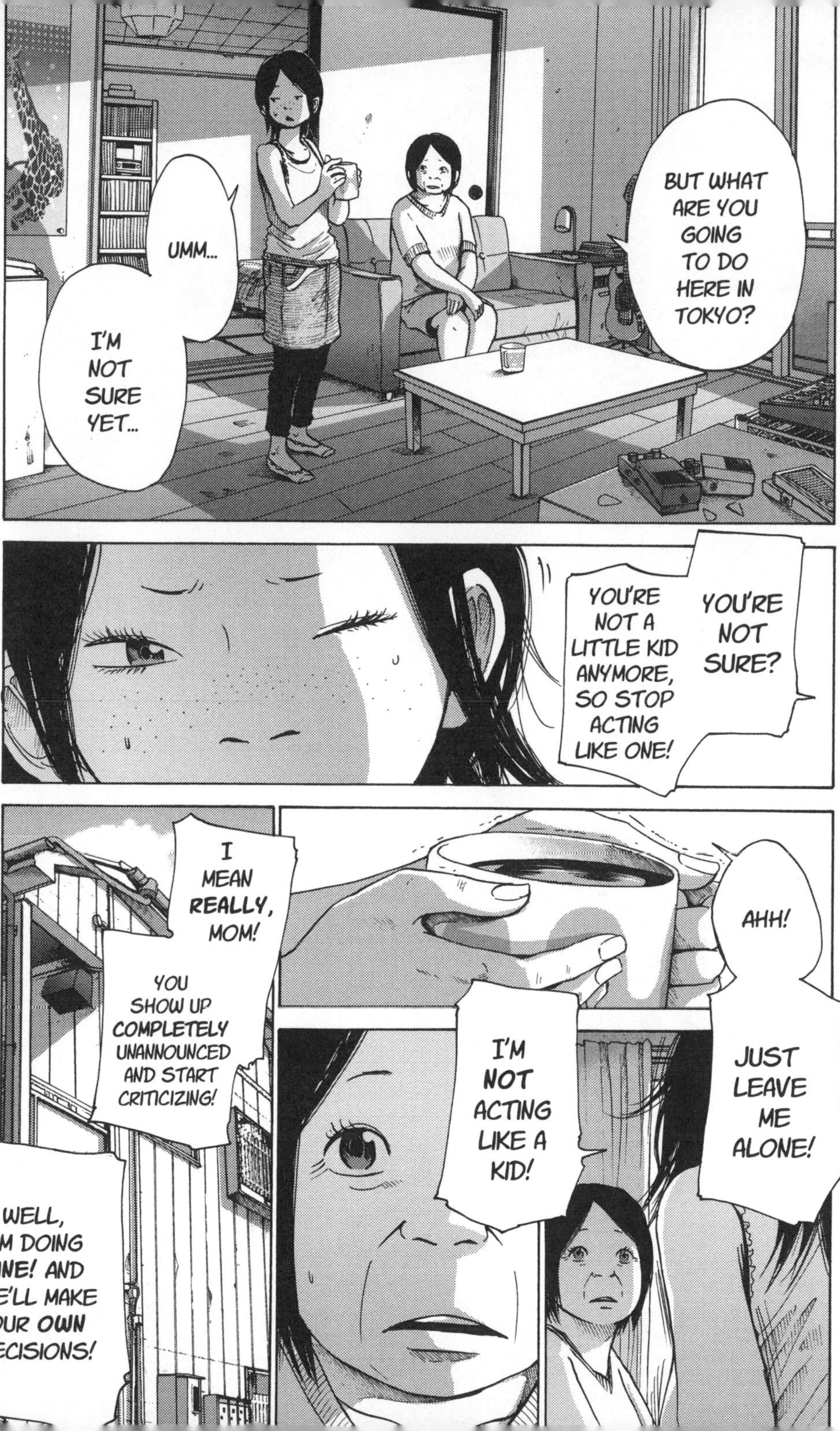
BUT WHAT ARE YOU GOING TO DO HERE IN TOKYO?
UMM...
I'M NOT SURE YET...
YOU'RE NOT SURE?
YOU'RE NOT A LITTLE KID ANYMORE, SO STOP ACTING LIKE ONE!
AHH!
JUST LEAVE ME ALONE!
I'M NOT ACTING LIKE A KID!
I MEAN REALLY, MOM!
YOU SHOW UP COMPLETELY UNANNOUNCED AND START CRITICIZING!
WELL, I'M DOING FINE! AND WE'LL MAKE OUR OWN DECISIONS!

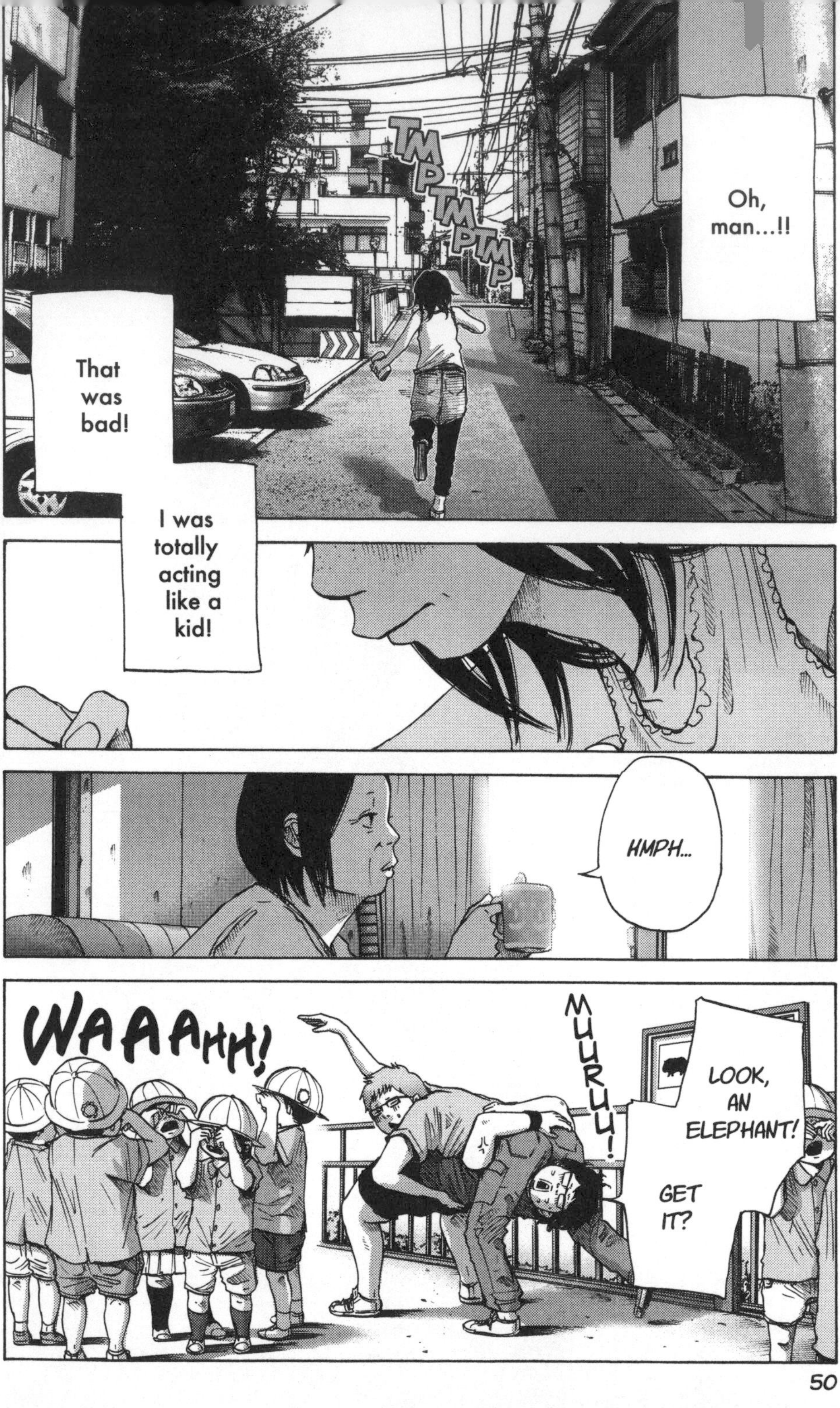
Oh, man...!!
TMPTMPTMPTMP
That was bad!
I was totally acting like a kid!
HMPH...
LOOK, AN ELEPHANT!
GET IT?
MUURUUU!
WAAAHH!

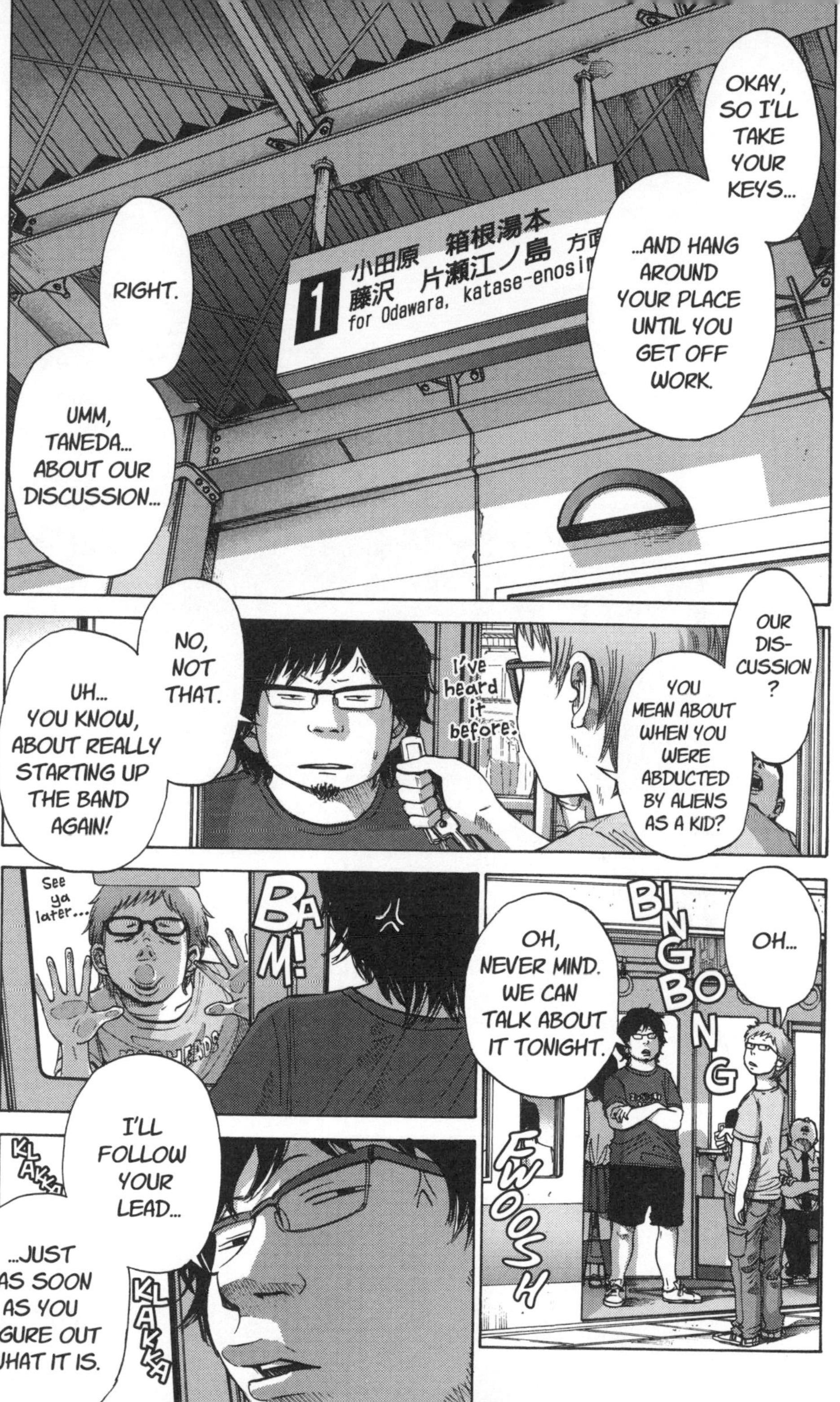
OKAY, SO I'LL TAKE YOUR KEYS...
...AND HANG AROUND YOUR PLACE UNTIL YOU GET OFF WORK.
1 小田原 箱根湯本
藤沢 片瀬江ノ島 方面
for Odawara, katase-enosi
RIGHT.
UMM, TANEDA... ABOUT OUR DISCUSSION...
OUR DIS-CUSSION?
YOU MEAN ABOUT WHEN YOU WERE ABDUCTED BY ALIENS AS A KID?
I've heard it before.
NO, NOT THAT.
UH... YOU KNOW, ABOUT REALLY STARTING UP THE BAND AGAIN!
OH...
BING BONG
OH, NEVER MIND. WE CAN TALK ABOUT IT TONIGHT.
FWOOSH
BAM!
See ya later...
KLAKKA
I'LL FOLLOW YOUR LEAD...
...JUST AS SOON AS YOU FIGURE OUT WHAT IT IS.
KLAKKA

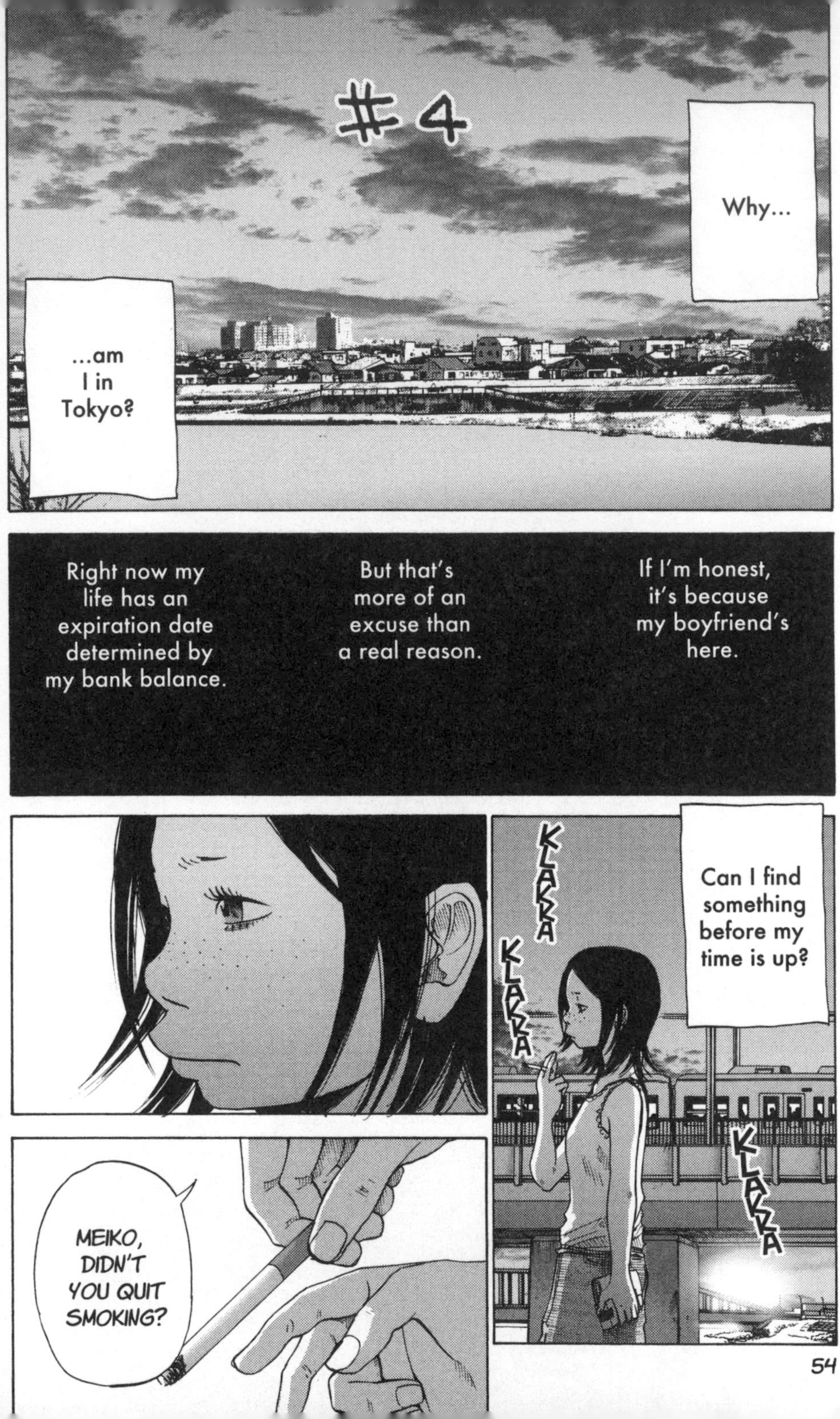
#4
Why...
...am I in Tokyo?
Right now my life has an expiration date determined by my bank balance.
But that's more of an excuse than a real reason.
If I'm honest, it's because my boyfriend's here.
KLAKKA
KLAKKA
Can I find something before my time is up?
KLAKKA
MEIKO, DIDN'T YOU QUIT SMOKING?

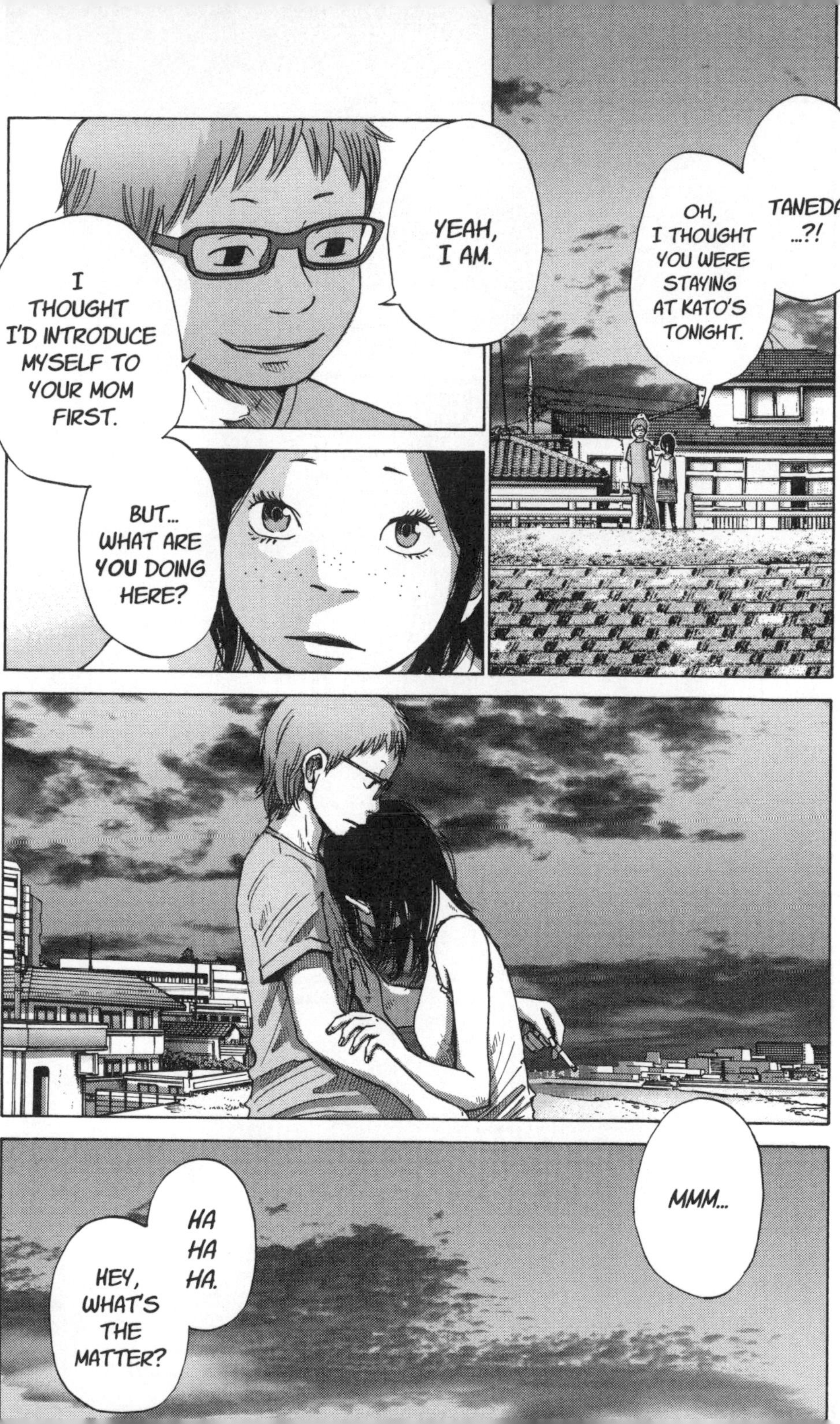
TANEDA ...?!
OH, I THOUGHT YOU WERE STAYING AT KATO'S TONIGHT.
YEAH, I AM.
I THOUGHT I'D INTRODUCE MYSELF TO YOUR MOM FIRST.
BUT... WHAT ARE YOU DOING HERE?
MMM...
HA HA HA.
HEY, WHAT'S THE MATTER?

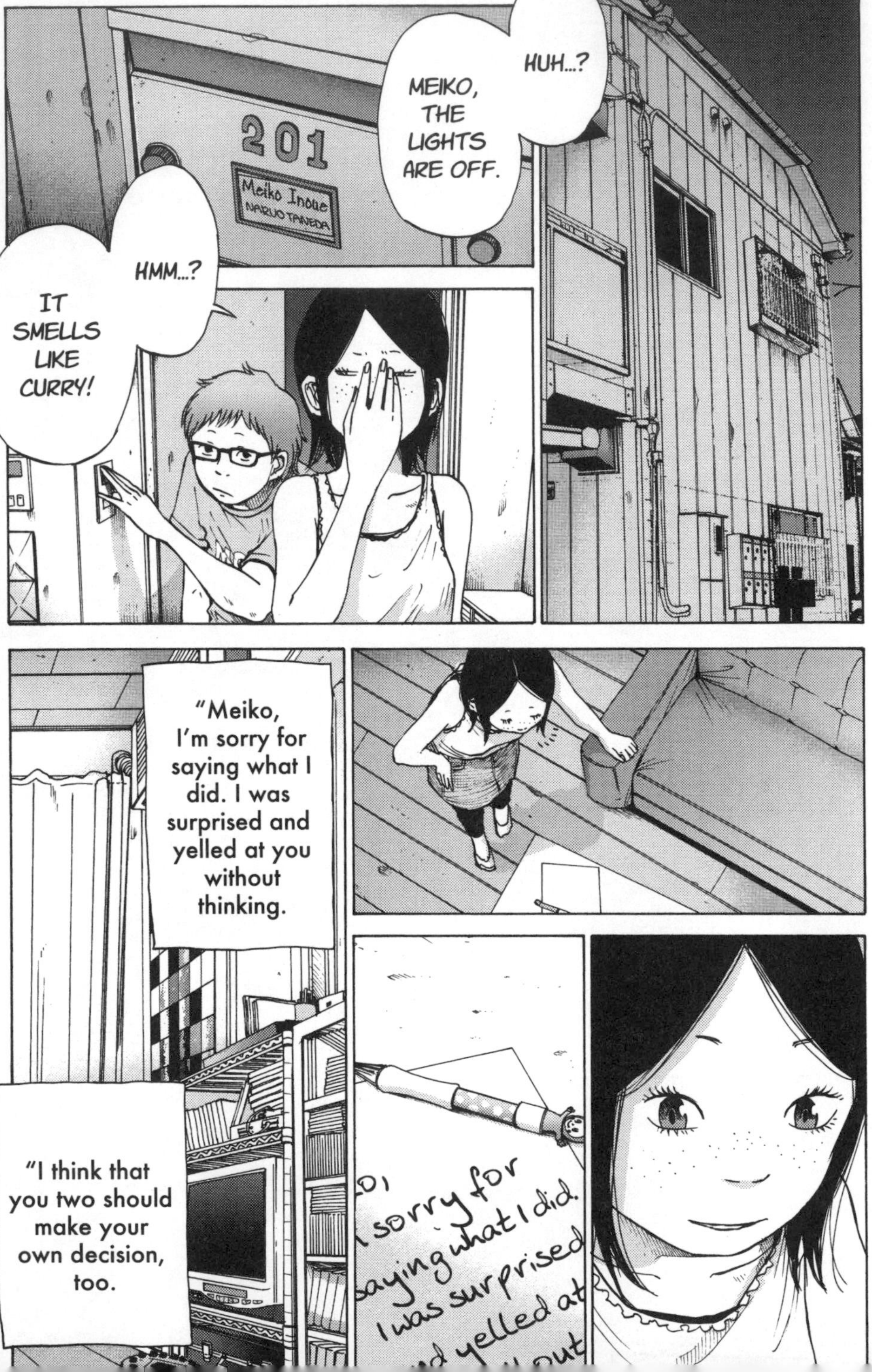
HUH...?
MEIKO, THE LIGHTS ARE OFF.
201
Meiko Inoue
NARUO TANEDA
HMM...?
IT SMELLS LIKE CURRY!
sorry for
saying what I did.
I was surprised
yelled at
"Meiko, I'm sorry for saying what I did. I was surprised and yelled at you without thinking.
"I think that you two should make your own decision, too.

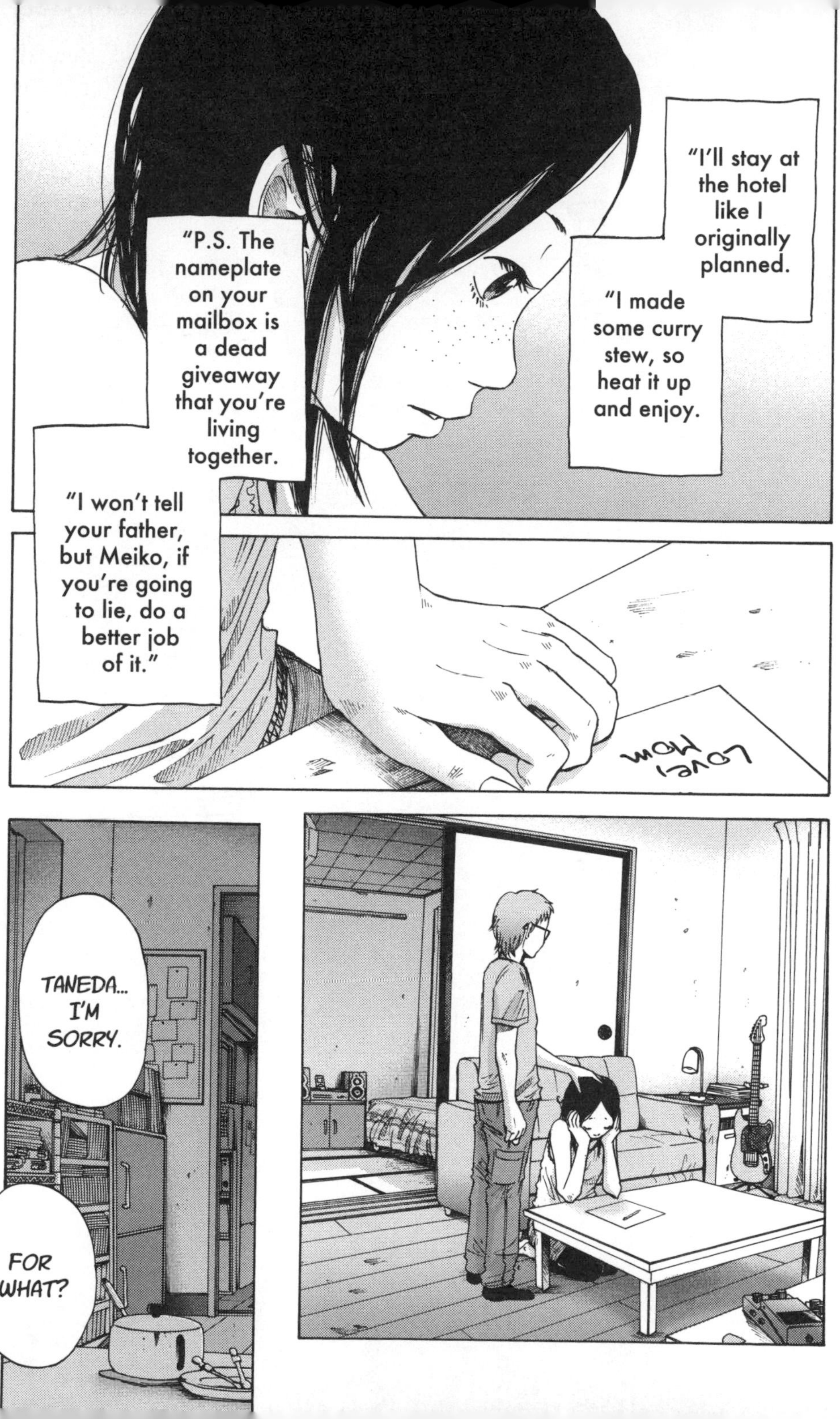
"I'll stay at the hotel like I originally planned.
"I made some curry stew, so heat it up and enjoy.
"P.S. The nameplate on your mailbox is a dead giveaway that you're living together.
"I won't tell your father, but Meiko, if you're going to lie, do a better job of it."
LOVE! MOM
TANEDA... I'M SORRY.
FOR WHAT?

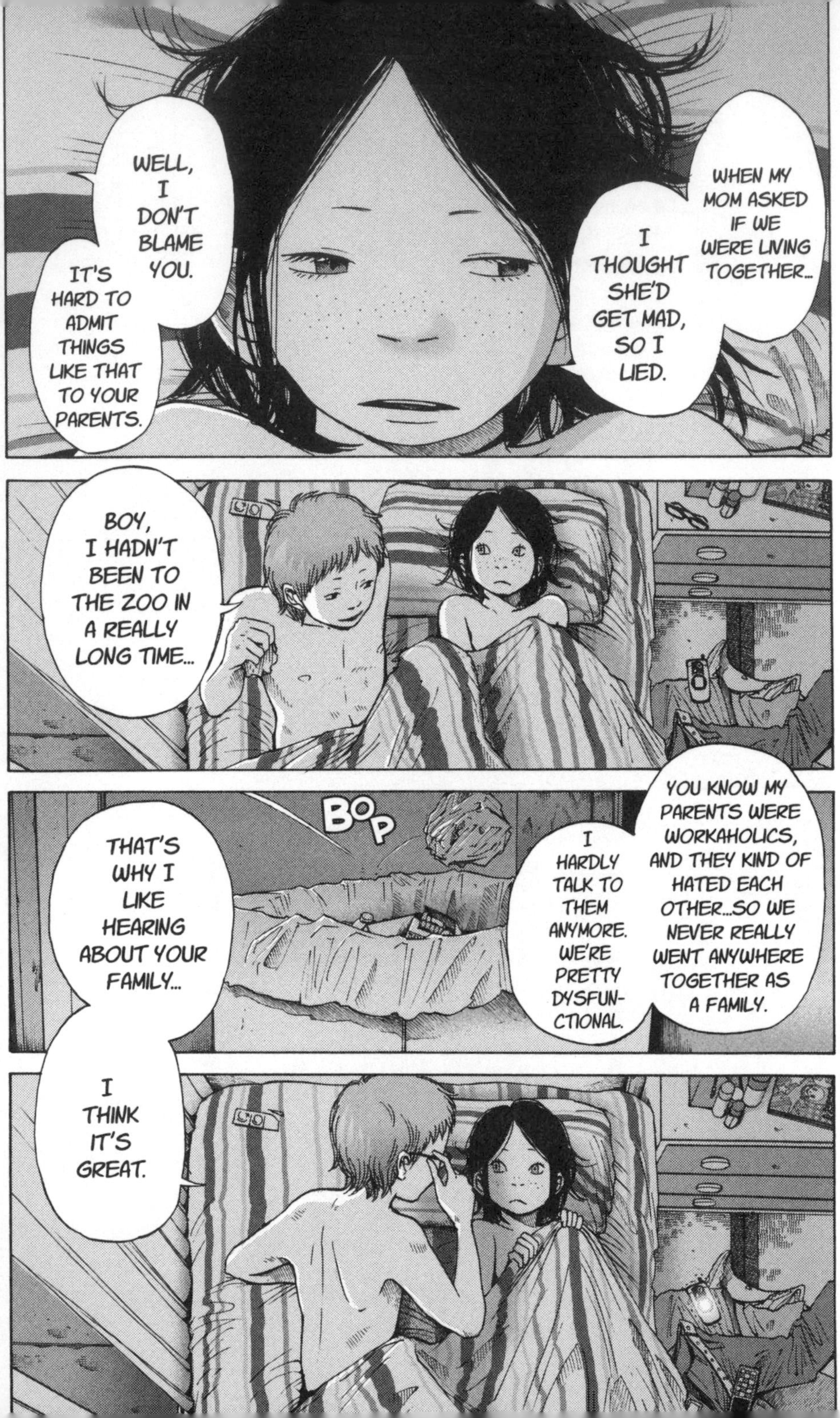
WHEN MY MOM ASKED IF WE WERE LIVING TOGETHER...
I THOUGHT SHE'D GET MAD, SO I LIED.
WELL, I DON'T BLAME YOU.
IT'S HARD TO ADMIT THINGS LIKE THAT TO YOUR PARENTS.
BOY, I HADN'T BEEN TO THE ZOO IN A REALLY LONG TIME...
YOU KNOW MY PARENTS WERE WORKAHOLICS, AND THEY KIND OF HATED EACH OTHER...SO WE NEVER REALLY WENT ANYWHERE TOGETHER AS A FAMILY.
I HARDLY TALK TO THEM ANYMORE. WE'RE PRETTY DYSFUNCTIONAL.
BOP
THAT'S WHY I LIKE HEARING ABOUT YOUR FAMILY...
I THINK IT'S GREAT.

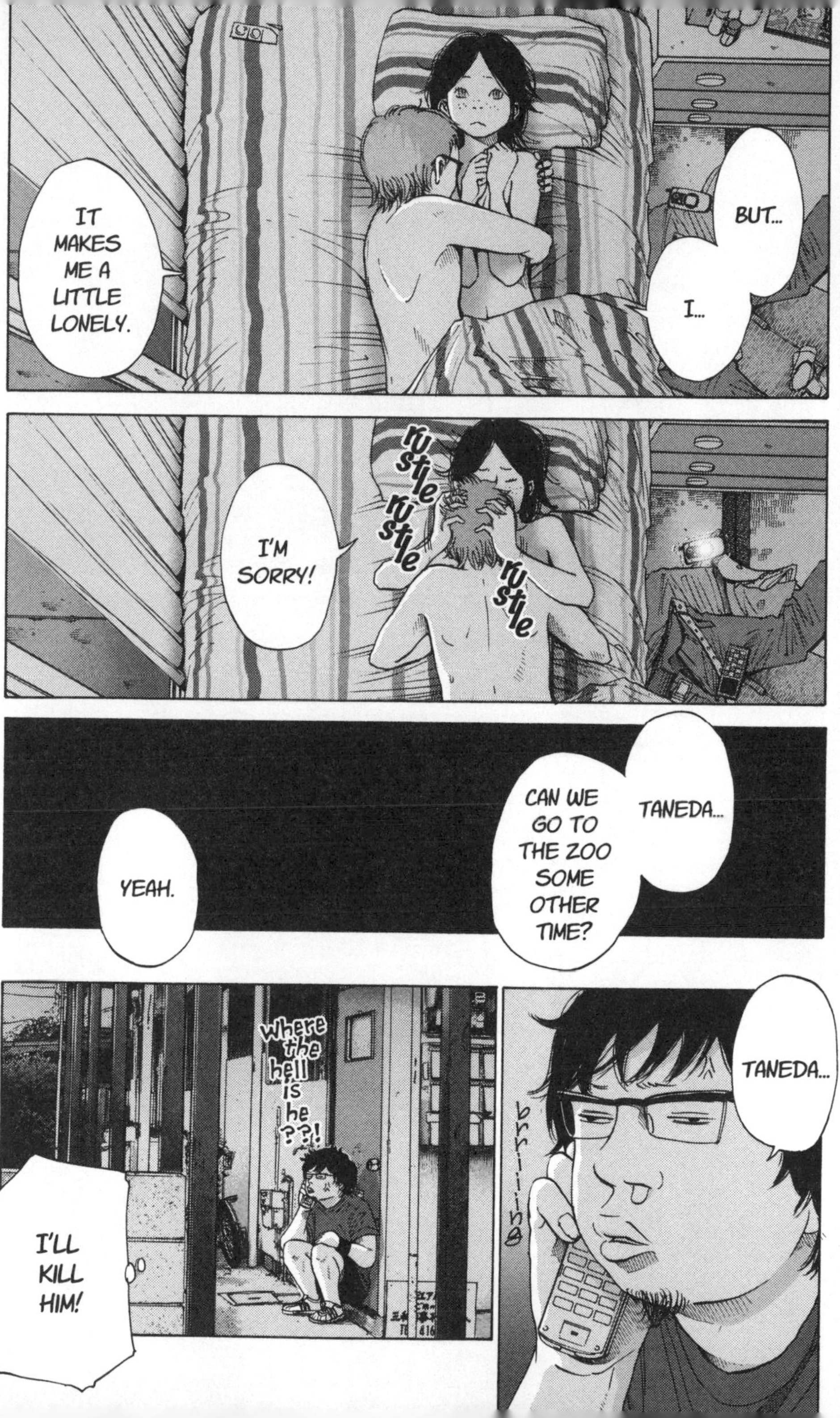
BUT...
I...
IT MAKES ME A LITTLE LONELY.
rustle
rustle
rustle
I'M SORRY!
TANEDA...
CAN WE GO TO THE ZOO SOME OTHER TIME?
YEAH.
TANEDA...
brriing
where the hell is he ??!
I'LL KILL HIM!

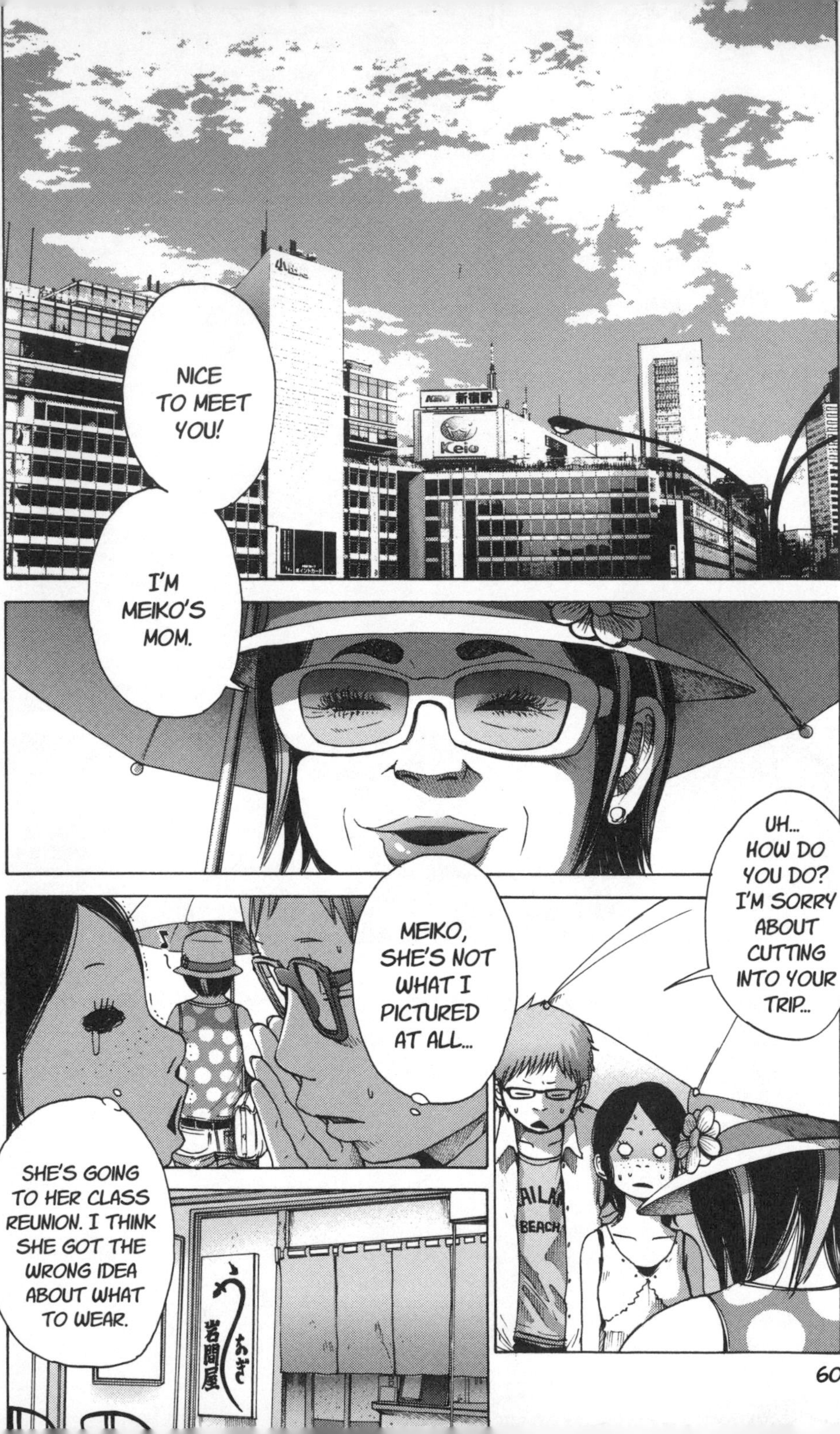
NICE TO MEET YOU!
I'M MEIKO'S MOM.
新宿駅
Keio
UH... HOW DO YOU DO? I'M SORRY ABOUT CUTTING INTO YOUR TRIP...
MEIKO, SHE'S NOT WHAT I PICTURED AT ALL...
SHE'S GOING TO HER CLASS REUNION. I THINK SHE GOT THE WRONG IDEA ABOUT WHAT TO WEAR.
岩間屋

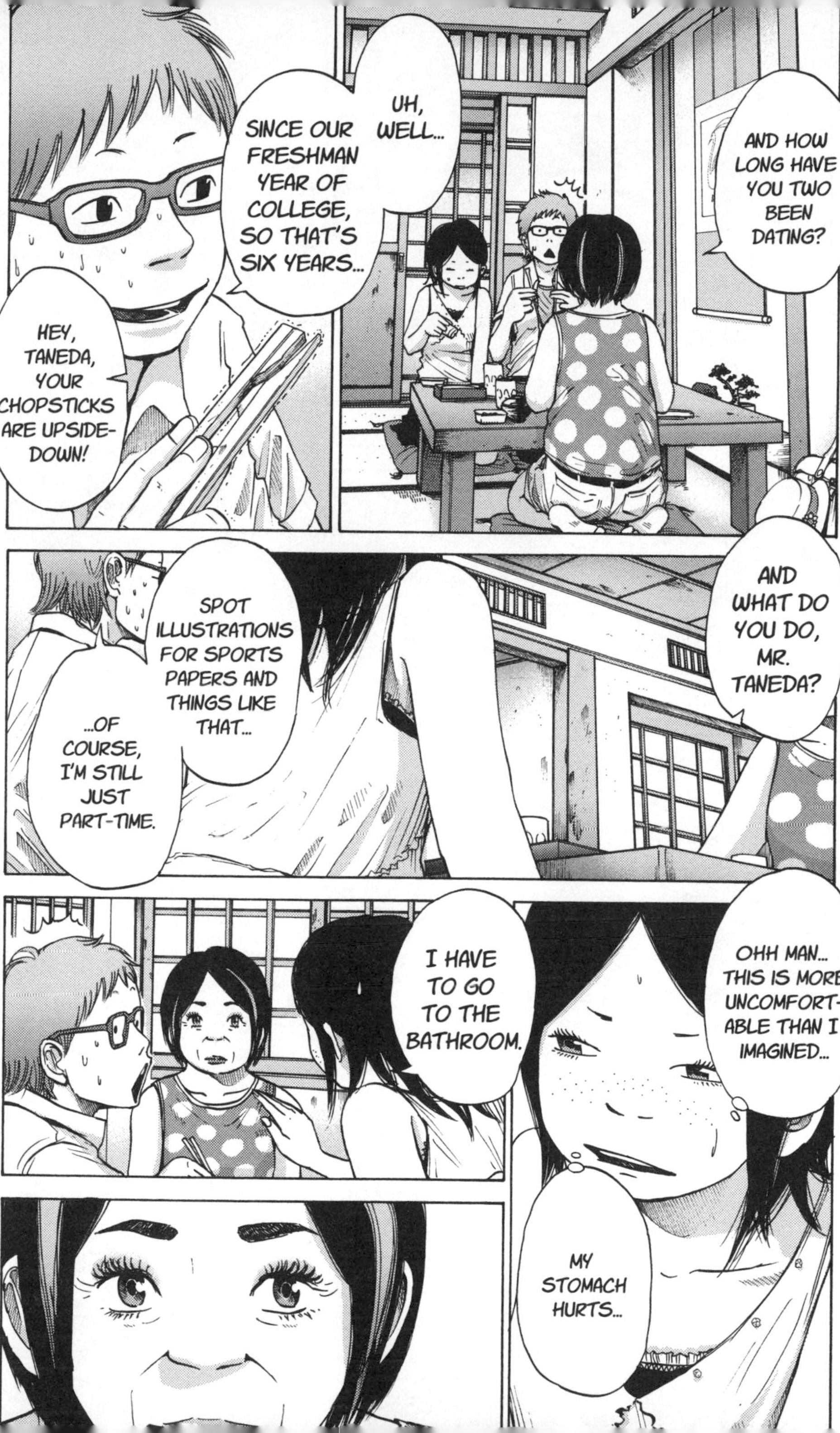
AND HOW LONG HAVE YOU TWO BEEN DATING?
UH, WELL...
SINCE OUR FRESHMAN YEAR OF COLLEGE, SO THAT'S SIX YEARS...
HEY, TANEDA, YOUR CHOPSTICKS ARE UPSIDE-DOWN!
AND WHAT DO YOU DO, MR. TANEDA?
SPOT ILLUSTRATIONS FOR SPORTS PAPERS AND THINGS LIKE THAT...
...OF COURSE, I'M STILL JUST PART-TIME.
OHH MAN... THIS IS MORE UNCOMFORT-ABLE THAN I IMAGINED...
MY STOMACH HURTS...
I HAVE TO GO TO THE BATHROOM.

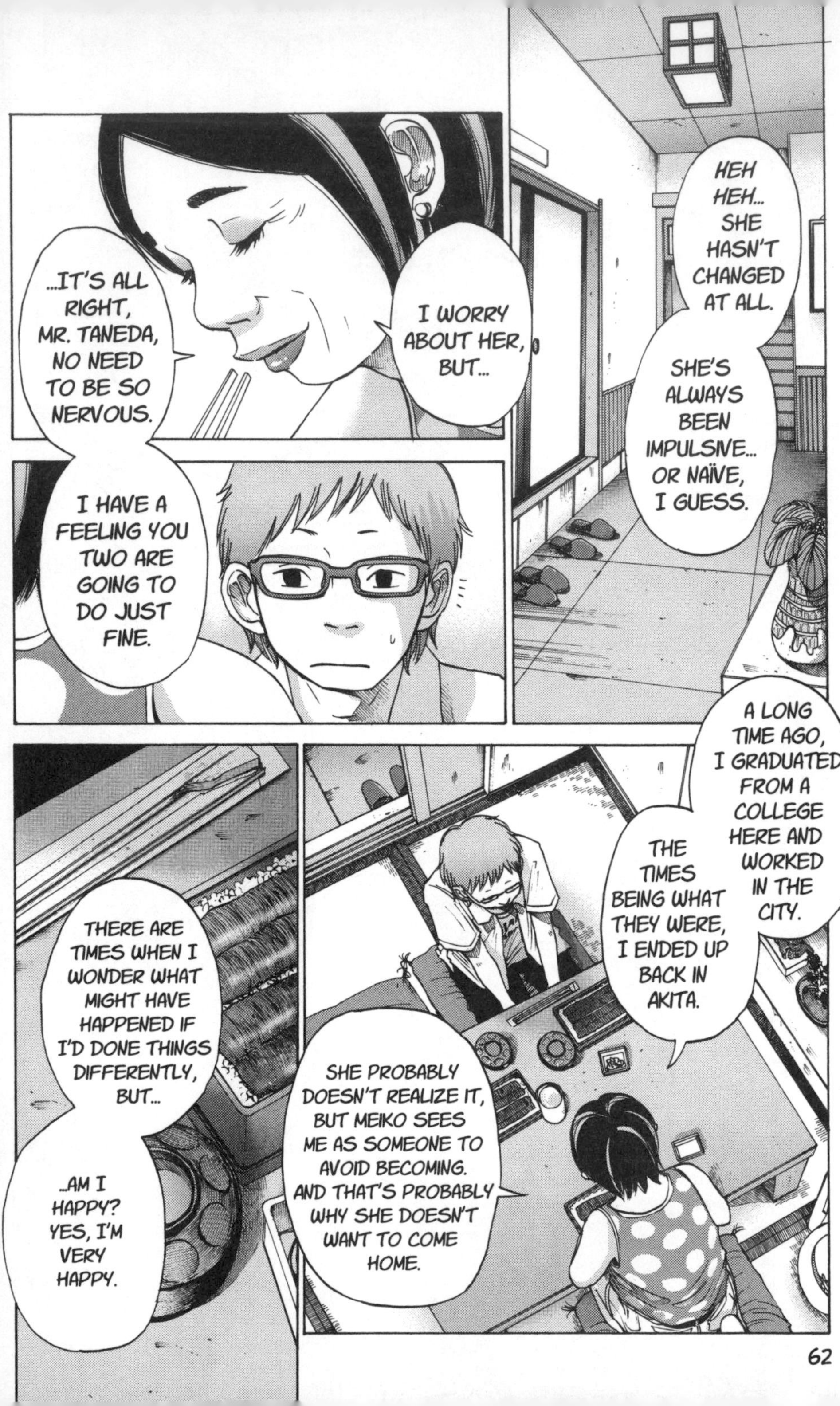
HEH HEH... SHE HASN'T CHANGED AT ALL.
SHE'S ALWAYS BEEN IMPULSIVE... OR NAÏVE, I GUESS.
I WORRY ABOUT HER, BUT...
...IT'S ALL RIGHT, MR. TANEDA, NO NEED TO BE SO NERVOUS.
I HAVE A FEELING YOU TWO ARE GOING TO DO JUST FINE.
A LONG TIME AGO, I GRADUATED FROM A COLLEGE HERE AND WORKED IN THE CITY.
THE TIMES BEING WHAT THEY WERE, I ENDED UP BACK IN AKITA.
SHE PROBABLY DOESN'T REALIZE IT, BUT MEIKO SEES ME AS SOMEONE TO AVOID BECOMING. AND THAT'S PROBABLY WHY SHE DOESN'T WANT TO COME HOME.
THERE ARE TIMES WHEN I WONDER WHAT MIGHT HAVE HAPPENED IF I'D DONE THINGS DIFFERENTLY, BUT...
...AM I HAPPY? YES, I'M VERY HAPPY.

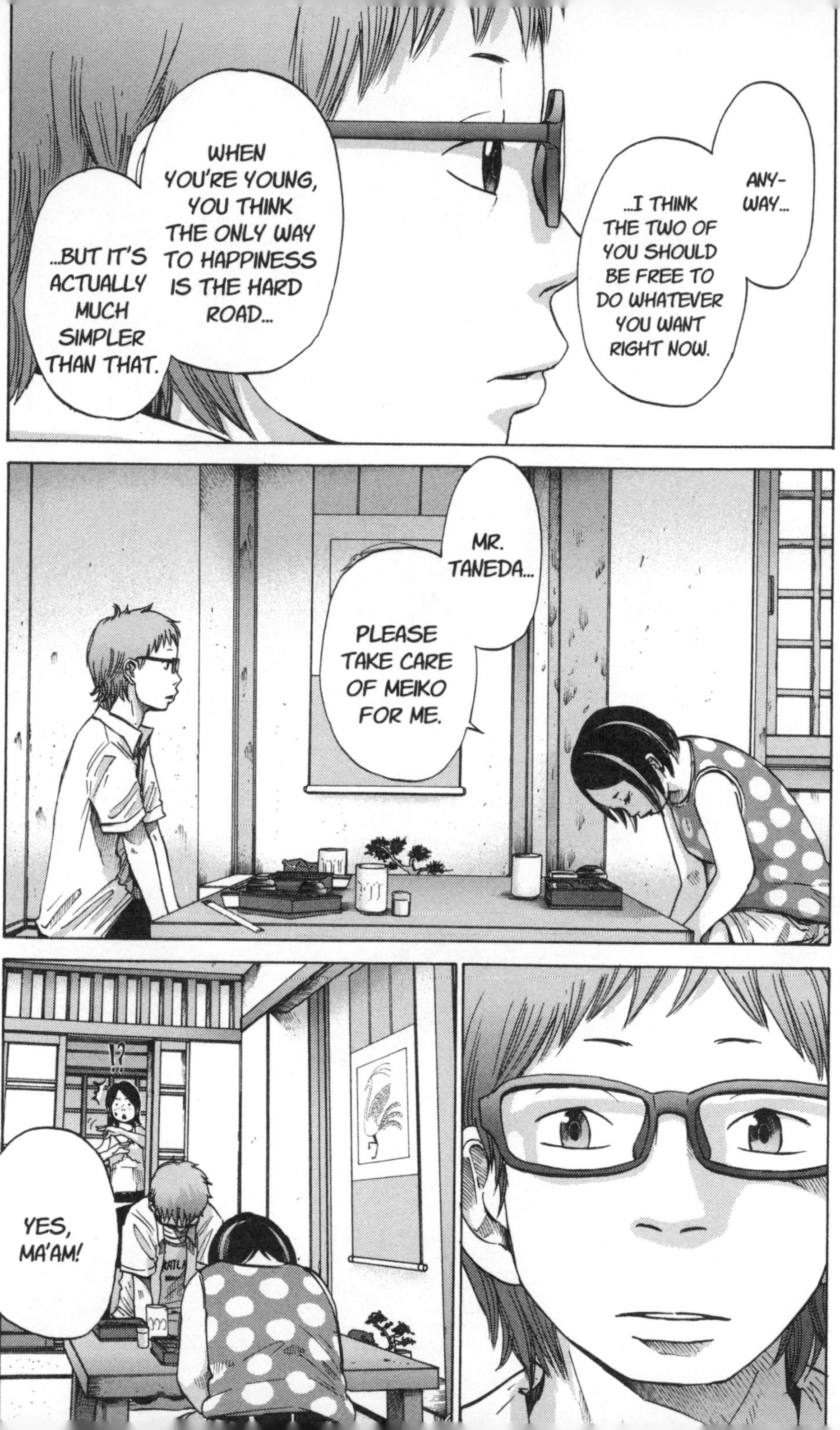
ANY-WAY...
...I THINK THE TWO OF YOU SHOULD BE FREE TO DO WHATEVER YOU WANT RIGHT NOW.
WHEN YOU'RE YOUNG, YOU THINK THE ONLY WAY TO HAPPINESS IS THE HARD ROAD...
...BUT IT'S ACTUALLY MUCH SIMPLER THAN THAT.
MR. TANEDA...
PLEASE TAKE CARE OF MEIKO FOR ME.
!?
YES, MA'AM!

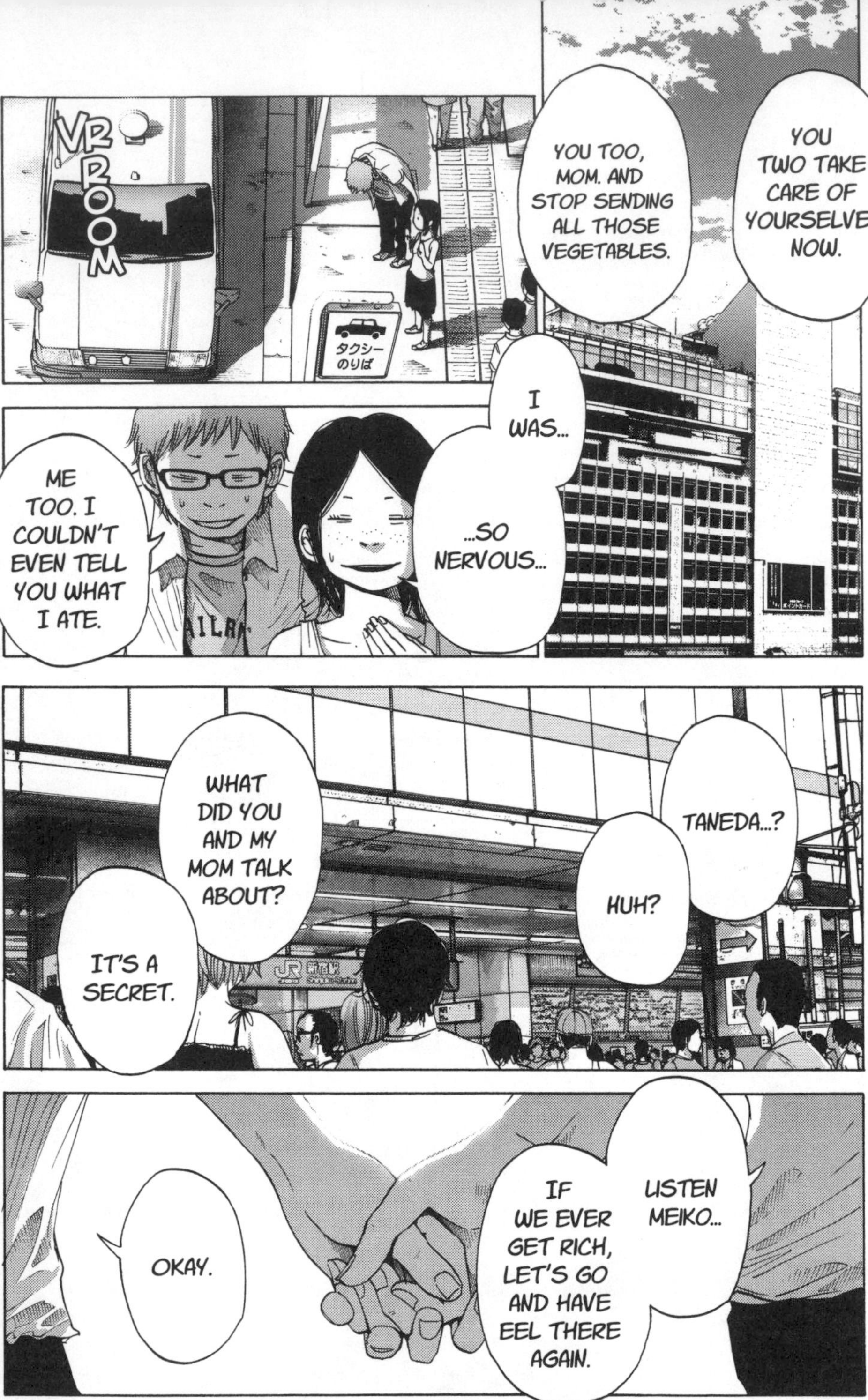
YOU TWO TAKE CARE OF YOURSELVES NOW.
YOU TOO, MOM. AND STOP SENDING ALL THOSE VEGETABLES.
VRROOM
タクシーのりば
I WAS...
...SO NERVOUS...
ME TOO. I COULDN'T EVEN TELL YOU WHAT I ATE.
TANEDA...?
HUH?
WHAT DID YOU AND MY MOM TALK ABOUT?
IT'S A SECRET.
LISTEN MEIKO...
IF WE EVER GET RICH, LET'S GO AND HAVE EEL THERE AGAIN.
OKAY.

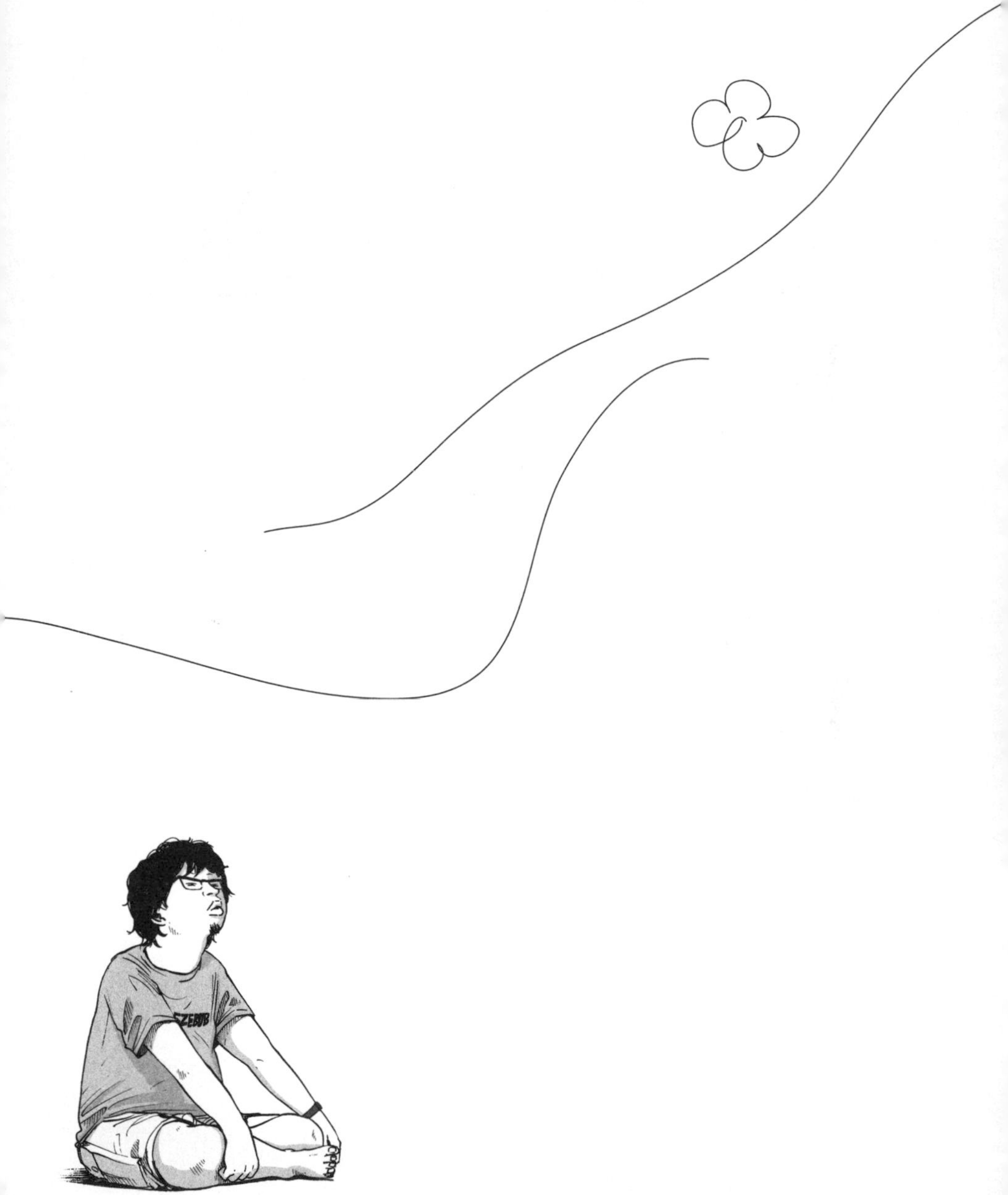

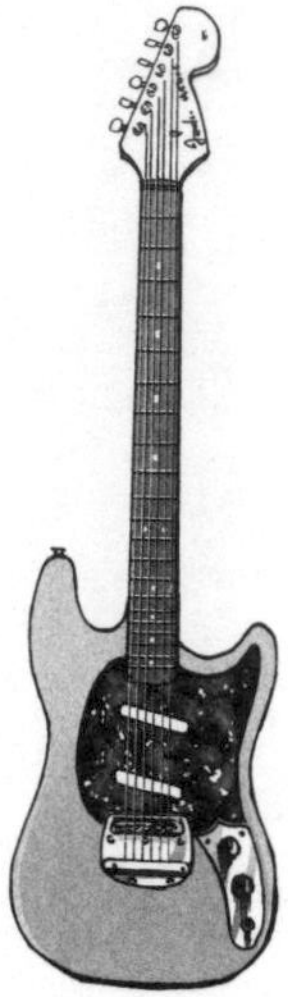

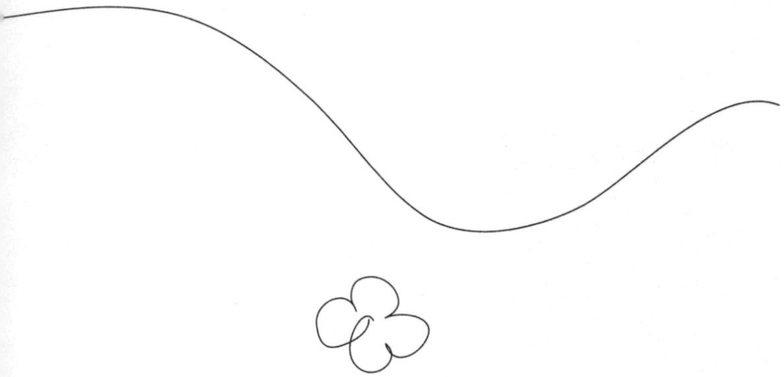

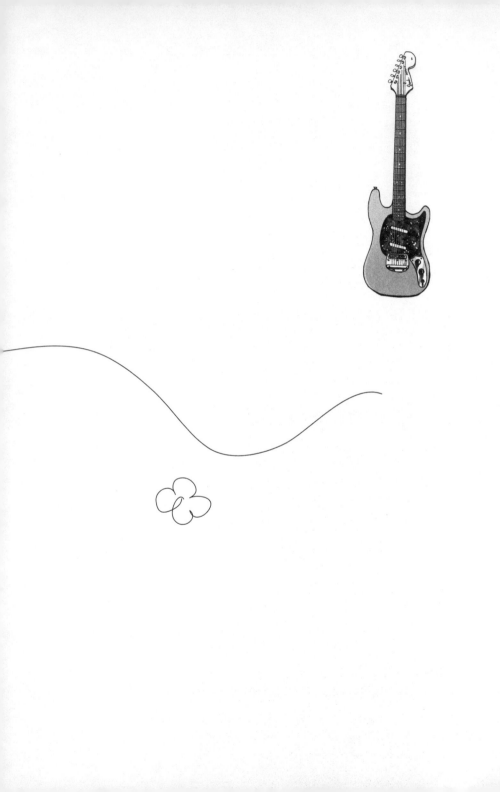

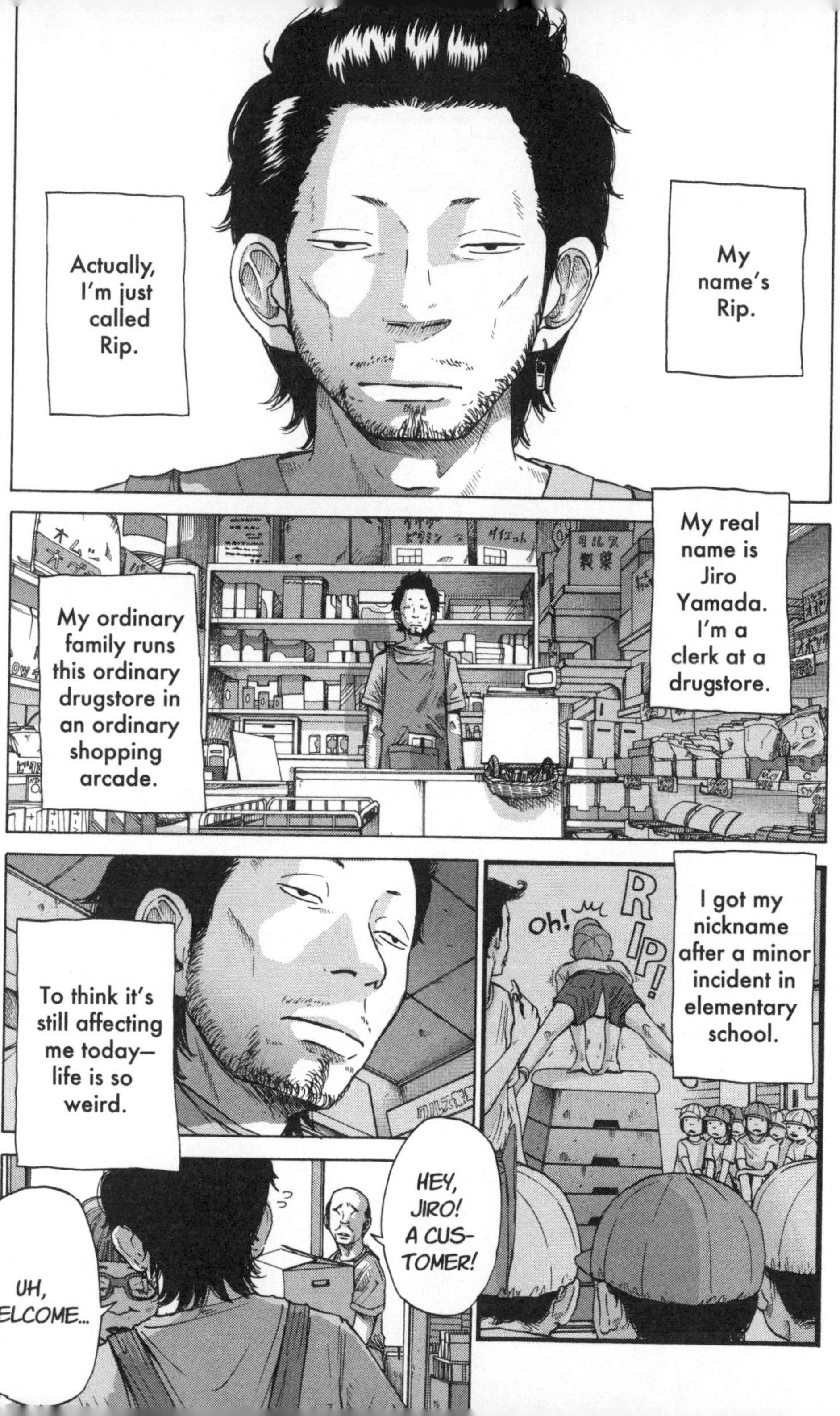

My name's Rip.
Actually, I'm just called Rip.
My real name is Jiro Yamada. I'm a clerk at a drugstore.
My ordinary family runs this ordinary drugstore in an ordinary shopping arcade.
I got my nickname after a minor incident in elementary school.
RIP!
Oh!
To think it's still affecting me today—life is so weird.
HEY, JIRO! A CUS-TOMER!
UH, WELCOME...

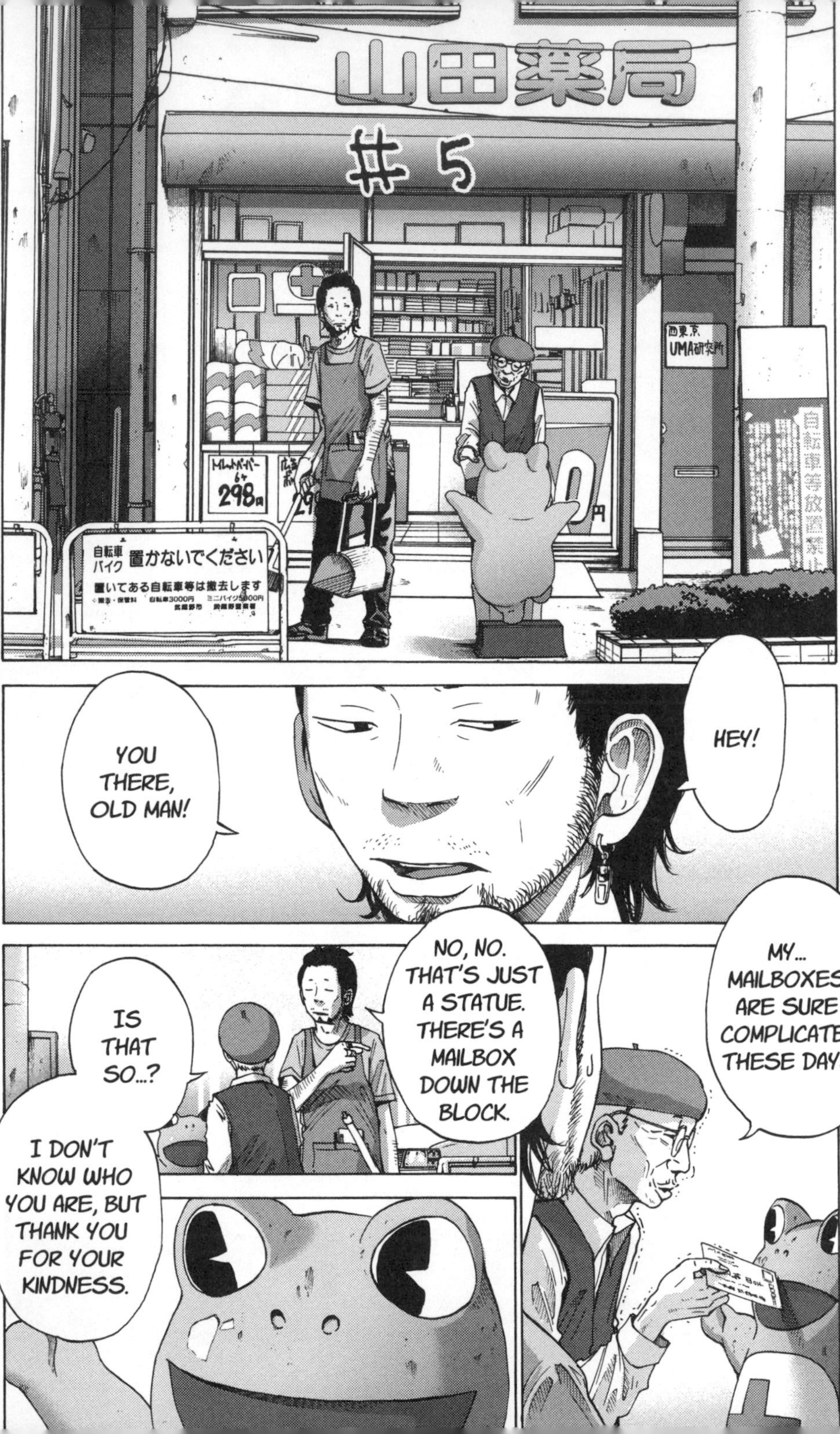
山田薬局
西東京 UMA研究所
298円
自転車 バイク 置かないでください
置いてある自転車等は撤去します
HEY!
YOU THERE, OLD MAN!
MY... MAILBOXES ARE SURE COMPLICATED THESE DAYS.
NO, NO. THAT'S JUST A STATUE. THERE'S A MAILBOX DOWN THE BLOCK.
IS THAT SO...?
I DON'T KNOW WHO YOU ARE, BUT THANK YOU FOR YOUR KINDNESS.

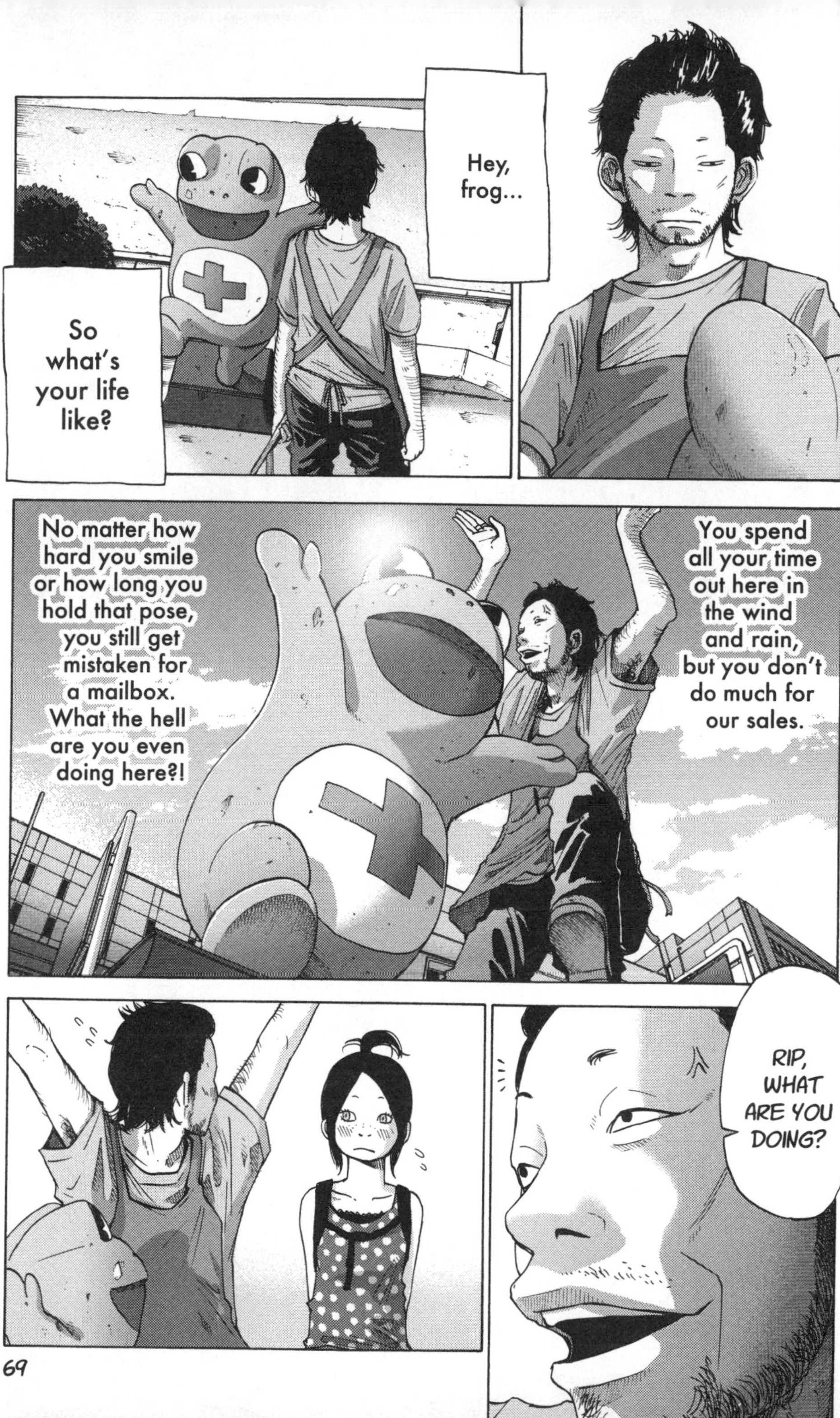
Hey, frog...
So what's your life like?
You spend all your time out here in the wind and rain, but you don't do much for our sales.
No matter how hard you smile or how long you hold that pose, you still get mistaken for a mailbox. What the hell are you even doing here?!
RIP, WHAT ARE YOU DOING?

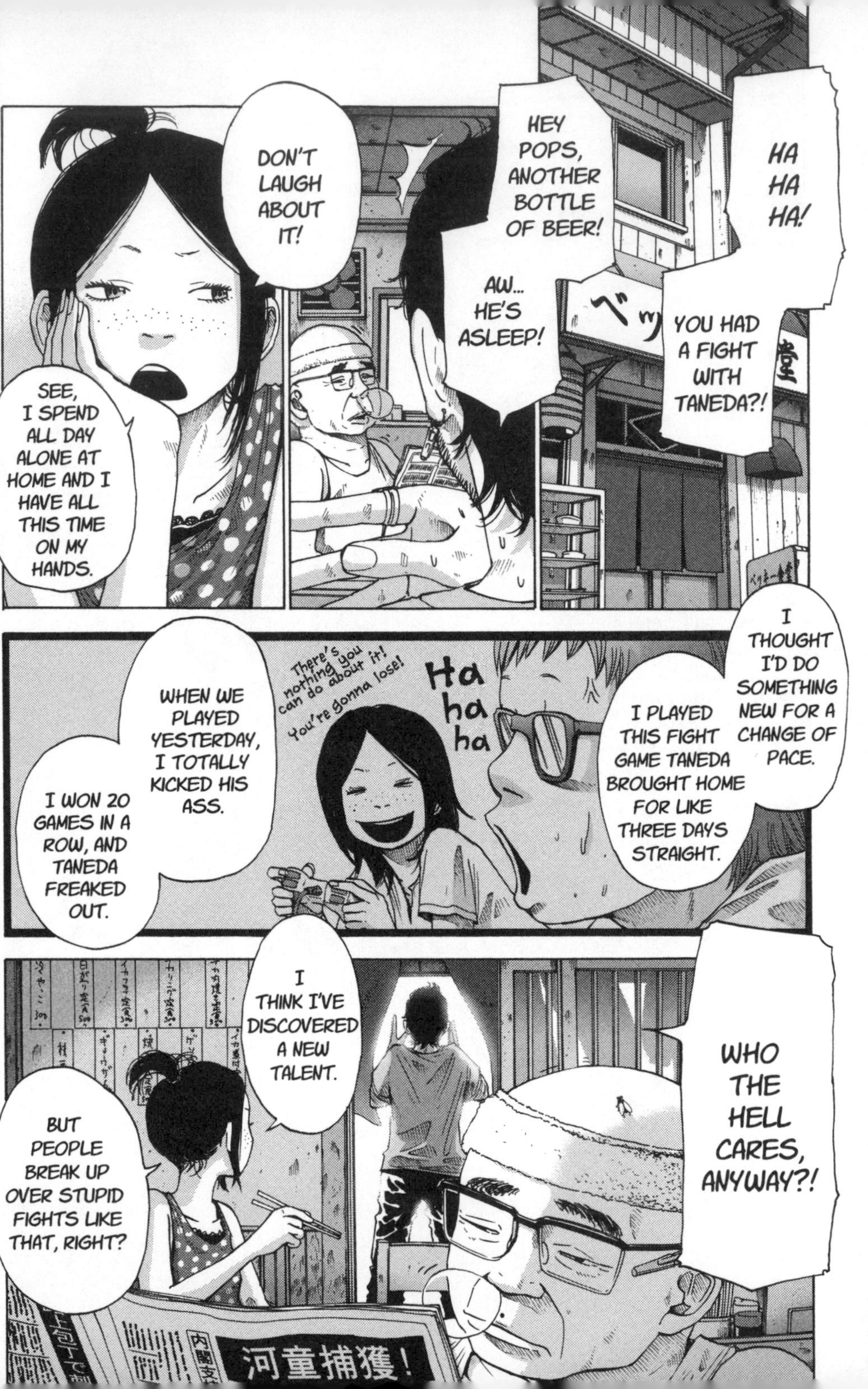
HA HA HA!
YOU HAD A FIGHT WITH TANEDA?!
HEY POPS, ANOTHER BOTTLE OF BEER!
AW... HE'S ASLEEP!
DON'T LAUGH ABOUT IT!
SEE, I SPEND ALL DAY ALONE AT HOME AND I HAVE ALL THIS TIME ON MY HANDS.
I THOUGHT I'D DO SOMETHING NEW FOR A CHANGE OF PACE.
I PLAYED THIS FIGHT GAME TANEDA BROUGHT HOME FOR LIKE THREE DAYS STRAIGHT.
Ha ha ha
There's nothing you can do about it! You're gonna lose!
WHEN WE PLAYED YESTERDAY, I TOTALLY KICKED HIS ASS.
I WON 20 GAMES IN A ROW, AND TANEDA FREAKED OUT.
WHO THE HELL CARES, ANYWAY?!
I THINK I'VE DISCOVERED A NEW TALENT.
BUT PEOPLE BREAK UP OVER STUPID FIGHTS LIKE THAT, RIGHT?
河童捕獲！

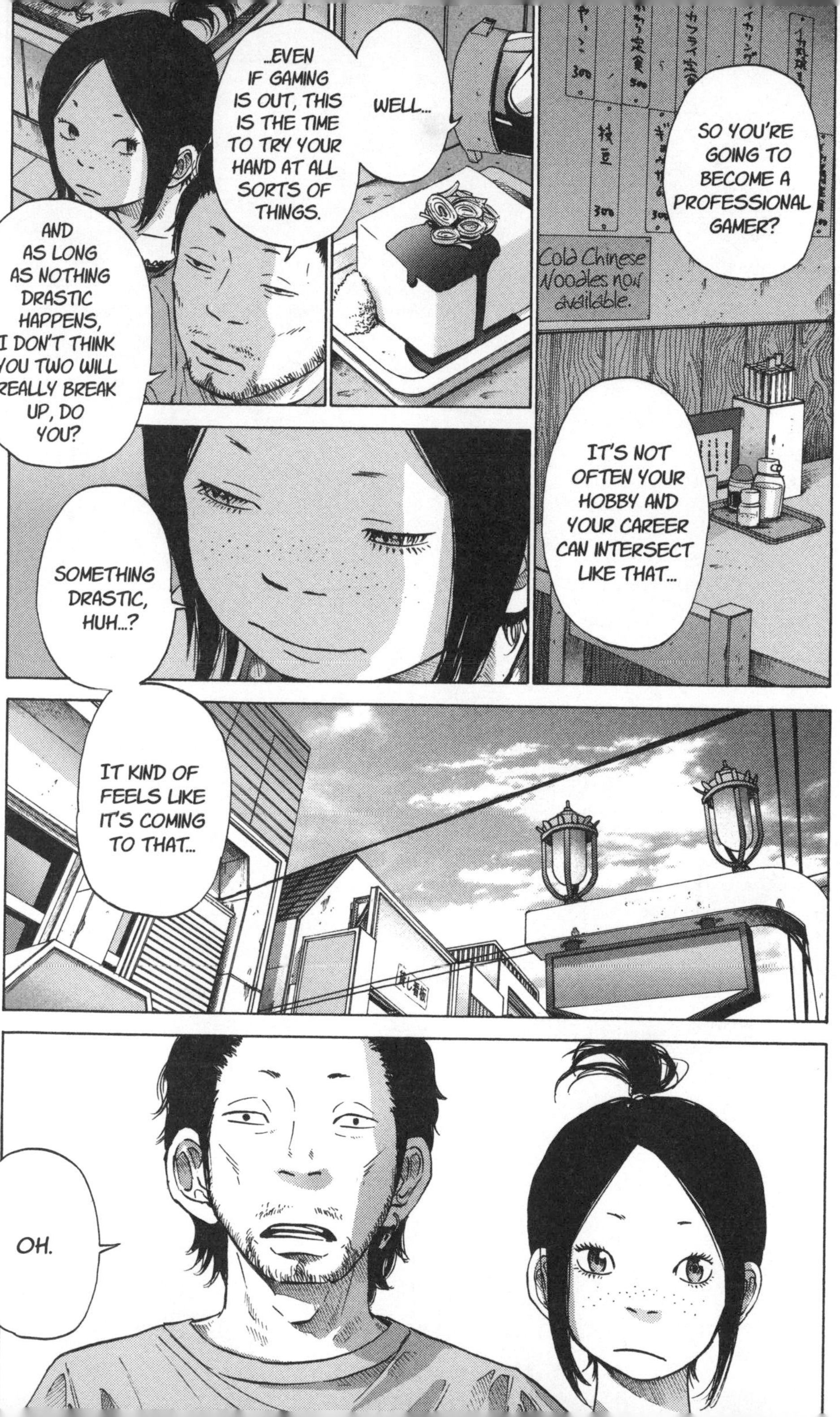
SO YOU'RE GOING TO BECOME A PROFESSIONAL GAMER?
Cold Chinese Noodles now available.
IT'S NOT OFTEN YOUR HOBBY AND YOUR CAREER CAN INTERSECT LIKE THAT...
WELL...
...EVEN IF GAMING IS OUT, THIS IS THE TIME TO TRY YOUR HAND AT ALL SORTS OF THINGS.
AND AS LONG AS NOTHING DRASTIC HAPPENS, I DON'T THINK YOU TWO WILL REALLY BREAK UP, DO YOU?
SOMETHING DRASTIC, HUH...?
IT KIND OF FEELS LIKE IT'S COMING TO THAT...
OH.

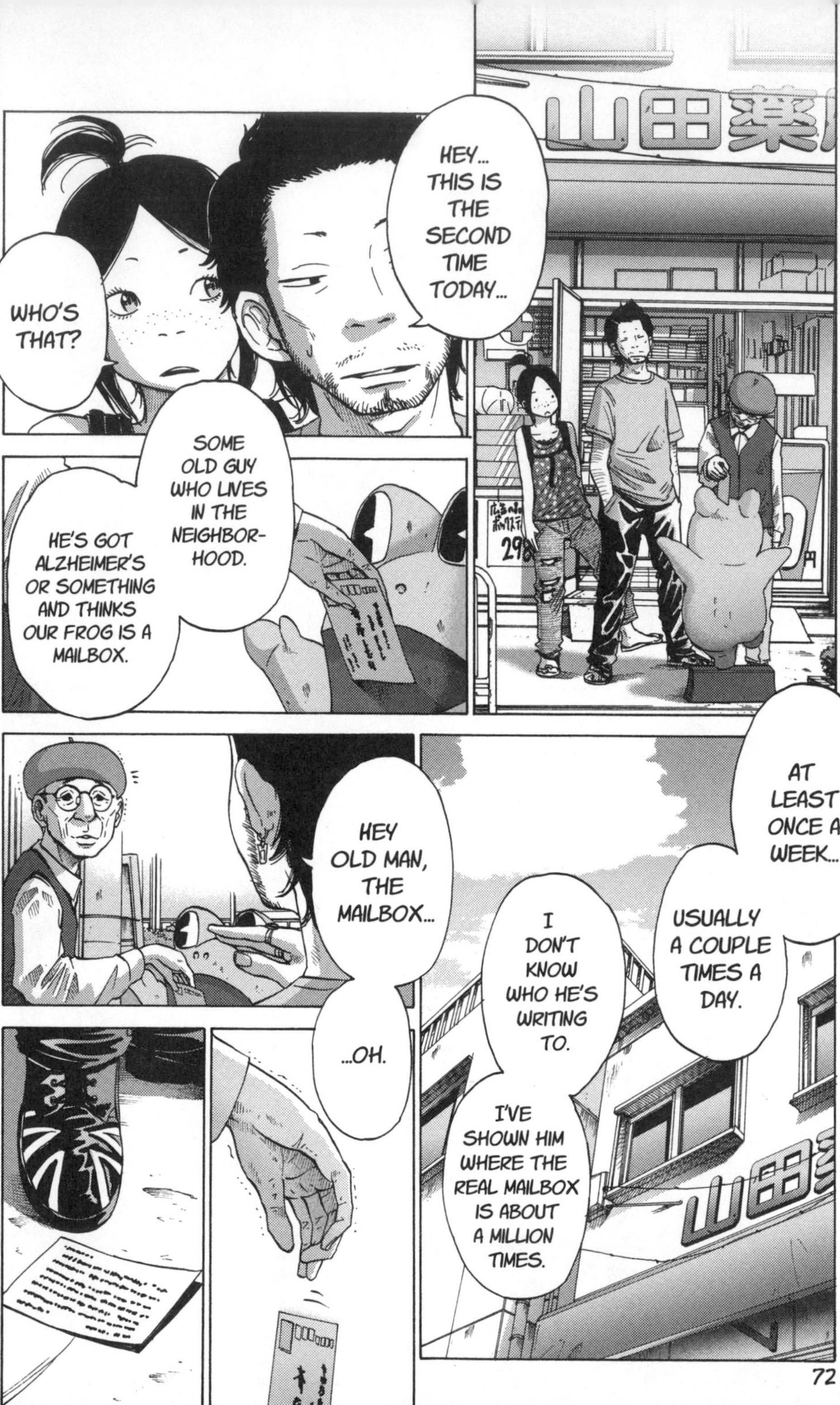
HEY... THIS IS THE SECOND TIME TODAY...
WHO'S THAT?
SOME OLD GUY WHO LIVES IN THE NEIGHBOR-HOOD.
HE'S GOT ALZHEIMER'S OR SOMETHING AND THINKS OUR FROG IS A MAILBOX.
AT LEAST ONCE A WEEK...
USUALLY A COUPLE TIMES A DAY.
I DON'T KNOW WHO HE'S WRITING TO.
I'VE SHOWN HIM WHERE THE REAL MAILBOX IS ABOUT A MILLION TIMES.
HEY OLD MAN, THE MAILBOX...
...OH.

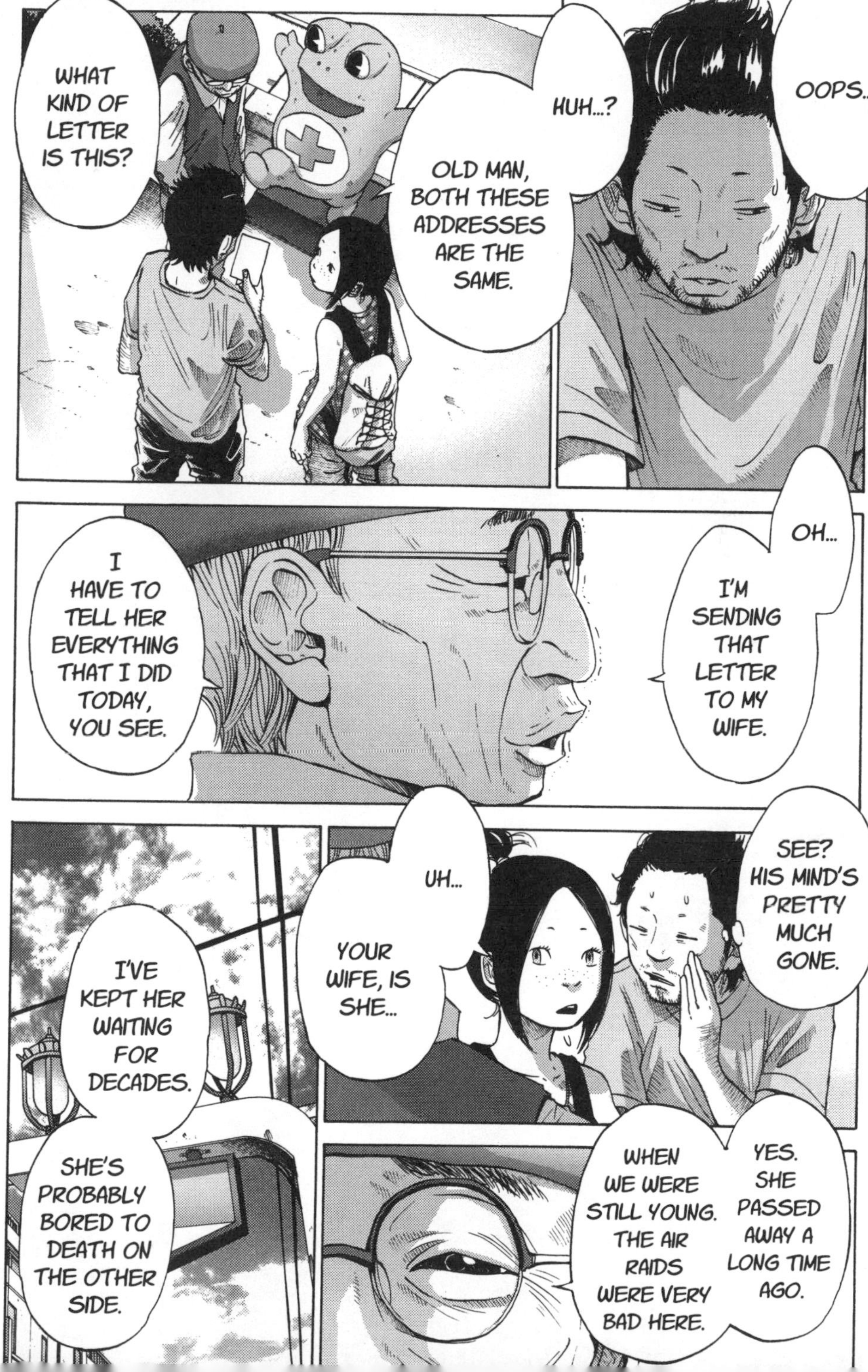
OOPS...
HUH...?
OLD MAN, BOTH THESE ADDRESSES ARE THE SAME.
WHAT KIND OF LETTER IS THIS?
OH...
I'M SENDING THAT LETTER TO MY WIFE.
I HAVE TO TELL HER EVERYTHING THAT I DID TODAY, YOU SEE.
SEE? HIS MIND'S PRETTY MUCH GONE.
UH...
YOUR WIFE, IS SHE...
I'VE KEPT HER WAITING FOR DECADES.
YES. SHE PASSED AWAY A LONG TIME AGO.
WHEN WE WERE STILL YOUNG. THE AIR RAIDS WERE VERY BAD HERE.
SHE'S PROBABLY BORED TO DEATH ON THE OTHER SIDE.

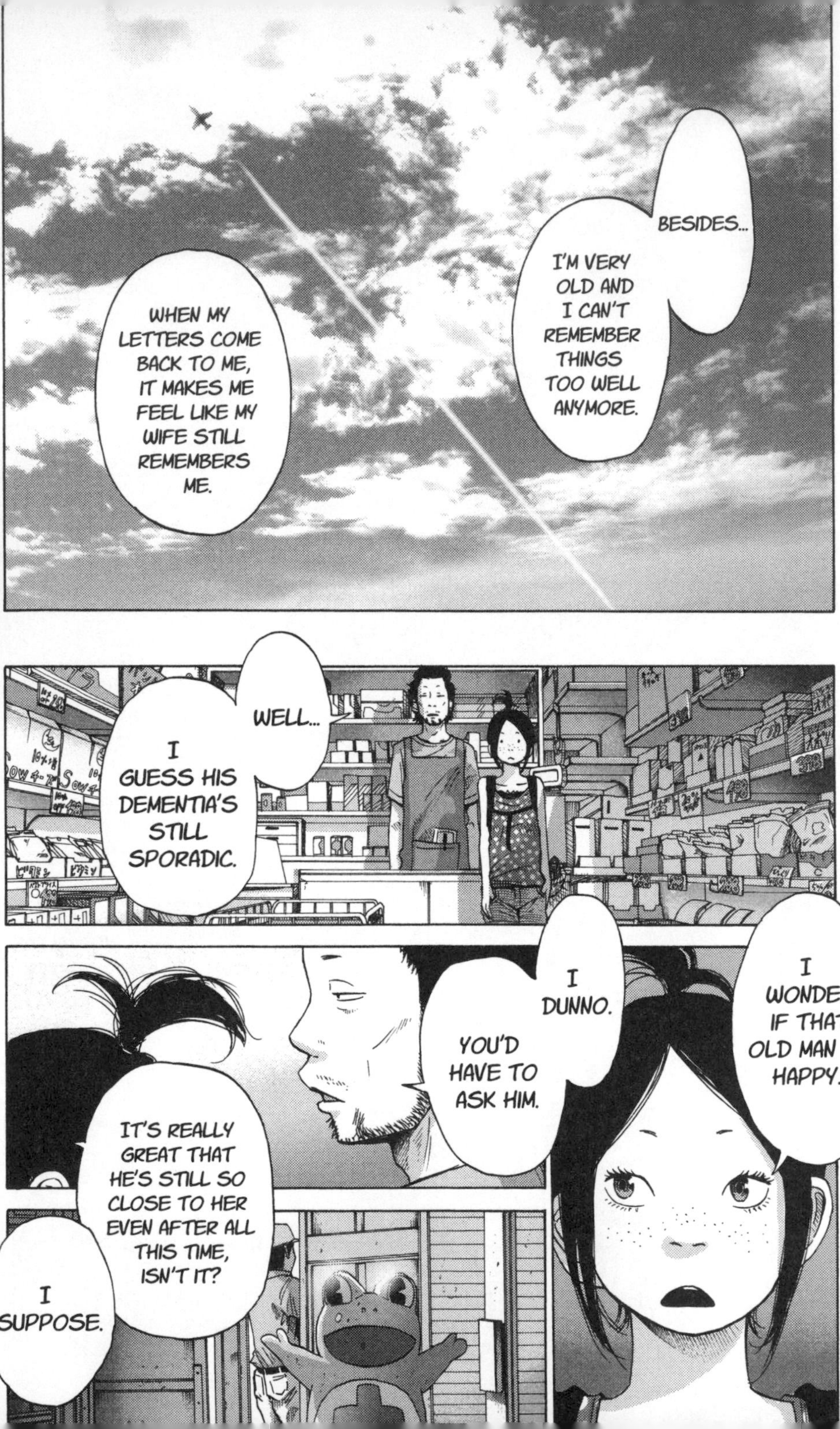
BESIDES...
I'M VERY OLD AND I CAN'T REMEMBER THINGS TOO WELL ANYMORE.
WHEN MY LETTERS COME BACK TO ME, IT MAKES ME FEEL LIKE MY WIFE STILL REMEMBERS ME.
WELL...
I GUESS HIS DEMENTIA'S STILL SPORADIC.
I WONDER IF THAT OLD MAN IS HAPPY.
I DUNNO.
YOU'D HAVE TO ASK HIM.
IT'S REALLY GREAT THAT HE'S STILL SO CLOSE TO HER EVEN AFTER ALL THIS TIME, ISN'T IT?
I SUPPOSE.

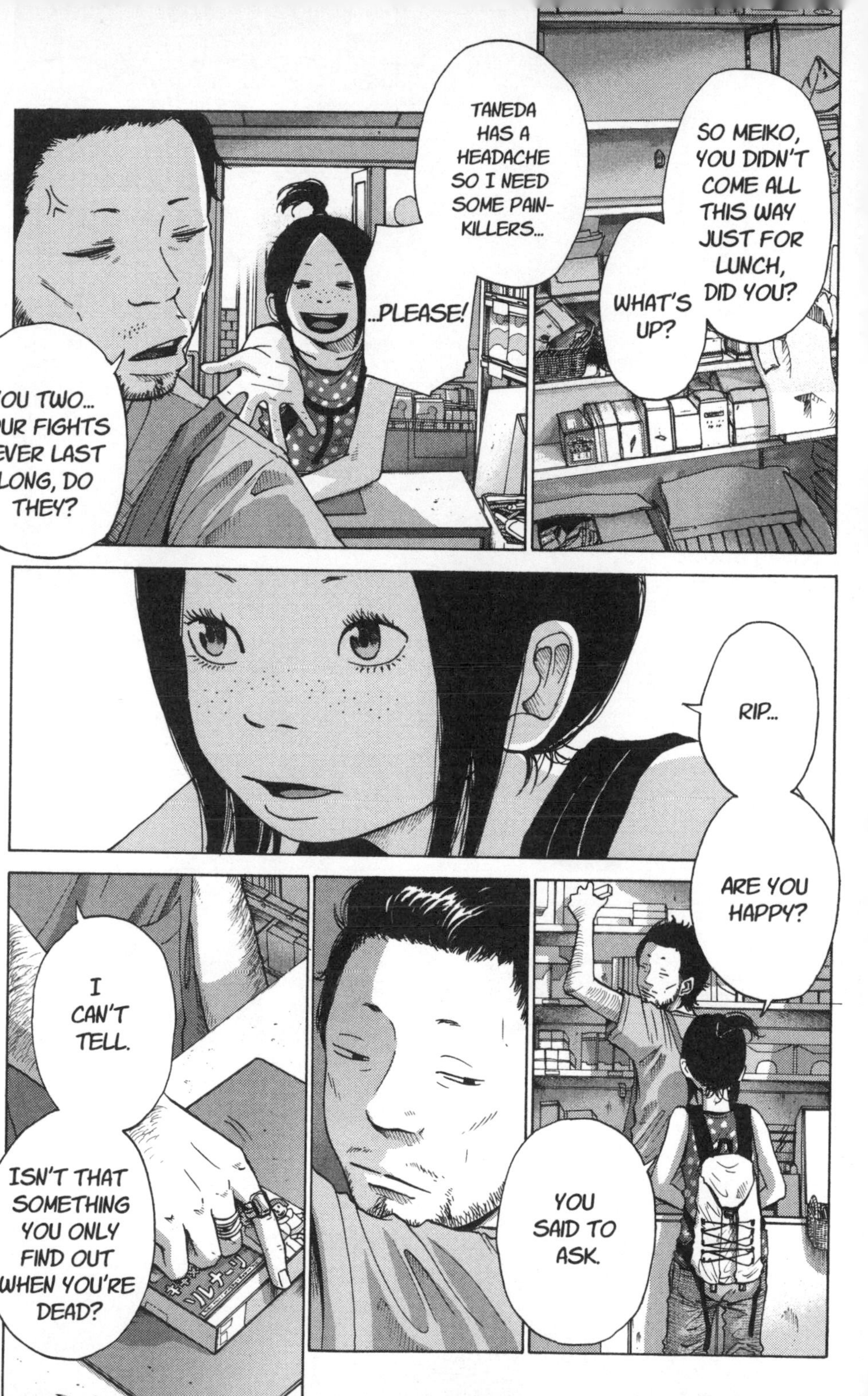
SO MEIKO, YOU DIDN'T COME ALL THIS WAY JUST FOR LUNCH, DID YOU?
WHAT'S UP?
TANEDA HAS A HEADACHE SO I NEED SOME PAIN-KILLERS...
...PLEASE!
YOU TWO... YOUR FIGHTS NEVER LAST LONG, DO THEY?
RIP...
ARE YOU HAPPY?
YOU SAID TO ASK.
I CAN'T TELL.
ISN'T THAT SOMETHING YOU ONLY FIND OUT WHEN YOU'RE DEAD?

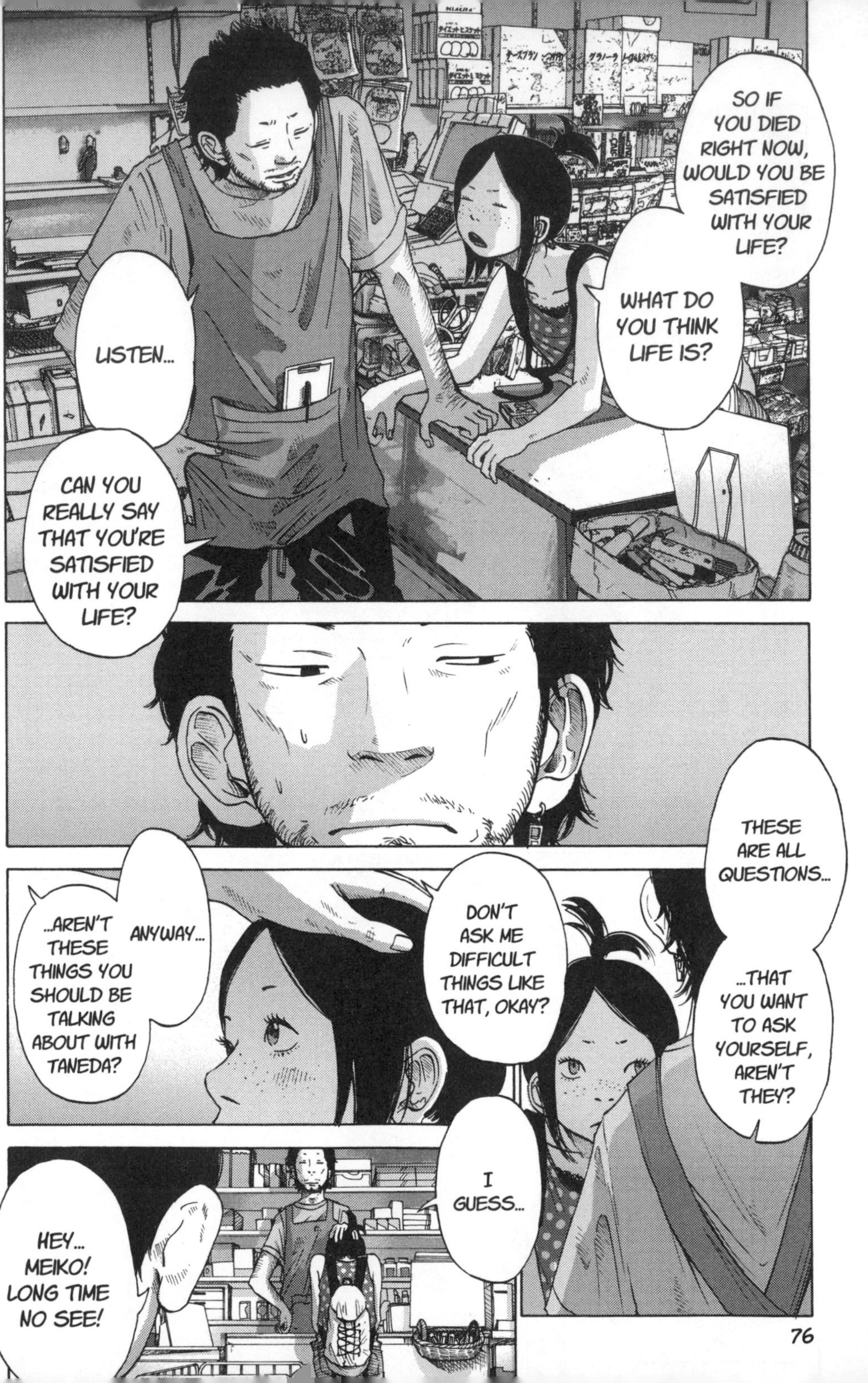
SO IF YOU DIED RIGHT NOW, WOULD YOU BE SATISFIED WITH YOUR LIFE?
WHAT DO YOU THINK LIFE IS?
LISTEN...
CAN YOU REALLY SAY THAT YOU'RE SATISFIED WITH YOUR LIFE?
THESE ARE ALL QUESTIONS...
...THAT YOU WANT TO ASK YOURSELF, AREN'T THEY?
DON'T ASK ME DIFFICULT THINGS LIKE THAT, OKAY?
ANYWAY...
...AREN'T THESE THINGS YOU SHOULD BE TALKING ABOUT WITH TANEDA?
I GUESS...
HEY... MEIKO! LONG TIME NO SEE!

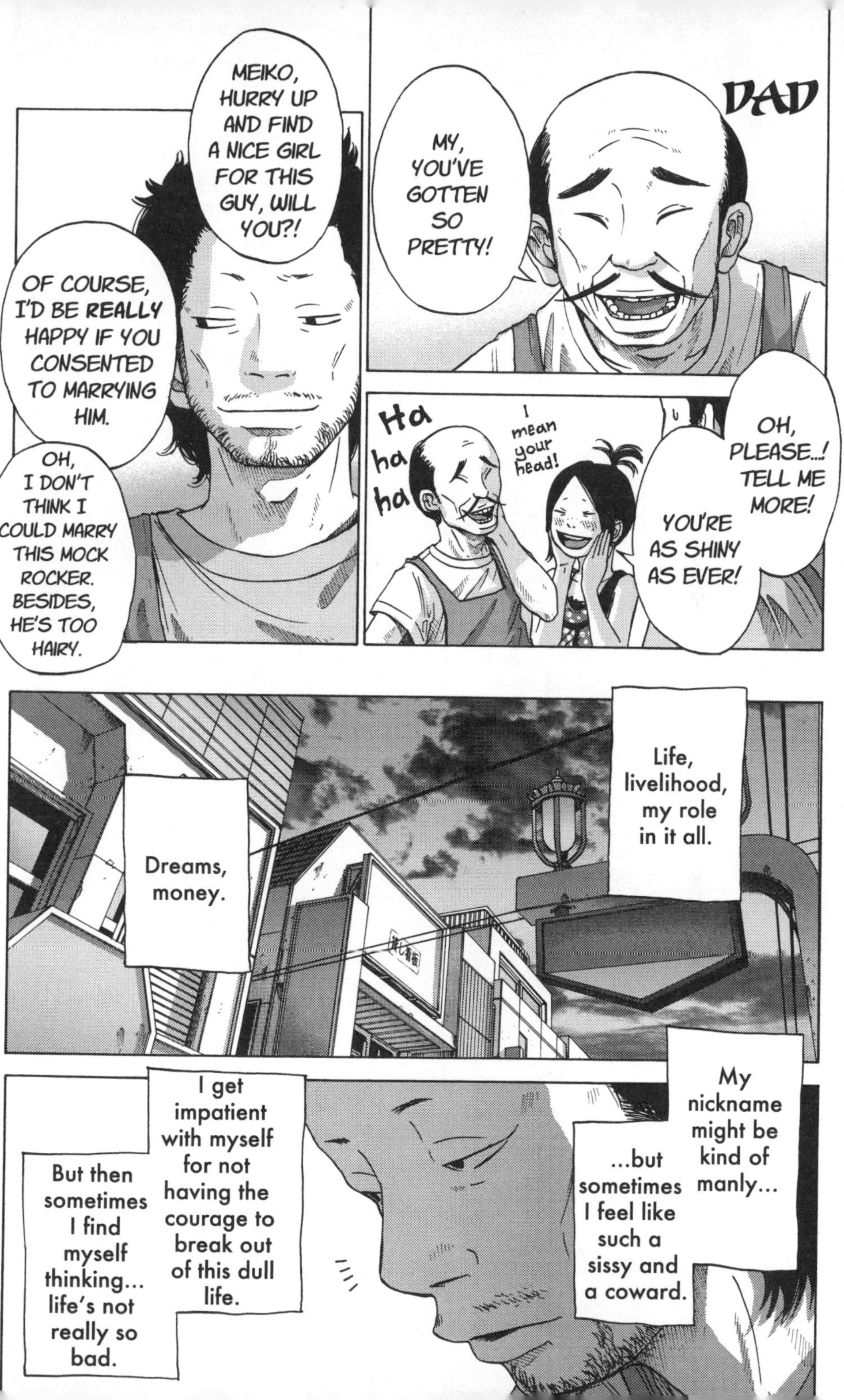
DAD
MY, YOU'VE GOTTEN SO PRETTY!
OH, PLEASE...! TELL ME MORE!
YOU'RE AS SHINY AS EVER!
I mean your head!
Ha ha ha
MEIKO, HURRY UP AND FIND A NICE GIRL FOR THIS GUY, WILL YOU?!
OF COURSE, I'D BE REALLY HAPPY IF YOU CONSENTED TO MARRYING HIM.
OH, I DON'T THINK I COULD MARRY THIS MOCK ROCKER. BESIDES, HE'S TOO HAIRY.
Life, livelihood, my role in it all.
Dreams, money.
My nickname might be kind of manly...
...but sometimes I feel like such a sissy and a coward.
I get impatient with myself for not having the courage to break out of this dull life.
But then sometimes I find myself thinking... life's not really so bad.

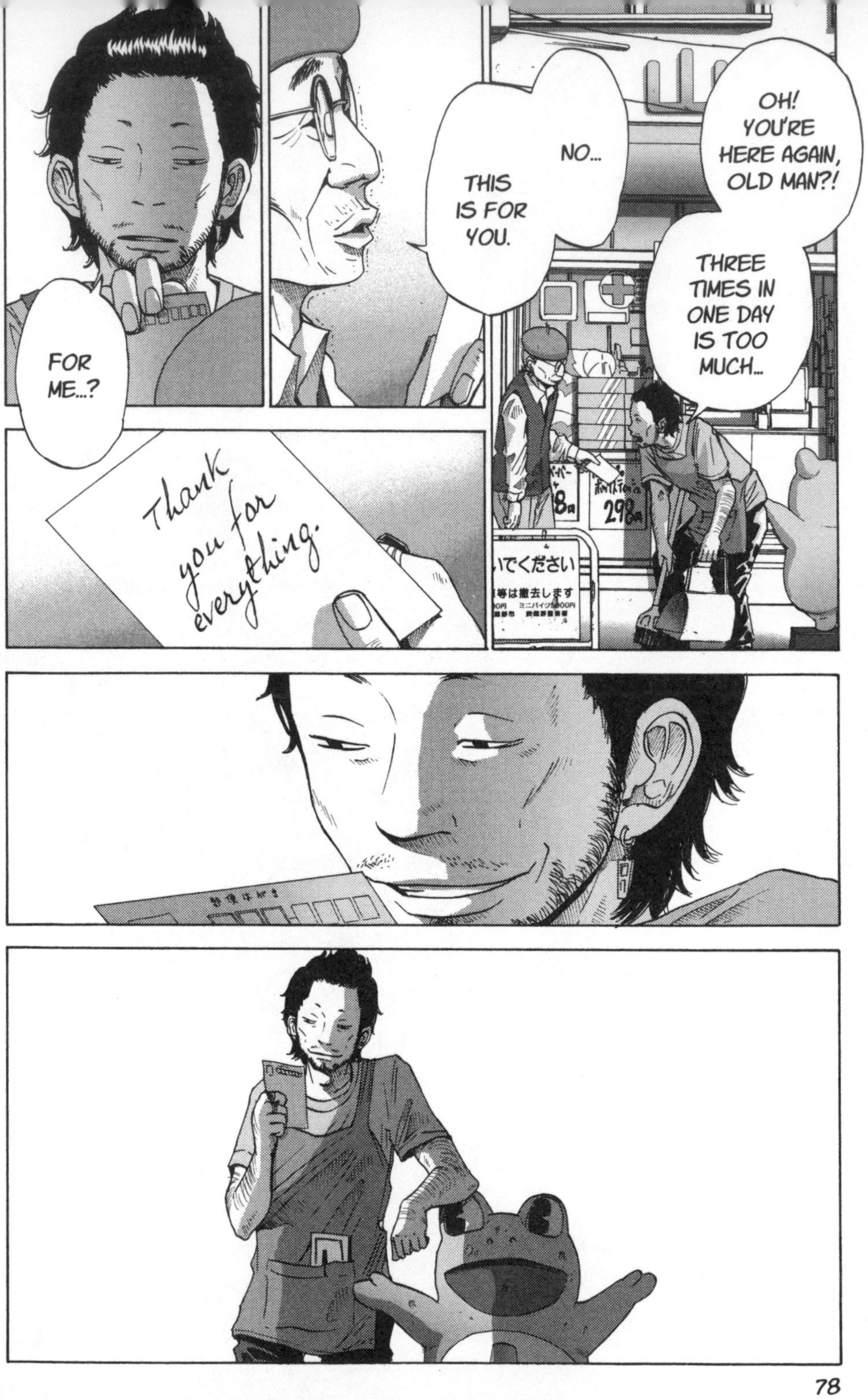
OH! YOU'RE HERE AGAIN, OLD MAN?!
THREE TIMES IN ONE DAY IS TOO MUCH...
いでください
等は撤去します
NO...
THIS IS FOR YOU.
FOR ME...?
Thank you for everything.

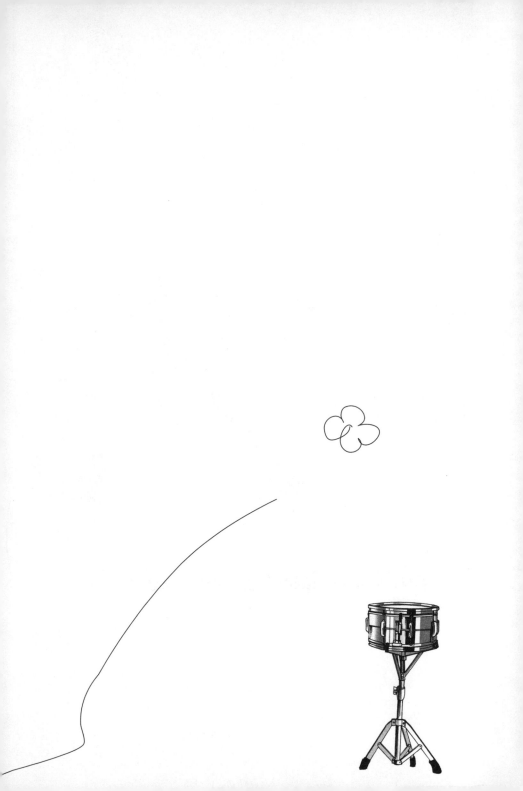

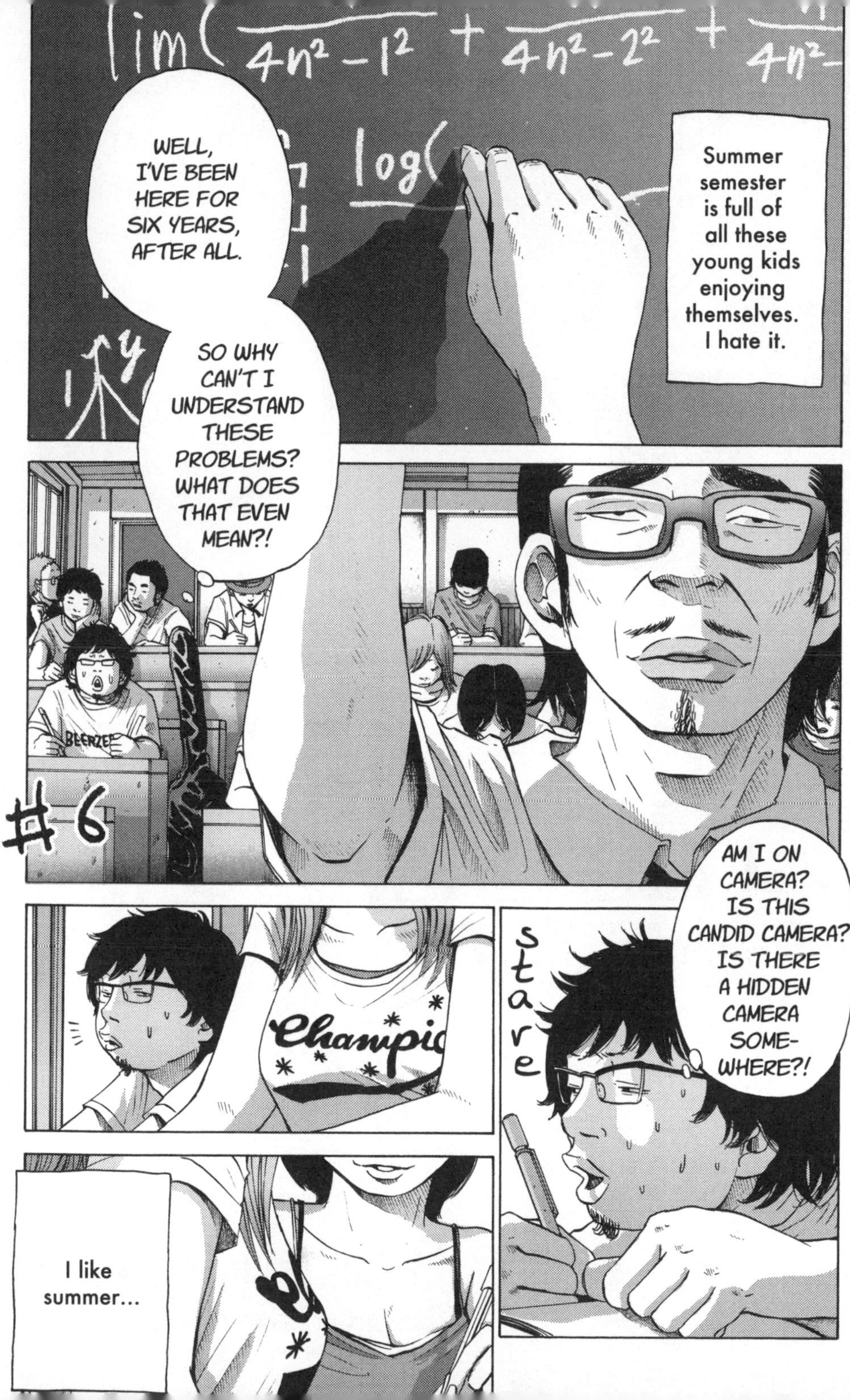
Summer semester is full of all these young kids enjoying themselves. I hate it.
WELL, I'VE BEEN HERE FOR SIX YEARS, AFTER ALL.
SO WHY CAN'T I UNDERSTAND THESE PROBLEMS? WHAT DOES THAT EVEN MEAN?!
#6
AM I ON CAMERA? IS THIS CANDID CAMERA? IS THERE A HIDDEN CAMERA SOME-WHERE?!
stare
I like summer...

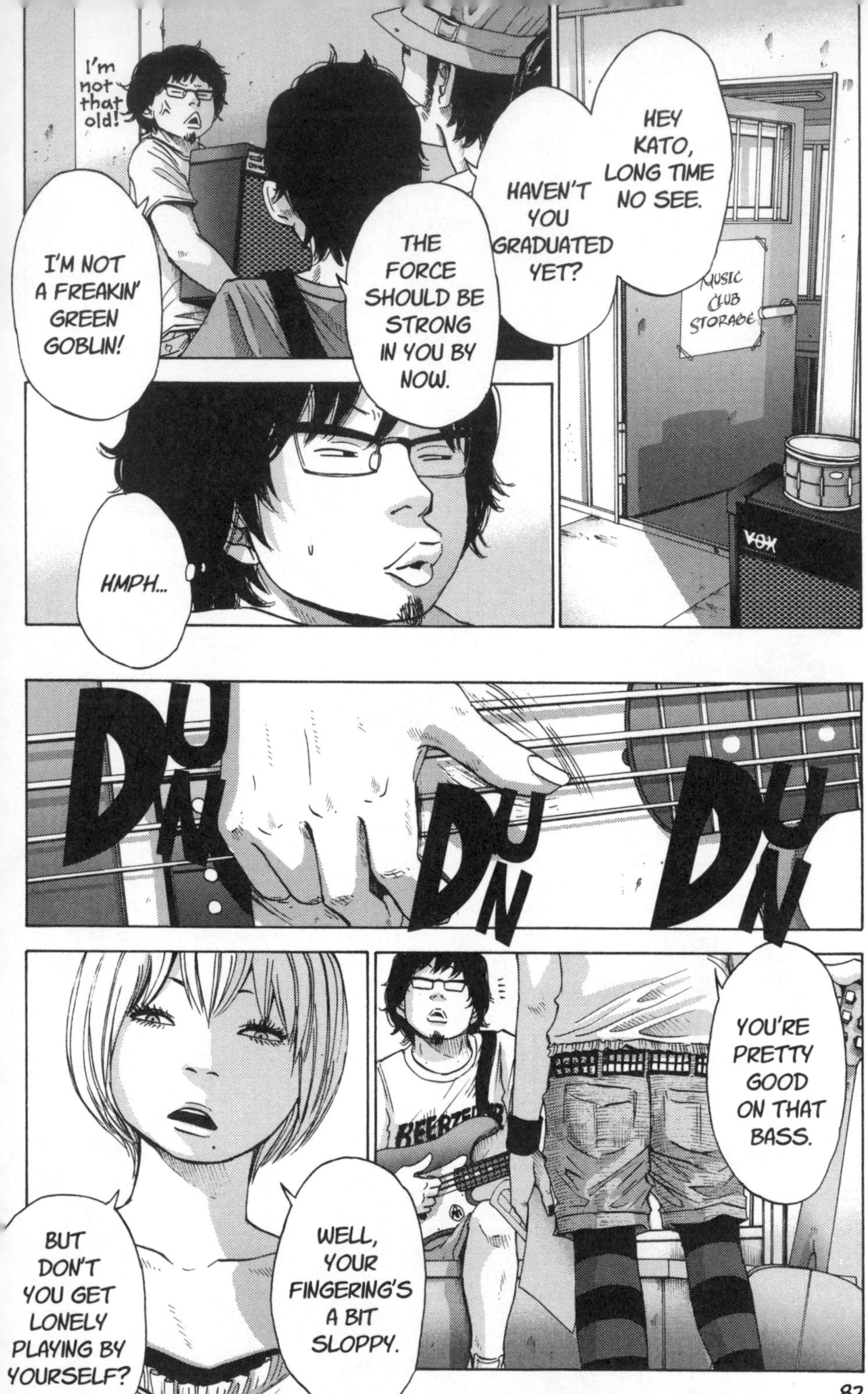
HEY KATO, LONG TIME NO SEE.
HAVEN'T YOU GRADUATED YET?
THE FORCE SHOULD BE STRONG IN YOU BY NOW.
I'm not that old!
I'M NOT A FREAKIN' GREEN GOBLIN!
MUSIC CLUB STORAGE
HMPH...
DUN
DUN
DUN
YOU'RE PRETTY GOOD ON THAT BASS.
WELL, YOUR FINGERING'S A BIT SLOPPY.
BUT DON'T YOU GET LONELY PLAYING BY YOURSELF?

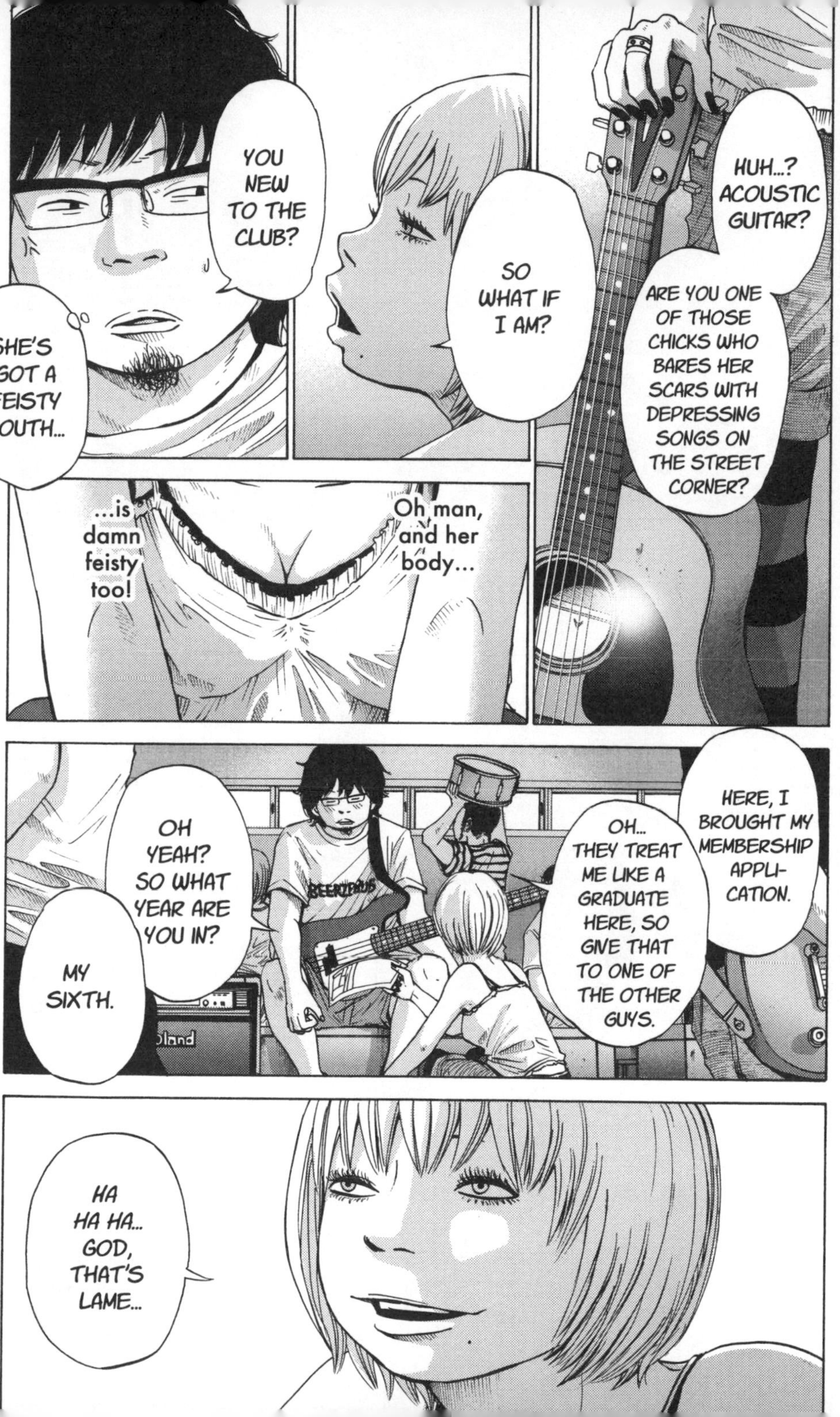

YOU NEW TO THE CLUB?
SHE'S GOT A FEISTY MOUTH...
SO WHAT IF I AM?
Oh man, and her body...
...is damn feisty too!
HUH...? ACOUSTIC GUITAR?
ARE YOU ONE OF THOSE CHICKS WHO BARES HER SCARS WITH DEPRESSING SONGS ON THE STREET CORNER?
HERE, I BROUGHT MY MEMBERSHIP APPLI-CATION.
OH... THEY TREAT ME LIKE A GRADUATE HERE, SO GIVE THAT TO ONE OF THE OTHER GUYS.
OH YEAH? SO WHAT YEAR ARE YOU IN?
MY SIXTH.
HA HA HA... GOD, THAT'S LAME...

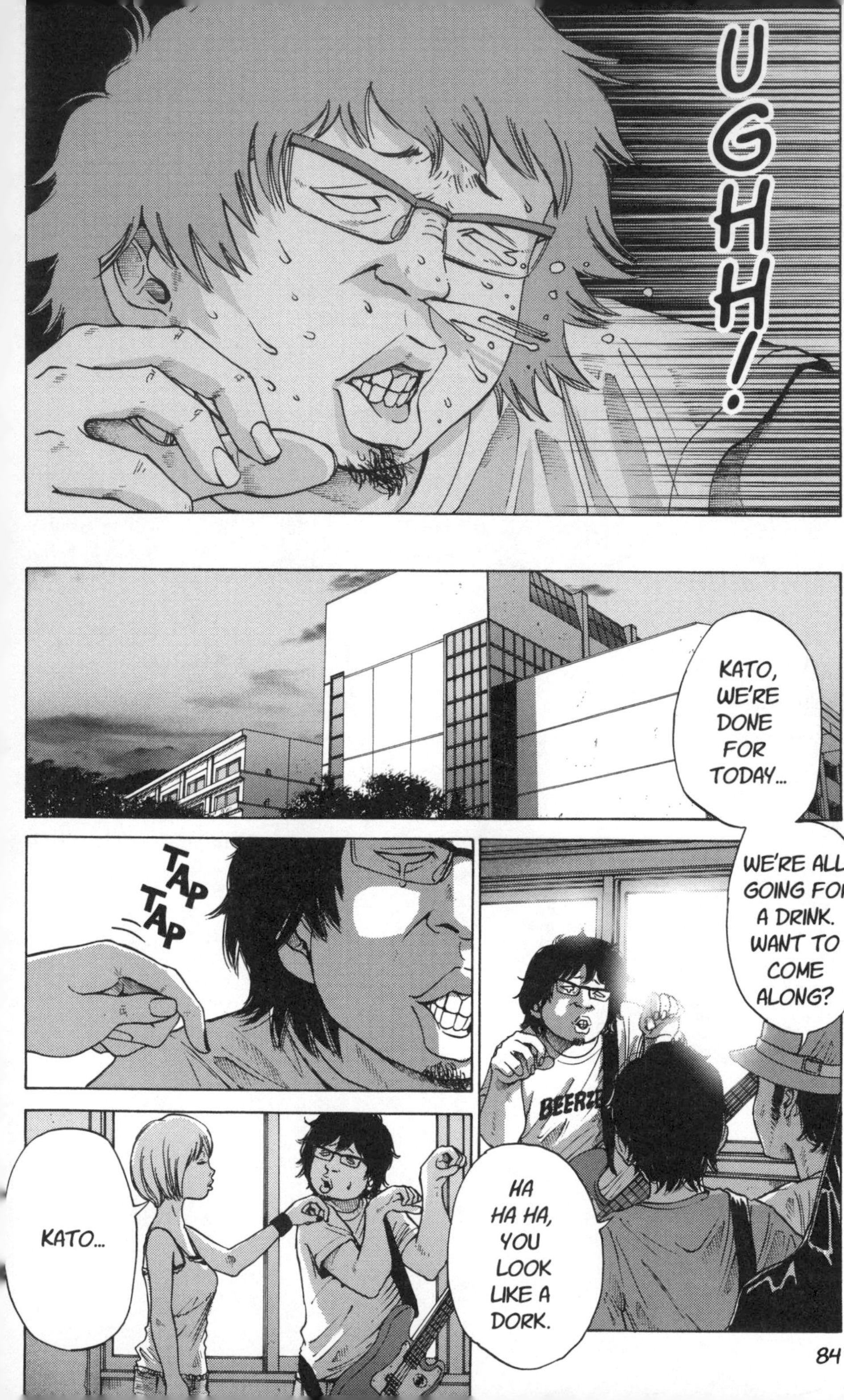
UGHH!
KATO, WE'RE DONE FOR TODAY...
WE'RE ALL GOING FOR A DRINK. WANT TO COME ALONG?
TAP TAP
HA HA HA, YOU LOOK LIKE A DORK.
KATO...

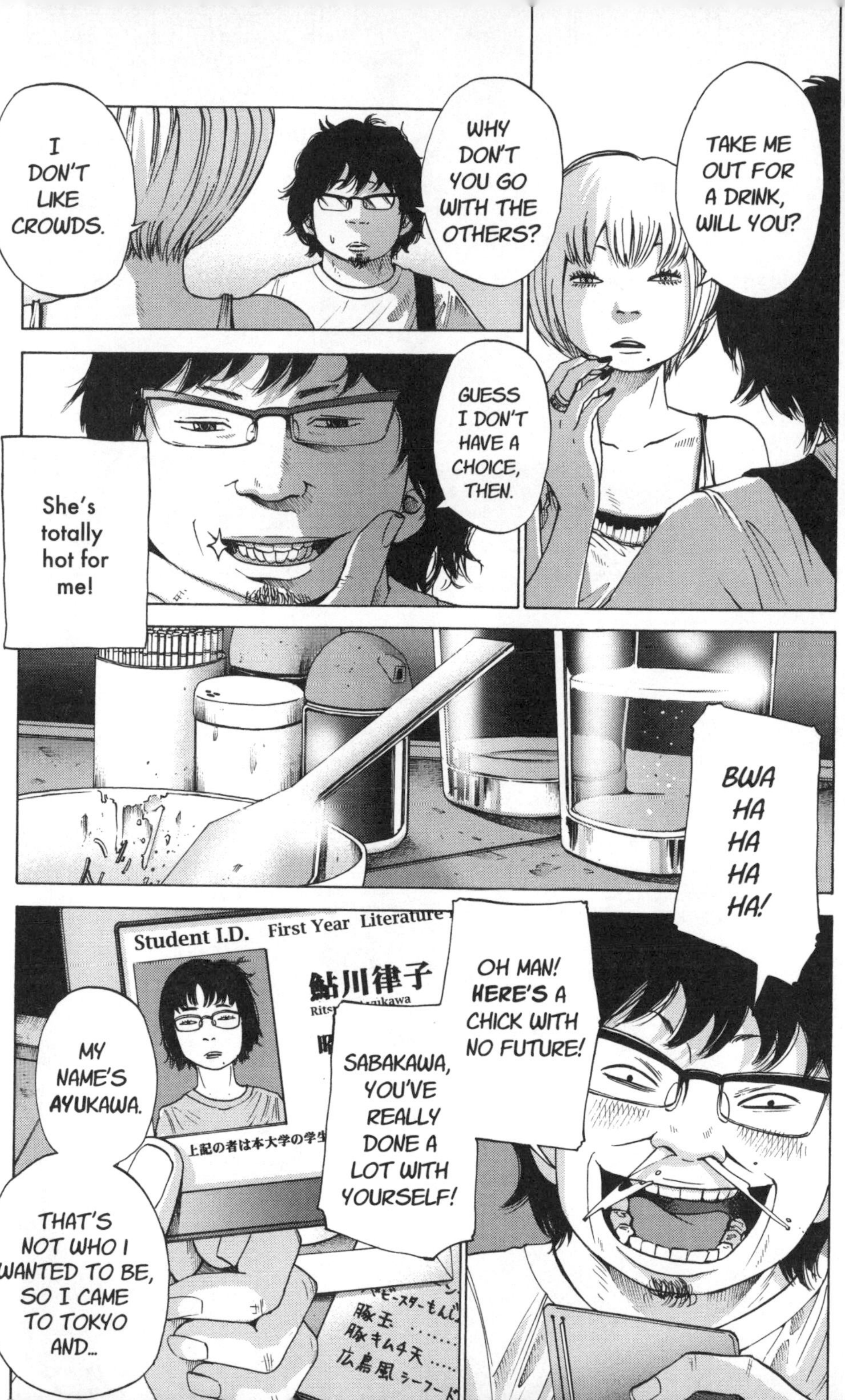

TAKE ME OUT FOR A DRINK, WILL YOU?
WHY DON'T YOU GO WITH THE OTHERS?
I DON'T LIKE CROWDS.
GUESS I DON'T HAVE A CHOICE, THEN.
She's totally hot for me!
BWA HA HA HA HA!
OH MAN! HERE'S A CHICK WITH NO FUTURE!
SABAKAWA, YOU'VE REALLY DONE A LOT WITH YOURSELF!
Student I.D. First Year
鮎川律子
MY NAME'S AYUKAWA.
THAT'S NOT WHO I WANTED TO BE, SO I CAME TO TOKYO AND...
豚玉
豚キムチ天

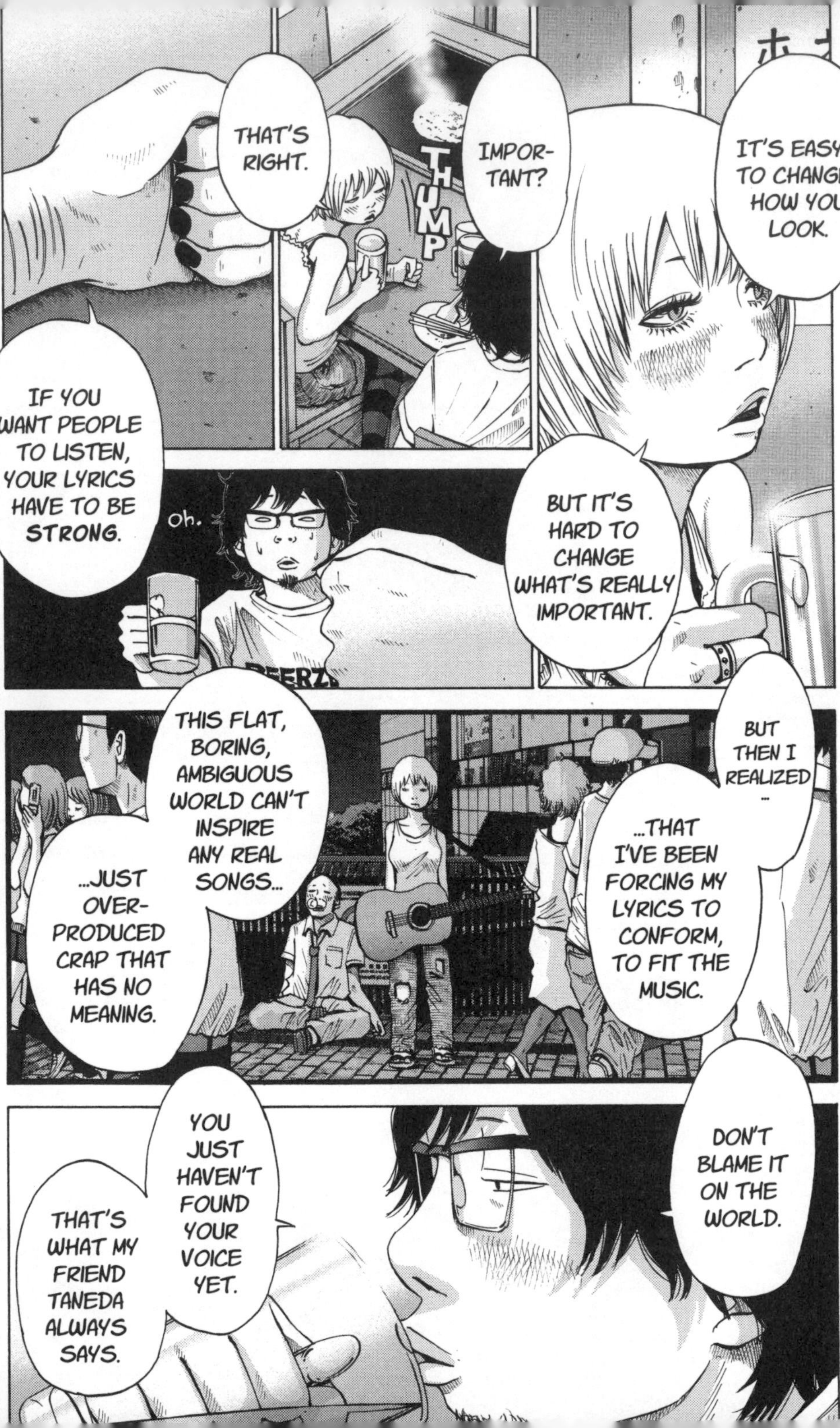
IT'S EASY TO CHANGE HOW YOU LOOK.
BUT IT'S HARD TO CHANGE WHAT'S REALLY IMPORTANT.
IMPOR-TANT?
THUMP
THAT'S RIGHT.
IF YOU WANT PEOPLE TO LISTEN, YOUR LYRICS HAVE TO BE **STRONG**.
Oh.
BUT THEN I REALIZED ...
...THAT I'VE BEEN FORCING MY LYRICS TO CONFORM, TO FIT THE MUSIC.
THIS FLAT, BORING, AMBIGUOUS WORLD CAN'T INSPIRE ANY REAL SONGS...
...JUST OVER-PRODUCED CRAP THAT HAS NO MEANING.
DON'T BLAME IT ON THE WORLD.
YOU JUST HAVEN'T FOUND YOUR VOICE YET.
THAT'S WHAT MY FRIEND TANEDA ALWAYS SAYS.

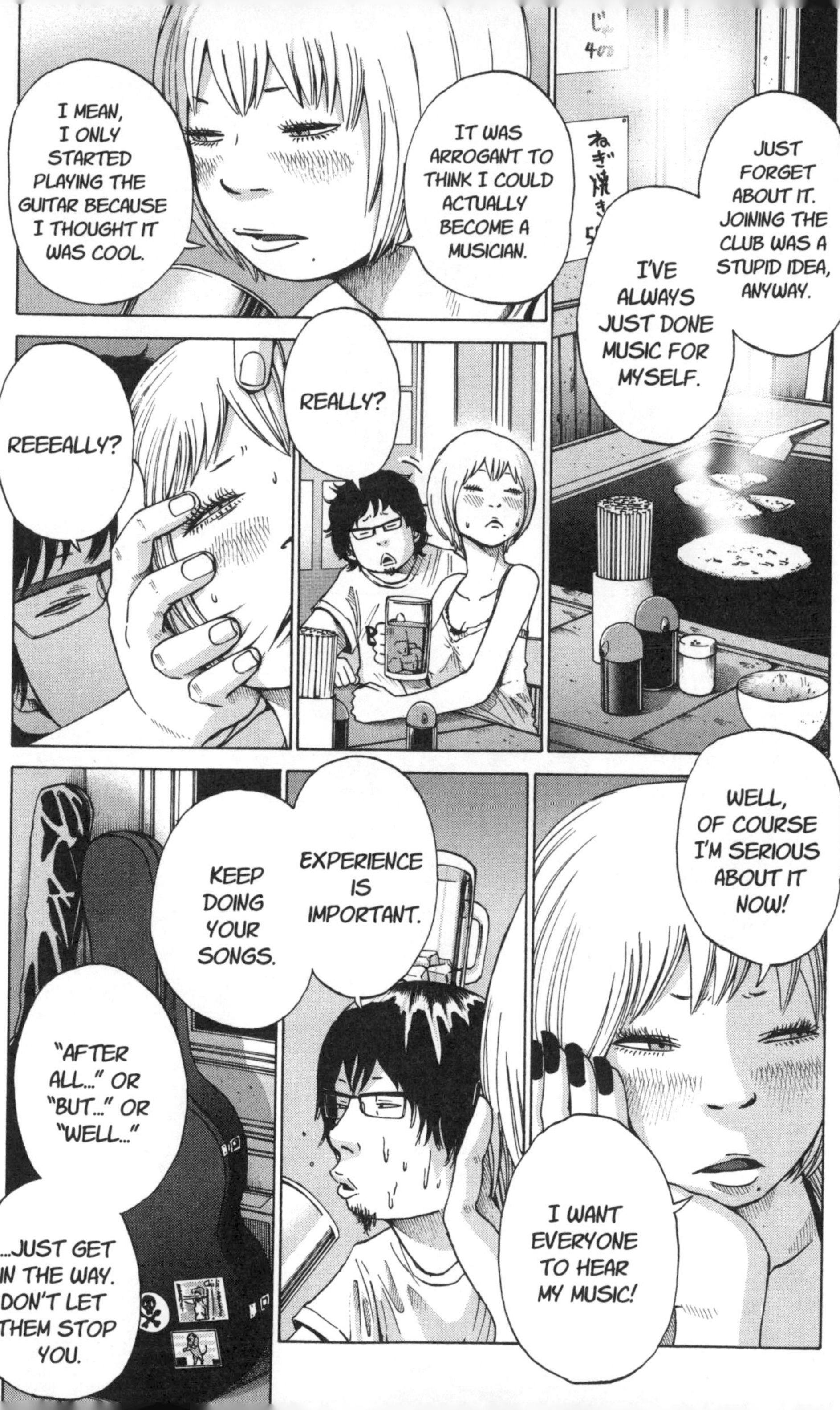
JUST FORGET ABOUT IT. JOINING THE CLUB WAS A STUPID IDEA, ANYWAY.
IT WAS ARROGANT TO THINK I COULD ACTUALLY BECOME A MUSICIAN.
I MEAN, I ONLY STARTED PLAYING THE GUITAR BECAUSE I THOUGHT IT WAS COOL.
I'VE ALWAYS JUST DONE MUSIC FOR MYSELF.
REALLY?
REEEALLY?
WELL, OF COURSE I'M SERIOUS ABOUT IT NOW!
I WANT EVERYONE TO HEAR MY MUSIC!
EXPERIENCE IS IMPORTANT.
KEEP DOING YOUR SONGS.
"AFTER ALL..." OR "BUT..." OR "WELL..."
...JUST GET IN THE WAY. DON'T LET THEM STOP YOU.

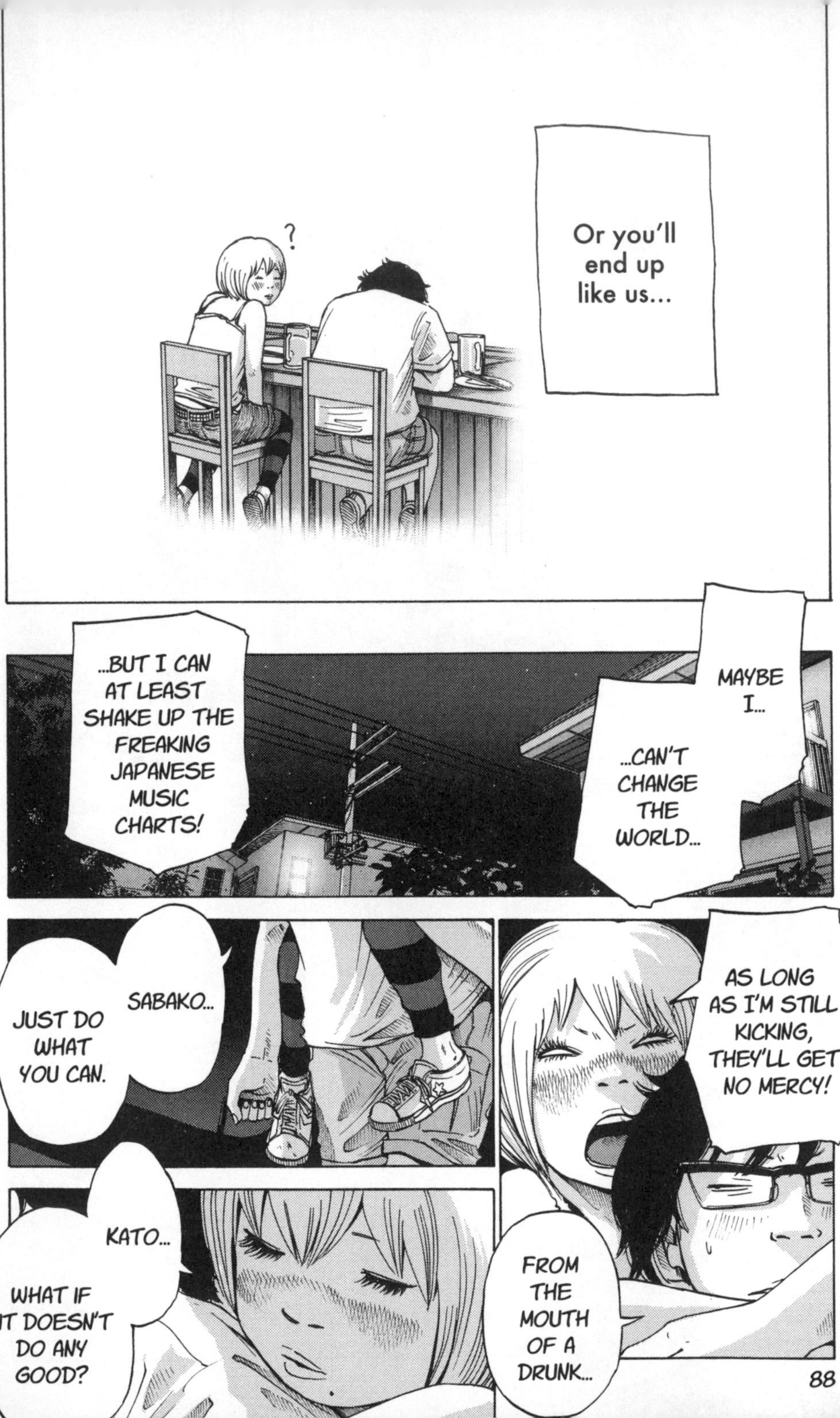
?
Or you'll end up like us...
MAYBE I...
...CAN'T CHANGE THE WORLD...
...BUT I CAN AT LEAST SHAKE UP THE FREAKING JAPANESE MUSIC CHARTS!
AS LONG AS I'M STILL KICKING, THEY'LL GET NO MERCY!
FROM THE MOUTH OF A DRUNK...
SABAKO...
JUST DO WHAT YOU CAN.
KATO...
WHAT IF IT DOESN'T DO ANY GOOD?

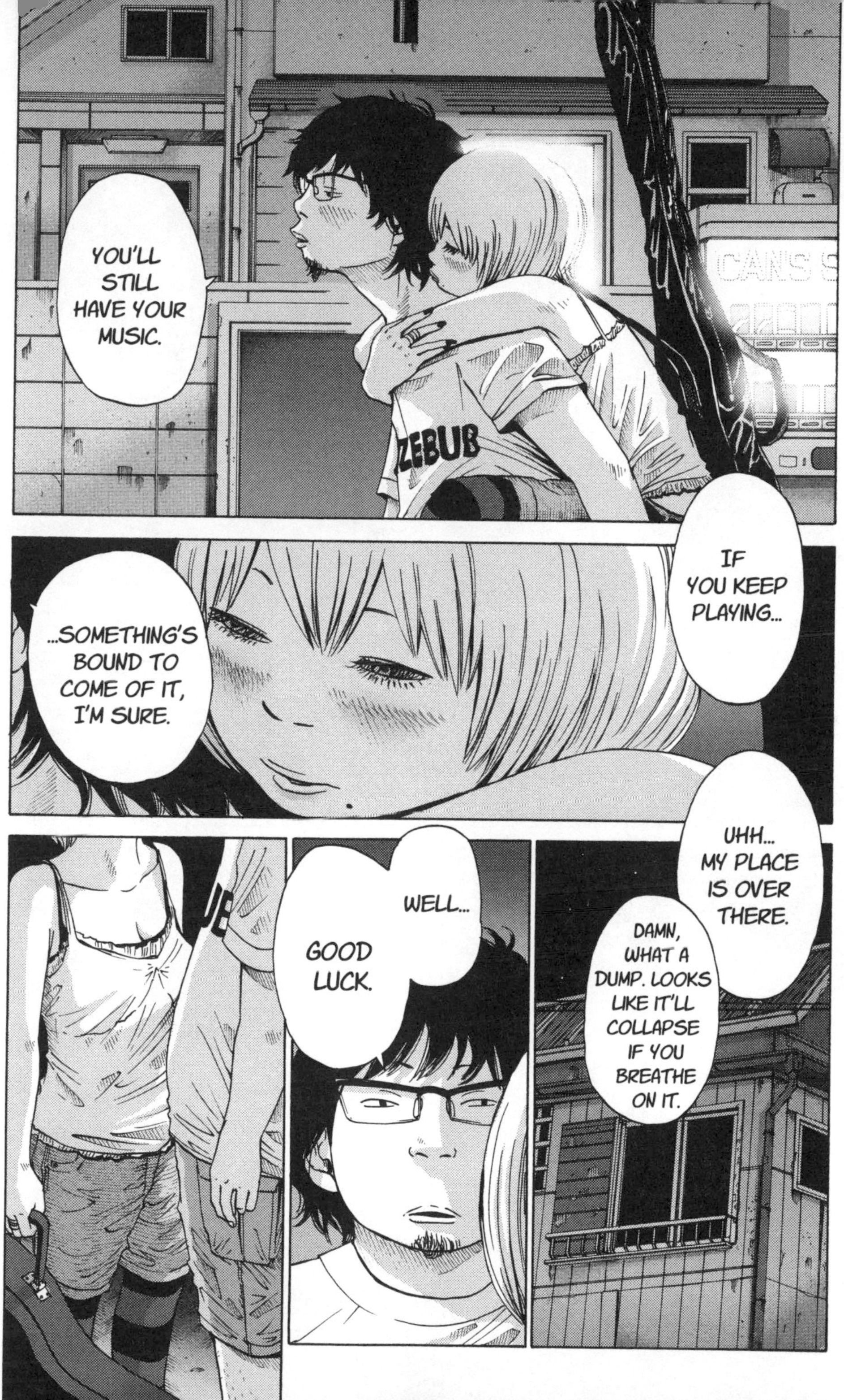
YOU'LL STILL HAVE YOUR MUSIC.
IF YOU KEEP PLAYING...
...SOMETHING'S BOUND TO COME OF IT, I'M SURE.
UHH... MY PLACE IS OVER THERE.
DAMN, WHAT A DUMP. LOOKS LIKE IT'LL COLLAPSE IF YOU BREATHE ON IT.
WELL...
GOOD LUCK.

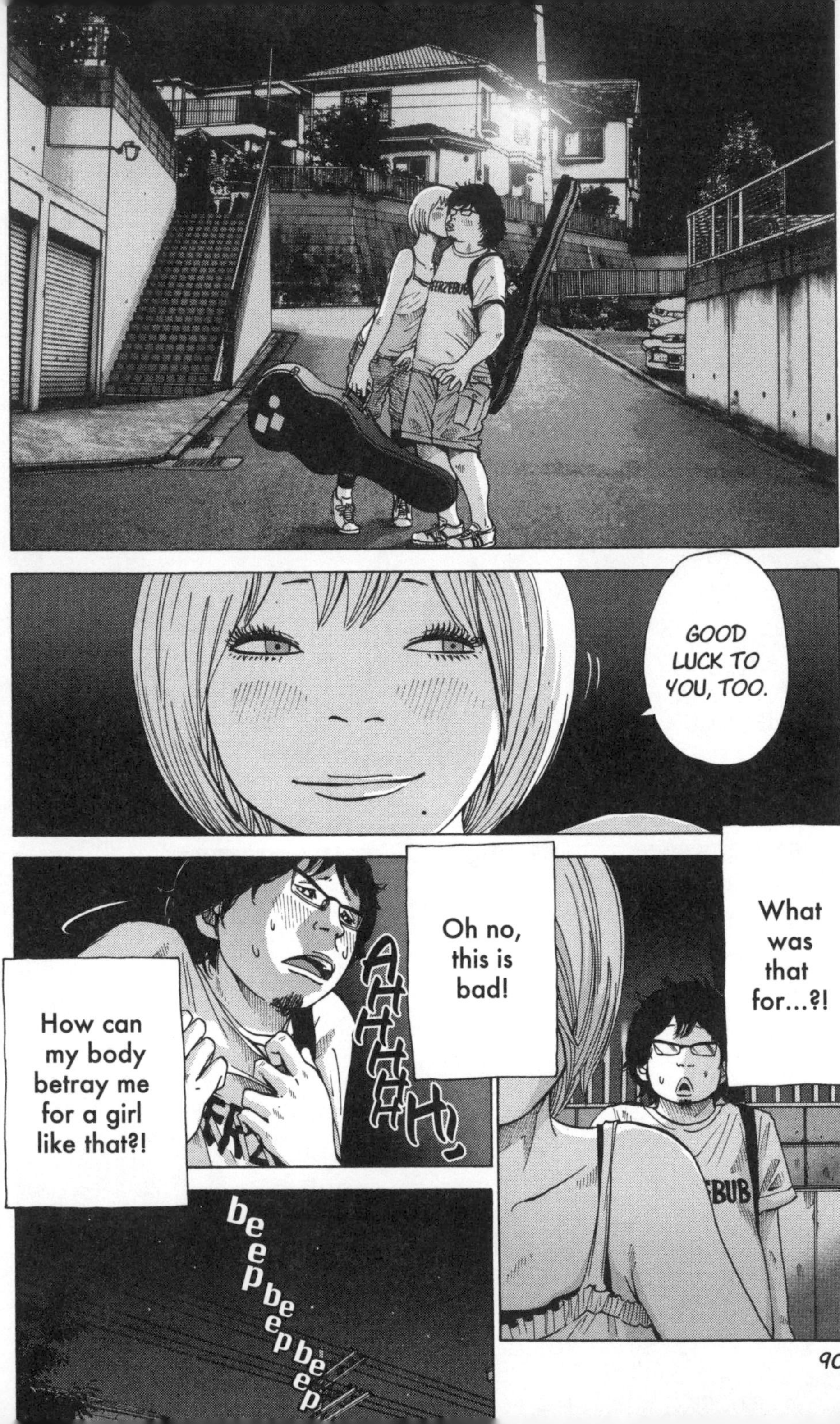

GOOD LUCK TO YOU, TOO.
What was that for...?!
Oh no, this is bad!
AHHHHH!
How can my body betray me for a girl like that?!
beep beep beep

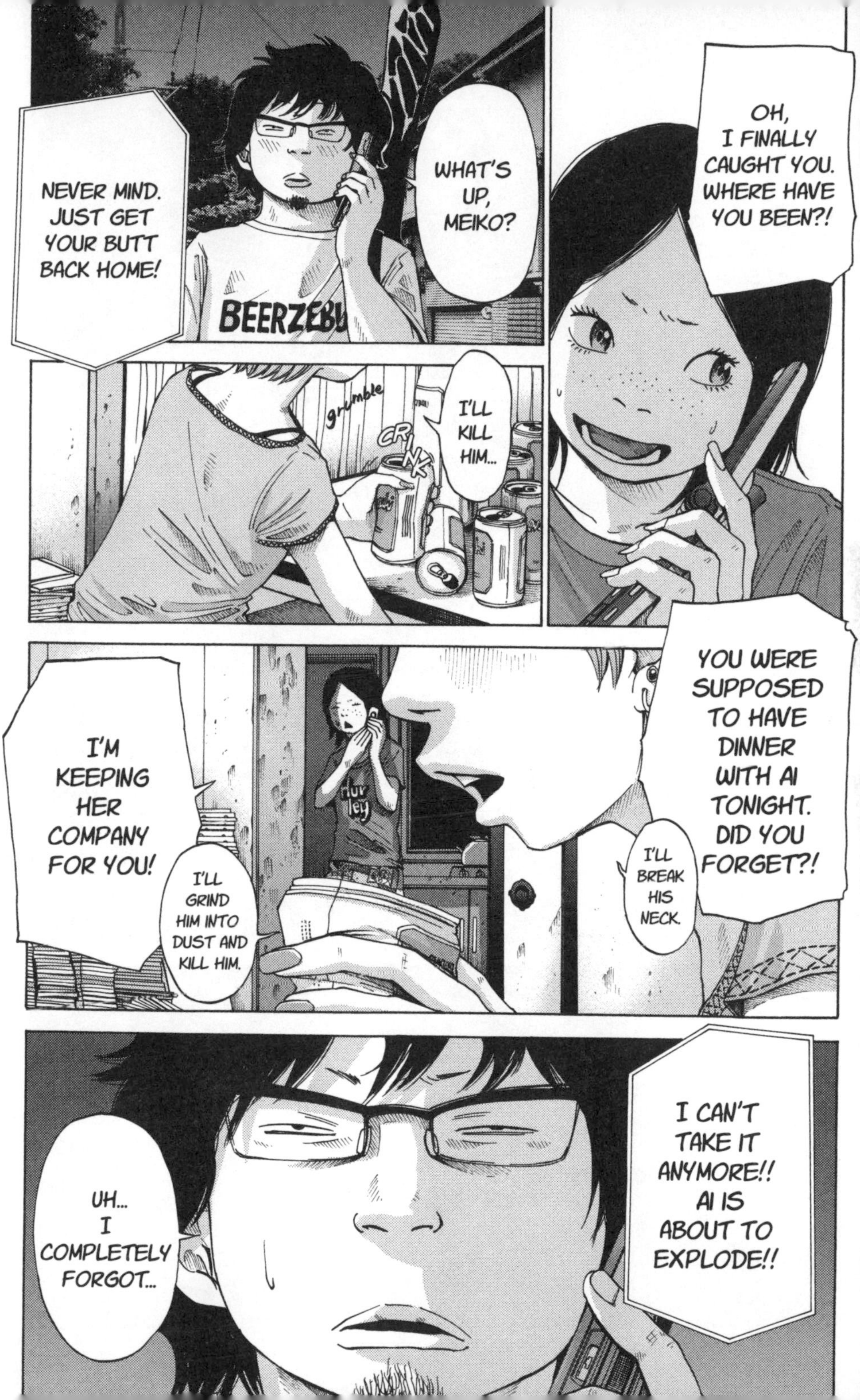
OH, I FINALLY CAUGHT YOU. WHERE HAVE YOU BEEN?!
WHAT'S UP, MEIKO?
NEVER MIND. JUST GET YOUR BUTT BACK HOME!
BEERZEBU
grumble
CRINK
I'LL KILL HIM...
YOU WERE SUPPOSED TO HAVE DINNER WITH AI TONIGHT. DID YOU FORGET?!
I'LL BREAK HIS NECK.
I'LL GRIND HIM INTO DUST AND KILL HIM.
I'M KEEPING HER COMPANY FOR YOU!
I CAN'T TAKE IT ANYMORE!! AI IS ABOUT TO EXPLODE!!
UH... I COMPLETELY FORGOT...

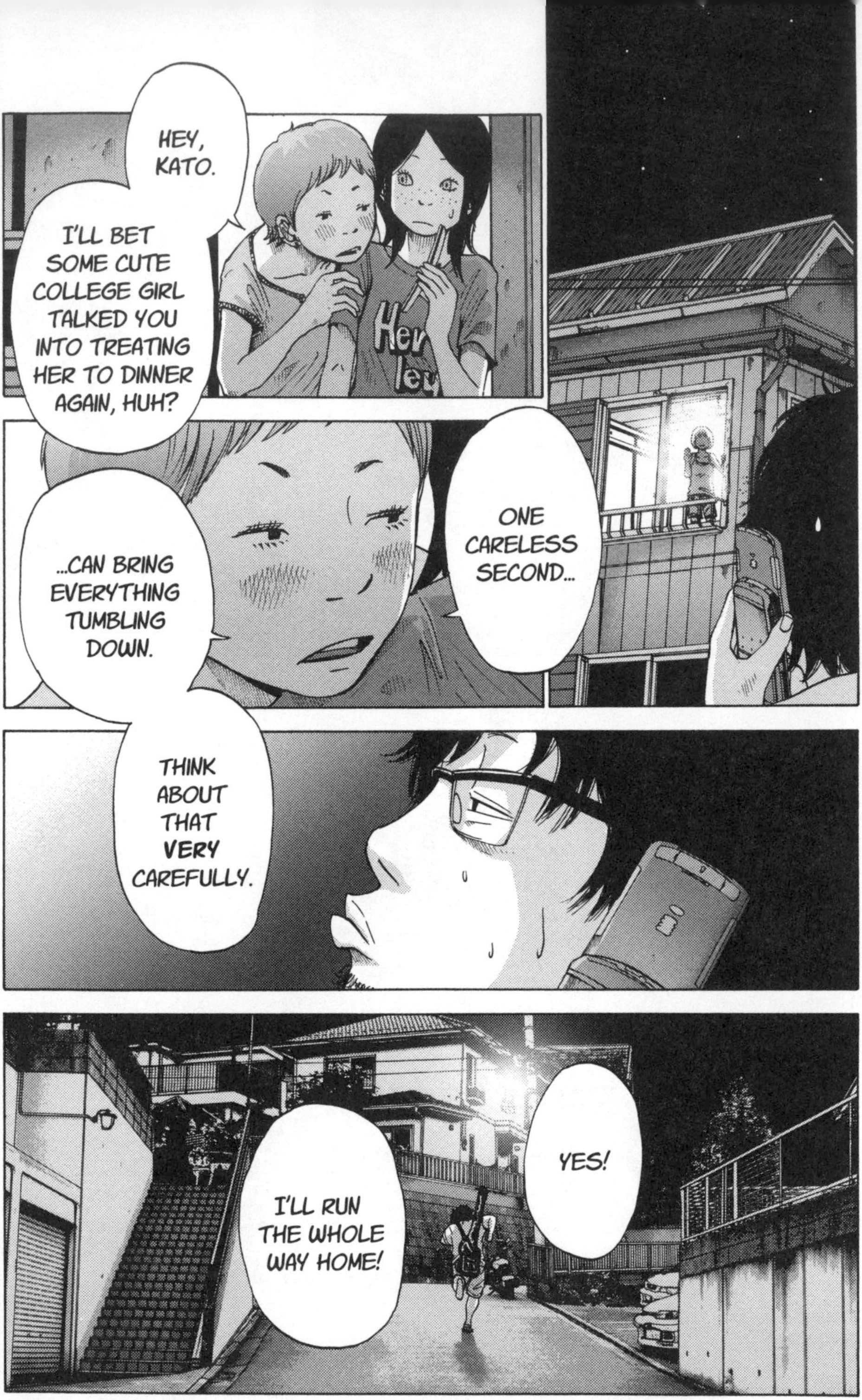
HEY, KATO.
I'LL BET SOME CUTE COLLEGE GIRL TALKED YOU INTO TREATING HER TO DINNER AGAIN, HUH?
ONE CARELESS SECOND...
...CAN BRING EVERYTHING TUMBLING DOWN.
THINK ABOUT THAT **VERY** CAREFULLY.
YES!
I'LL RUN THE WHOLE WAY HOME!

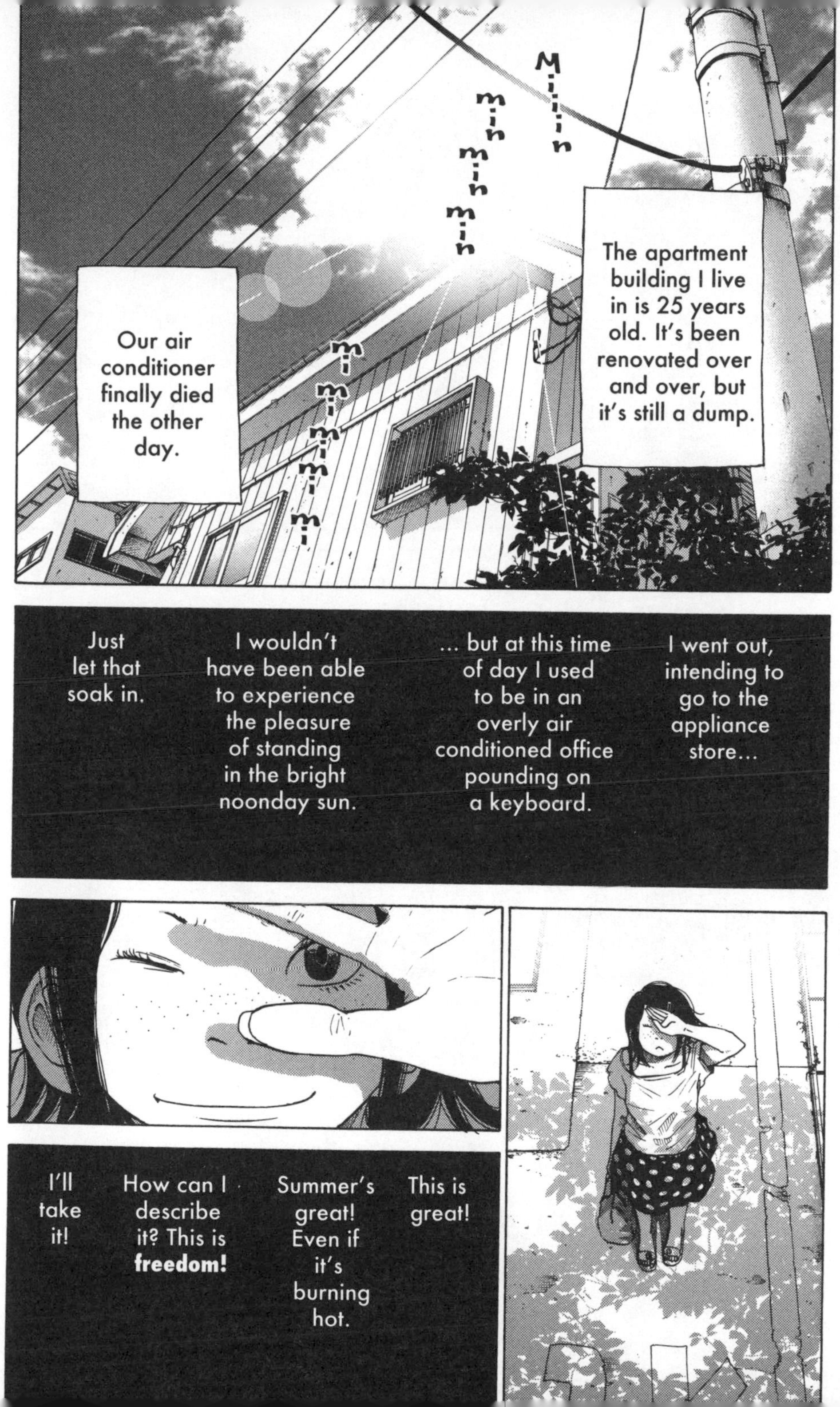

The apartment building I live in is 25 years old. It's been renovated over and over, but it's still a dump.
Miiiin
min min min
mimimimimi
Our air conditioner finally died the other day.
I went out, intending to go to the appliance store...
... but at this time of day I used to be in an overly air conditioned office pounding on a keyboard.
I wouldn't have been able to experience the pleasure of standing in the bright noonday sun.
Just let that soak in.
This is great!
Summer's great! Even if it's burning hot.
How can I describe it? This is **freedom!**
I'll take it!

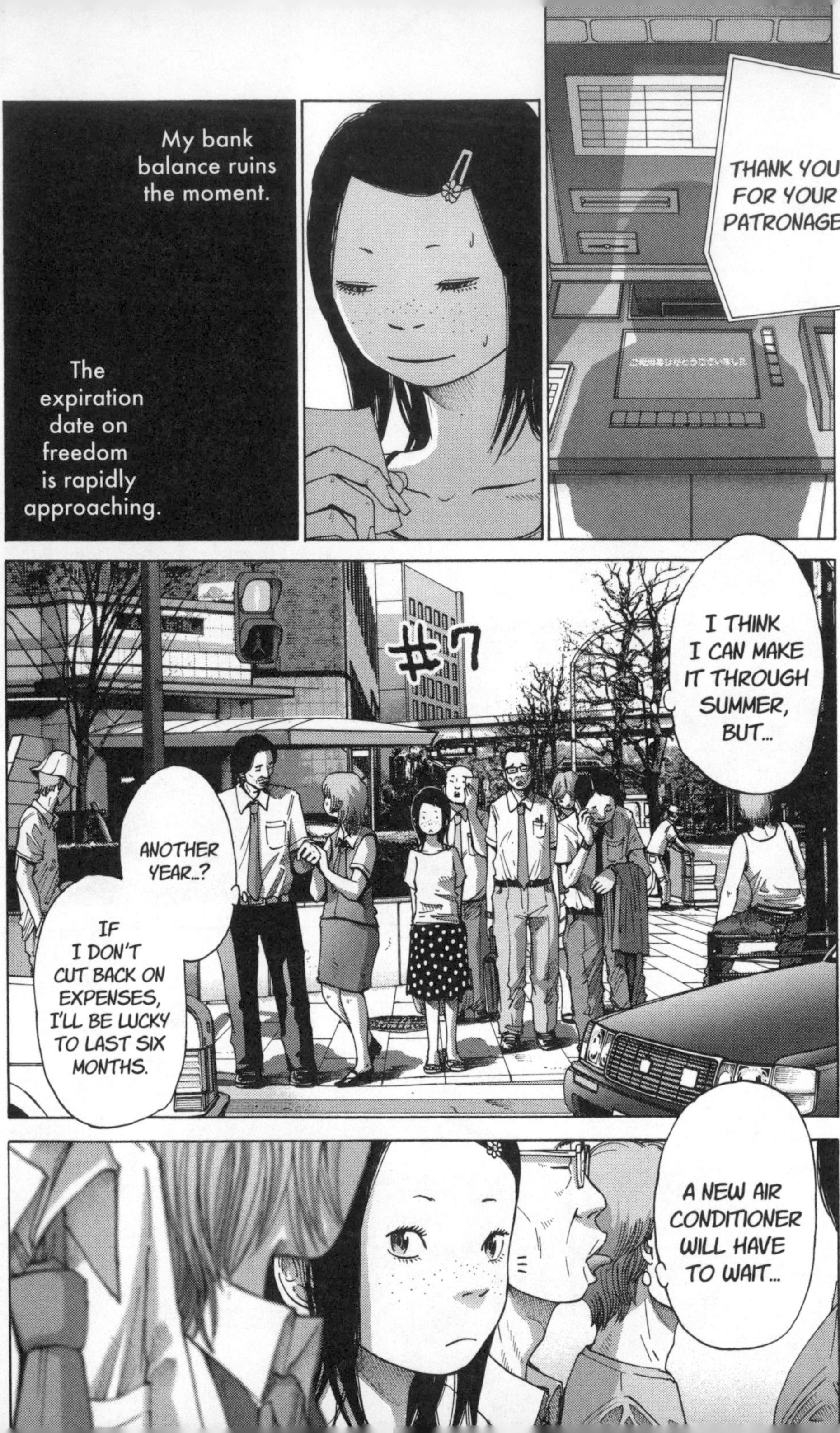

THANK YOU FOR YOUR PATRONAGE.
My bank balance ruins the moment.
The expiration date on freedom is rapidly approaching.
I THINK I CAN MAKE IT THROUGH SUMMER, BUT...
ANOTHER YEAR...?
IF I DON'T CUT BACK ON EXPENSES, I'LL BE LUCKY TO LAST SIX MONTHS.
A NEW AIR CONDITIONER WILL HAVE TO WAIT...

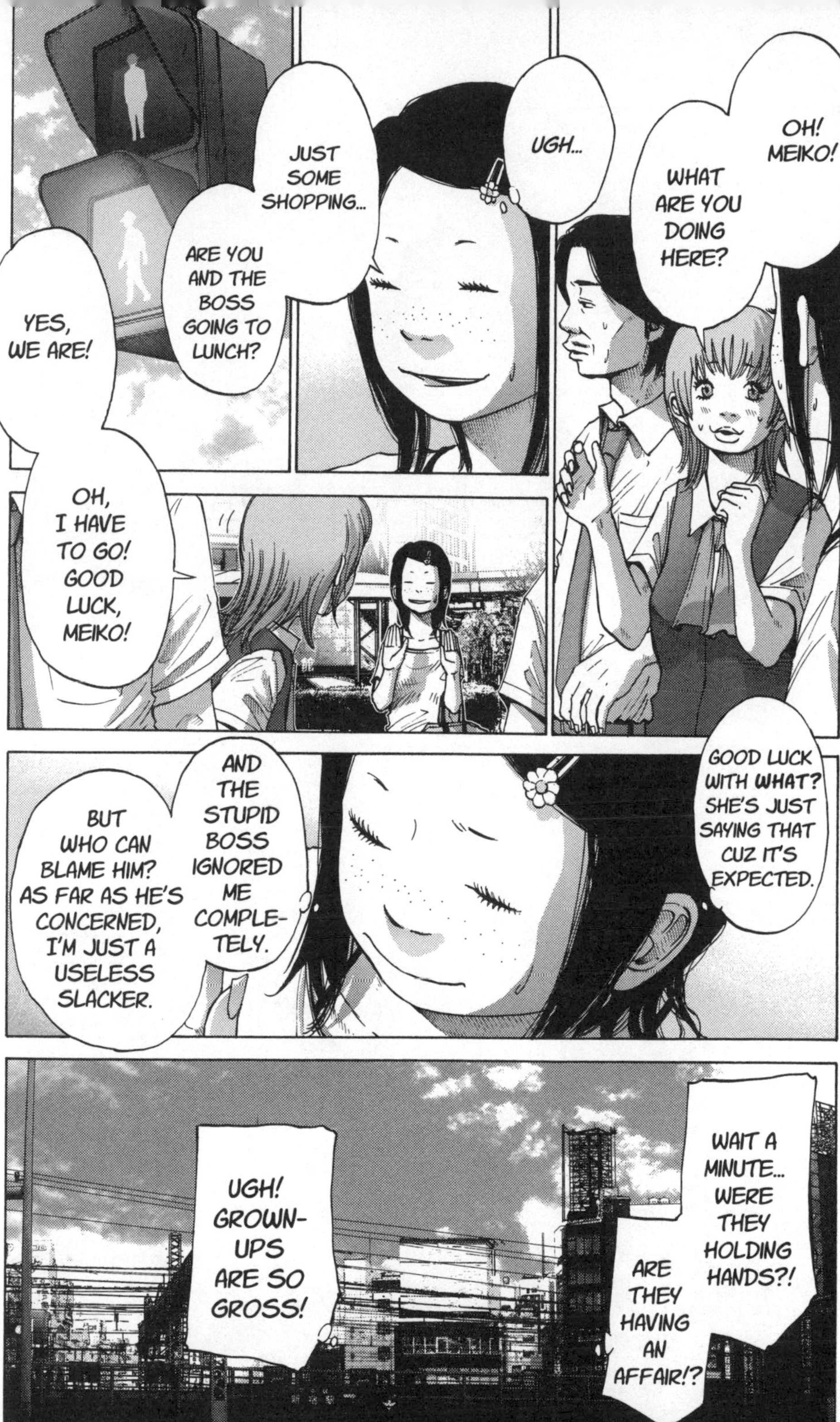

OH! MEIKO!
WHAT ARE YOU DOING HERE?
UGH...
JUST SOME SHOPPING...
ARE YOU AND THE BOSS GOING TO LUNCH?
YES, WE ARE!
OH, I HAVE TO GO! GOOD LUCK, MEIKO!
GOOD LUCK WITH WHAT? SHE'S JUST SAYING THAT CUZ IT'S EXPECTED.
AND THE STUPID BOSS IGNORED ME COMPLETELY.
BUT WHO CAN BLAME HIM? AS FAR AS HE'S CONCERNED, I'M JUST A USELESS SLACKER.
WAIT A MINUTE... WERE THEY HOLDING HANDS?!
ARE THEY HAVING AN AFFAIR!?
UGH! GROWN-UPS ARE SO GROSS!

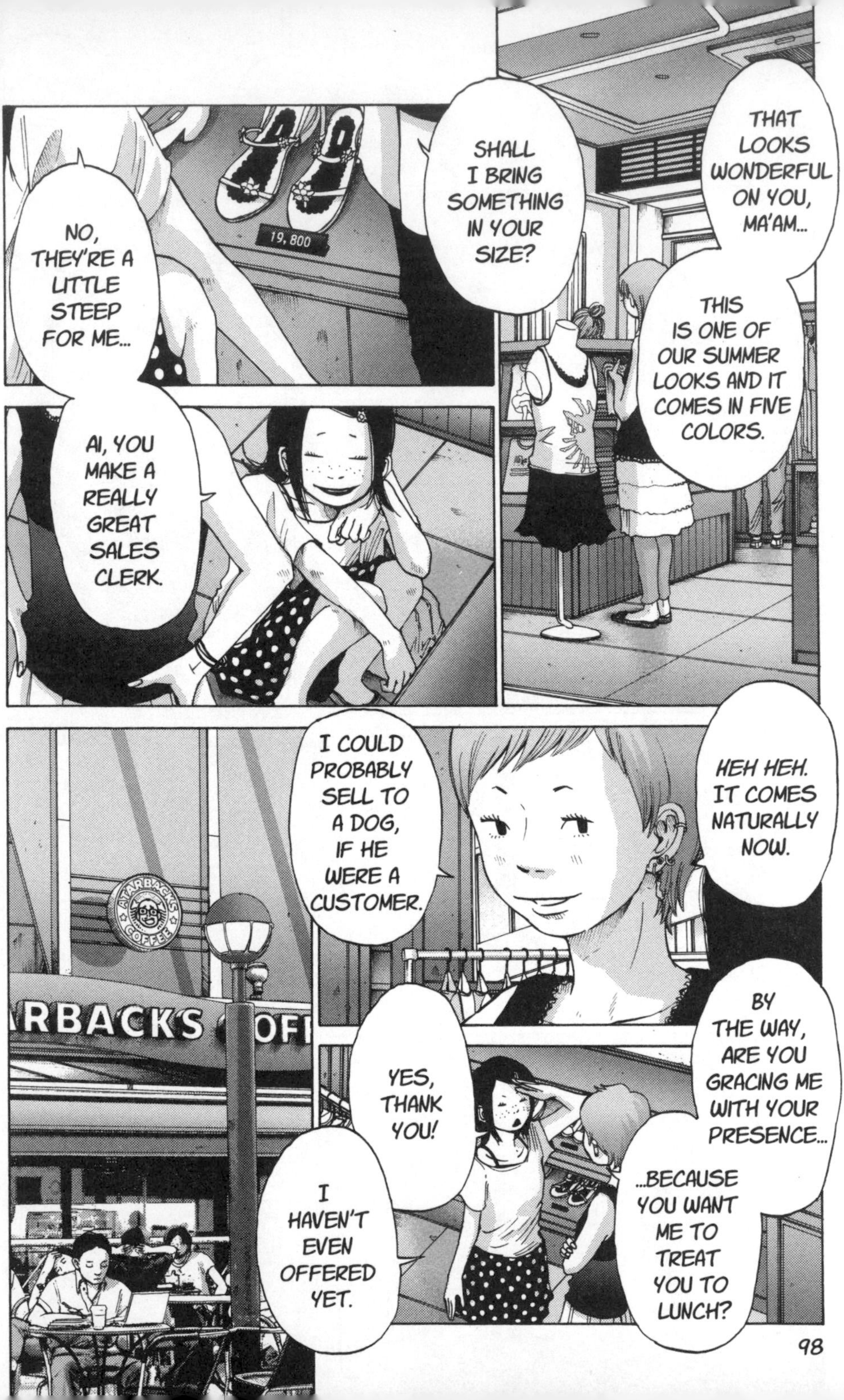
THAT LOOKS WONDERFUL ON YOU, MA'AM...
THIS IS ONE OF OUR SUMMER LOOKS AND IT COMES IN FIVE COLORS.
SHALL I BRING SOMETHING IN YOUR SIZE?
19,800
NO, THEY'RE A LITTLE STEEP FOR ME...
AI, YOU MAKE A REALLY GREAT SALES CLERK.
HEH HEH. IT COMES NATURALLY NOW.
I COULD PROBABLY SELL TO A DOG, IF HE WERE A CUSTOMER.
BY THE WAY, ARE YOU GRACING ME WITH YOUR PRESENCE...
...BECAUSE YOU WANT ME TO TREAT YOU TO LUNCH?
YES, THANK YOU!
I HAVEN'T EVEN OFFERED YET.
ATARBACKS COFFEE
RBACKS OFF

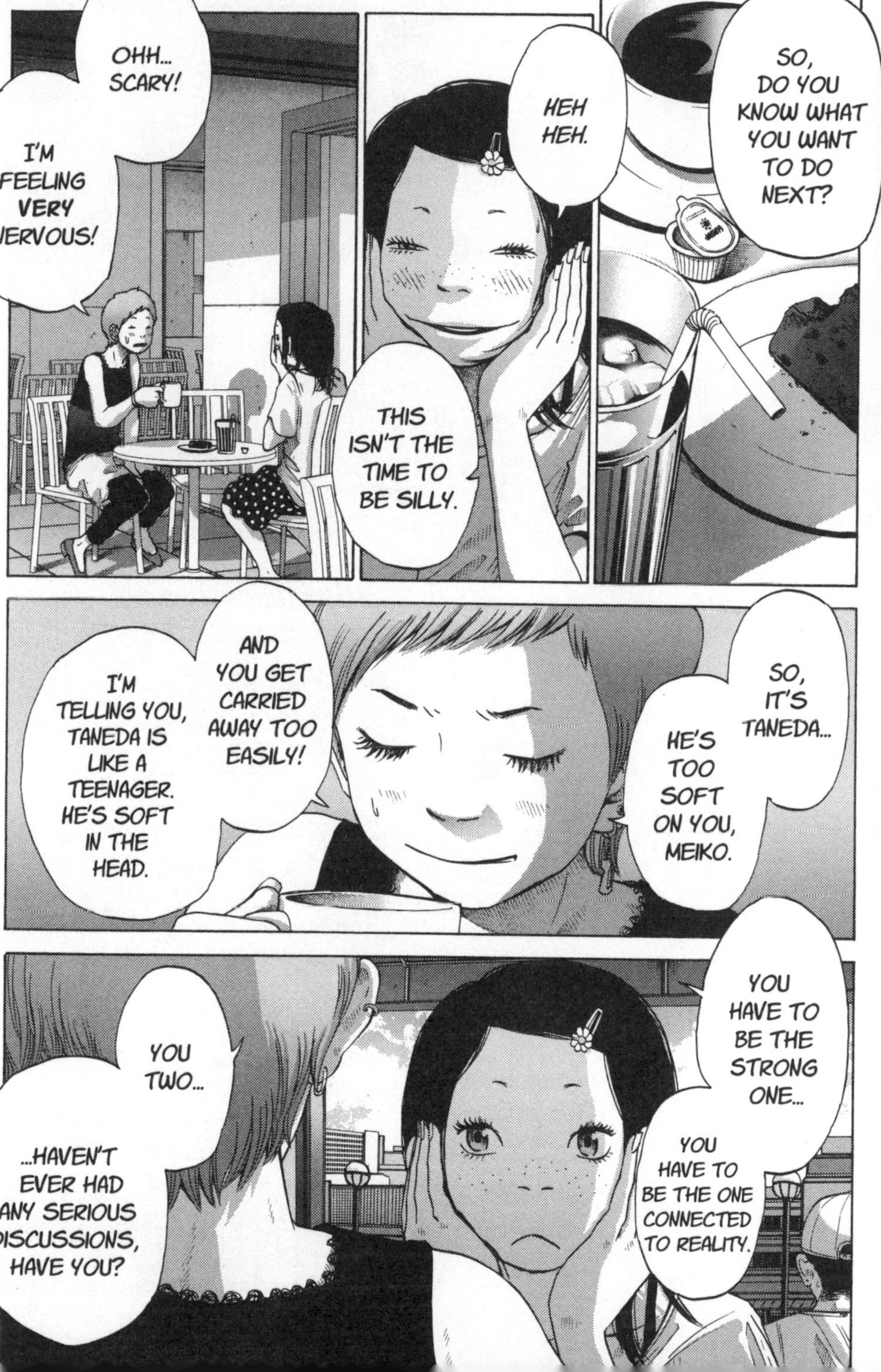
SO, DO YOU KNOW WHAT YOU WANT TO DO NEXT?
HEH HEH.
THIS ISN'T THE TIME TO BE SILLY.
OHH... SCARY!
I'M FEELING VERY NERVOUS!
SO, IT'S TANEDA...
HE'S TOO SOFT ON YOU, MEIKO.
AND YOU GET CARRIED AWAY TOO EASILY!
I'M TELLING YOU, TANEDA IS LIKE A TEENAGER. HE'S SOFT IN THE HEAD.
YOU HAVE TO BE THE STRONG ONE...
YOU HAVE TO BE THE ONE CONNECTED TO REALITY.
YOU TWO...
...HAVEN'T EVER HAD ANY SERIOUS DISCUSSIONS, HAVE YOU?

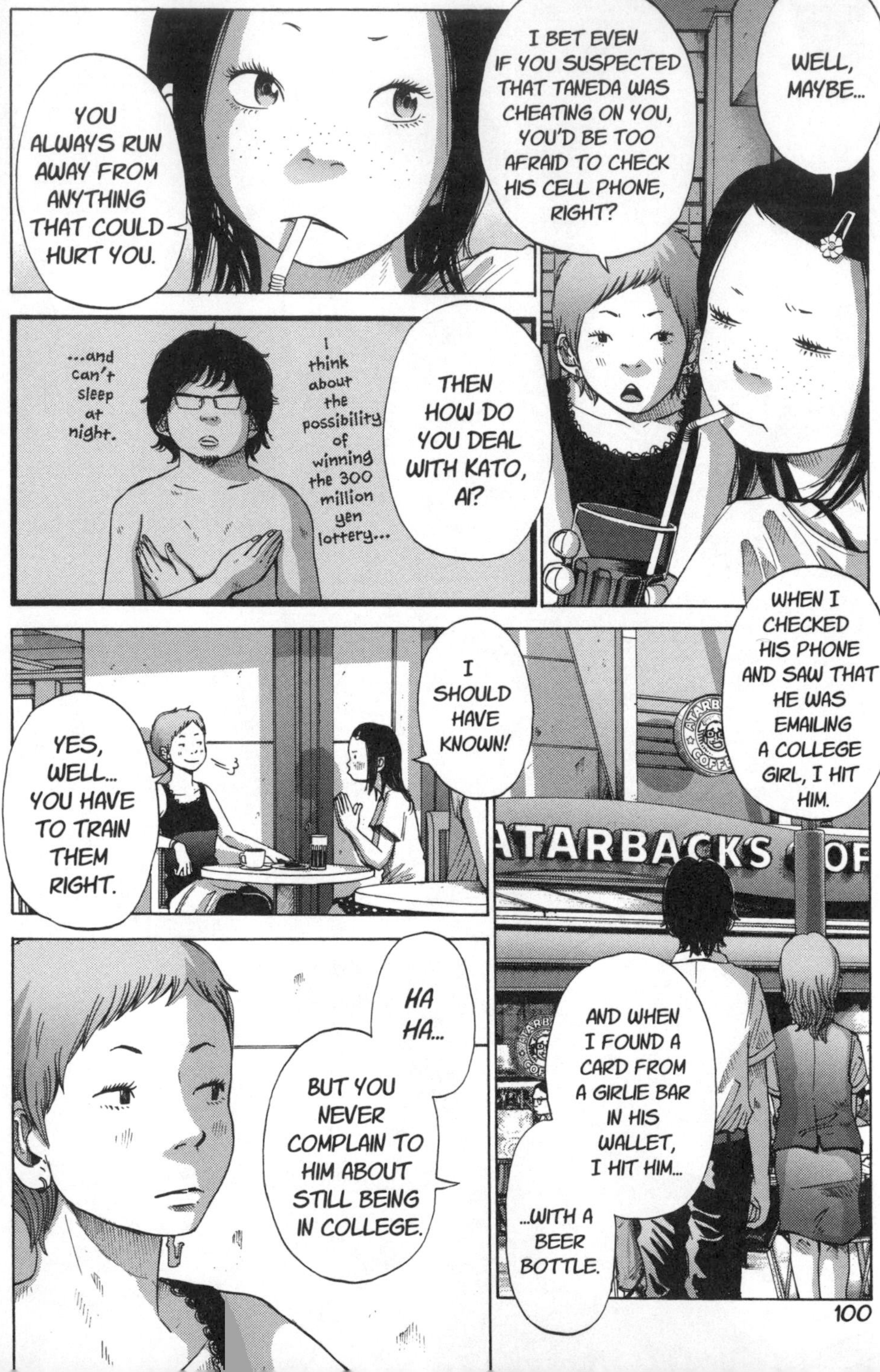

I BET EVEN IF YOU SUSPECTED THAT TANEDA WAS CHEATING ON YOU, YOU'D BE TOO AFRAID TO CHECK HIS CELL PHONE, RIGHT?
WELL, MAYBE...
YOU ALWAYS RUN AWAY FROM ANYTHING THAT COULD HURT YOU.
THEN HOW DO YOU DEAL WITH KATO, AI?
I think about the possibility of winning the 300 million yen lottery...
...and can't sleep at night.
WHEN I CHECKED HIS PHONE AND SAW THAT HE WAS EMAILING A COLLEGE GIRL, I HIT HIM.
ATARBACKS COF
AND WHEN I FOUND A CARD FROM A GIRLIE BAR IN HIS WALLET, I HIT HIM...
...WITH A BEER BOTTLE.
I SHOULD HAVE KNOWN!
YES, WELL... YOU HAVE TO TRAIN THEM RIGHT.
HA HA...
BUT YOU NEVER COMPLAIN TO HIM ABOUT STILL BEING IN COLLEGE.

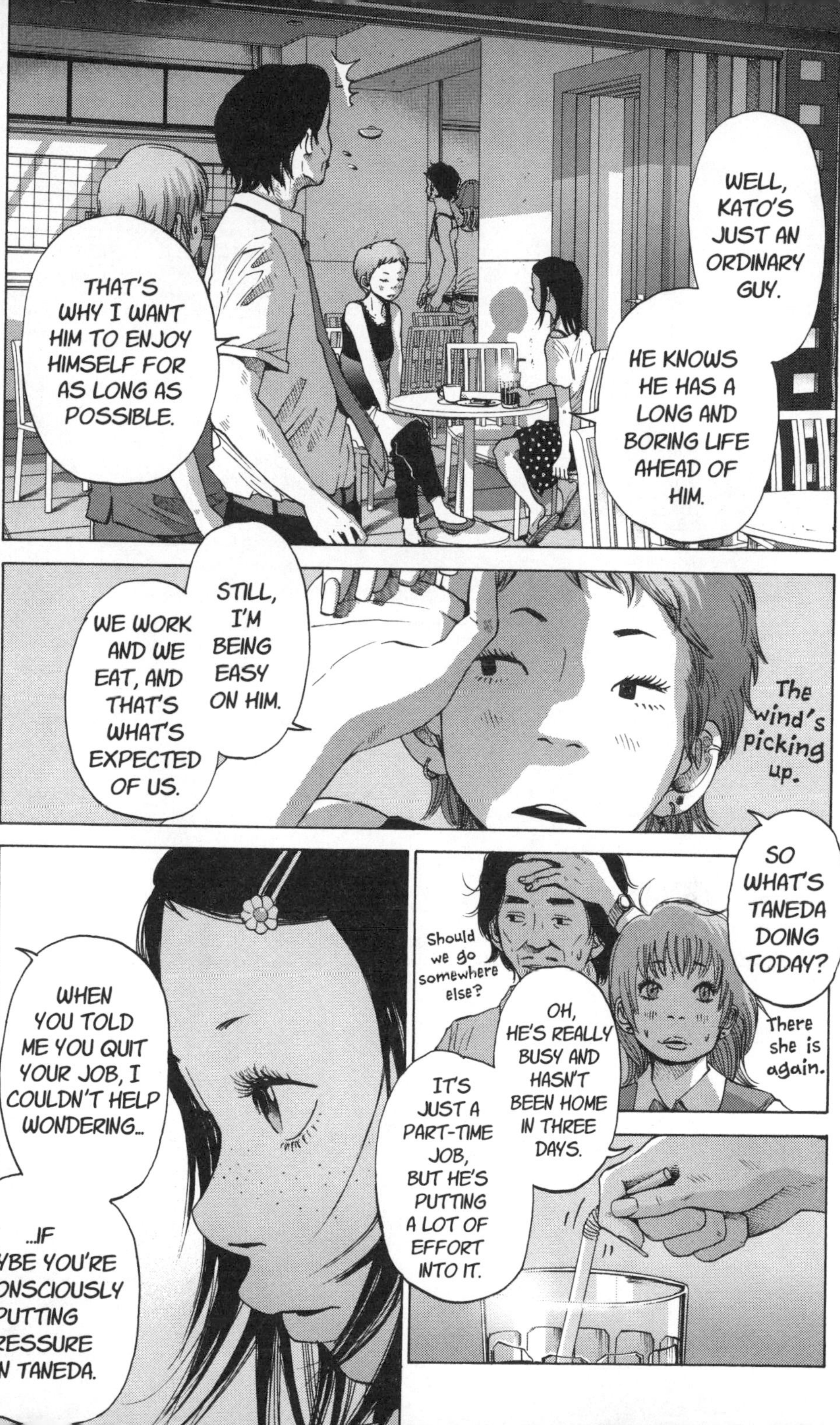
WELL, KATO'S JUST AN ORDINARY GUY.
HE KNOWS HE HAS A LONG AND BORING LIFE AHEAD OF HIM.
THAT'S WHY I WANT HIM TO ENJOY HIMSELF FOR AS LONG AS POSSIBLE.
The wind's picking up.
STILL, I'M BEING EASY ON HIM.
WE WORK AND WE EAT, AND THAT'S WHAT'S EXPECTED OF US.
SO WHAT'S TANEDA DOING TODAY?
There she is again.
Should we go somewhere else?
OH, HE'S REALLY BUSY AND HASN'T BEEN HOME IN THREE DAYS.
IT'S JUST A PART-TIME JOB, BUT HE'S PUTTING A LOT OF EFFORT INTO IT.
WHEN YOU TOLD ME YOU QUIT YOUR JOB, I COULDN'T HELP WONDERING...
...IF MAYBE YOU'RE UNCONSCIOUSLY PUTTING PRESSURE ON TANEDA.

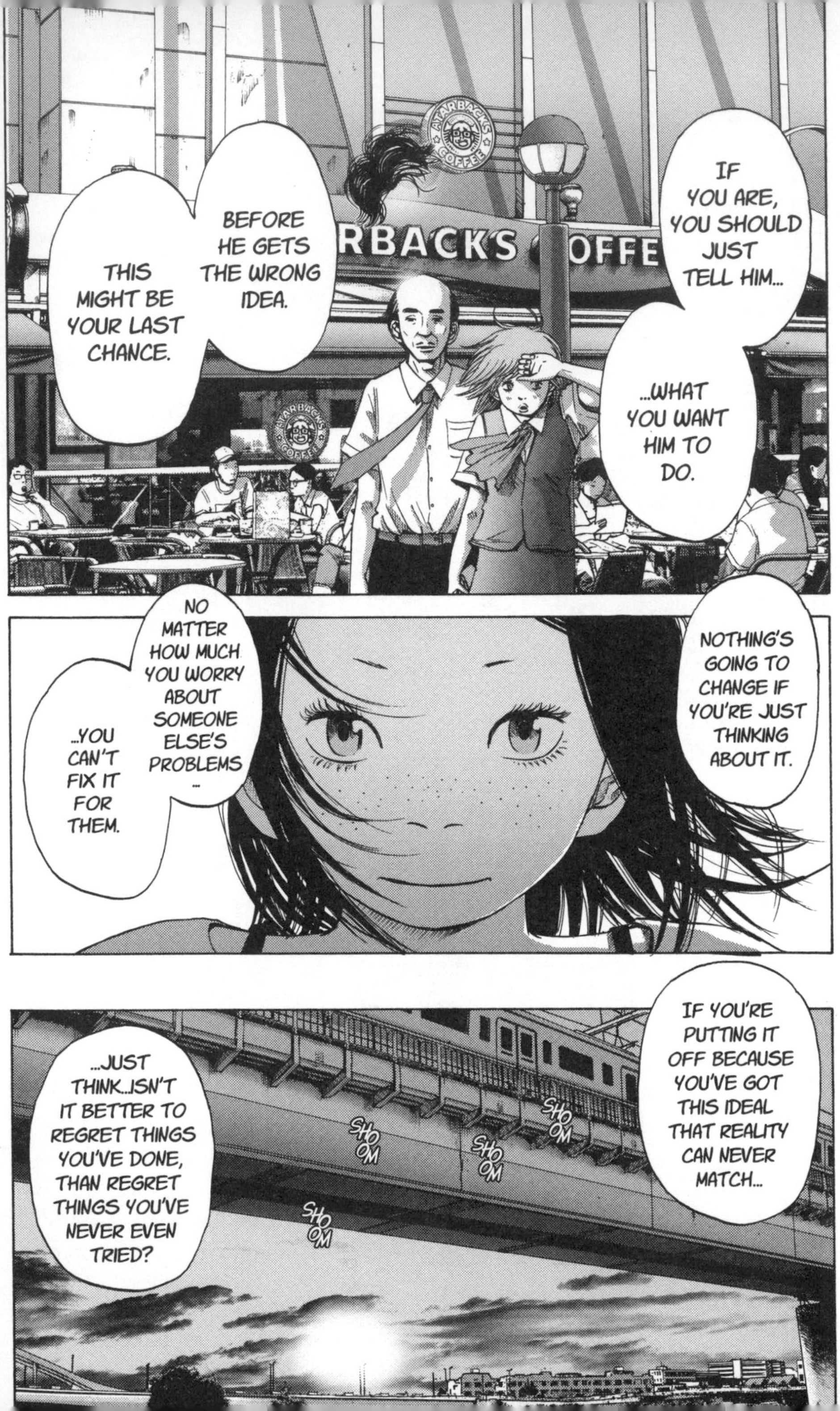
IF YOU ARE, YOU SHOULD JUST TELL HIM...
...WHAT YOU WANT HIM TO DO.
BEFORE HE GETS THE WRONG IDEA.
THIS MIGHT BE YOUR LAST CHANCE.
NOTHING'S GOING TO CHANGE IF YOU'RE JUST THINKING ABOUT IT.
NO MATTER HOW MUCH YOU WORRY ABOUT SOMEONE ELSE'S PROBLEMS...
...YOU CAN'T FIX IT FOR THEM.
IF YOU'RE PUTTING IT OFF BECAUSE YOU'VE GOT THIS IDEAL THAT REALITY CAN NEVER MATCH...
SHOOM
SHOOM
SHOOM
SHOOM
...JUST THINK...ISN'T IT BETTER TO REGRET THINGS YOU'VE DONE, THAN REGRET THINGS YOU'VE NEVER EVEN TRIED?

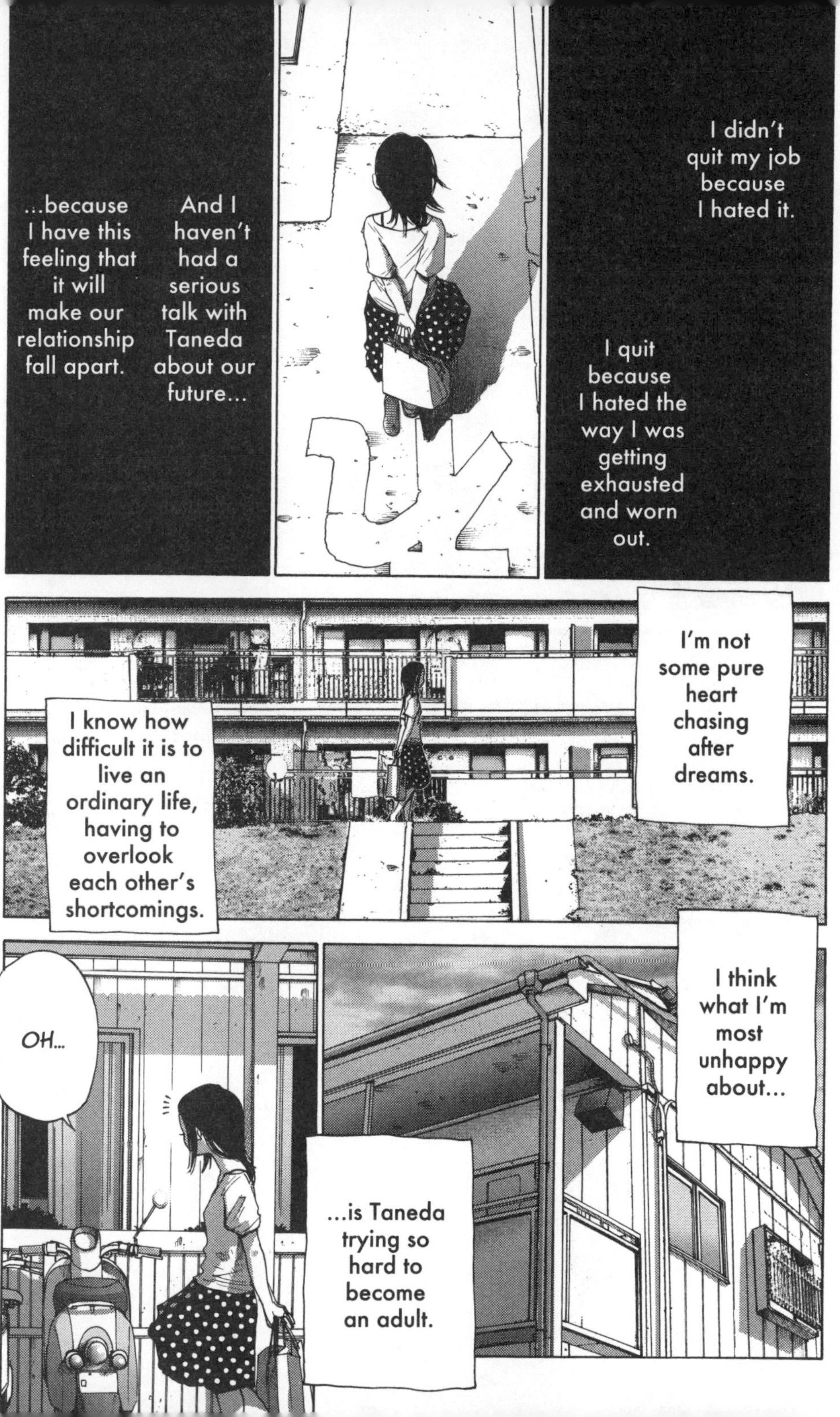
I didn't quit my job because I hated it.
I quit because I hated the way I was getting exhausted and worn out.
And I haven't had a serious talk with Taneda about our future...
...because I have this feeling that it will make our relationship fall apart.
I'm not some pure heart chasing after dreams.
I know how difficult it is to live an ordinary life, having to overlook each other's shortcomings.
I think what I'm most unhappy about...
...is Taneda trying so hard to become an adult.
OH...

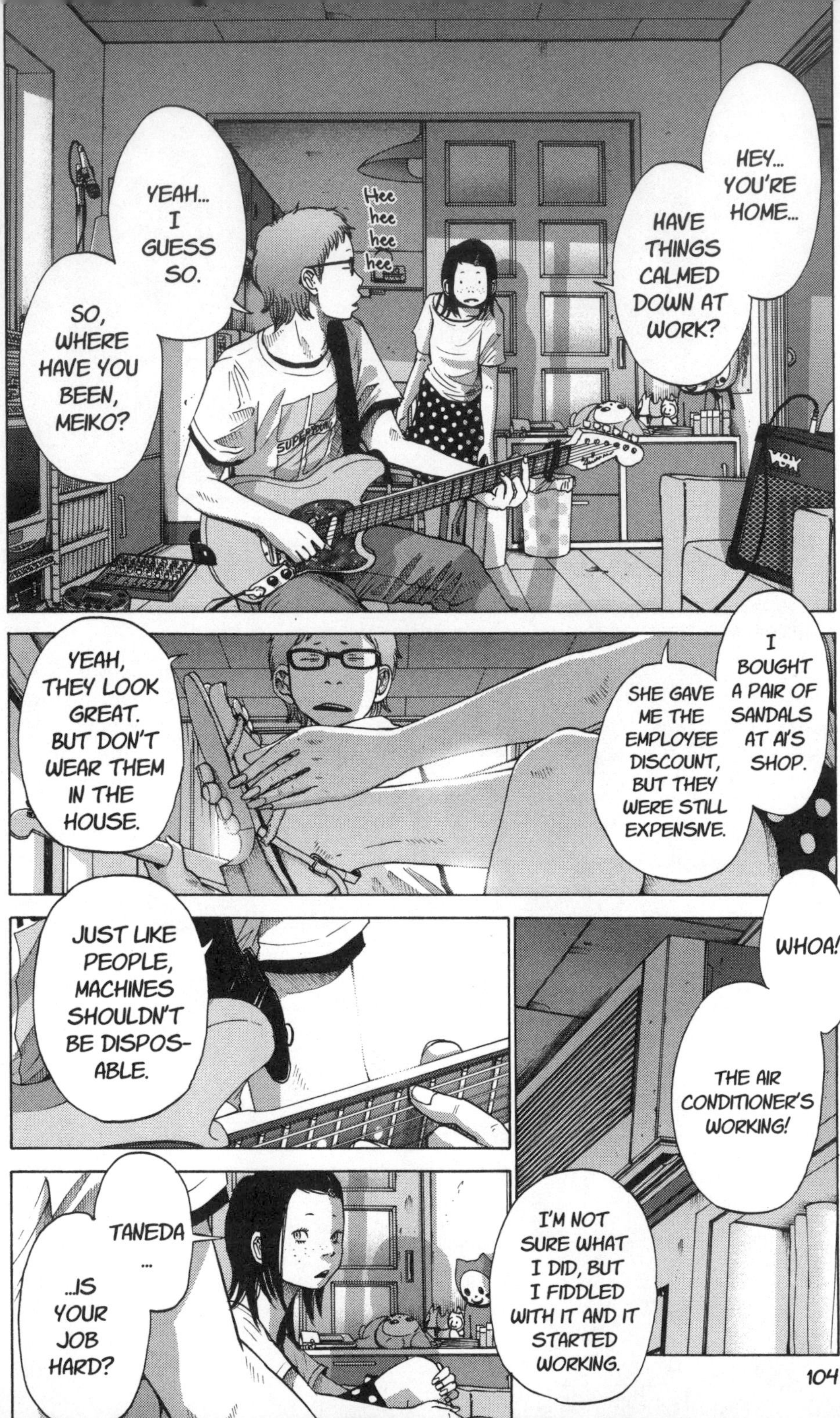
HEY... YOU'RE HOME...
HAVE THINGS CALMED DOWN AT WORK?
Hee hee hee hee
YEAH... I GUESS SO.
SO, WHERE HAVE YOU BEEN, MEIKO?
I BOUGHT A PAIR OF SANDALS AT AI'S SHOP.
SHE GAVE ME THE EMPLOYEE DISCOUNT, BUT THEY WERE STILL EXPENSIVE.
YEAH, THEY LOOK GREAT. BUT DON'T WEAR THEM IN THE HOUSE.
WHOA!
THE AIR CONDITIONER'S WORKING!
I'M NOT SURE WHAT I DID, BUT I FIDDLED WITH IT AND IT STARTED WORKING.
JUST LIKE PEOPLE, MACHINES SHOULDN'T BE DISPOS-ABLE.
TANEDA ...
...IS YOUR JOB HARD?

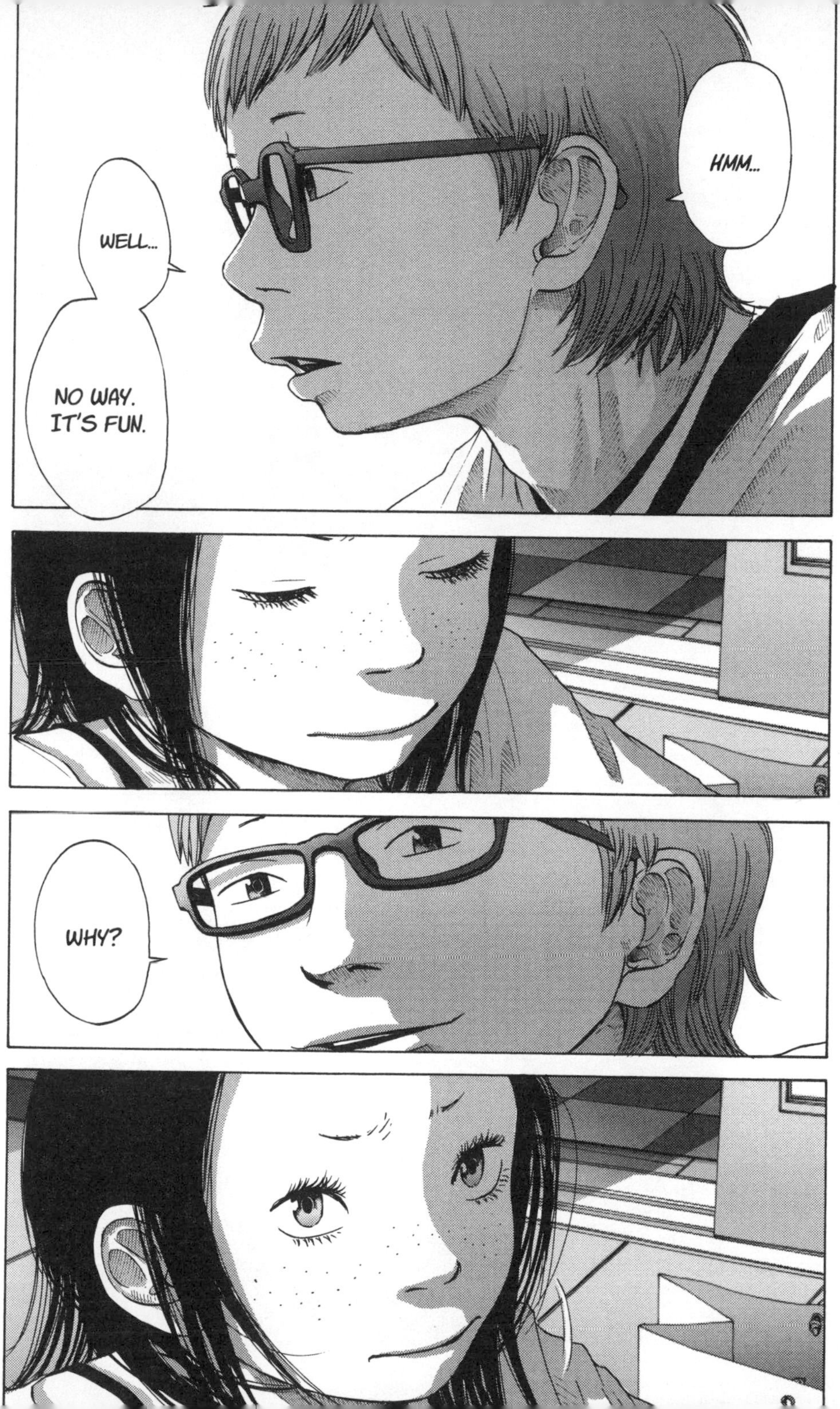
HMM...
WELL...
NO WAY. IT'S FUN.
WHY?

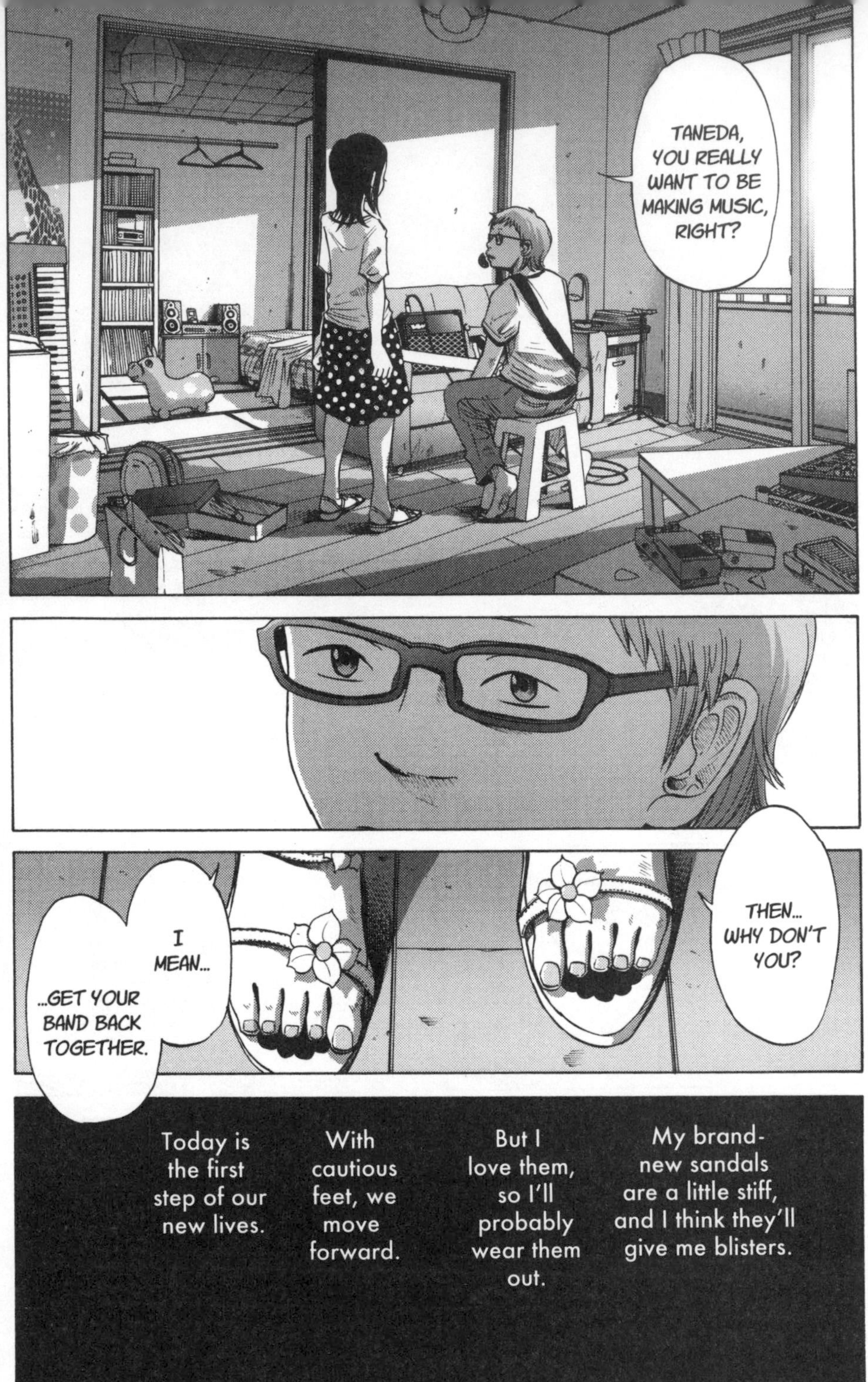
TANEDA, YOU REALLY WANT TO BE MAKING MUSIC, RIGHT?
THEN... WHY DON'T YOU?
I MEAN...
...GET YOUR BAND BACK TOGETHER.
My brand-new sandals are a little stiff, and I think they'll give me blisters.
But I love them, so I'll probably wear them out.
With cautious feet, we move forward.
Today is the first step of our new lives.

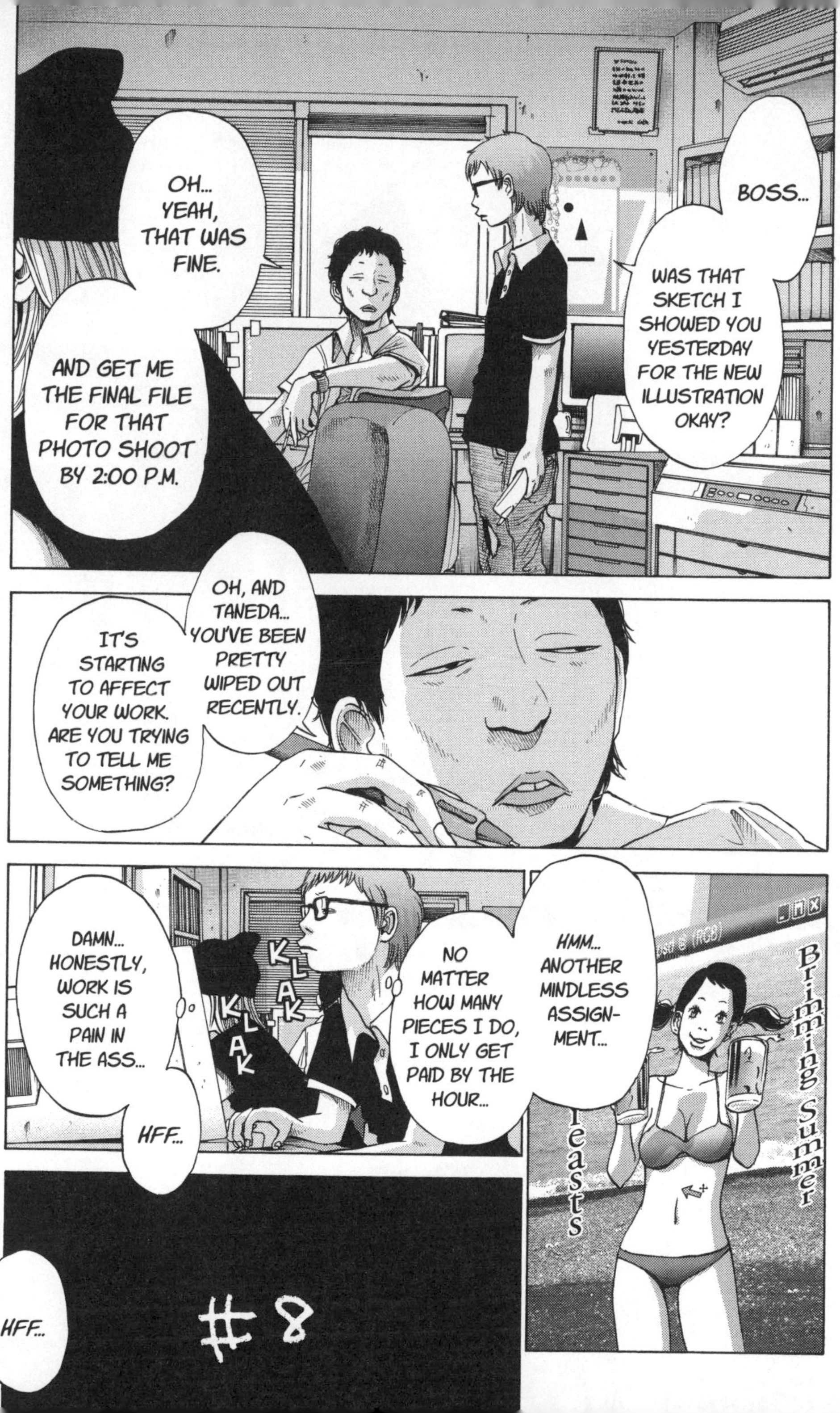
BOSS...
WAS THAT SKETCH I SHOWED YOU YESTERDAY FOR THE NEW ILLUSTRATION OKAY?
OH... YEAH, THAT WAS FINE.
AND GET ME THE FINAL FILE FOR THAT PHOTO SHOOT BY 2:00 P.M.
OH, AND TANEDA... YOU'VE BEEN PRETTY WIPED OUT RECENTLY.
IT'S STARTING TO AFFECT YOUR WORK. ARE YOU TRYING TO TELL ME SOMETHING?
Brimming Summer
HMM... ANOTHER MINDLESS ASSIGNMENT...
NO MATTER HOW MANY PIECES I DO, I ONLY GET PAID BY THE HOUR...
KLAK KLAK
DAMN... HONESTLY, WORK IS SUCH A PAIN IN THE ASS...
HFF...
#8
HFF...

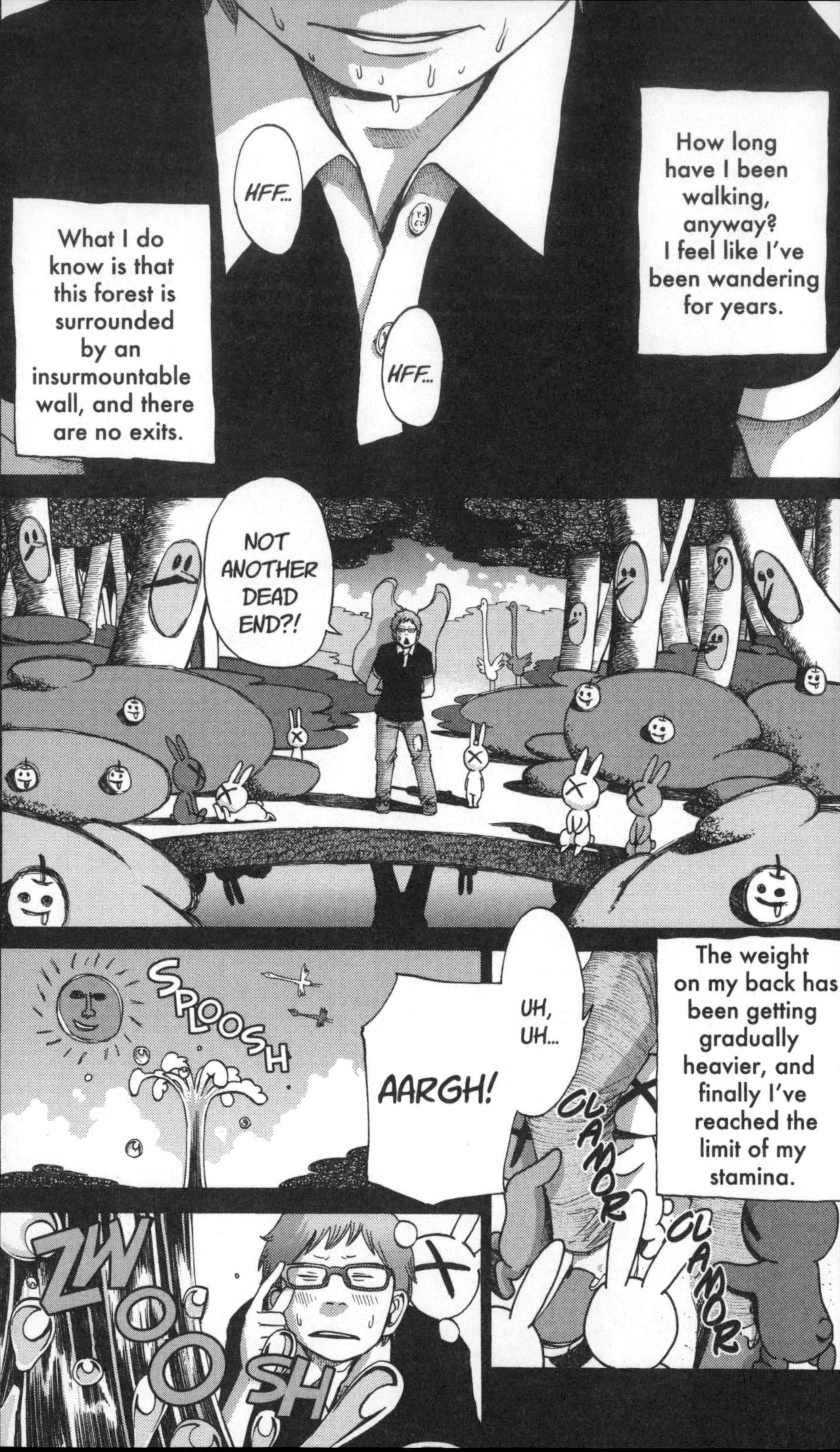
How long have I been walking, anyway? I feel like I've been wandering for years.
HFF...
HFF...
What I do know is that this forest is surrounded by an insurmountable wall, and there are no exits.
NOT ANOTHER DEAD END?!
The weight on my back has been getting gradually heavier, and finally I've reached the limit of my stamina.
CLAMOR
CLAMOR
UH, UH...
AARGH!
SPLOOSH
ZWOOOSH

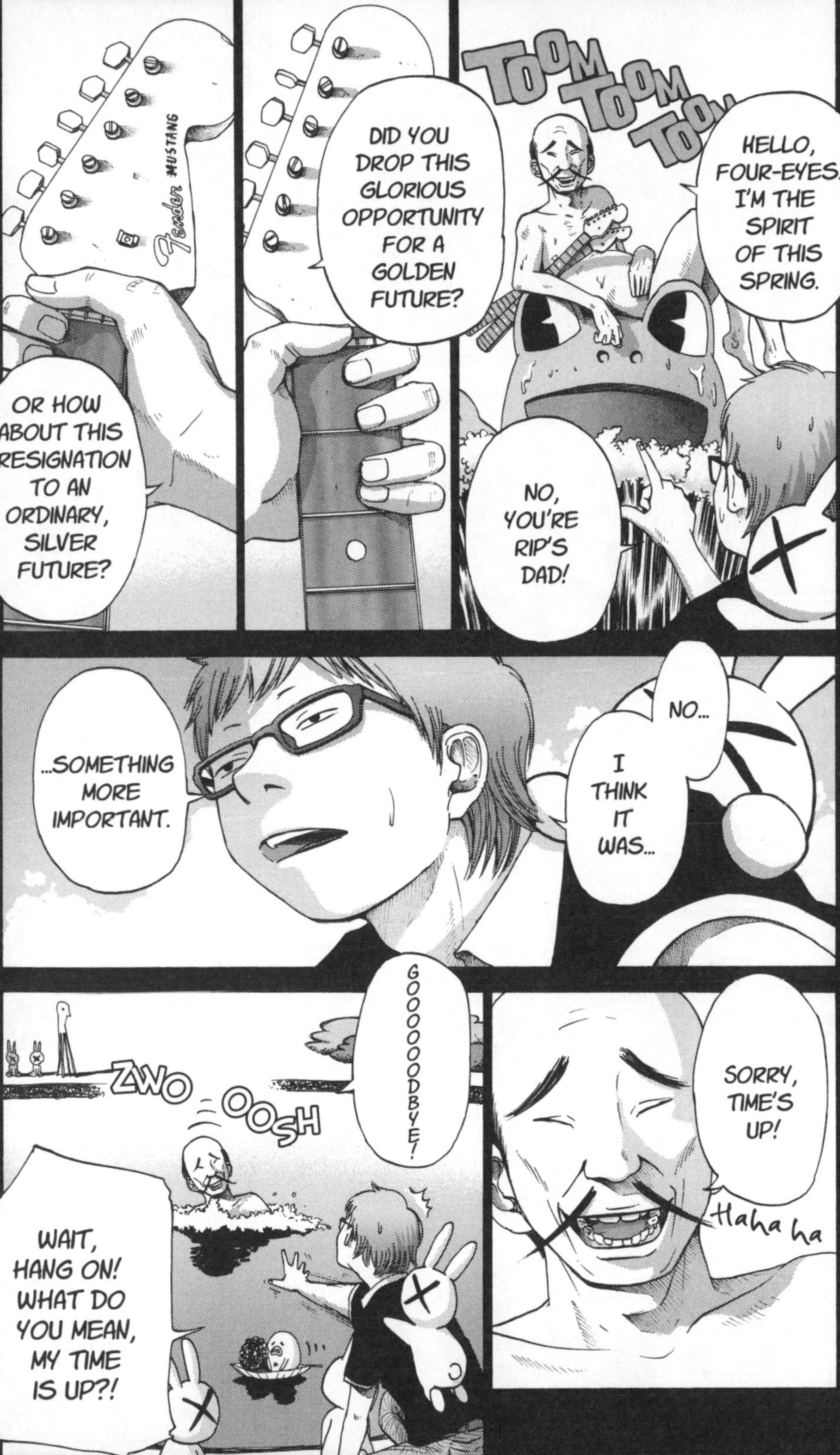
TOOM TOOM TOO
HELLO, FOUR-EYES. I'M THE SPIRIT OF THIS SPRING.
NO, YOU'RE RIP'S DAD!
Fender MUSTANG
DID YOU DROP THIS GLORIOUS OPPORTUNITY FOR A GOLDEN FUTURE?
OR HOW ABOUT THIS RESIGNATION TO AN ORDINARY, SILVER FUTURE?
NO...
I THINK IT WAS...
...SOMETHING MORE IMPORTANT.
SORRY, TIME'S UP!
Haha ha
GOOOOOOODBYE!
ZWO OOSH
WAIT, HANG ON! WHAT DO YOU MEAN, MY TIME IS UP?!

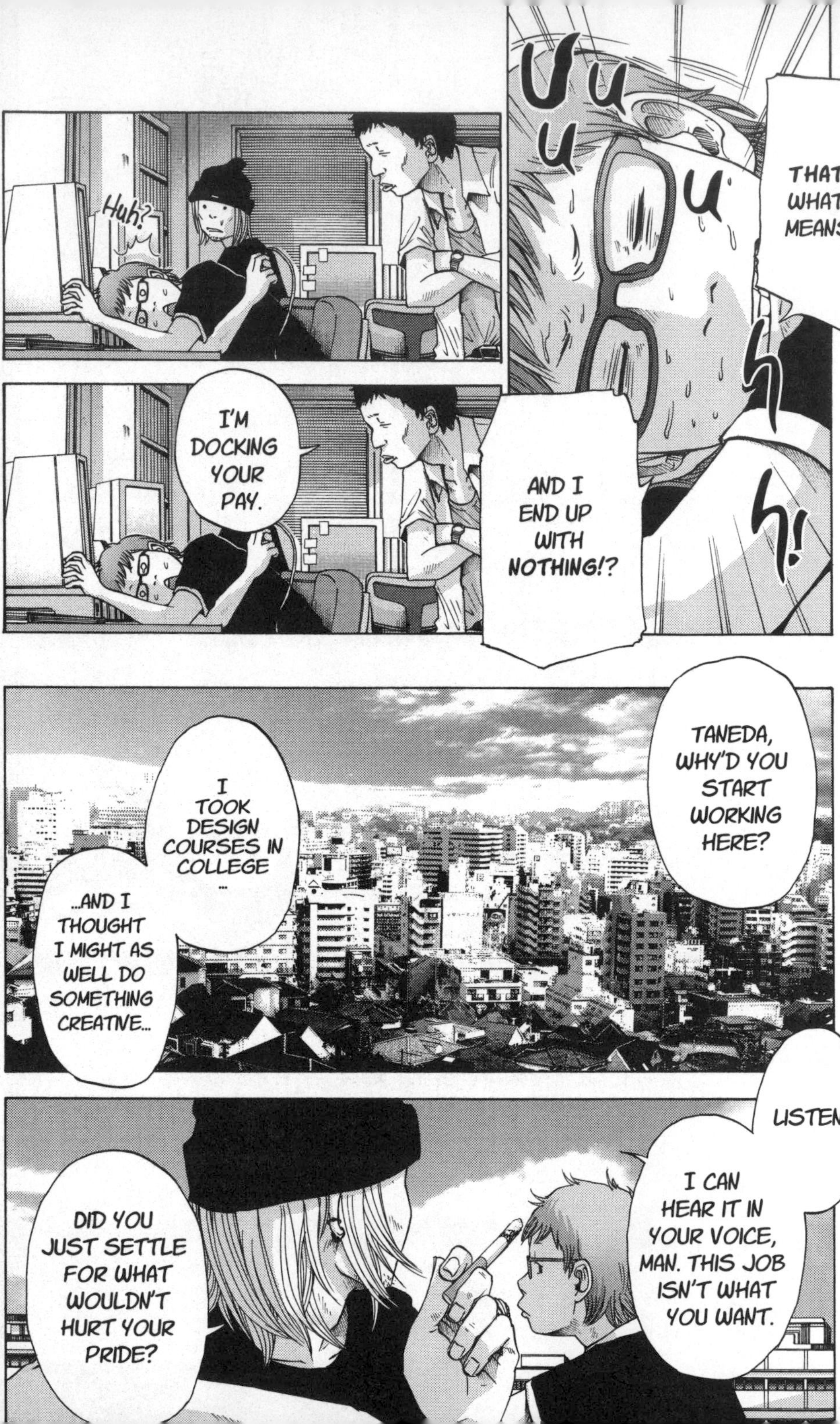
Uuuuhh!
THAT'S WHAT IT MEANS?!
AND I END UP WITH NOTHING!?
Huh?
I'M DOCKING YOUR PAY.
TANEDA, WHY'D YOU START WORKING HERE?
I TOOK DESIGN COURSES IN COLLEGE ...
...AND I THOUGHT I MIGHT AS WELL DO SOMETHING CREATIVE...
LISTEN.
I CAN HEAR IT IN YOUR VOICE, MAN. THIS JOB ISN'T WHAT YOU WANT.
DID YOU JUST SETTLE FOR WHAT WOULDN'T HURT YOUR PRIDE?

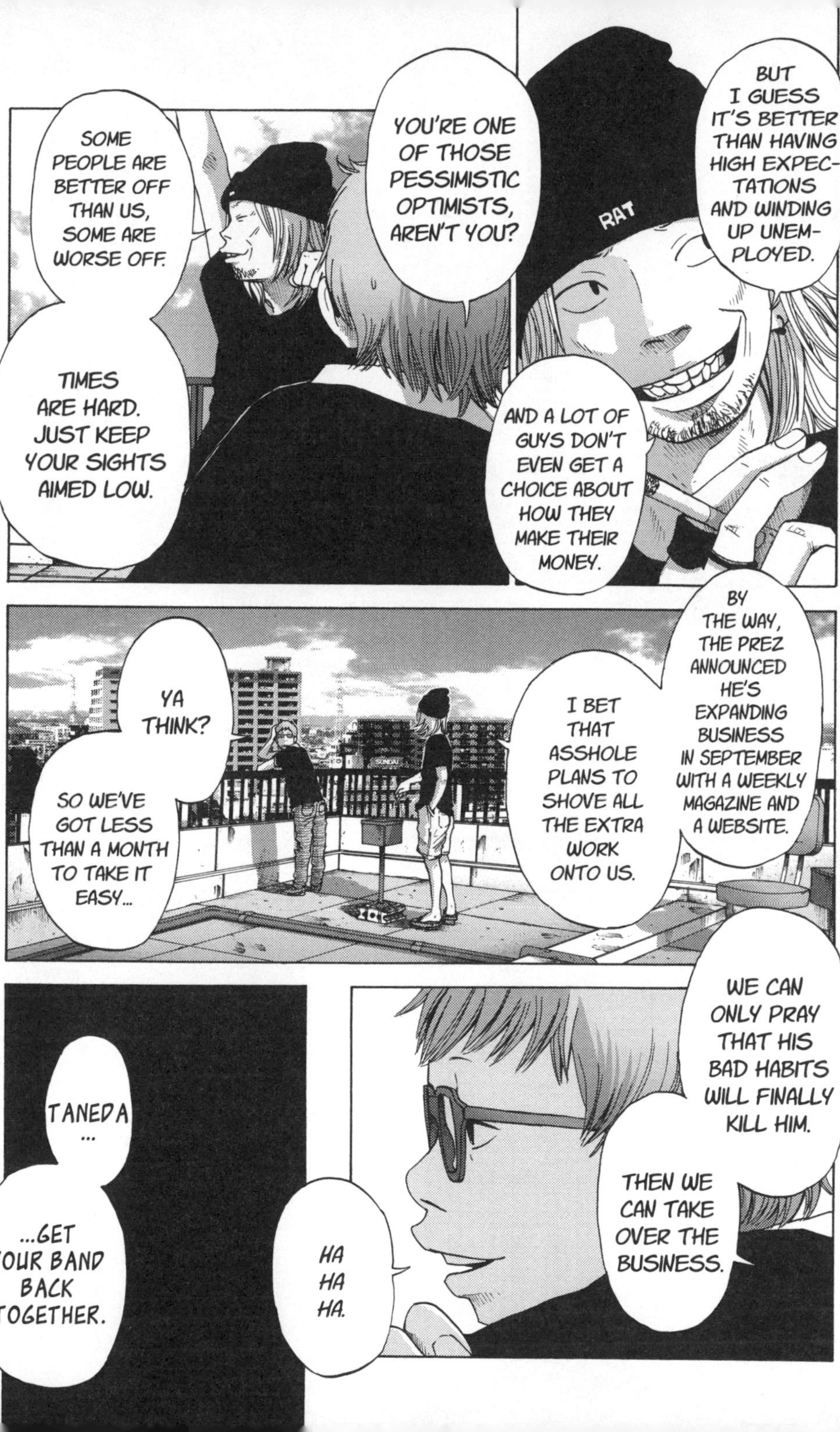
BUT I GUESS IT'S BETTER THAN HAVING HIGH EXPEC-TATIONS AND WINDING UP UNEM-PLOYED.
RAT
AND A LOT OF GUYS DON'T EVEN GET A CHOICE ABOUT HOW THEY MAKE THEIR MONEY.
YOU'RE ONE OF THOSE PESSIMISTIC OPTIMISTS, AREN'T YOU?
SOME PEOPLE ARE BETTER OFF THAN US, SOME ARE WORSE OFF.
TIMES ARE HARD. JUST KEEP YOUR SIGHTS AIMED LOW.
BY THE WAY, THE PREZ ANNOUNCED HE'S EXPANDING BUSINESS IN SEPTEMBER WITH A WEEKLY MAGAZINE AND A WEBSITE.
I BET THAT ASSHOLE PLANS TO SHOVE ALL THE EXTRA WORK ONTO US.
YA THINK?
SO WE'VE GOT LESS THAN A MONTH TO TAKE IT EASY...
WE CAN ONLY PRAY THAT HIS BAD HABITS WILL FINALLY KILL HIM.
THEN WE CAN TAKE OVER THE BUSINESS.
HA HA HA.
TANEDA...
...GET YOUR BAND BACK TOGETHER.

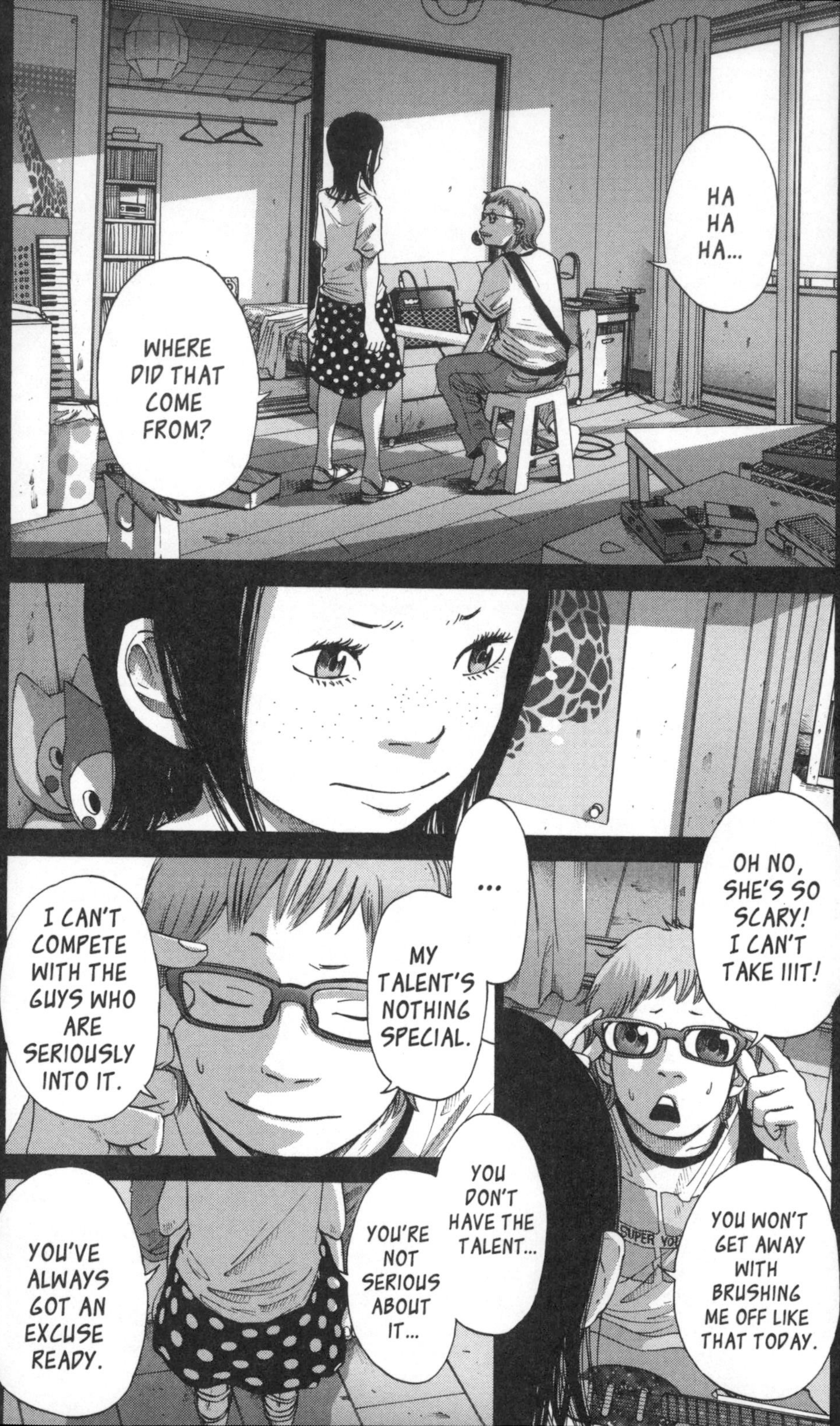
HA HA HA...
WHERE DID THAT COME FROM?
OH NO, SHE'S SO SCARY! I CAN'T TAKE IIIT!
...
MY TALENT'S NOTHING SPECIAL.
I CAN'T COMPETE WITH THE GUYS WHO ARE SERIOUSLY INTO IT.
YOU WON'T GET AWAY WITH BRUSHING ME OFF LIKE THAT TODAY.
YOU DON'T HAVE THE TALENT...
YOU'RE NOT SERIOUS ABOUT IT...
YOU'VE ALWAYS GOT AN EXCUSE READY.

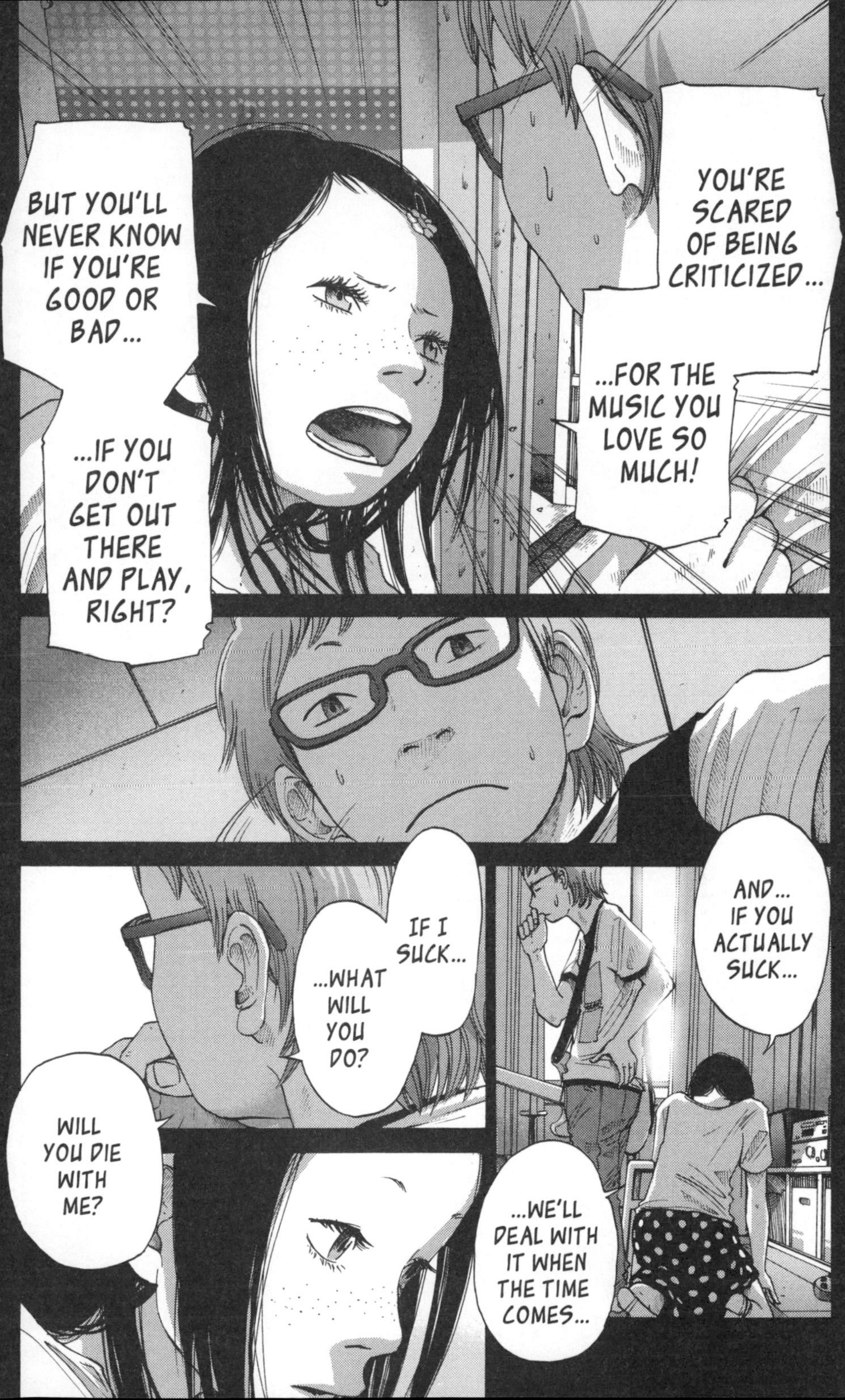
YOU'RE SCARED OF BEING CRITICIZED...
...FOR THE MUSIC YOU LOVE SO MUCH!
BUT YOU'LL NEVER KNOW IF YOU'RE GOOD OR BAD...
...IF YOU DON'T GET OUT THERE AND PLAY, RIGHT?
AND... IF YOU ACTUALLY SUCK...
...WE'LL DEAL WITH IT WHEN THE TIME COMES...
IF I SUCK...
...WHAT WILL YOU DO?
WILL YOU DIE WITH ME?

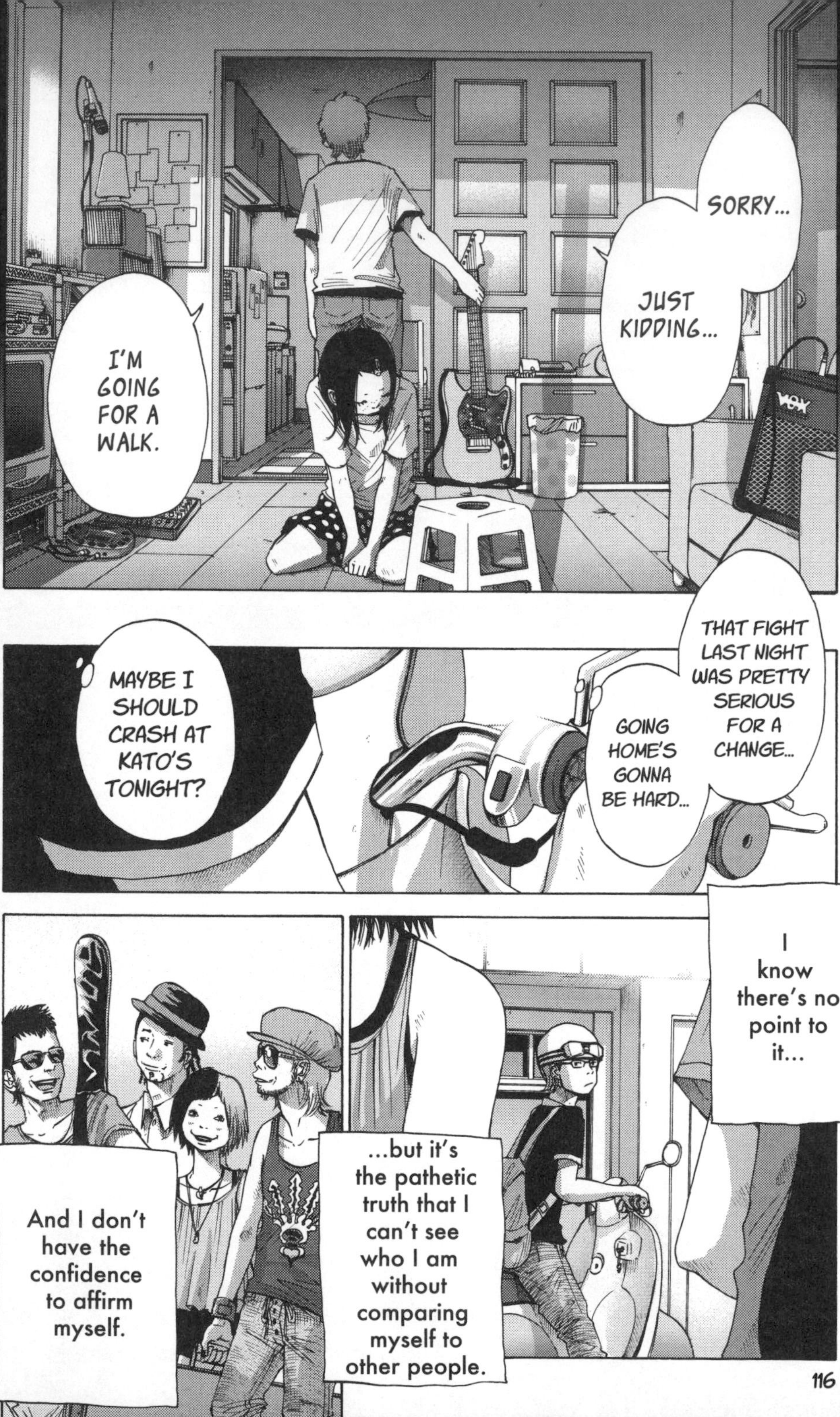
SORRY...
JUST KIDDING...
I'M GOING FOR A WALK.
THAT FIGHT LAST NIGHT WAS PRETTY SERIOUS FOR A CHANGE...
GOING HOME'S GONNA BE HARD...
MAYBE I SHOULD CRASH AT KATO'S TONIGHT?
I know there's no point to it...
...but it's the pathetic truth that I can't see who I am without comparing myself to other people.
And I don't have the confidence to affirm myself.

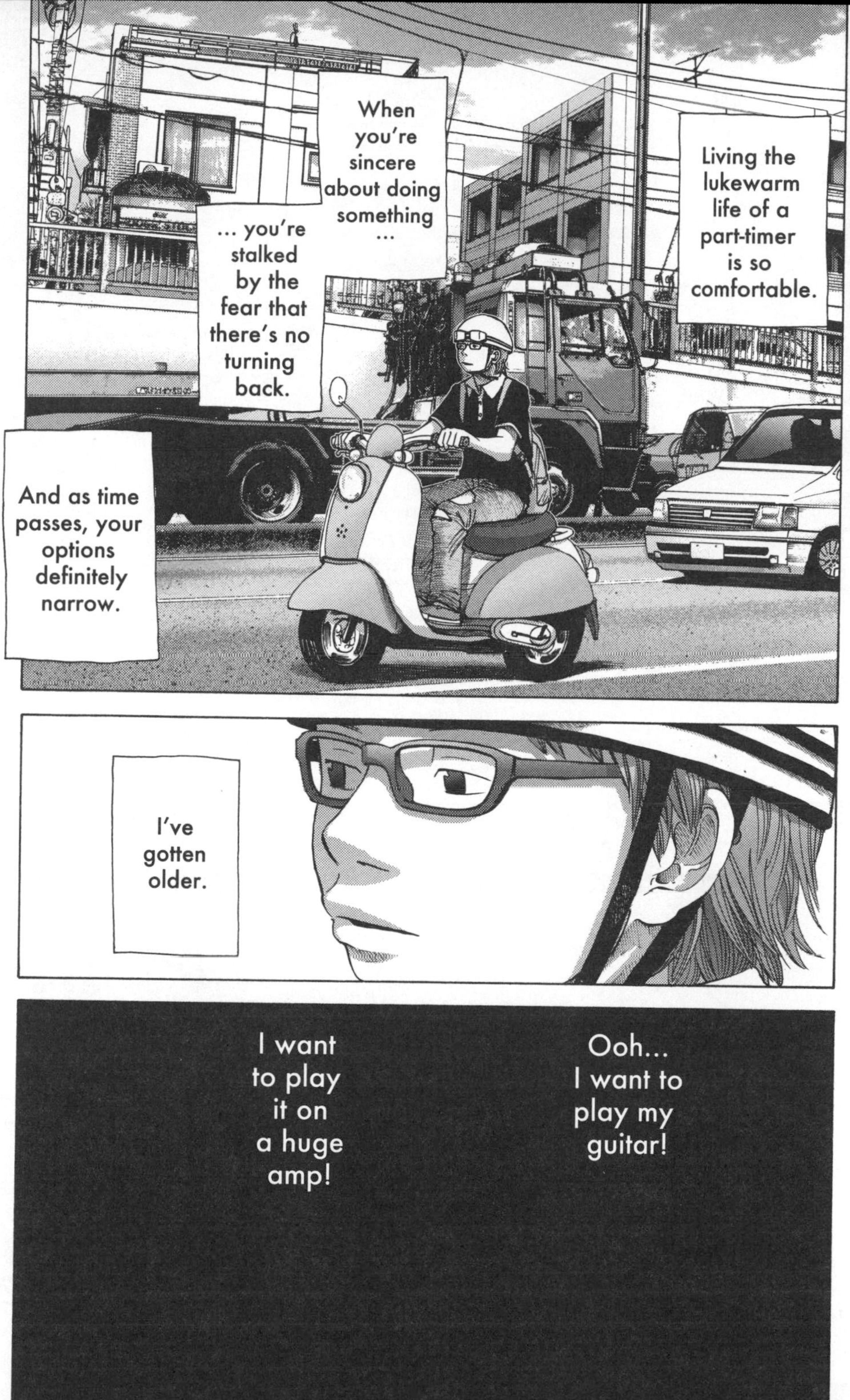

Living the lukewarm life of a part-timer is so comfortable.
When you're sincere about doing something ...
... you're stalked by the fear that there's no turning back.
And as time passes, your options definitely narrow.
I've gotten older.
Ooh... I want to play my guitar!
I want to play it on a huge amp!

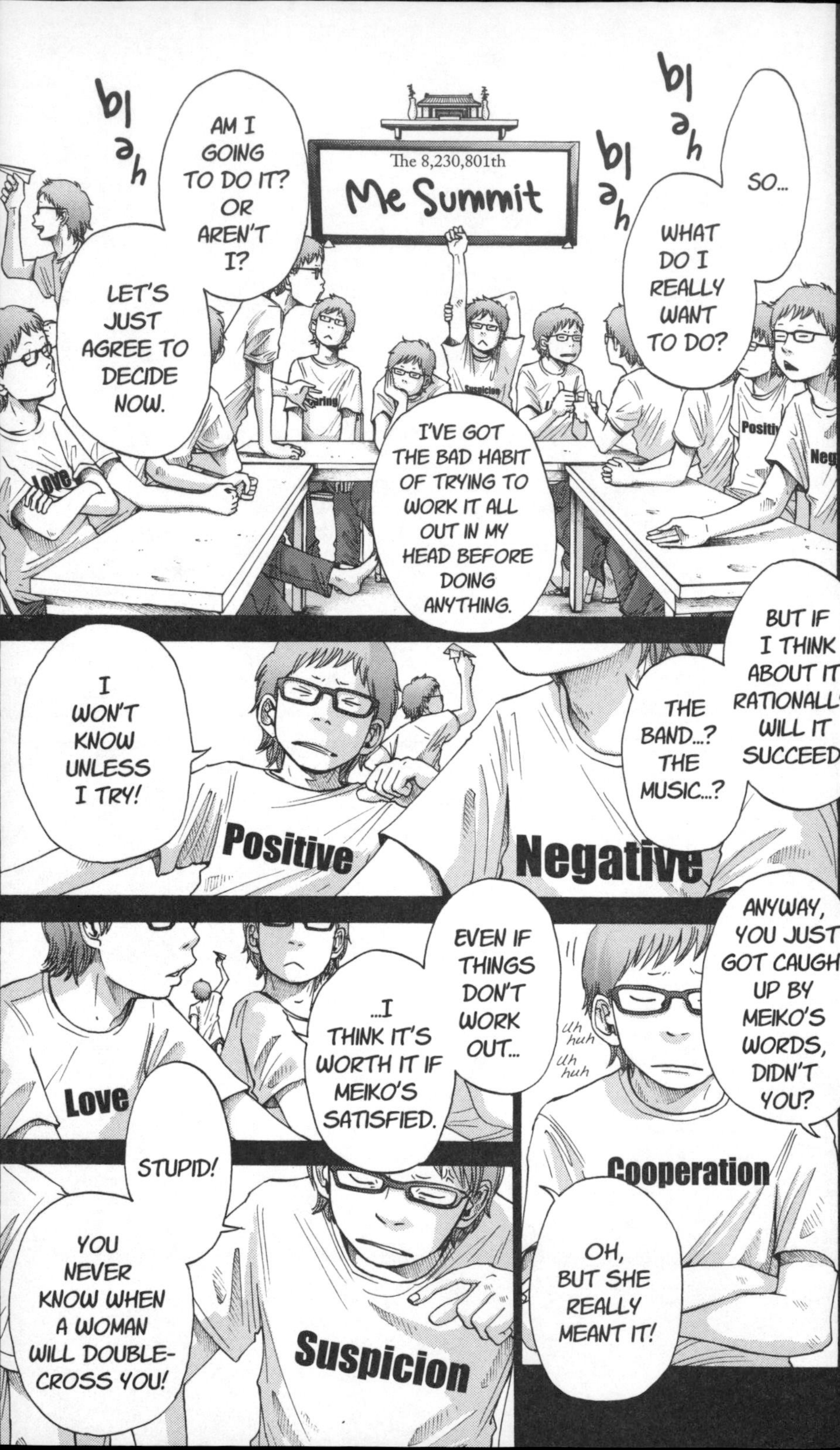
SO...
WHAT DO I REALLY WANT TO DO?
blah
blah
The 8,230,801th
Me Summit
blah
AM I GOING TO DO IT? OR AREN'T I?
LET'S JUST AGREE TO DECIDE NOW.
I'VE GOT THE BAD HABIT OF TRYING TO WORK IT ALL OUT IN MY HEAD BEFORE DOING ANYTHING.
BUT IF I THINK ABOUT IT RATIONALLY, WILL IT SUCCEED?
THE BAND...? THE MUSIC...?
Negative
I WON'T KNOW UNLESS I TRY!
Positive
ANYWAY, YOU JUST GOT CAUGHT UP BY MEIKO'S WORDS, DIDN'T YOU?
uh huh
uh huh
Cooperation
OH, BUT SHE REALLY MEANT IT!
EVEN IF THINGS DON'T WORK OUT...
...I THINK IT'S WORTH IT IF MEIKO'S SATISFIED.
Love
STUPID!
YOU NEVER KNOW WHEN A WOMAN WILL DOUBLE-CROSS YOU!
Suspicion

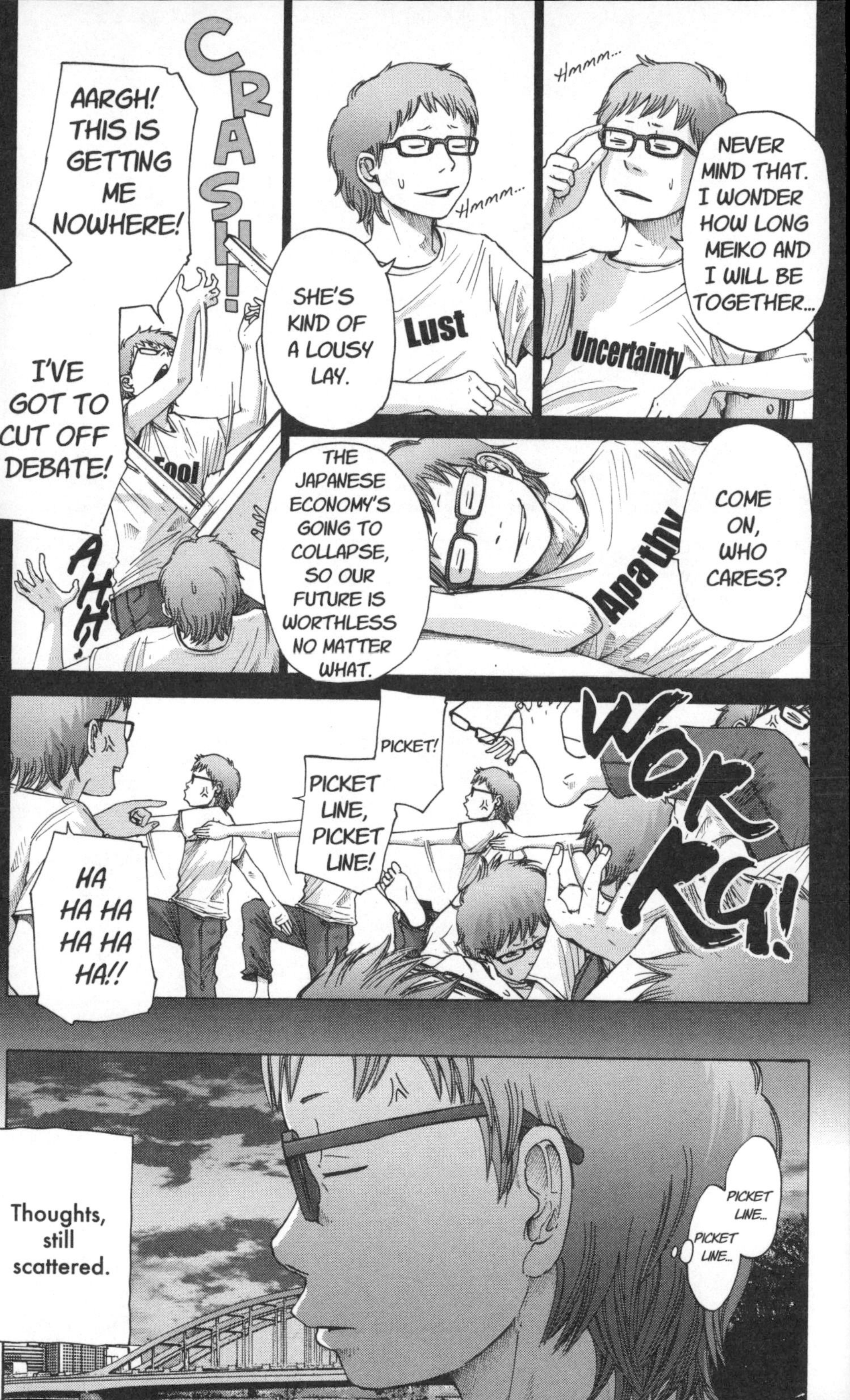
Hmmm...
NEVER MIND THAT. I WONDER HOW LONG MEIKO AND I WILL BE TOGETHER...
Uncertainty
Hmmm...
SHE'S KIND OF A LOUSY LAY.
Lust
COME ON, WHO CARES?
Apathy
THE JAPANESE ECONOMY'S GOING TO COLLAPSE, SO OUR FUTURE IS WORTHLESS NO MATTER WHAT.
CRASH!
AARGH! THIS IS GETTING ME NOWHERE!
I'VE GOT TO CUT OFF DEBATE!
Fool
AHH!?
WORK!
PICKET!
PICKET LINE, PICKET LINE!
HA HA HA HA HA HA HA!!
Thoughts, still scattered.
PICKET LINE...
PICKET LINE...

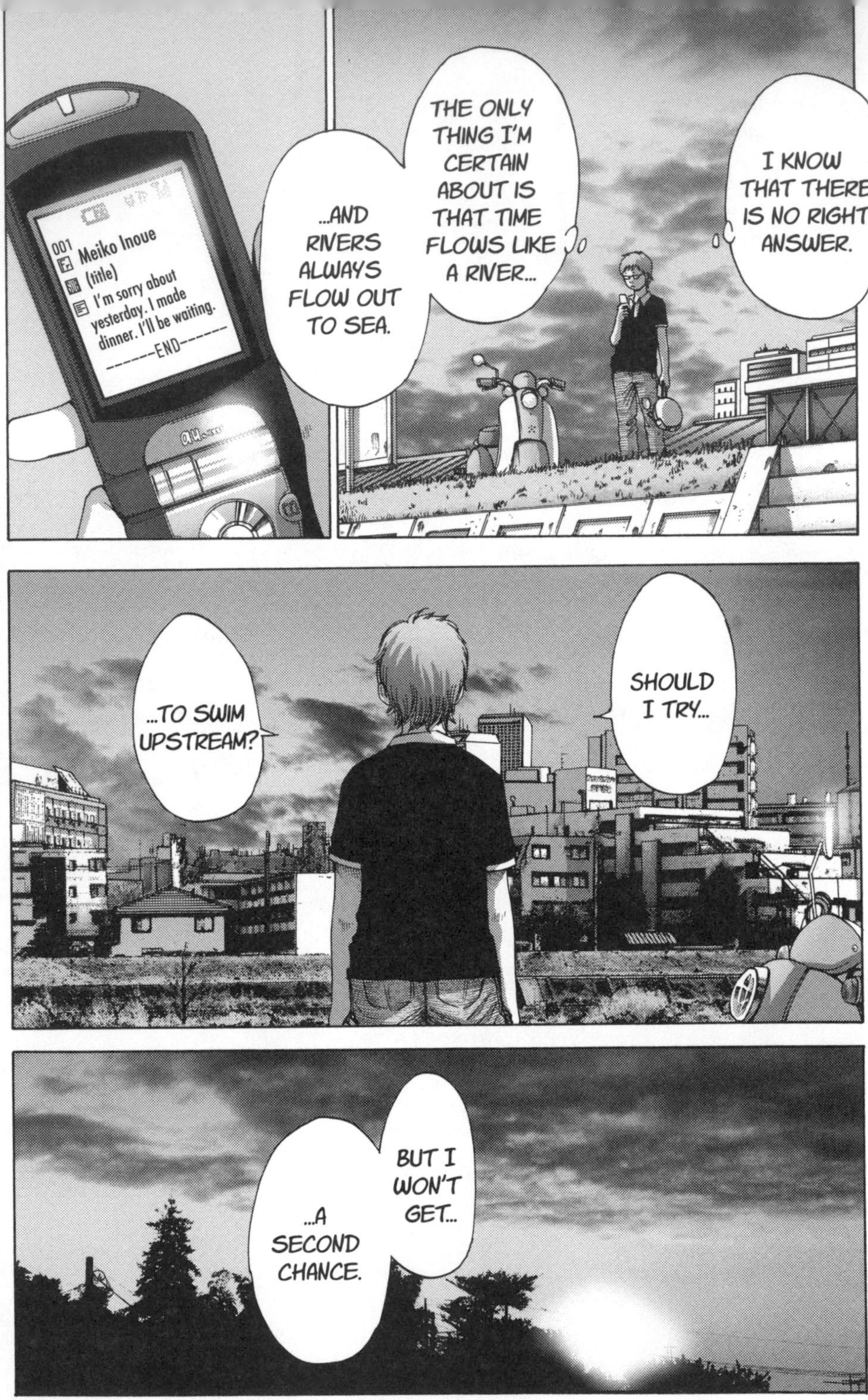
I KNOW THAT THERE IS NO RIGHT ANSWER.
THE ONLY THING I'M CERTAIN ABOUT IS THAT TIME FLOWS LIKE A RIVER...
...AND RIVERS ALWAYS FLOW OUT TO SEA.
001
Meiko Inoue
(title)
I'm sorry about yesterday. I made dinner. I'll be waiting.
------END------
SHOULD I TRY...
...TO SWIM UPSTREAM?
BUT I WON'T GET...
...A SECOND CHANCE.

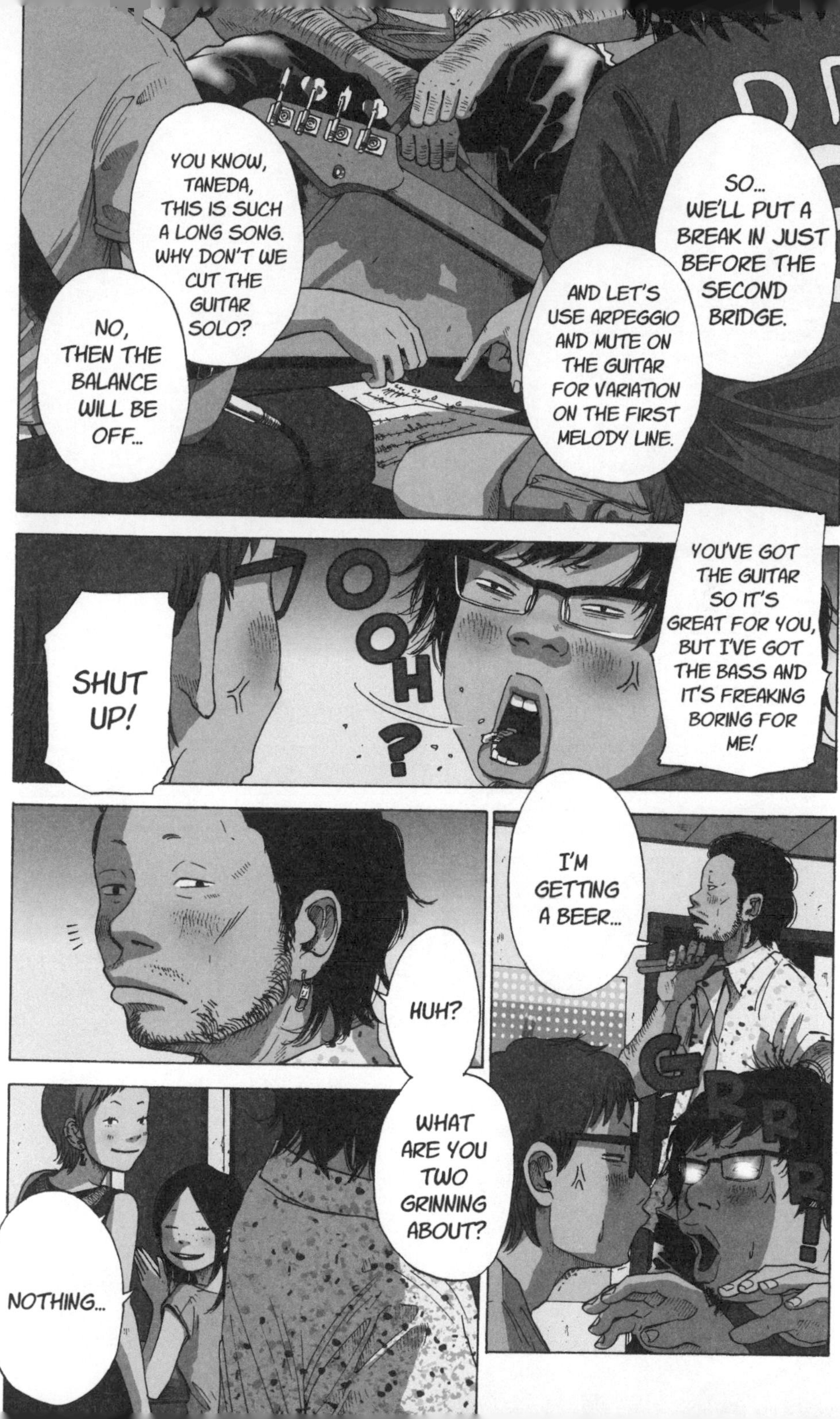
SO... WE'LL PUT A BREAK IN JUST BEFORE THE SECOND BRIDGE.
AND LET'S USE ARPEGGIO AND MUTE ON THE GUITAR FOR VARIATION ON THE FIRST MELODY LINE.
YOU KNOW, TANEDA, THIS IS SUCH A LONG SONG. WHY DON'T WE CUT THE GUITAR SOLO?
NO, THEN THE BALANCE WILL BE OFF...
YOU'VE GOT THE GUITAR SO IT'S GREAT FOR YOU, BUT I'VE GOT THE BASS AND IT'S FREAKING BORING FOR ME!
OOH?
SHUT UP!
I'M GETTING A BEER...
GRRR!
HUH?
WHAT ARE YOU TWO GRINNING ABOUT?
NOTHING...

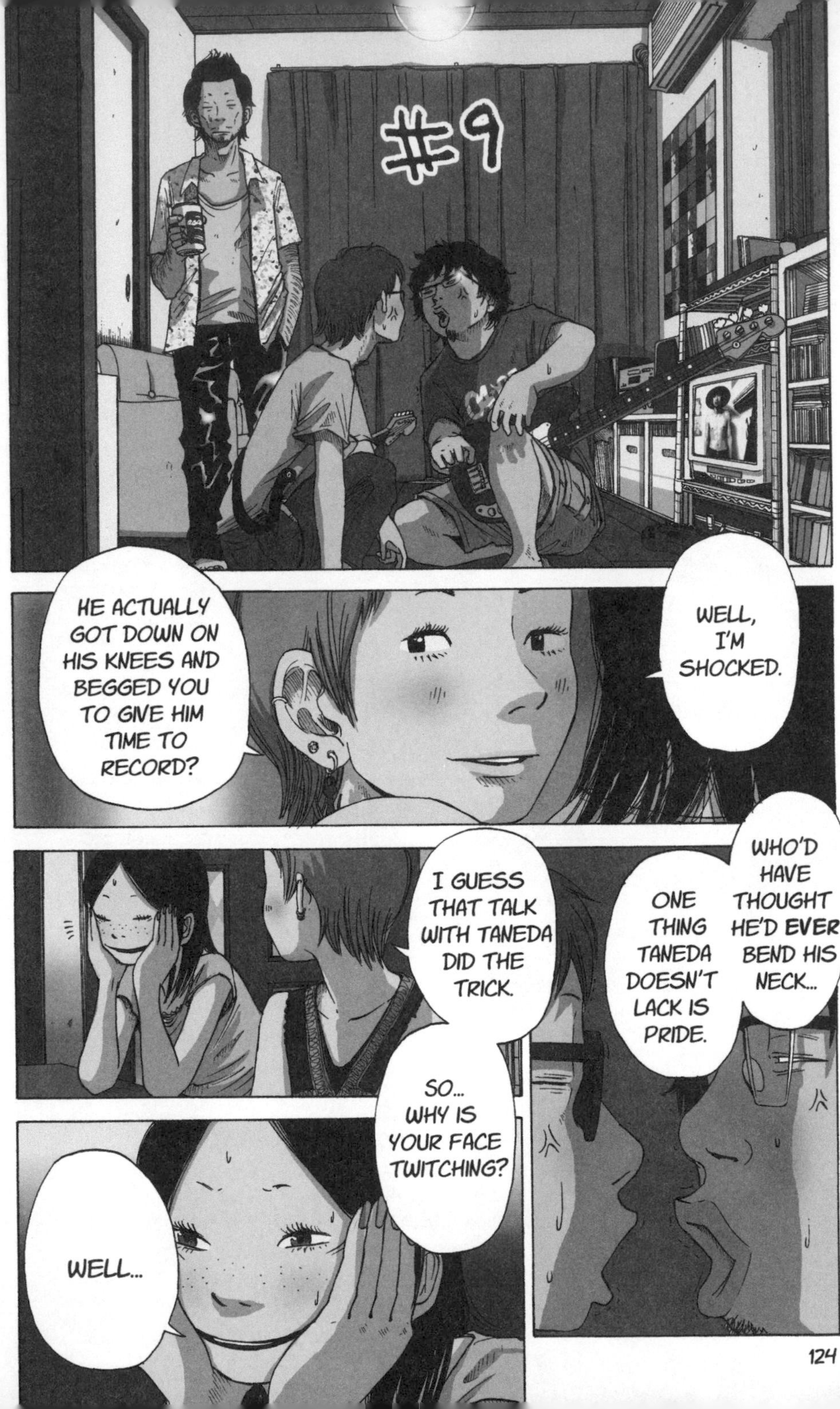
#9
WELL, I'M SHOCKED.
HE ACTUALLY GOT DOWN ON HIS KNEES AND BEGGED YOU TO GIVE HIM TIME TO RECORD?
WHO'D HAVE THOUGHT HE'D EVER BEND HIS NECK...
ONE THING TANEDA DOESN'T LACK IS PRIDE.
I GUESS THAT TALK WITH TANEDA DID THE TRICK.
SO... WHY IS YOUR FACE TWITCHING?
WELL...

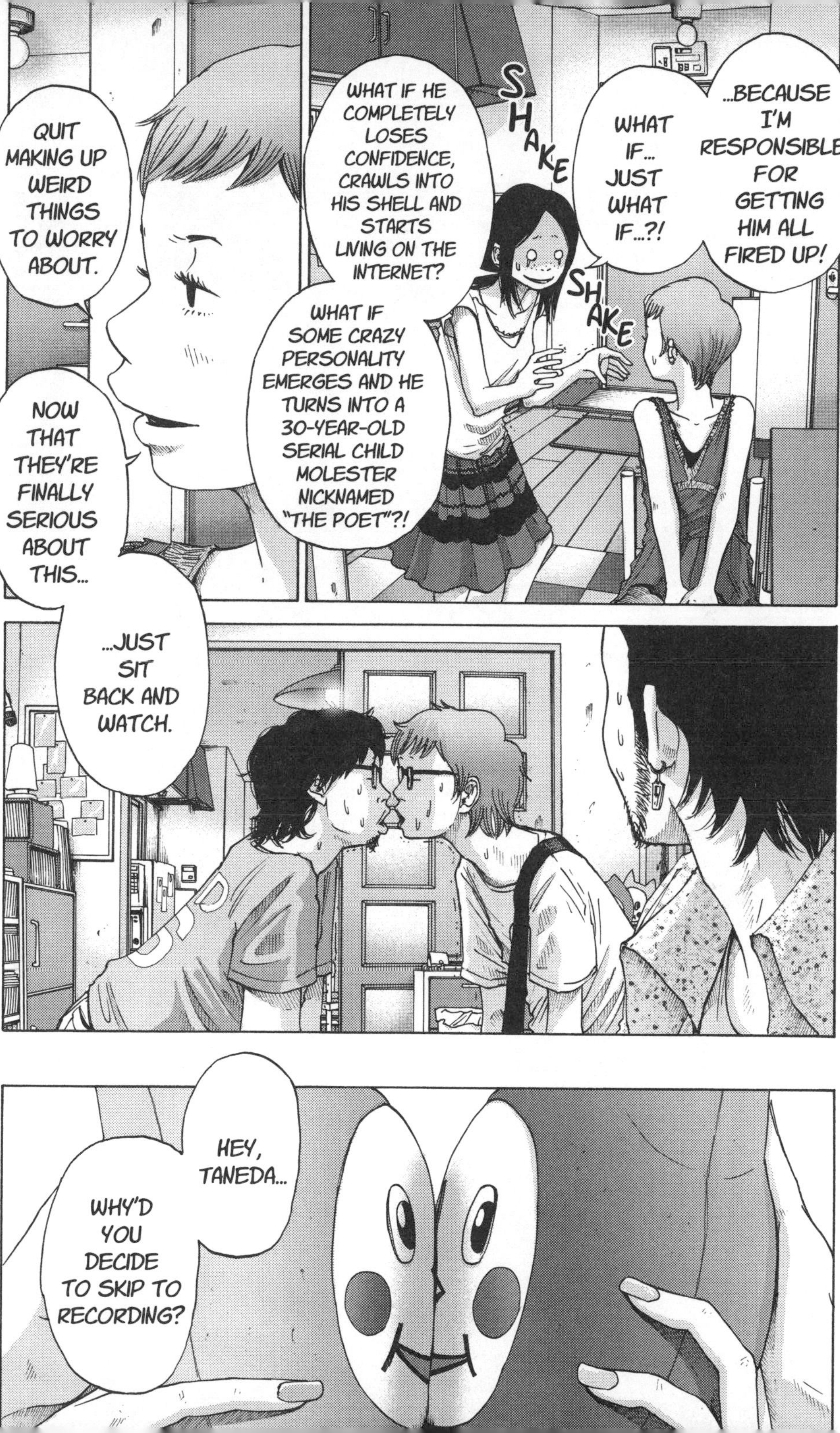
...BECAUSE I'M RESPONSIBLE FOR GETTING HIM ALL FIRED UP!
WHAT IF... JUST WHAT IF...?!
SHAKE
WHAT IF HE COMPLETELY LOSES CONFIDENCE, CRAWLS INTO HIS SHELL AND STARTS LIVING ON THE INTERNET?
SHAKE
WHAT IF SOME CRAZY PERSONALITY EMERGES AND HE TURNS INTO A 30-YEAR-OLD SERIAL CHILD MOLESTER NICKNAMED "THE POET"?!
QUIT MAKING UP WEIRD THINGS TO WORRY ABOUT.
NOW THAT THEY'RE FINALLY SERIOUS ABOUT THIS...
...JUST SIT BACK AND WATCH.
HEY, TANEDA...
WHY'D YOU DECIDE TO SKIP TO RECORDING?

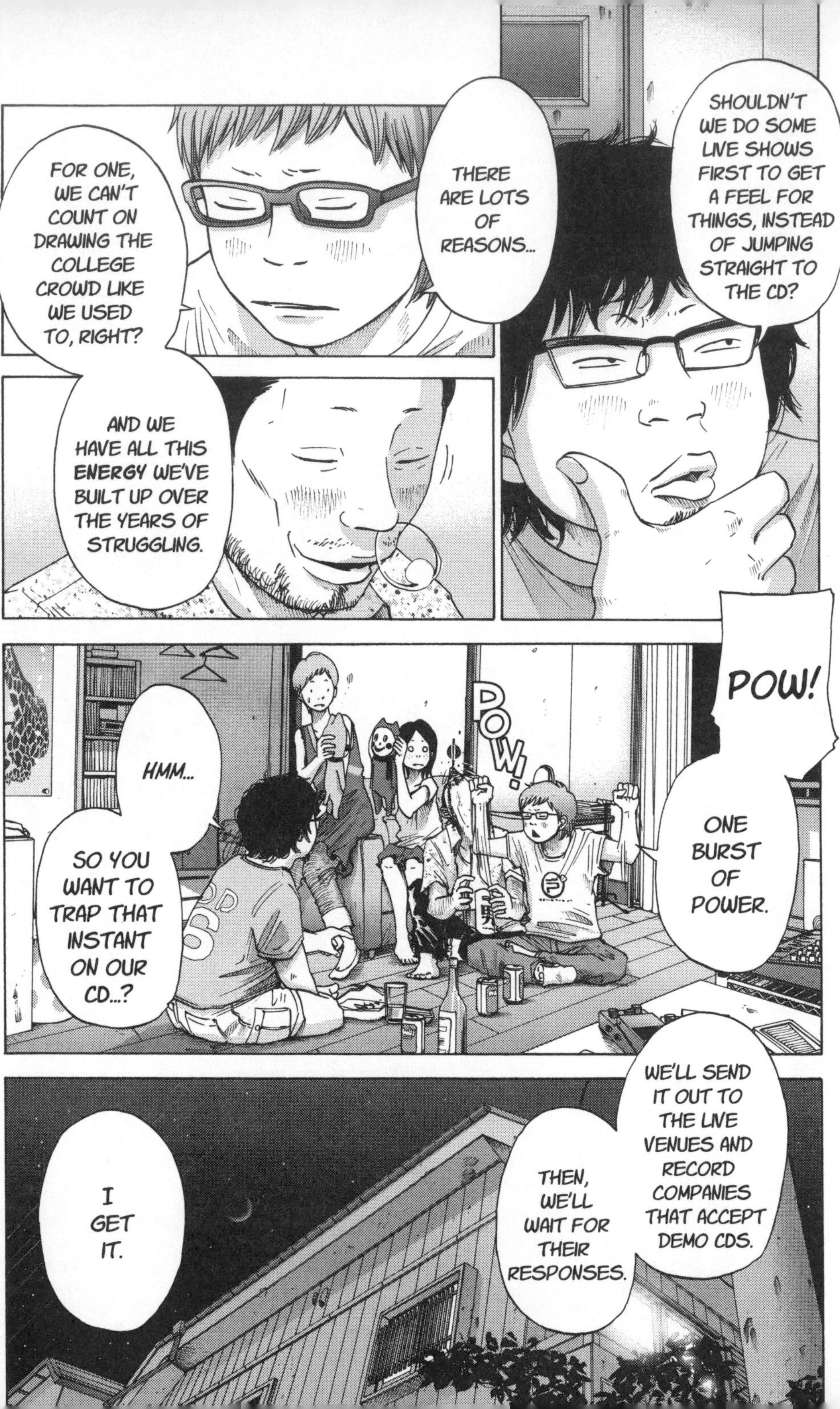
SHOULDN'T WE DO SOME LIVE SHOWS FIRST TO GET A FEEL FOR THINGS, INSTEAD OF JUMPING STRAIGHT TO THE CD?
THERE ARE LOTS OF REASONS...
FOR ONE, WE CAN'T COUNT ON DRAWING THE COLLEGE CROWD LIKE WE USED TO, RIGHT?
AND WE HAVE ALL THIS ENERGY WE'VE BUILT UP OVER THE YEARS OF STRUGGLING.
POW!
POW!
ONE BURST OF POWER.
HMM...
SO YOU WANT TO TRAP THAT INSTANT ON OUR CD...?
WE'LL SEND IT OUT TO THE LIVE VENUES AND RECORD COMPANIES THAT ACCEPT DEMO CDS.
THEN, WE'LL WAIT FOR THEIR RESPONSES.
I GET IT.

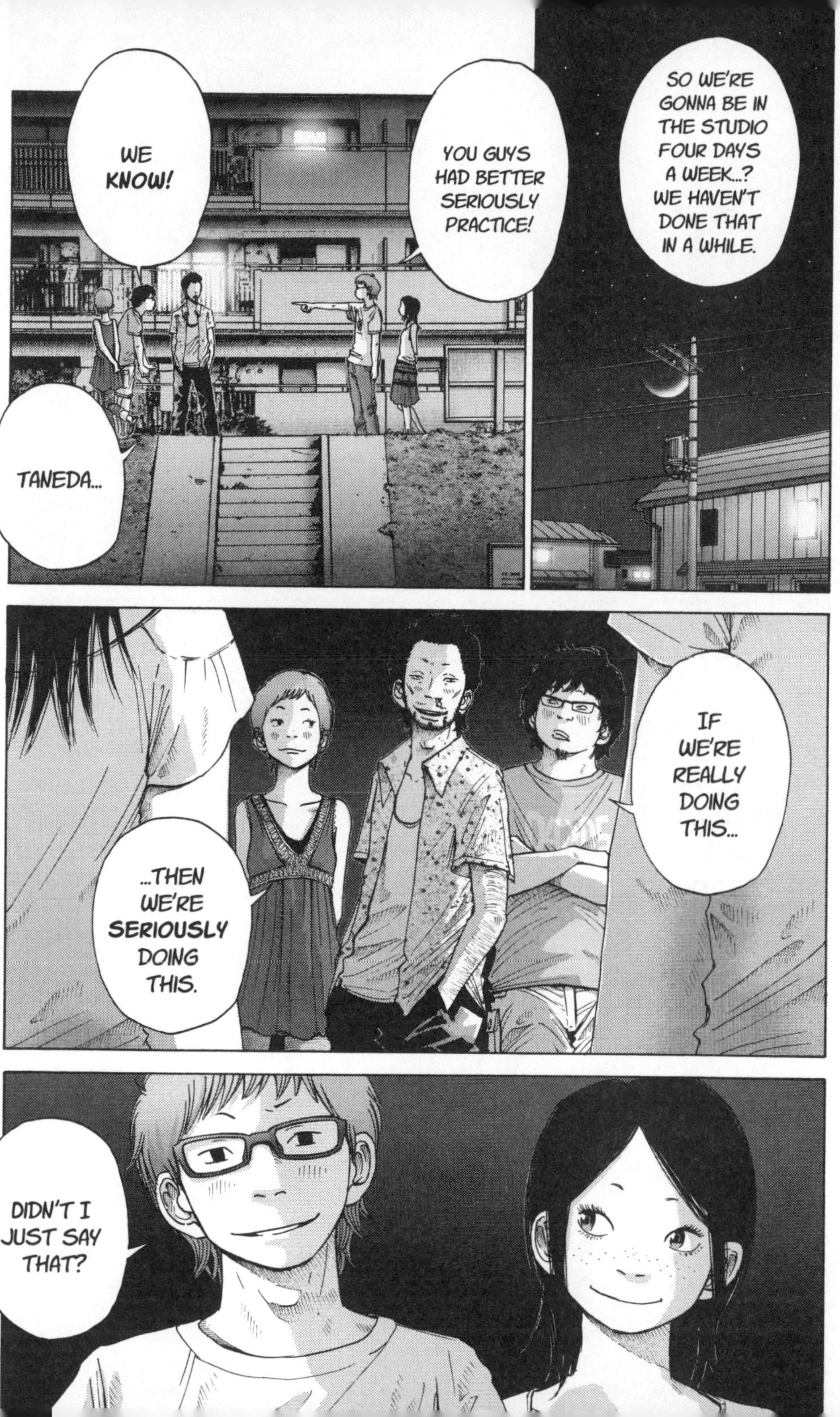
SO WE'RE GONNA BE IN THE STUDIO FOUR DAYS A WEEK...? WE HAVEN'T DONE THAT IN A WHILE.
YOU GUYS HAD BETTER SERIOUSLY PRACTICE!
WE KNOW!
TANEDA...
IF WE'RE REALLY DOING THIS...
...THEN WE'RE SERIOUSLY DOING THIS.
DIDN'T I JUST SAY THAT?

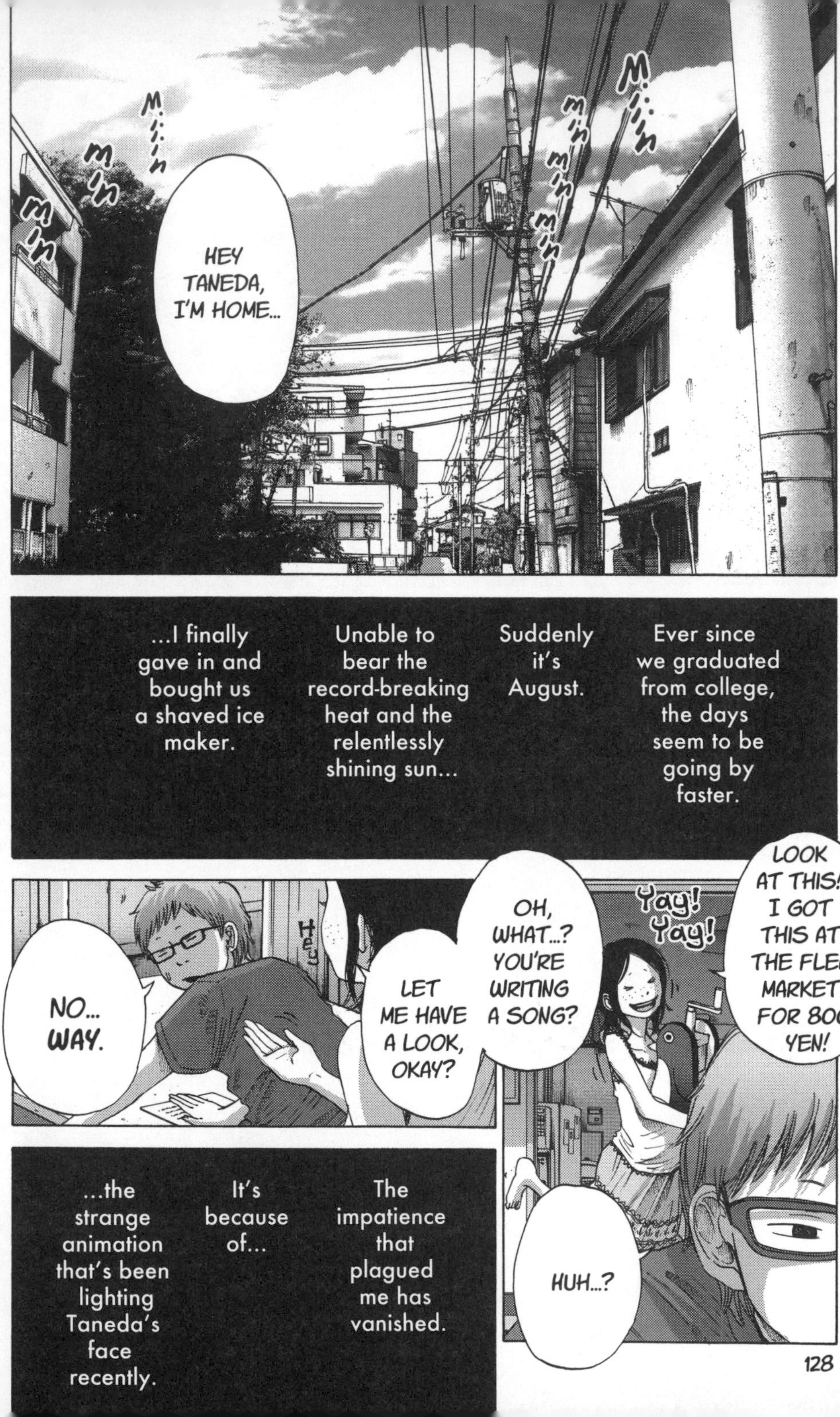
Miiin
min min min
Miiin
min min
HEY TANEDA, I'M HOME...
Ever since we graduated from college, the days seem to be going by faster.
Suddenly it's August.
Unable to bear the record-breaking heat and the relentlessly shining sun...
...I finally gave in and bought us a shaved ice maker.
LOOK AT THIS! I GOT THIS AT THE FLEA MARKET FOR 800 YEN!
Yay! Yay!
HUH...?
OH, WHAT...? YOU'RE WRITING A SONG?
LET ME HAVE A LOOK, OKAY?
Hey
NO... WAY.
The impatience that plagued me has vanished.
It's because of...
...the strange animation that's been lighting Taneda's face recently.

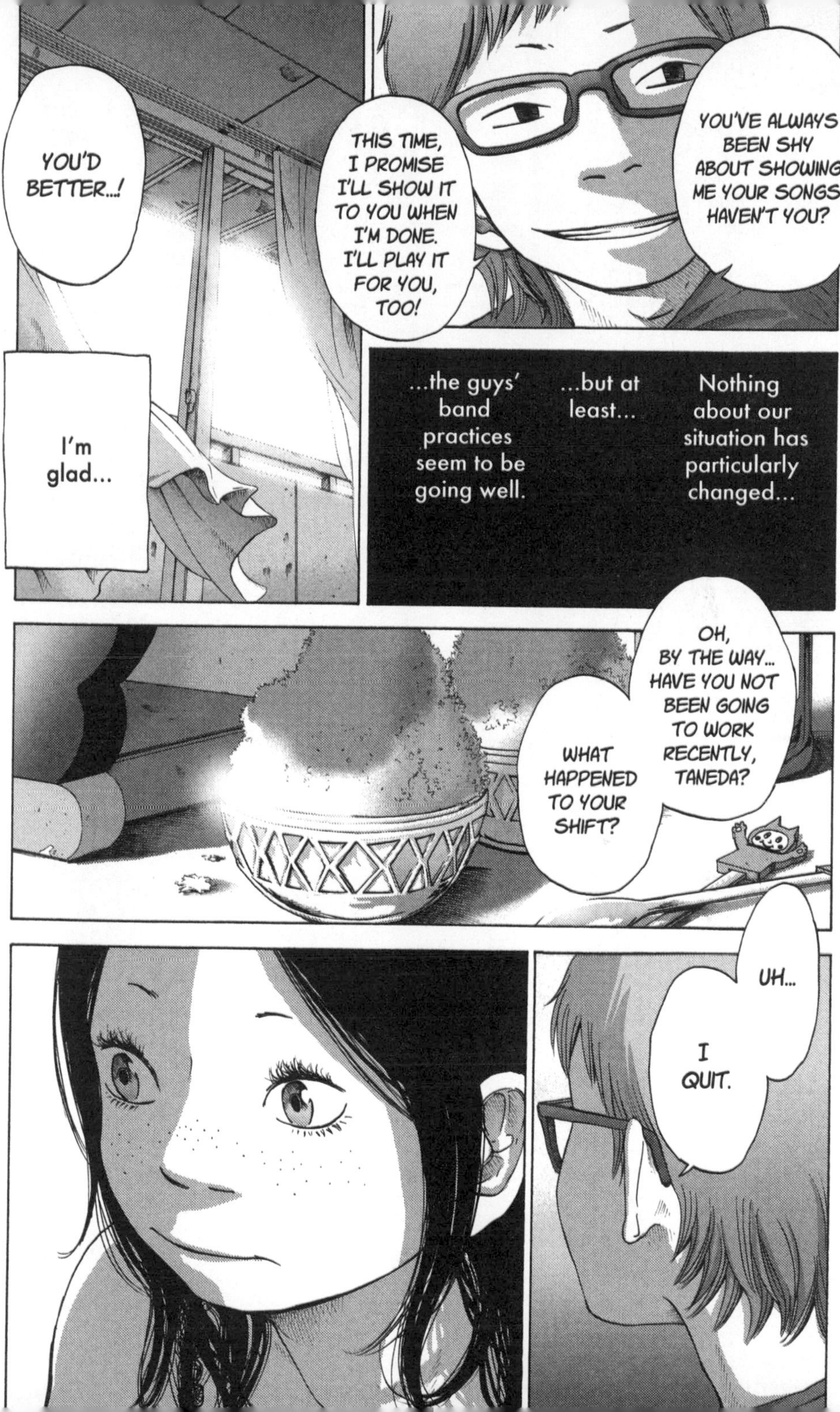
YOU'VE ALWAYS BEEN SHY ABOUT SHOWING ME YOUR SONGS, HAVEN'T YOU?
THIS TIME, I PROMISE I'LL SHOW IT TO YOU WHEN I'M DONE. I'LL PLAY IT FOR YOU, TOO!
Nothing about our situation has particularly changed...
...but at least...
...the guys' band practices seem to be going well.
YOU'D BETTER...!
I'm glad...
OH, BY THE WAY... HAVE YOU NOT BEEN GOING TO WORK RECENTLY, TANEDA?
WHAT HAPPENED TO YOUR SHIFT?
UH...
I QUIT.

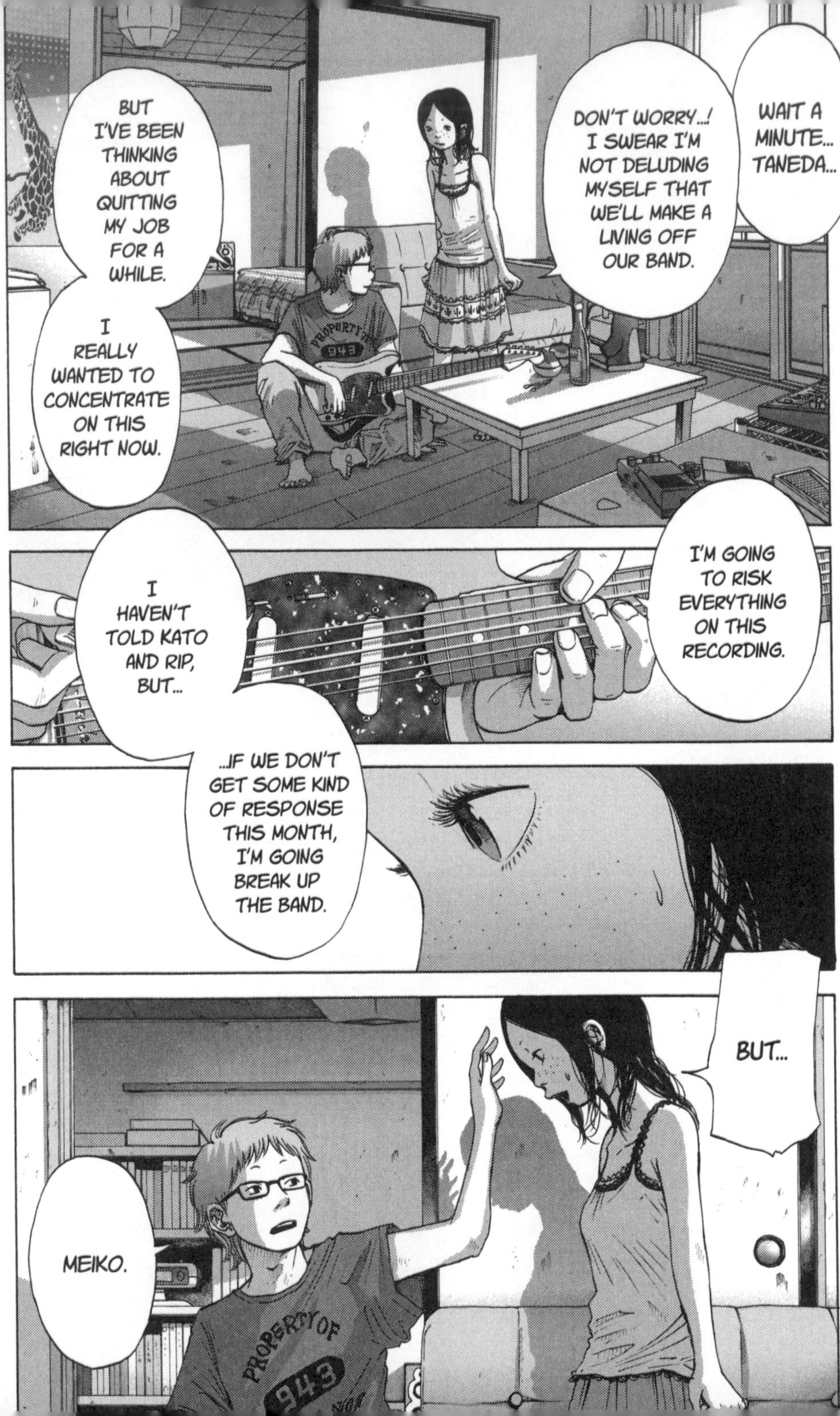
WAIT A MINUTE... TANEDA...
DON'T WORRY...! I SWEAR I'M NOT DELUDING MYSELF THAT WE'LL MAKE A LIVING OFF OUR BAND.
BUT I'VE BEEN THINKING ABOUT QUITTING MY JOB FOR A WHILE.
I REALLY WANTED TO CONCENTRATE ON THIS RIGHT NOW.
I'M GOING TO RISK EVERYTHING ON THIS RECORDING.
I HAVEN'T TOLD KATO AND RIP, BUT...
...IF WE DON'T GET SOME KIND OF RESPONSE THIS MONTH, I'M GOING BREAK UP THE BAND.
BUT...
MEIKO.

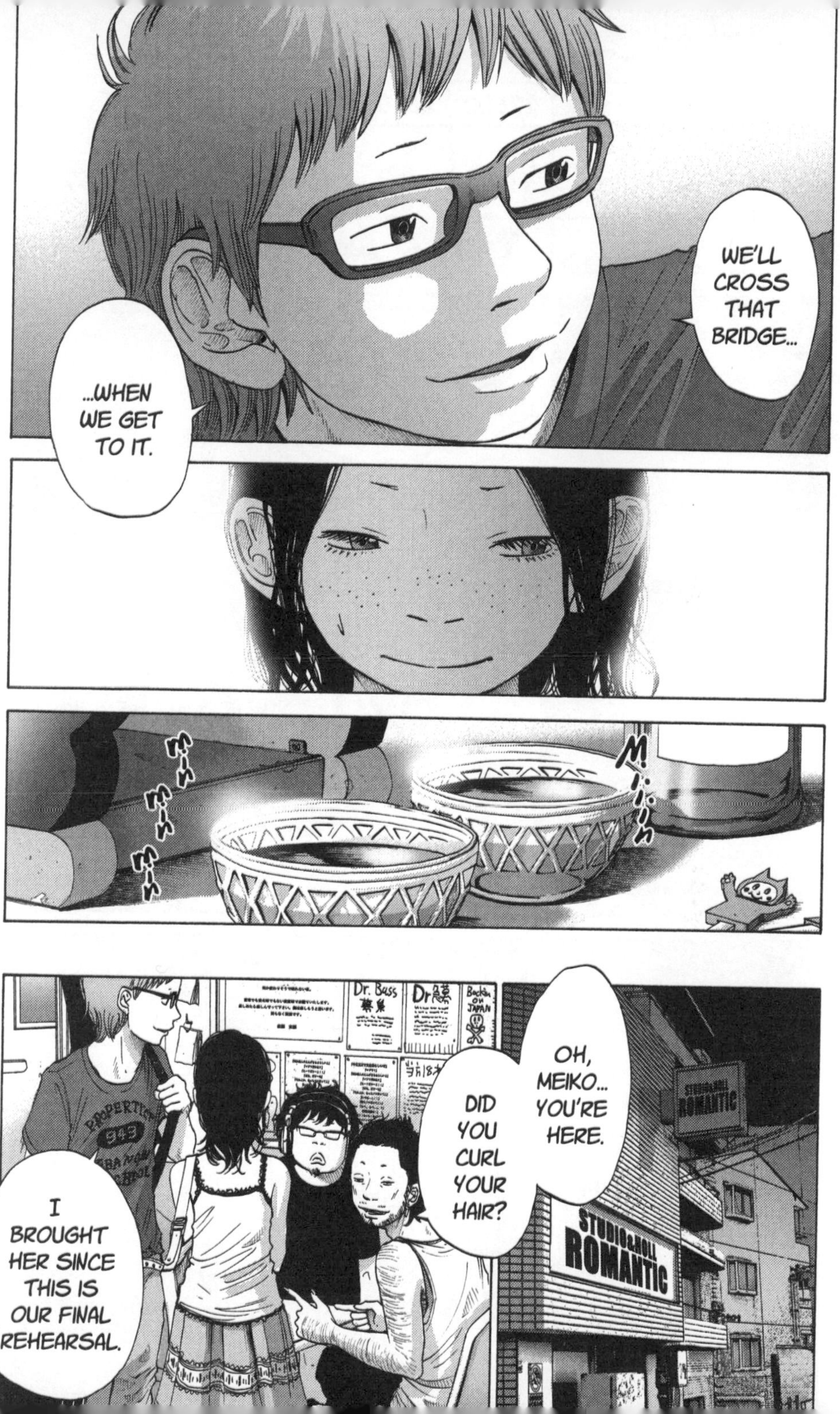
WE'LL CROSS THAT BRIDGE...
...WHEN WE GET TO IT.
min min min
OH, MEIKO... YOU'RE HERE.
DID YOU CURL YOUR HAIR?
STUDIO&ROLL ROMANTIC
I BROUGHT HER SINCE THIS IS OUR FINAL REHEARSAL.

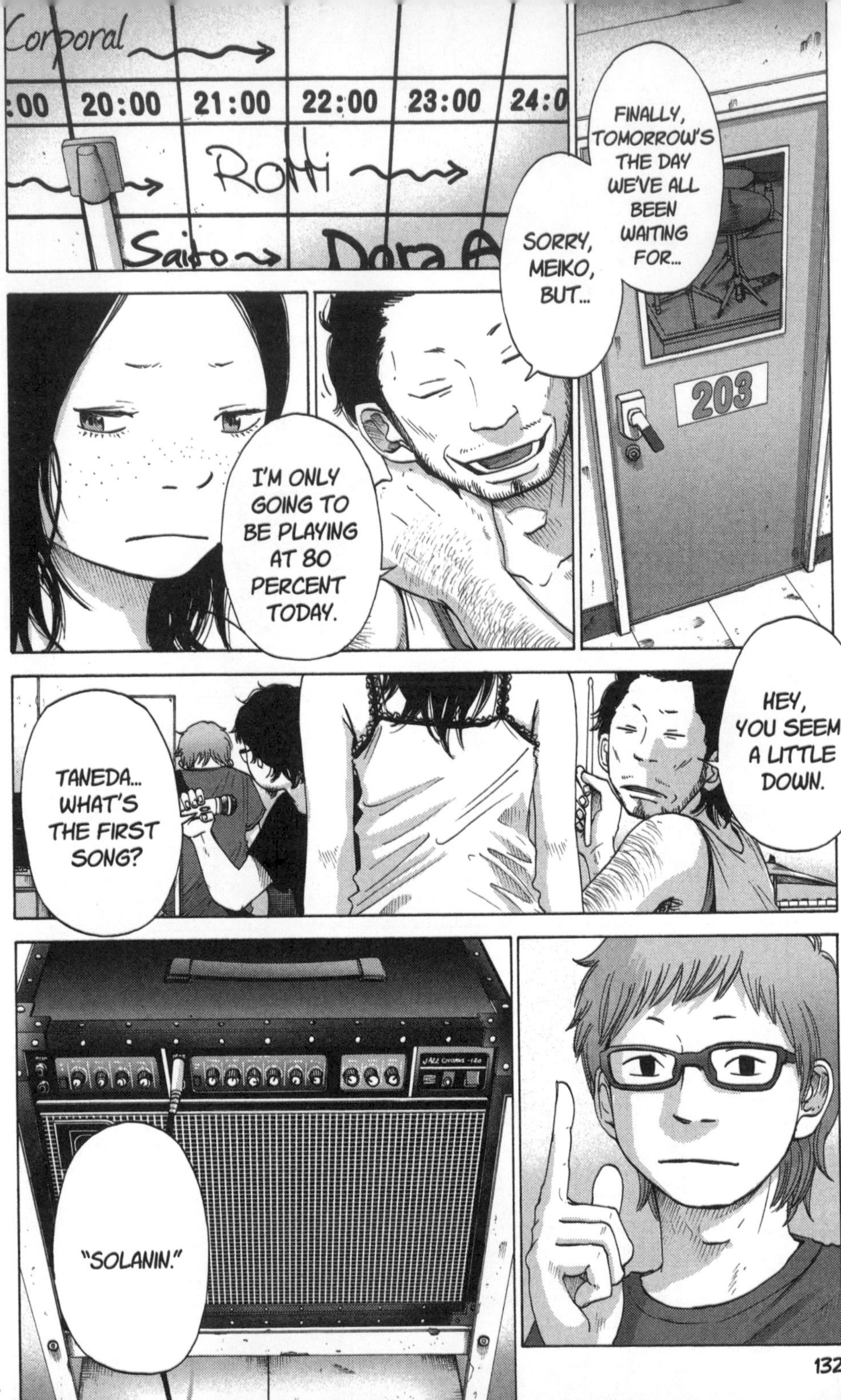
FINALLY, TOMORROW'S THE DAY WE'VE ALL BEEN WAITING FOR...
SORRY, MEIKO, BUT...
Corporal
20:00
21:00
22:00
23:00
Rotti
Saito
I'M ONLY GOING TO BE PLAYING AT 80 PERCENT TODAY.
HEY, YOU SEEM A LITTLE DOWN.
TANEDA... WHAT'S THE FIRST SONG?
"SOLANIN."

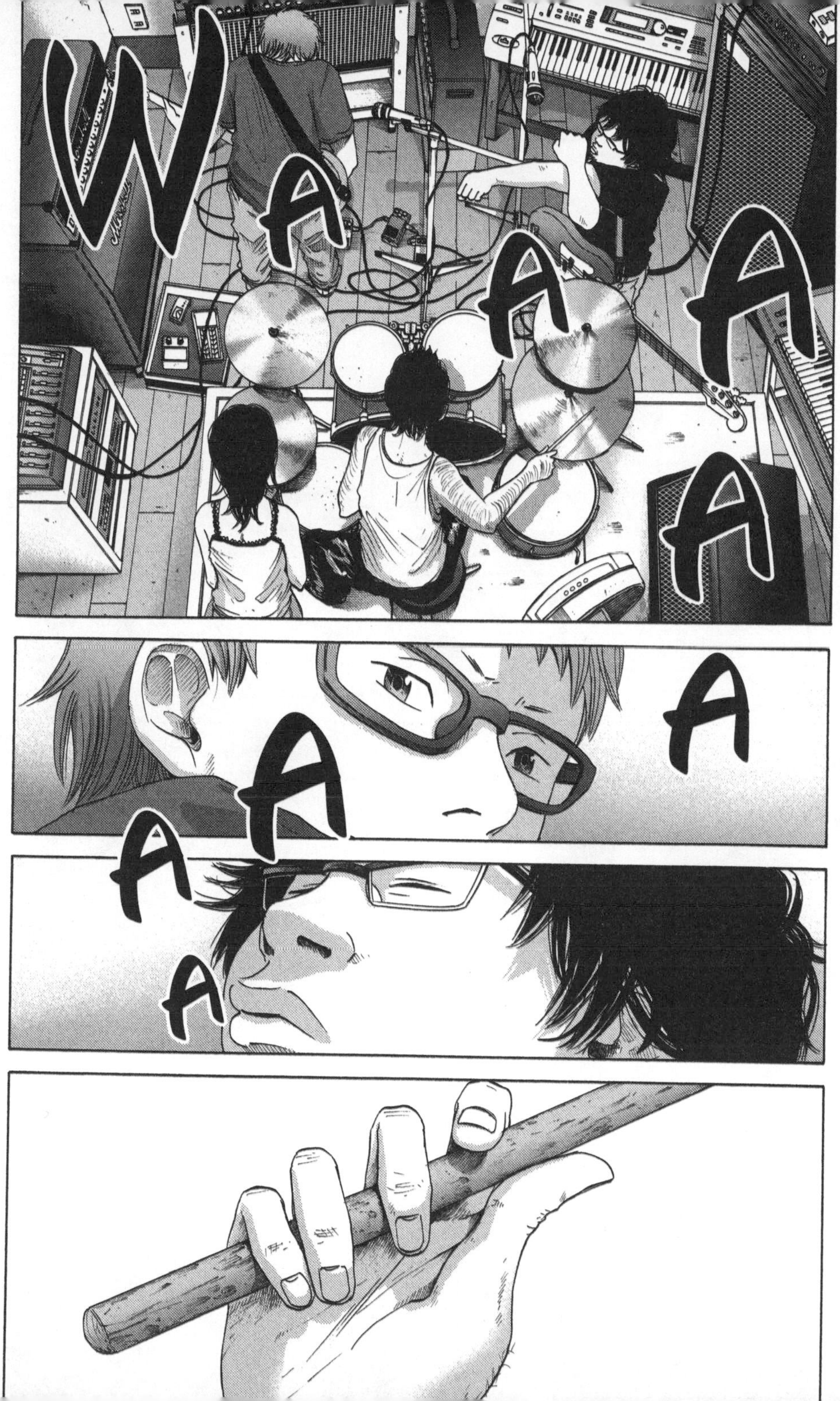
WAAAA
AAA
A

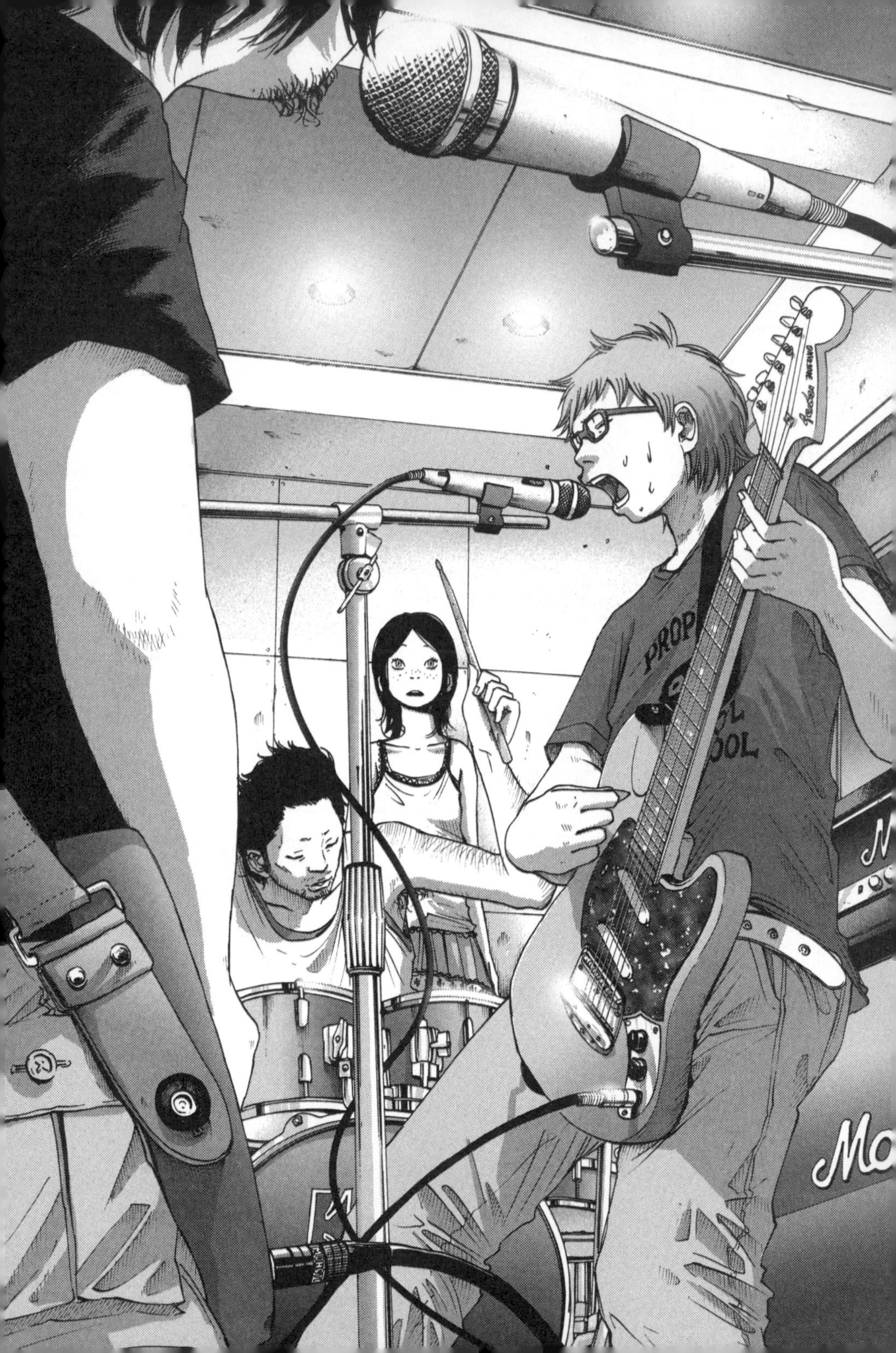

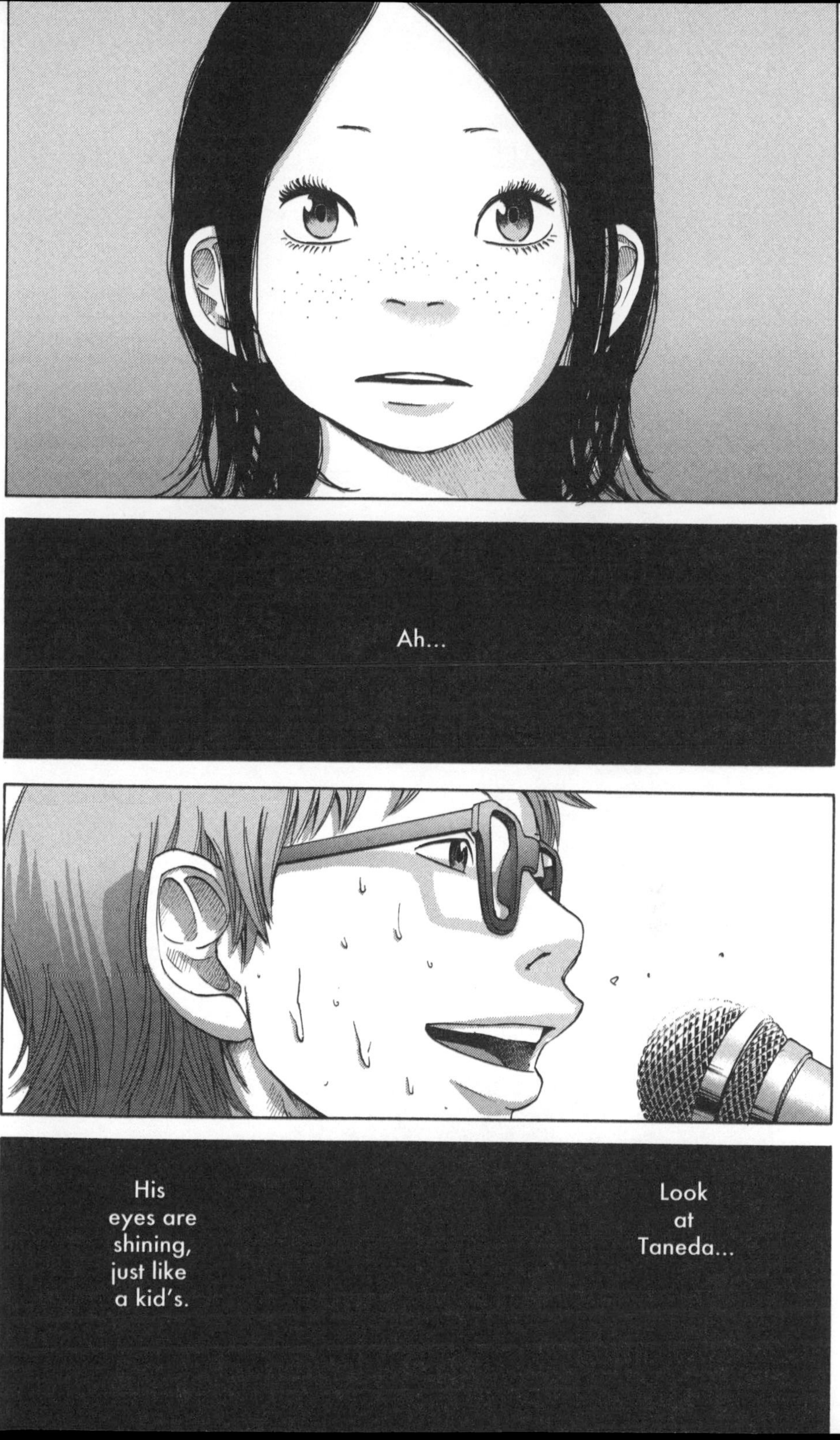
Ah...
Look at Taneda...
His eyes are shining, just like a kid's.

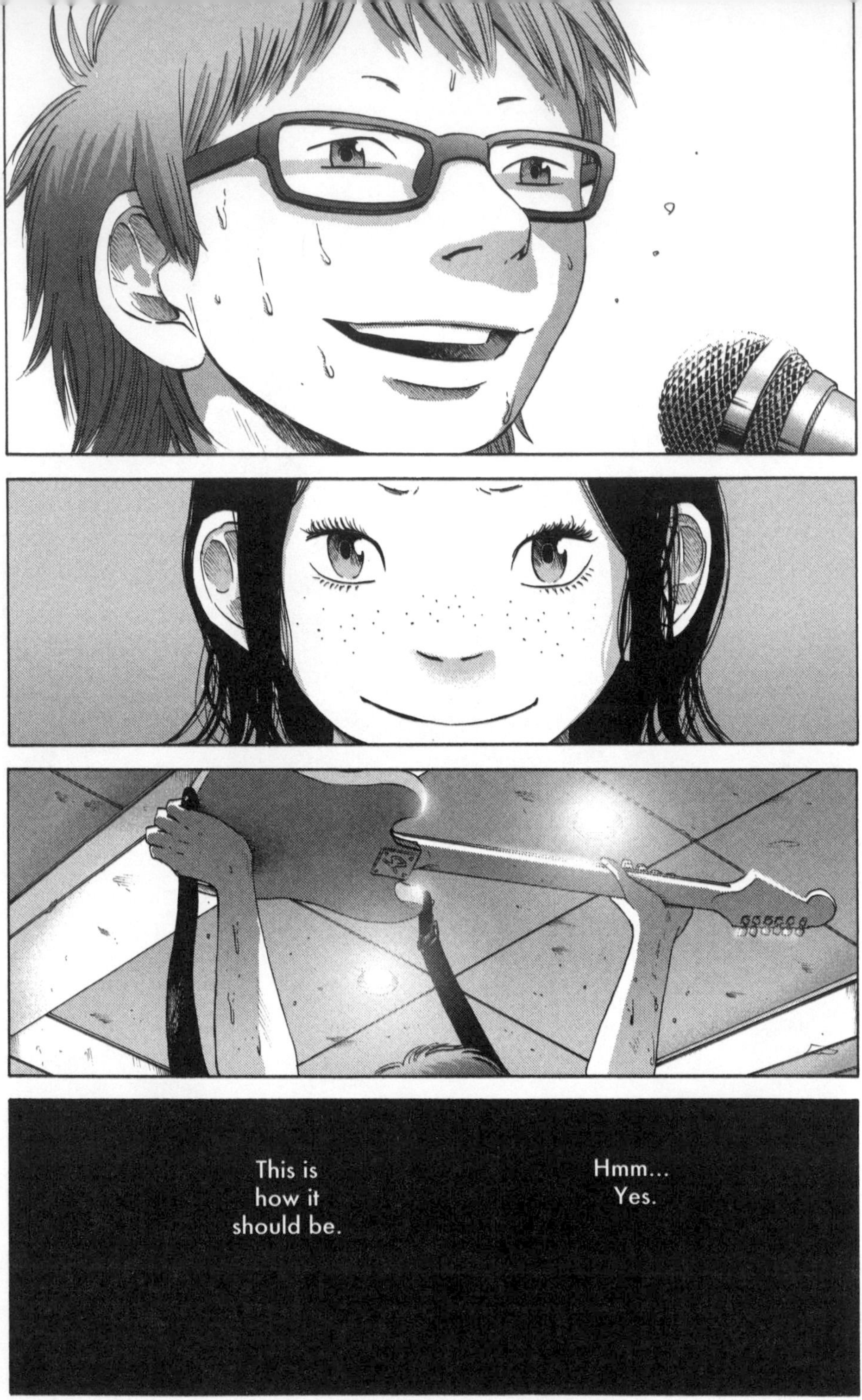
Hmm... Yes.
This is how it should be.

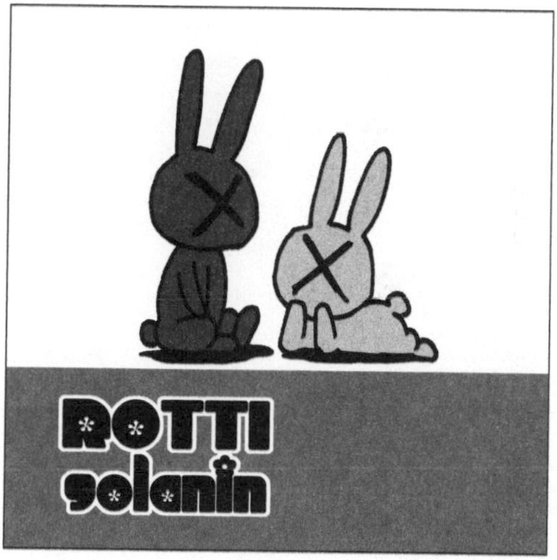
ROTTI
solanin

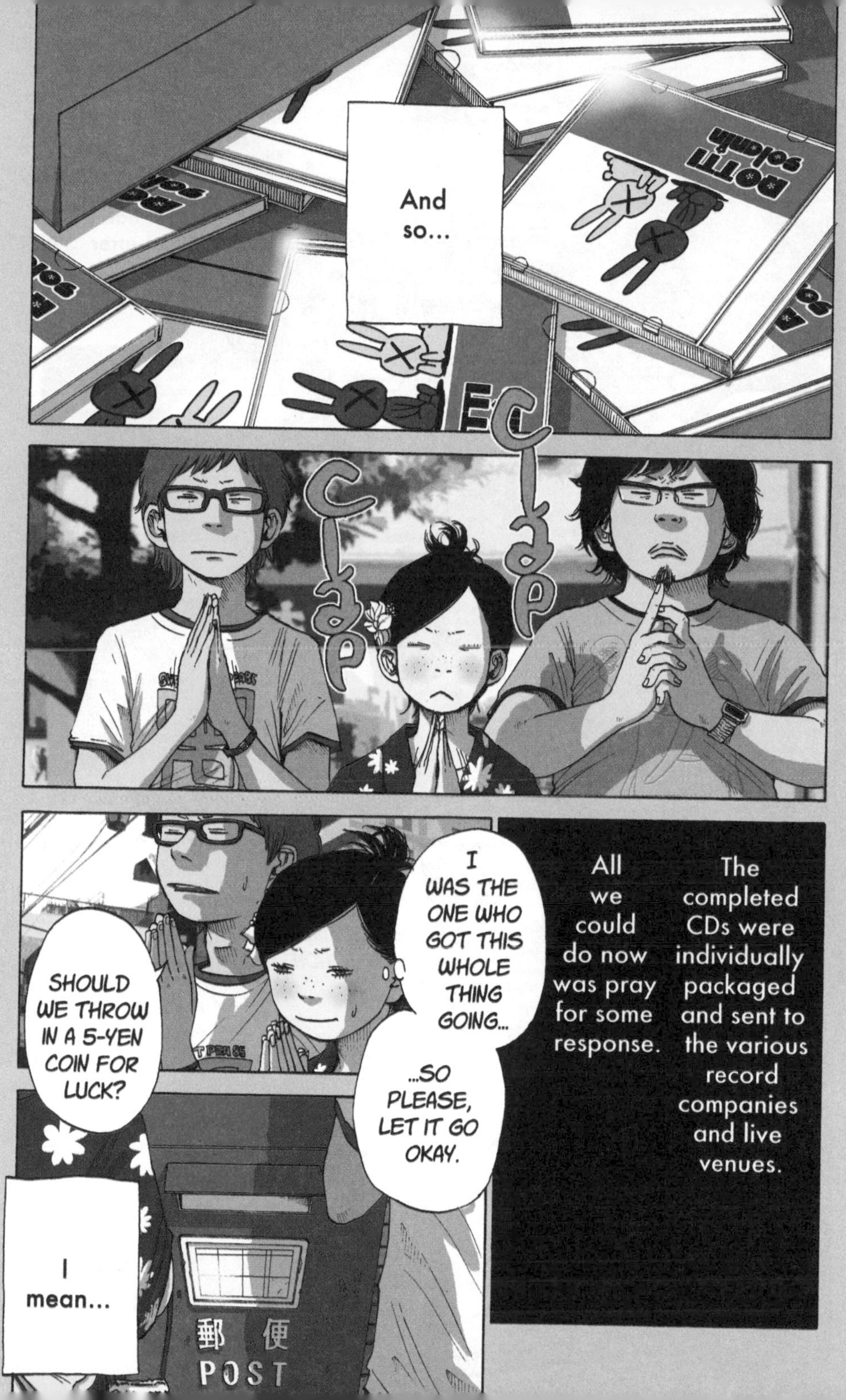
And so...
CLAP
CLAP
The completed CDs were individually packaged and sent to the various record companies and live venues.
All we could do now was pray for some response.
I WAS THE ONE WHO GOT THIS WHOLE THING GOING...
...SO PLEASE, LET IT GO OKAY.
SHOULD WE THROW IN A 5-YEN COIN FOR LUCK?
I mean...
郵便
POST

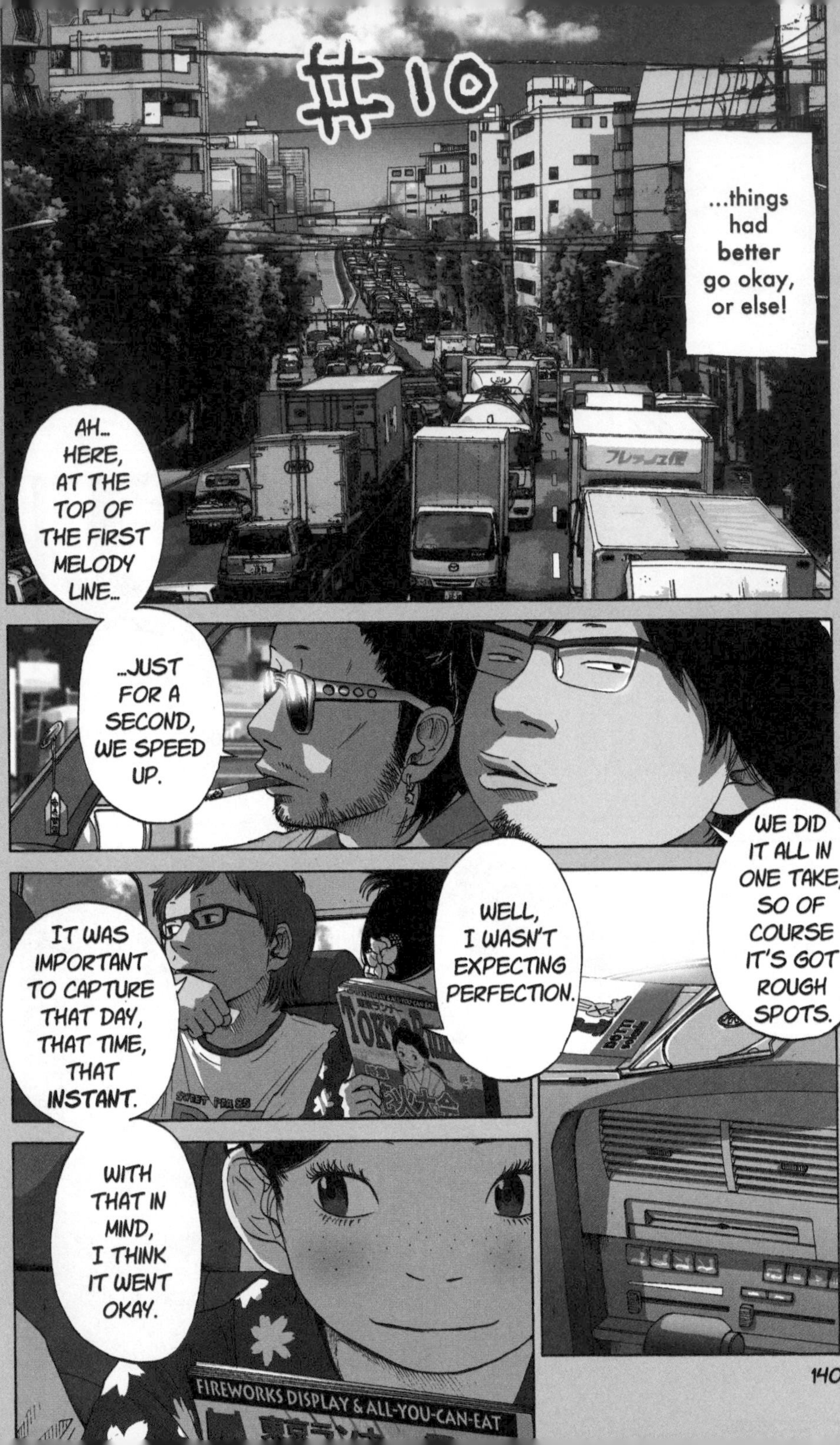
#10
...things had better go okay, or else!
AH... HERE, AT THE TOP OF THE FIRST MELODY LINE...
...JUST FOR A SECOND, WE SPEED UP.
WE DID IT ALL IN ONE TAKE, SO OF COURSE IT'S GOT ROUGH SPOTS.
WELL, I WASN'T EXPECTING PERFECTION.
IT WAS IMPORTANT TO CAPTURE THAT DAY, THAT TIME, THAT INSTANT.
WITH THAT IN MIND, I THINK IT WENT OKAY.
FIREWORKS DISPLAY & ALL-YOU-CAN-EAT

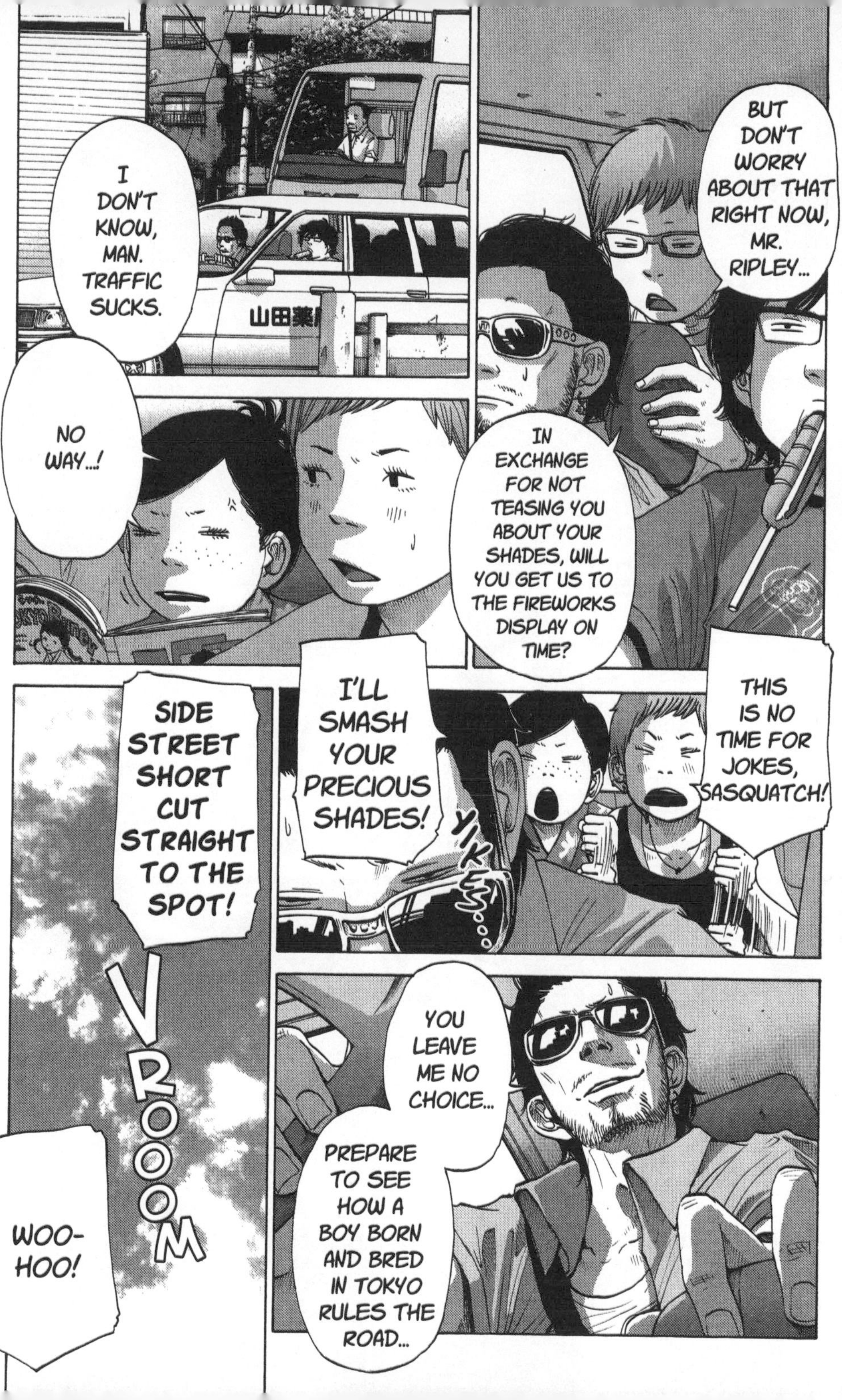

BUT DON'T WORRY ABOUT THAT RIGHT NOW, MR. RIPLEY...
IN EXCHANGE FOR NOT TEASING YOU ABOUT YOUR SHADES, WILL YOU GET US TO THE FIREWORKS DISPLAY ON TIME?
I DON'T KNOW, MAN. TRAFFIC SUCKS.
NO WAY...!
THIS IS NO TIME FOR JOKES, SASQUATCH!
I'LL SMASH YOUR PRECIOUS SHADES!
YIKESooo
YOU LEAVE ME NO CHOICE...
PREPARE TO SEE HOW A BOY BORN AND BRED IN TOKYO RULES THE ROAD...
SIDE STREET SHORT CUT STRAIGHT TO THE SPOT!
VROOOOM
WOO-HOO!

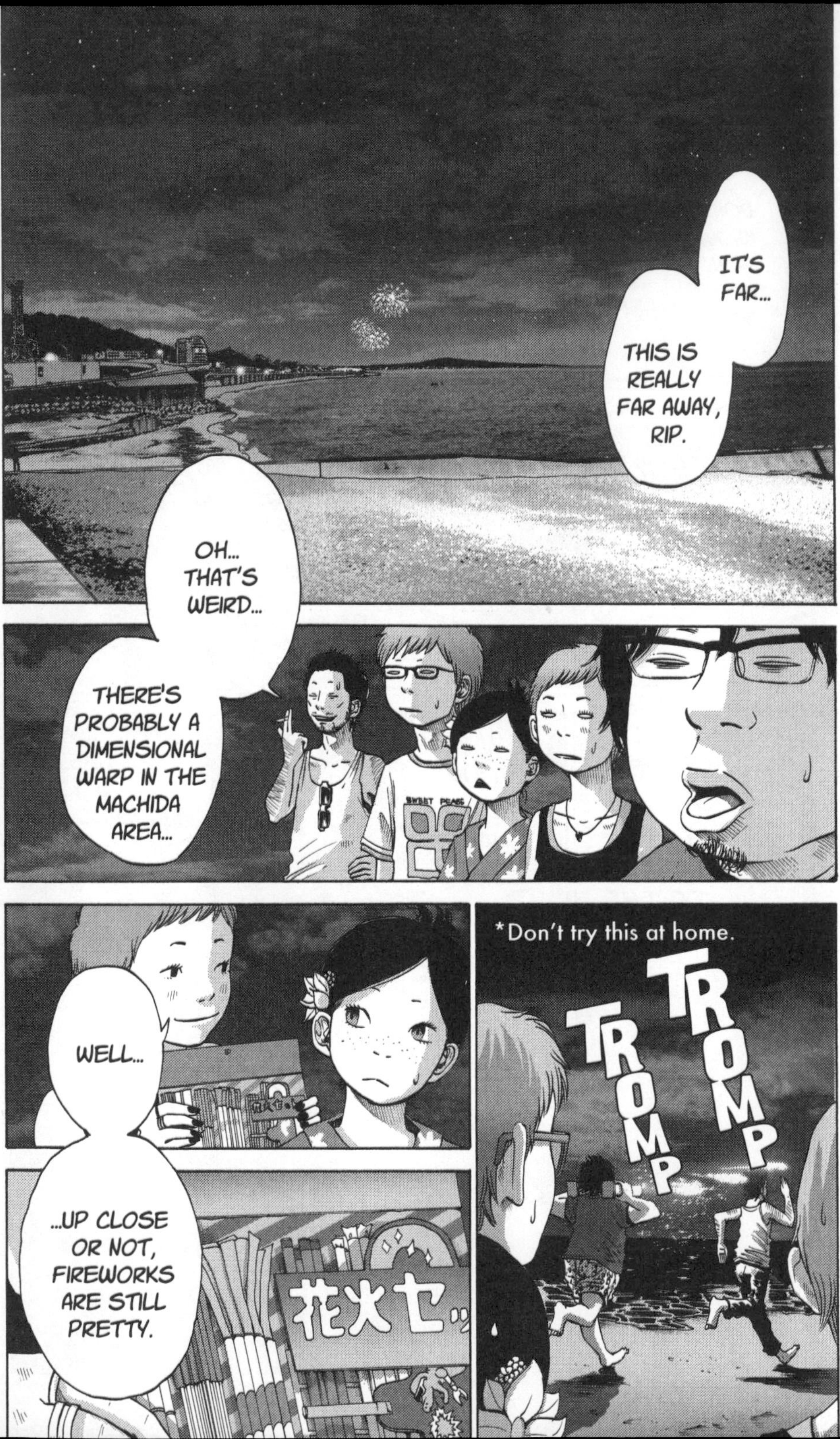
IT'S FAR...
THIS IS REALLY FAR AWAY, RIP.
OH... THAT'S WEIRD...
THERE'S PROBABLY A DIMENSIONAL WARP IN THE MACHIDA AREA...
*Don't try this at home.
TROMP
TROMP
WELL...
...UP CLOSE OR NOT, FIREWORKS ARE STILL PRETTY.
花火セッ

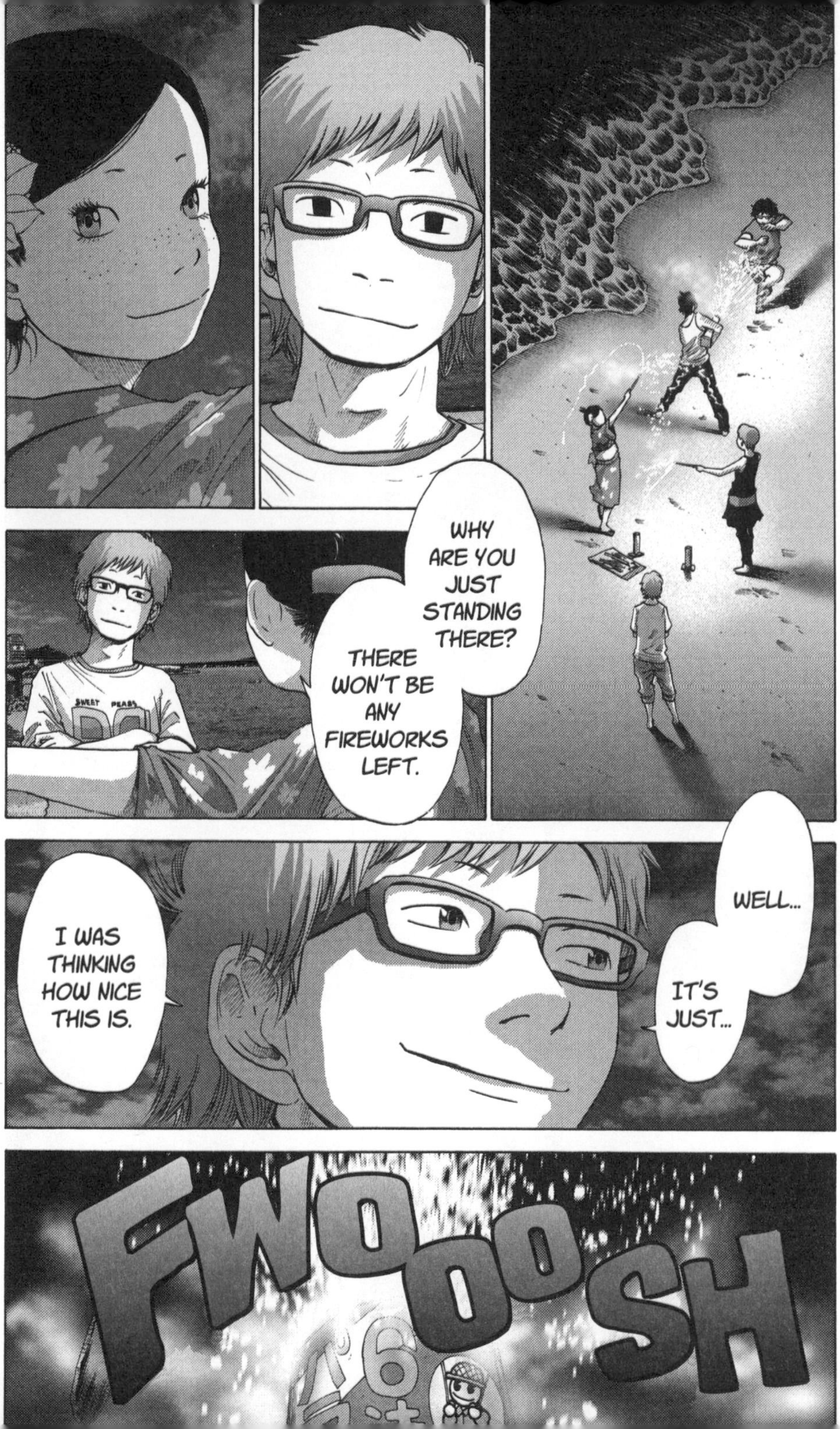
WHY ARE YOU JUST STANDING THERE?
THERE WON'T BE ANY FIREWORKS LEFT.
WELL...
IT'S JUST...
I WAS THINKING HOW NICE THIS IS.
FWOOOSH

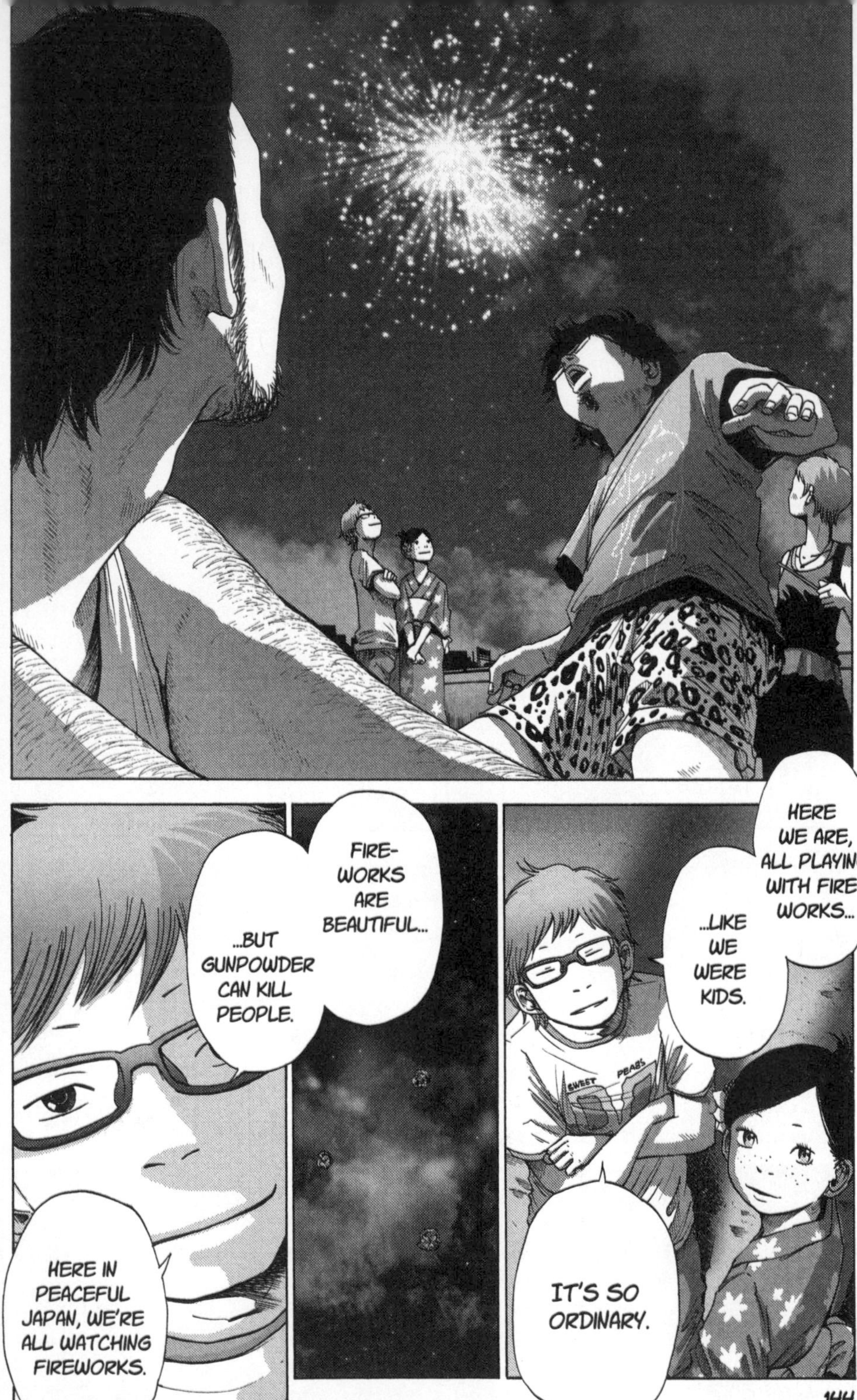
HERE WE ARE, ALL PLAYING WITH FIRE-WORKS...
...LIKE WE WERE KIDS.
IT'S SO ORDINARY.
FIRE-WORKS ARE BEAUTIFUL...
...BUT GUNPOWDER CAN KILL PEOPLE.
HERE IN PEACEFUL JAPAN, WE'RE ALL WATCHING FIREWORKS.
SWEET PEAS

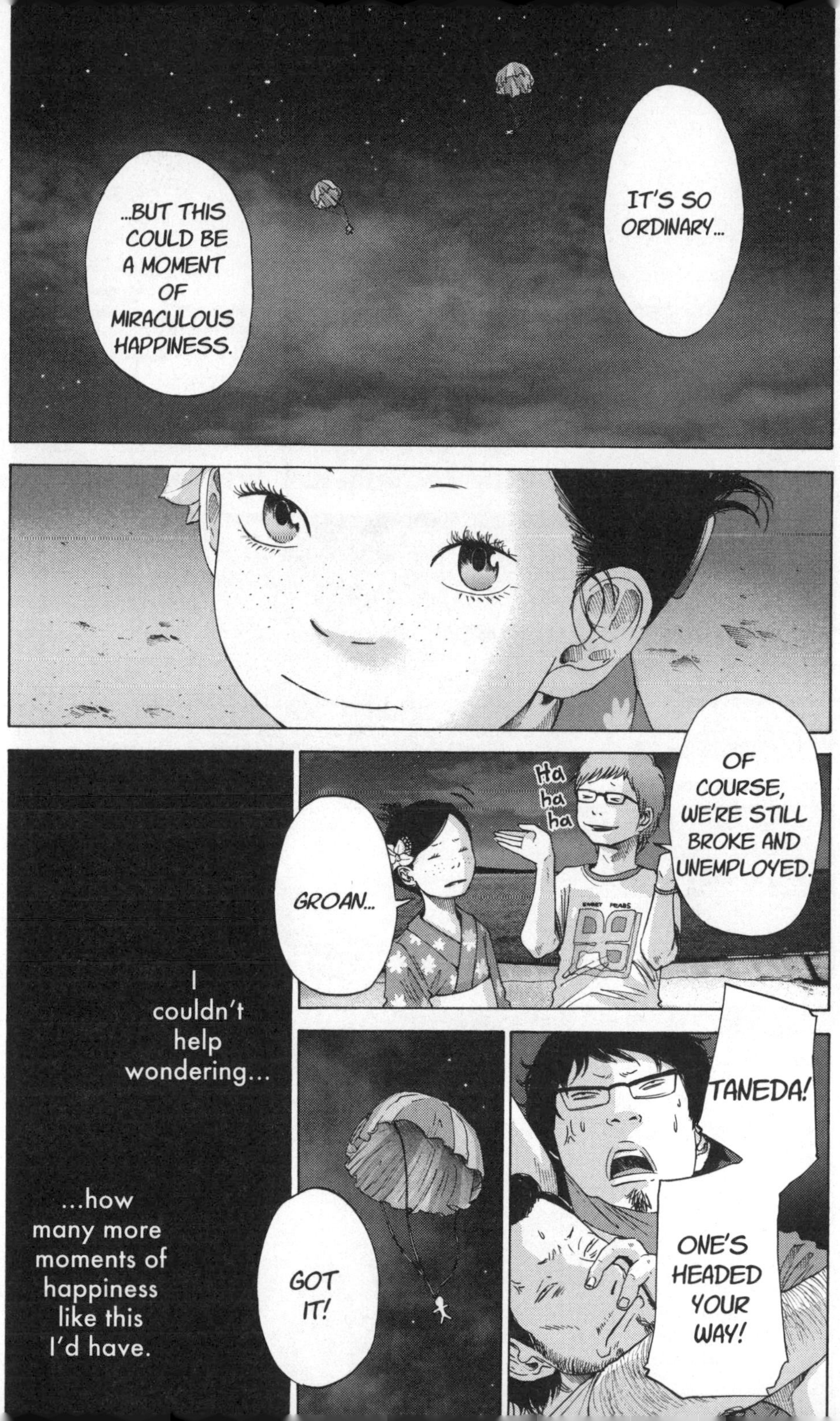
IT'S SO ORDINARY...
...BUT THIS COULD BE A MOMENT OF MIRACULOUS HAPPINESS.
OF COURSE, WE'RE STILL BROKE AND UNEMPLOYED.
Ha ha ha
GROAN...
TANEDA!
ONE'S HEADED YOUR WAY!
GOT IT!
I couldn't help wondering...
...how many more moments of happiness like this I'd have.

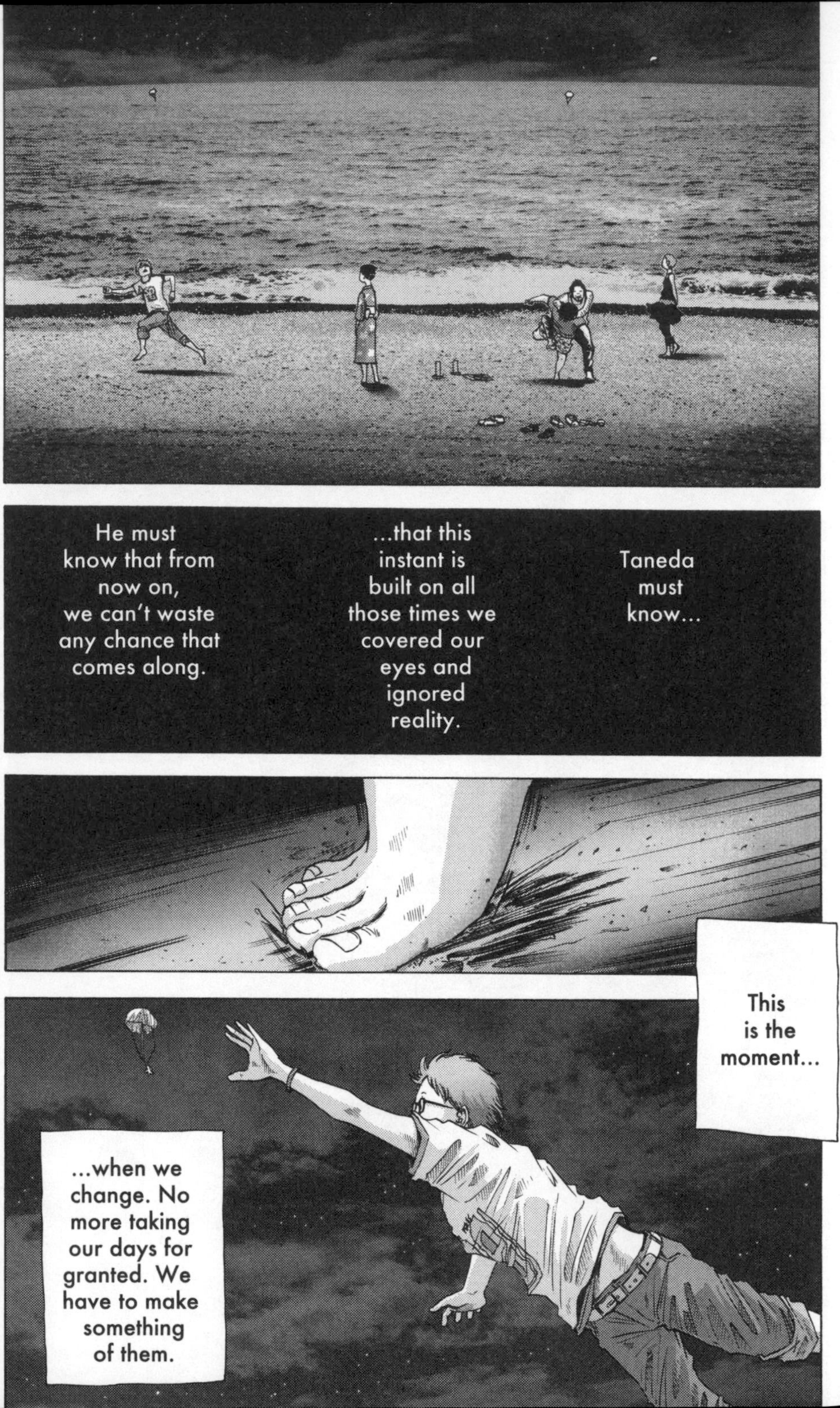
Taneda must know...
...that this instant is built on all those times we covered our eyes and ignored reality.
He must know that from now on, we can't waste any chance that comes along.
This is the moment...
...when we change. No more taking our days for granted. We have to make something of them.

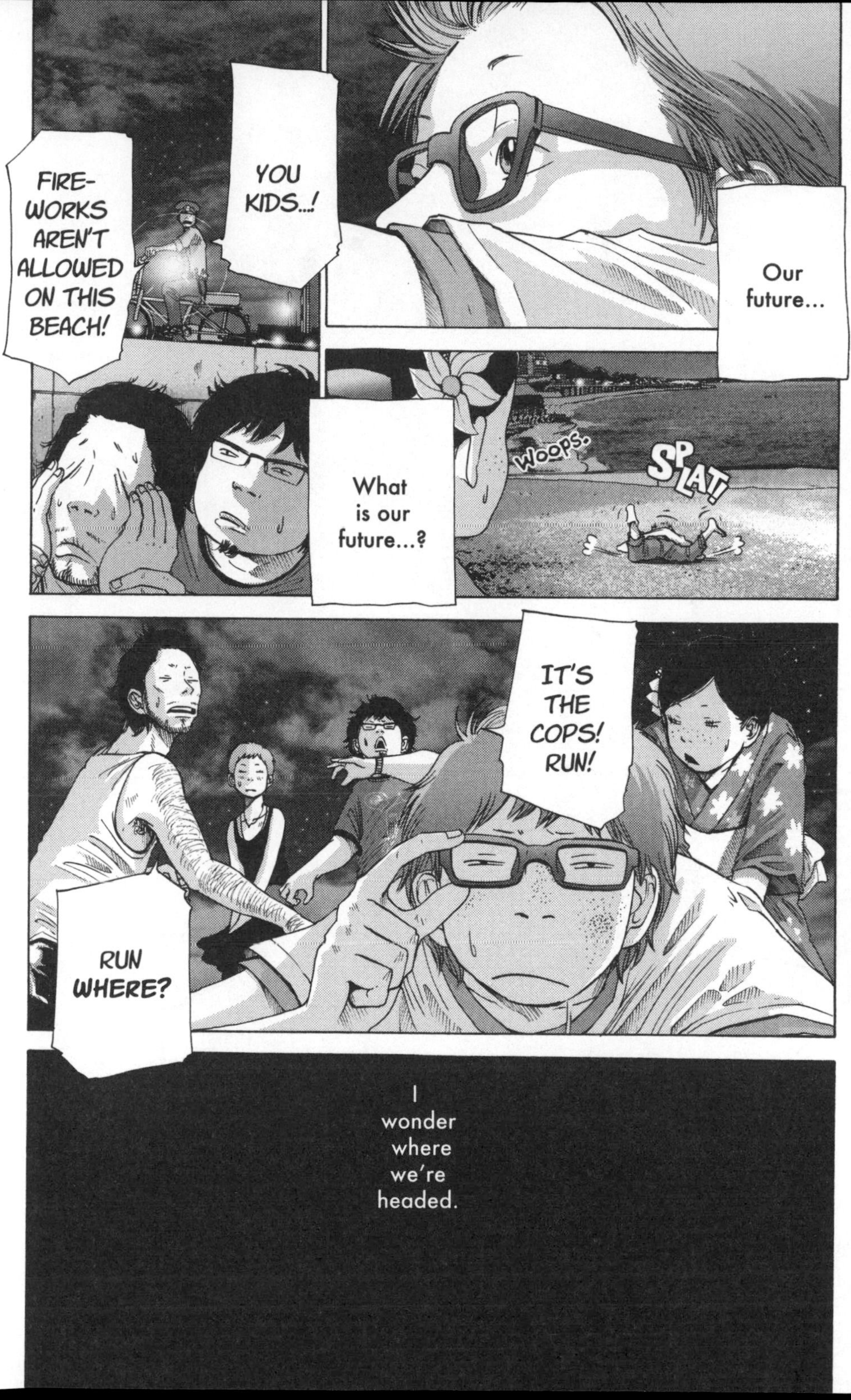
Our future...
YOU KIDS...!
FIRE-WORKS AREN'T ALLOWED ON THIS BEACH!
WOOPS.
SPLAT!
What is our future...?
IT'S THE COPS! RUN!
RUN WHERE?
I wonder where we're headed.

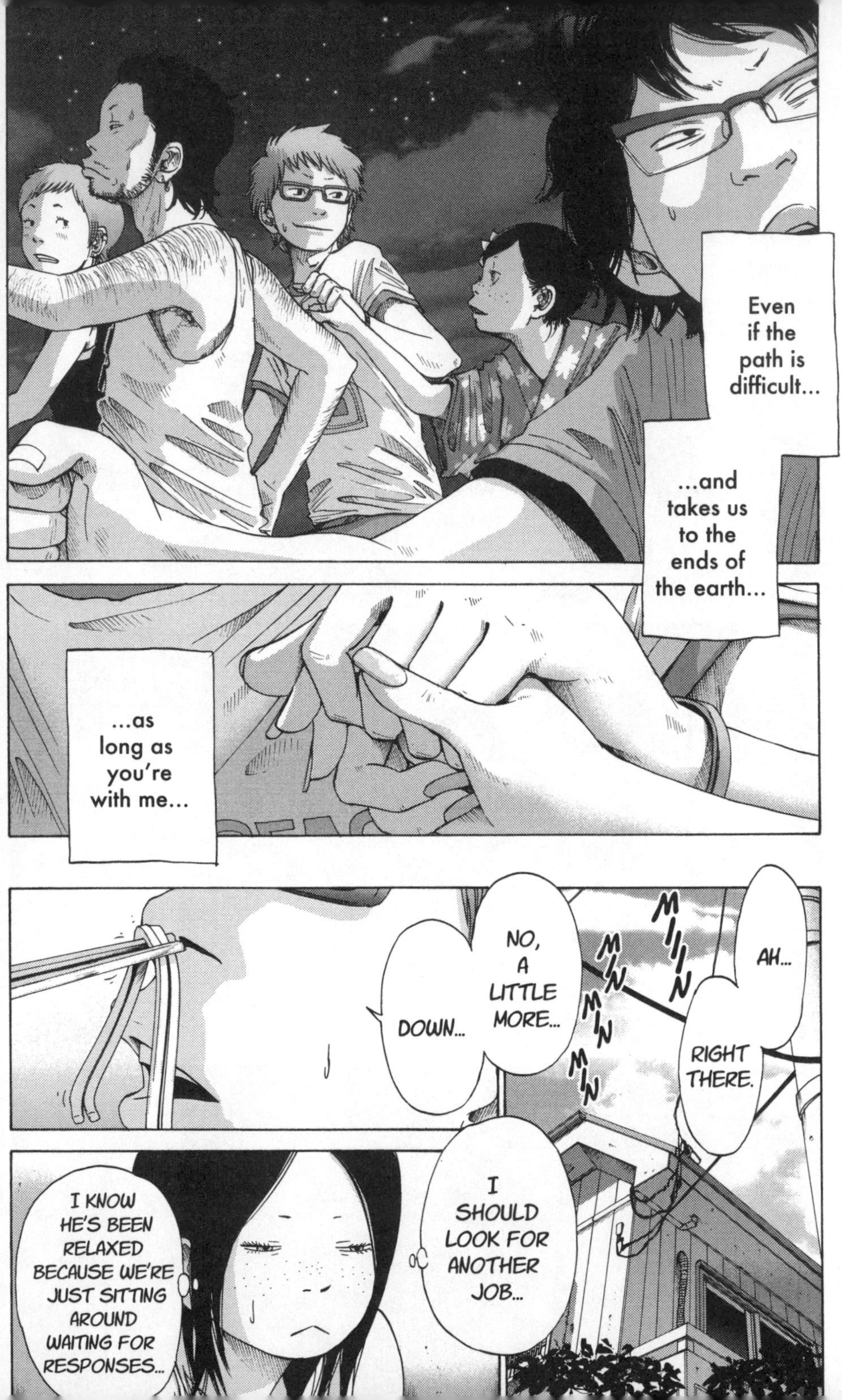
Even if the path is difficult...
...and takes us to the ends of the earth...
...as long as you're with me...
AH...
RIGHT THERE.
MIIIN
MIN MIN MIN
NO, A LITTLE MORE...
DOWN...
I SHOULD LOOK FOR ANOTHER JOB...
I KNOW HE'S BEEN RELAXED BECAUSE WE'RE JUST SITTING AROUND WAITING FOR RESPONSES...

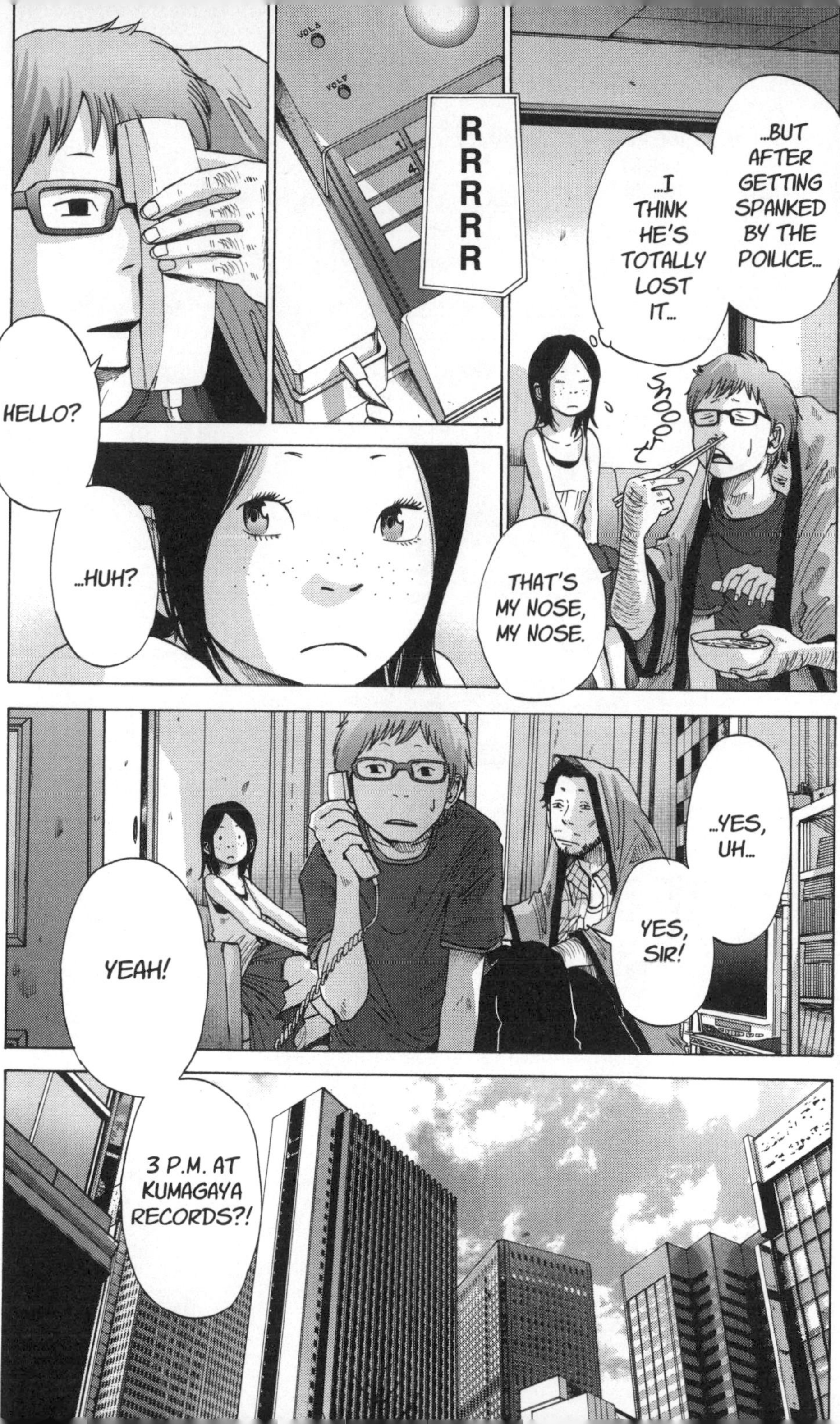

...BUT AFTER GETTING SPANKED BY THE POILICE...
...I THINK HE'S TOTALLY LOST IT...
SNOOORT
THAT'S MY NOSE, MY NOSE.
RRRRR
HELLO?
...HUH?
...YES, UH...
YES, SIR!
YEAH!
3 P.M. AT KUMAGAYA RECORDS?!

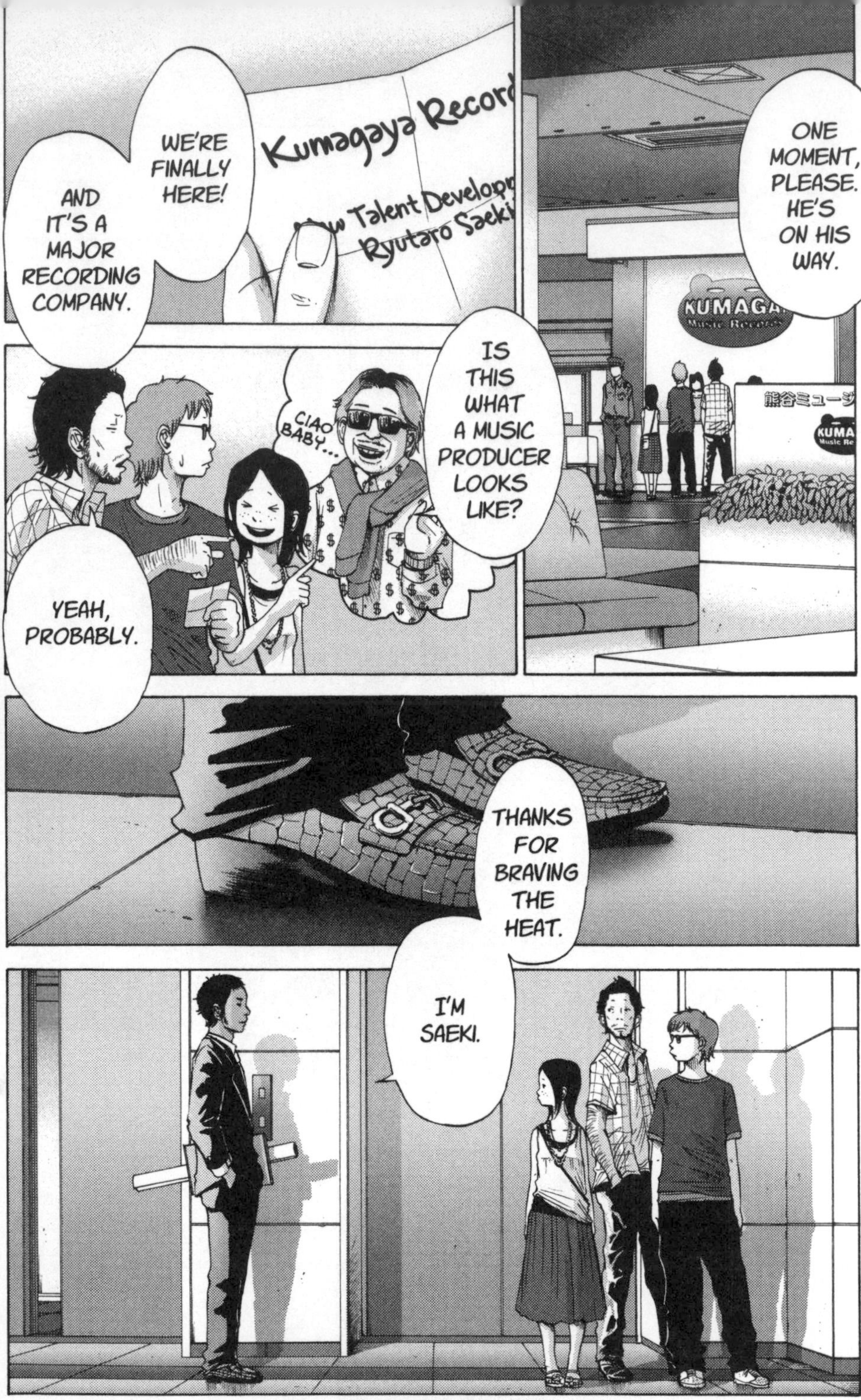
ONE MOMENT, PLEASE. HE'S ON HIS WAY.
Ryutaro Saeki
WE'RE FINALLY HERE!
AND IT'S A MAJOR RECORDING COMPANY.
IS THIS WHAT A MUSIC PRODUCER LOOKS LIKE?
CIAO BABY...
YEAH, PROBABLY.
THANKS FOR BRAVING THE HEAT.
I'M SAEKI.

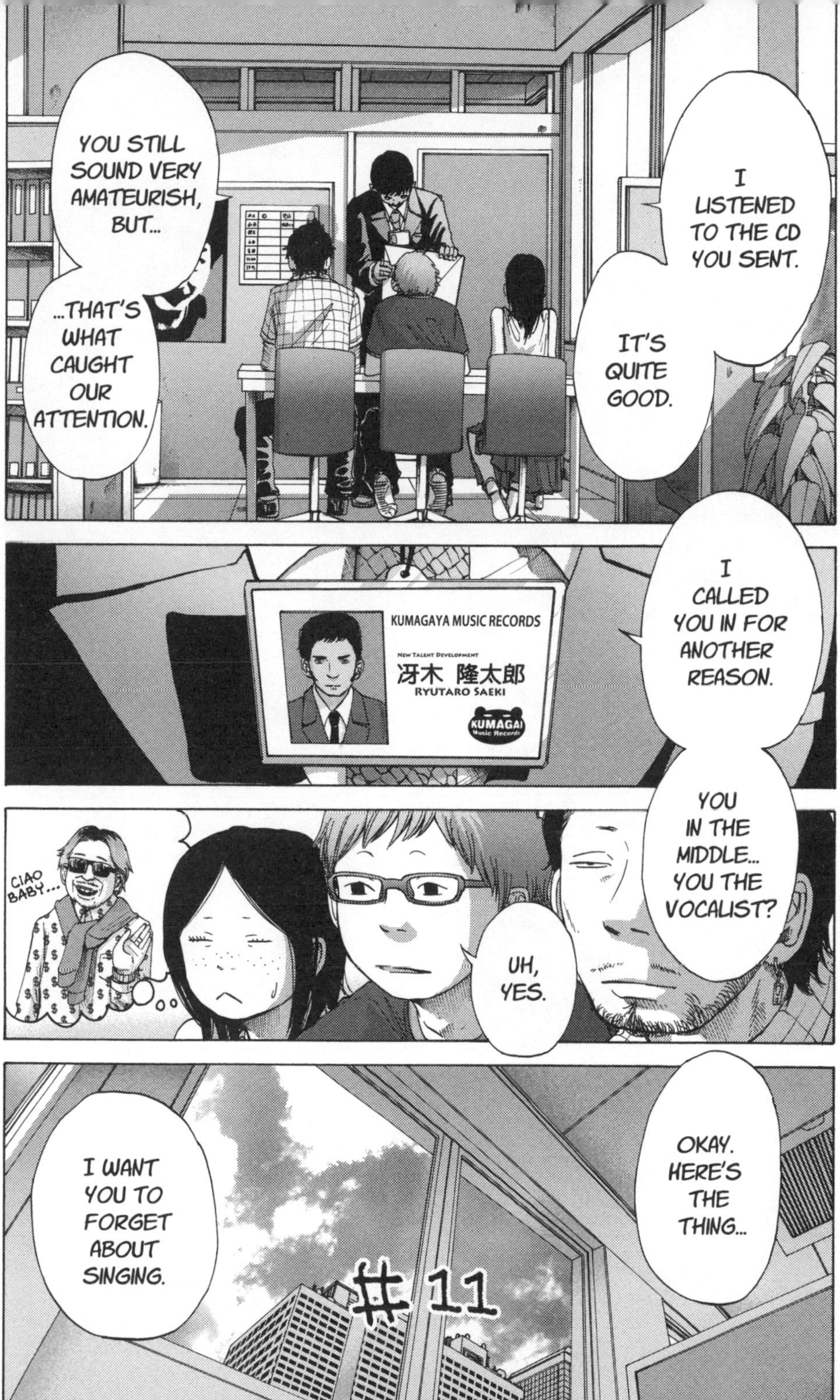
I LISTENED TO THE CD YOU SENT.
IT'S QUITE GOOD.
YOU STILL SOUND VERY AMATEURISH, BUT...
...THAT'S WHAT CAUGHT OUR ATTENTION.
I CALLED YOU IN FOR ANOTHER REASON.
KUMAGAYA MUSIC RECORDS
NEW TALENT DEVELOPMENT
冴木 隆太郎
RYUTARO SAEKI
KUMAGAI Music Records
YOU IN THE MIDDLE... YOU THE VOCALIST?
UH, YES.
CIAO BABY...
OKAY. HERE'S THE THING...
I WANT YOU TO FORGET ABOUT SINGING.
11

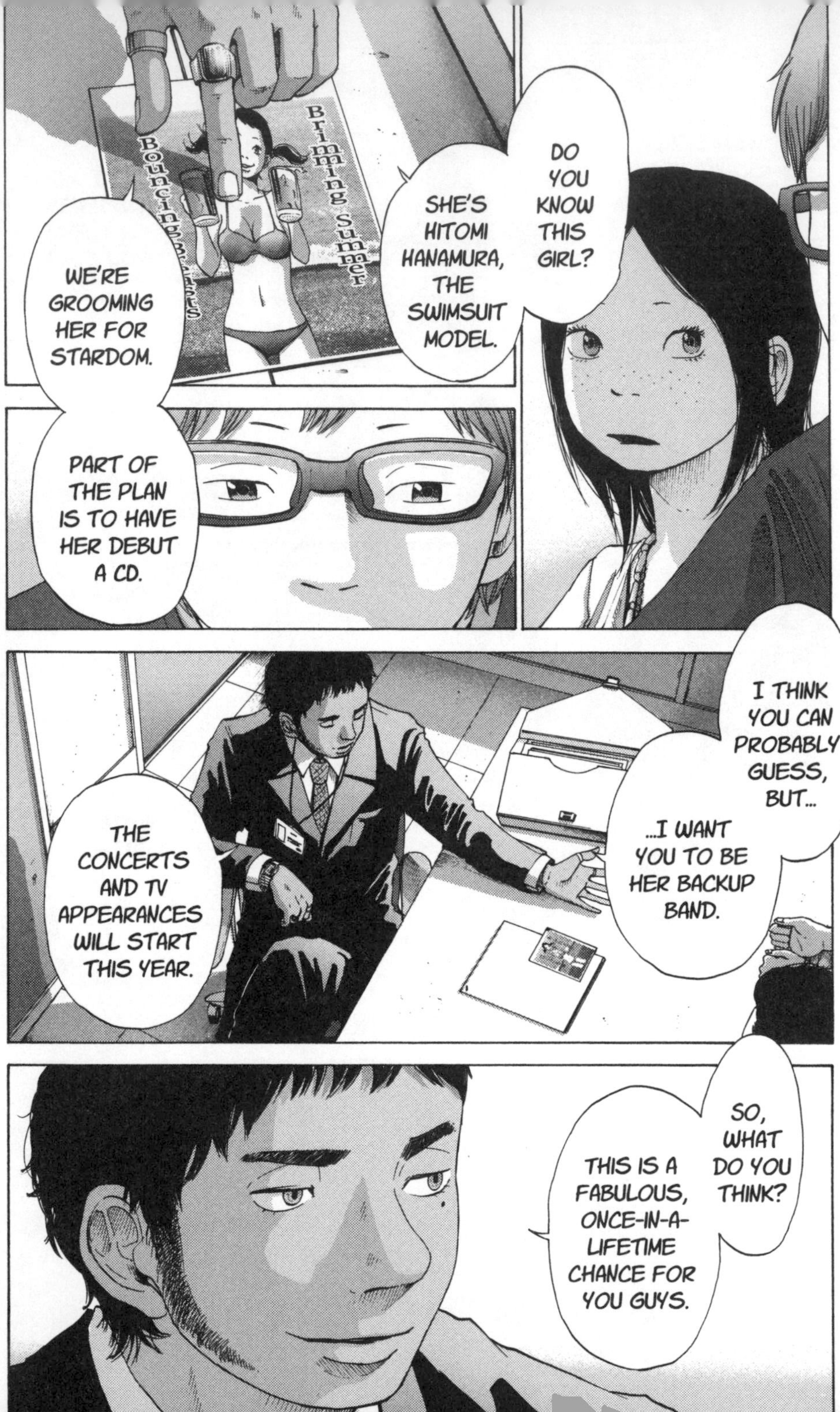
DO YOU KNOW THIS GIRL?
SHE'S HITOMI HANAMURA, THE SWIMSUIT MODEL.
Brimming Summer
Bouncing
WE'RE GROOMING HER FOR STARDOM.
PART OF THE PLAN IS TO HAVE HER DEBUT A CD.
I THINK YOU CAN PROBABLY GUESS, BUT...
...I WANT YOU TO BE HER BACKUP BAND.
THE CONCERTS AND TV APPEARANCES WILL START THIS YEAR.
SO, WHAT DO YOU THINK?
THIS IS A FABULOUS, ONCE-IN-A-LIFETIME CHANCE FOR YOU GUYS.

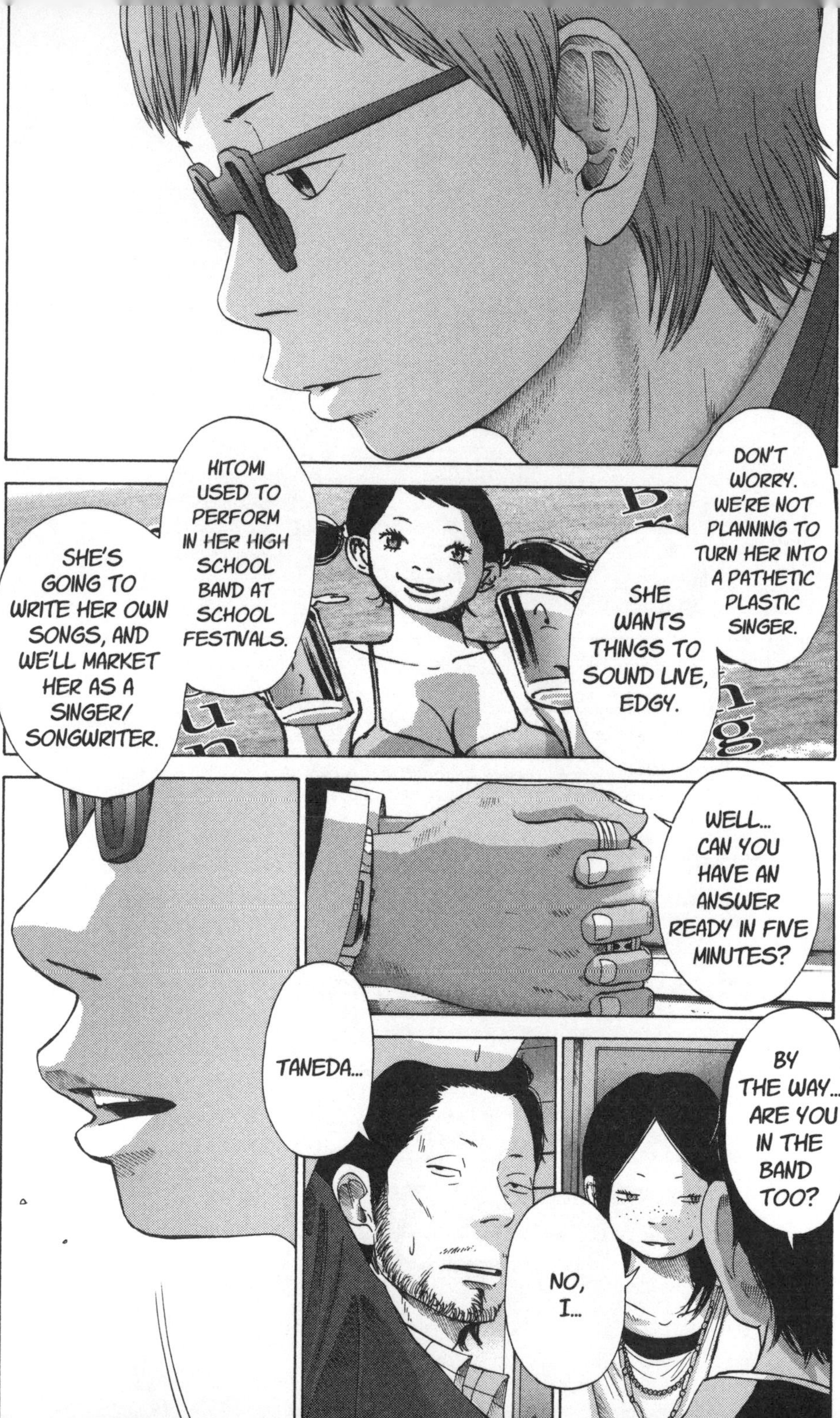
DON'T WORRY. WE'RE NOT PLANNING TO TURN HER INTO A PATHETIC PLASTIC SINGER.
SHE WANTS THINGS TO SOUND LIVE, EDGY.
HITOMI USED TO PERFORM IN HER HIGH SCHOOL BAND AT SCHOOL FESTIVALS.
SHE'S GOING TO WRITE HER OWN SONGS, AND WE'LL MARKET HER AS A SINGER/ SONGWRITER.
WELL... CAN YOU HAVE AN ANSWER READY IN FIVE MINUTES?
BY THE WAY... ARE YOU IN THE BAND TOO?
TANEDA...
NO, I...

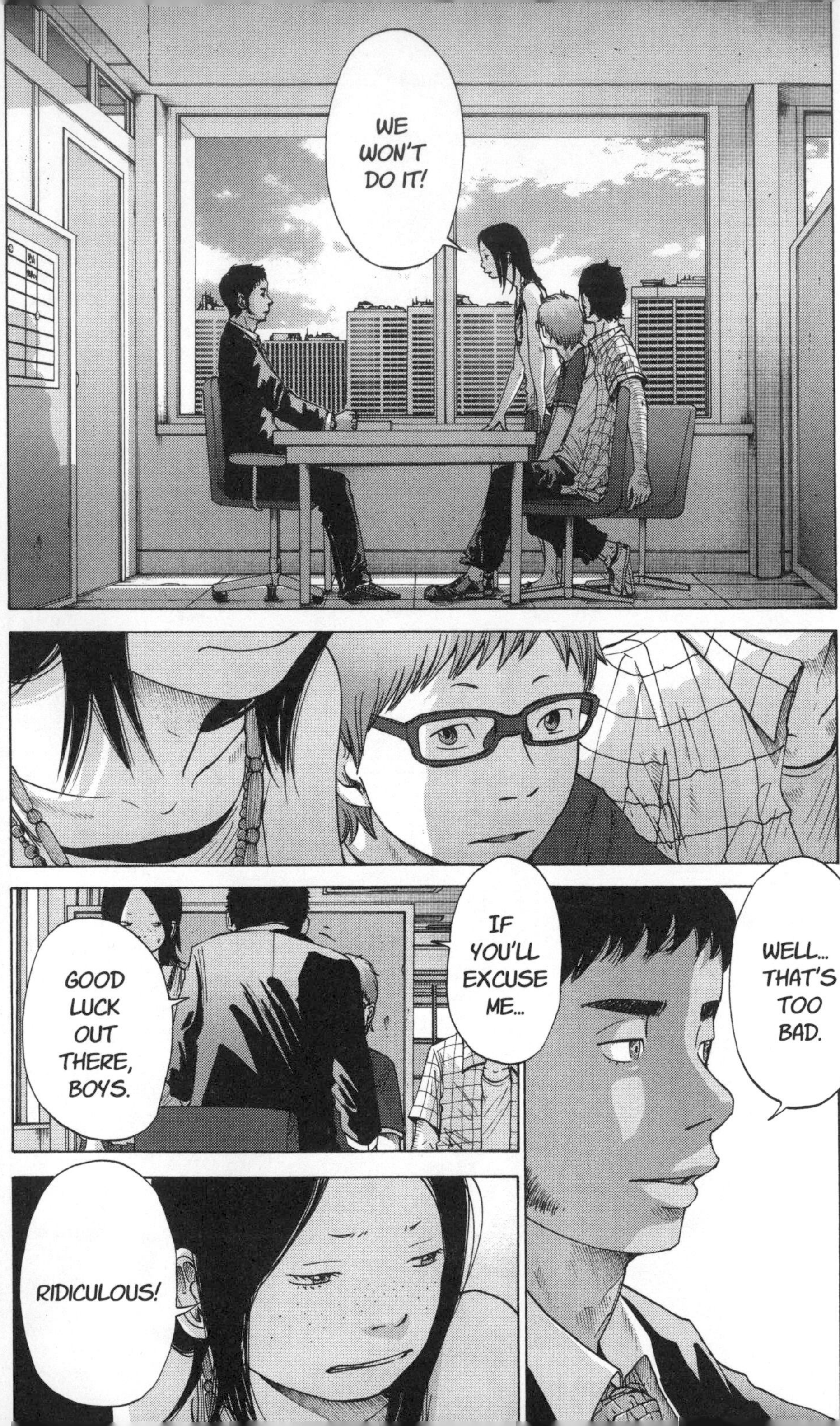
WE WON'T DO IT!
WELL... THAT'S TOO BAD.
IF YOU'LL EXCUSE ME...
GOOD LUCK OUT THERE, BOYS.
RIDICULOUS!

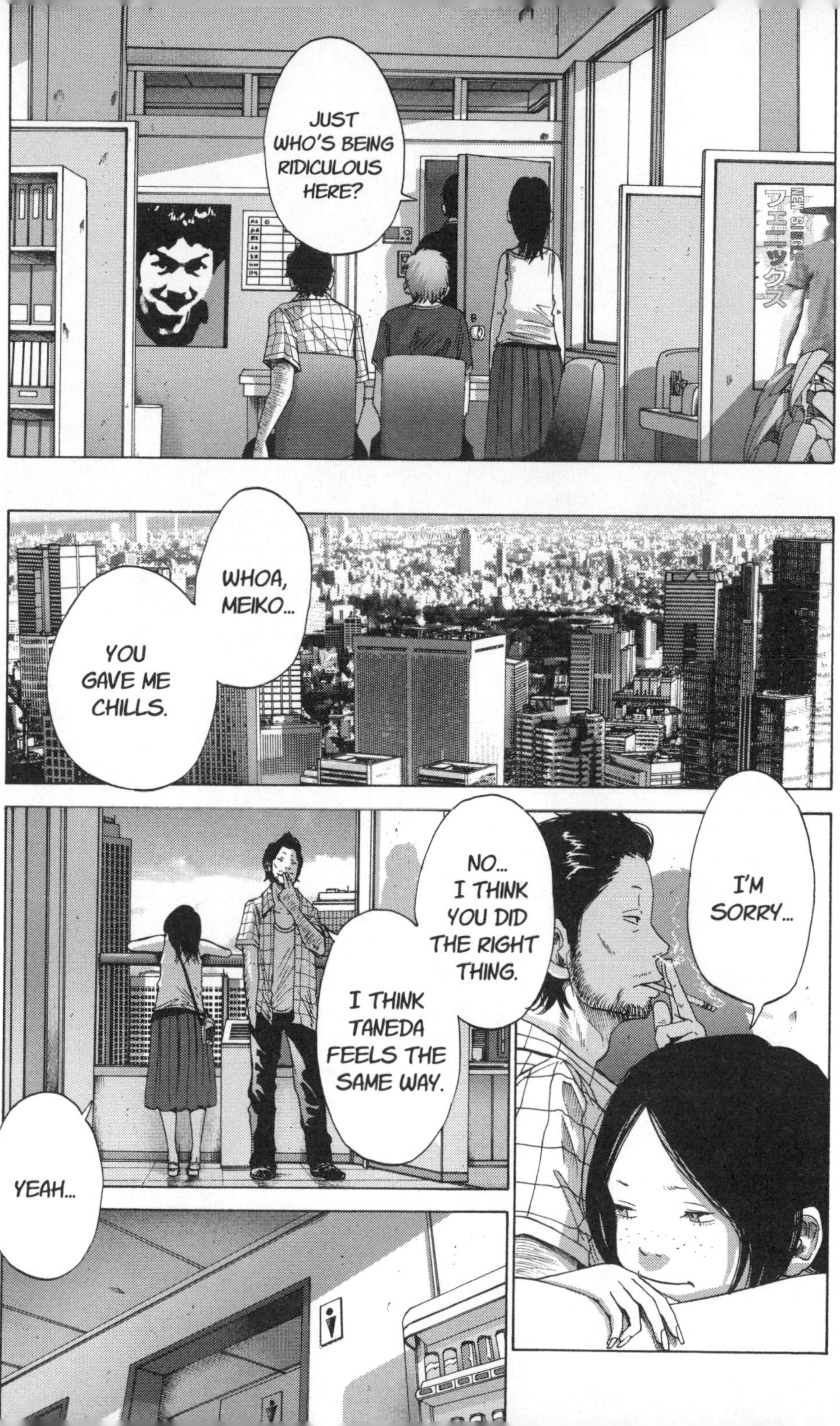
JUST WHO'S BEING RIDICULOUS HERE?
フェニックス
WHOA, MEIKO...
YOU GAVE ME CHILLS.
I'M SORRY...
NO... I THINK YOU DID THE RIGHT THING.
I THINK TANEDA FEELS THE SAME WAY.
YEAH...

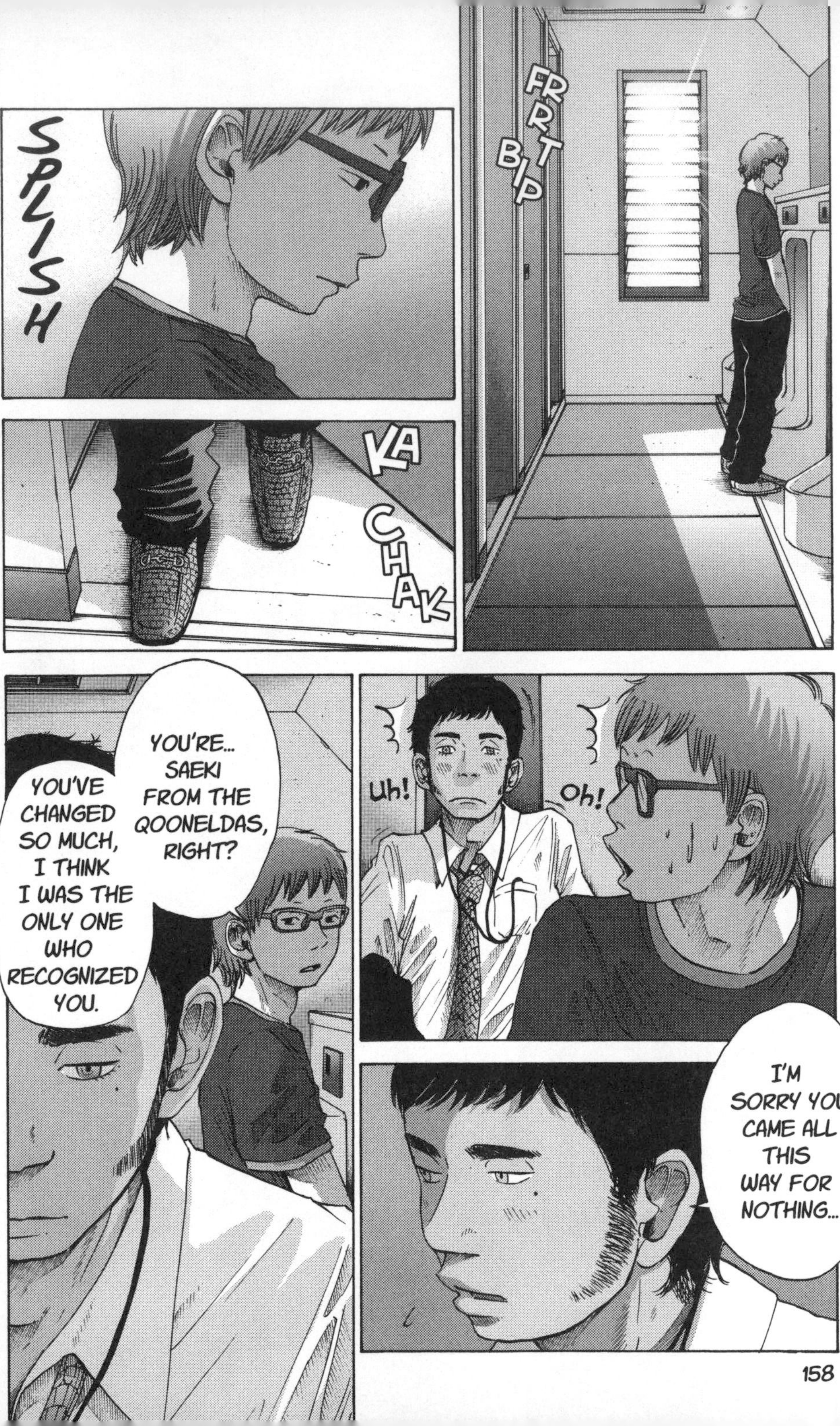
FRRT
BIP
SPLISH
KA
CHAK
Uh!
Oh!
I'M SORRY YOU CAME ALL THIS WAY FOR NOTHING...
YOU'RE... SAEKI FROM THE QOONELDAS, RIGHT?
YOU'VE CHANGED SO MUCH, I THINK I WAS THE ONLY ONE WHO RECOGNIZED YOU.

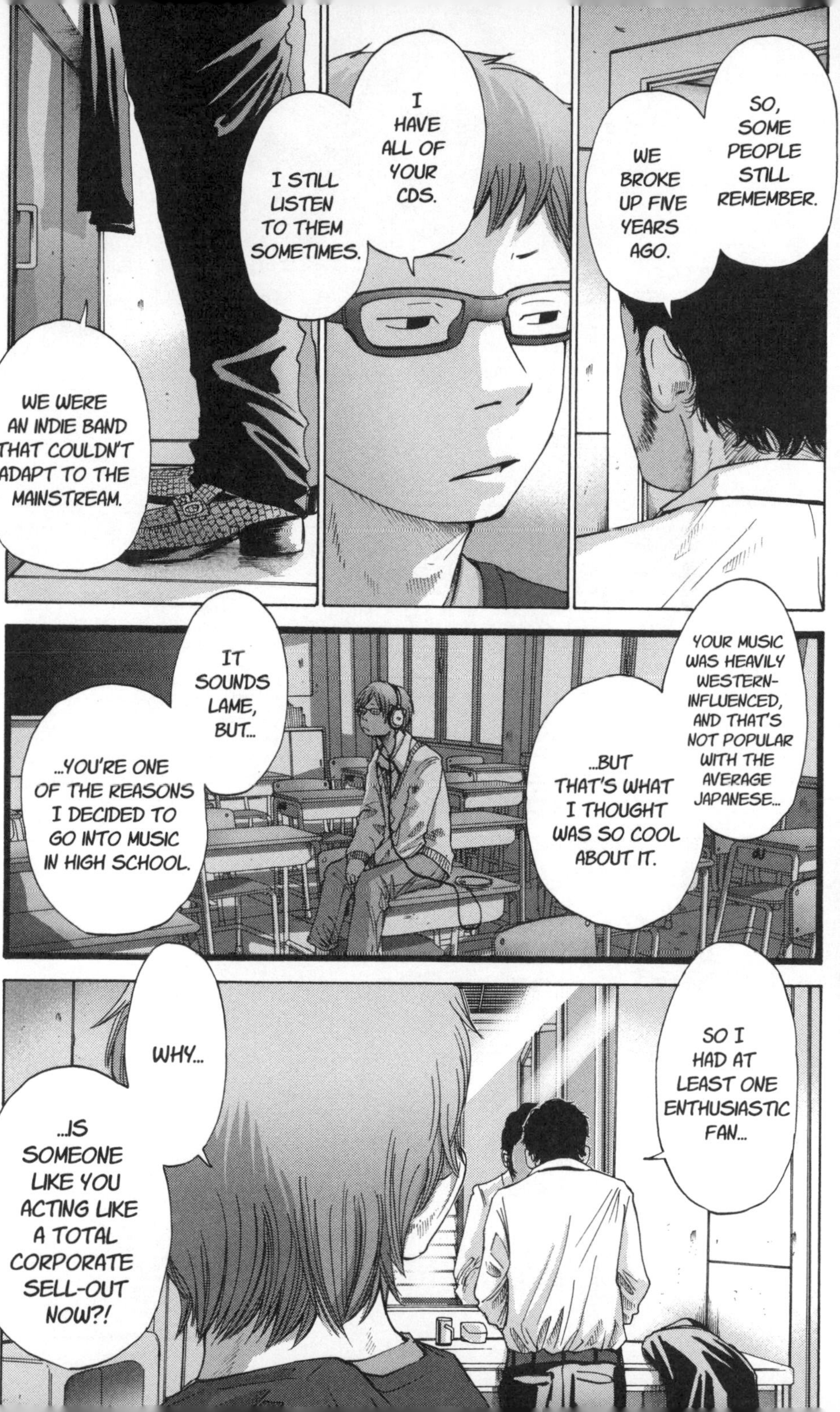
SO, SOME PEOPLE STILL REMEMBER.
WE BROKE UP FIVE YEARS AGO.
I HAVE ALL OF YOUR CDS.
I STILL LISTEN TO THEM SOMETIMES.
WE WERE AN INDIE BAND THAT COULDN'T ADAPT TO THE MAINSTREAM.
YOUR MUSIC WAS HEAVILY WESTERN-INFLUENCED, AND THAT'S NOT POPULAR WITH THE AVERAGE JAPANESE...
...BUT THAT'S WHAT I THOUGHT WAS SO COOL ABOUT IT.
IT SOUNDS LAME, BUT...
...YOU'RE ONE OF THE REASONS I DECIDED TO GO INTO MUSIC IN HIGH SCHOOL.
SO I HAD AT LEAST ONE ENTHUSIASTIC FAN...
WHY...
...IS SOMEONE LIKE YOU ACTING LIKE A TOTAL CORPORATE SELL-OUT NOW?!

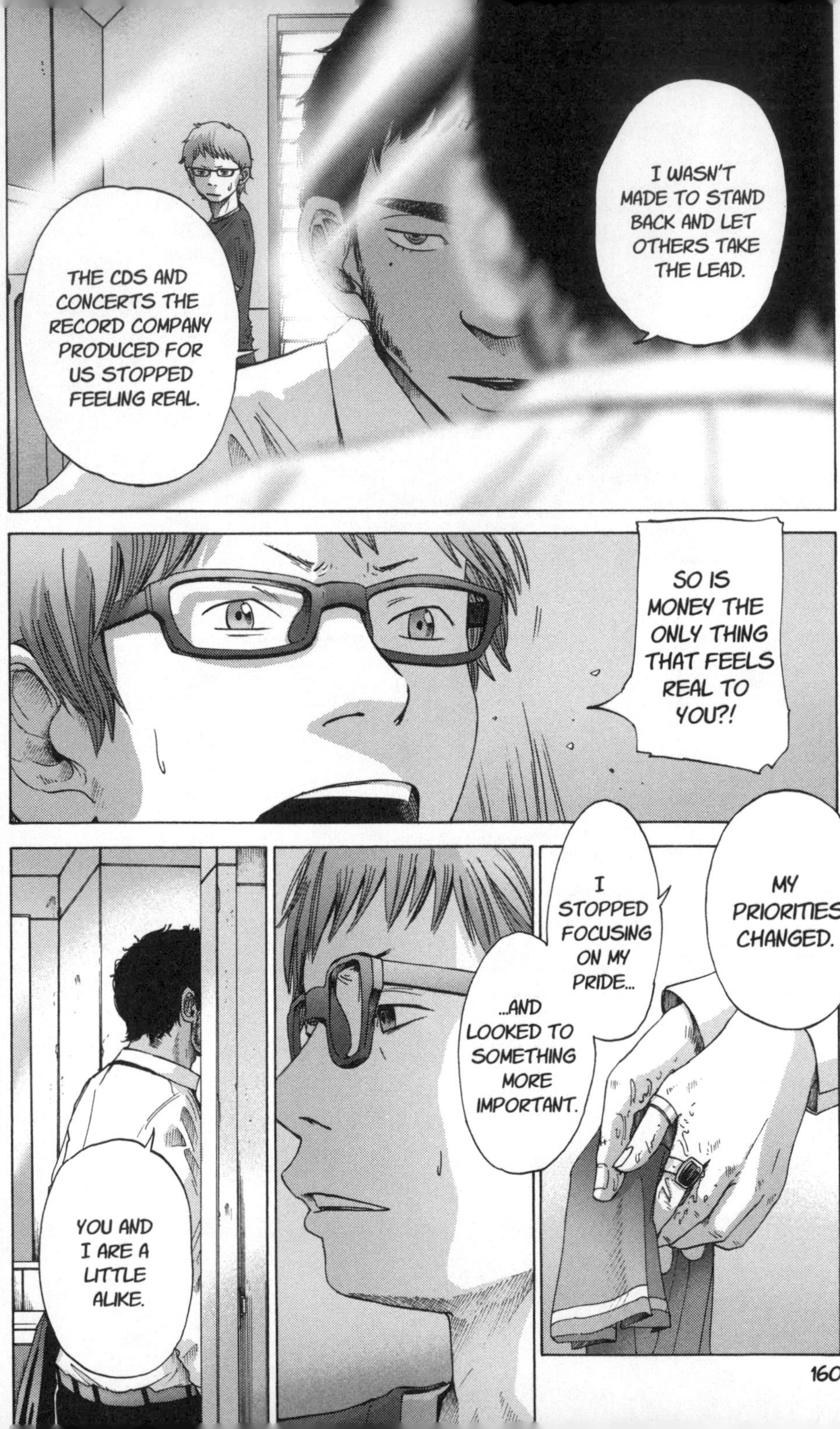
I WASN'T MADE TO STAND BACK AND LET OTHERS TAKE THE LEAD.
THE CDS AND CONCERTS THE RECORD COMPANY PRODUCED FOR US STOPPED FEELING REAL.
SO IS MONEY THE ONLY THING THAT FEELS REAL TO YOU?!
MY PRIORITIES CHANGED.
I STOPPED FOCUSING ON MY PRIDE...
...AND LOOKED TO SOMETHING MORE IMPORTANT.
YOU AND I ARE A LITTLE ALIKE.

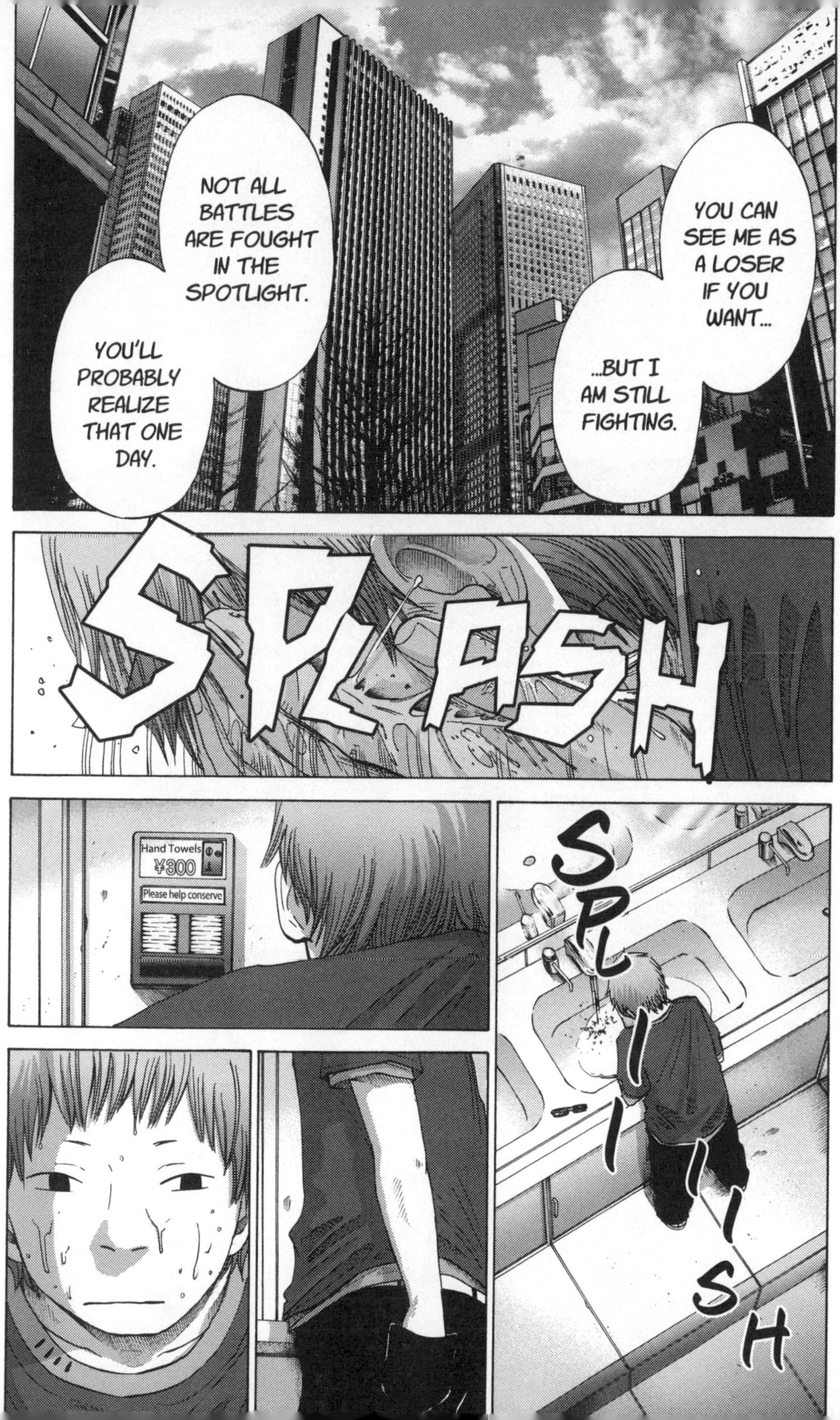
YOU CAN SEE ME AS A LOSER IF YOU WANT...
...BUT I AM STILL FIGHTING.
NOT ALL BATTLES ARE FOUGHT IN THE SPOTLIGHT.
YOU'LL PROBABLY REALIZE THAT ONE DAY.
SPLASH
SPLIIIIISH
Hand Towels ¥300
Please help conserve

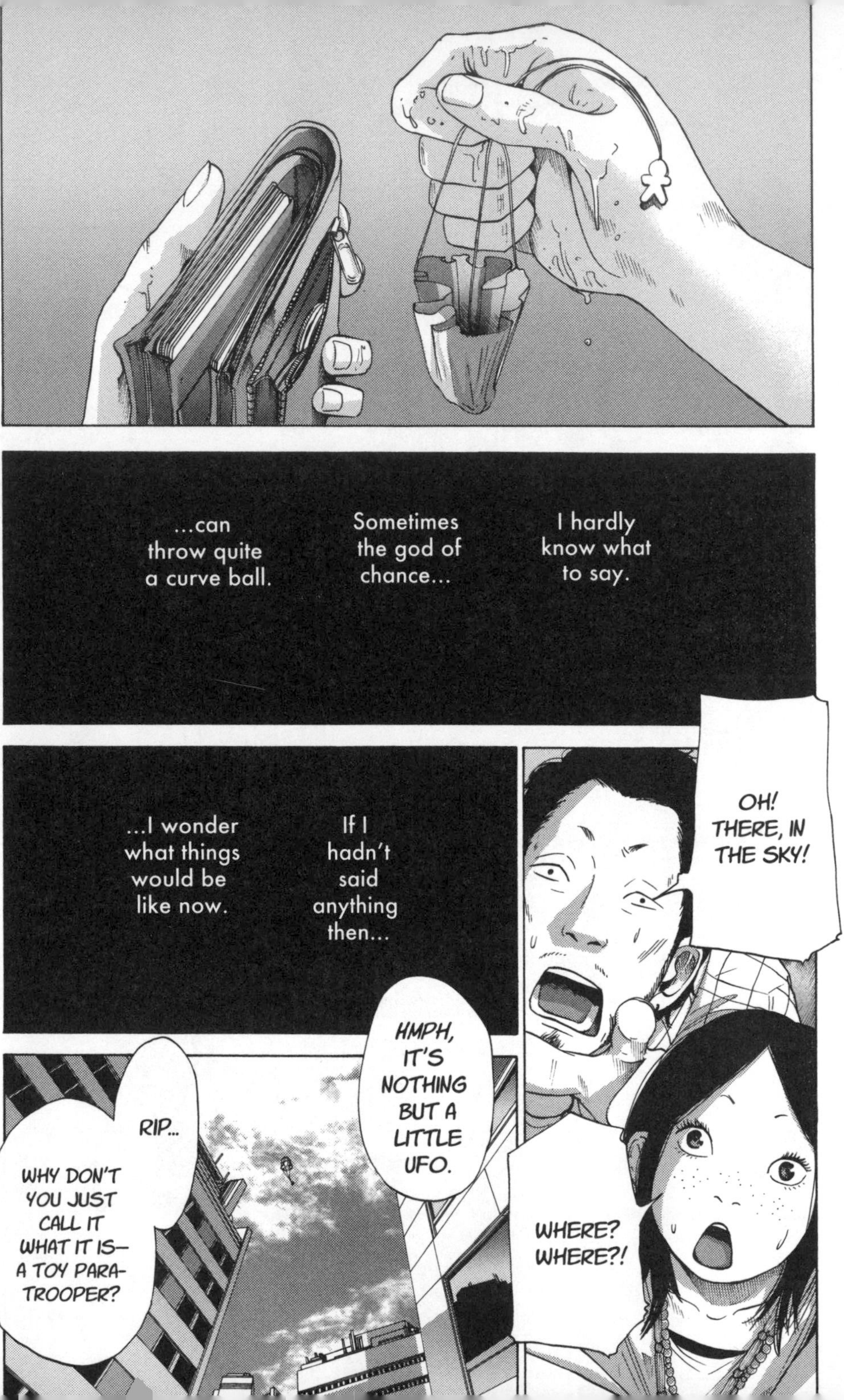

I hardly know what to say.
Sometimes the god of chance...
...can throw quite a curve ball.
OH! THERE, IN THE SKY!
If I hadn't said anything then...
...I wonder what things would be like now.
WHERE? WHERE?!
HMPH, IT'S NOTHING BUT A LITTLE UFO.
RIP...
WHY DON'T YOU JUST CALL IT WHAT IT IS— A TOY PARA-TROOPER?

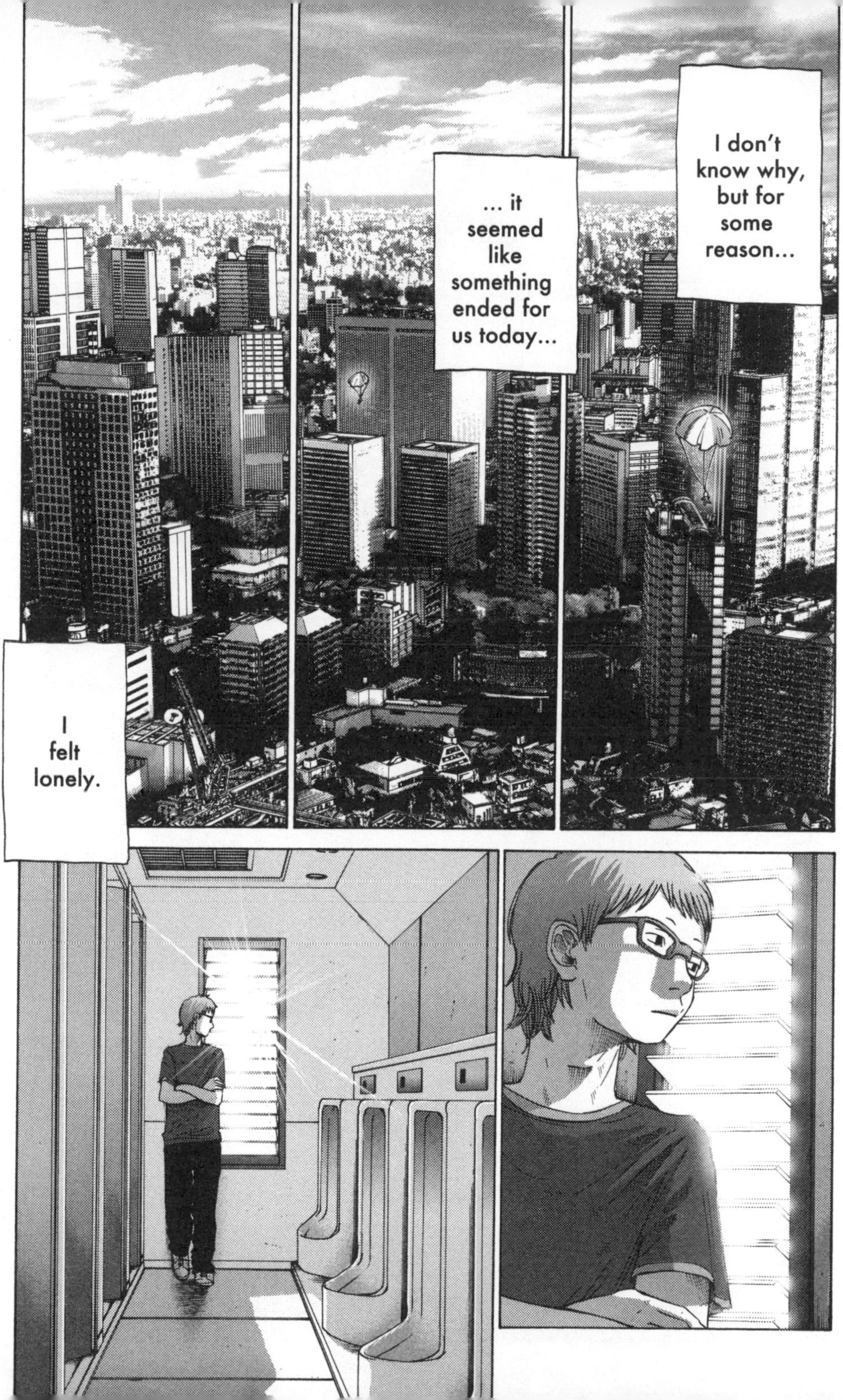
I don't know why, but for some reason...
... it seemed like something ended for us today...
I felt lonely.

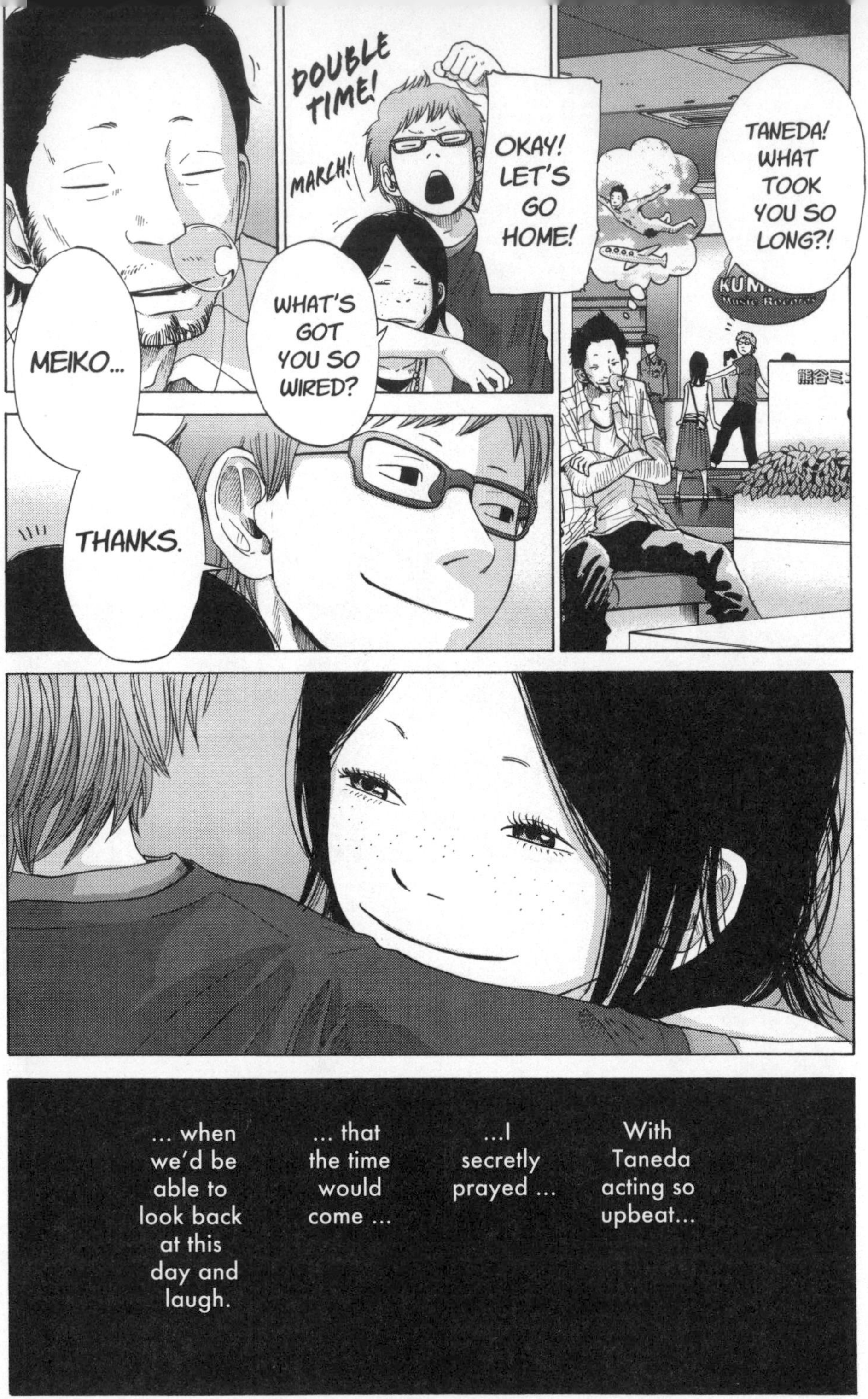
TANEDA! WHAT TOOK YOU SO LONG?!
DOUBLE TIME!
MARCH!
OKAY! LET'S GO HOME!
WHAT'S GOT YOU SO WIRED?
MEIKO...
THANKS.
With Taneda acting so upbeat...
...I secretly prayed ...
... that the time would come ...
... when we'd be able to look back at this day and laugh.

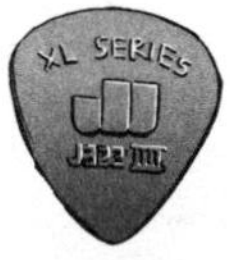
XL SERIES
JAZZ III

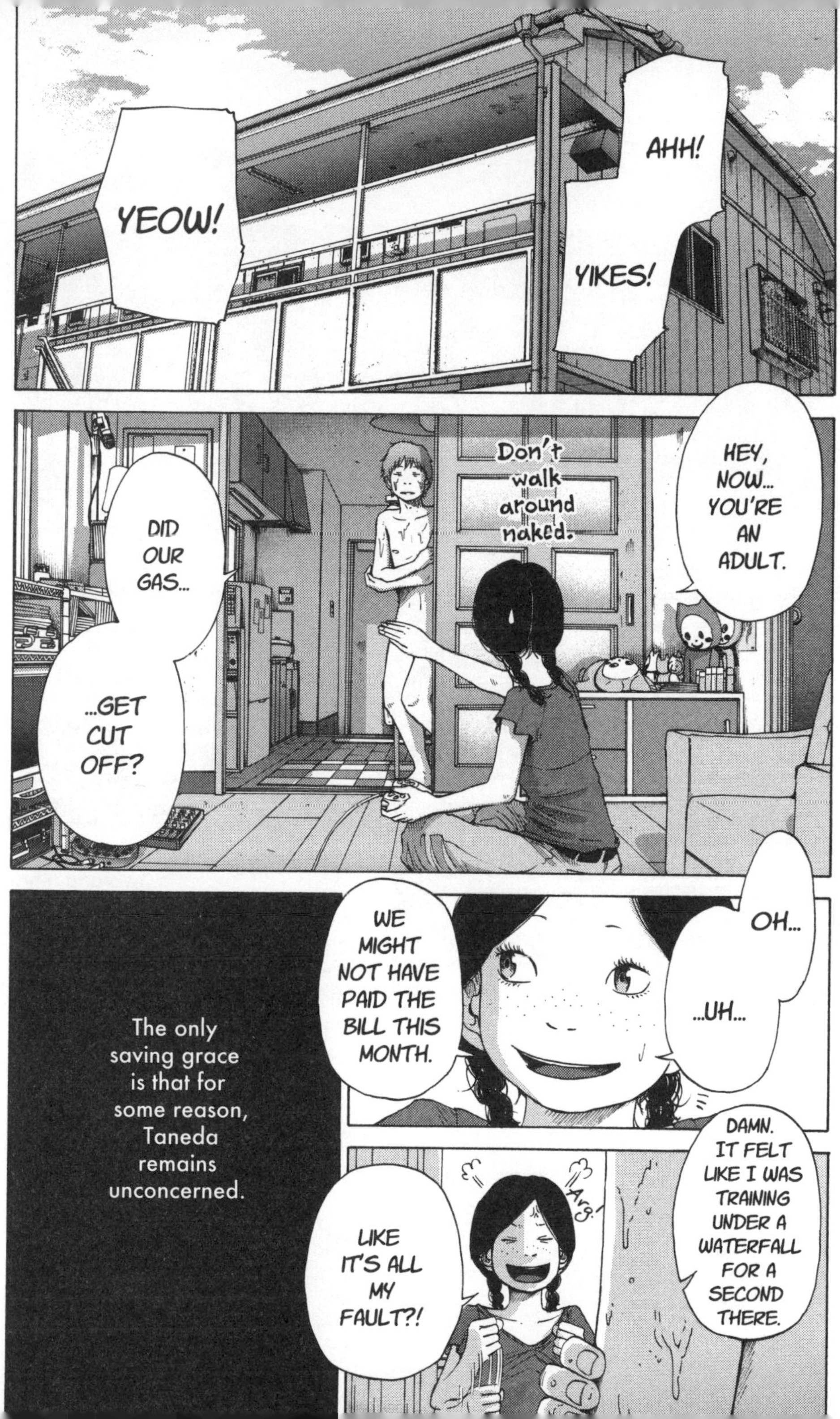
AHH!
YIKES!
YEOW!
HEY, NOW... YOU'RE AN ADULT.
Don't walk around naked.
DID OUR GAS...
...GET CUT OFF?
OH...
...UH...
WE MIGHT NOT HAVE PAID THE BILL THIS MONTH.
DAMN. IT FELT LIKE I WAS TRAINING UNDER A WATERFALL FOR A SECOND THERE.
Arg.
LIKE IT'S ALL MY FAULT?!
The only saving grace is that for some reason, Taneda remains unconcerned.

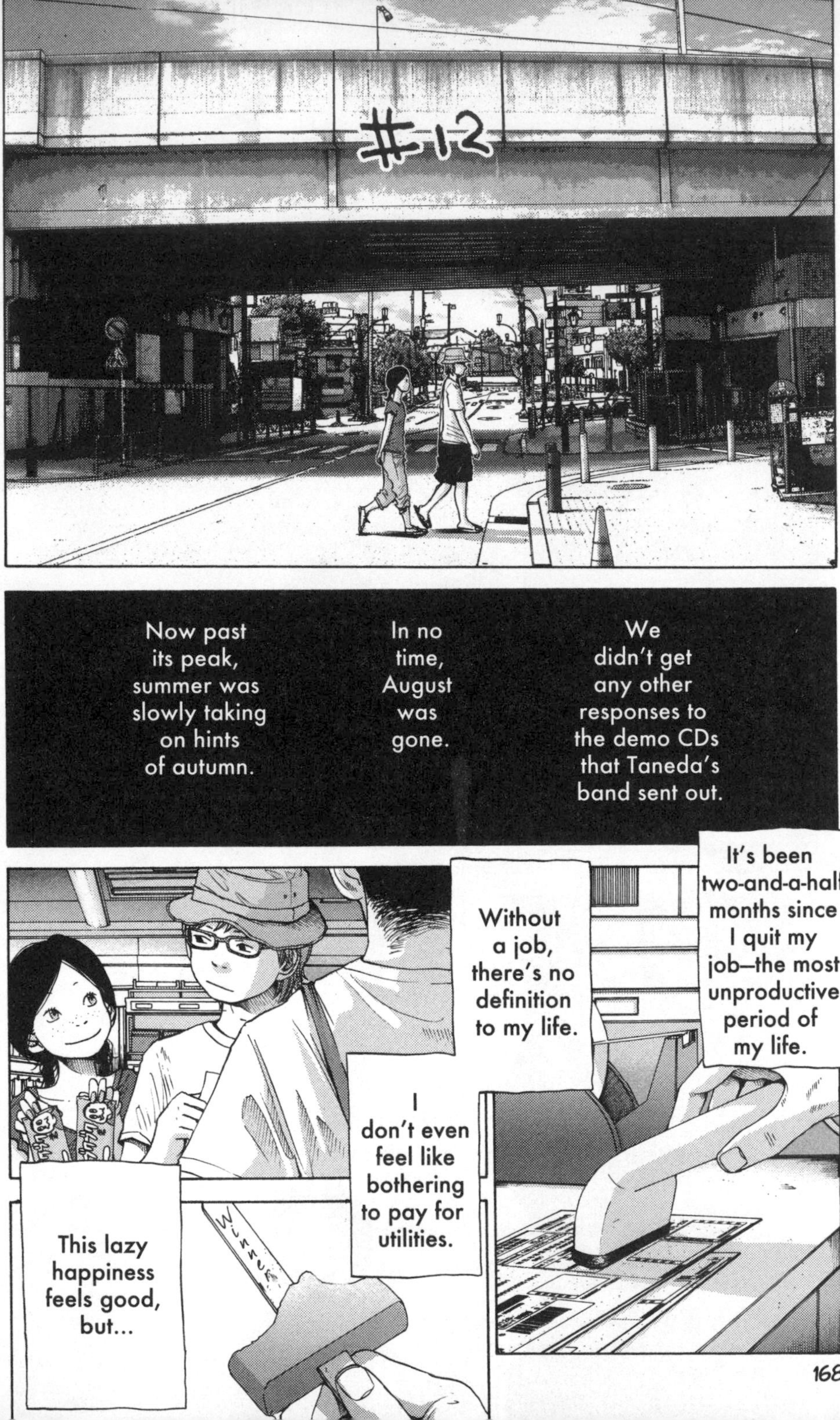
#12
Now past its peak, summer was slowly taking on hints of autumn.
In no time, August was gone.
We didn't get any other responses to the demo CDs that Taneda's band sent out.
It's been two-and-a-half months since I quit my job—the most unproductive period of my life.
Without a job, there's no definition to my life.
I don't even feel like bothering to pay for utilities.
This lazy happiness feels good, but...
Winner

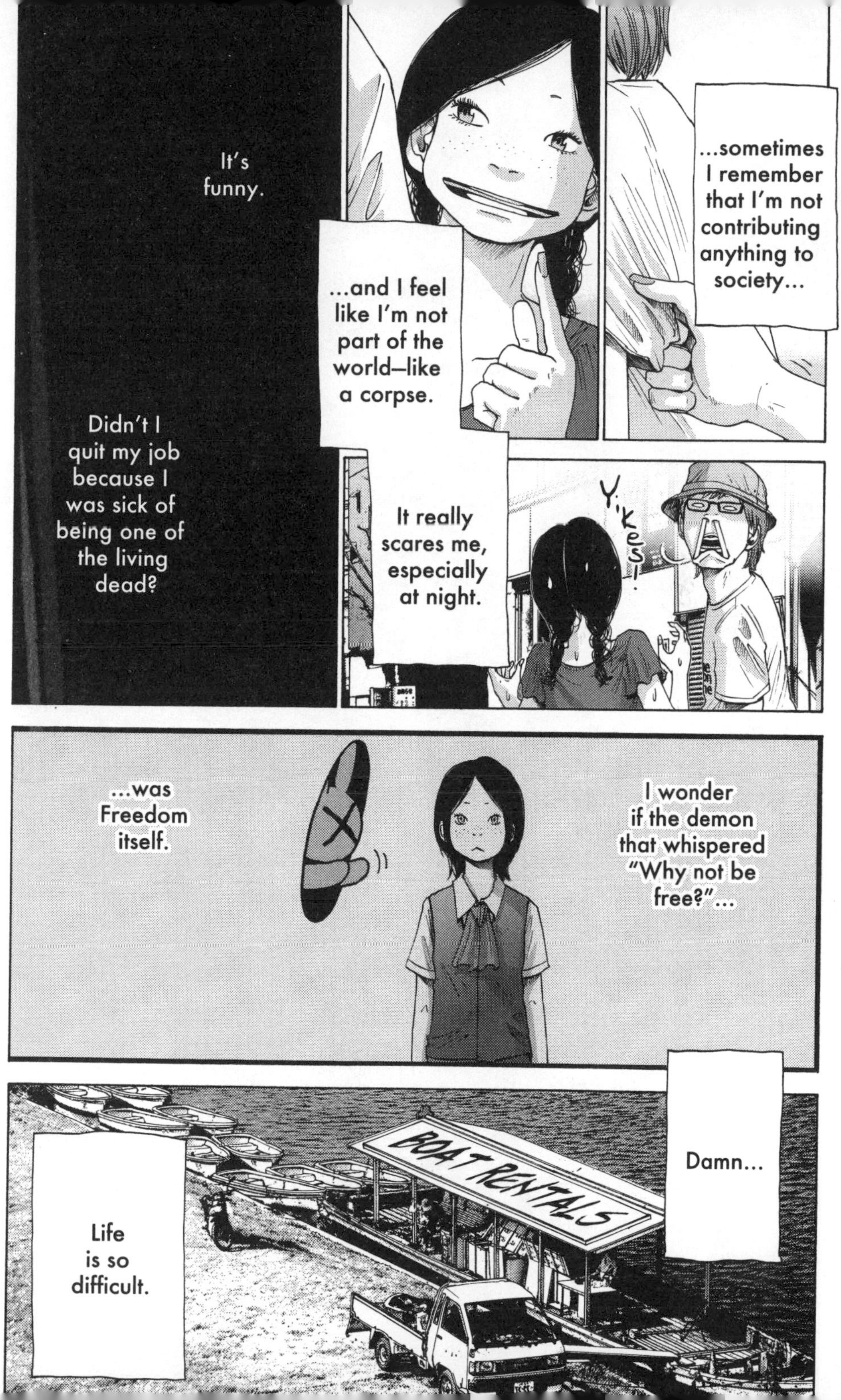
...sometimes I remember that I'm not contributing anything to society...
...and I feel like I'm not part of the world—like a corpse.
It really scares me, especially at night.
Yikes!
It's funny.
Didn't I quit my job because I was sick of being one of the living dead?
I wonder if the demon that whispered "Why not be free?"...
...was Freedom itself.
Damn...
BOAT RENTALS
Life is so difficult.

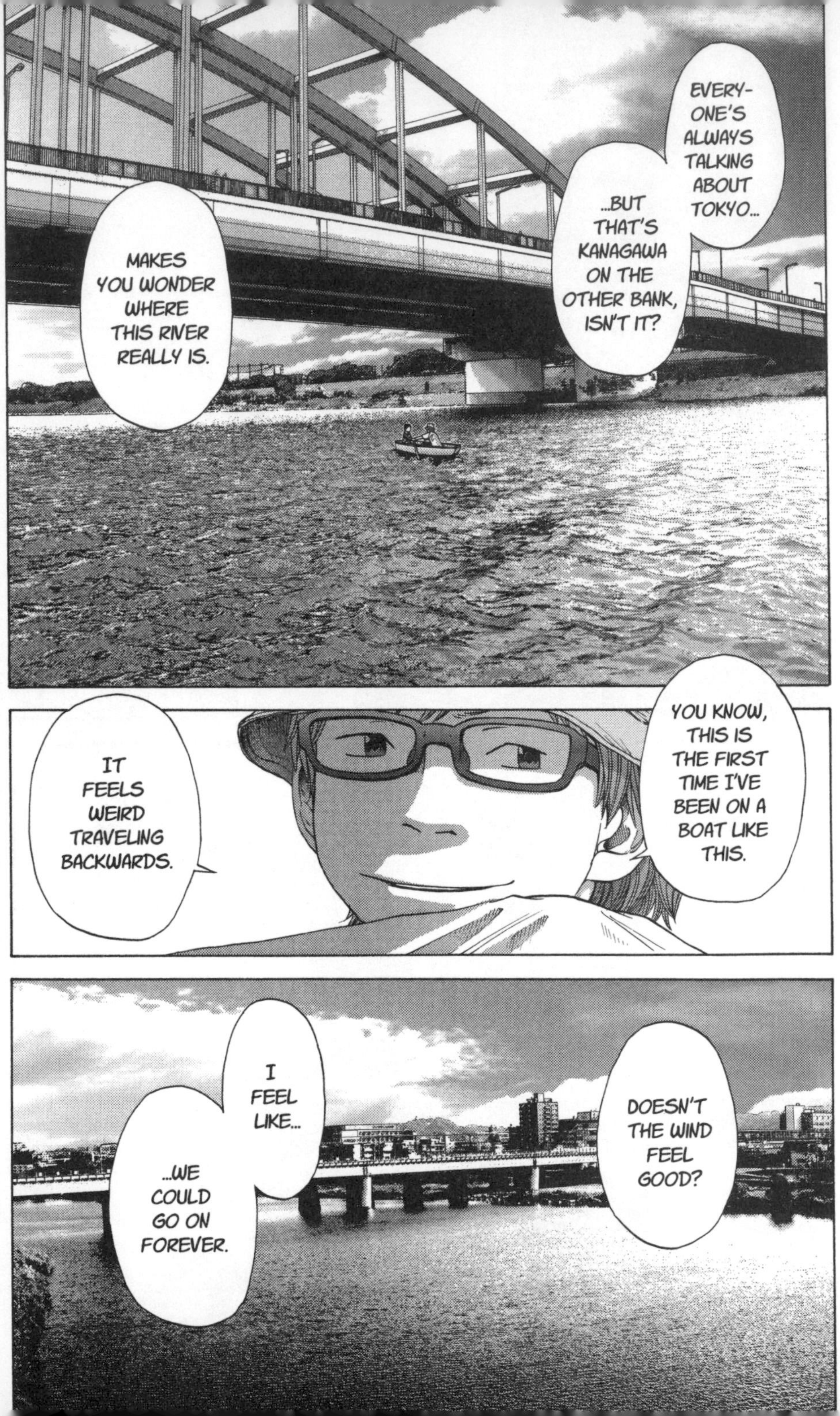
EVERYONE'S ALWAYS TALKING ABOUT TOKYO...
...BUT THAT'S KANAGAWA ON THE OTHER BANK, ISN'T IT?
MAKES YOU WONDER WHERE THIS RIVER REALLY IS.
YOU KNOW, THIS IS THE FIRST TIME I'VE BEEN ON A BOAT LIKE THIS.
IT FEELS WEIRD TRAVELING BACKWARDS.
DOESN'T THE WIND FEEL GOOD?
I FEEL LIKE...
...WE COULD GO ON FOREVER.

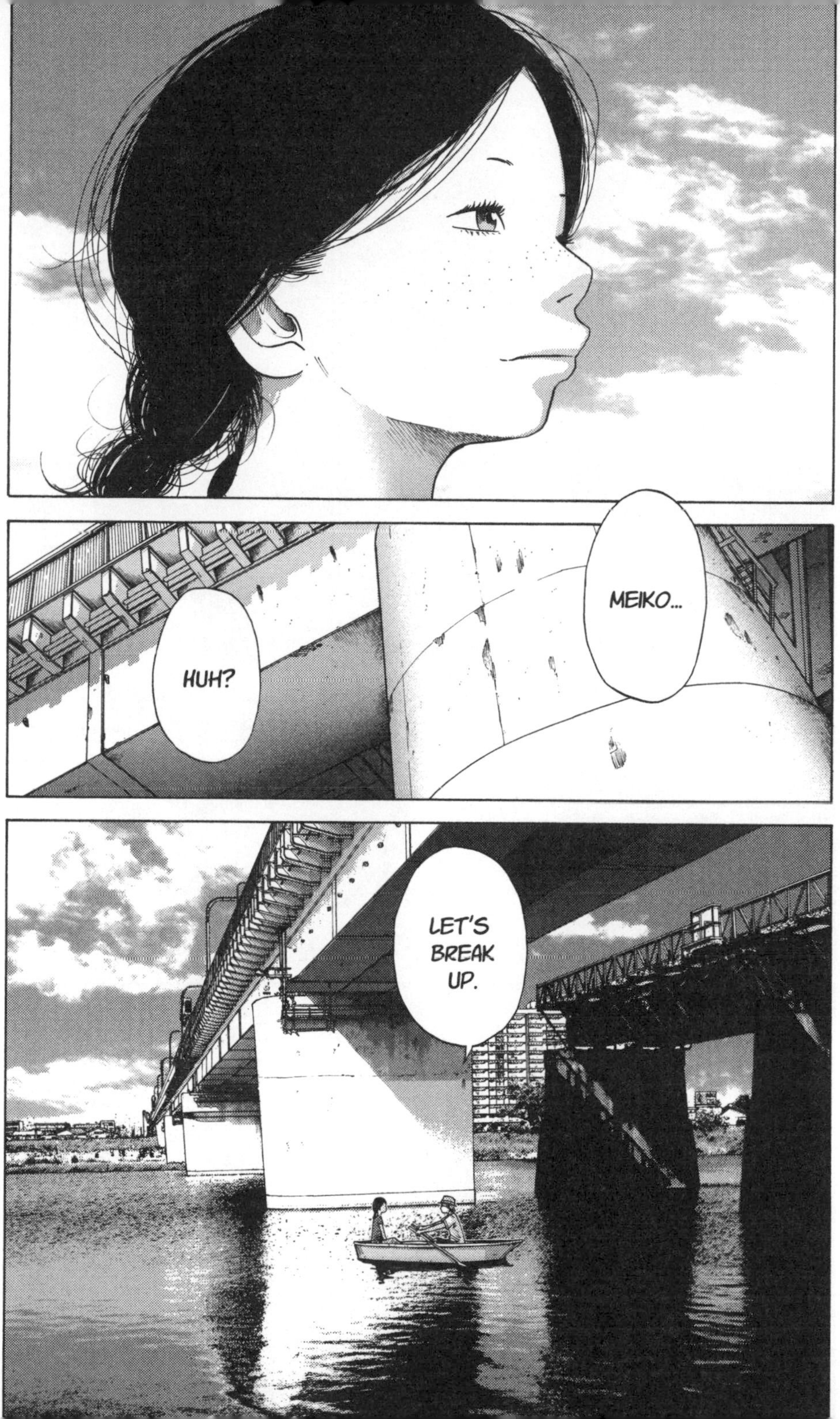
MEIKO...
HUH?
LET'S BREAK UP.

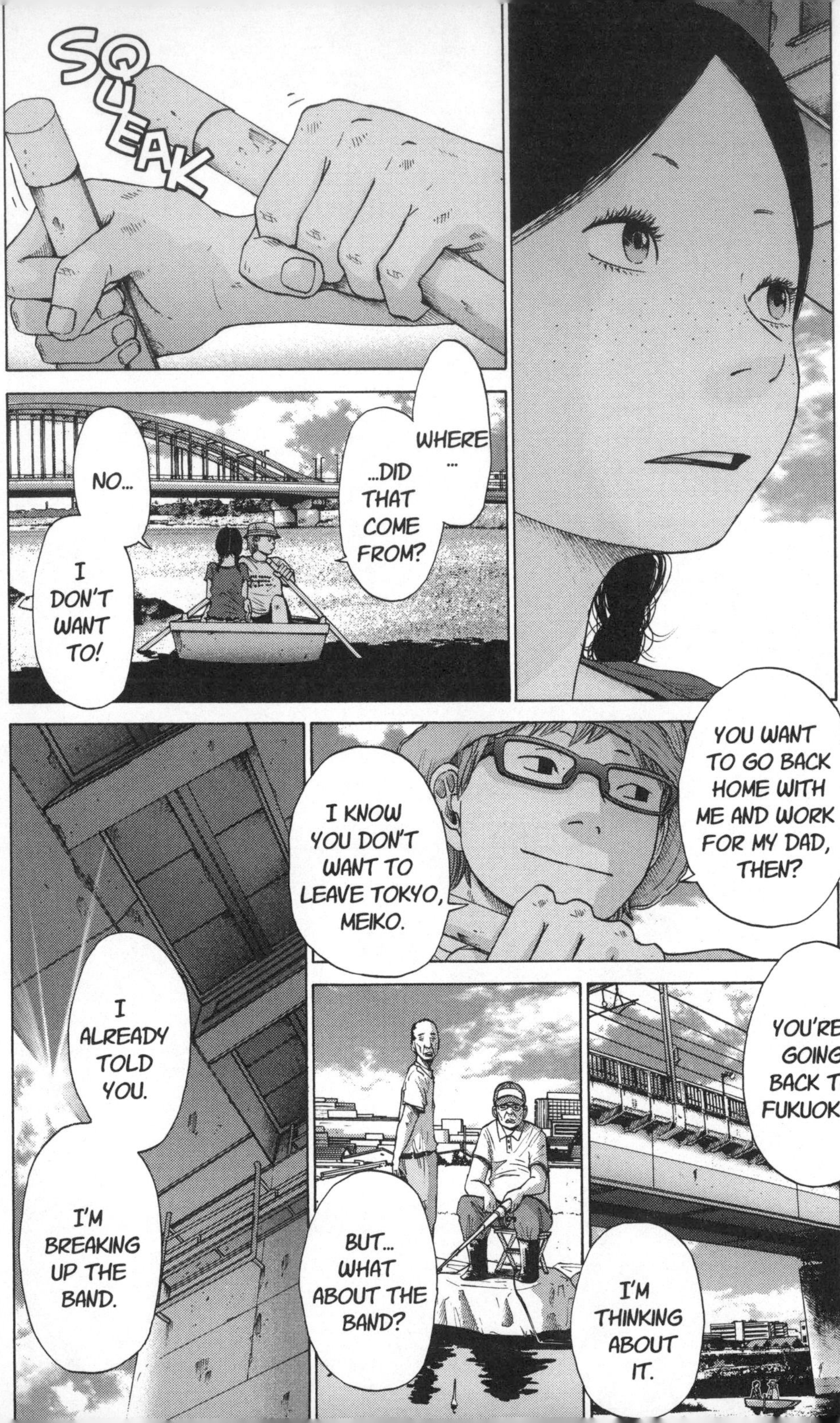
SQUEAK
WHERE ...
...DID THAT COME FROM?
NO...
I DON'T WANT TO!
YOU WANT TO GO BACK HOME WITH ME AND WORK FOR MY DAD, THEN?
I KNOW YOU DON'T WANT TO LEAVE TOKYO, MEIKO.
YOU'RE GOING BACK TO FUKUOKA?
I'M THINKING ABOUT IT.
BUT... WHAT ABOUT THE BAND?
I ALREADY TOLD YOU.
I'M BREAKING UP THE BAND.

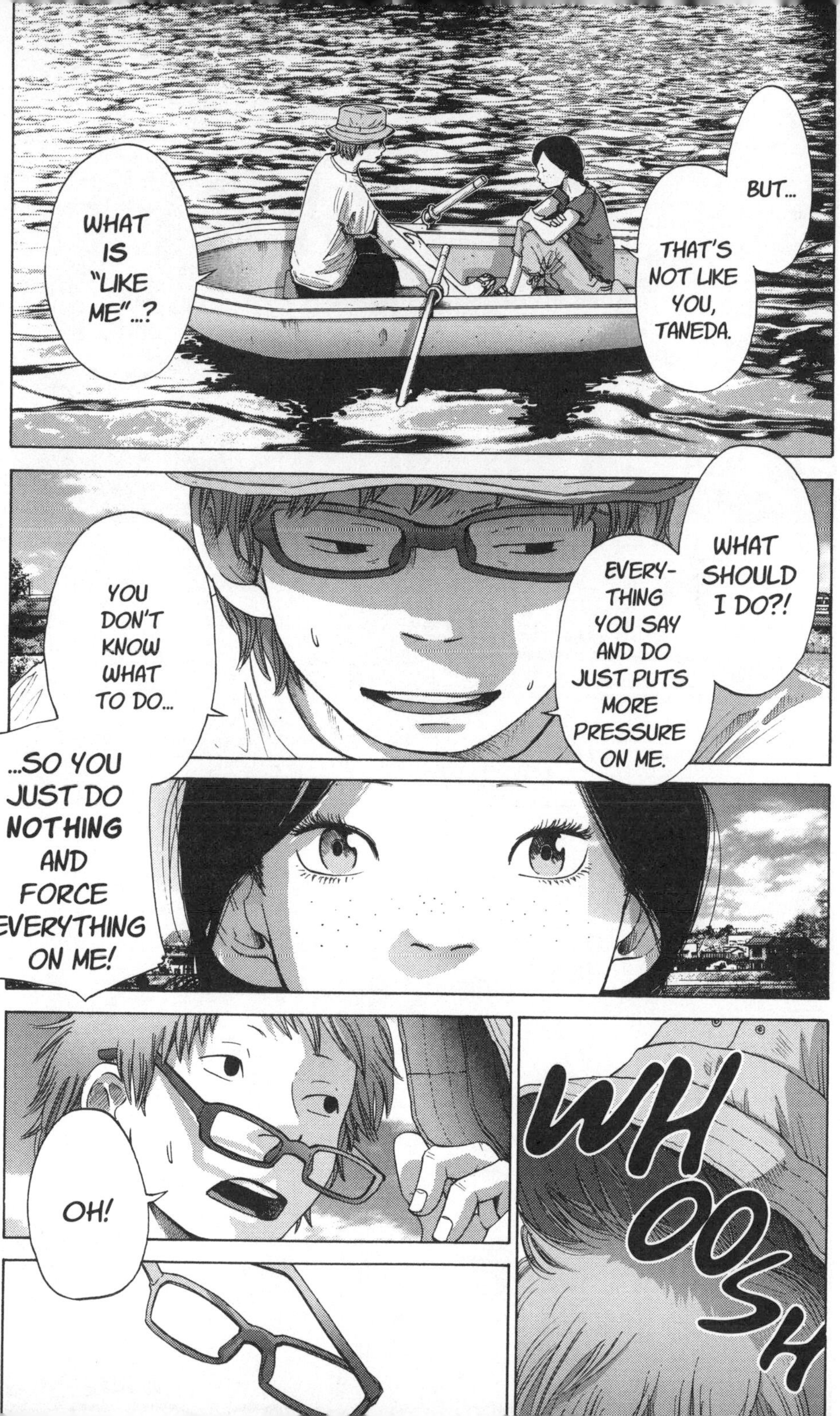
BUT...
THAT'S NOT LIKE YOU, TANEDA.
WHAT IS "LIKE ME"...?
WHAT SHOULD I DO?!
EVERY-THING YOU SAY AND DO JUST PUTS MORE PRESSURE ON ME.
YOU DON'T KNOW WHAT TO DO...
...SO YOU JUST DO NOTHING AND FORCE EVERYTHING ON ME!
WHOOSH
OH!

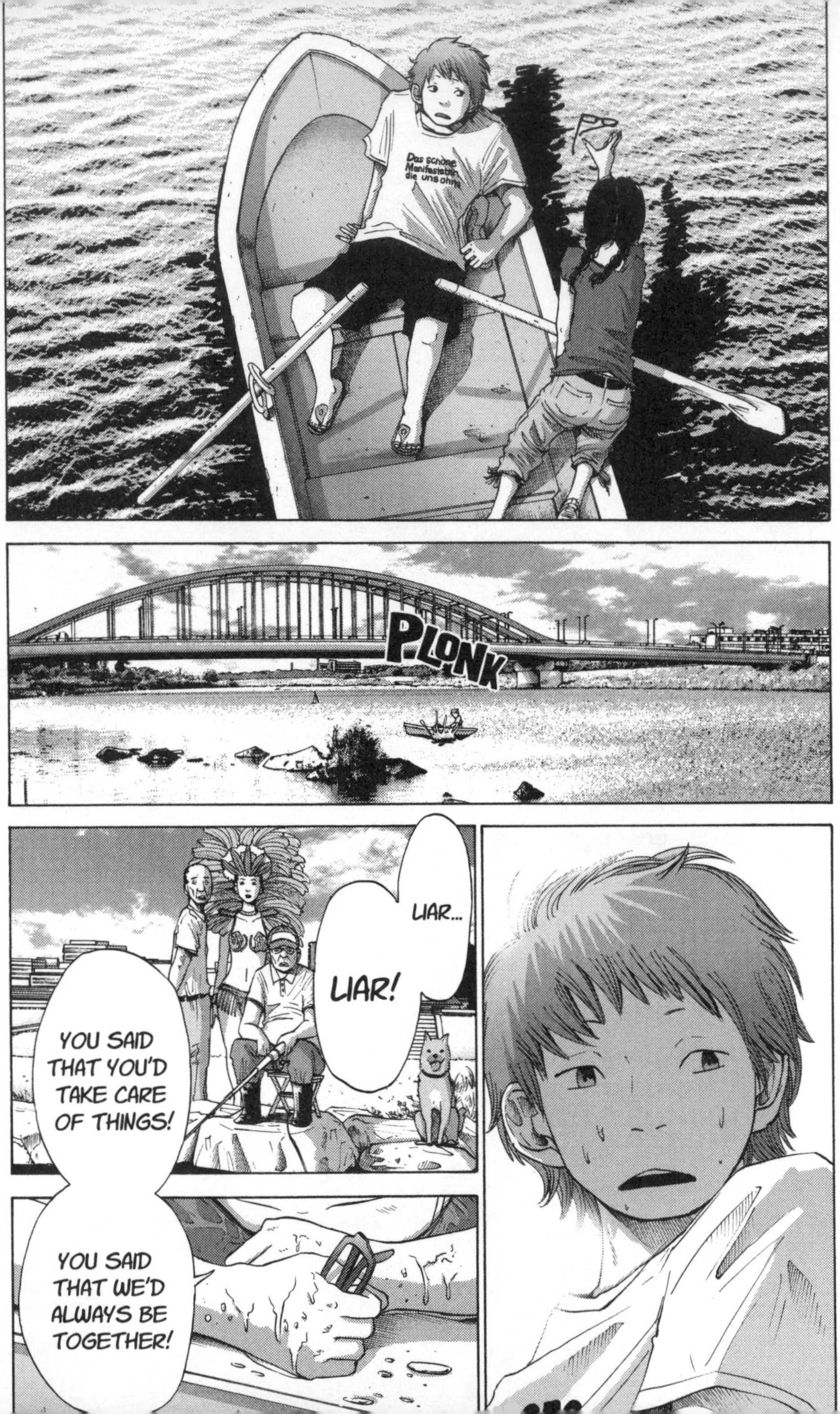
PLONK
LIAR...
LIAR!
YOU SAID THAT YOU'D TAKE CARE OF THINGS!
YOU SAID THAT WE'D ALWAYS BE TOGETHER!

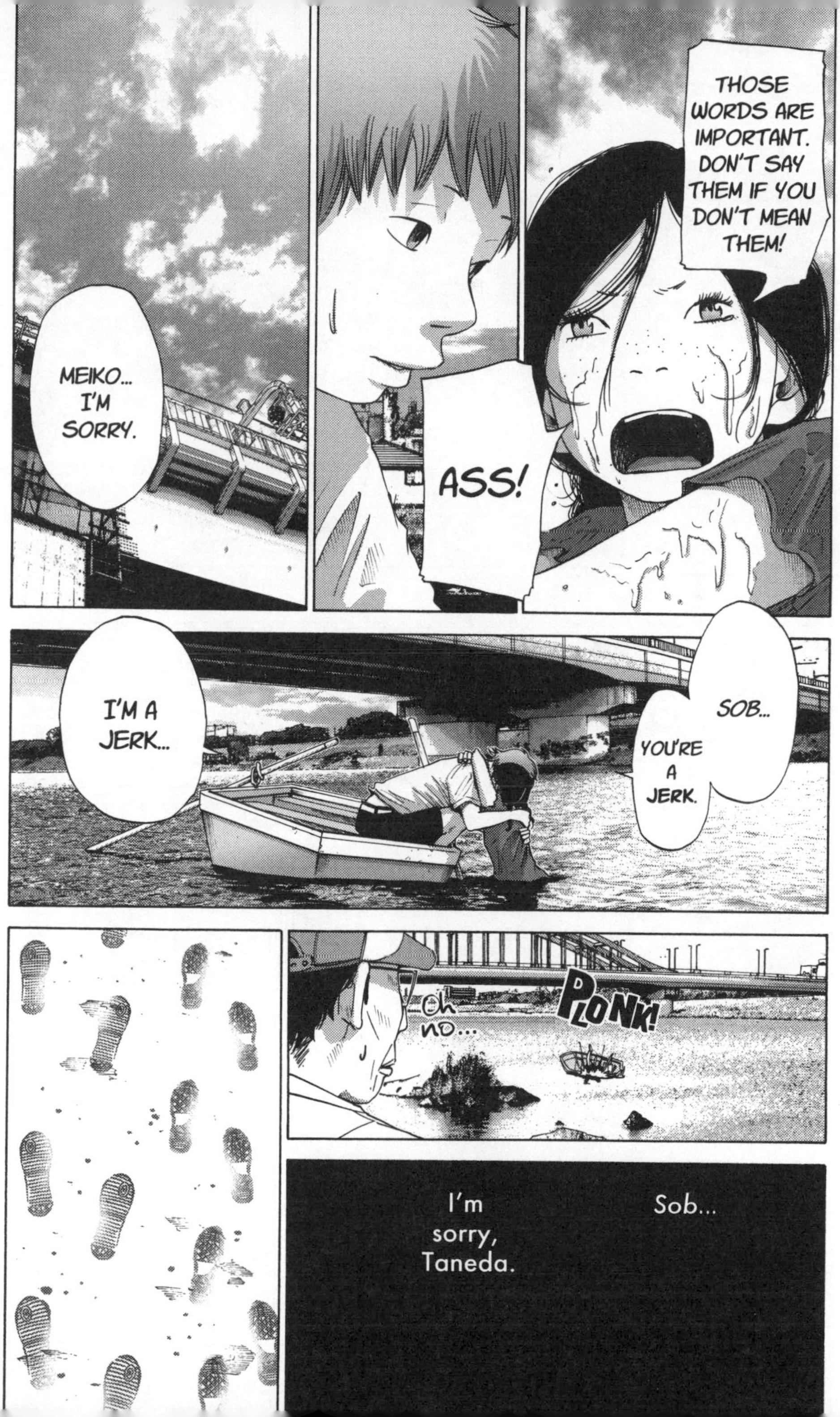
THOSE WORDS ARE IMPORTANT. DON'T SAY THEM IF YOU DON'T MEAN THEM!
ASS!
MEIKO... I'M SORRY.
SOB...
YOU'RE A JERK.
I'M A JERK...
PLONK!
Oh no...
Sob...
I'm sorry, Taneda.

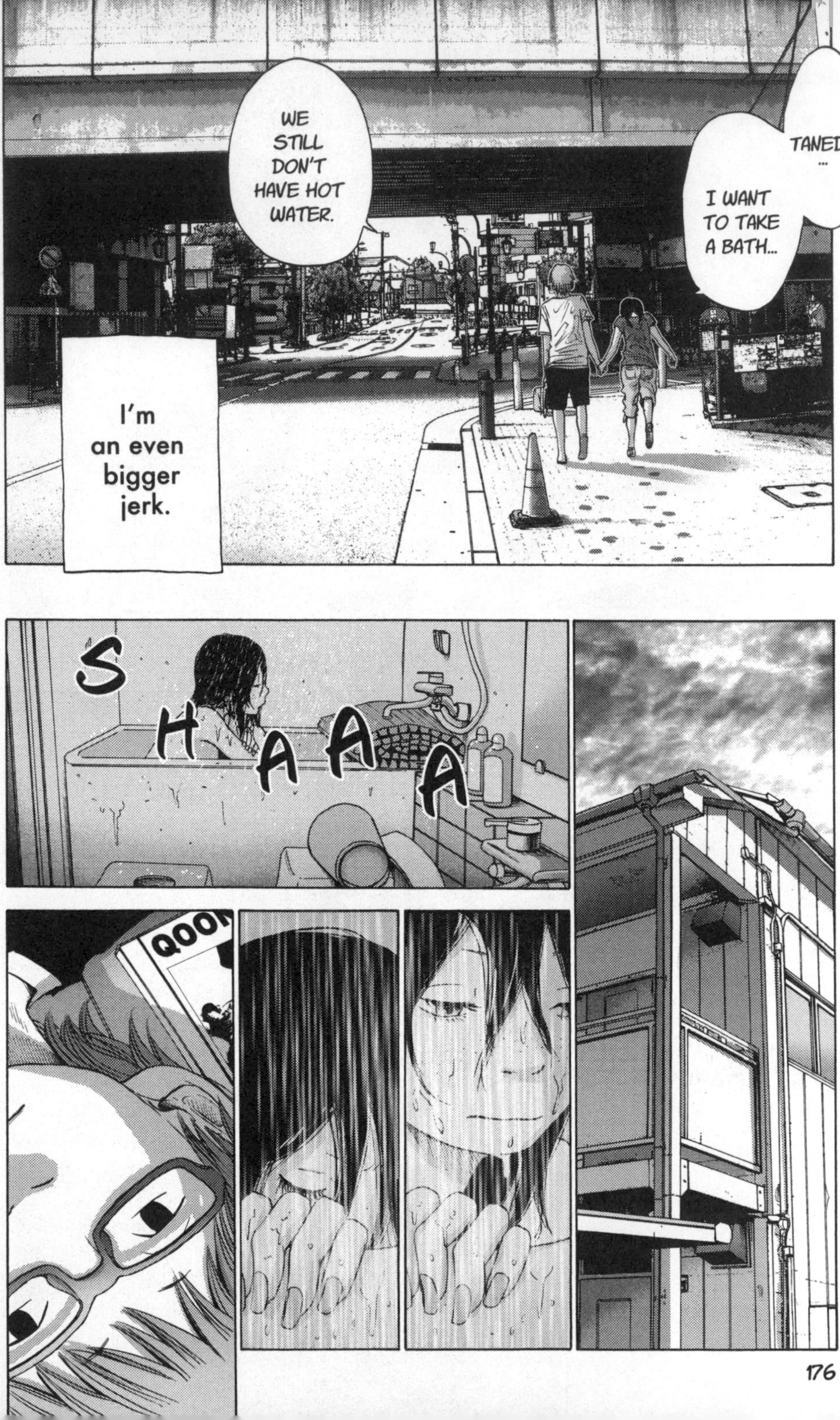
TANEDA ... I WANT TO TAKE A BATH...
WE STILL DON'T HAVE HOT WATER.
I'm an even bigger jerk.
SHAAA

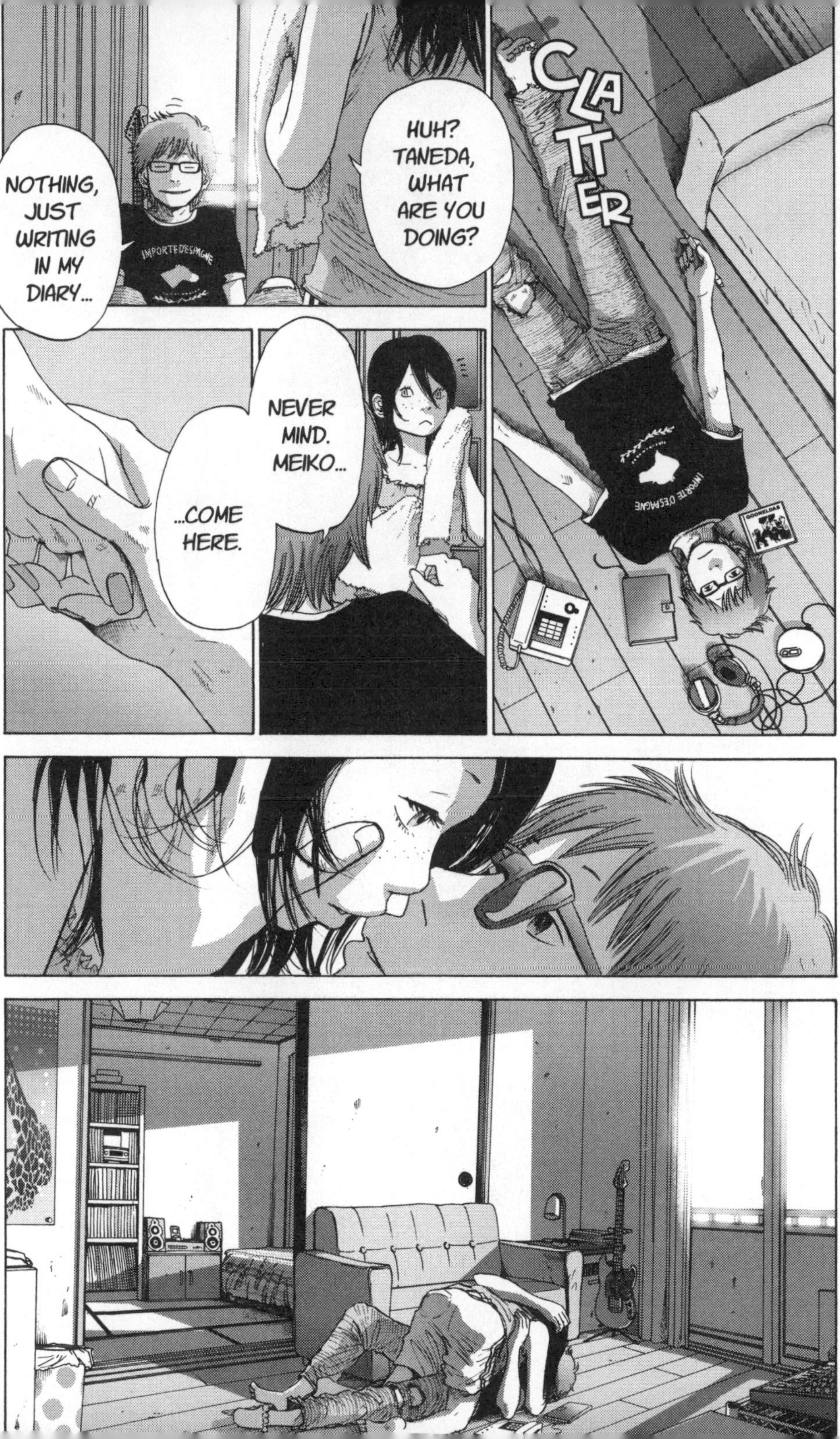
CLATTER
HUH? TANEDA, WHAT ARE YOU DOING?
NOTHING, JUST WRITING IN MY DIARY...
NEVER MIND. MEIKO...
...COME HERE.

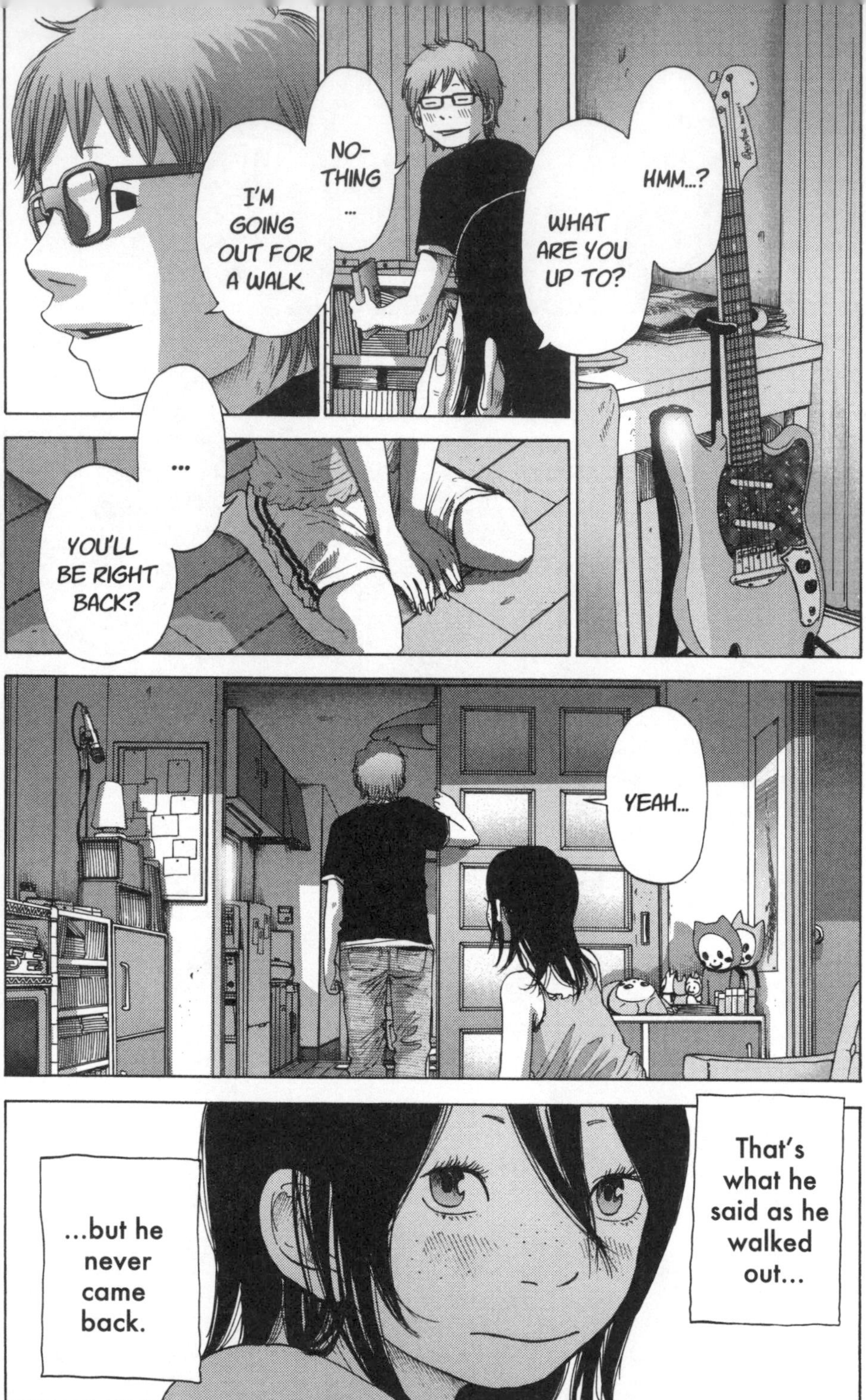
HMM...?
WHAT ARE YOU UP TO?
NO-THING...
I'M GOING OUT FOR A WALK.
...
YOU'LL BE RIGHT BACK?
YEAH...
That's what he said as he walked out...
...but he never came back.

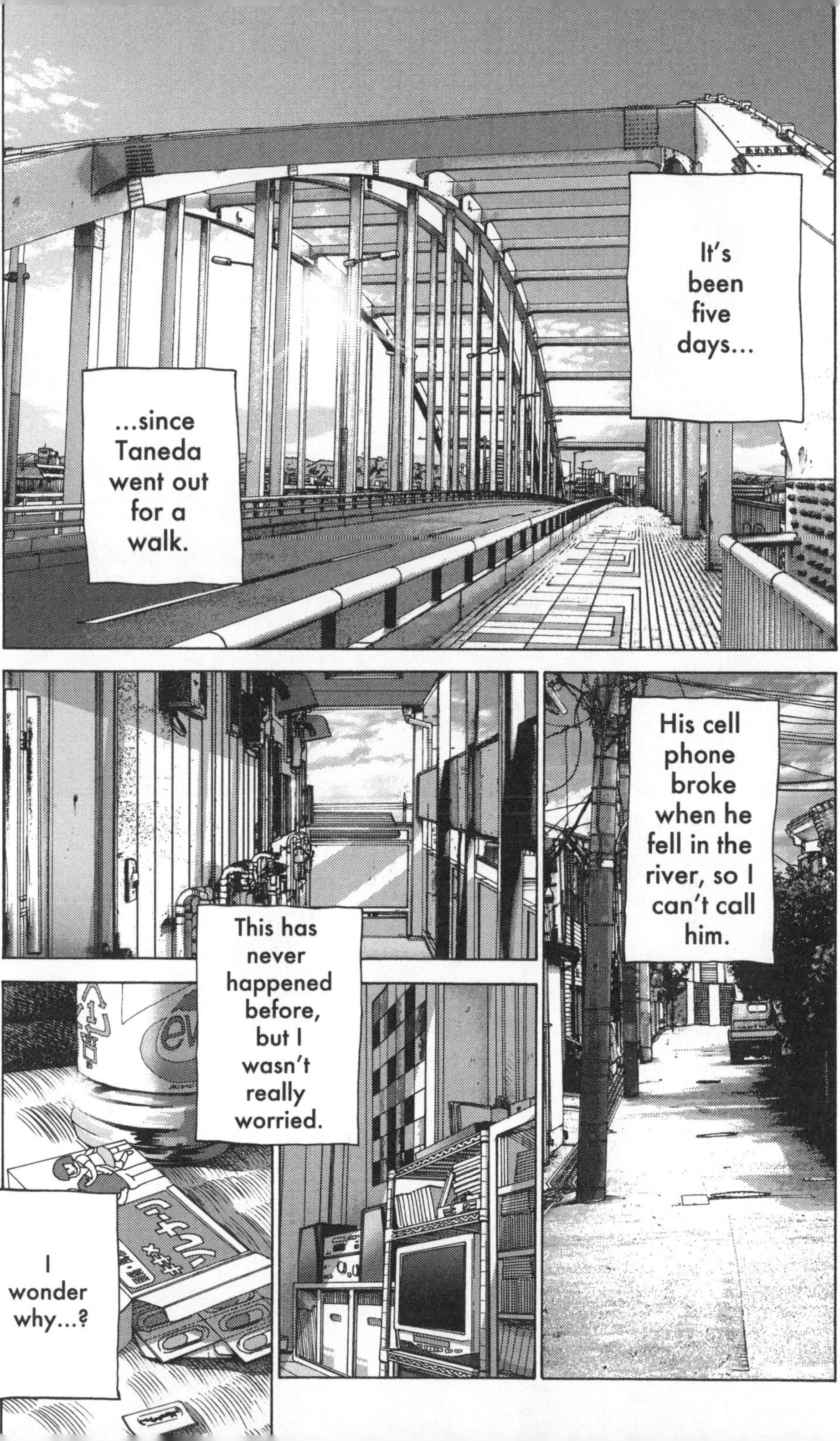
It's been five days...
...since Taneda went out for a walk.
His cell phone broke when he fell in the river, so I can't call him.
This has never happened before, but I wasn't really worried.
I wonder why...?

Then,
I caught
a cold.

While I
was sick,
I dreamed
that Taneda
was back,
acting the
same as
always...

...and I
acted the
same as
always, not
realizing it
was a
dream.

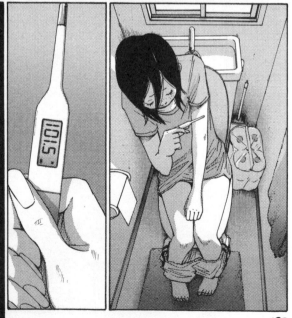

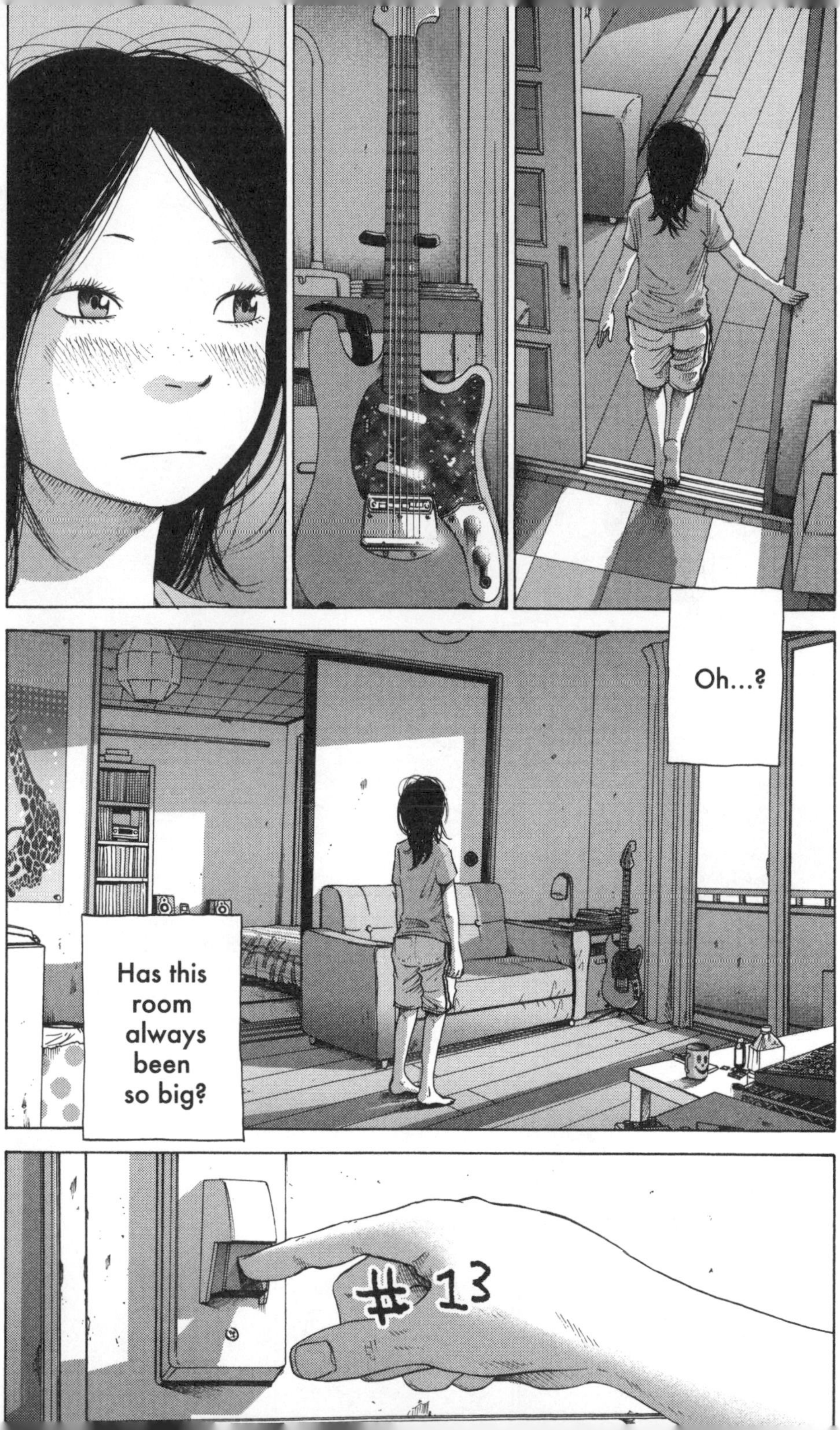
Oh...?
Has this room always been so big?
#13

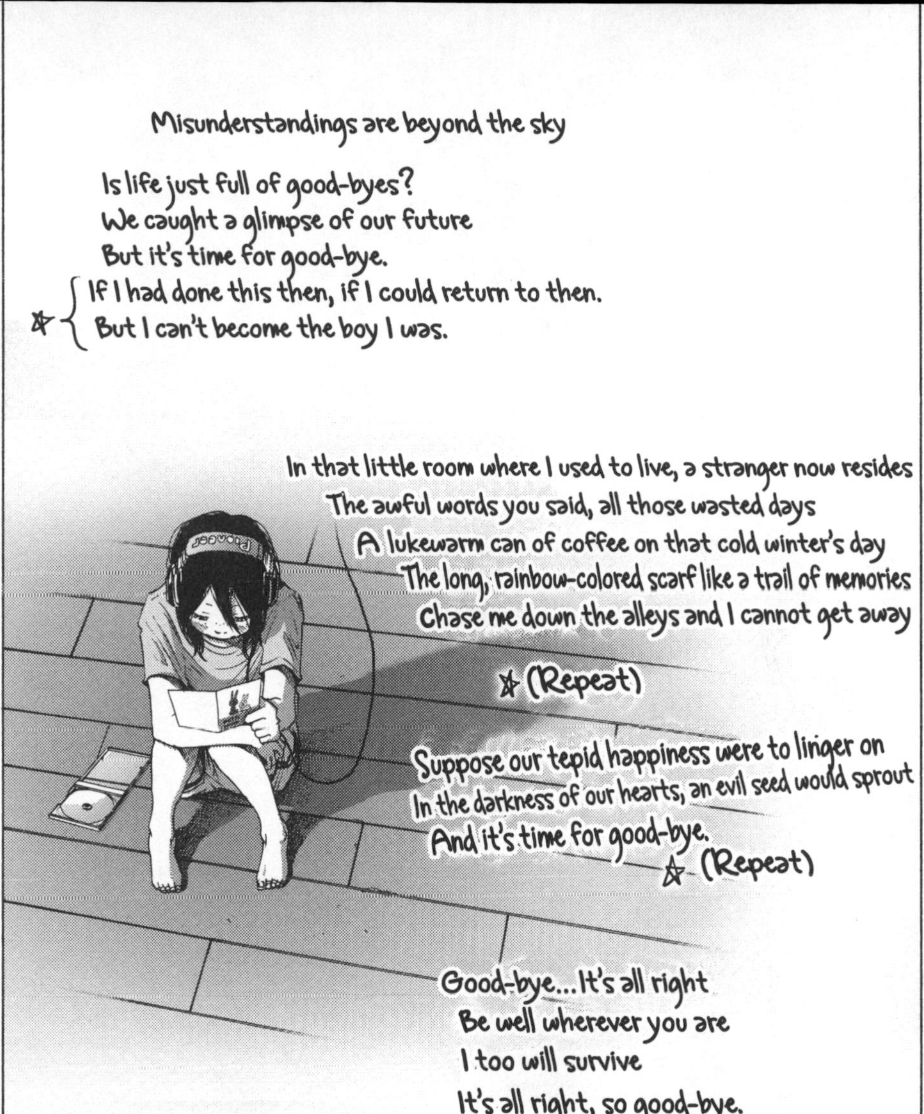
Misunderstandings are beyond the sky
Is life just full of good-byes?
We caught a glimpse of our future
But it's time for good-bye.
☆ If I had done this then, if I could return to then.
But I can't become the boy I was.
In that little room where I used to live, a stranger now resides
The awful words you said, all those wasted days
A lukewarm can of coffee on that cold winter's day
The long, rainbow-colored scarf like a trail of memories
Chase me down the alleys and I cannot get away
☆ (Repeat)
Suppose our tepid happiness were to linger on
In the darkness of our hearts, an evil seed would sprout
And it's time for good-bye.
☆ (Repeat)
Good-bye... It's all right
Be well wherever you are
I too will survive
It's all right, so good-bye.

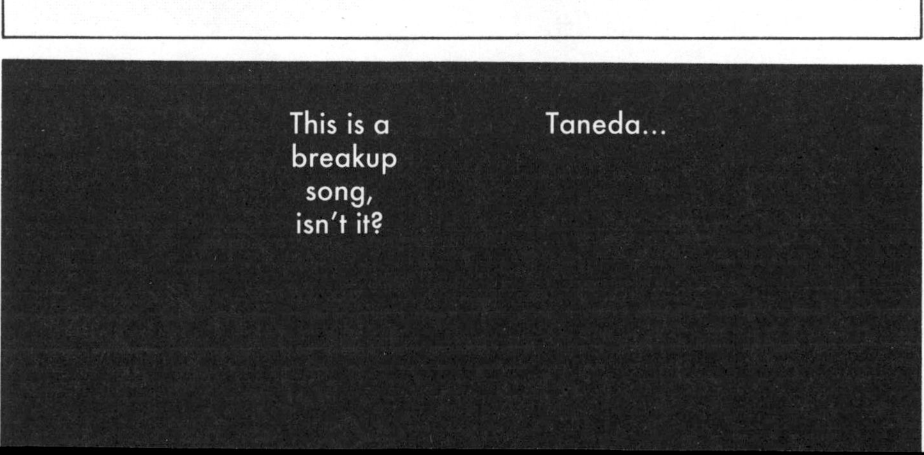
Taneda...
This is a breakup song, isn't it?

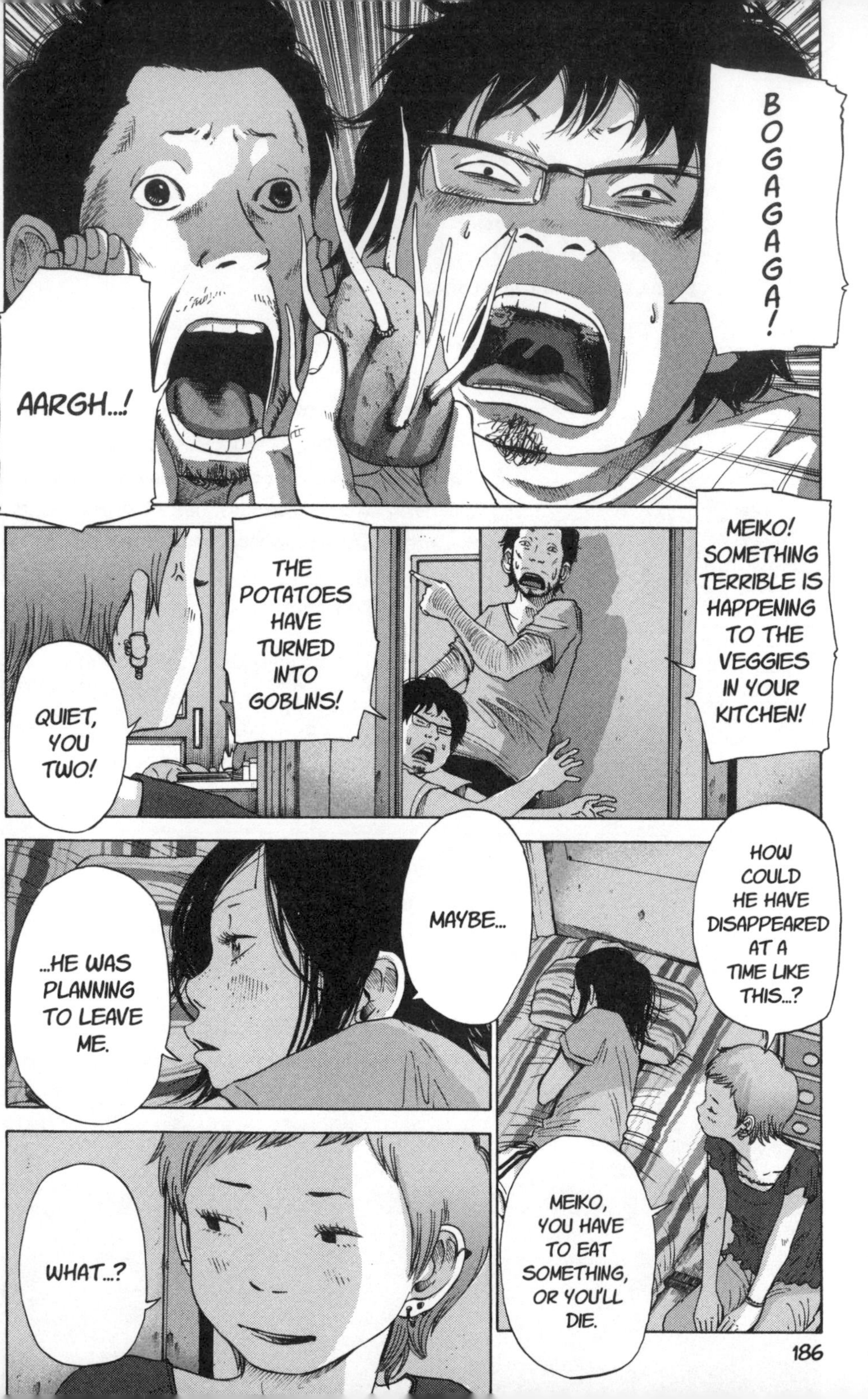
BOGAGAGA!
AARGH...!
MEIKO! SOMETHING TERRIBLE IS HAPPENING TO THE VEGGIES IN YOUR KITCHEN!
THE POTATOES HAVE TURNED INTO GOBLINS!
QUIET, YOU TWO!
HOW COULD HE HAVE DISAPPEARED AT A TIME LIKE THIS...?
MEIKO, YOU HAVE TO EAT SOMETHING, OR YOU'LL DIE.
MAYBE...
...HE WAS PLANNING TO LEAVE ME.
WHAT...?

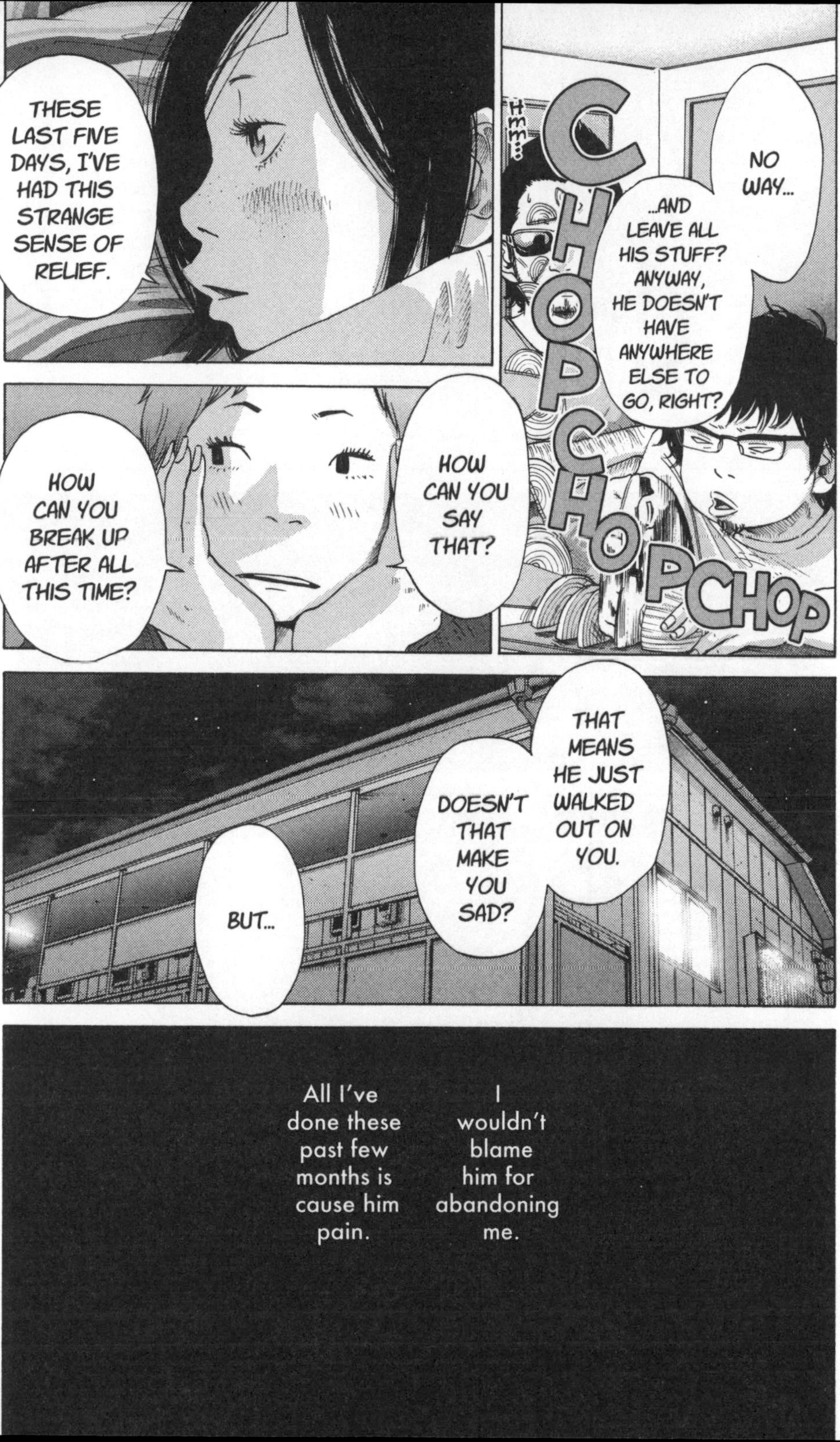
NO WAY...
Hmm...
...AND LEAVE ALL HIS STUFF? ANYWAY, HE DOESN'T HAVE ANYWHERE ELSE TO GO, RIGHT?
CHOP CHOP CHOP CHOP
THESE LAST FIVE DAYS, I'VE HAD THIS STRANGE SENSE OF RELIEF.
HOW CAN YOU SAY THAT?
HOW CAN YOU BREAK UP AFTER ALL THIS TIME?
THAT MEANS HE JUST WALKED OUT ON YOU.
DOESN'T THAT MAKE YOU SAD?
BUT...
I wouldn't blame him for abandoning me.
All I've done these past few months is cause him pain.

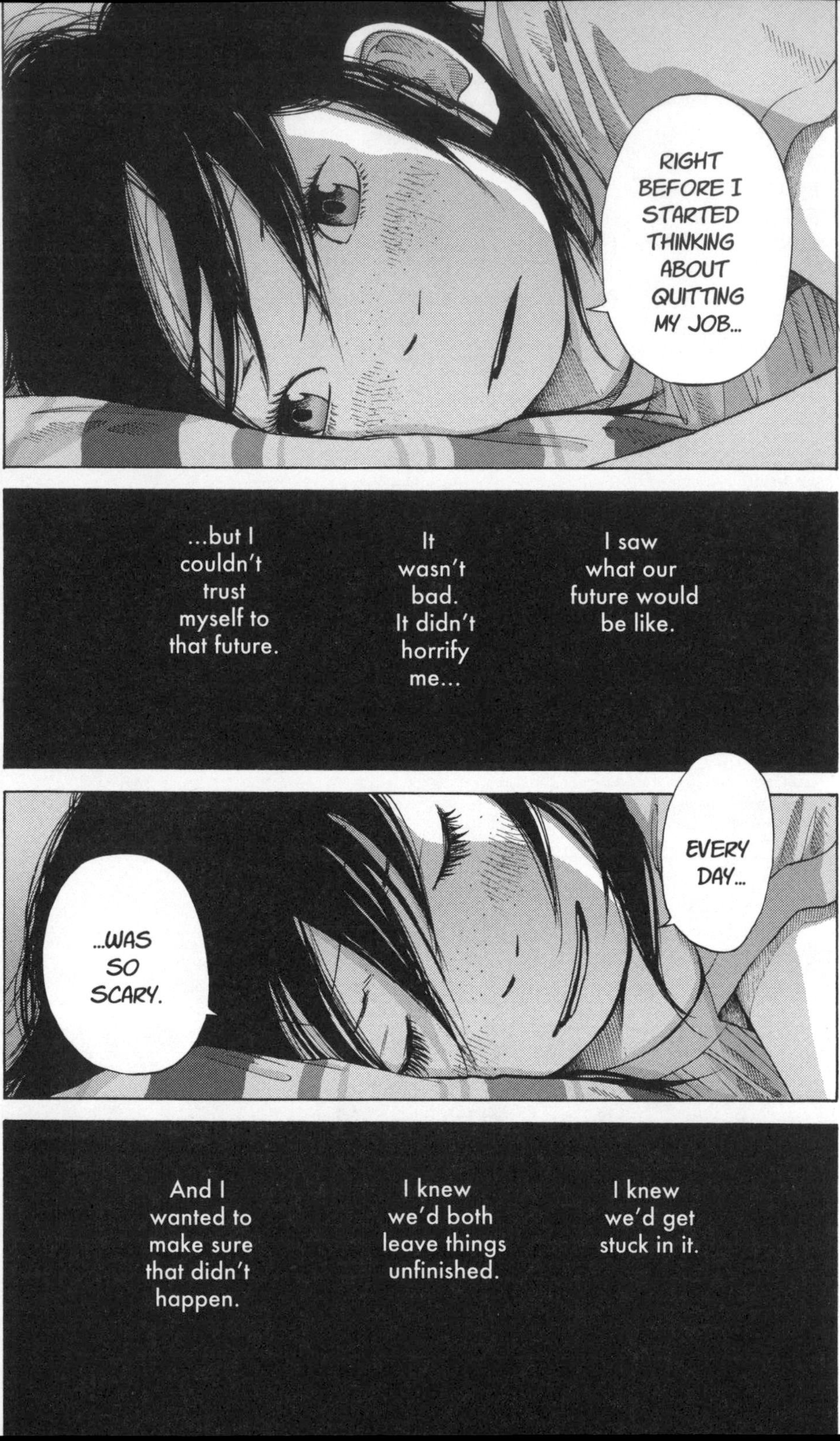
RIGHT BEFORE I STARTED THINKING ABOUT QUITTING MY JOB...
I saw what our future would be like.
It wasn't bad. It didn't horrify me...
...but I couldn't trust myself to that future.
EVERY DAY...
...WAS SO SCARY.
I knew we'd get stuck in it.
I knew we'd both leave things unfinished.
And I wanted to make sure that didn't happen.

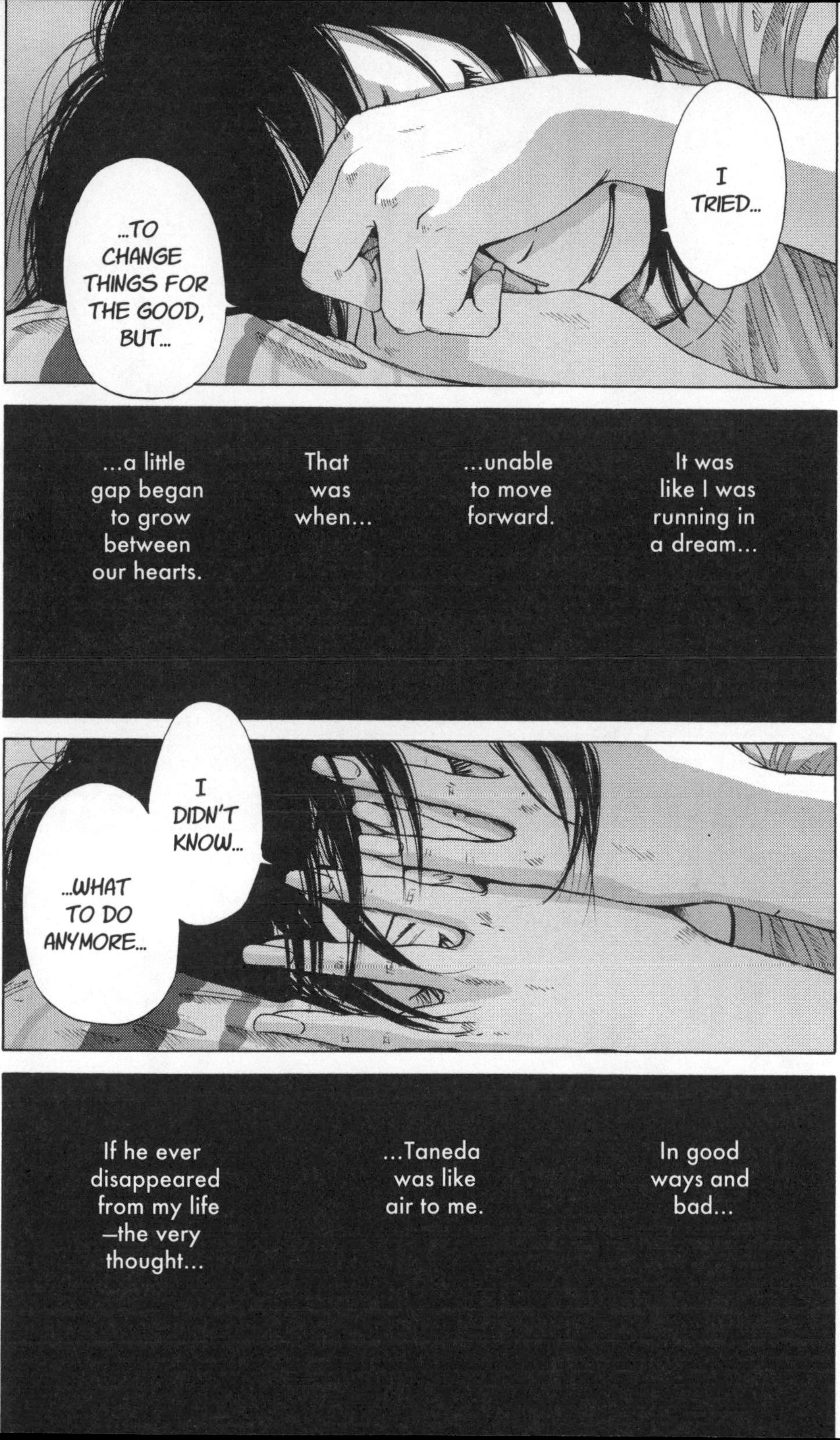
I TRIED...
...TO CHANGE THINGS FOR THE GOOD, BUT...
It was like I was running in a dream...
...unable to move forward.
That was when...
...a little gap began to grow between our hearts.
I DIDN'T KNOW...
...WHAT TO DO ANYMORE...
In good ways and bad...
...Taneda was like air to me.
If he ever disappeared from my life —the very thought...

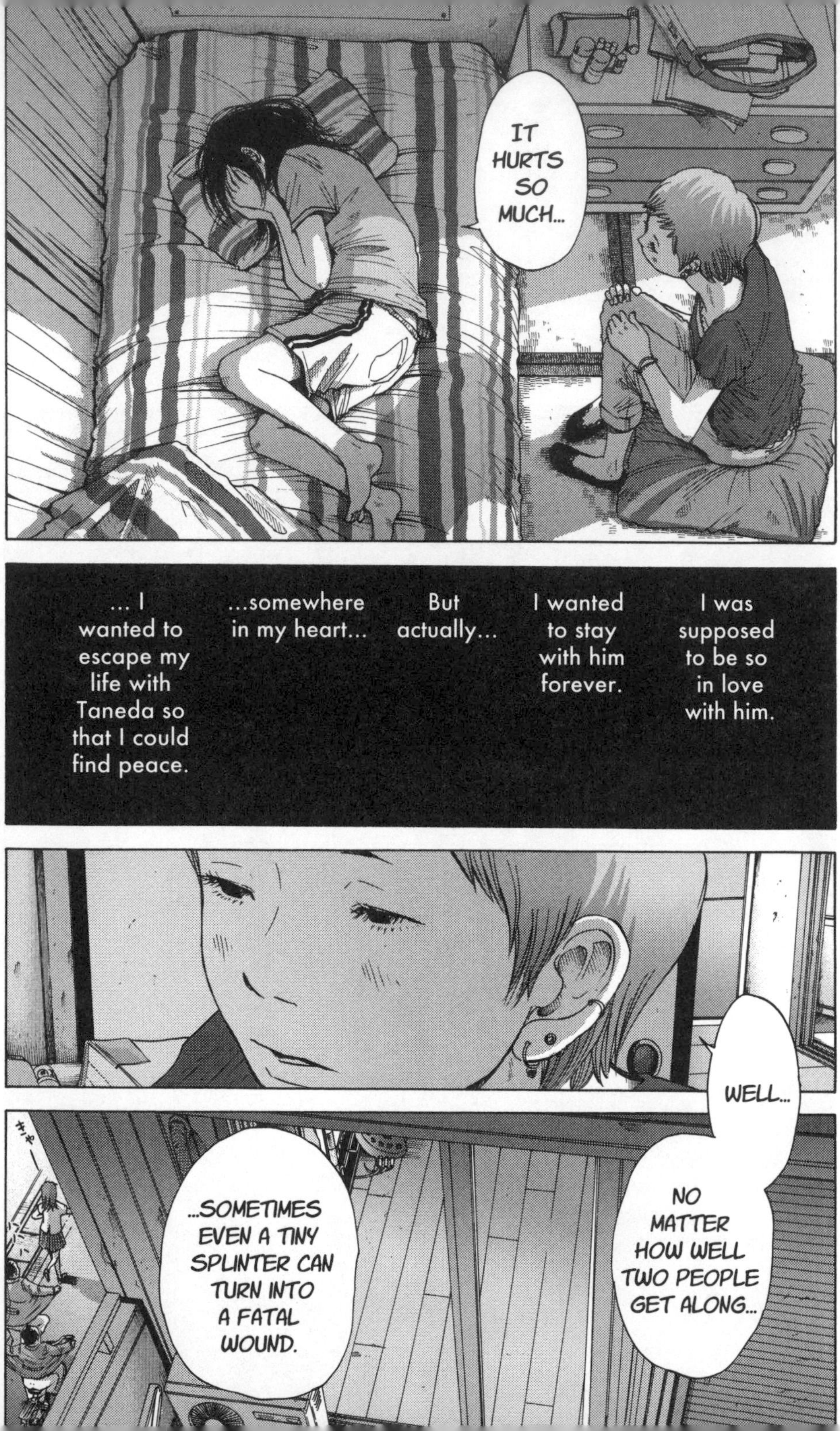
IT HURTS SO MUCH...
I was supposed to be so in love with him.
I wanted to stay with him forever.
But actually...
...somewhere in my heart...
... I wanted to escape my life with Taneda so that I could find peace.
WELL...
NO MATTER HOW WELL TWO PEOPLE GET ALONG...
...SOMETIMES EVEN A TINY SPLINTER CAN TURN INTO A FATAL WOUND.
きゃー

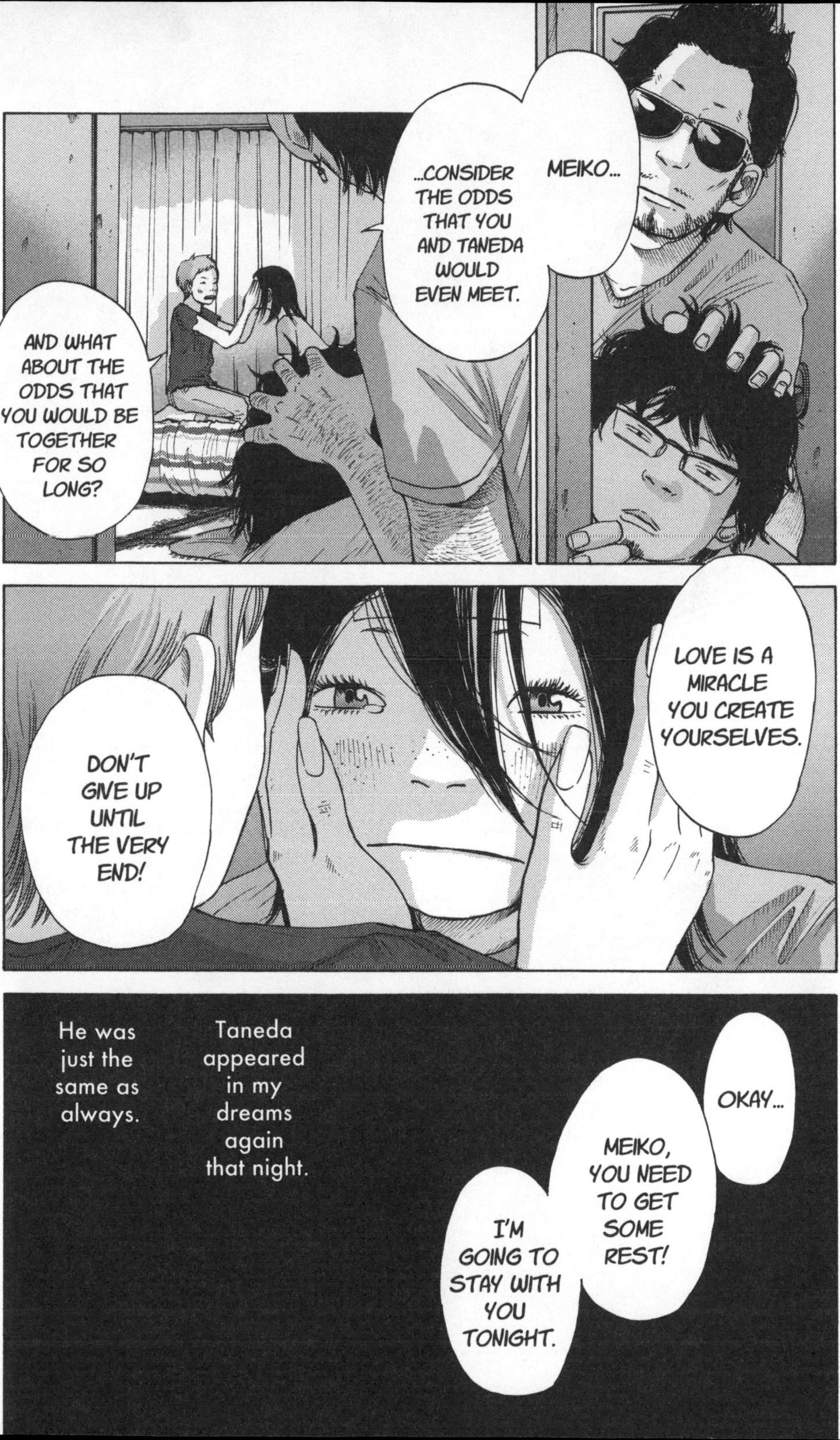
MEIKO...
...CONSIDER THE ODDS THAT YOU AND TANEDA WOULD EVEN MEET.
AND WHAT ABOUT THE ODDS THAT YOU WOULD BE TOGETHER FOR SO LONG?
LOVE IS A MIRACLE YOU CREATE YOURSELVES.
DON'T GIVE UP UNTIL THE VERY END!
OKAY...
MEIKO, YOU NEED TO GET SOME REST!
I'M GOING TO STAY WITH YOU TONIGHT.
Taneda appeared in my dreams again that night.
He was just the same as always.

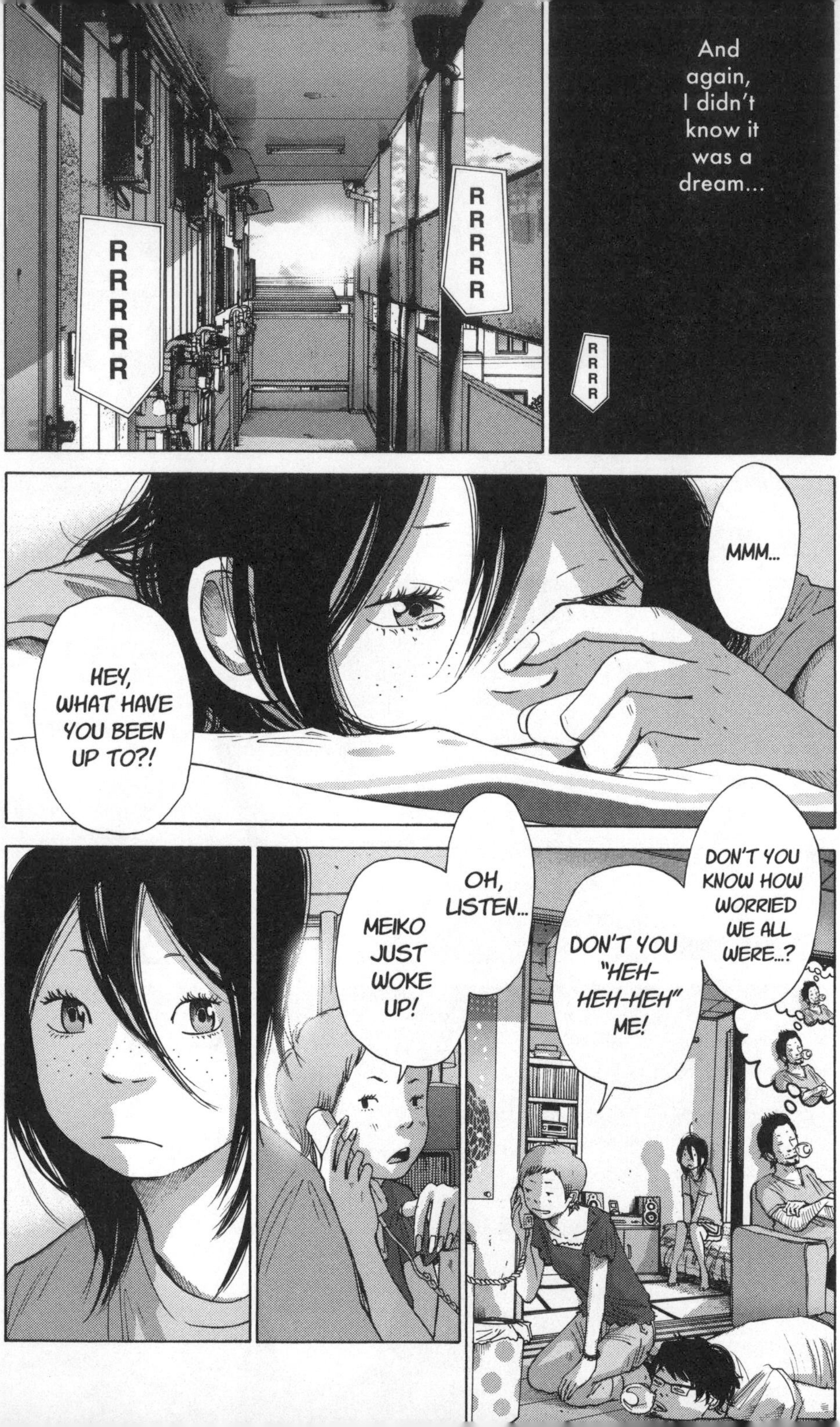
And again, I didn't know it was a dream...
RRRR
RRRRR
RRRRR
MMM...
HEY, WHAT HAVE YOU BEEN UP TO?!
DON'T YOU KNOW HOW WORRIED WE ALL WERE...?
DON'T YOU "HEH-HEH-HEH" ME!
OH, LISTEN...
MEIKO JUST WOKE UP!

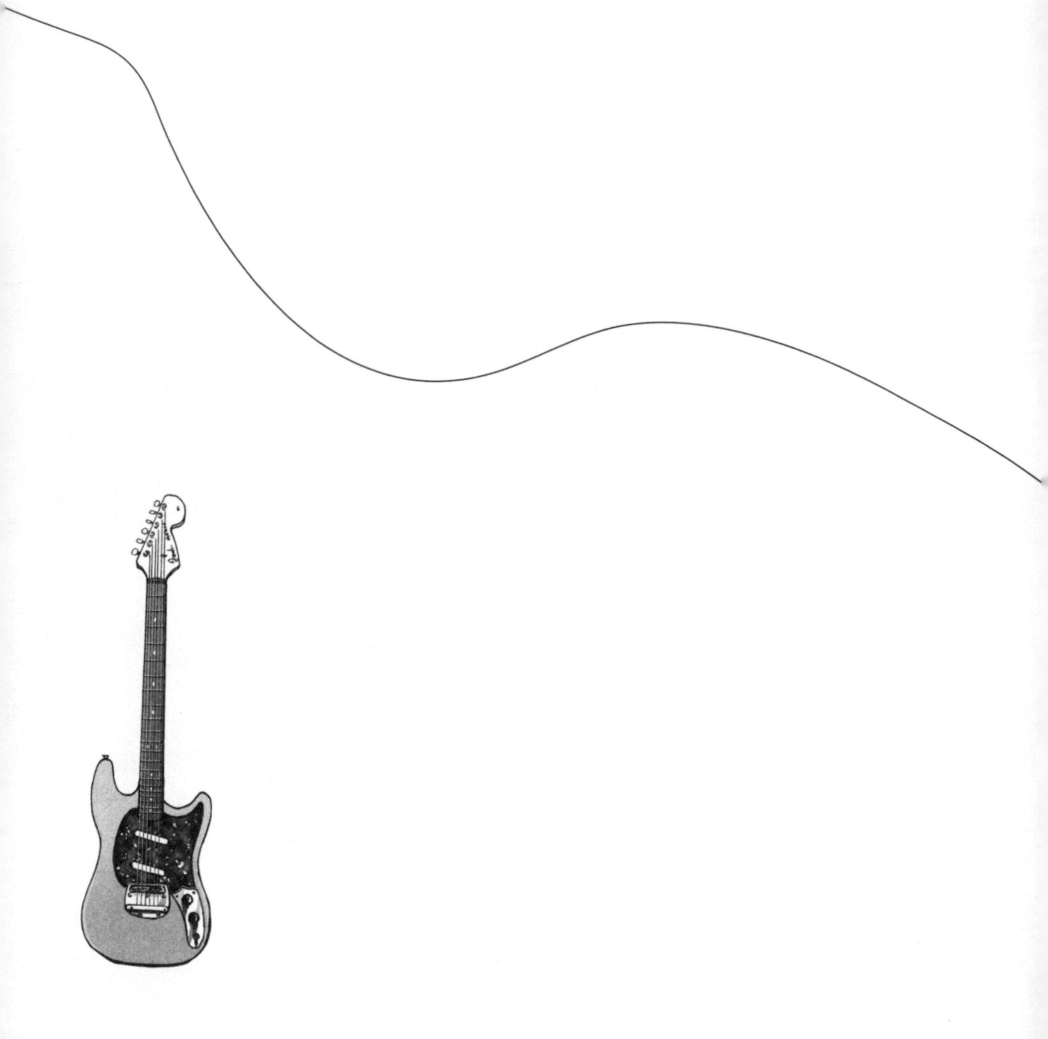

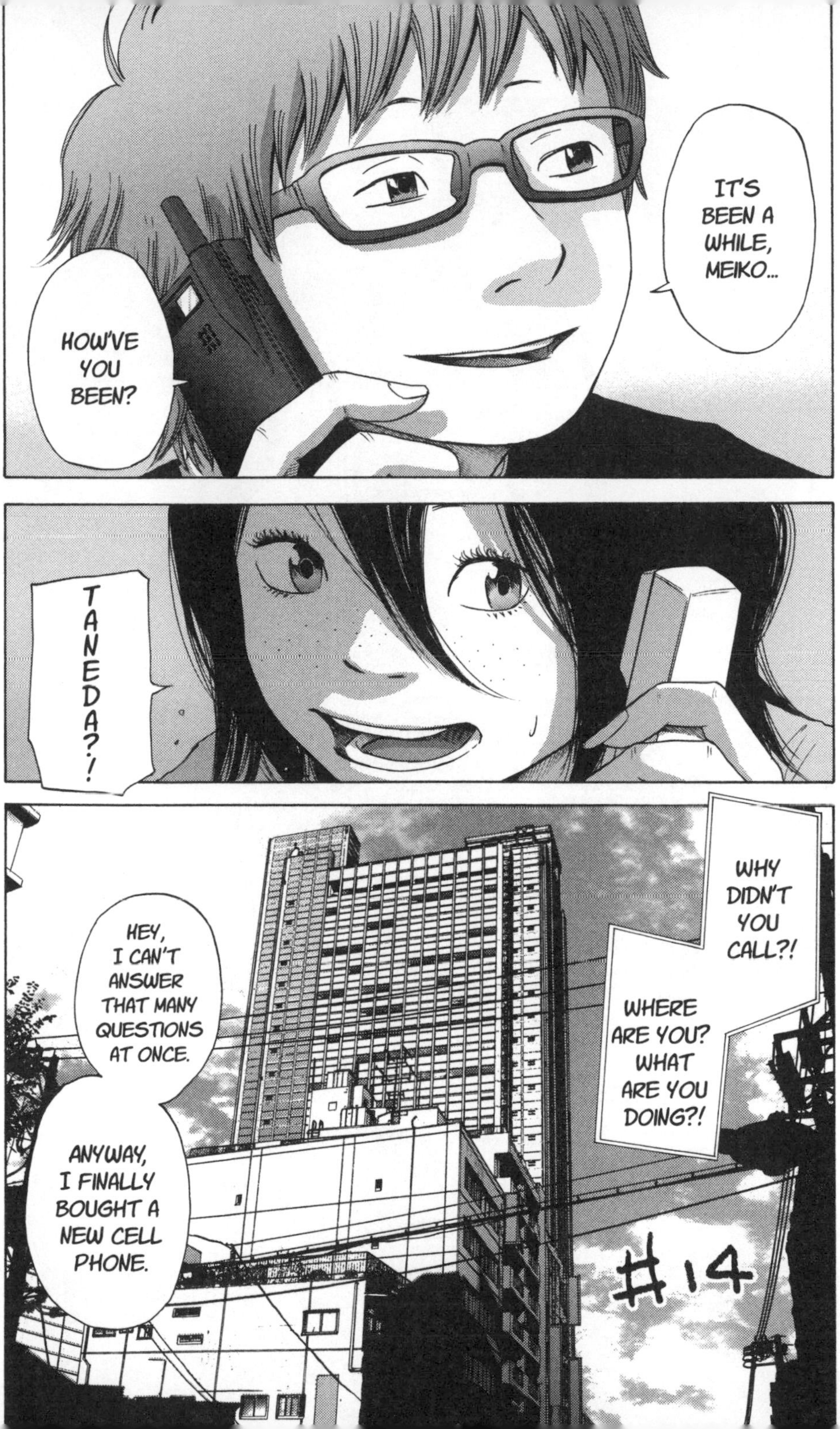
IT'S BEEN A WHILE, MEIKO...
HOW'VE YOU BEEN?
TANEDA?!
WHY DIDN'T YOU CALL?!
WHERE ARE YOU? WHAT ARE YOU DOING?!
HEY, I CAN'T ANSWER THAT MANY QUESTIONS AT ONCE.
ANYWAY, I FINALLY BOUGHT A NEW CELL PHONE.
#14

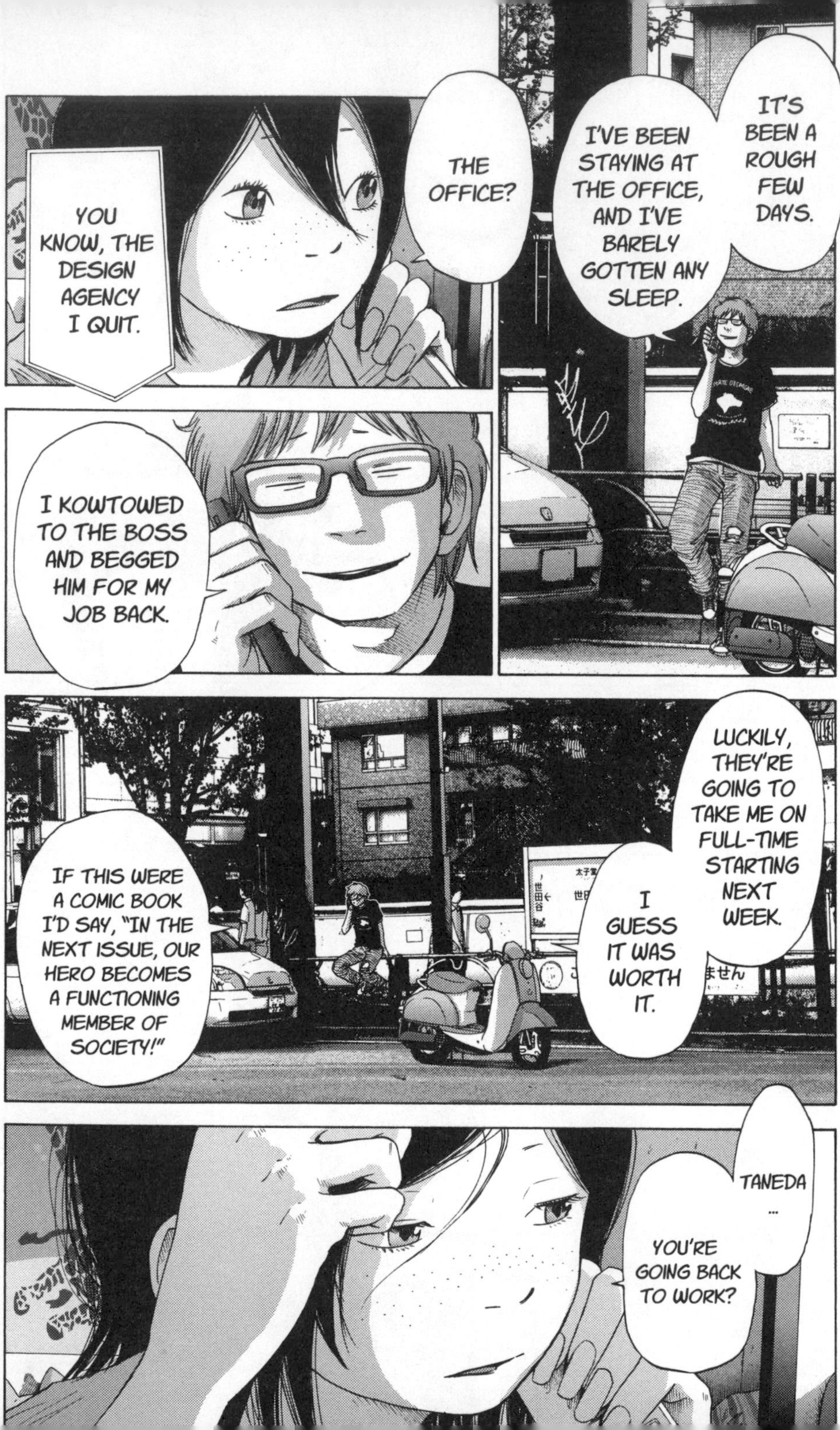
IT'S BEEN A ROUGH FEW DAYS.
I'VE BEEN STAYING AT THE OFFICE, AND I'VE BARELY GOTTEN ANY SLEEP.
THE OFFICE?
YOU KNOW, THE DESIGN AGENCY I QUIT.
I KOWTOWED TO THE BOSS AND BEGGED HIM FOR MY JOB BACK.
LUCKILY, THEY'RE GOING TO TAKE ME ON FULL-TIME STARTING NEXT WEEK.
I GUESS IT WAS WORTH IT.
IF THIS WERE A COMIC BOOK I'D SAY, "IN THE NEXT ISSUE, OUR HERO BECOMES A FUNCTIONING MEMBER OF SOCIETY!"
TANEDA ...
YOU'RE GOING BACK TO WORK?

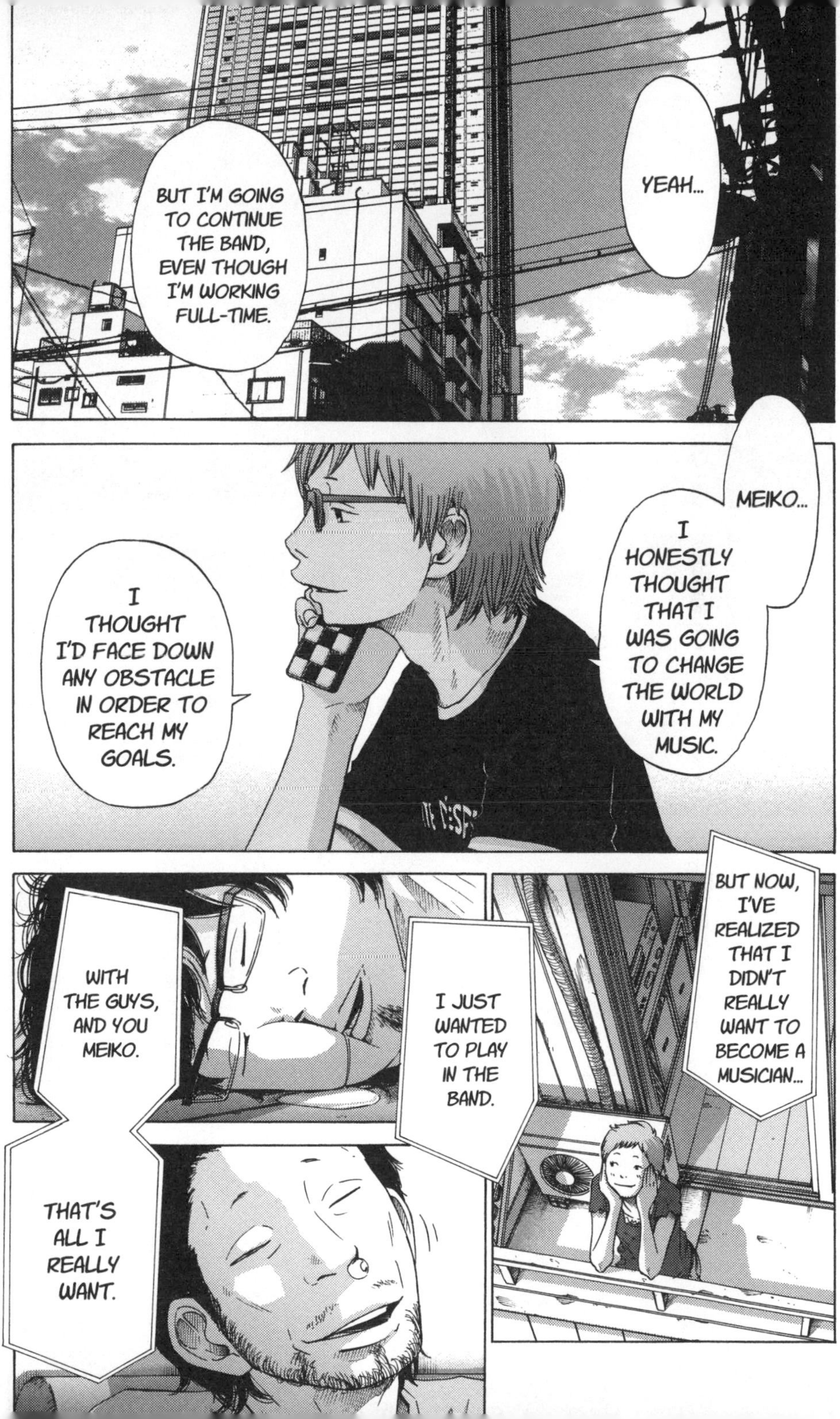
YEAH...
BUT I'M GOING TO CONTINUE THE BAND, EVEN THOUGH I'M WORKING FULL-TIME.
MEIKO...
I HONESTLY THOUGHT THAT I WAS GOING TO CHANGE THE WORLD WITH MY MUSIC.
I THOUGHT I'D FACE DOWN ANY OBSTACLE IN ORDER TO REACH MY GOALS.
BUT NOW, I'VE REALIZED THAT I DIDN'T REALLY WANT TO BECOME A MUSICIAN...
I JUST WANTED TO PLAY IN THE BAND.
WITH THE GUYS, AND YOU MEIKO.
THAT'S ALL I REALLY WANT.

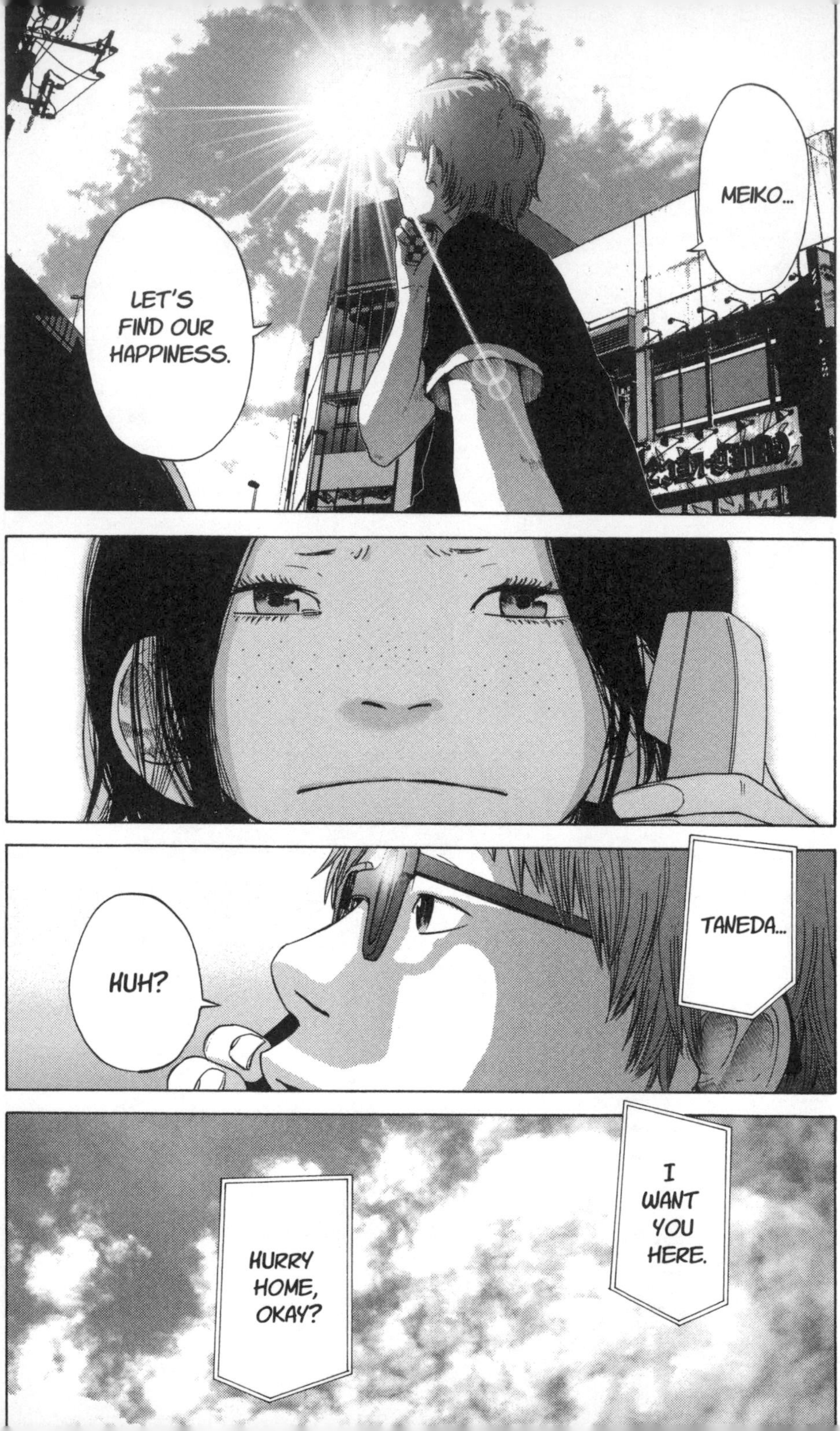
MEIKO...
LET'S FIND OUR HAPPINESS.
TANEDA...
HUH?
I WANT YOU HERE.
HURRY HOME, OKAY?

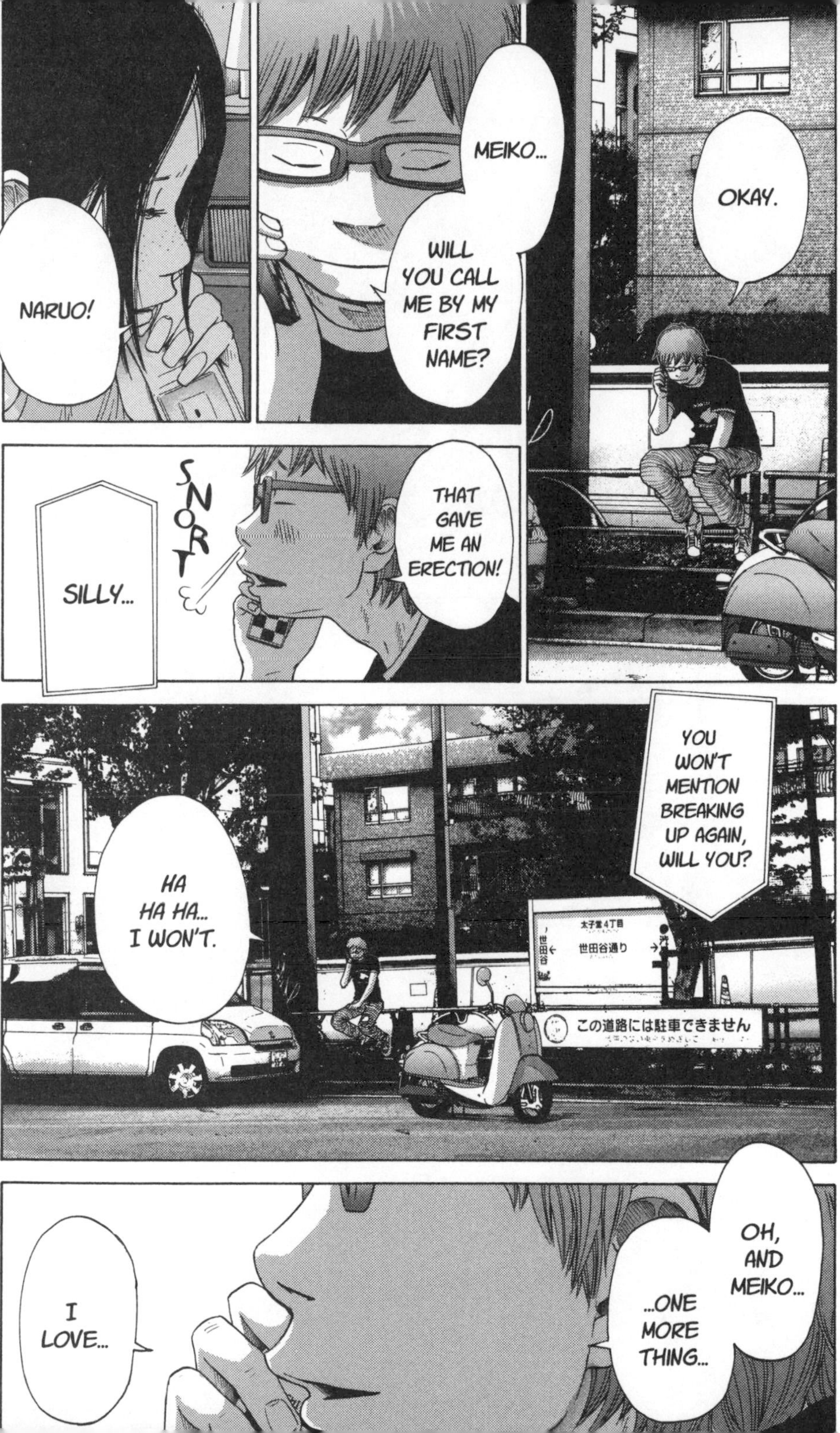
OKAY.
MEIKO...
WILL YOU CALL ME BY MY FIRST NAME?
NARUO!
THAT GAVE ME AN ERECTION!
SNORT
SILLY...
YOU WON'T MENTION BREAKING UP AGAIN, WILL YOU?
HA HA HA... I WON'T.
太子堂4丁目
世田谷
世田谷通り
この道路には駐車できません
OH, AND MEIKO...
...ONE MORE THING...
I LOVE...

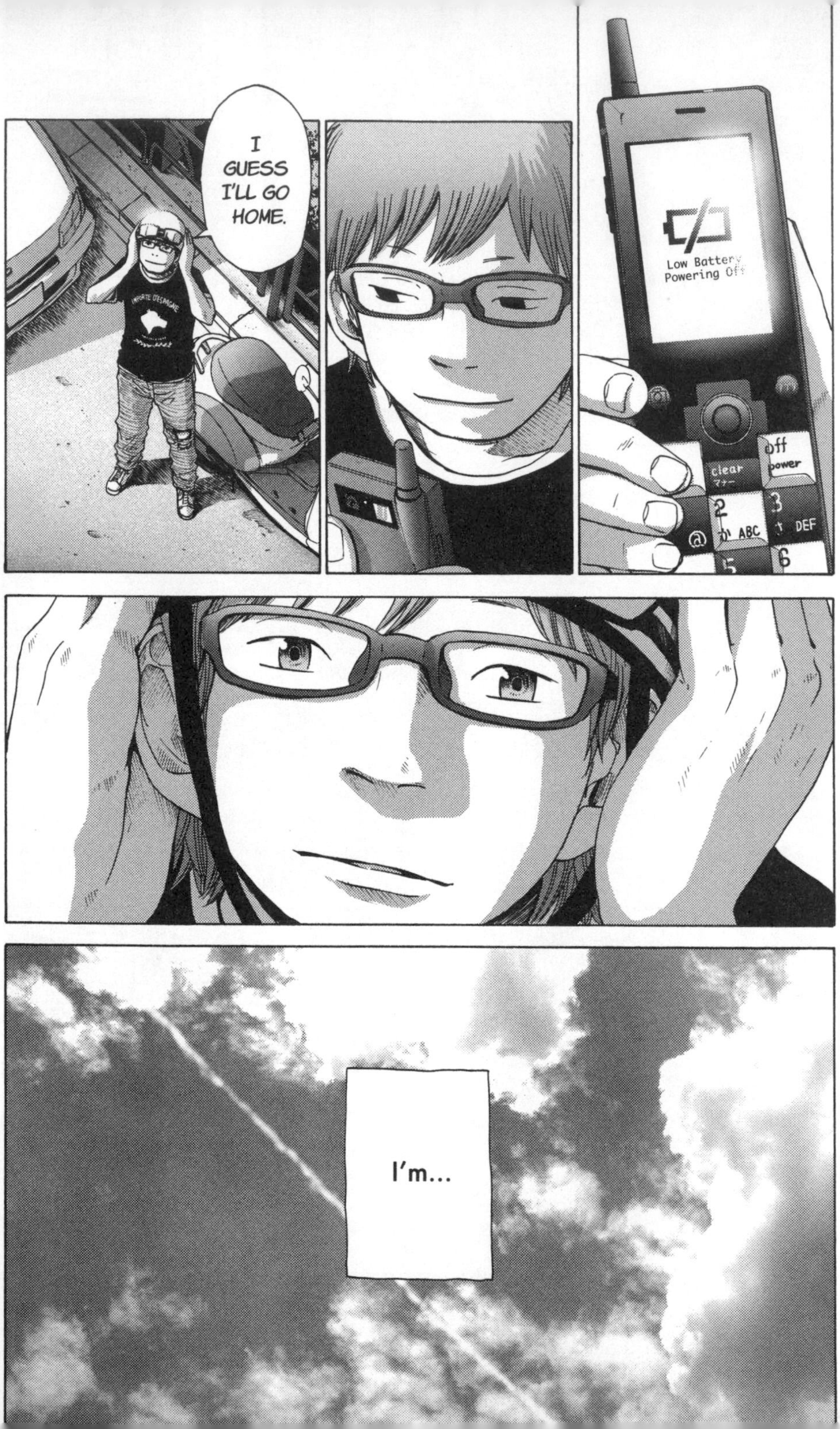
Low Batter
Powering Of
I GUESS I'LL GO HOME.
I'm...

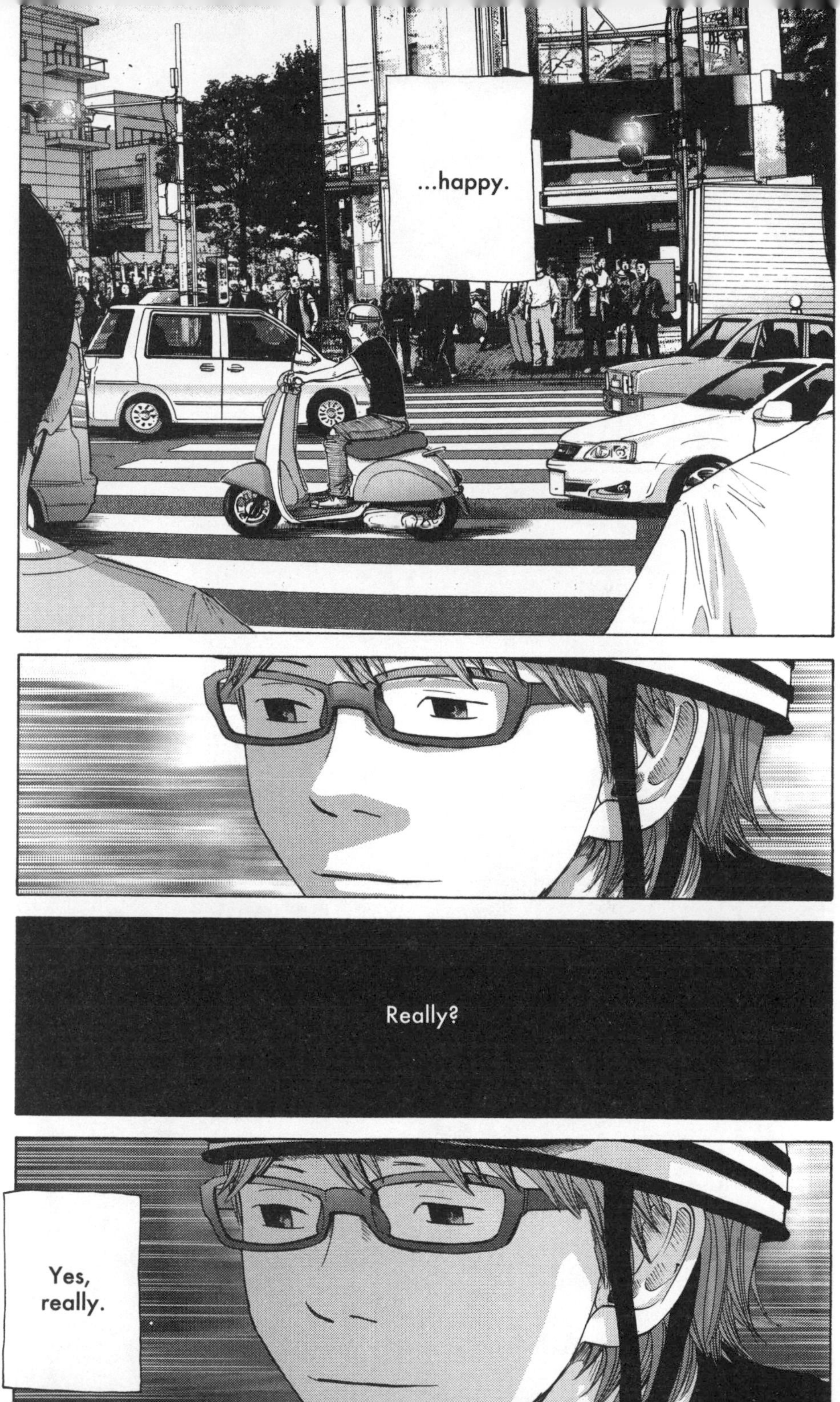
...happy.
Really?
Yes, really.

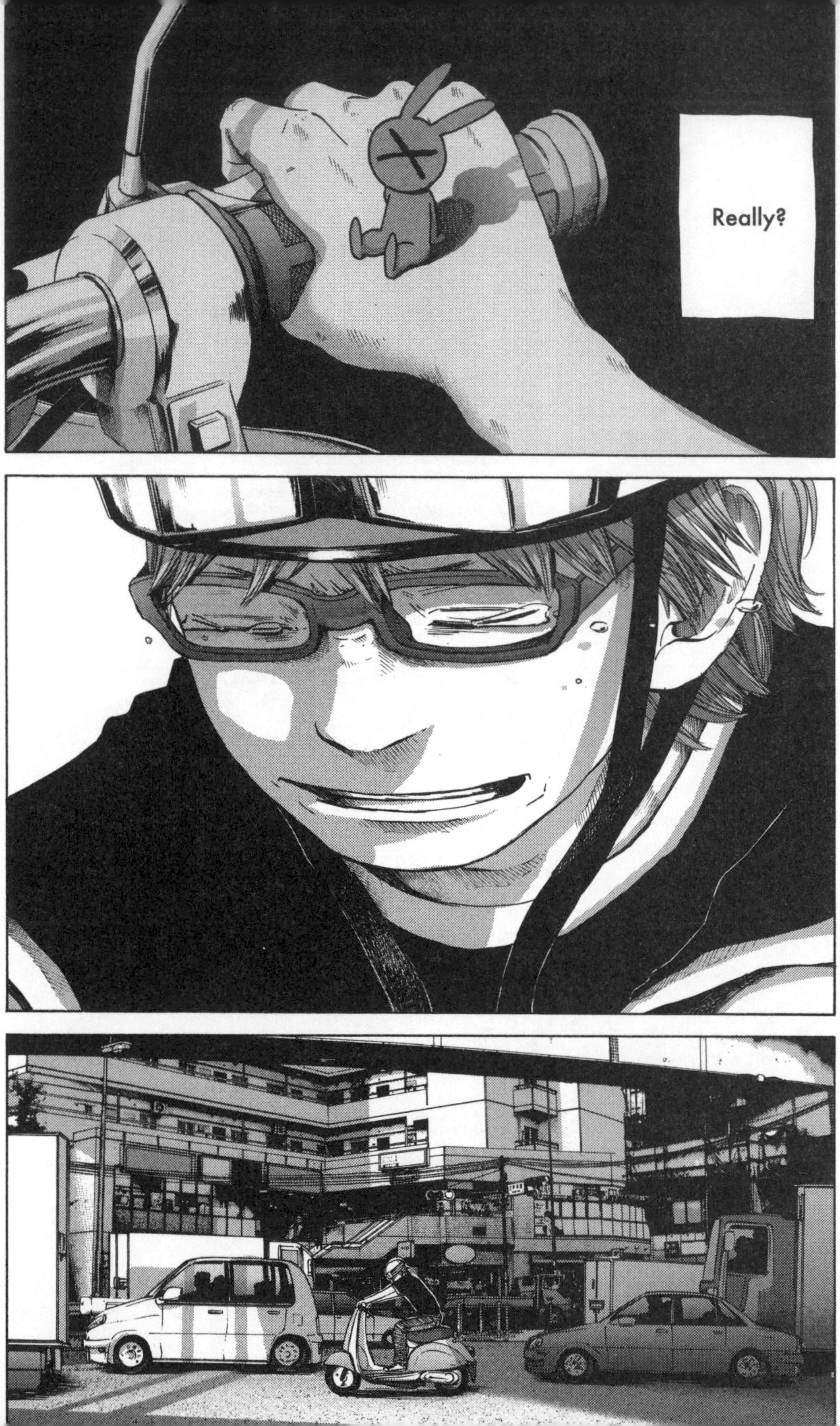
Really?

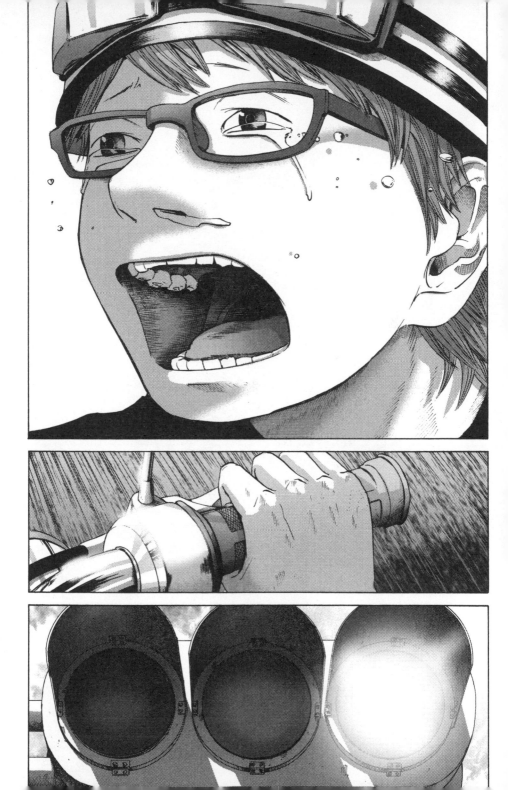

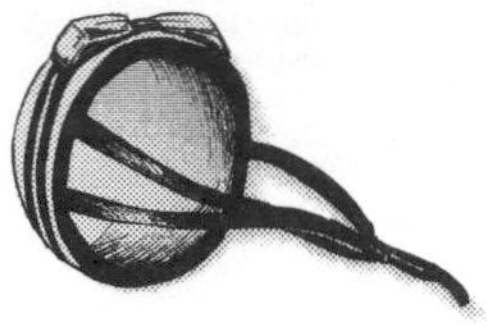

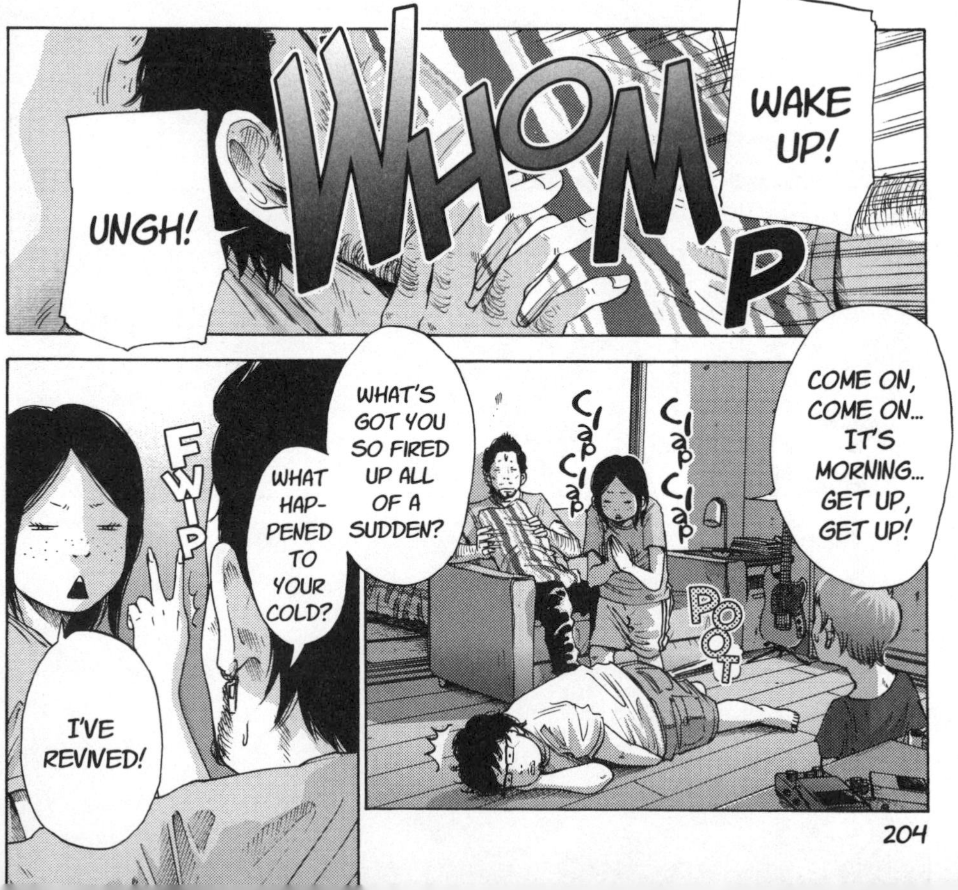
WAKE UP!
WHOMP
UNGH!
COME ON, COME ON... IT'S MORNING... GET UP, GET UP!
Clap Clap
Clap Clap
POOT
WHAT'S GOT YOU SO FIRED UP ALL OF A SUDDEN?
WHAT HAP-PENED TO YOUR COLD?
FWIP
I'VE REVIVED!

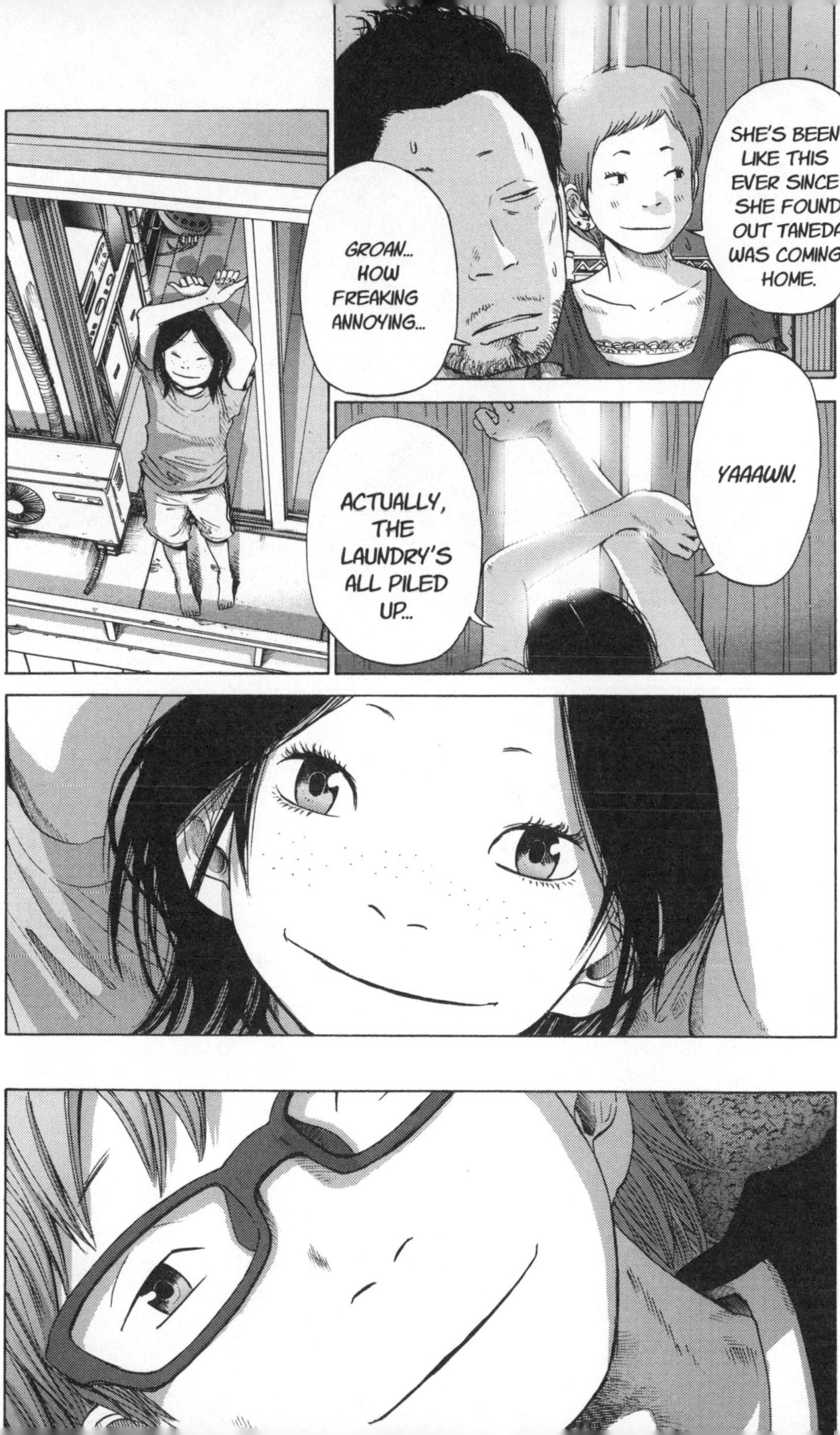
SHE'S BEEN LIKE THIS EVER SINCE SHE FOUND OUT TANEDA WAS COMING HOME.
GROAN... HOW FREAKING ANNOYING...
YAAAWN.
ACTUALLY, THE LAUNDRY'S ALL PILED UP...

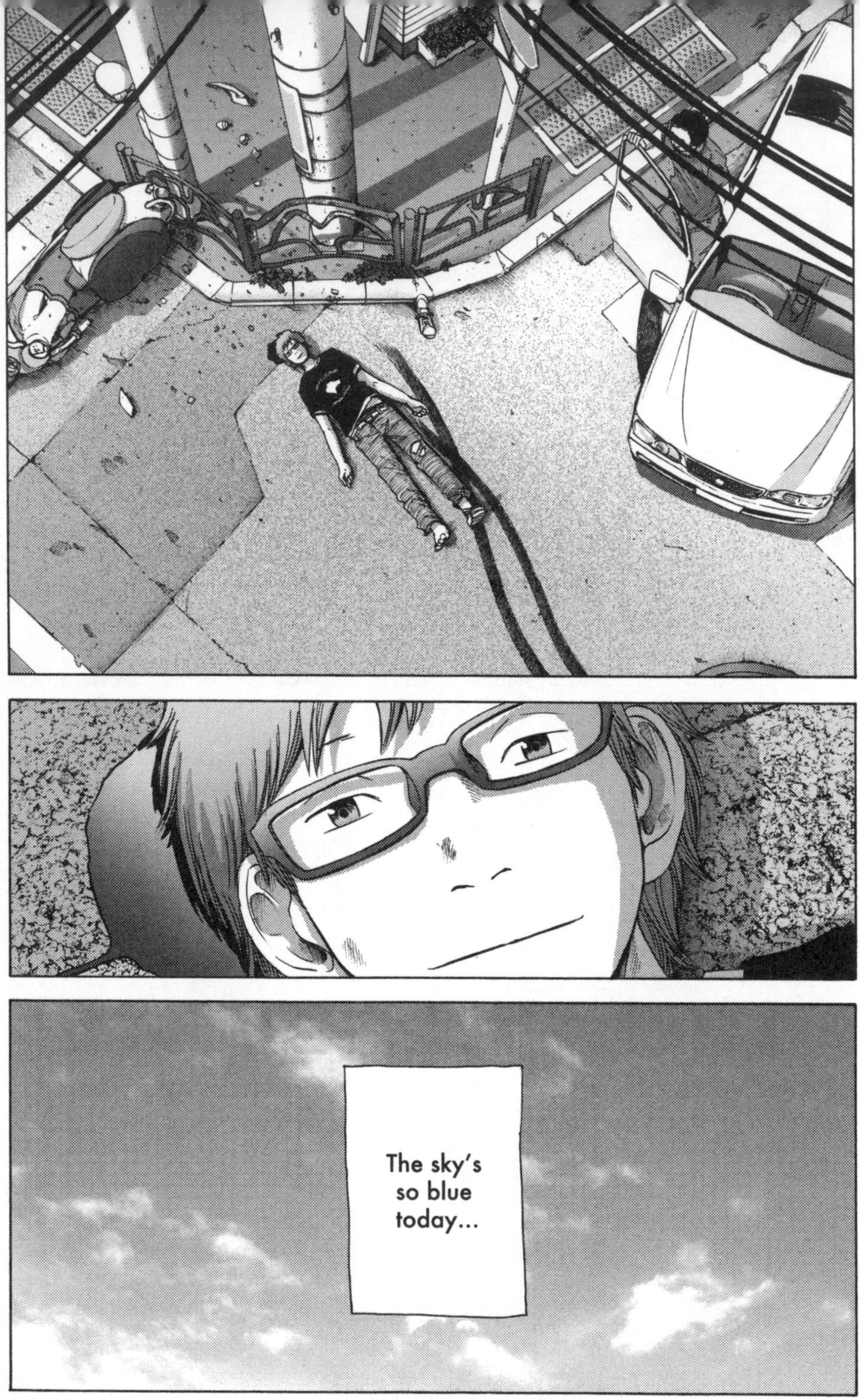
The sky's
so blue
today...

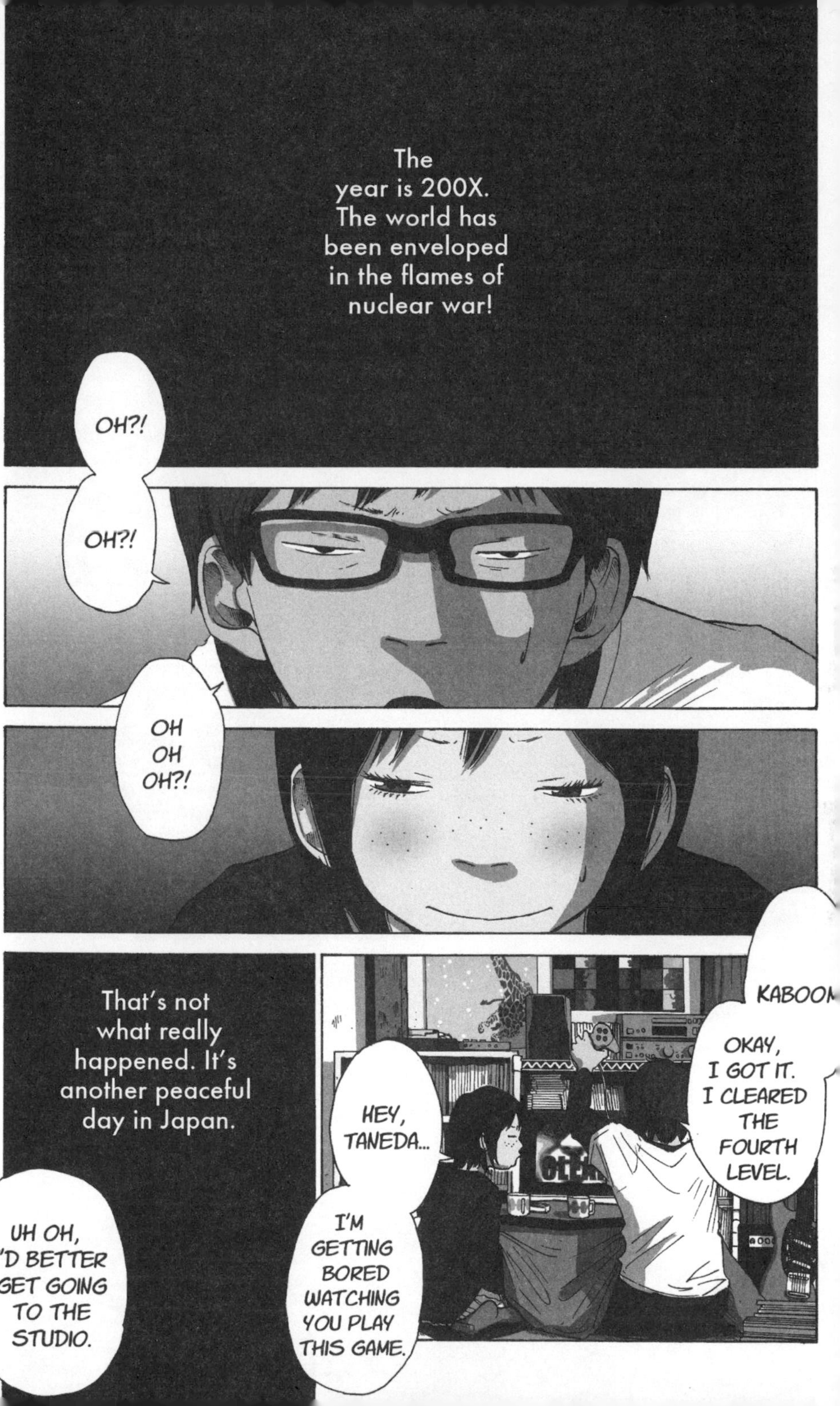
The year is 200X. The world has been enveloped in the flames of nuclear war!
OH?!
OH?!
OH OH OH?!
KABOOM
OKAY, I GOT IT. I CLEARED THE FOURTH LEVEL.
HEY, TANEDA...
I'M GETTING BORED WATCHING YOU PLAY THIS GAME.
That's not what really happened. It's another peaceful day in Japan.
UH OH, I'D BETTER GET GOING TO THE STUDIO.

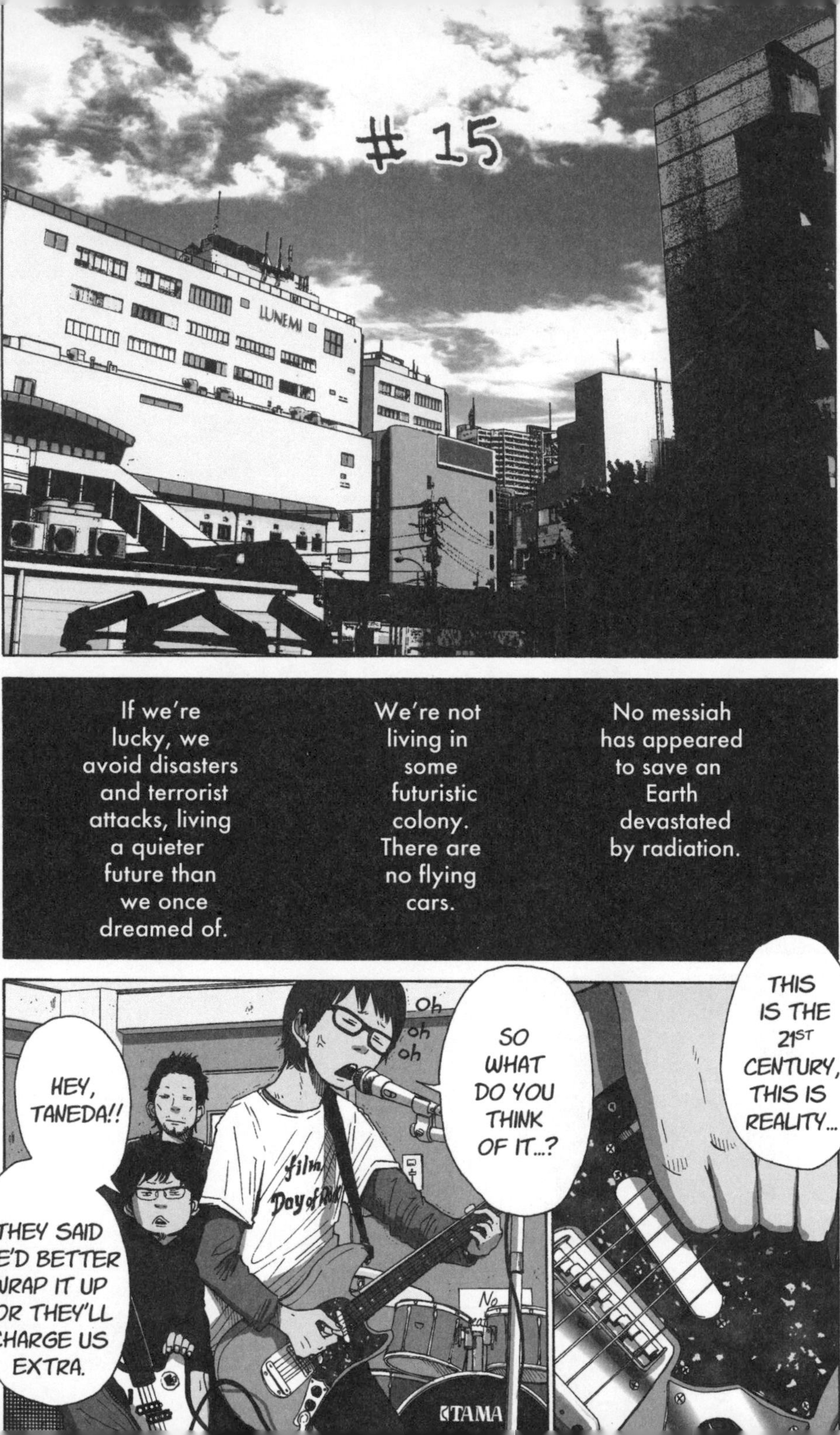
#15
LUNEMI
No messiah has appeared to save an Earth devastated by radiation.
We're not living in some futuristic colony. There are no flying cars.
If we're lucky, we avoid disasters and terrorist attacks, living a quieter future than we once dreamed of.
THIS IS THE 21ST CENTURY, THIS IS REALITY...
SO WHAT DO YOU THINK OF IT...?
oh oh oh
HEY, TANEDA!!
THEY SAID WE'D BETTER WRAP IT UP OR THEY'LL CHARGE US EXTRA.
TAMA

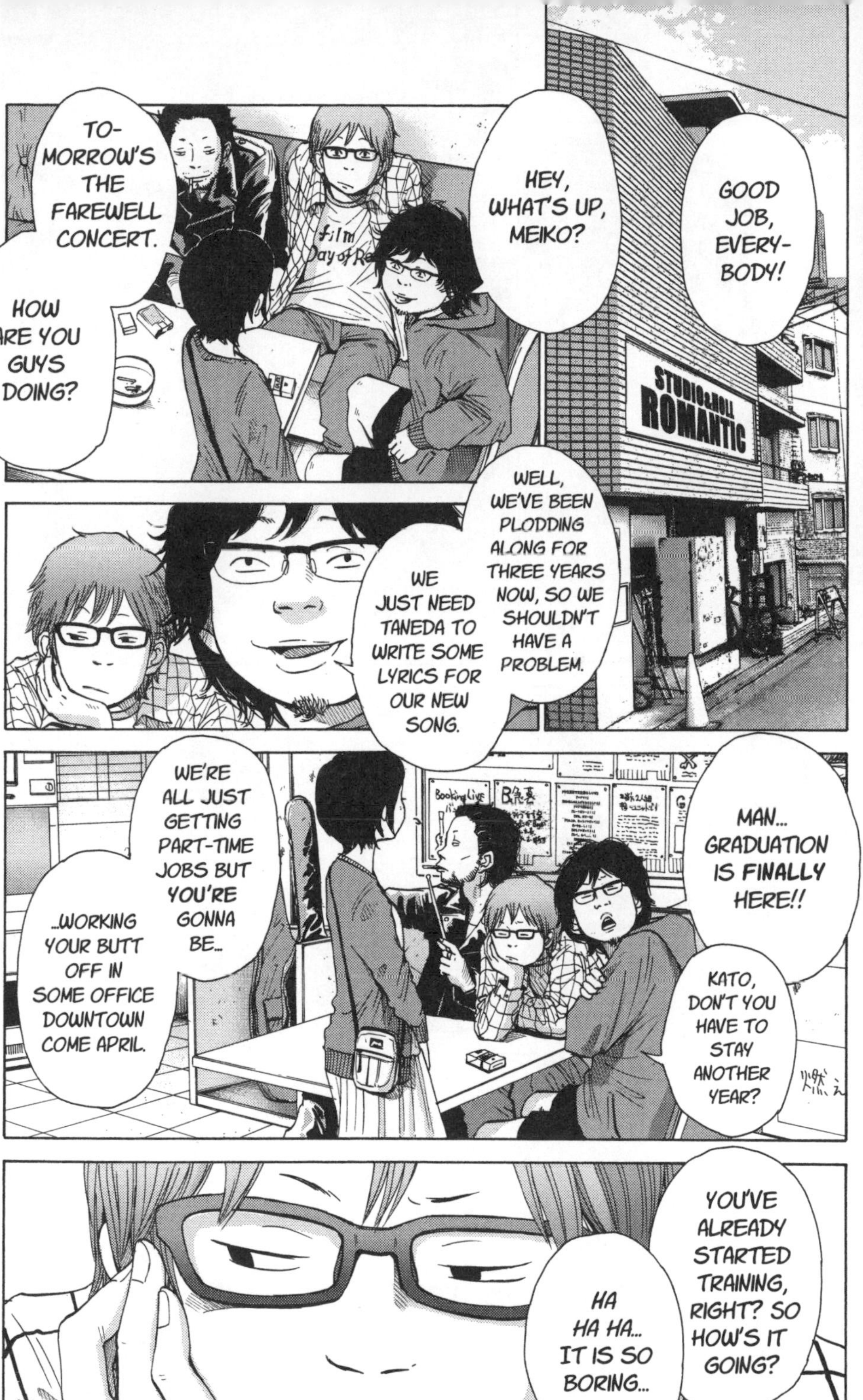
GOOD JOB, EVERYBODY!
HEY, WHAT'S UP, MEIKO?
STUDIO&ROLL ROMANTIC
TO-MORROW'S THE FAREWELL CONCERT.
HOW ARE YOU GUYS DOING?
WELL, WE'VE BEEN PLODDING ALONG FOR THREE YEARS NOW, SO WE SHOULDN'T HAVE A PROBLEM.
WE JUST NEED TANEDA TO WRITE SOME LYRICS FOR OUR NEW SONG.
MAN... GRADUATION IS FINALLY HERE!!
KATO, DON'T YOU HAVE TO STAY ANOTHER YEAR?
WE'RE ALL JUST GETTING PART-TIME JOBS BUT YOU'RE GONNA BE...
...WORKING YOUR BUTT OFF IN SOME OFFICE DOWNTOWN COME APRIL.
YOU'VE ALREADY STARTED TRAINING, RIGHT? SO HOW'S IT GOING?
HA HA HA... IT IS SO BORING...

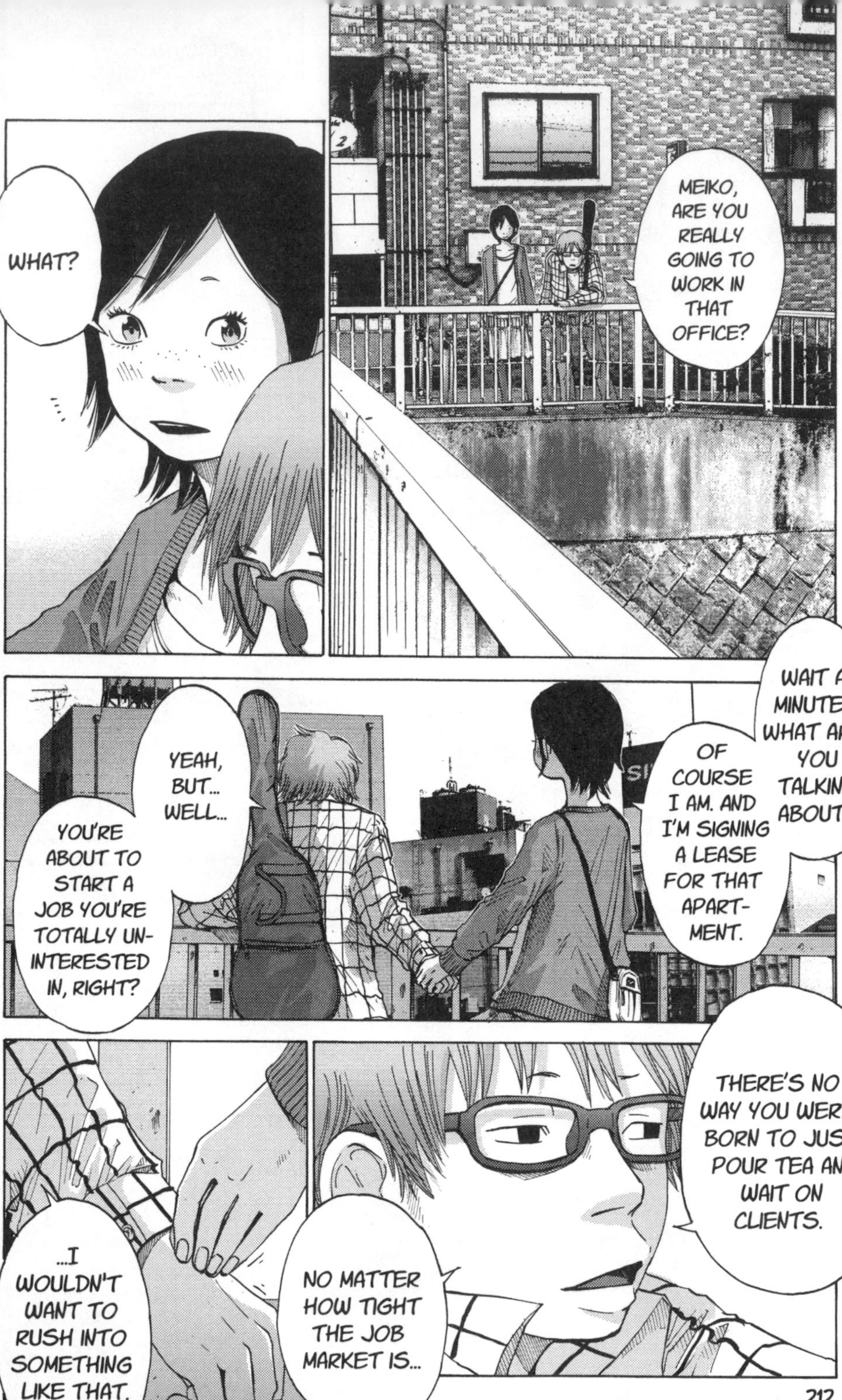
MEIKO, ARE YOU REALLY GOING TO WORK IN THAT OFFICE?
WHAT?
WAIT A MINUTE... WHAT ARE YOU TALKING ABOUT?
OF COURSE I AM. AND I'M SIGNING A LEASE FOR THAT APART-MENT.
YEAH, BUT... WELL...
YOU'RE ABOUT TO START A JOB YOU'RE TOTALLY UN-INTERESTED IN, RIGHT?
THERE'S NO WAY YOU WERE BORN TO JUST POUR TEA AND WAIT ON CLIENTS.
NO MATTER HOW TIGHT THE JOB MARKET IS...
...I WOULDN'T WANT TO RUSH INTO SOMETHING LIKE THAT.

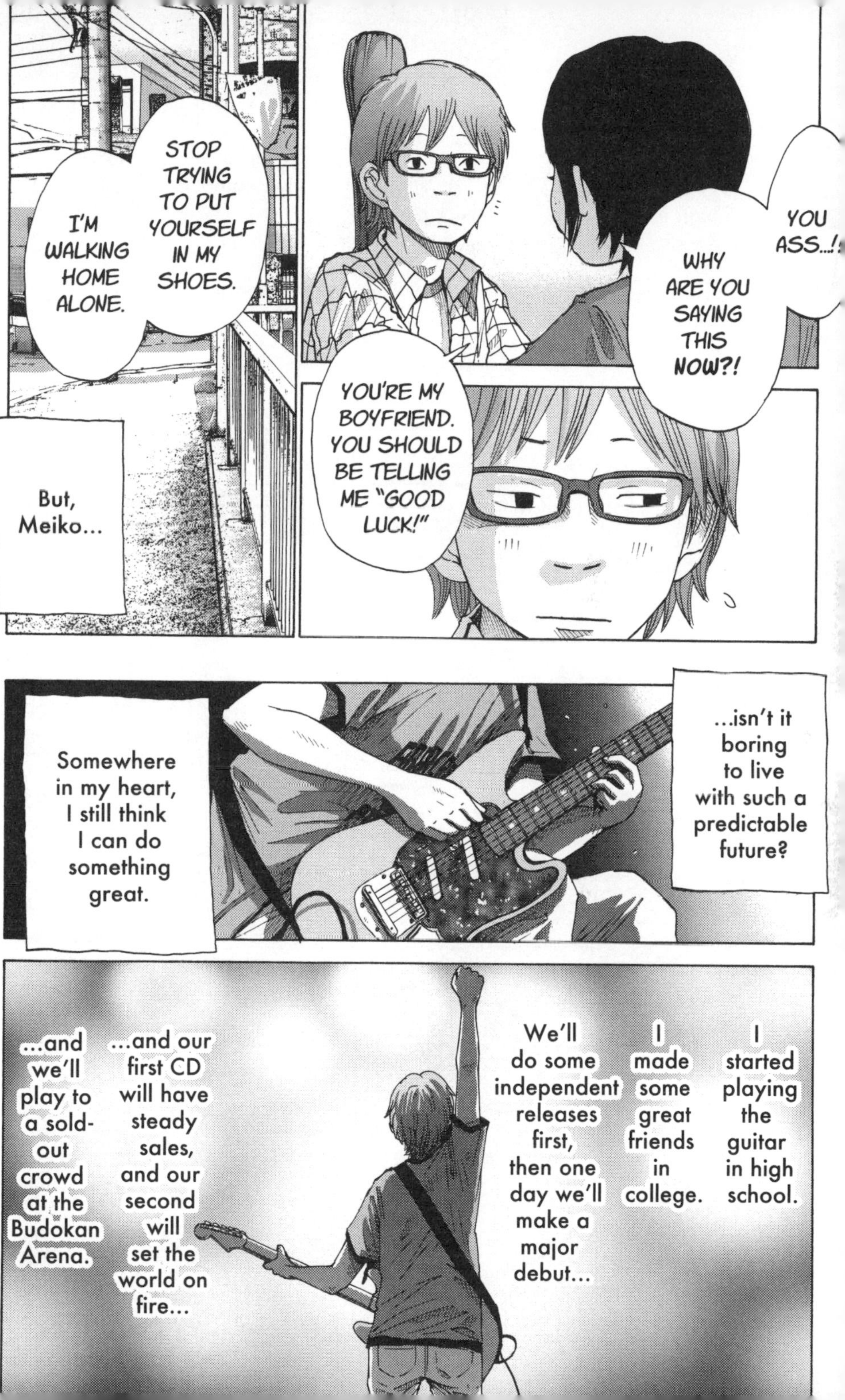
YOU ASS...!
WHY ARE YOU SAYING THIS NOW?!
YOU'RE MY BOYFRIEND. YOU SHOULD BE TELLING ME "GOOD LUCK!"
STOP TRYING TO PUT YOURSELF IN MY SHOES.
I'M WALKING HOME ALONE.
But, Meiko...
...isn't it boring to live with such a predictable future?
Somewhere in my heart, I still think I can do something great.
I started playing the guitar in high school.
I made some great friends in college.
We'll do some independent releases first, then one day we'll make a major debut...
...and our first CD will have steady sales, and our second will set the world on fire...
...and we'll play to a sold-out crowd at the Budokan Arena.

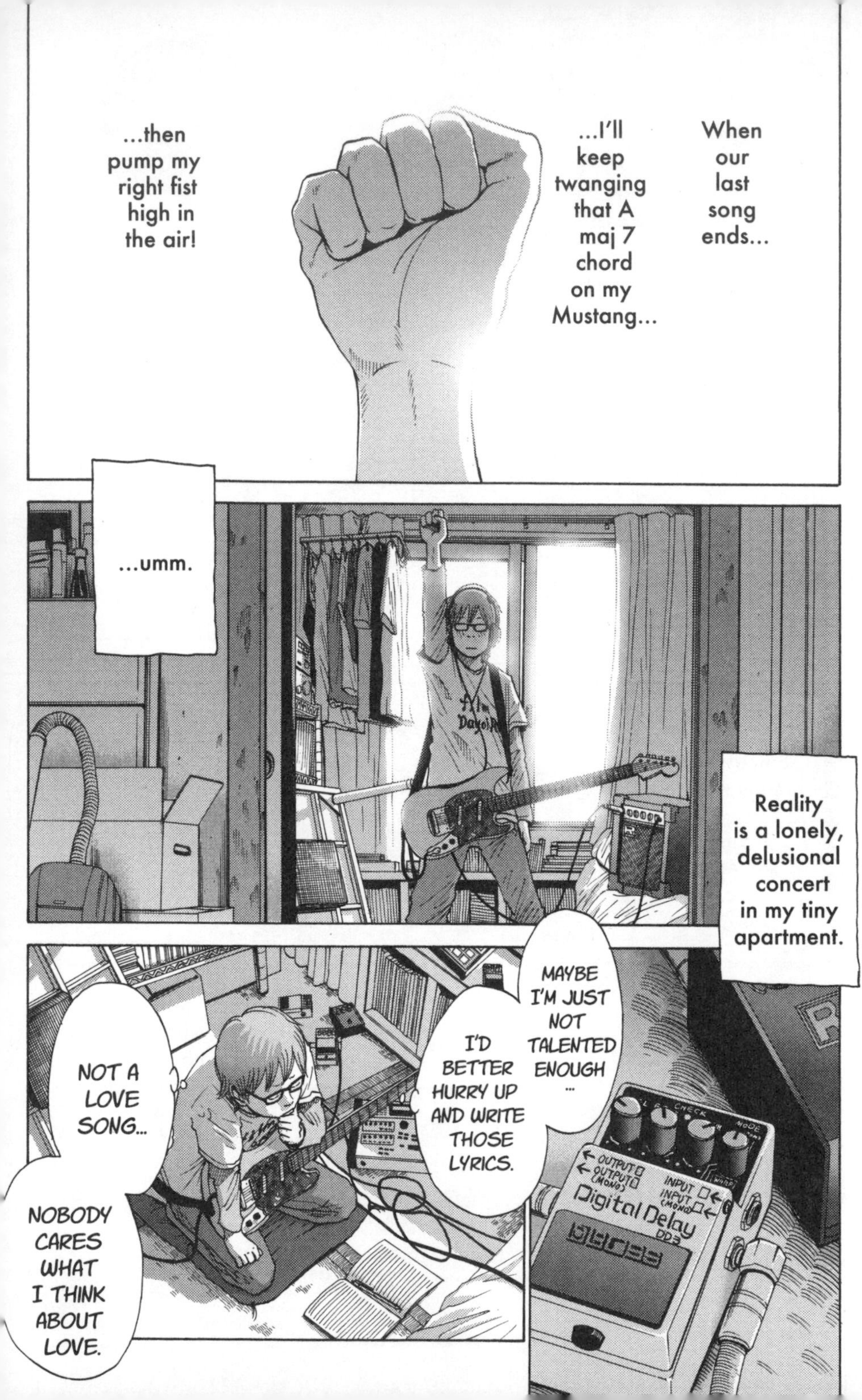
When our last song ends...
...I'll keep twanging that A maj 7 chord on my Mustang...
...then pump my right fist high in the air!
...umm.
Reality is a lonely, delusional concert in my tiny apartment.
MAYBE I'M JUST NOT TALENTED ENOUGH ...
I'D BETTER HURRY UP AND WRITE THOSE LYRICS.
NOT A LOVE SONG...
NOBODY CARES WHAT I THINK ABOUT LOVE.
Digital Delay DD3

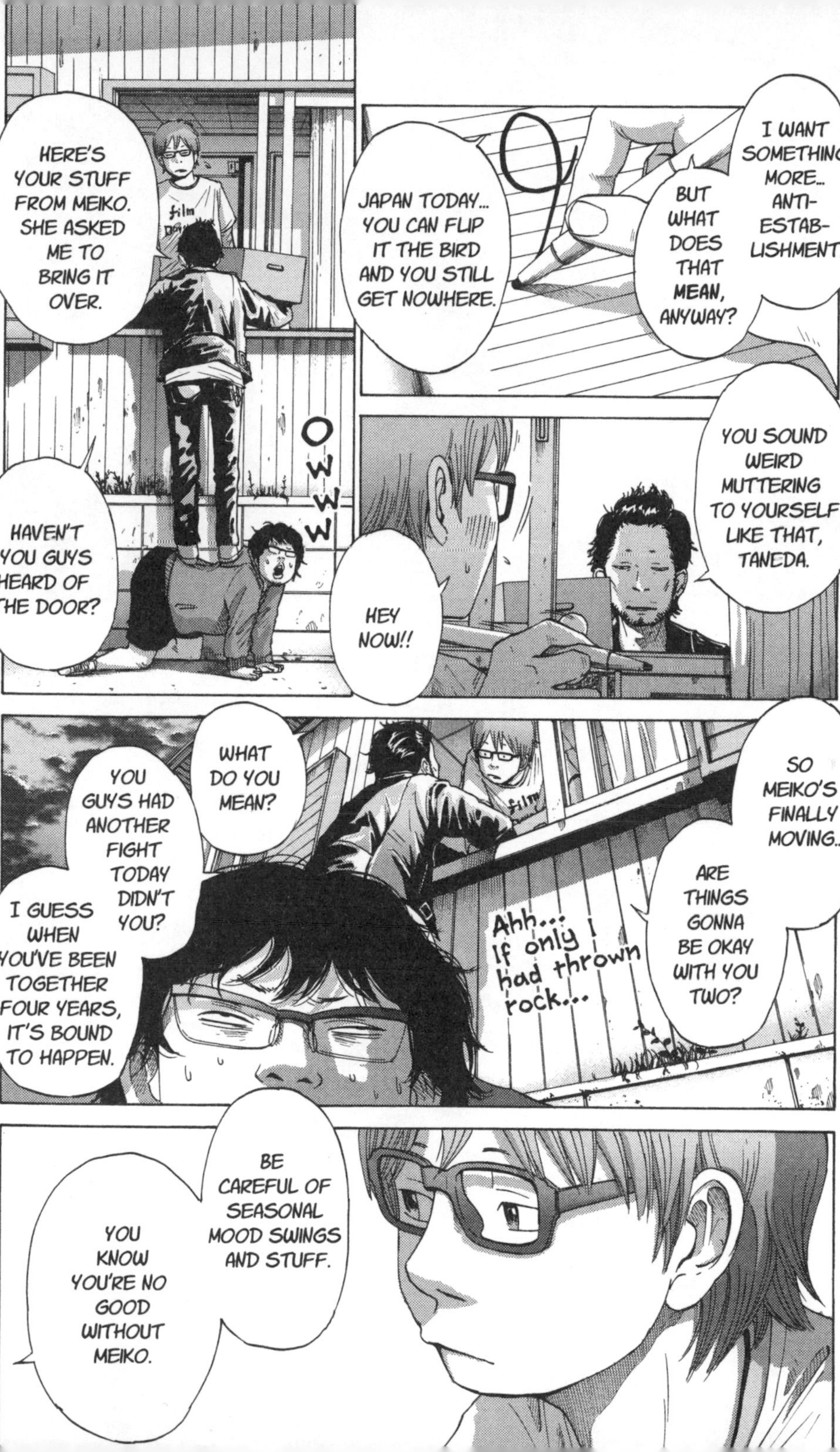
I WANT SOMETHING MORE... ANTI-ESTABLISHMENT...
BUT WHAT DOES THAT MEAN, ANYWAY?
JAPAN TODAY... YOU CAN FLIP IT THE BIRD AND YOU STILL GET NOWHERE.
YOU SOUND WEIRD MUTTERING TO YOURSELF LIKE THAT, TANEDA.
HEY NOW!!
HERE'S YOUR STUFF FROM MEIKO. SHE ASKED ME TO BRING IT OVER.
OWWW
HAVEN'T YOU GUYS HEARD OF THE DOOR?
SO MEIKO'S FINALLY MOVING...
ARE THINGS GONNA BE OKAY WITH YOU TWO?
Ahh... If only I had thrown rock...
WHAT DO YOU MEAN?
YOU GUYS HAD ANOTHER FIGHT TODAY DIDN'T YOU?
I GUESS WHEN YOU'VE BEEN TOGETHER FOUR YEARS, IT'S BOUND TO HAPPEN.
BE CAREFUL OF SEASONAL MOOD SWINGS AND STUFF.
YOU KNOW YOU'RE NO GOOD WITHOUT MEIKO.

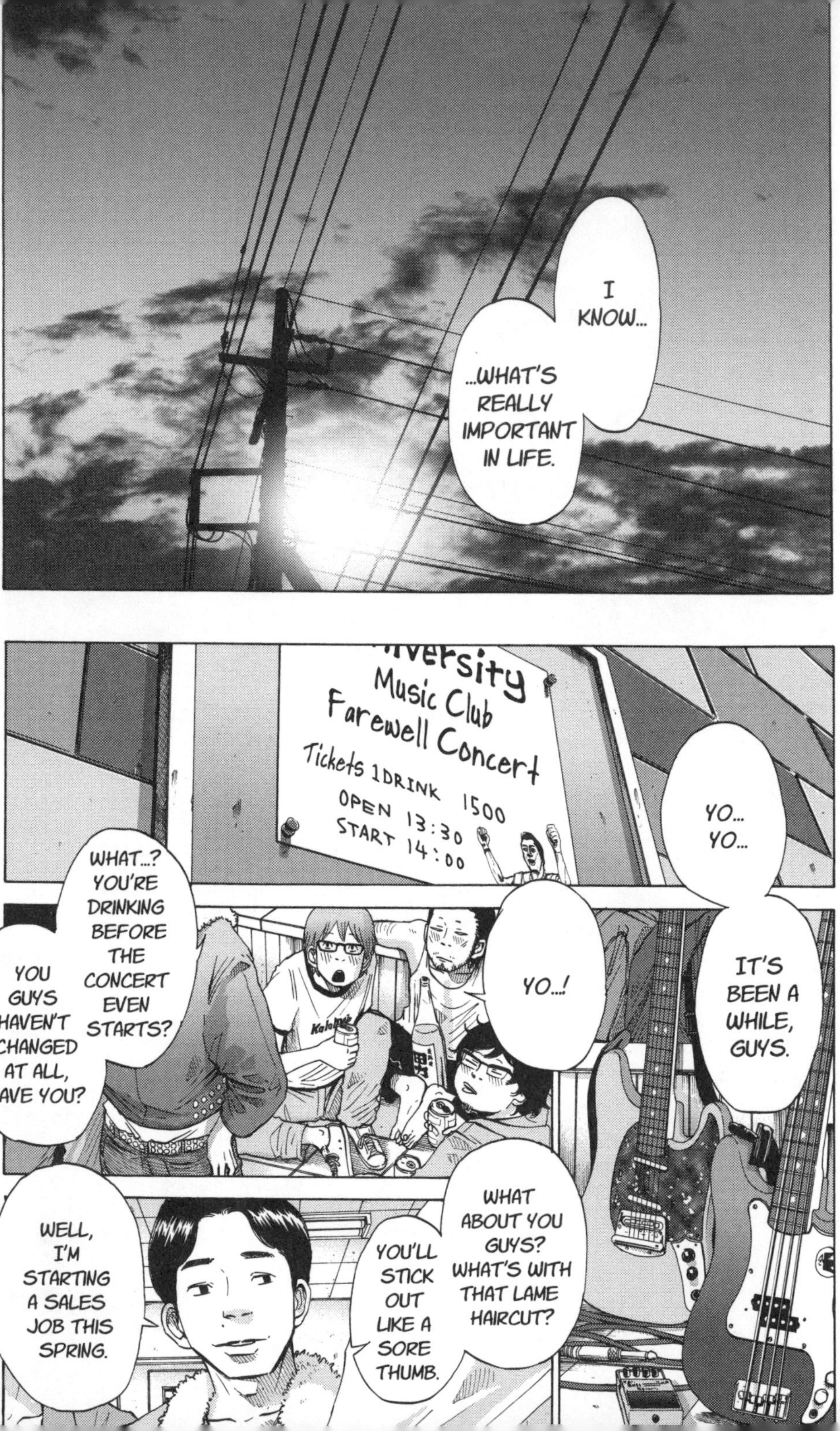
I KNOW...
...WHAT'S REALLY IMPORTANT IN LIFE.
iversity
Music Club
Farewell Concert
Tickets 1DRINK 1500
OPEN 13:30
START 14:00
YO... YO...
IT'S BEEN A WHILE, GUYS.
YO...!
WHAT...? YOU'RE DRINKING BEFORE THE CONCERT EVEN STARTS?
YOU GUYS HAVEN'T CHANGED AT ALL, HAVE YOU?
WHAT ABOUT YOU GUYS? WHAT'S WITH THAT LAME HAIRCUT?
YOU'LL STICK OUT LIKE A SORE THUMB.
WELL, I'M STARTING A SALES JOB THIS SPRING.

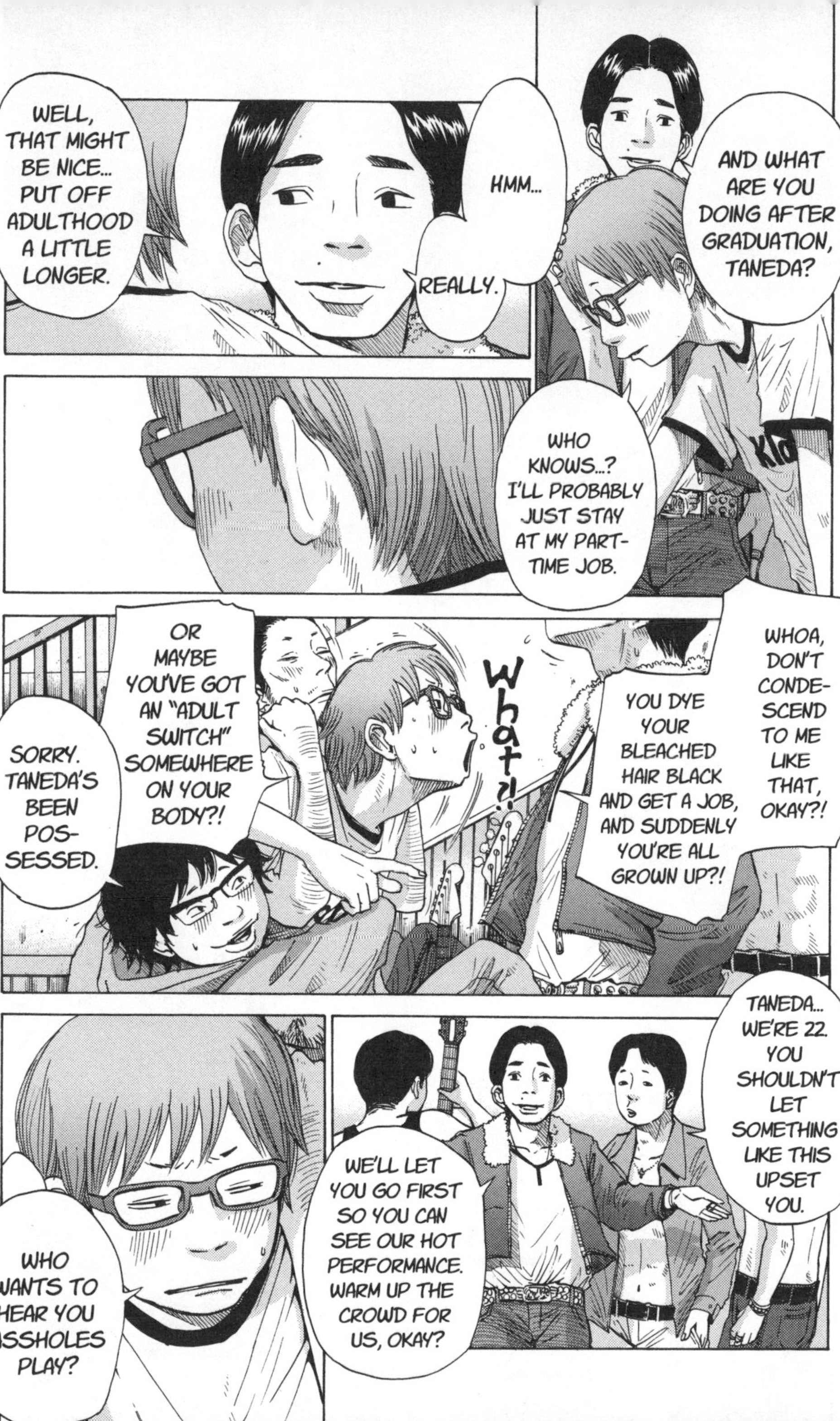
AND WHAT ARE YOU DOING AFTER GRADUATION, TANEDA?
HMM...
REALLY.
WELL, THAT MIGHT BE NICE... PUT OFF ADULTHOOD A LITTLE LONGER.
WHO KNOWS...? I'LL PROBABLY JUST STAY AT MY PART-TIME JOB.
WHOA, DON'T CONDE-SCEND TO ME LIKE THAT, OKAY?!
YOU DYE YOUR BLEACHED HAIR BLACK AND GET A JOB, AND SUDDENLY YOU'RE ALL GROWN UP?!
What?!
OR MAYBE YOU'VE GOT AN "ADULT SWITCH" SOMEWHERE ON YOUR BODY?!
SORRY. TANEDA'S BEEN POS-SESSED.
TANEDA... WE'RE 22. YOU SHOULDN'T LET SOMETHING LIKE THIS UPSET YOU.
WE'LL LET YOU GO FIRST SO YOU CAN SEE OUR HOT PERFORMANCE. WARM UP THE CROWD FOR US, OKAY?
WHO WANTS TO HEAR YOU ASSHOLES PLAY?

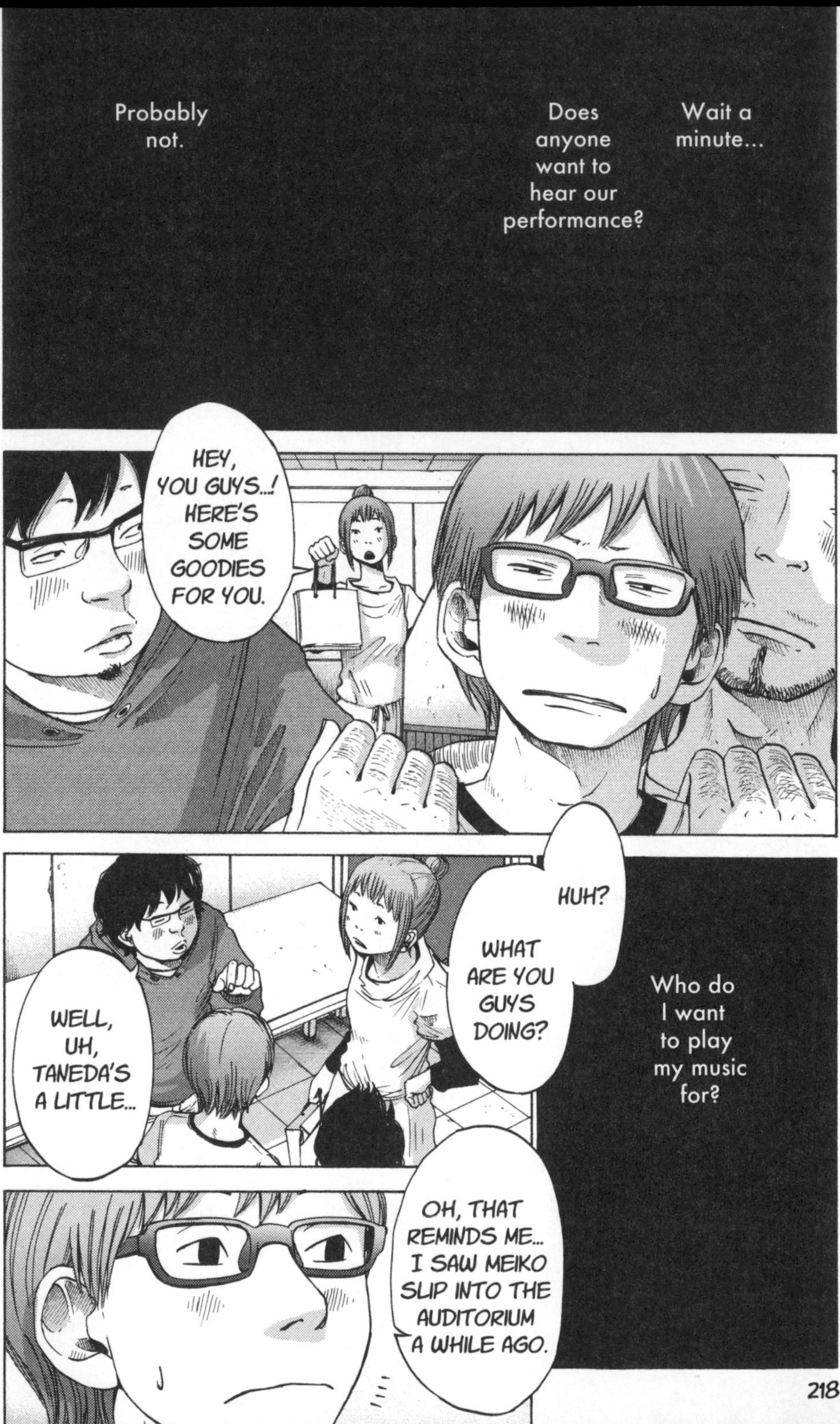
Wait a minute...
Does anyone want to hear our performance?
Probably not.
HEY, YOU GUYS...! HERE'S SOME GOODIES FOR YOU.
Who do I want to play my music for?
HUH?
WHAT ARE YOU GUYS DOING?
WELL, UH, TANEDA'S A LITTLE...
OH, THAT REMINDS ME... I SAW MEIKO SLIP INTO THE AUDITORIUM A WHILE AGO.

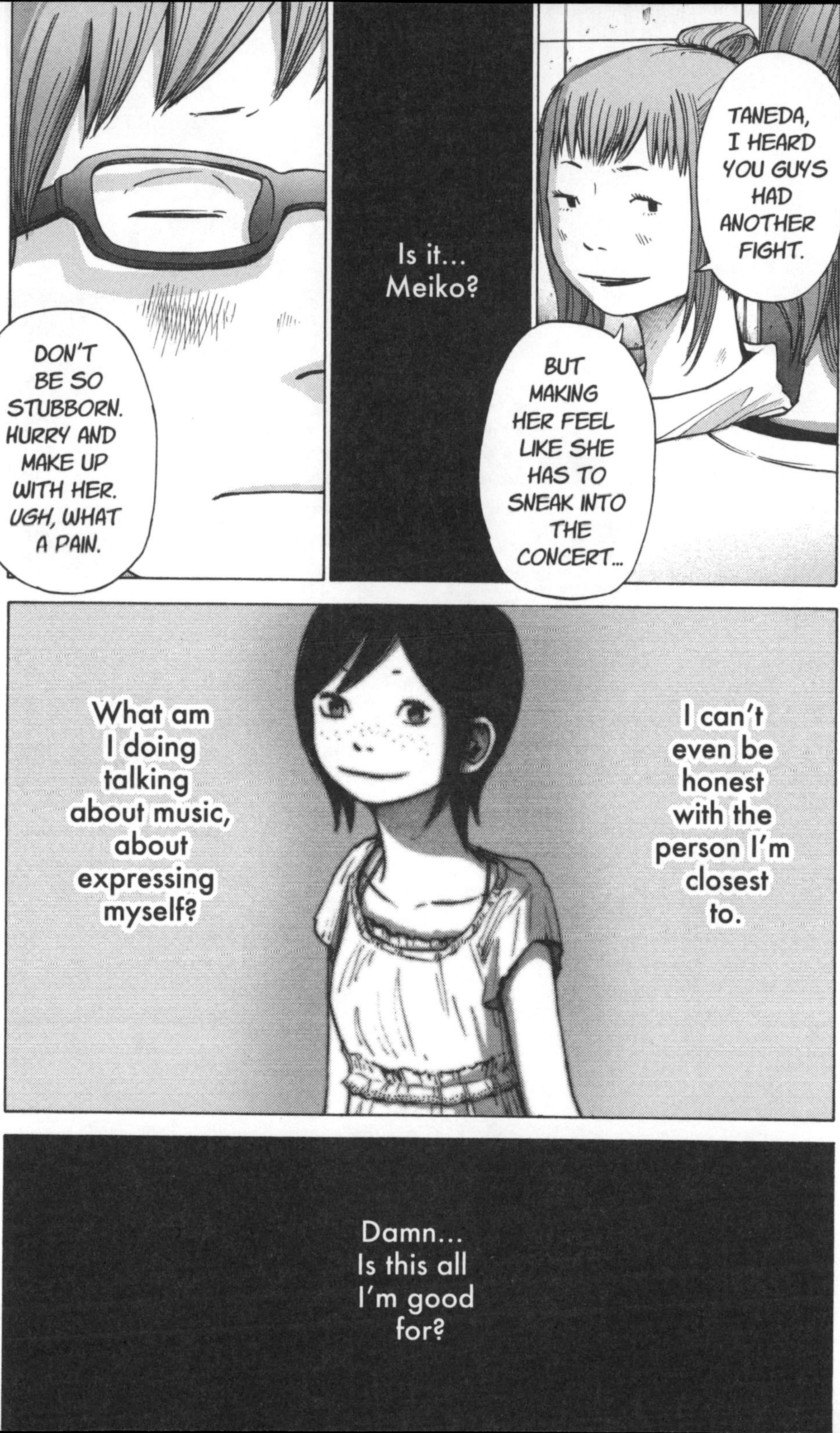
TANEDA, I HEARD YOU GUYS HAD ANOTHER FIGHT.
BUT MAKING HER FEEL LIKE SHE HAS TO SNEAK INTO THE CONCERT...
Is it... Meiko?
DON'T BE SO STUBBORN. HURRY AND MAKE UP WITH HER. UGH, WHAT A PAIN.
I can't even be honest with the person I'm closest to.
What am I doing talking about music, about expressing myself?
Damn... Is this all I'm good for?

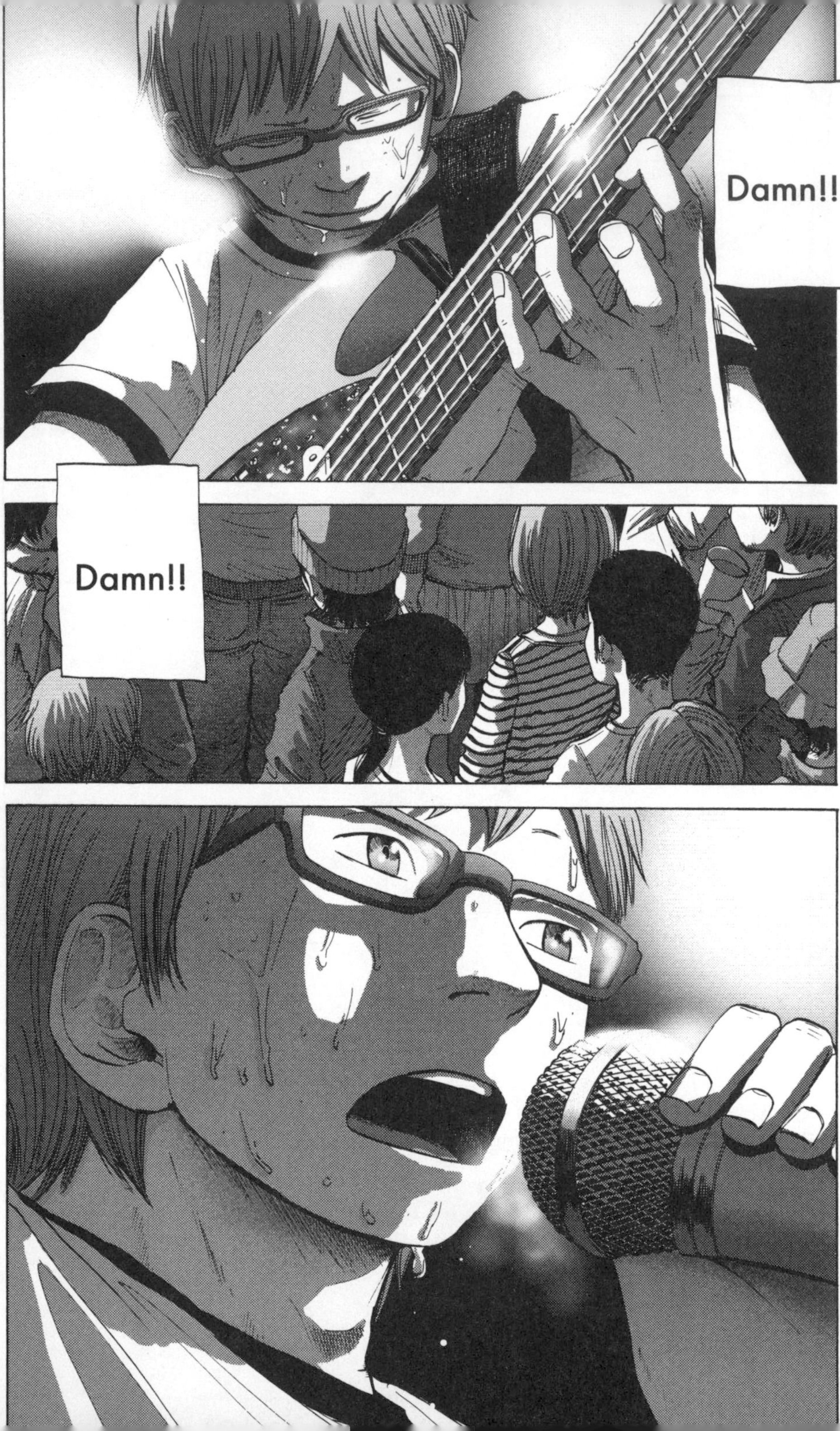
Damn!!
Damn!!

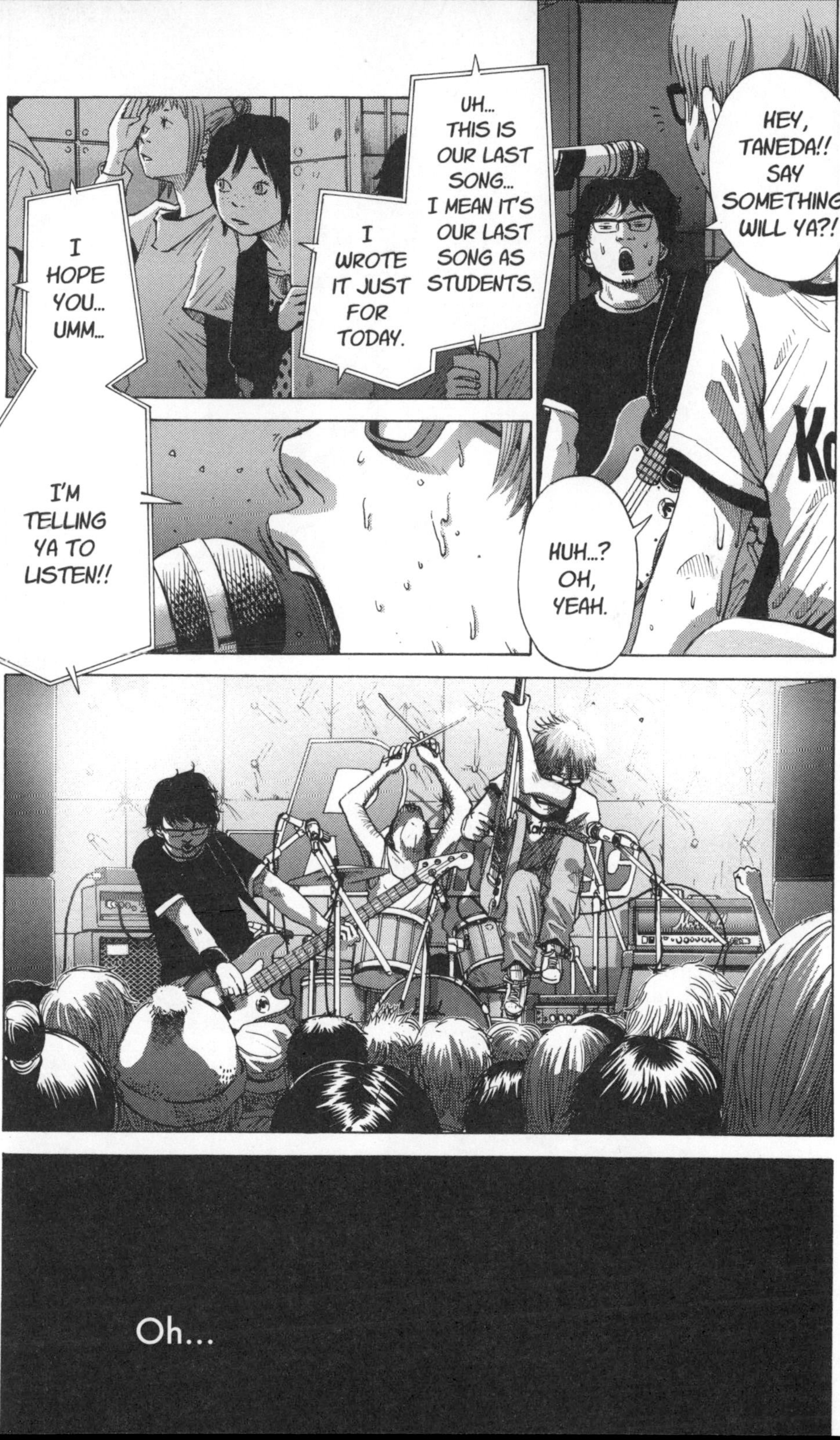
HEY, TANEDA!! SAY SOMETHING, WILL YA?!
HUH...? OH, YEAH.
UH... THIS IS OUR LAST SONG... I MEAN IT'S OUR LAST SONG AS STUDENTS.
I WROTE IT JUST FOR TODAY.
I HOPE YOU... UMM...
I'M TELLING YA TO LISTEN!!
Oh...

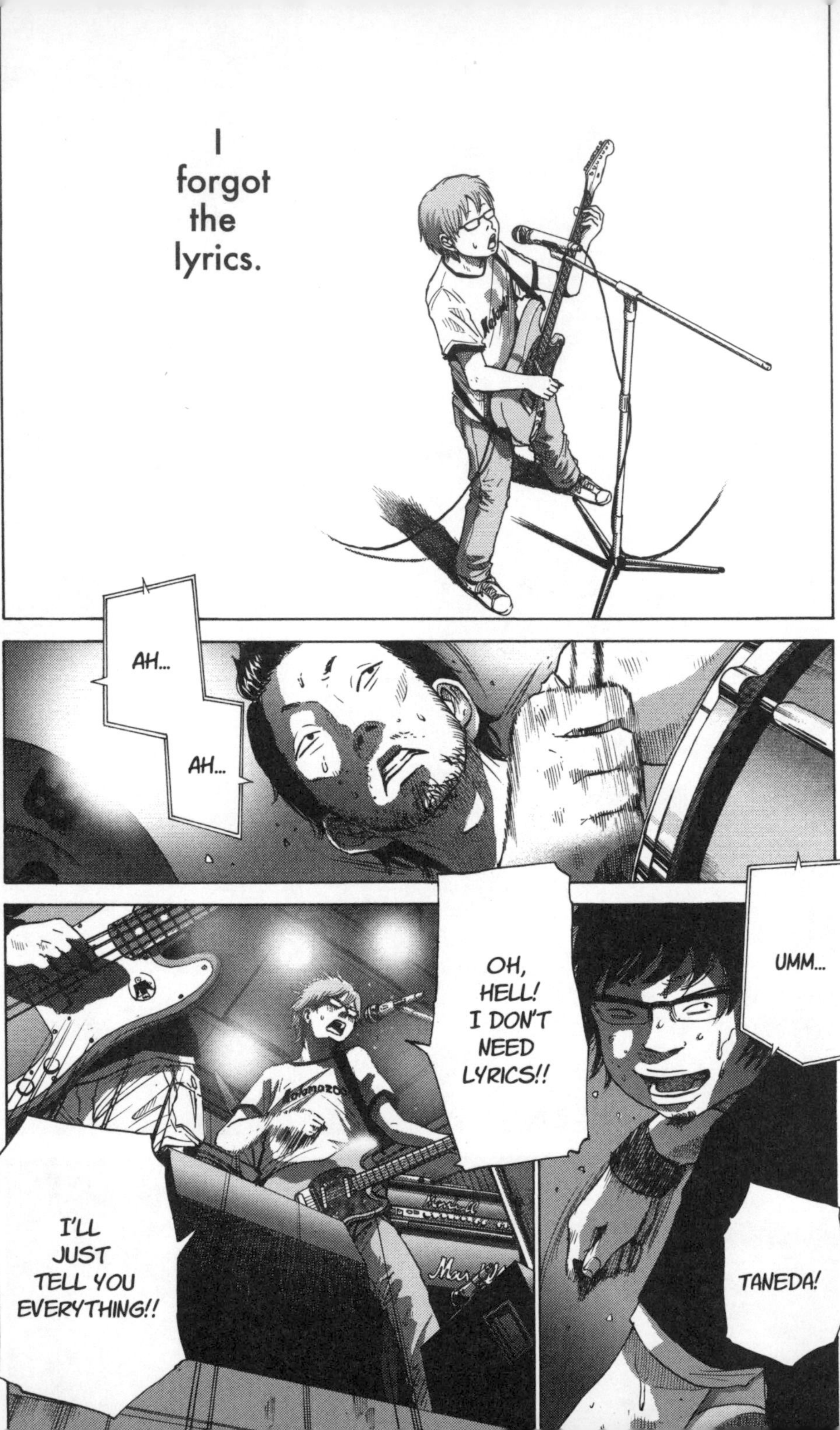
I forgot the lyrics.
AH...
AH...
UMM...
TANEDA!
OH, HELL! I DON'T NEED LYRICS!!
I'LL JUST TELL YOU EVERYTHING!!

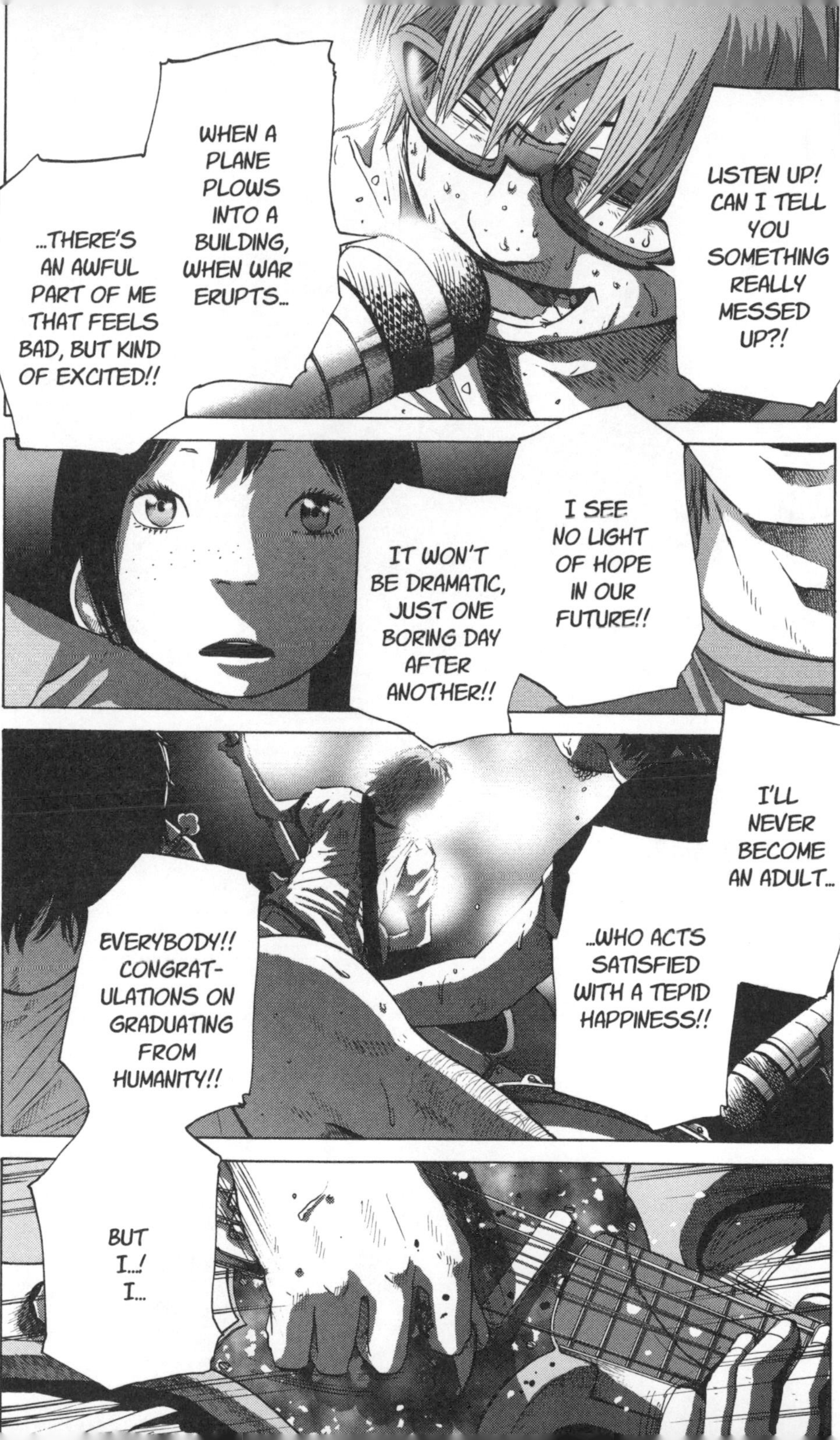
LISTEN UP! CAN I TELL YOU SOMETHING REALLY MESSED UP?!
WHEN A PLANE PLOWS INTO A BUILDING, WHEN WAR ERUPTS...
...THERE'S AN AWFUL PART OF ME THAT FEELS BAD, BUT KIND OF EXCITED!!
I SEE NO LIGHT OF HOPE IN OUR FUTURE!!
IT WON'T BE DRAMATIC, JUST ONE BORING DAY AFTER ANOTHER!!
I'LL NEVER BECOME AN ADULT...
...WHO ACTS SATISFIED WITH A TEPID HAPPINESS!!
EVERYBODY!! CONGRAT-ULATIONS ON GRADUATING FROM HUMANITY!!
BUT I...! I...

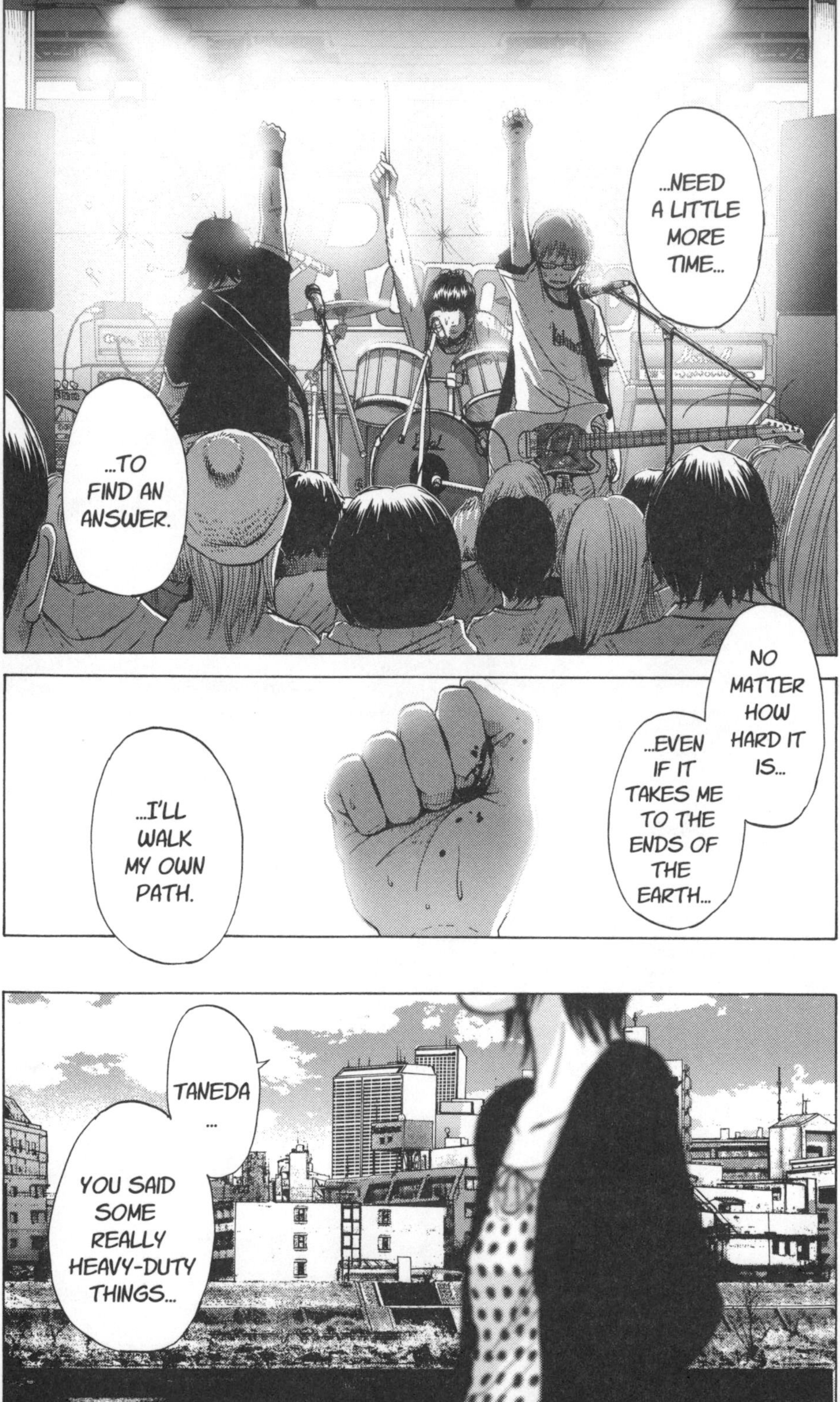
...NEED A LITTLE MORE TIME...
...TO FIND AN ANSWER.
NO MATTER HOW HARD IT IS...
...EVEN IF IT TAKES ME TO THE ENDS OF THE EARTH...
...I'LL WALK MY OWN PATH.
TANEDA ...
YOU SAID SOME REALLY HEAVY-DUTY THINGS...

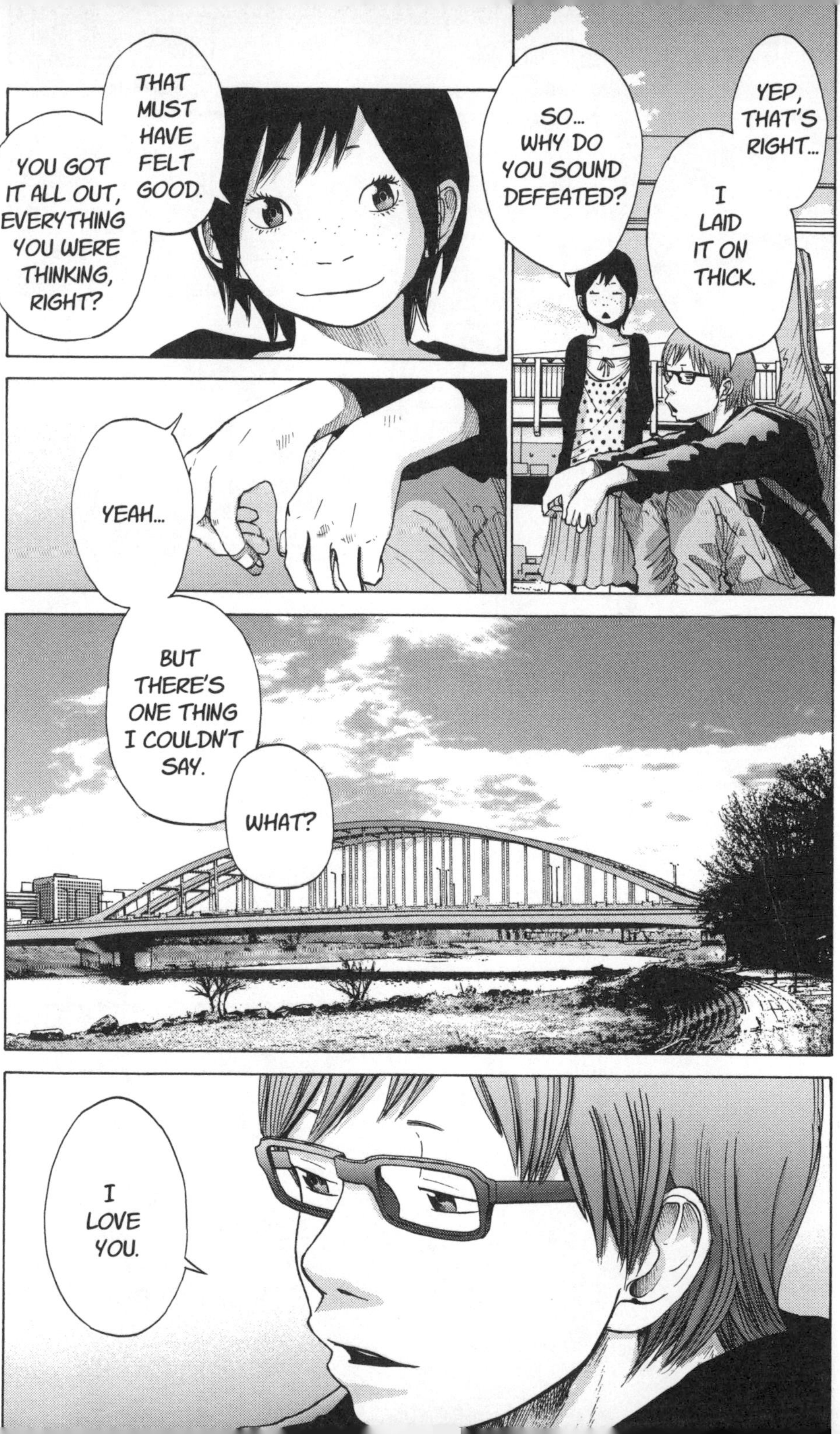
YEP, THAT'S RIGHT...
I LAID IT ON THICK.
SO... WHY DO YOU SOUND DEFEATED?
THAT MUST HAVE FELT GOOD.
YOU GOT IT ALL OUT, EVERYTHING YOU WERE THINKING, RIGHT?
YEAH...
BUT THERE'S ONE THING I COULDN'T SAY.
WHAT?
I LOVE YOU.

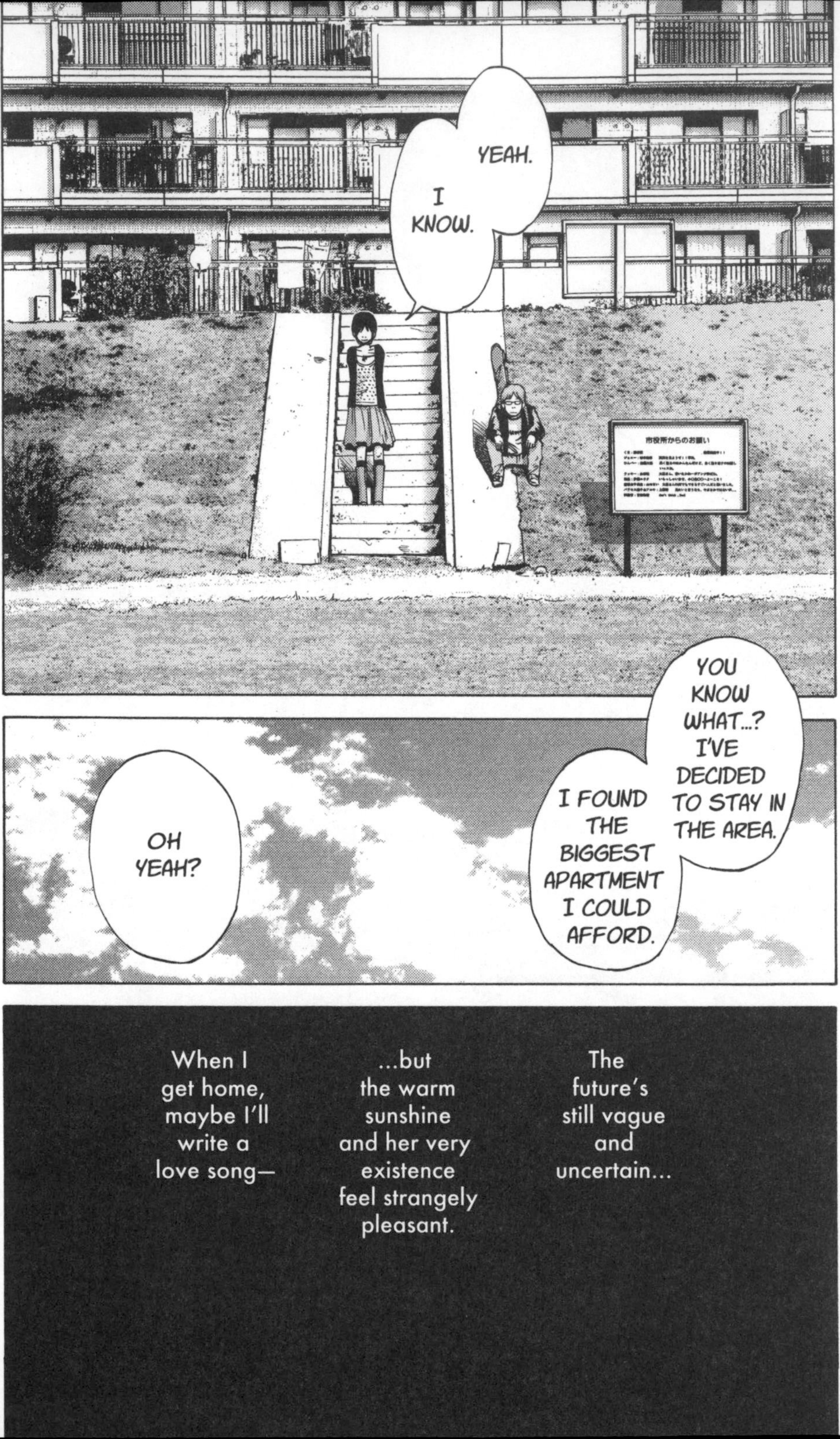
YEAH.
I KNOW.
市役所からのお願い
YOU KNOW WHAT...? I'VE DECIDED TO STAY IN THE AREA.
I FOUND THE BIGGEST APARTMENT I COULD AFFORD.
OH YEAH?
The future's still vague and uncertain...
...but the warm sunshine and her very existence feel strangely pleasant.
When I get home, maybe I'll write a love song—

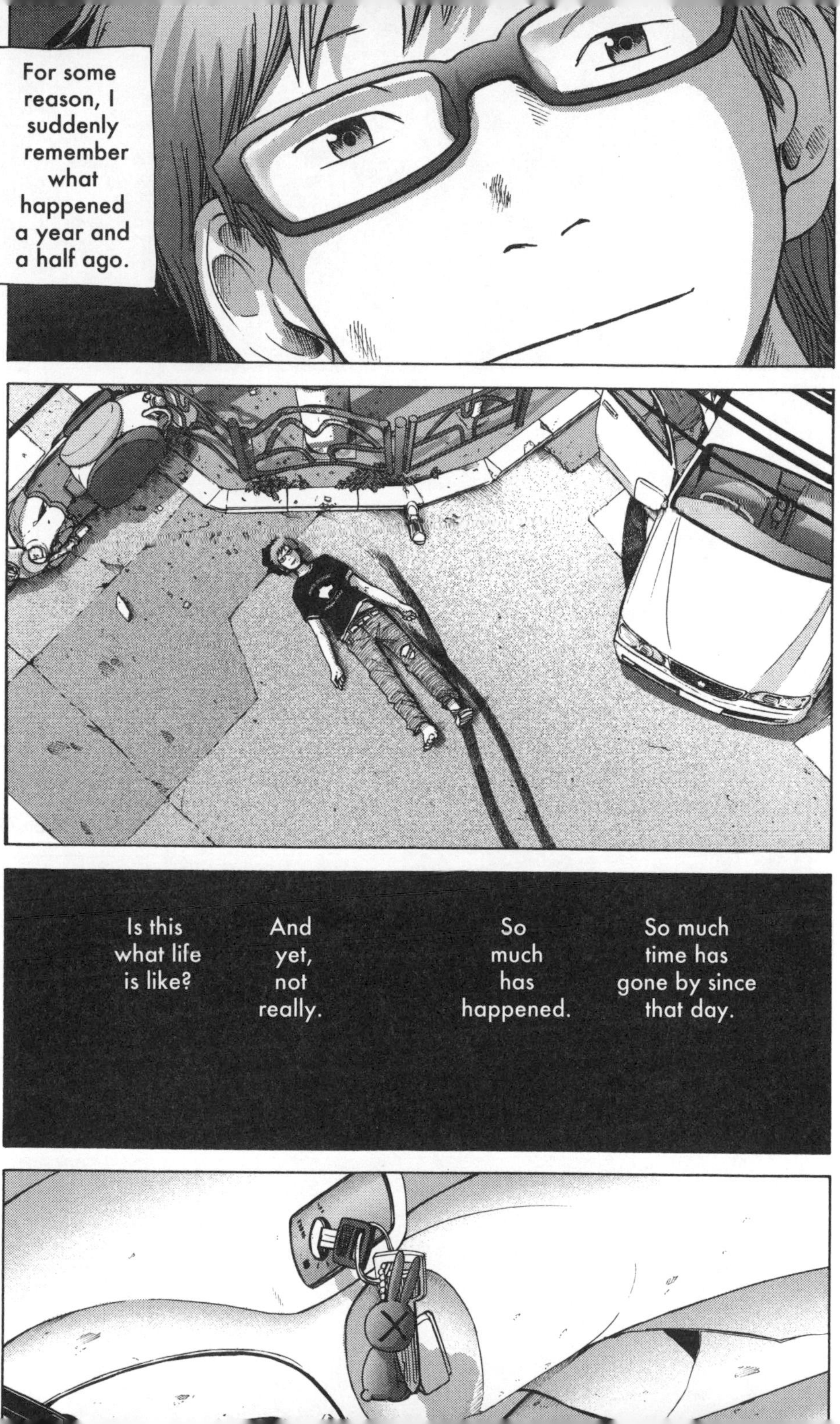

For some reason, I suddenly remember what happened a year and a half ago.
So much time has gone by since that day.
So much has happened.
And yet, not really.
Is this what life is like?

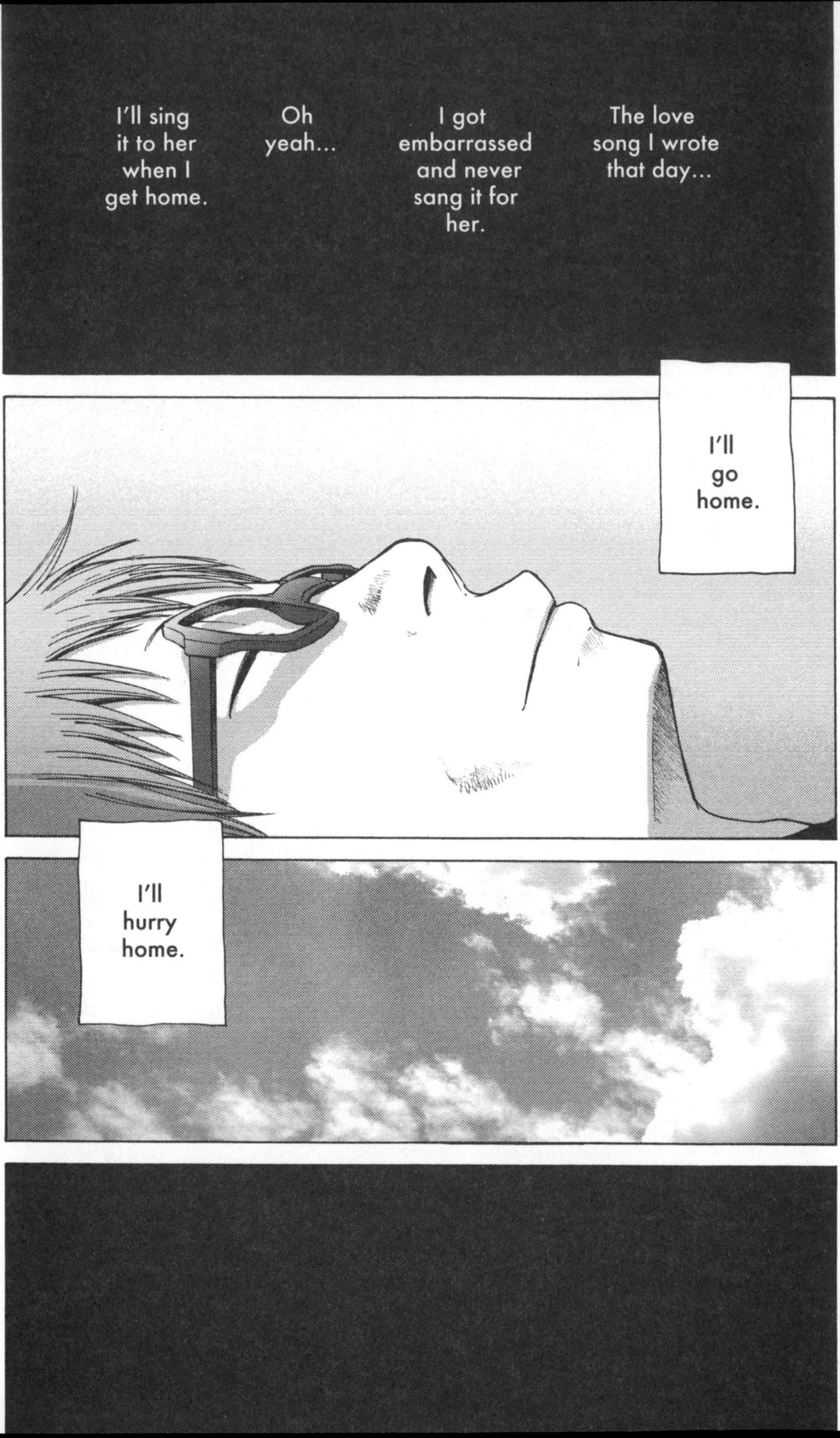
The love song I wrote that day...
I got embarrassed and never sang it for her.
Oh yeah...
I'll sing it to her when I get home.
I'll go home.
I'll hurry home.

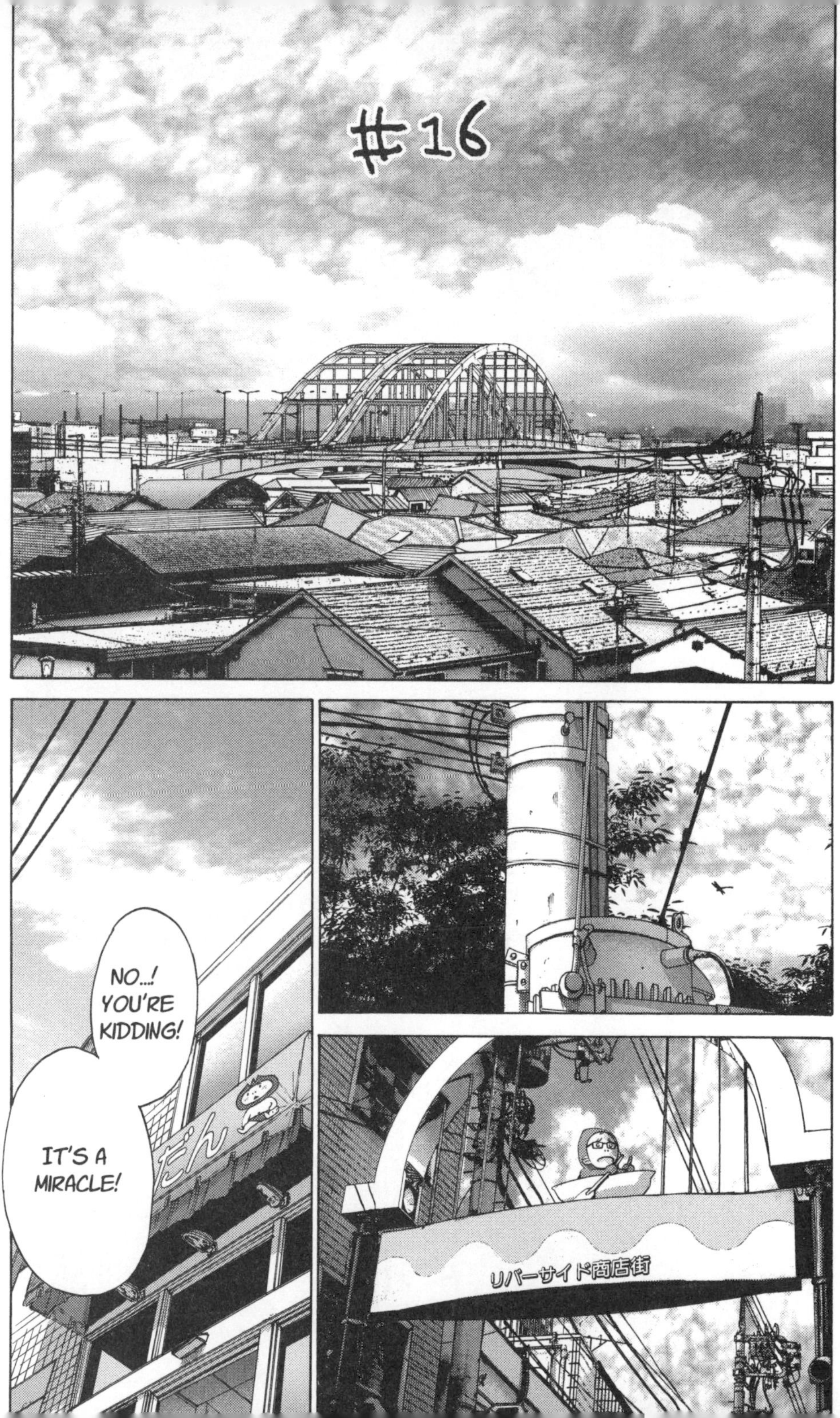
#16
リバーサイド商店街
NO...! YOU'RE KIDDING!
IT'S A MIRACLE!

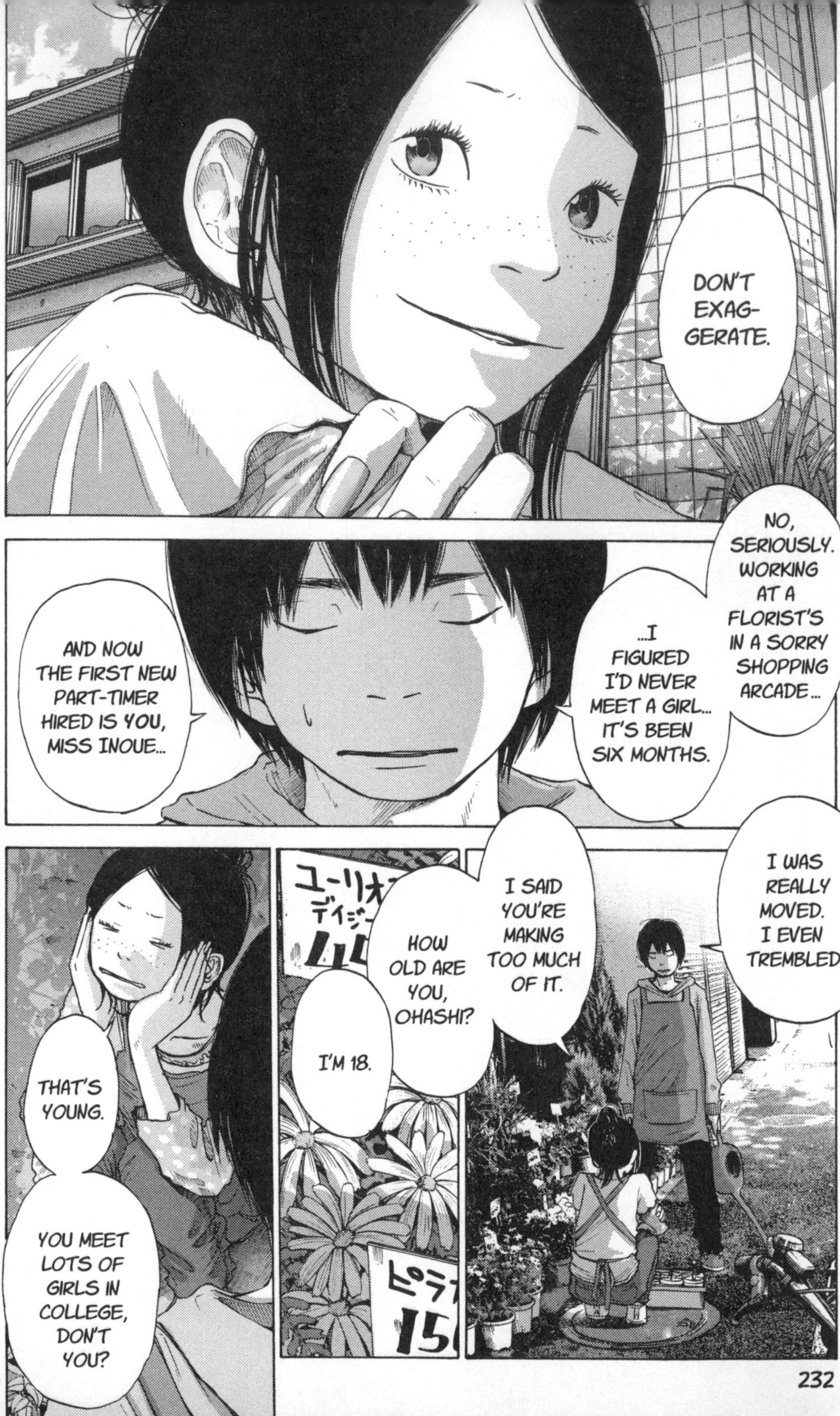
DON'T EXAG-GERATE.
NO, SERIOUSLY. WORKING AT A FLORIST'S IN A SORRY SHOPPING ARCADE...
...I FIGURED I'D NEVER MEET A GIRL... IT'S BEEN SIX MONTHS.
AND NOW THE FIRST NEW PART-TIMER HIRED IS YOU, MISS INOUE...
I WAS REALLY MOVED. I EVEN TREMBLED.
I SAID YOU'RE MAKING TOO MUCH OF IT.
HOW OLD ARE YOU, OHASHI?
I'M 18.
THAT'S YOUNG.
YOU MEET LOTS OF GIRLS IN COLLEGE, DON'T YOU?

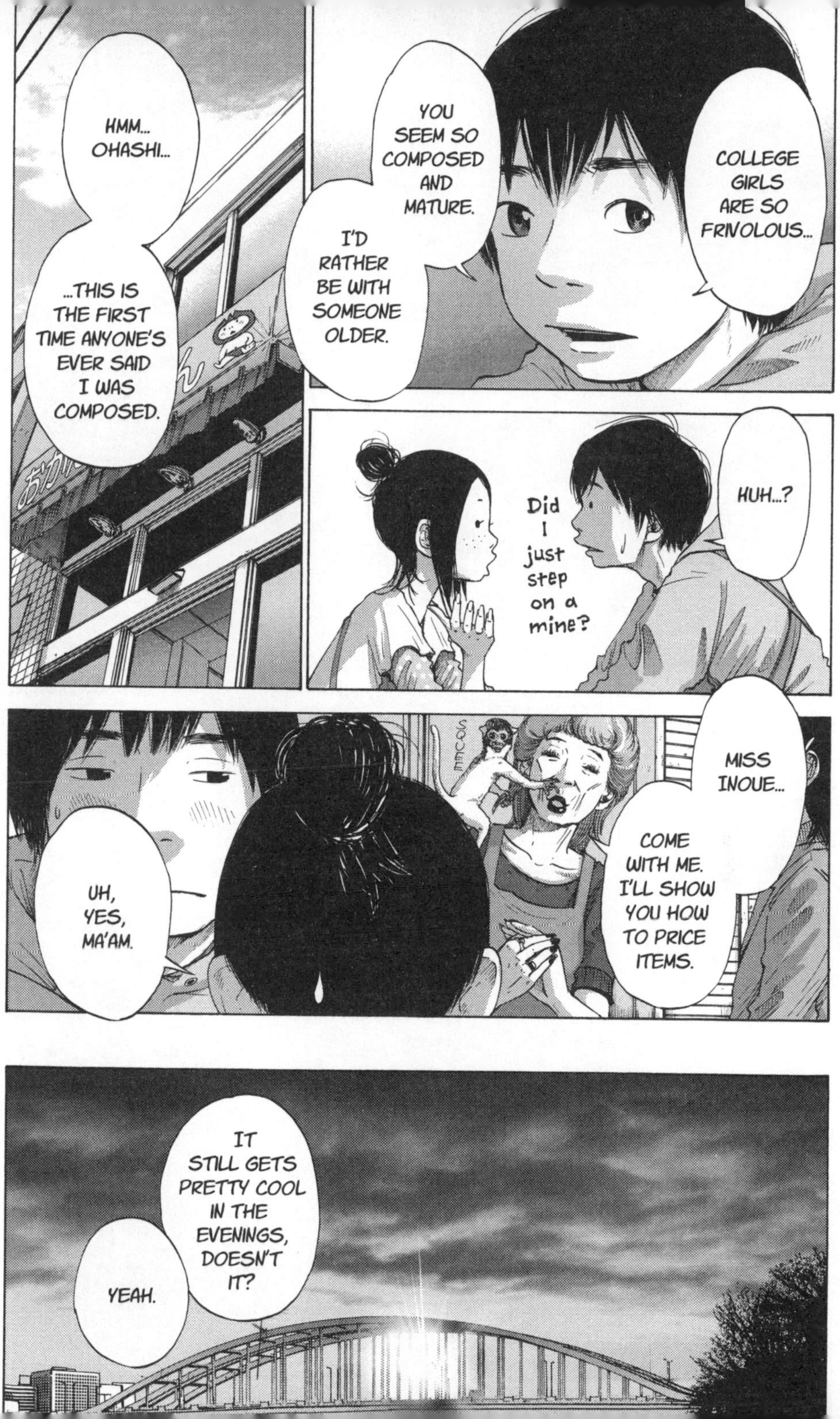
COLLEGE GIRLS ARE SO FRIVOLOUS...
YOU SEEM SO COMPOSED AND MATURE.
I'D RATHER BE WITH SOMEONE OLDER.
HUH...?
Did I just step on a mine?
HMM... OHASHI...
...THIS IS THE FIRST TIME ANYONE'S EVER SAID I WAS COMPOSED.
MISS INOUE...
COME WITH ME. I'LL SHOW YOU HOW TO PRICE ITEMS.
SQUEE
UH, YES, MA'AM.
IT STILL GETS PRETTY COOL IN THE EVENINGS, DOESN'T IT?
YEAH.

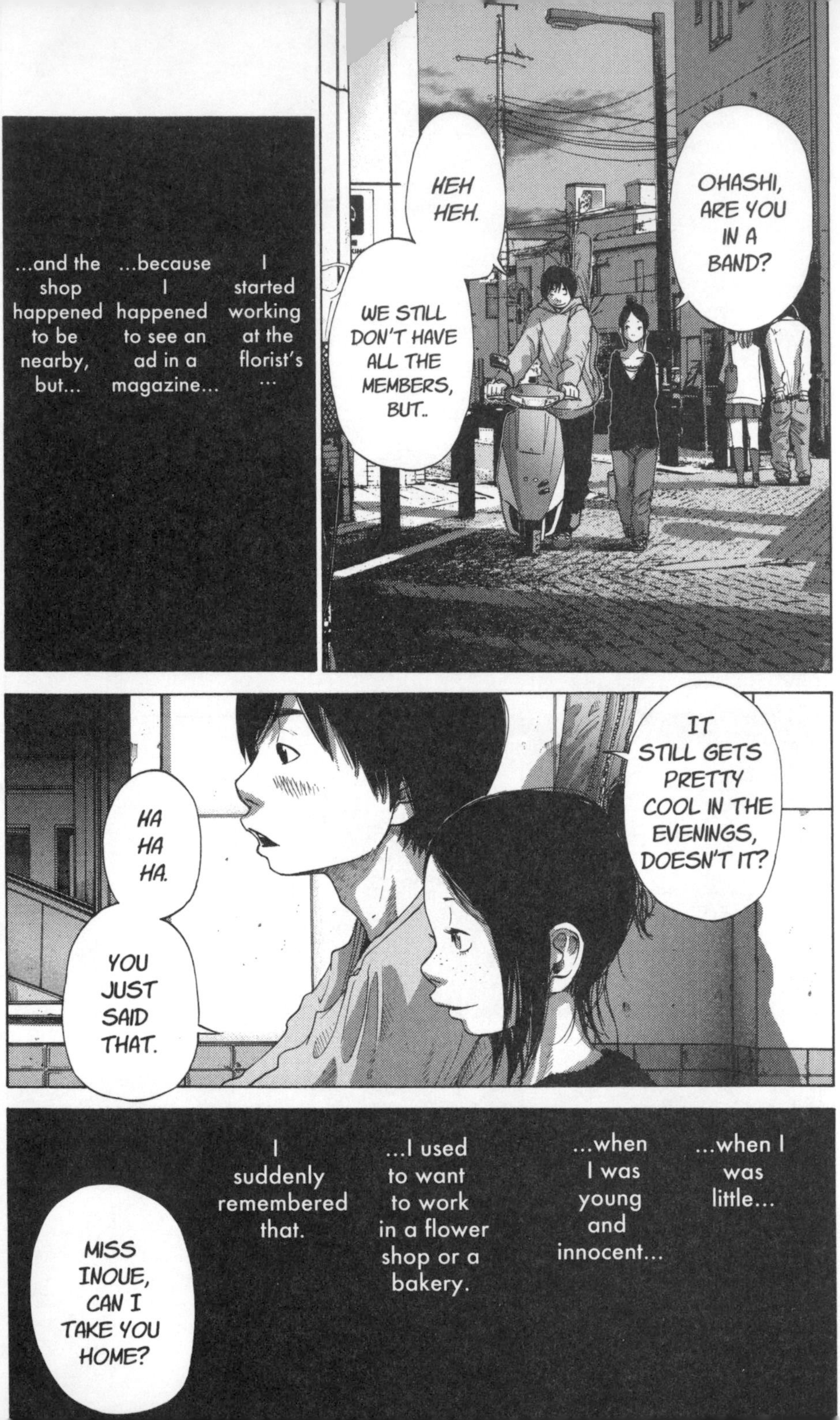
OHASHI, ARE YOU IN A BAND?
HEH HEH.
WE STILL DON'T HAVE ALL THE MEMBERS, BUT..
I started working at the florist's...
...because I happened to see an ad in a magazine...
...and the shop happened to be nearby, but...
IT STILL GETS PRETTY COOL IN THE EVENINGS, DOESN'T IT?
HA HA HA.
YOU JUST SAID THAT.
...when I was little...
...when I was young and innocent...
...I used to want to work in a flower shop or a bakery.
I suddenly remembered that.
MISS INOUE, CAN I TAKE YOU HOME?

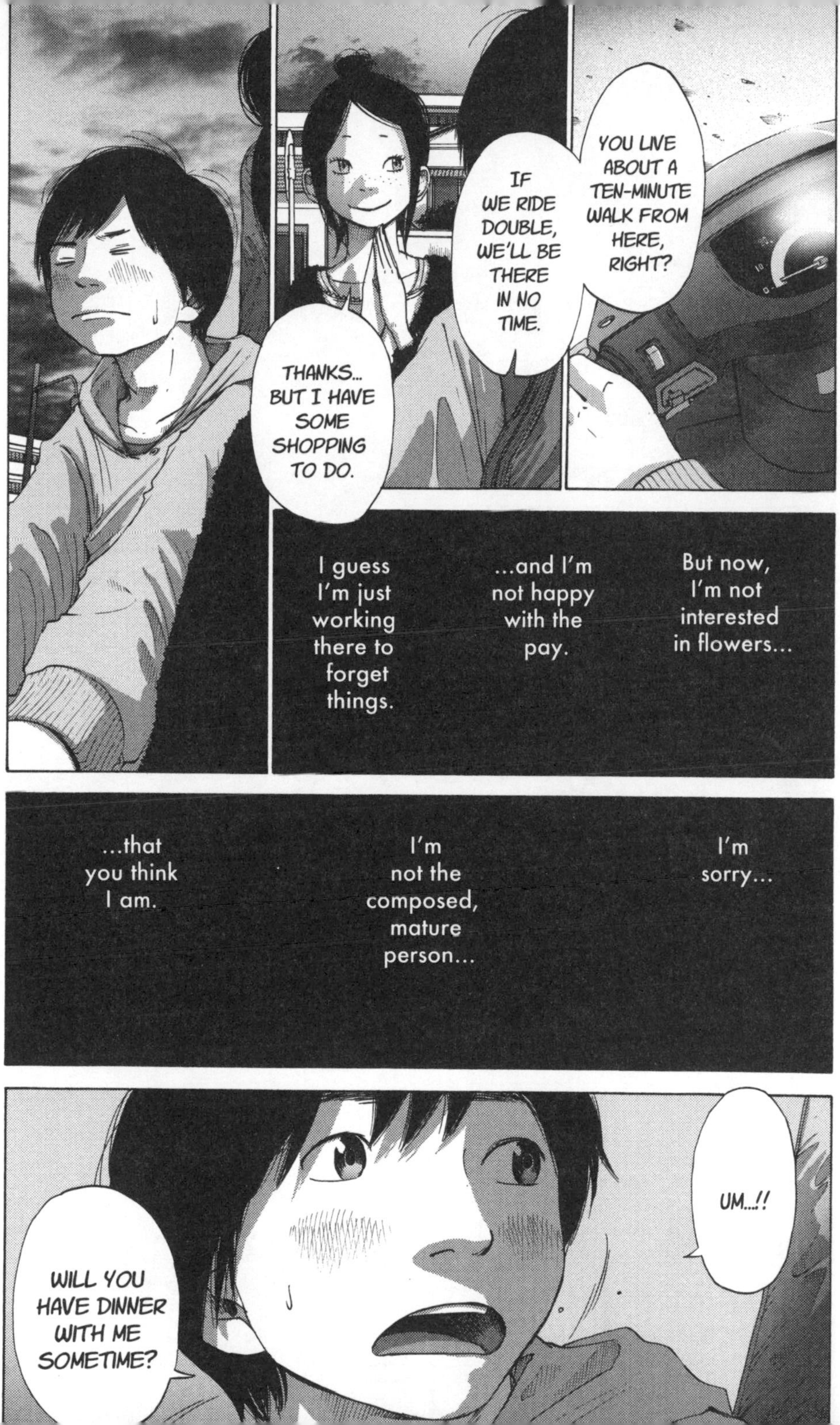
YOU LIVE ABOUT A TEN-MINUTE WALK FROM HERE, RIGHT?
IF WE RIDE DOUBLE, WE'LL BE THERE IN NO TIME.
THANKS... BUT I HAVE SOME SHOPPING TO DO.
But now, I'm not interested in flowers...
...and I'm not happy with the pay.
I guess I'm just working there to forget things.
I'm sorry...
I'm not the composed, mature person...
...that you think I am.
UM...!!
WILL YOU HAVE DINNER WITH ME SOMETIME?

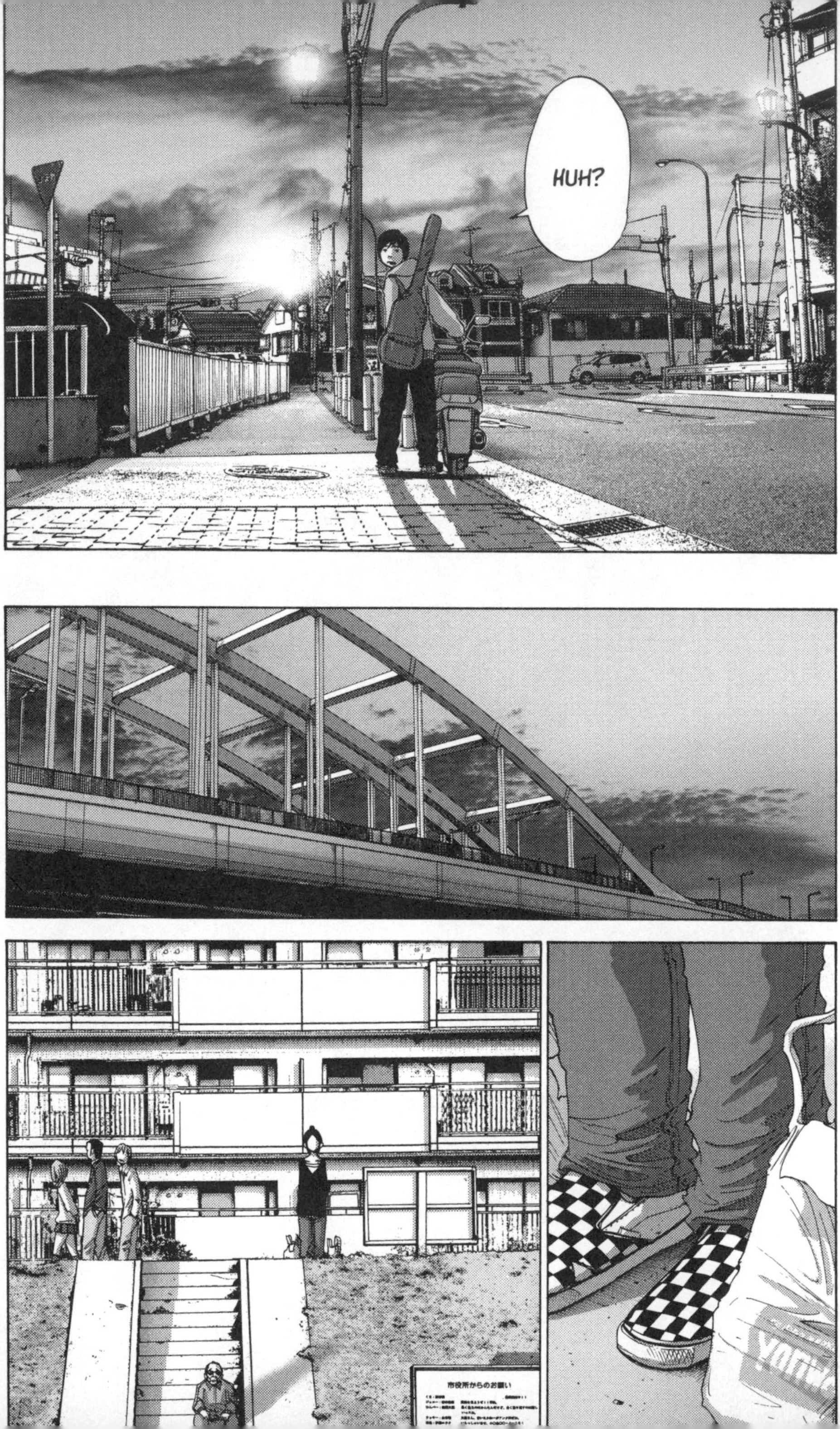
HUH?
市役所からのお願い

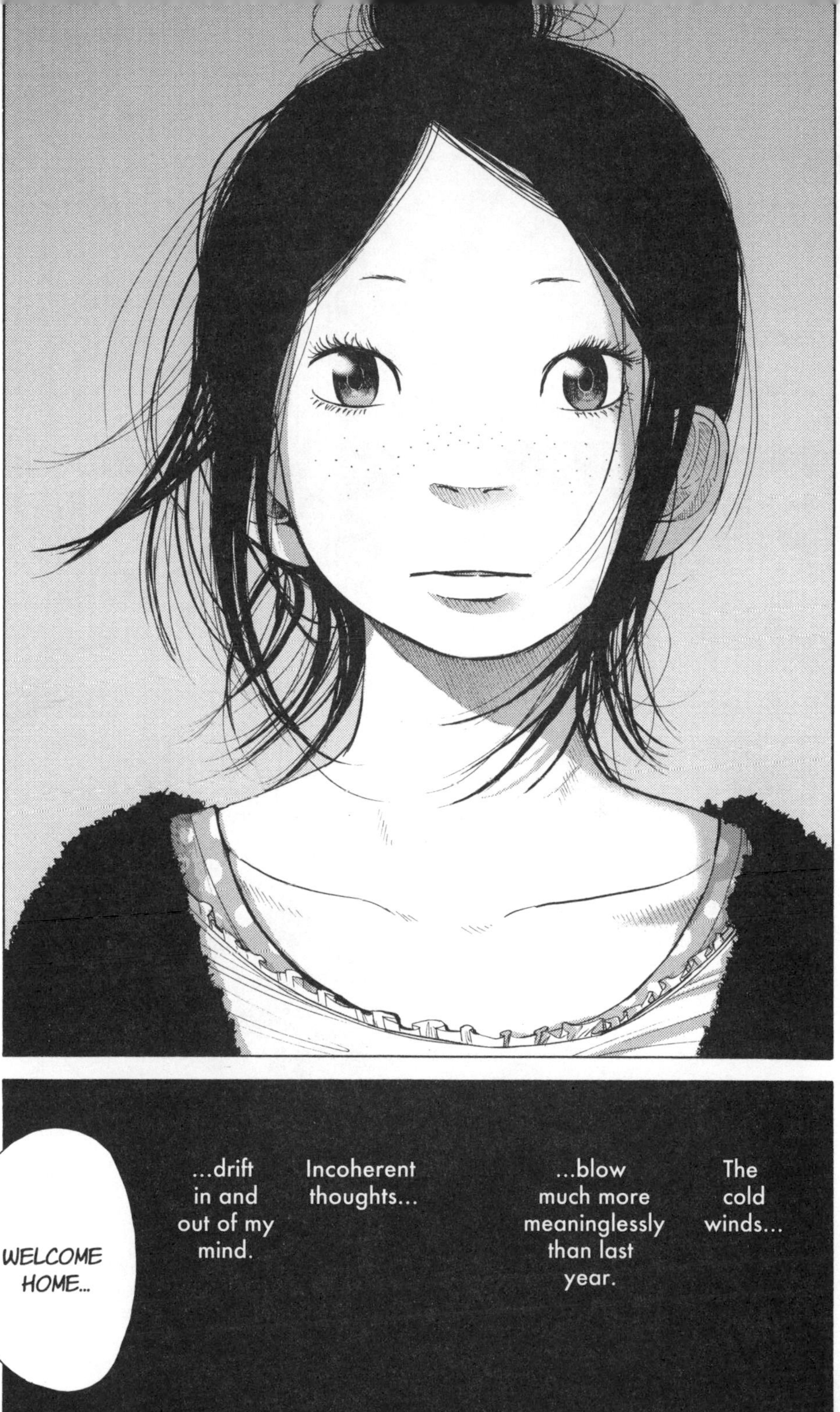
The cold winds...
...blow much more meaninglessly than last year.
Incoherent thoughts...
...drift in and out of my mind.
WELCOME HOME...

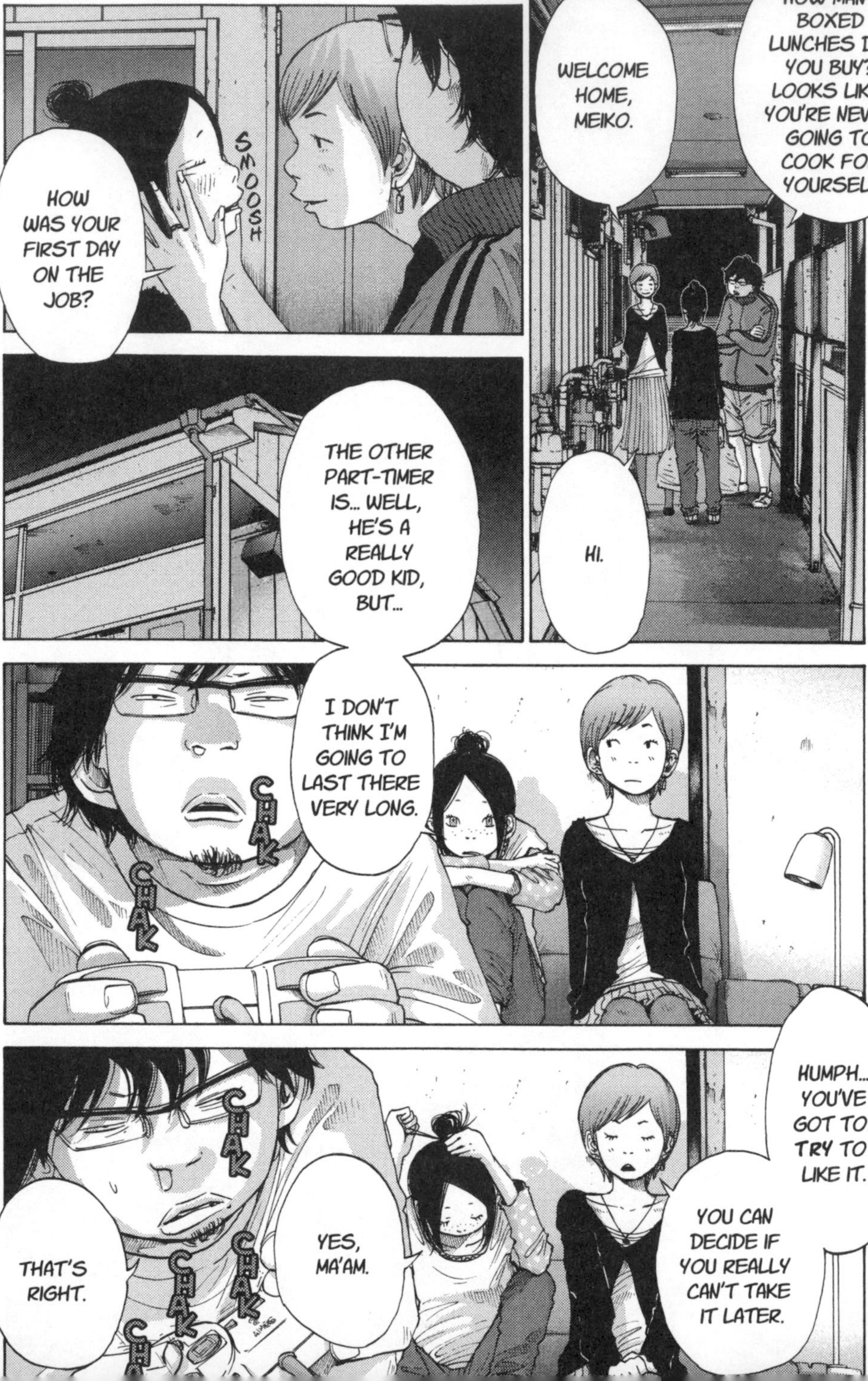
WOW... HOW MANY BOXED LUNCHES DID YOU BUY? LOOKS LIKE YOU'RE NEVER GOING TO COOK FOR YOURSELF.
WELCOME HOME, MEIKO.
HI.
SMOOSH
HOW WAS YOUR FIRST DAY ON THE JOB?
THE OTHER PART-TIMER IS... WELL, HE'S A REALLY GOOD KID, BUT...
I DON'T THINK I'M GOING TO LAST THERE VERY LONG.
CHAK
CHAK
HUMPH... YOU'VE GOT TO TRY TO LIKE IT.
YOU CAN DECIDE IF YOU REALLY CAN'T TAKE IT LATER.
CHAK
YES, MA'AM.
CHAK
CHAK
THAT'S RIGHT.

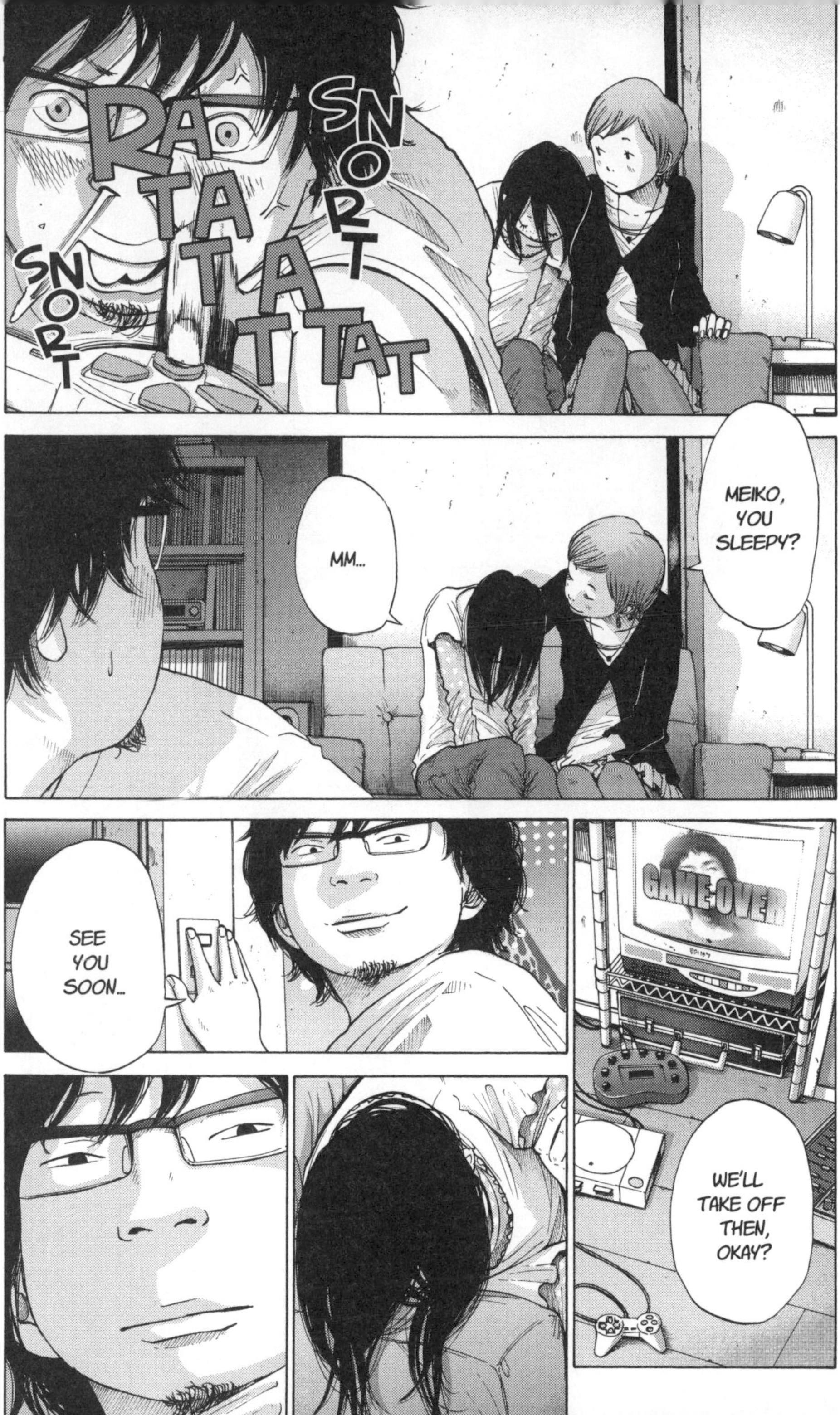
SNORT
RATATATTAT
SNORT
MEIKO, YOU SLEEPY?
MM...
GAME OVER
WE'LL TAKE OFF THEN, OKAY?
SEE YOU SOON...

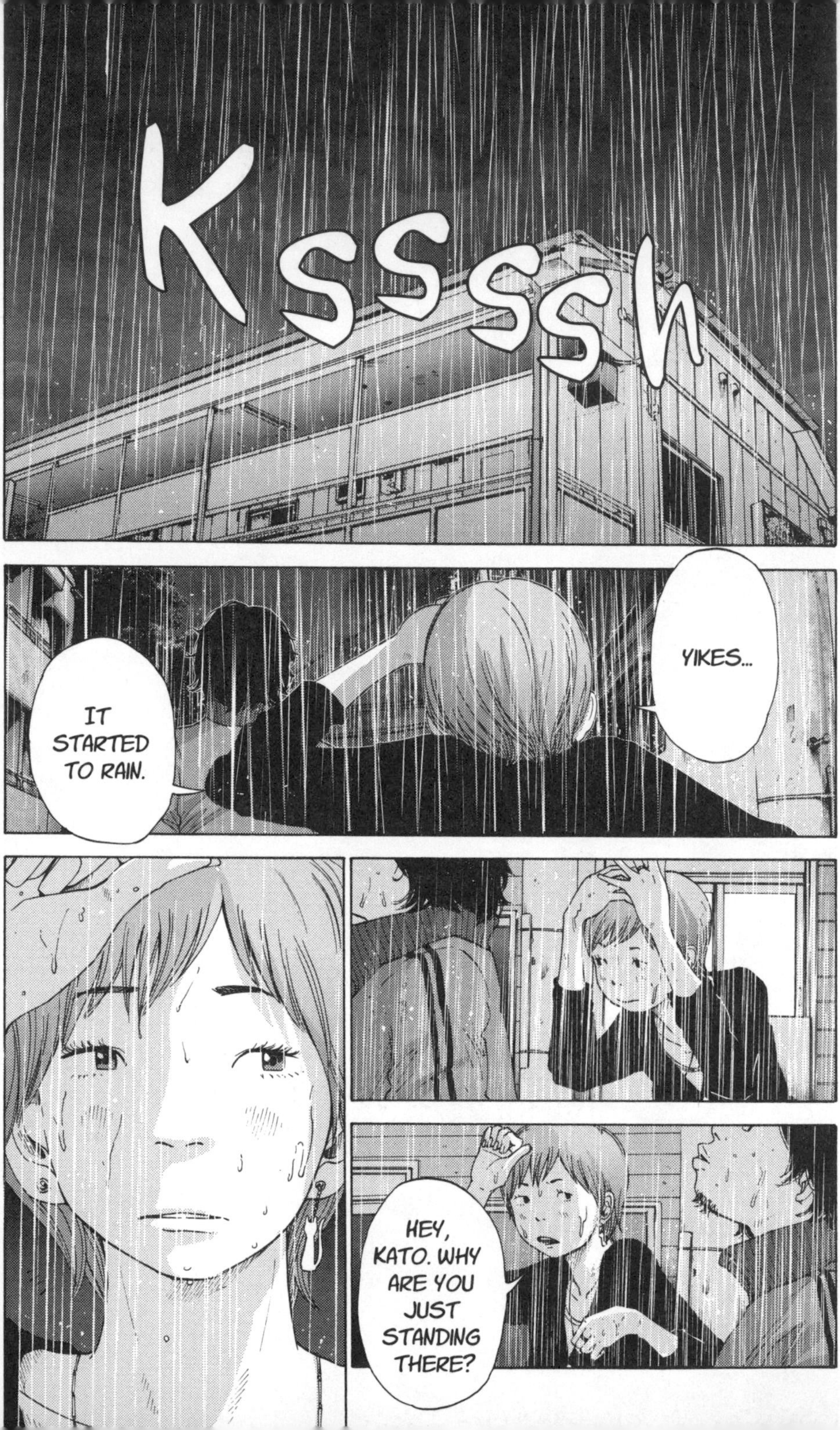
Kssssh
YIKES...
IT STARTED TO RAIN.
HEY, KATO. WHY ARE YOU JUST STANDING THERE?

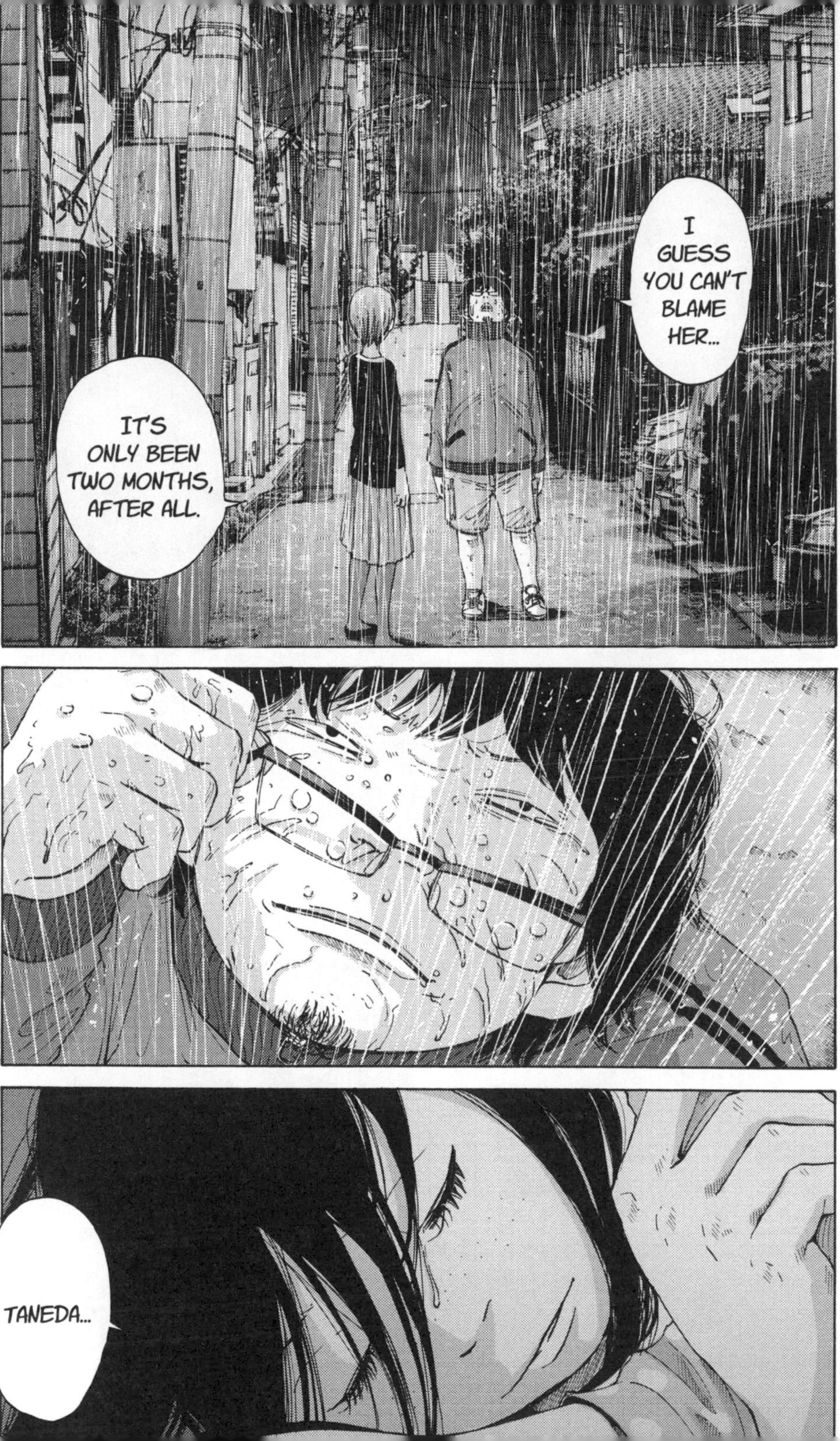
I GUESS YOU CAN'T BLAME HER...
IT'S ONLY BEEN TWO MONTHS, AFTER ALL.
TANEDA...

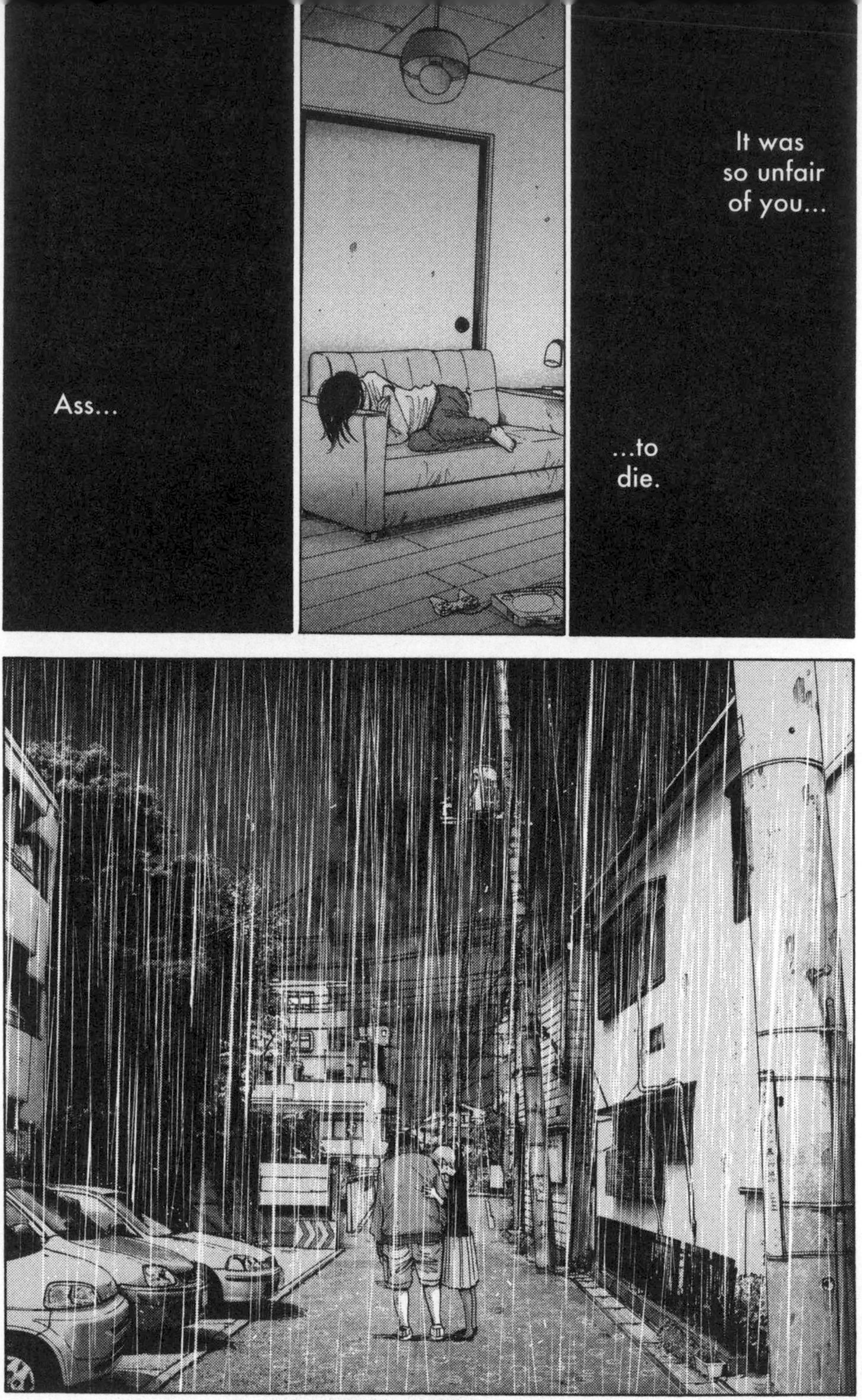
It was so unfair of you...
...to die.
Ass...

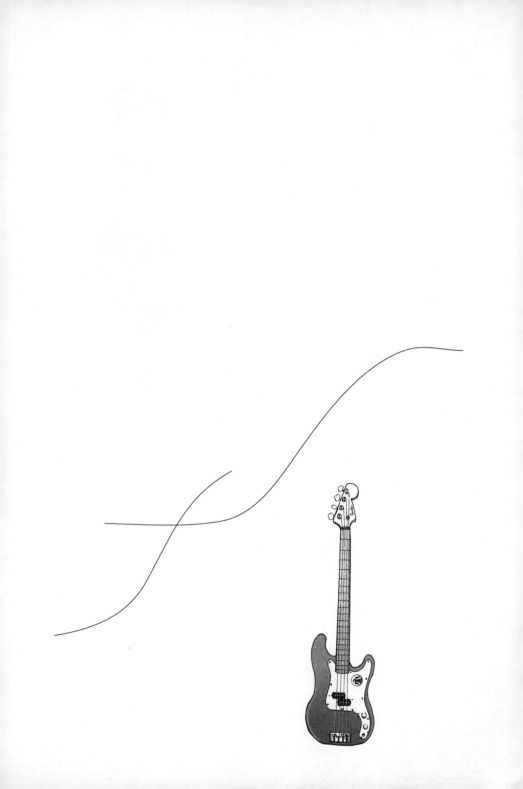

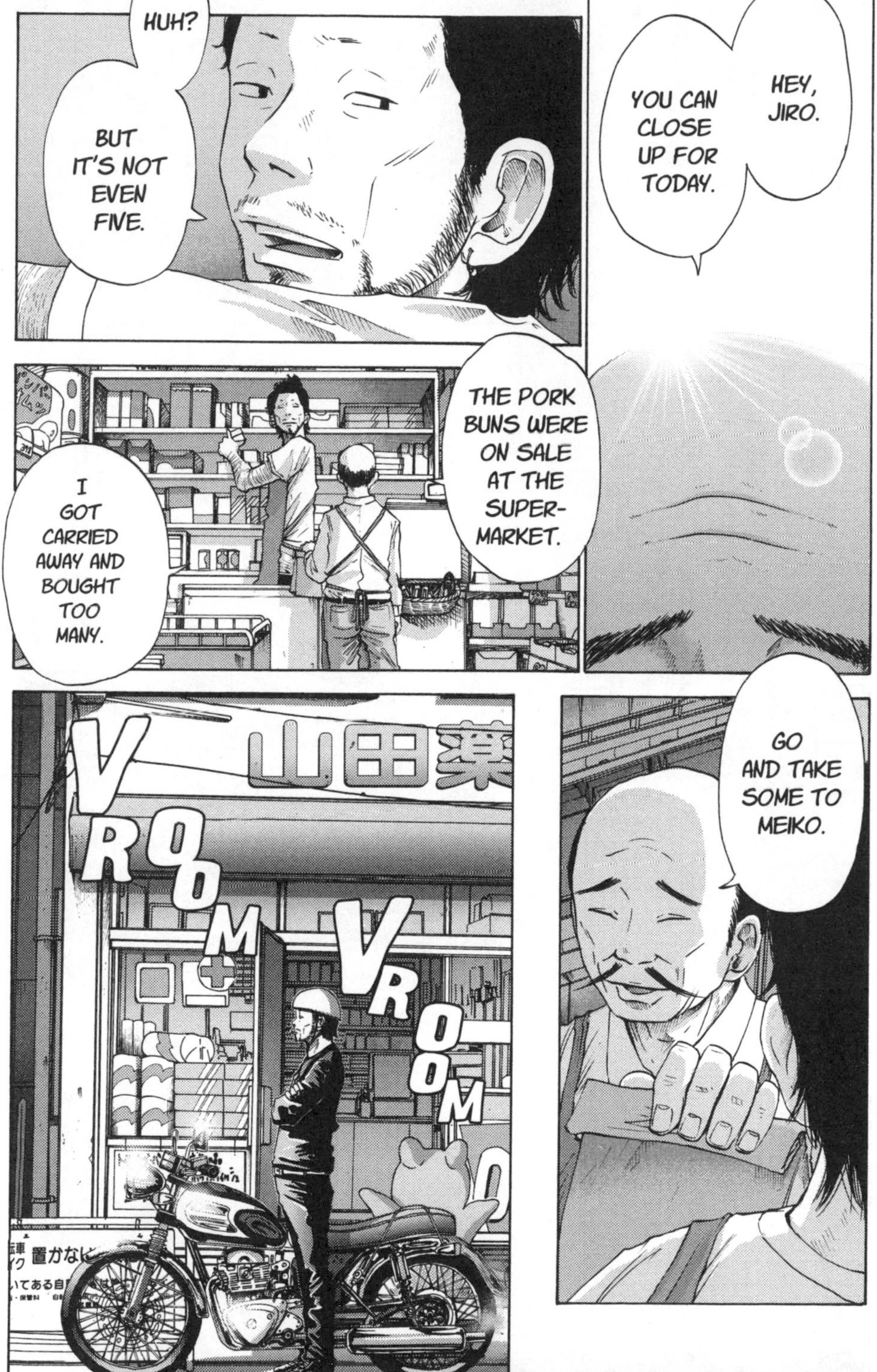
HEY, JIRO.
YOU CAN CLOSE UP FOR TODAY.
HUH?
BUT IT'S NOT EVEN FIVE.
THE PORK BUNS WERE ON SALE AT THE SUPER-MARKET.
I GOT CARRIED AWAY AND BOUGHT TOO MANY.
GO AND TAKE SOME TO MEIKO.
山田薬
VROOM
VROOM

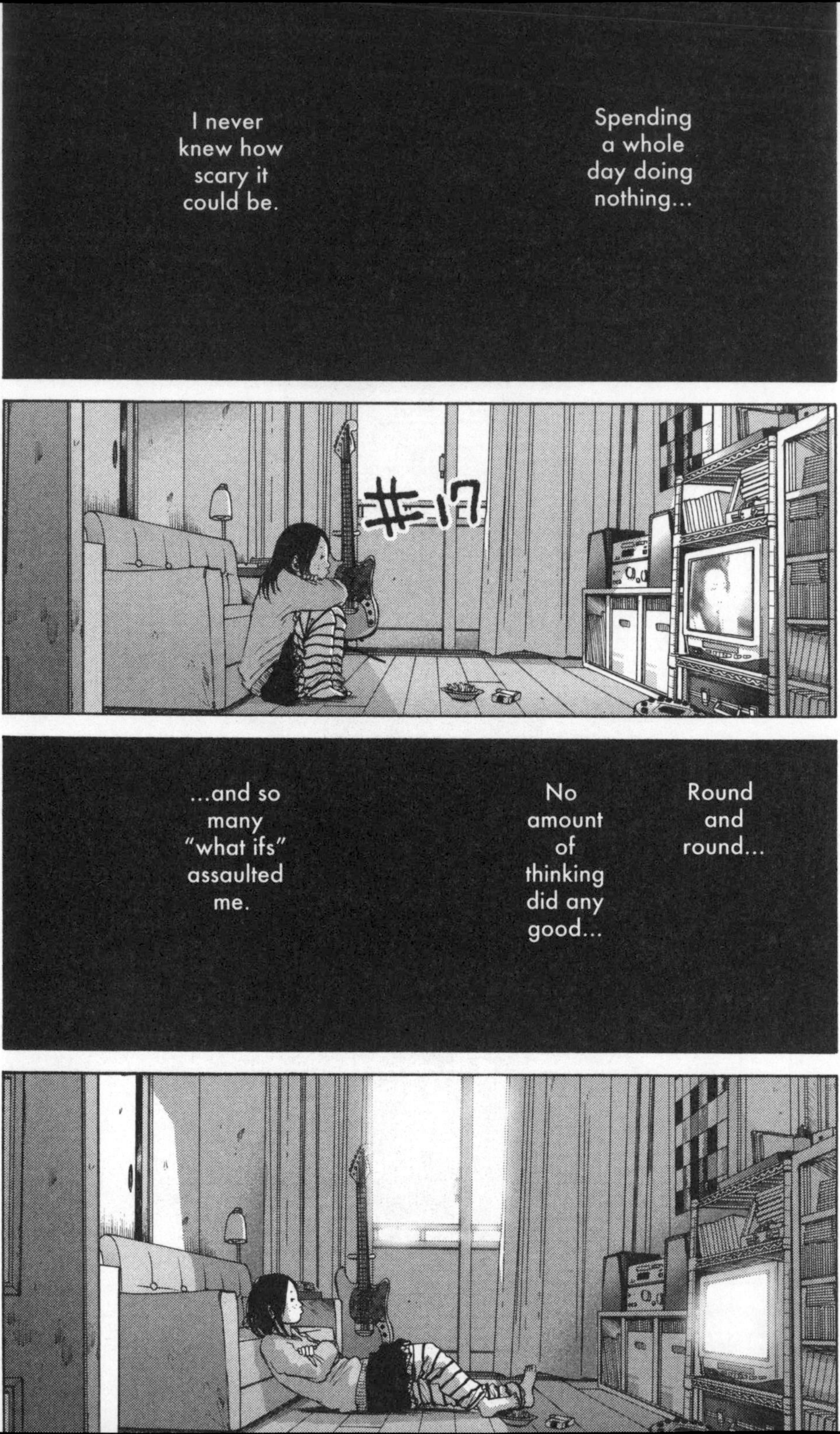
Spending a whole day doing nothing...
I never knew how scary it could be.
#17
Round and round...
No amount of thinking did any good...
...and so many "what ifs" assaulted me.

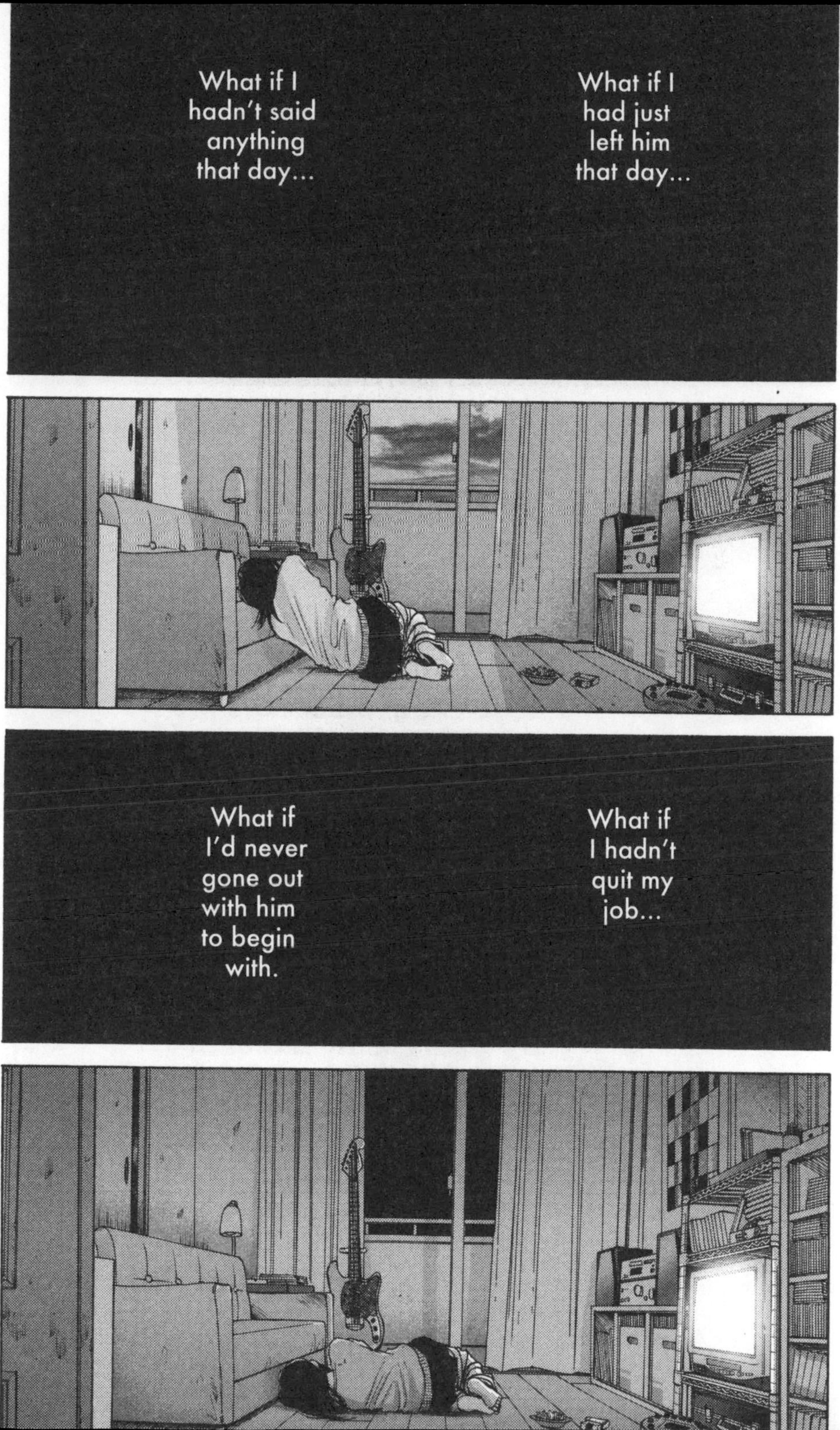
What if I had just left him that day...
What if I hadn't said anything that day...
What if I hadn't quit my job...
What if I'd never gone out with him to begin with.

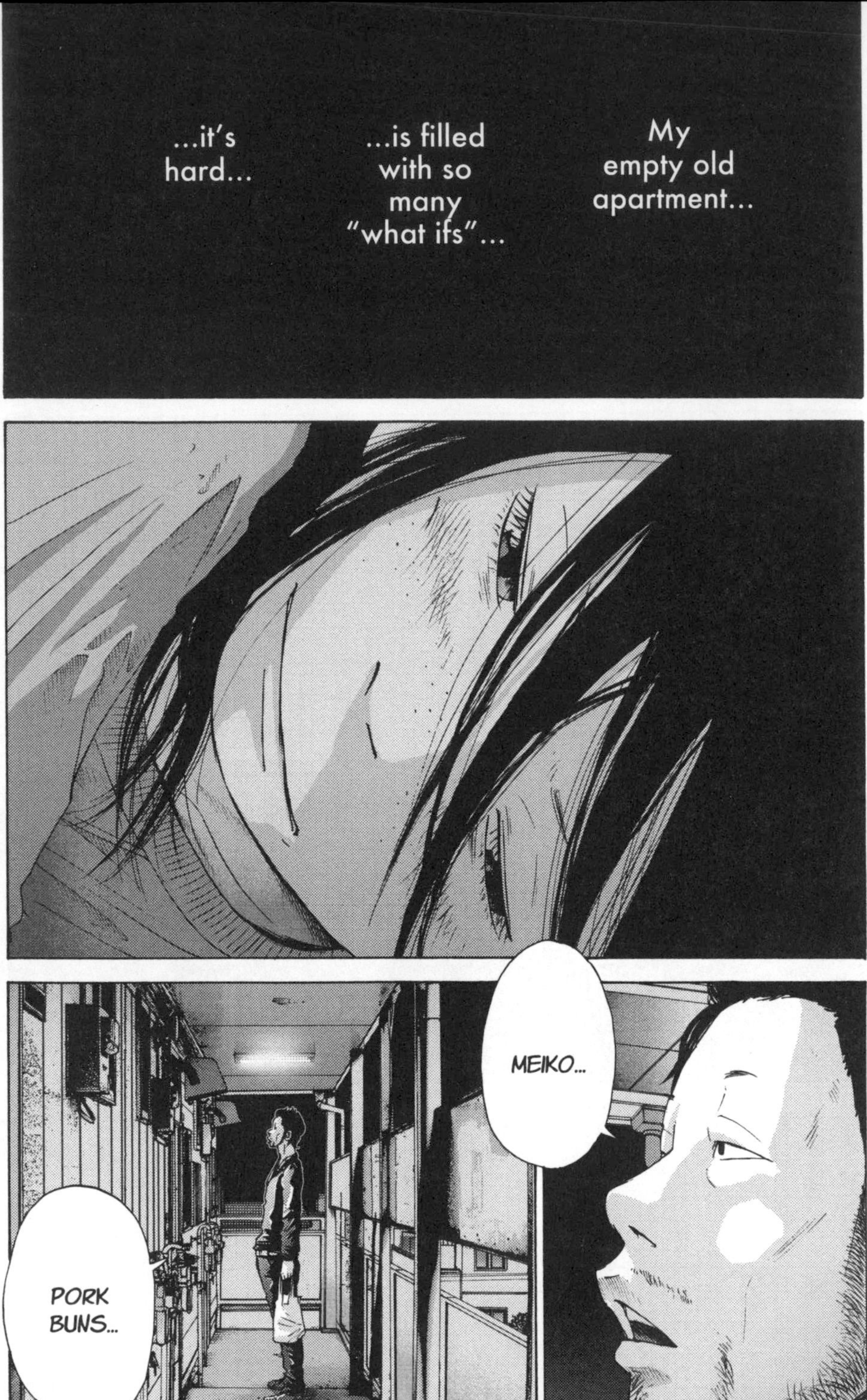
My empty old apartment...
...is filled with so many "what ifs"...
...it's hard...
MEIKO...
PORK BUNS...

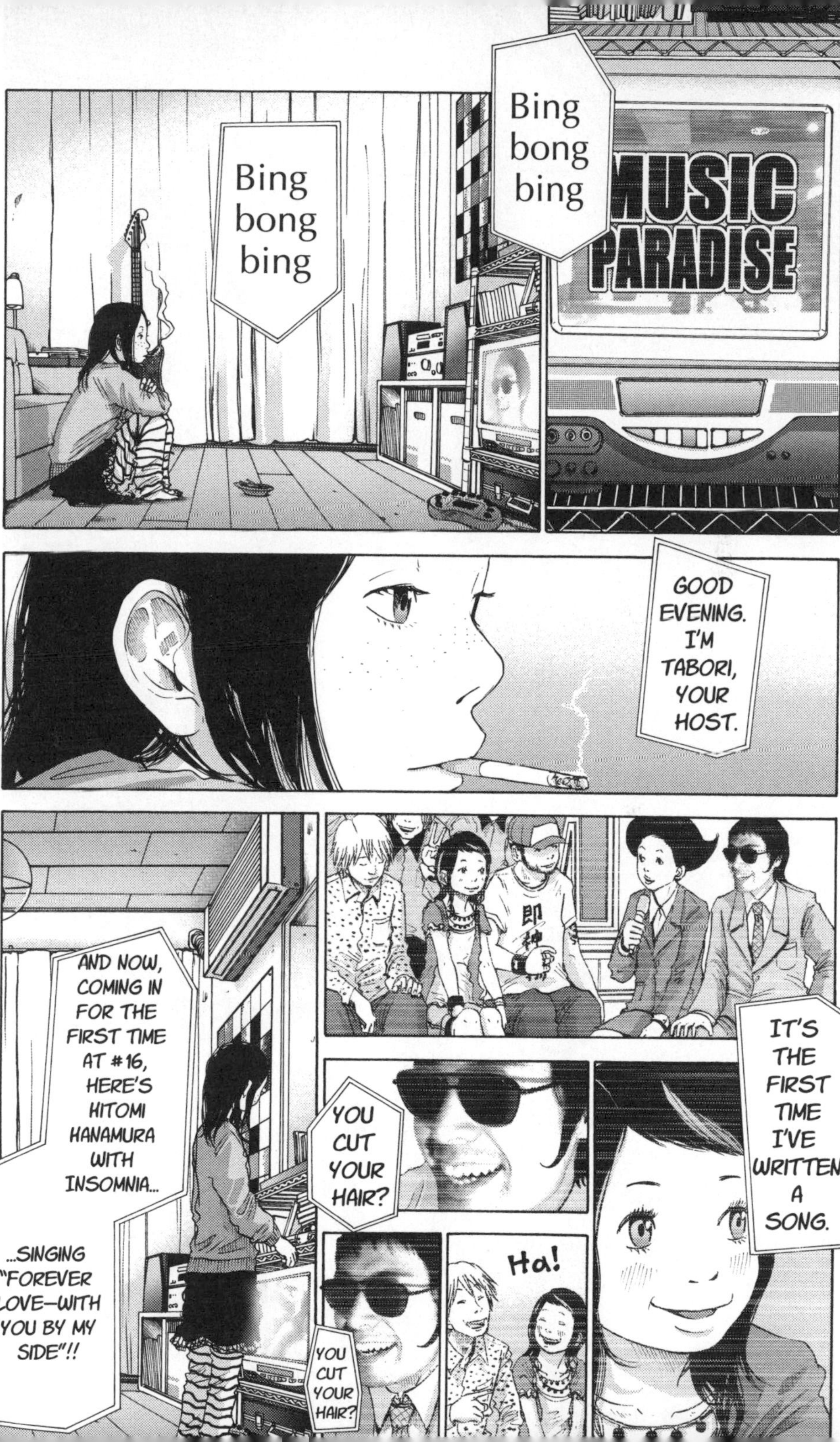

Bing bong bing
MUSIC PARADISE
Bing bong bing
GOOD EVENING. I'M TABORI, YOUR HOST.
IT'S THE FIRST TIME I'VE WRITTEN A SONG.
YOU CUT YOUR HAIR?
Ha!
YOU CUT YOUR HAIR?
AND NOW, COMING IN FOR THE FIRST TIME AT #16, HERE'S HITOMI HANAMURA WITH INSOMNIA...
...SINGING "FOREVER LOVE—WITH YOU BY MY SIDE"!!

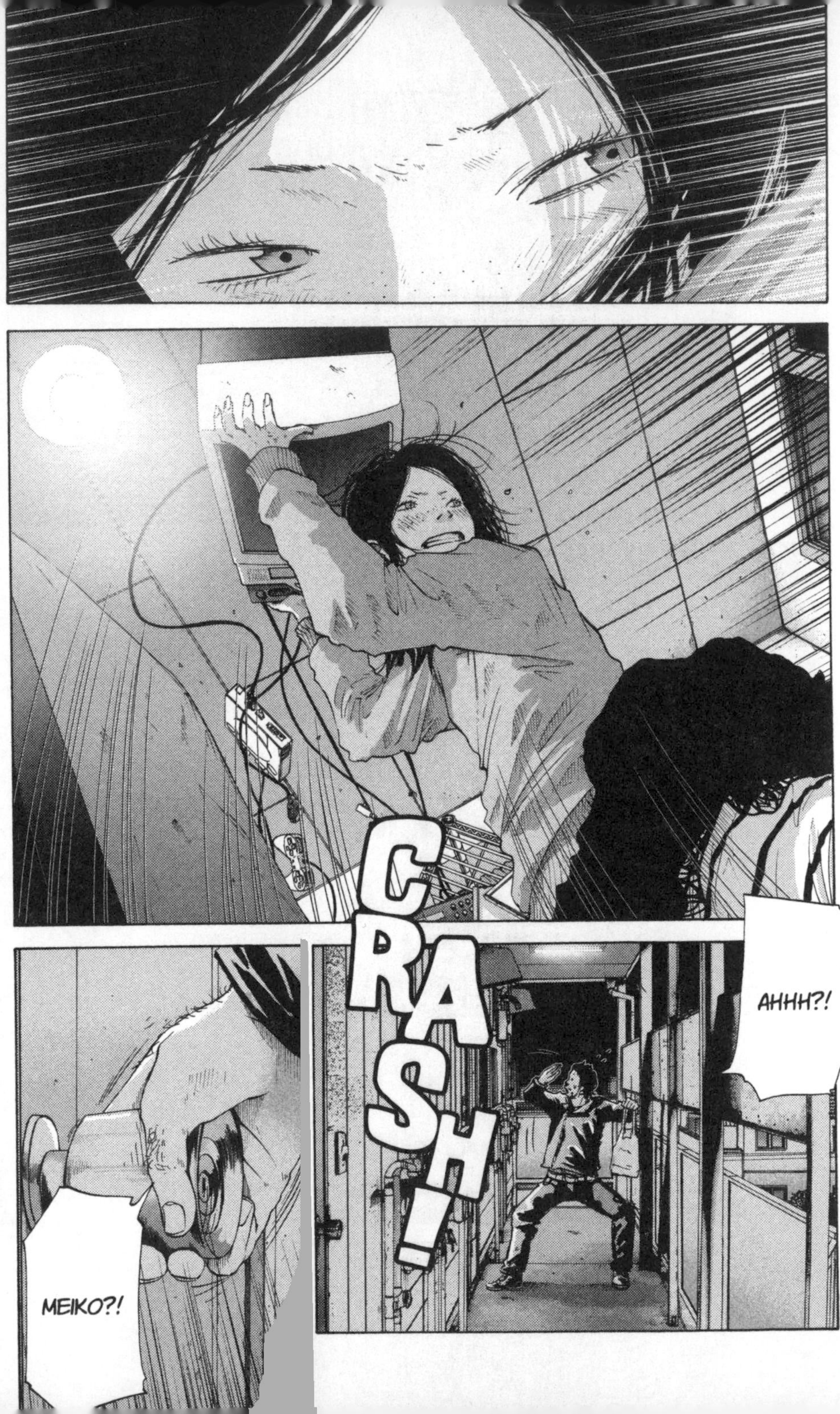
CRASH!
AHHH?!
MEIKO?!

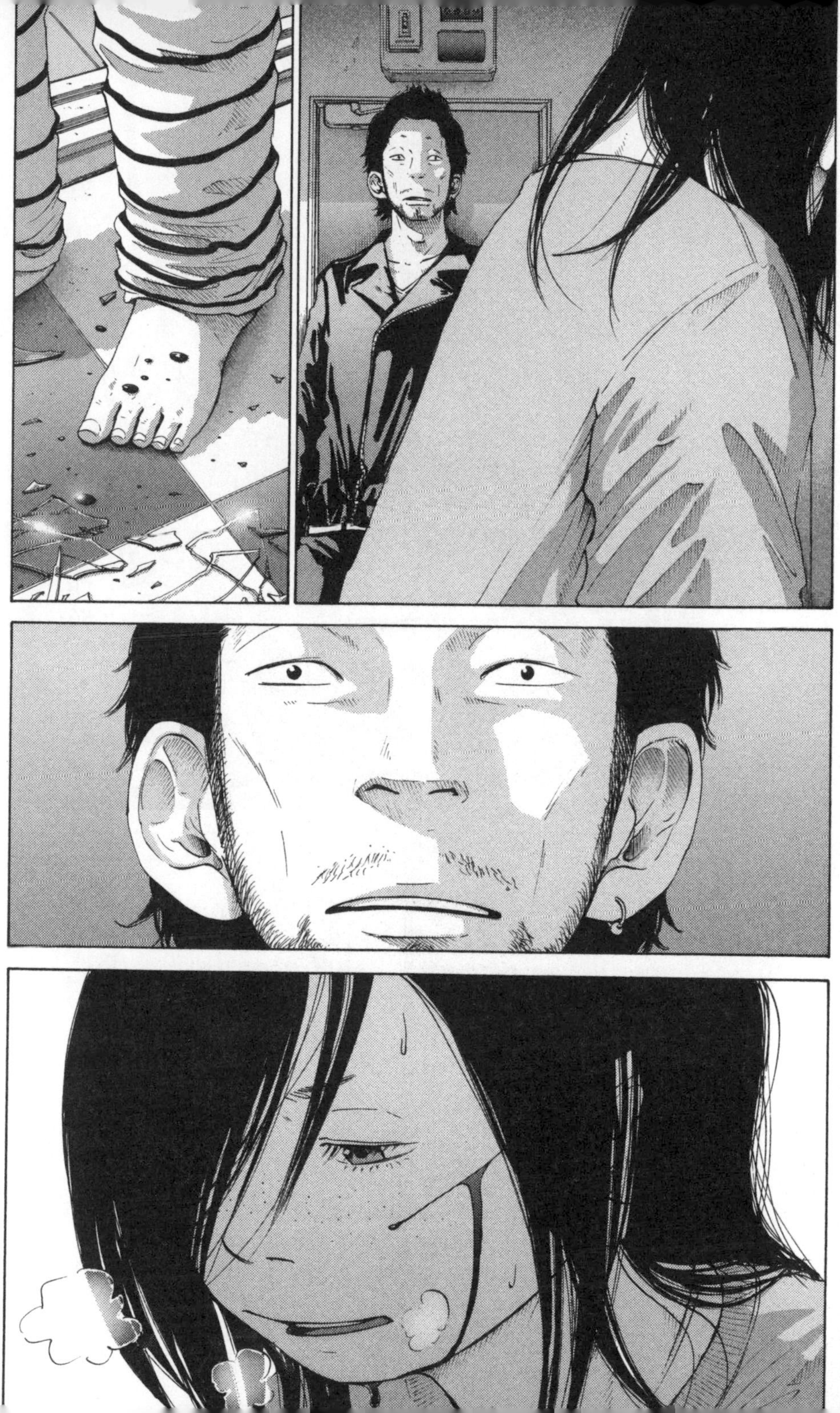

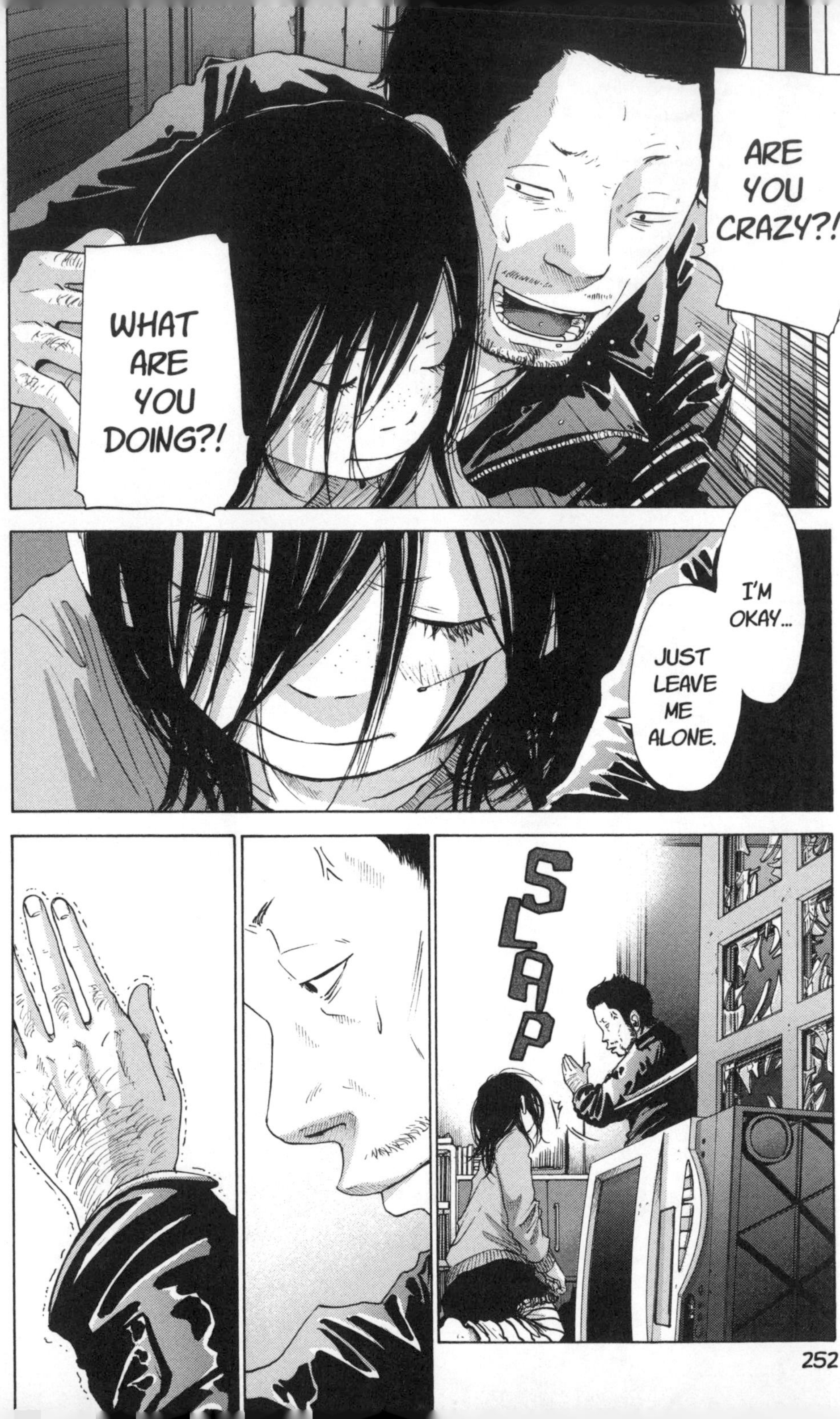
ARE YOU CRAZY?!
WHAT ARE YOU DOING?!
I'M OKAY... JUST LEAVE ME ALONE.
SLAP

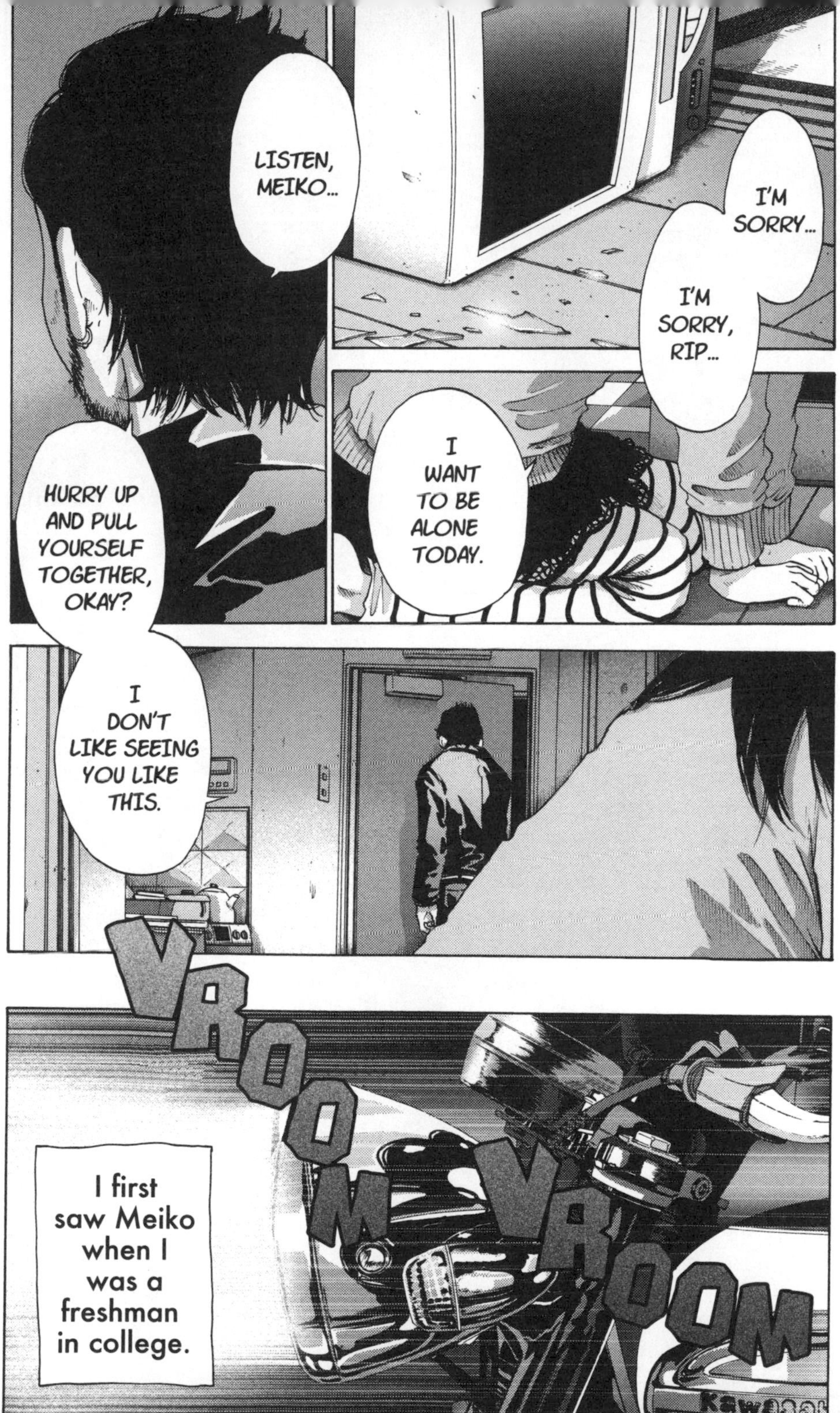
I'M SORRY...
I'M SORRY, RIP...
I WANT TO BE ALONE TODAY.
LISTEN, MEIKO...
HURRY UP AND PULL YOURSELF TOGETHER, OKAY?
I DON'T LIKE SEEING YOU LIKE THIS.
VROOM VROOM
I first saw Meiko when I was a freshman in college.

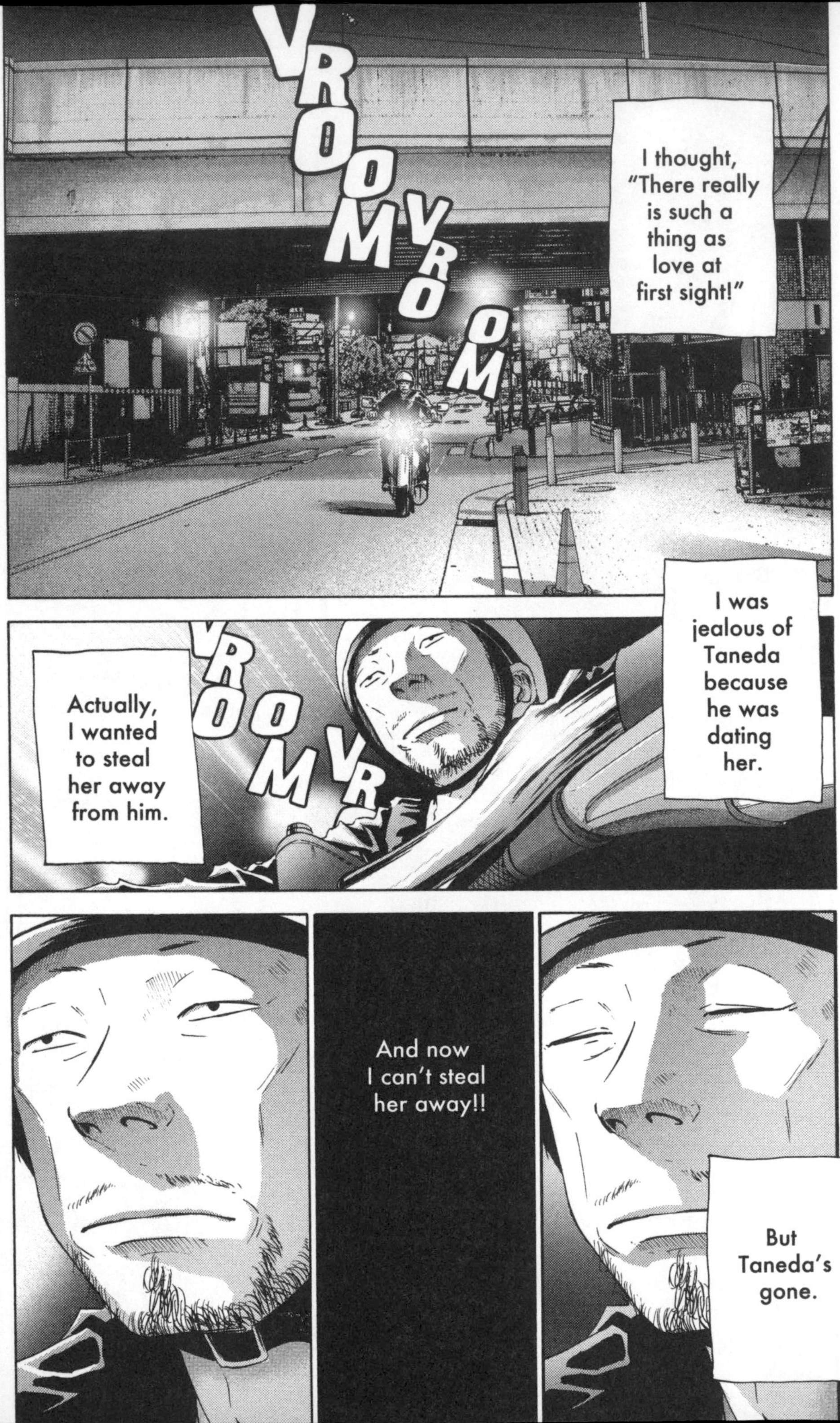
VROOOM
VROOM
I thought, "There really is such a thing as love at first sight!"
I was jealous of Taneda because he was dating her.
VROOOM
VR
Actually, I wanted to steal her away from him.
But Taneda's gone.
And now I can't steal her away!!

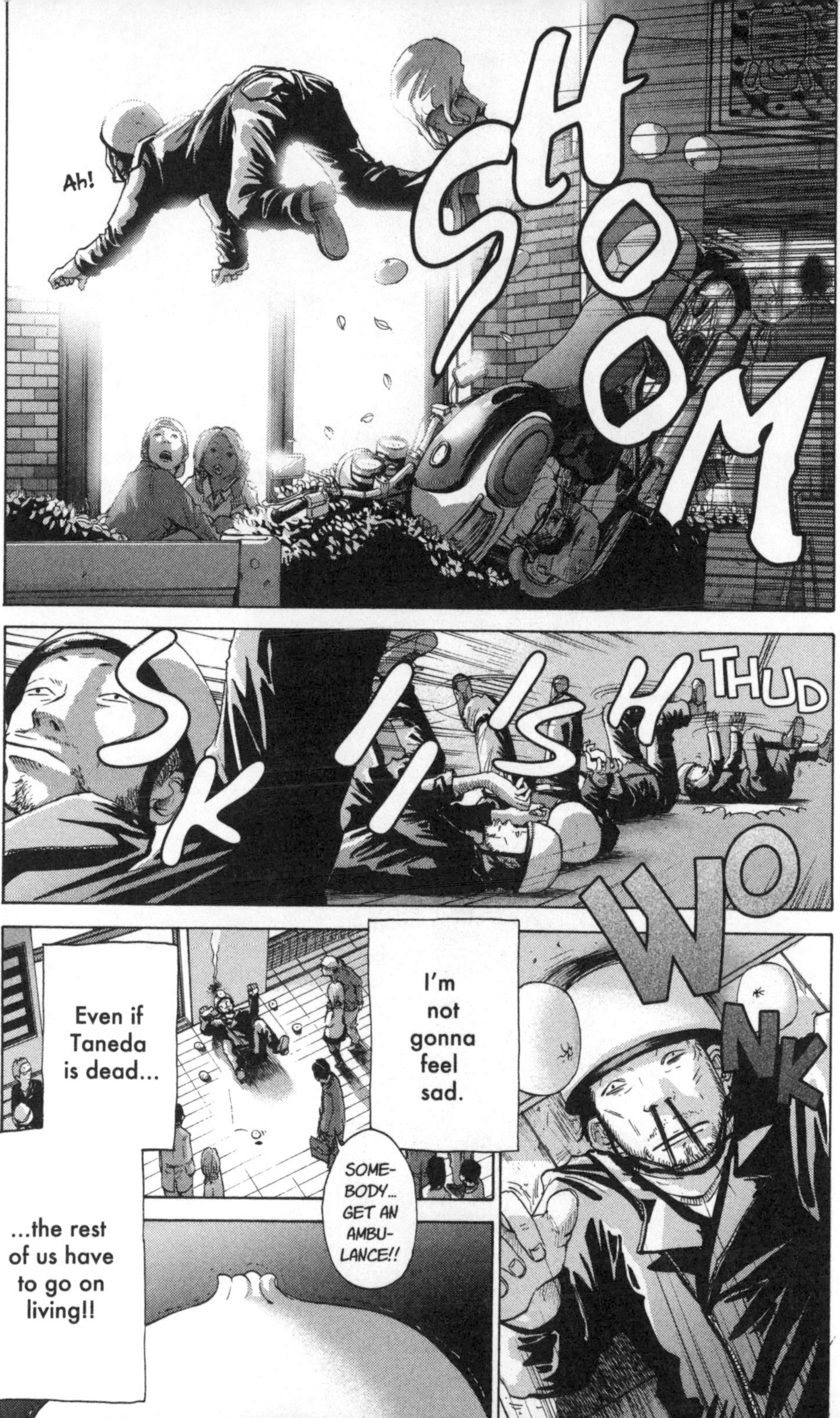
SHOOM
Ah!
THUD
SKIISH
WONK
I'm not gonna feel sad.
Even if Taneda is dead...
SOME-BODY... GET AN AMBU-LANCE!!
...the rest of us have to go on living!!

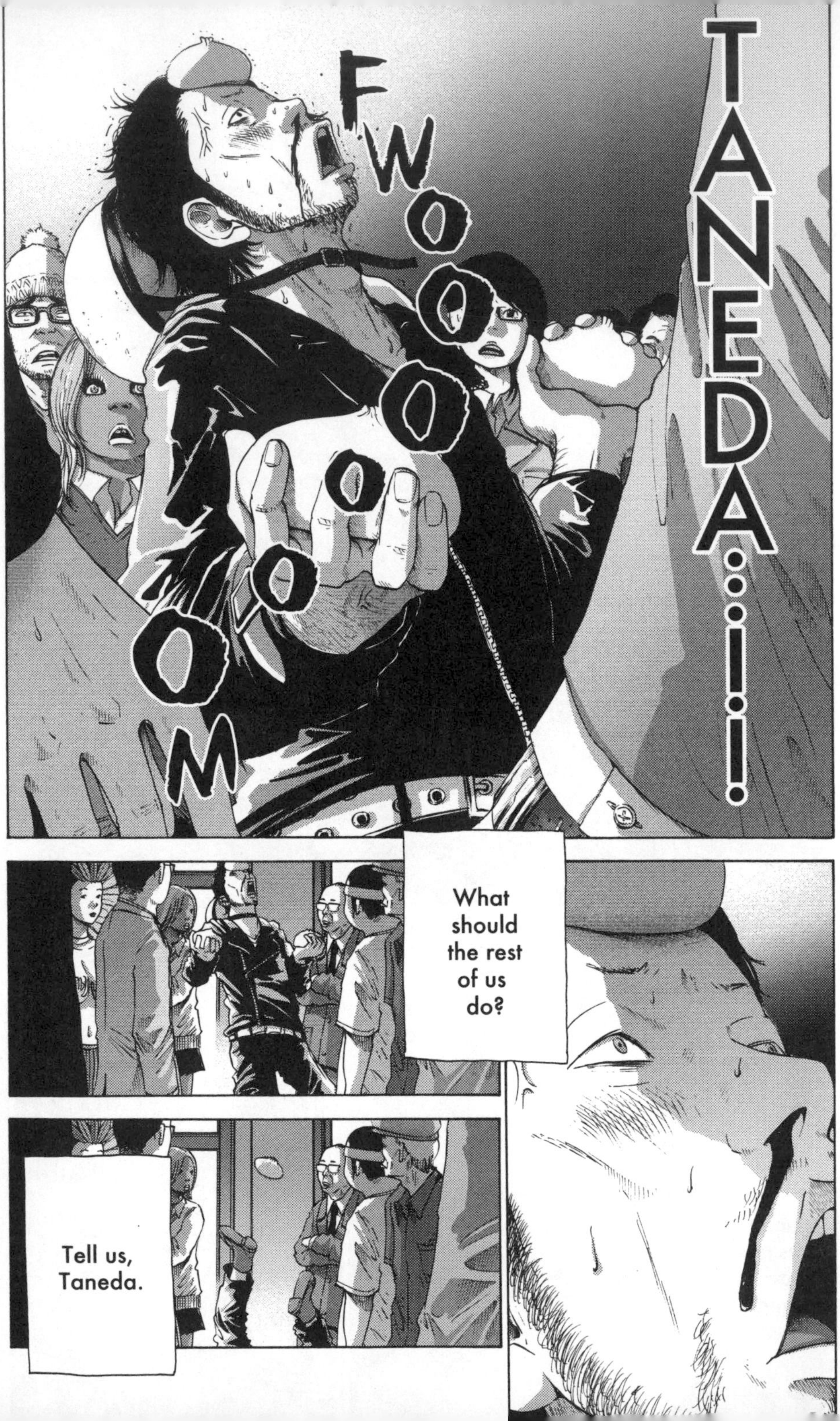
TANEDA...!!!
FWOOOOOOM
What should the rest of us do?
Tell us, Taneda.

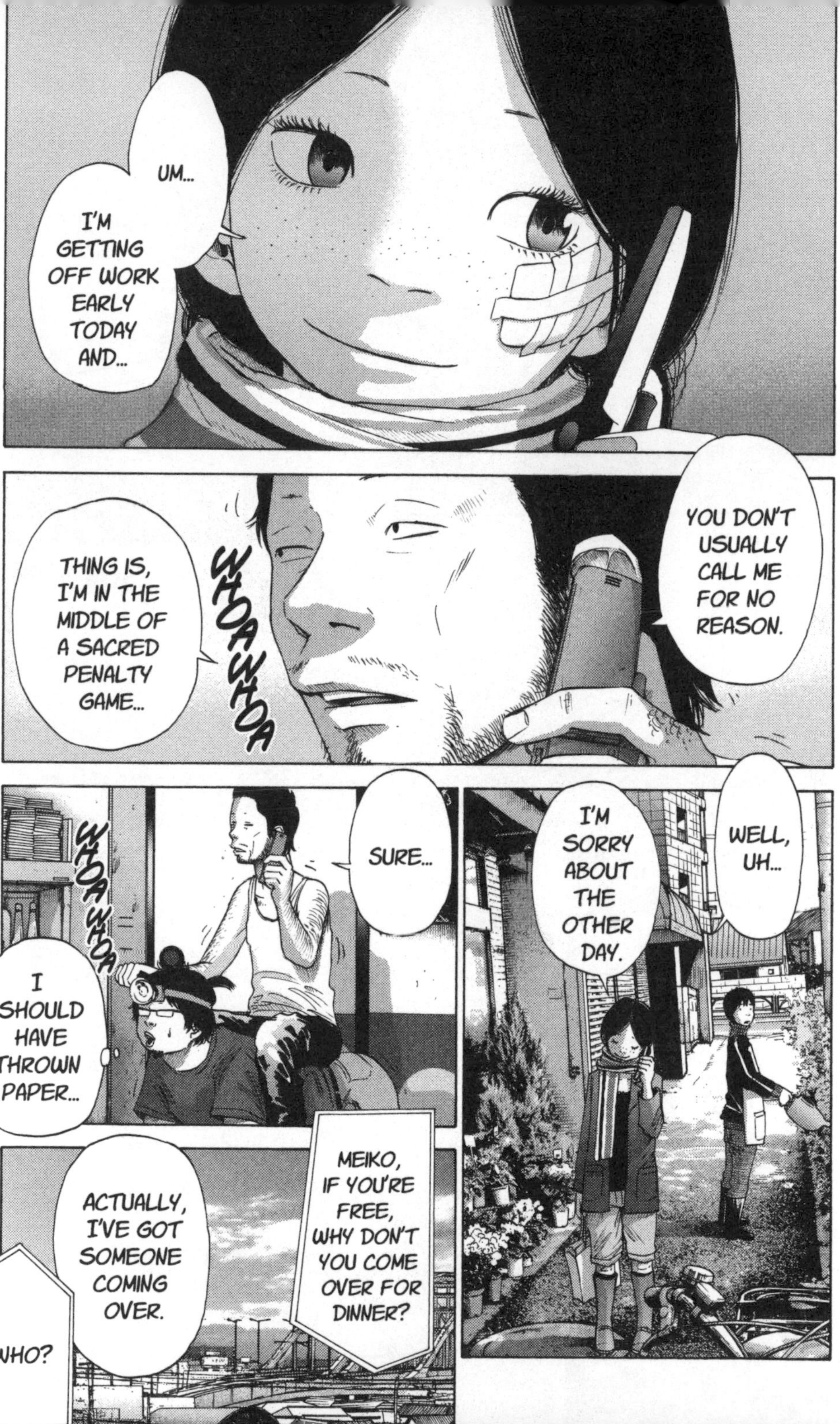
UM...
I'M GETTING OFF WORK EARLY TODAY AND...
YOU DON'T USUALLY CALL ME FOR NO REASON.
WHOAWHOA
THING IS, I'M IN THE MIDDLE OF A SACRED PENALTY GAME...
WELL, UH...
I'M SORRY ABOUT THE OTHER DAY.
SURE...
WHOAWHOA
I SHOULD HAVE THROWN PAPER...
MEIKO, IF YOU'RE FREE, WHY DON'T YOU COME OVER FOR DINNER?
ACTUALLY, I'VE GOT SOMEONE COMING OVER.
WHO?

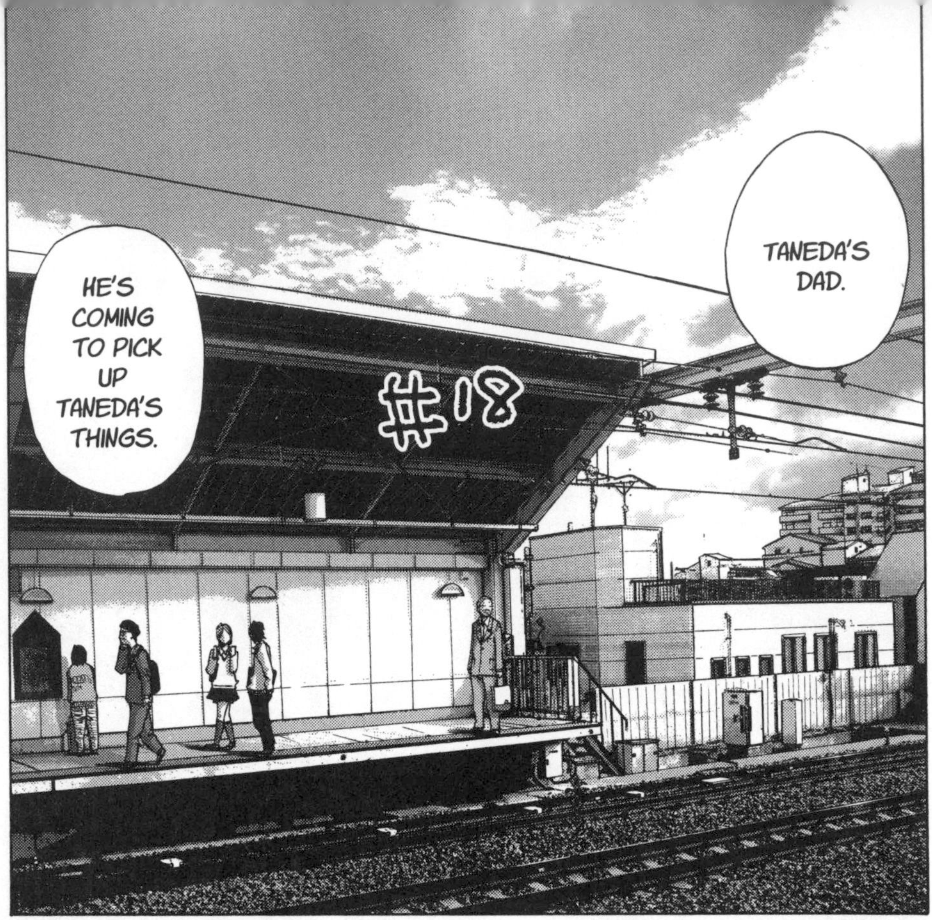
TANEDA'S DAD.
#18
HE'S COMING TO PICK UP TANEDA'S THINGS.

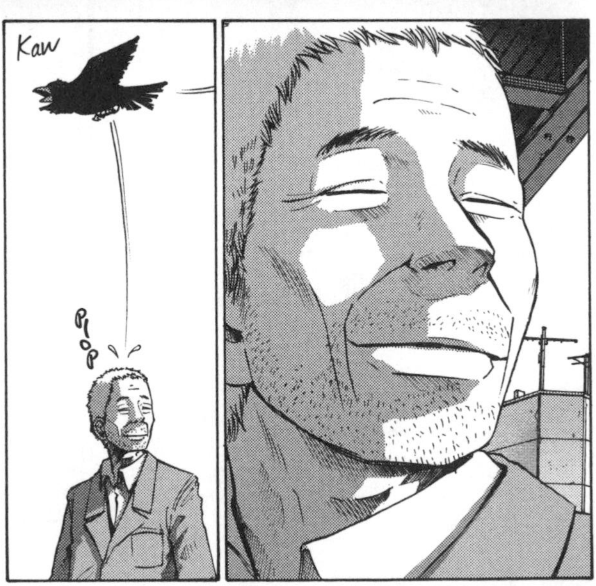
Kaw
PLOP

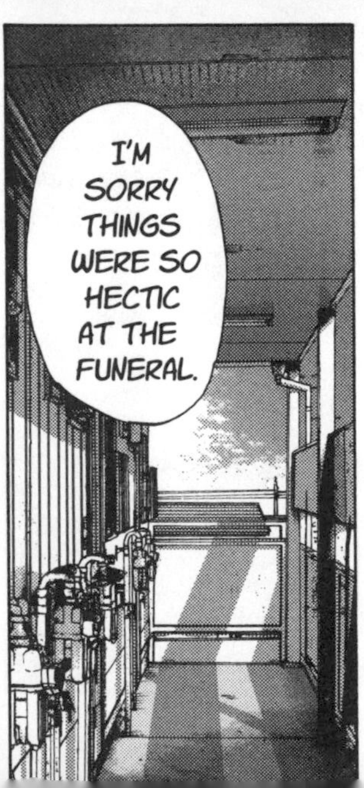
I'M SORRY THINGS WERE SO HECTIC AT THE FUNERAL.

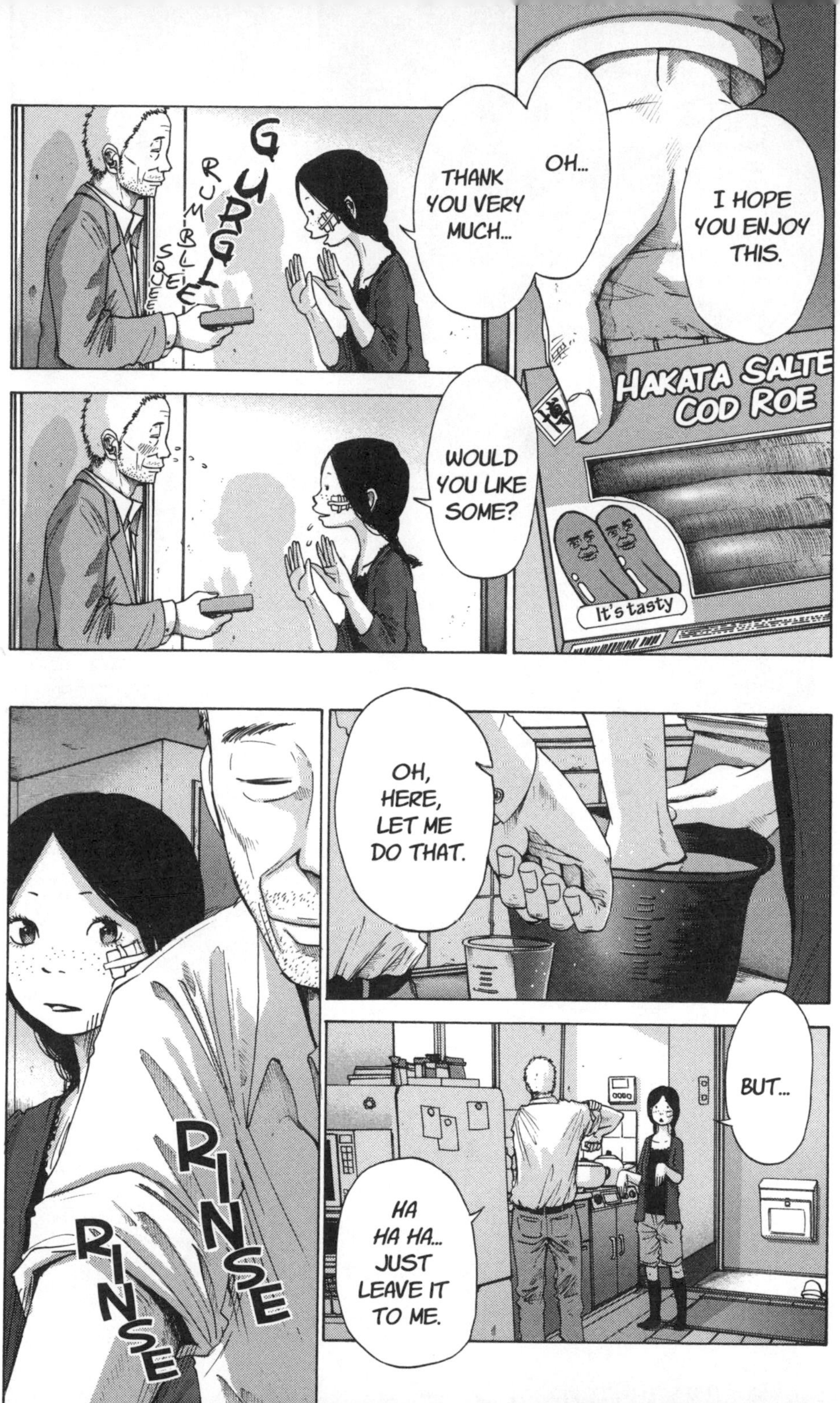
I HOPE YOU ENJOY THIS.
HAKATA SALTE COD ROE
It's tasty
OH...
THANK YOU VERY MUCH...
GURGLE
RUMBLE
SQUEE
WOULD YOU LIKE SOME?
OH, HERE, LET ME DO THAT.
BUT...
HA HA HA... JUST LEAVE IT TO ME.
RINSE
RINSE

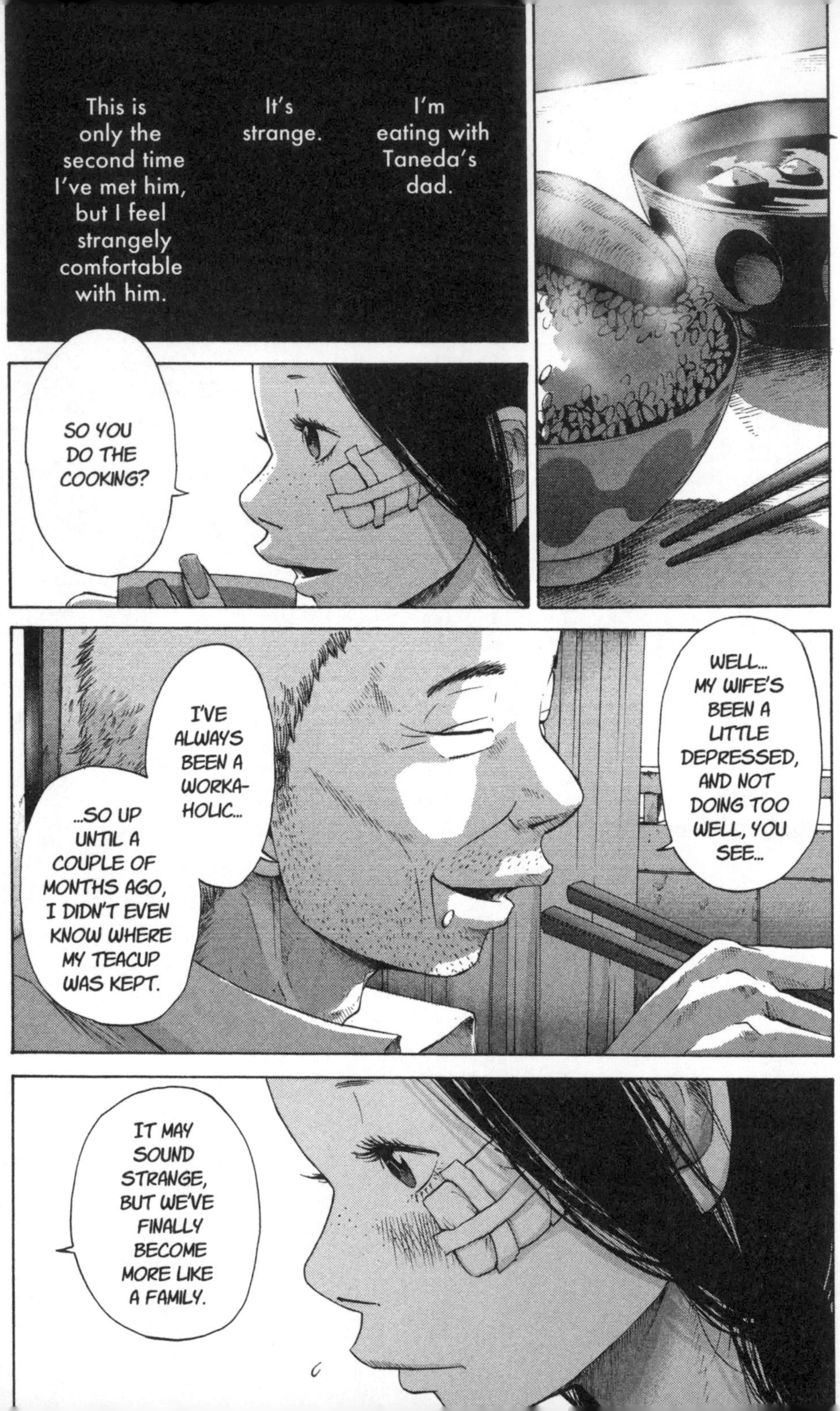
I'm eating with Taneda's dad.
It's strange.
This is only the second time I've met him, but I feel strangely comfortable with him.
SO YOU DO THE COOKING?
WELL... MY WIFE'S BEEN A LITTLE DEPRESSED, AND NOT DOING TOO WELL, YOU SEE...
I'VE ALWAYS BEEN A WORKA-HOLIC...
...SO UP UNTIL A COUPLE OF MONTHS AGO, I DIDN'T EVEN KNOW WHERE MY TEACUP WAS KEPT.
IT MAY SOUND STRANGE, BUT WE'VE FINALLY BECOME MORE LIKE A FAMILY.

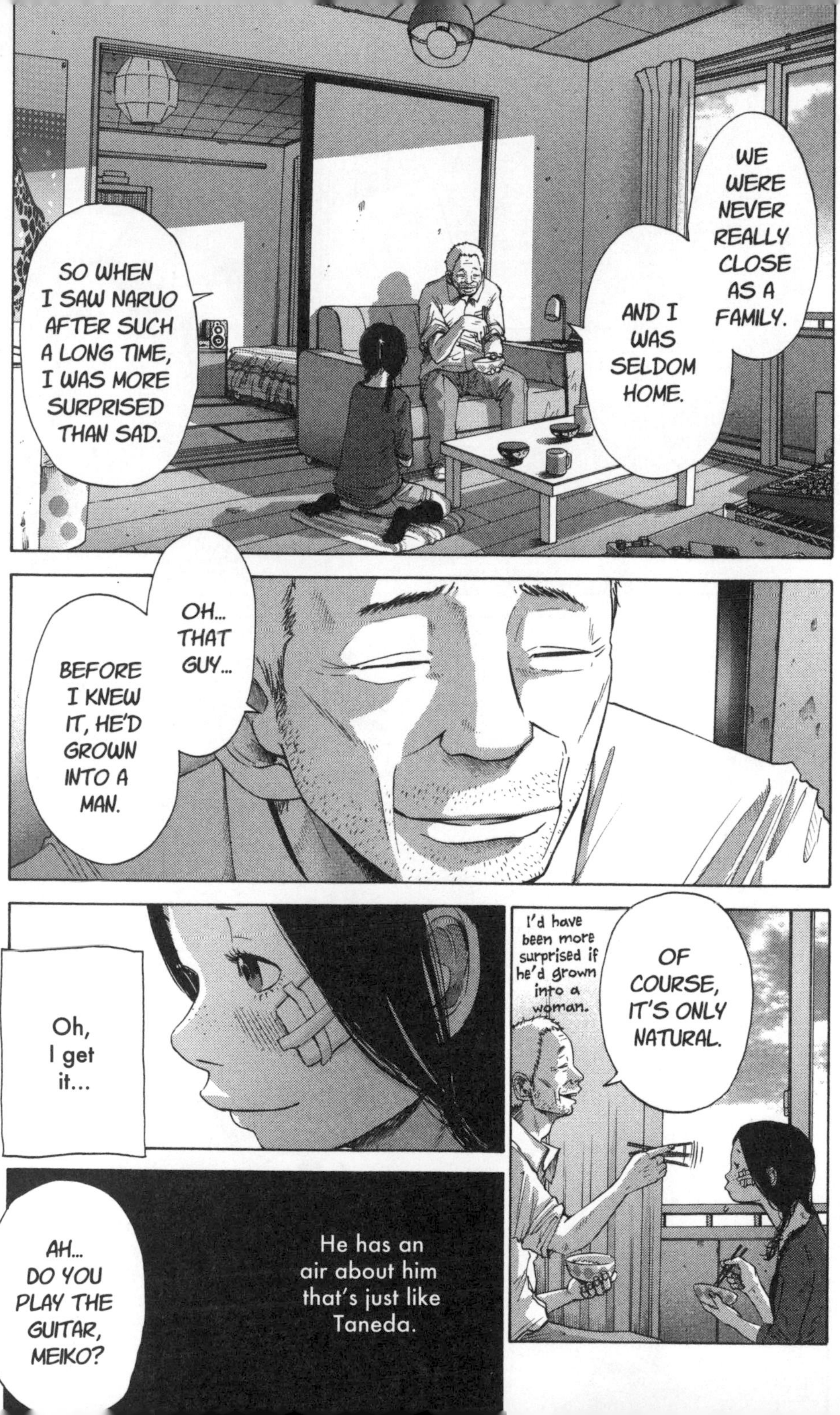
WE WERE NEVER REALLY CLOSE AS A FAMILY.
AND I WAS SELDOM HOME.
SO WHEN I SAW NARUO AFTER SUCH A LONG TIME, I WAS MORE SURPRISED THAN SAD.
OH... THAT GUY...
BEFORE I KNEW IT, HE'D GROWN INTO A MAN.
OF COURSE, IT'S ONLY NATURAL.
I'd have been more surprised if he'd grown into a woman.
Oh, I get it...
He has an air about him that's just like Taneda.
AH... DO YOU PLAY THE GUITAR, MEIKO?

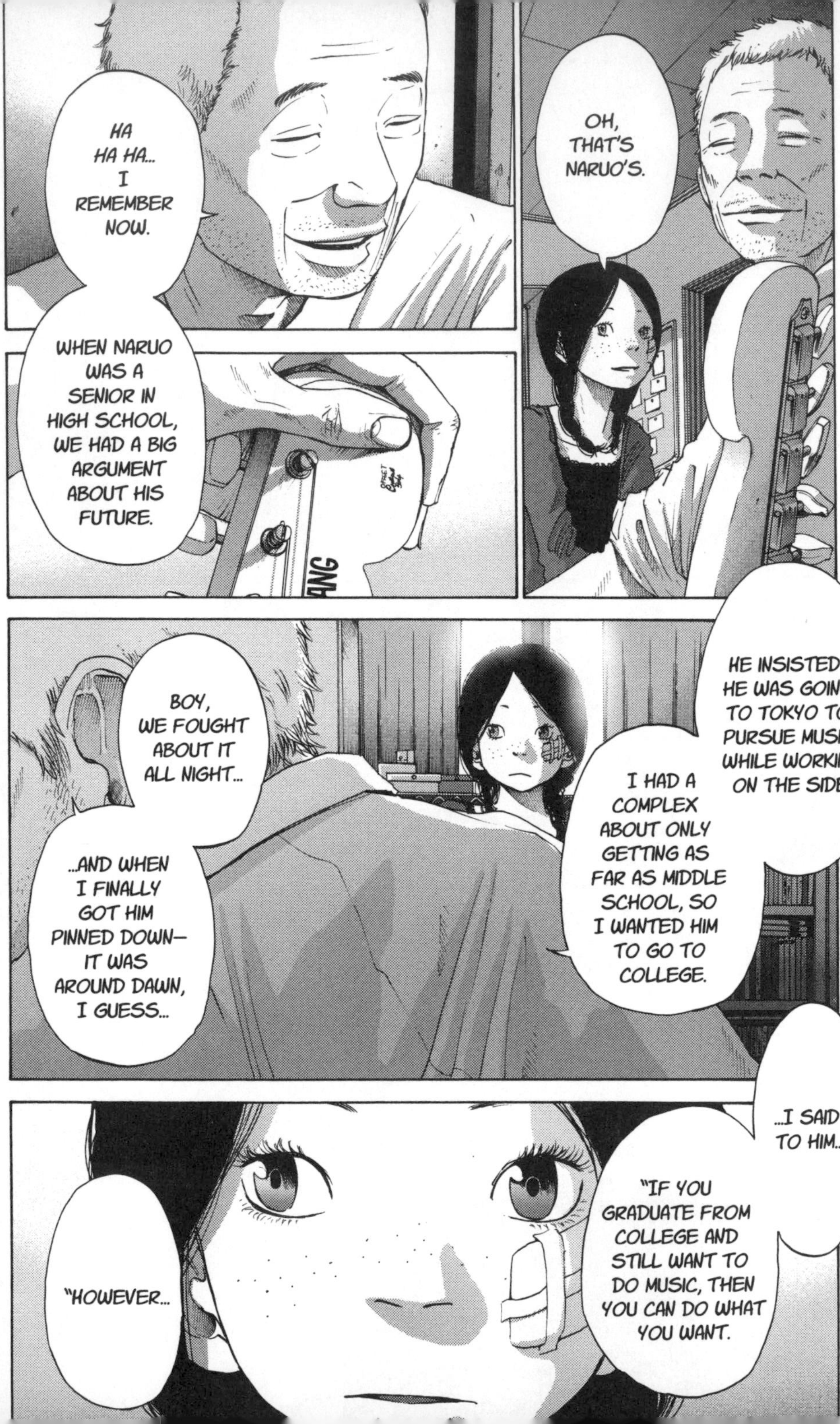
OH, THAT'S NARUO'S.
HA HA HA... I REMEMBER NOW.
WHEN NARUO WAS A SENIOR IN HIGH SCHOOL, WE HAD A BIG ARGUMENT ABOUT HIS FUTURE.
HE INSISTED HE WAS GOING TO TOKYO TO PURSUE MUSIC WHILE WORKING ON THE SIDE.
I HAD A COMPLEX ABOUT ONLY GETTING AS FAR AS MIDDLE SCHOOL, SO I WANTED HIM TO GO TO COLLEGE.
BOY, WE FOUGHT ABOUT IT ALL NIGHT...
...AND WHEN I FINALLY GOT HIM PINNED DOWN—IT WAS AROUND DAWN, I GUESS...
...I SAID TO HIM...
"IF YOU GRADUATE FROM COLLEGE AND STILL WANT TO DO MUSIC, THEN YOU CAN DO WHAT YOU WANT.
"HOWEVER...

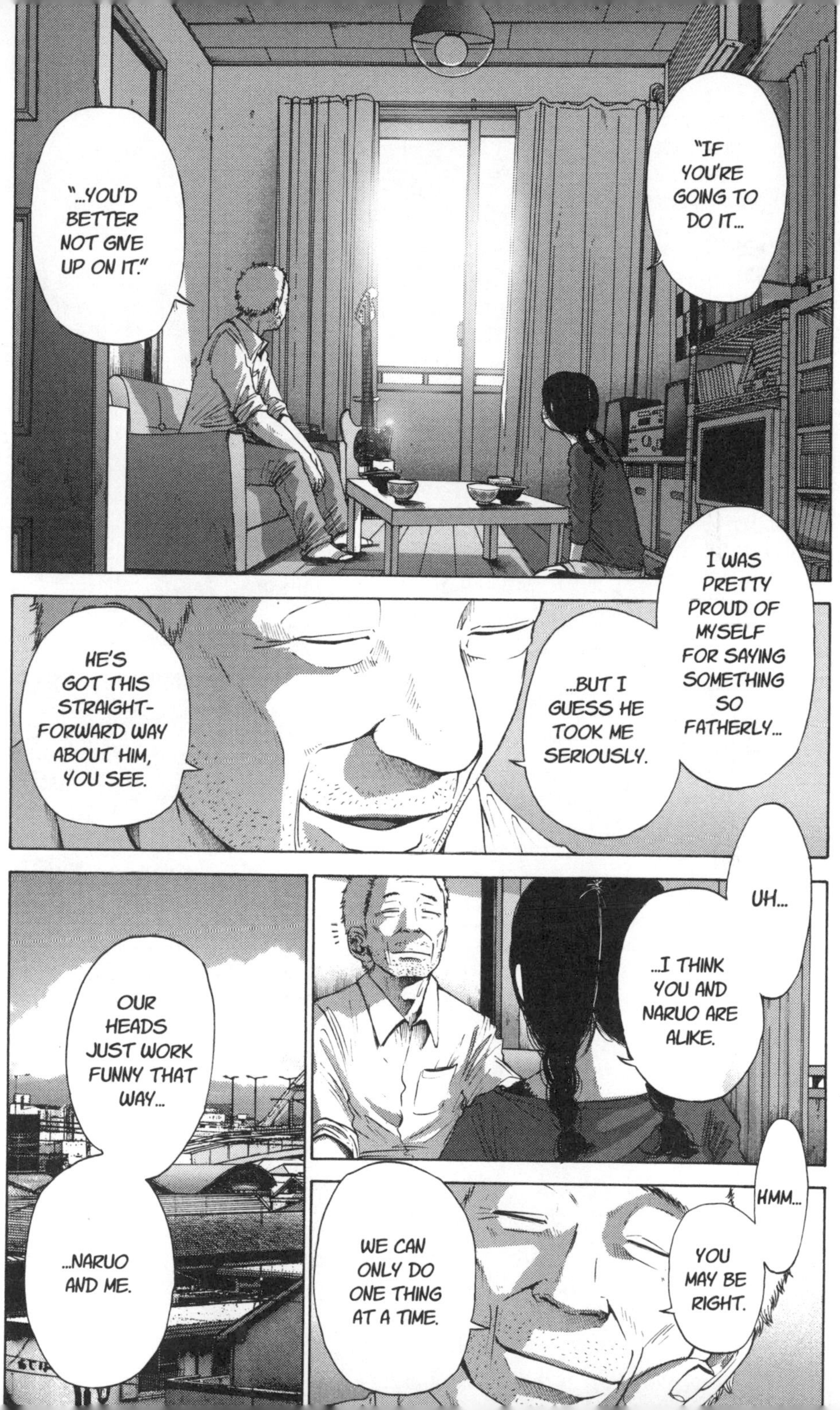
"IF YOU'RE GOING TO DO IT...
"...YOU'D BETTER NOT GIVE UP ON IT."
I WAS PRETTY PROUD OF MYSELF FOR SAYING SOMETHING SO FATHERLY...
...BUT I GUESS HE TOOK ME SERIOUSLY.
HE'S GOT THIS STRAIGHT-FORWARD WAY ABOUT HIM, YOU SEE.
UH...
...I THINK YOU AND NARUO ARE ALIKE.
HMM...
YOU MAY BE RIGHT.
WE CAN ONLY DO ONE THING AT A TIME.
OUR HEADS JUST WORK FUNNY THAT WAY...
...NARUO AND ME.

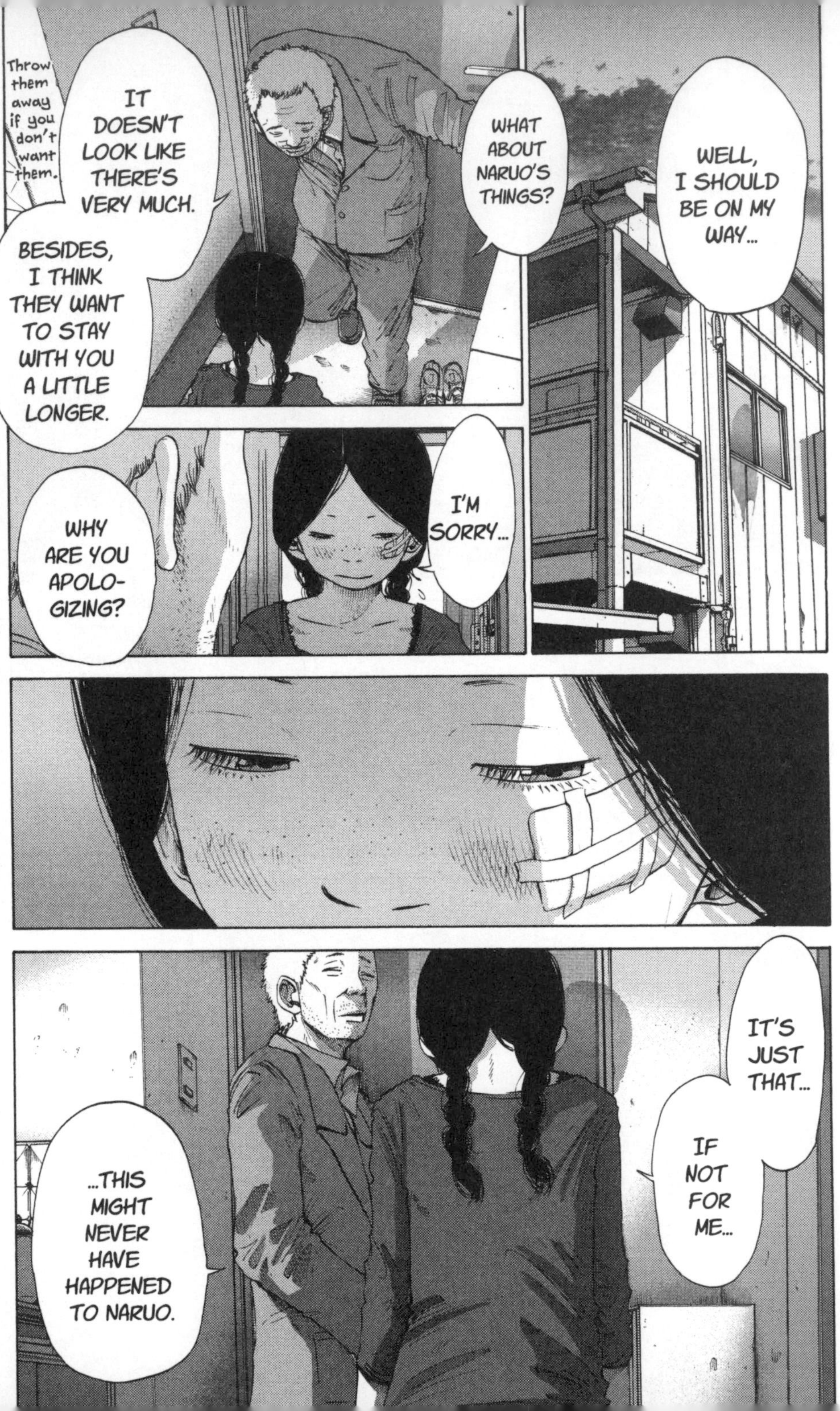
WELL, I SHOULD BE ON MY WAY...
WHAT ABOUT NARUO'S THINGS?
IT DOESN'T LOOK LIKE THERE'S VERY MUCH.
Throw them away if you don't want them.
BESIDES, I THINK THEY WANT TO STAY WITH YOU A LITTLE LONGER.
I'M SORRY...
WHY ARE YOU APOLO-GIZING?
IT'S JUST THAT...
IF NOT FOR ME...
...THIS MIGHT NEVER HAVE HAPPENED TO NARUO.

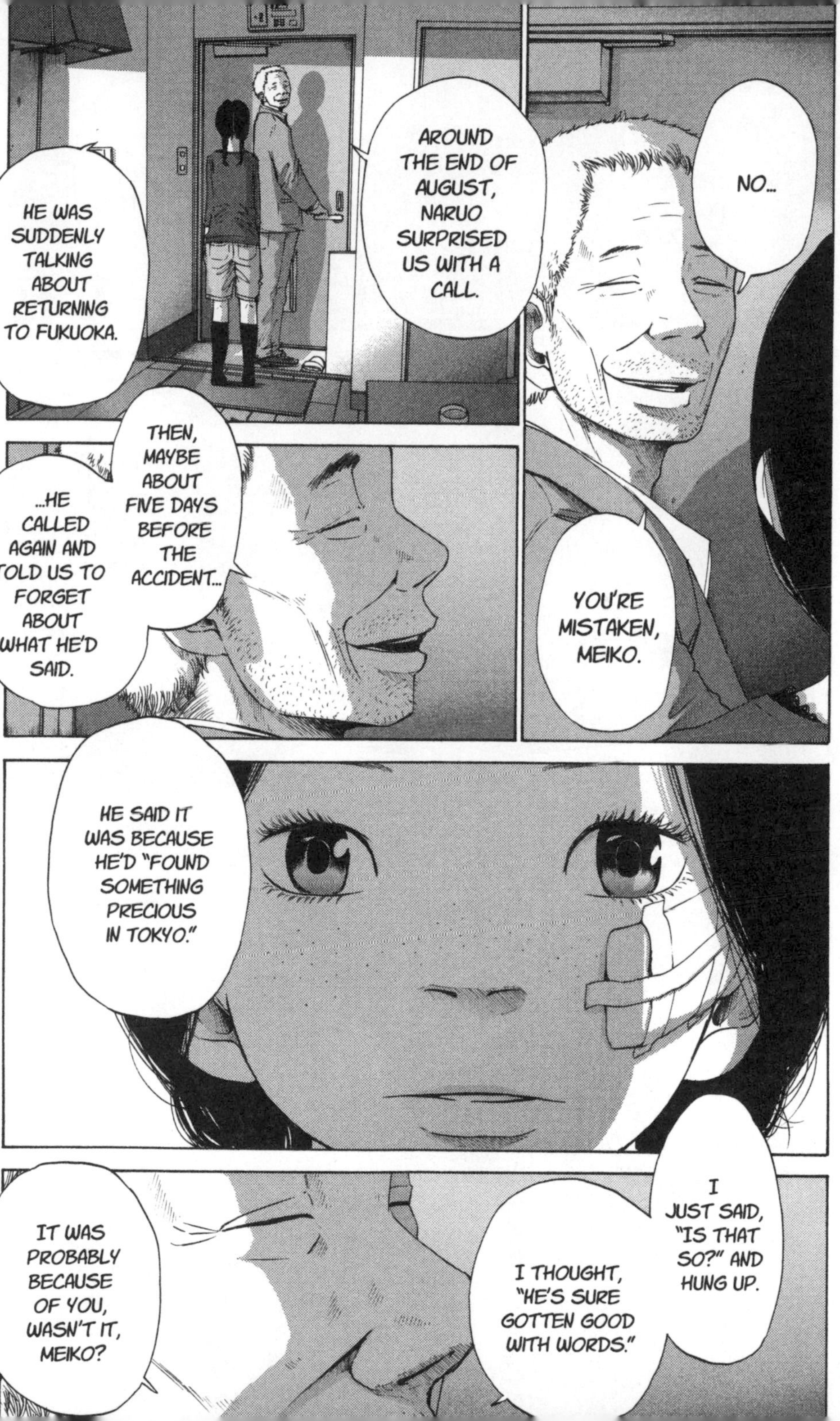
NO...
YOU'RE MISTAKEN, MEIKO.
AROUND THE END OF AUGUST, NARUO SURPRISED US WITH A CALL.
HE WAS SUDDENLY TALKING ABOUT RETURNING TO FUKUOKA.
THEN, MAYBE ABOUT FIVE DAYS BEFORE THE ACCIDENT...
...HE CALLED AGAIN AND TOLD US TO FORGET ABOUT WHAT HE'D SAID.
HE SAID IT WAS BECAUSE HE'D "FOUND SOMETHING PRECIOUS IN TOKYO."
I JUST SAID, "IS THAT SO?" AND HUNG UP.
I THOUGHT, "HE'S SURE GOTTEN GOOD WITH WORDS."
IT WAS PROBABLY BECAUSE OF YOU, WASN'T IT, MEIKO?

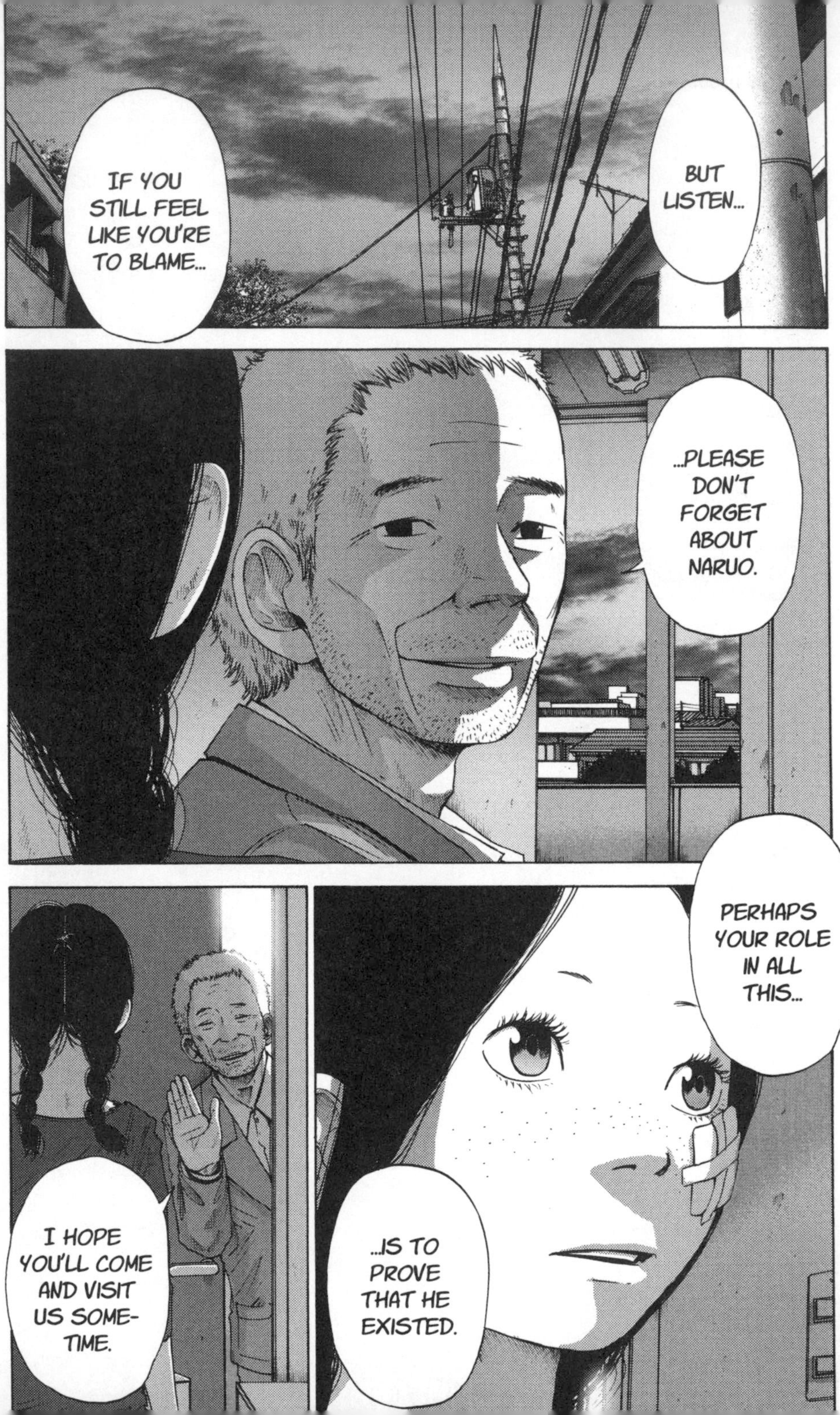
BUT LISTEN...
IF YOU STILL FEEL LIKE YOU'RE TO BLAME...
...PLEASE DON'T FORGET ABOUT NARUO.
PERHAPS YOUR ROLE IN ALL THIS...
...IS TO PROVE THAT HE EXISTED.
I HOPE YOU'LL COME AND VISIT US SOME-TIME.

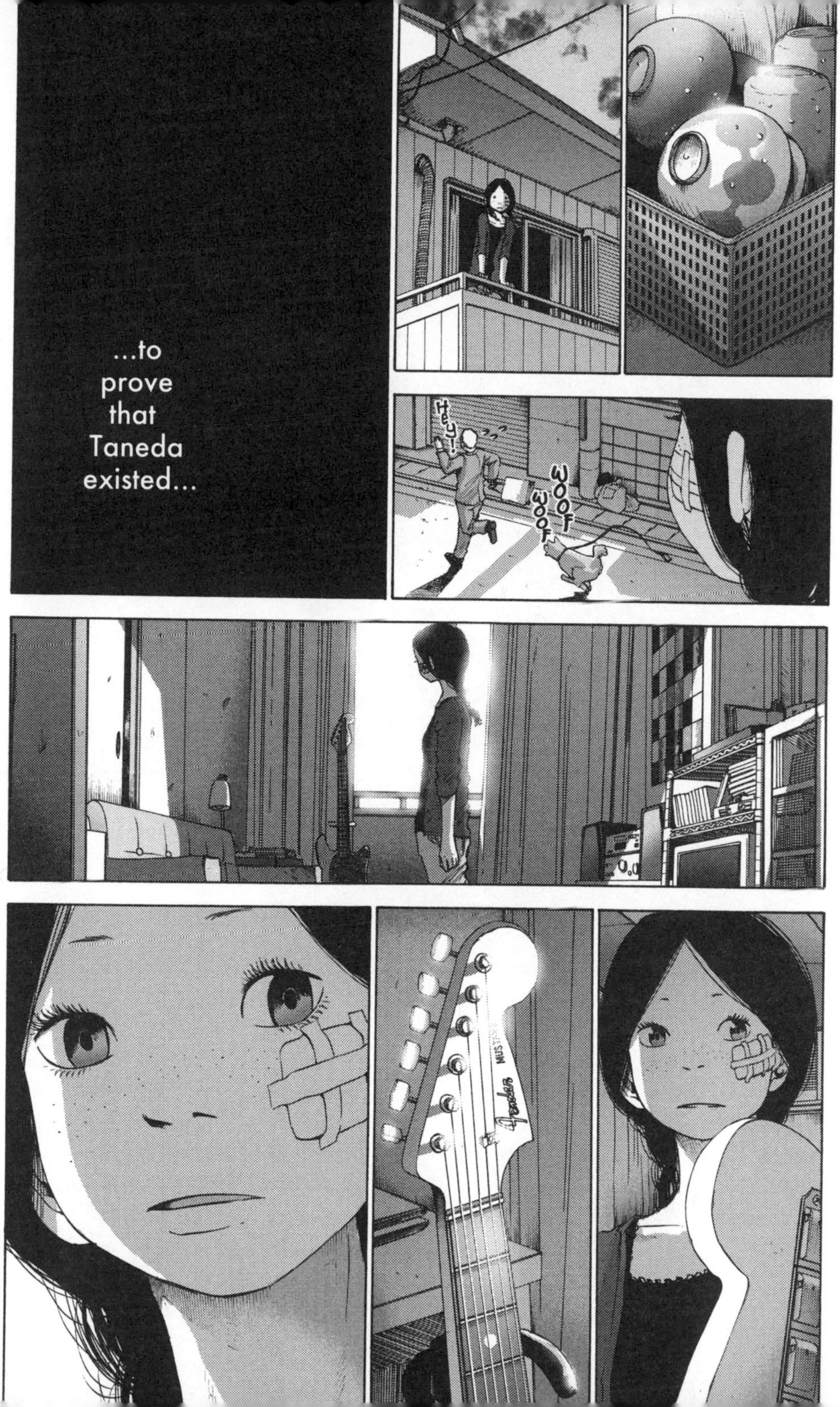
HEY!
WOOF
WOOF
...to prove that Taneda existed...

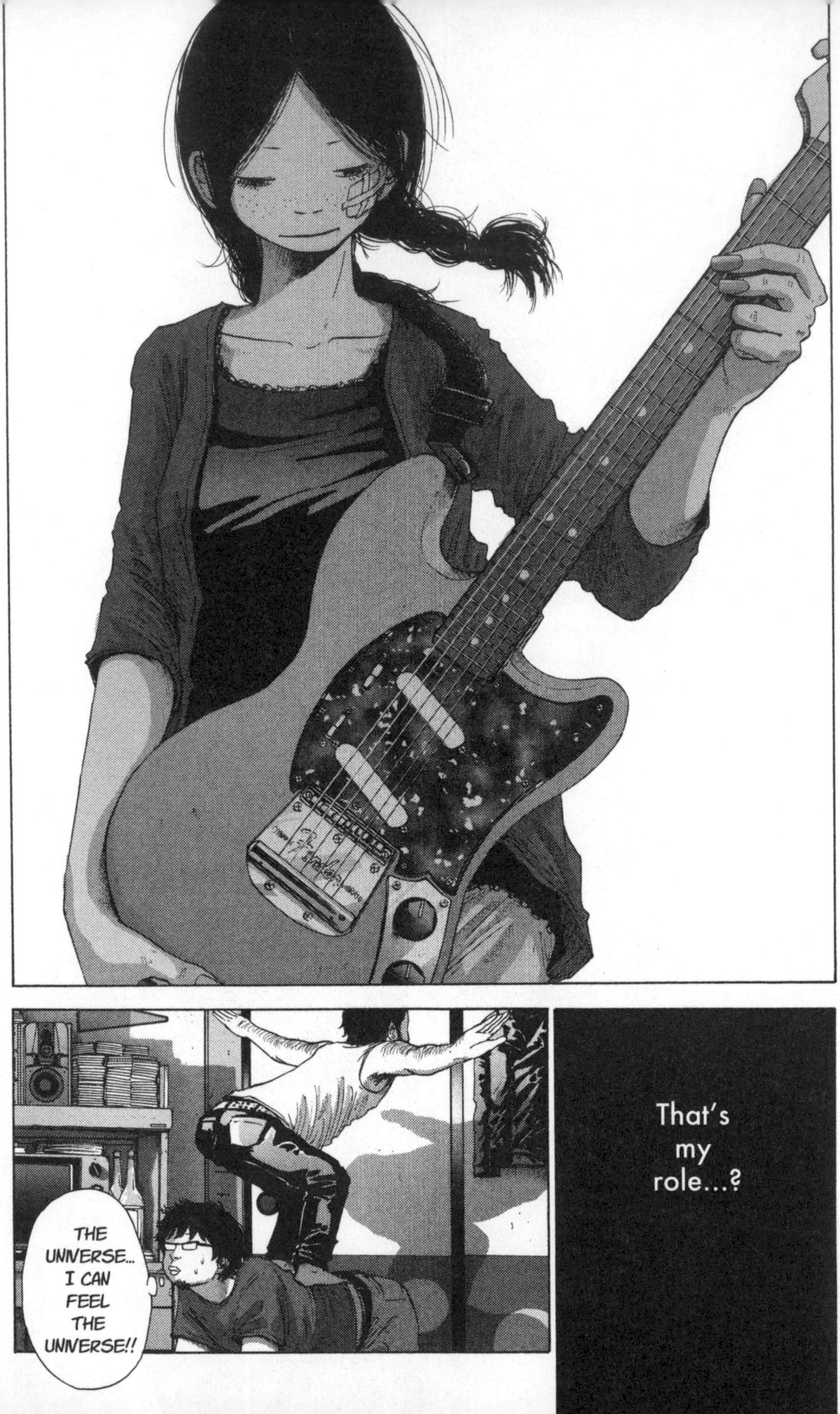
That's my role...?
THE UNIVERSE... I CAN FEEL THE UNIVERSE!!

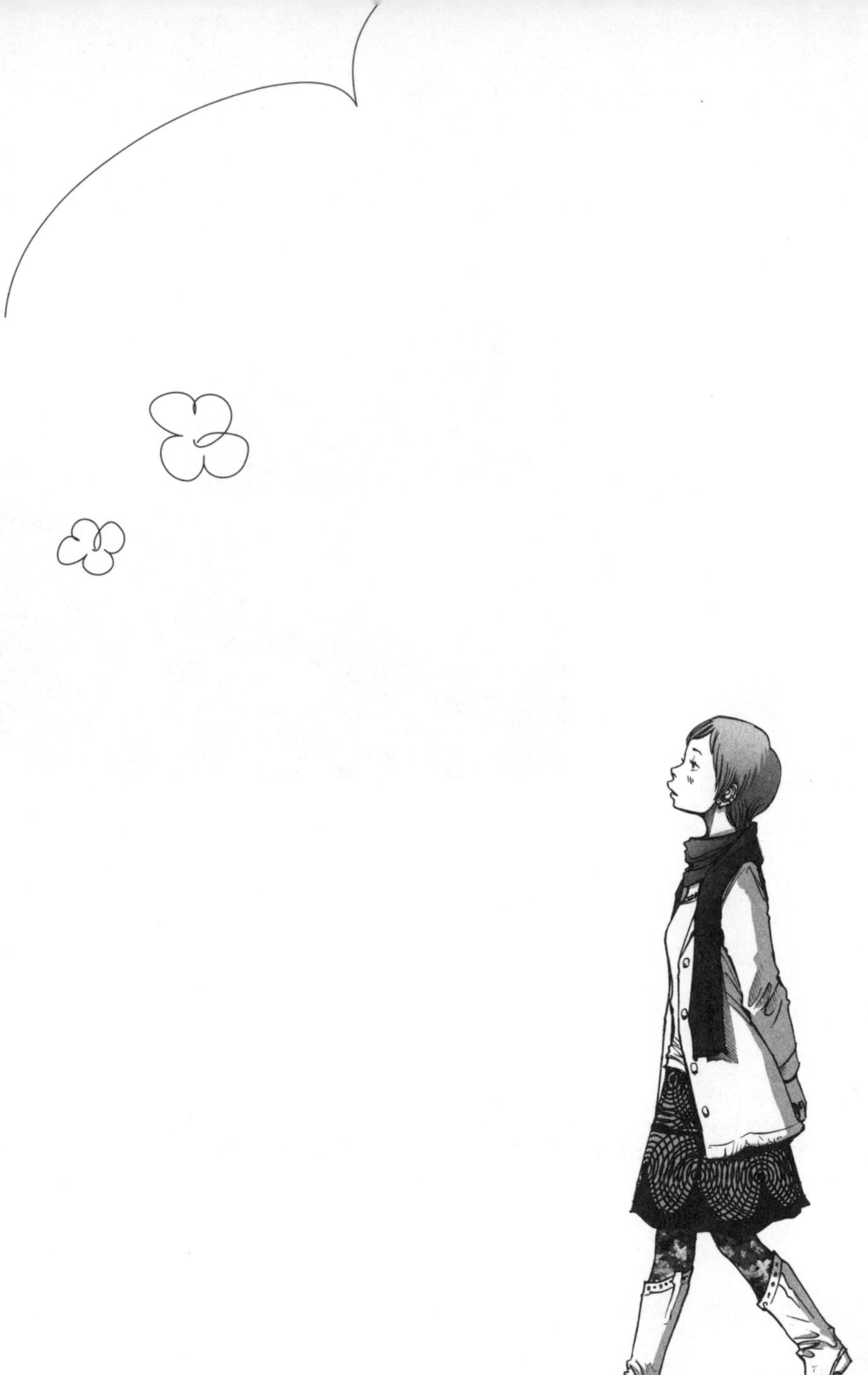

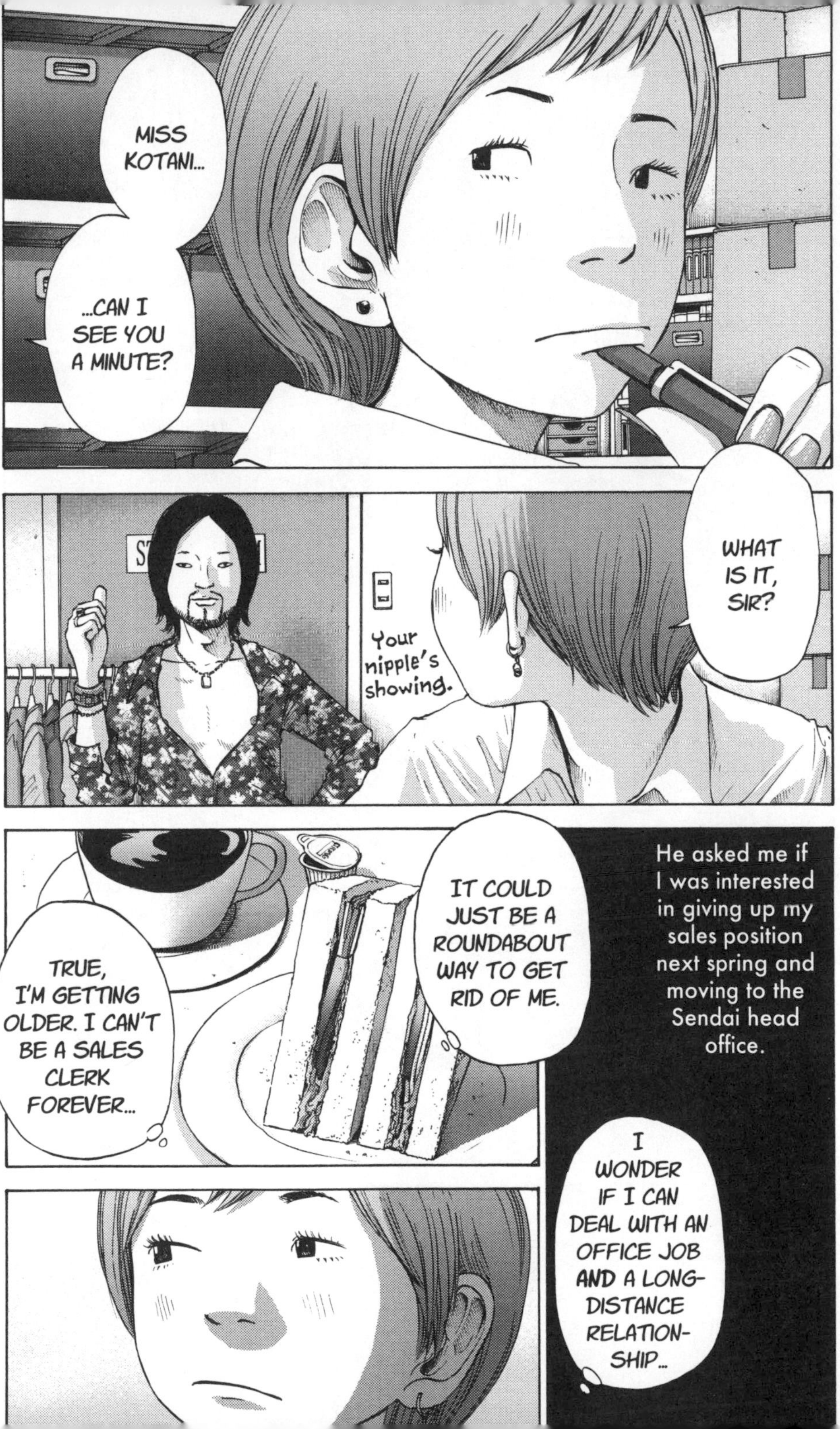

MISS KOTANI...
...CAN I SEE YOU A MINUTE?
WHAT IS IT, SIR?
Your nipple's showing.
He asked me if I was interested in giving up my sales position next spring and moving to the Sendai head office.
IT COULD JUST BE A ROUNDABOUT WAY TO GET RID OF ME.
TRUE, I'M GETTING OLDER. I CAN'T BE A SALES CLERK FOREVER...
I WONDER IF I CAN DEAL WITH AN OFFICE JOB AND A LONG-DISTANCE RELATIONSHIP...

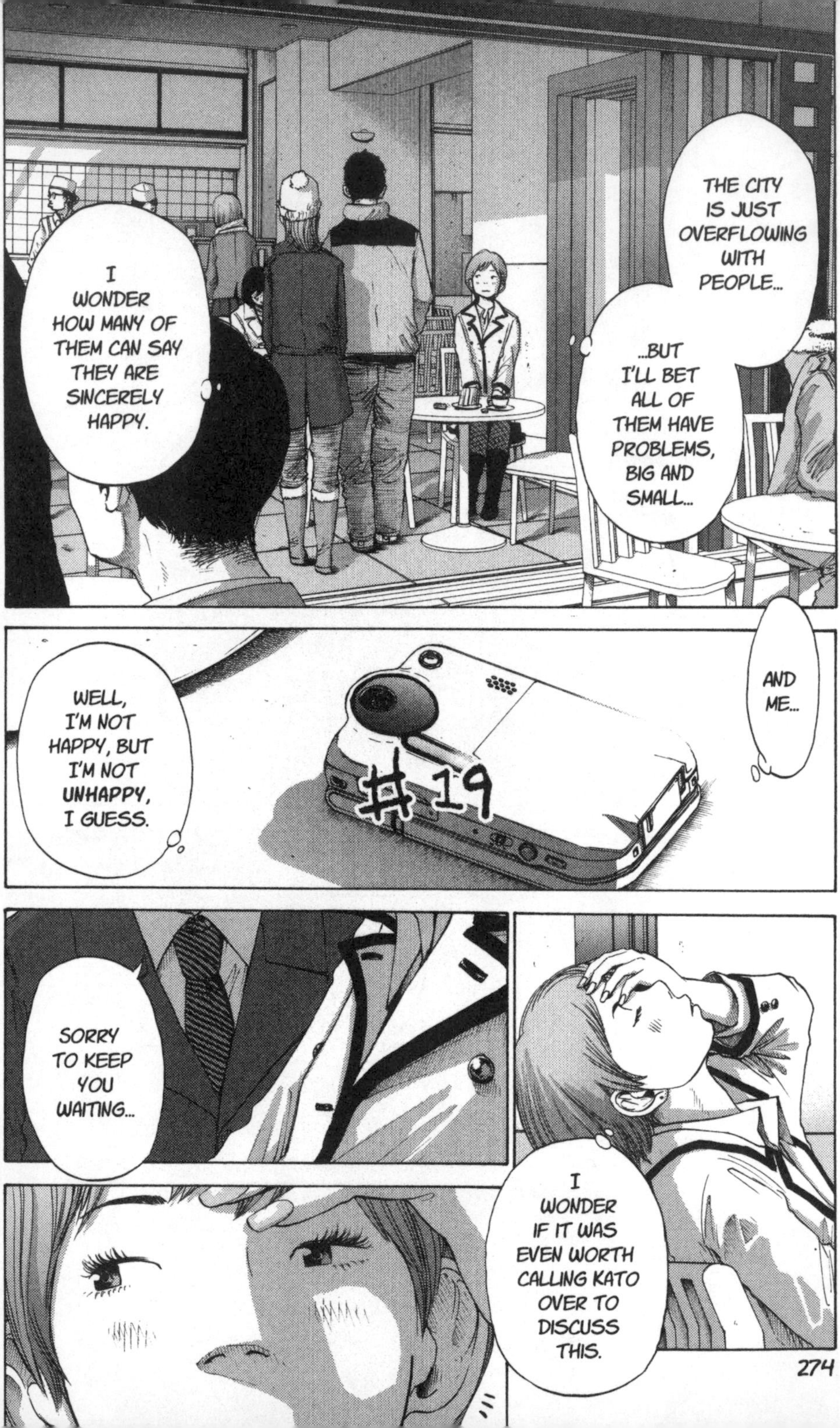
THE CITY IS JUST OVERFLOWING WITH PEOPLE...
...BUT I'LL BET ALL OF THEM HAVE PROBLEMS, BIG AND SMALL...
I WONDER HOW MANY OF THEM CAN SAY THEY ARE SINCERELY HAPPY.
AND ME...
#19
WELL, I'M NOT HAPPY, BUT I'M NOT UNHAPPY, I GUESS.
I WONDER IF IT WAS EVEN WORTH CALLING KATO OVER TO DISCUSS THIS.
SORRY TO KEEP YOU WAITING...

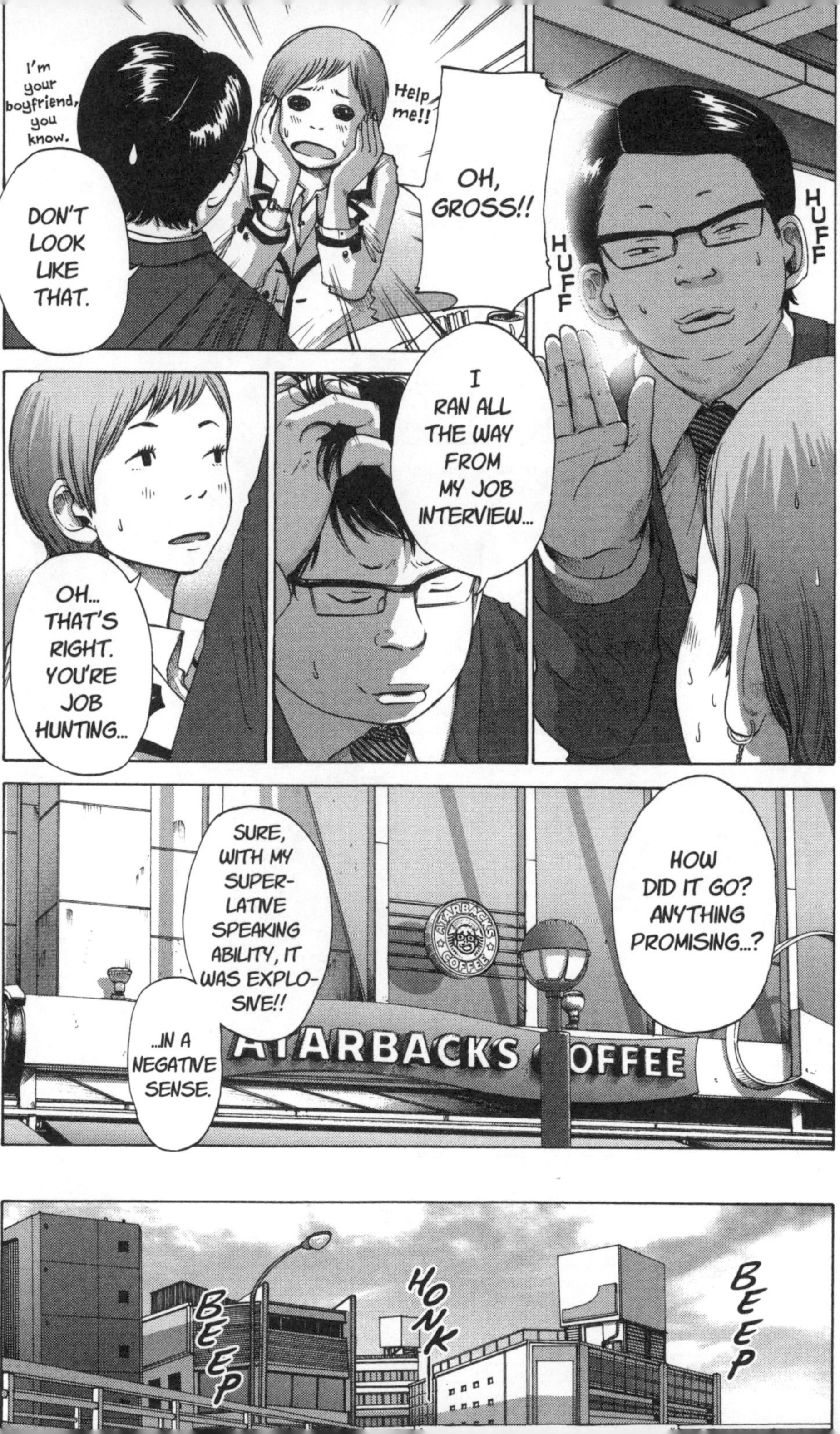
HUFF HUFF
I RAN ALL THE WAY FROM MY JOB INTERVIEW...
OH, GROSS!!
Help me!!
I'm your boyfriend, you know.
DON'T LOOK LIKE THAT.
OH... THAT'S RIGHT. YOU'RE JOB HUNTING...
HOW DID IT GO? ANYTHING PROMISING...?
ATARBACKS COFFEE
SURE, WITH MY SUPER-LATIVE SPEAKING ABILITY, IT WAS EXPLO-SIVE!!
...IN A NEGATIVE SENSE.
ATARBACKS OFFEE
BEEP
HONK
BEEP

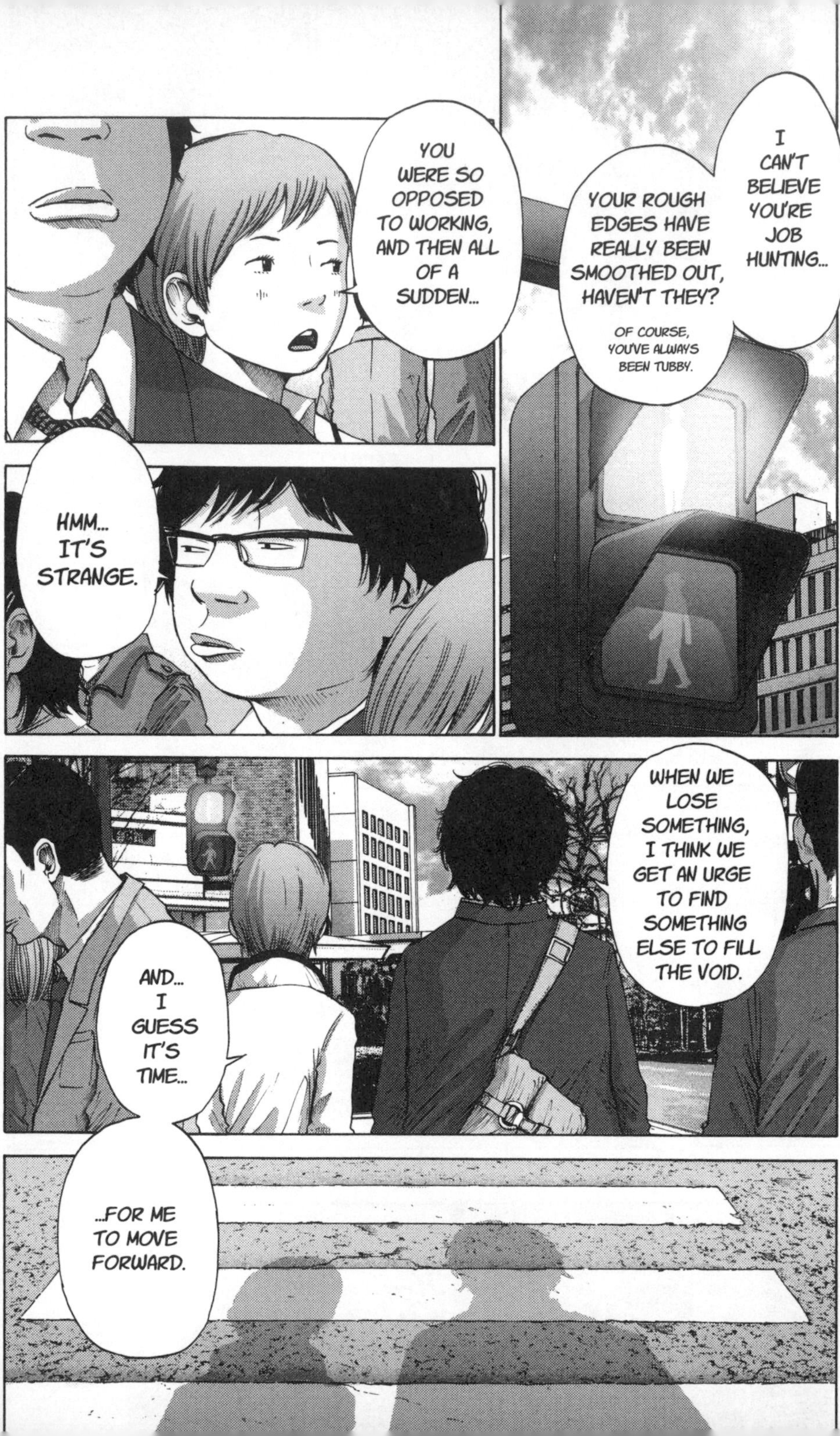
I CAN'T BELIEVE YOU'RE JOB HUNTING...
YOUR ROUGH EDGES HAVE REALLY BEEN SMOOTHED OUT, HAVEN'T THEY?
OF COURSE, YOU'VE ALWAYS BEEN TUBBY.
YOU WERE SO OPPOSED TO WORKING, AND THEN ALL OF A SUDDEN...
HMM... IT'S STRANGE.
WHEN WE LOSE SOMETHING, I THINK WE GET AN URGE TO FIND SOMETHING ELSE TO FILL THE VOID.
AND... I GUESS IT'S TIME...
...FOR ME TO MOVE FORWARD.

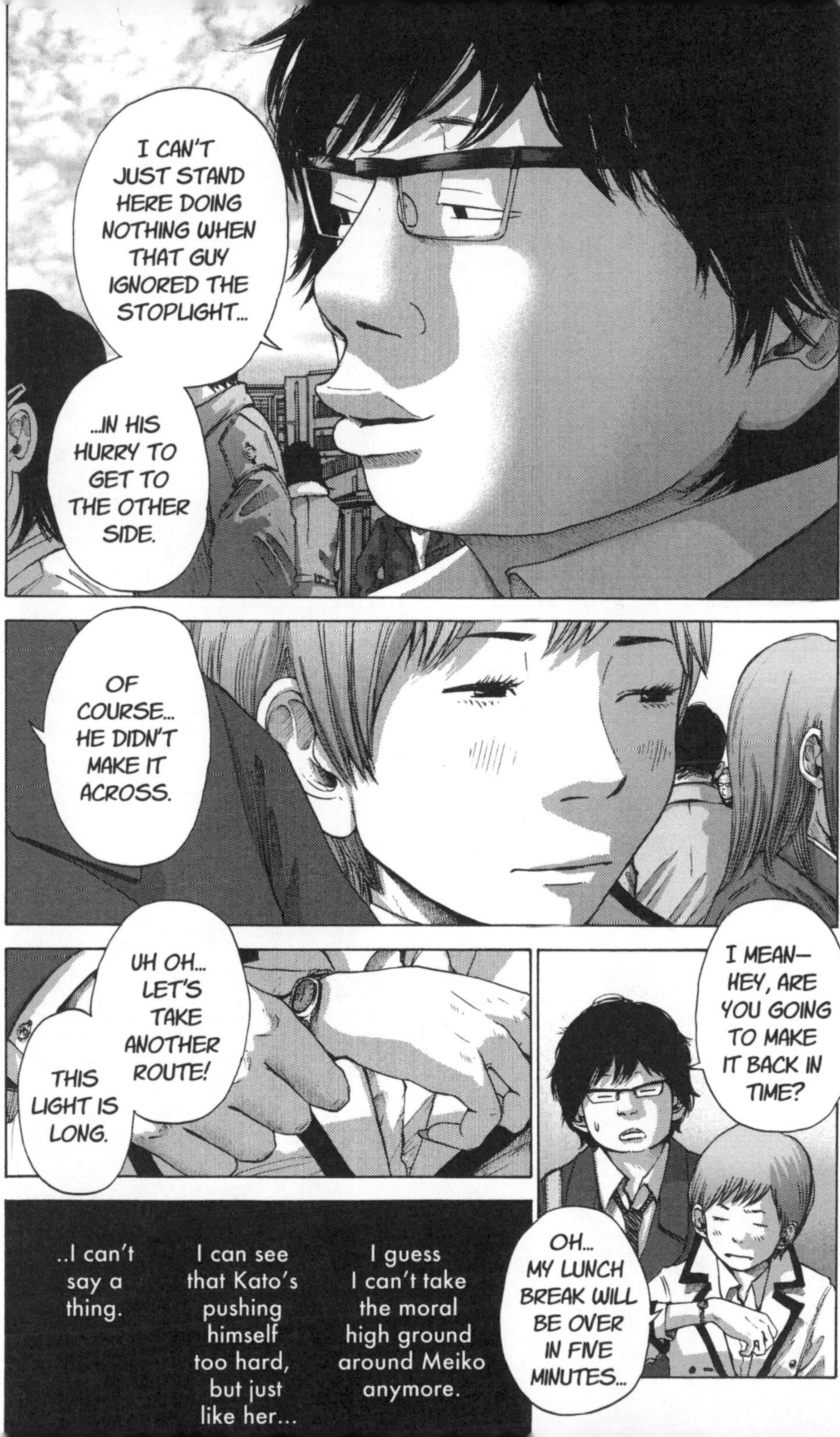
I CAN'T JUST STAND HERE DOING NOTHING WHEN THAT GUY IGNORED THE STOPLIGHT...
...IN HIS HURRY TO GET TO THE OTHER SIDE.
OF COURSE... HE DIDN'T MAKE IT ACROSS.
I MEAN— HEY, ARE YOU GOING TO MAKE IT BACK IN TIME?
OH... MY LUNCH BREAK WILL BE OVER IN FIVE MINUTES...
UH OH... LET'S TAKE ANOTHER ROUTE!
THIS LIGHT IS LONG.
I guess I can't take the moral high ground around Meiko anymore.
I can see that Kato's pushing himself too hard, but just like her...
..I can't say a thing.

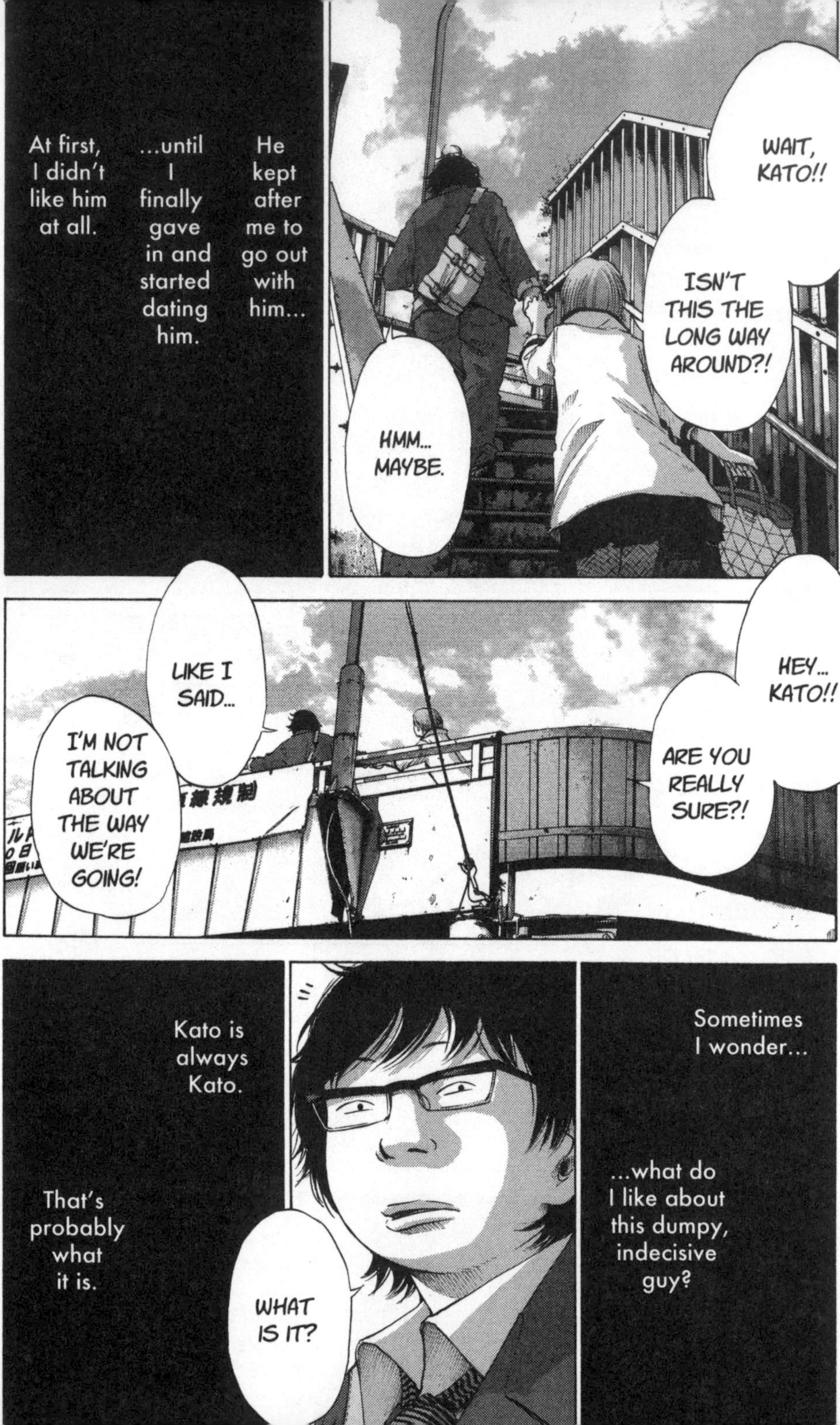
WAIT, KATO!!
ISN'T THIS THE LONG WAY AROUND?!
HMM... MAYBE.
He kept after me to go out with him...
...until I finally gave in and started dating him.
At first, I didn't like him at all.
HEY... KATO!!
ARE YOU REALLY SURE?!
LIKE I SAID...
I'M NOT TALKING ABOUT THE WAY WE'RE GOING!
Sometimes I wonder...
...what do I like about this dumpy, indecisive guy?
WHAT IS IT?
Kato is always Kato.
That's probably what it is.

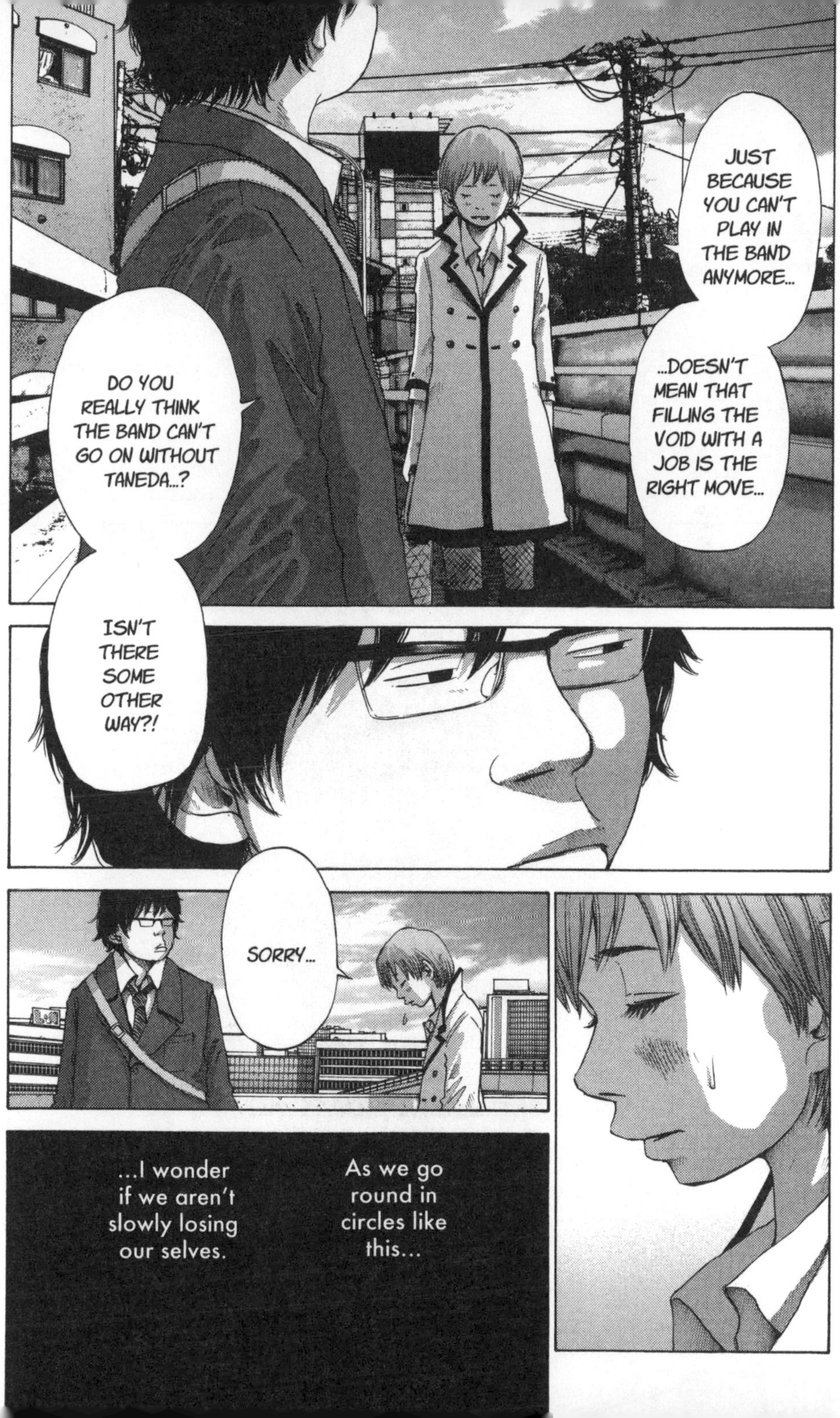
JUST BECAUSE YOU CAN'T PLAY IN THE BAND ANYMORE...
...DOESN'T MEAN THAT FILLING THE VOID WITH A JOB IS THE RIGHT MOVE...
DO YOU REALLY THINK THE BAND CAN'T GO ON WITHOUT TANEDA...?
ISN'T THERE SOME OTHER WAY?!
SORRY...
As we go round in circles like this...
...I wonder if we aren't slowly losing our selves.

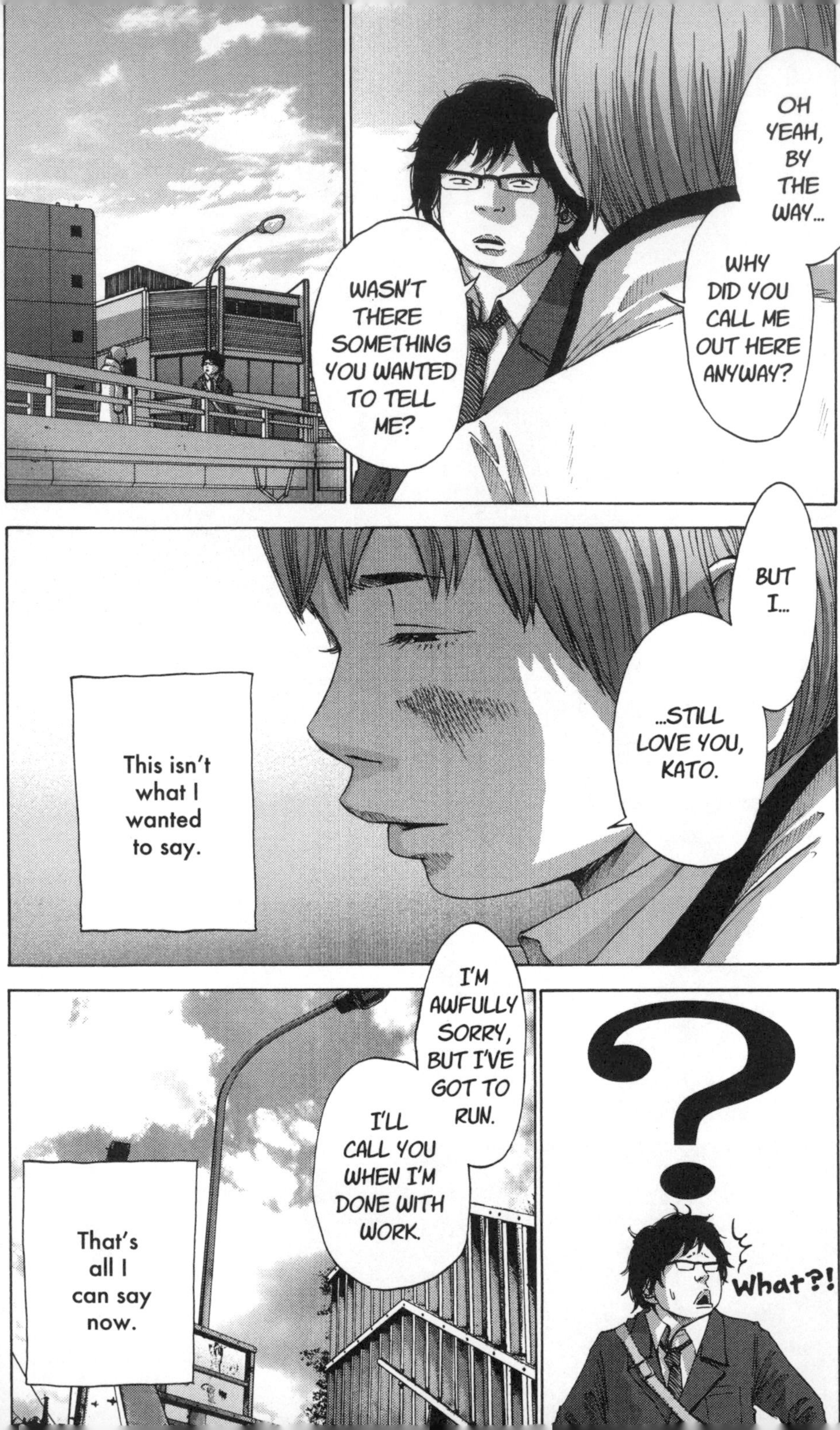
OH YEAH, BY THE WAY...
WHY DID YOU CALL ME OUT HERE ANYWAY?
WASN'T THERE SOMETHING YOU WANTED TO TELL ME?
BUT I...
...STILL LOVE YOU, KATO.
This isn't what I wanted to say.
?
What?!
I'M AWFULLY SORRY, BUT I'VE GOT TO RUN.
I'LL CALL YOU WHEN I'M DONE WITH WORK.
That's all I can say now.

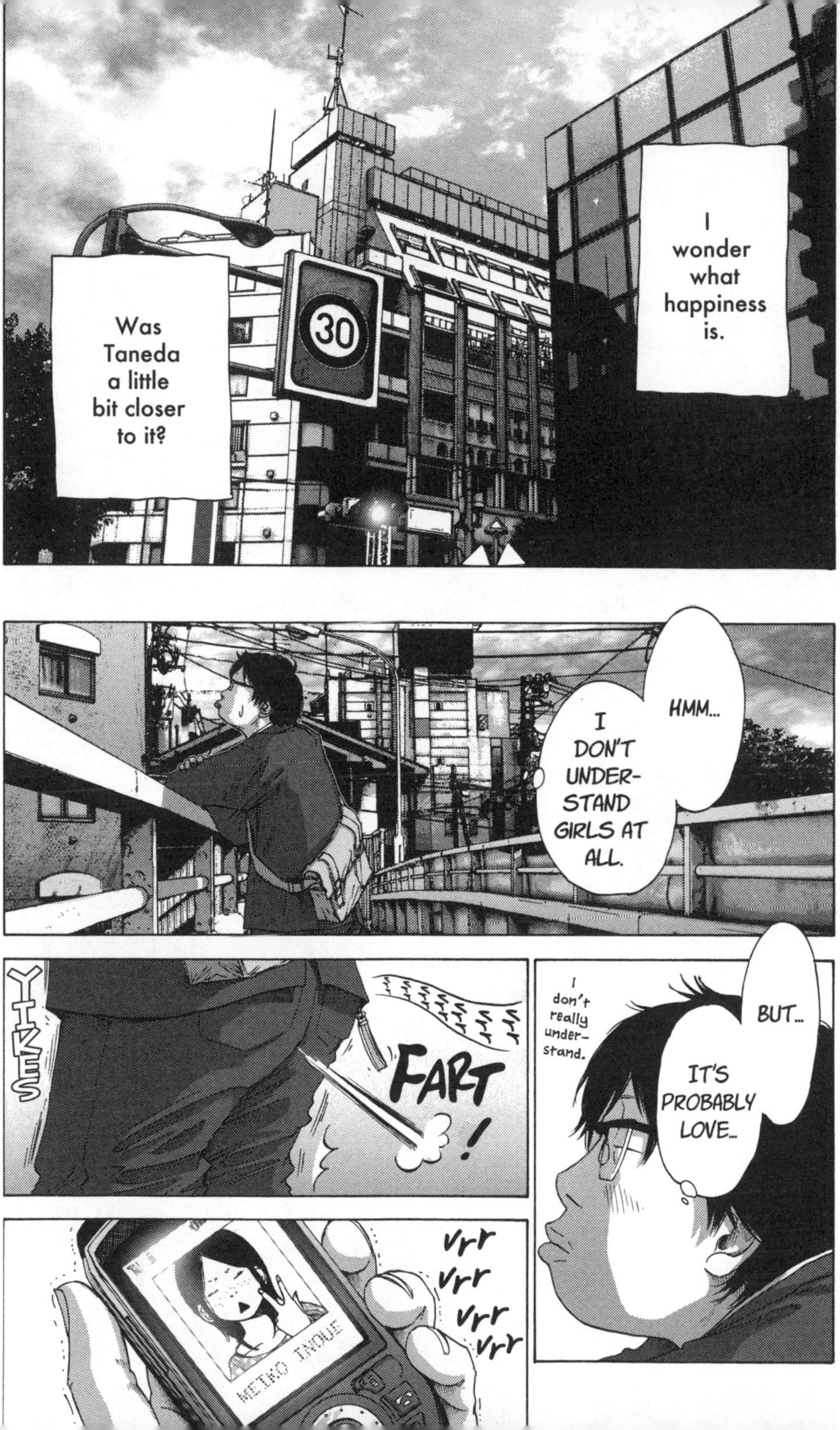
I wonder what happiness is.
Was Taneda a little bit closer to it?
HMM...
I DON'T UNDER-STAND GIRLS AT ALL.
BUT...
IT'S PROBABLY LOVE...
I don't really under-stand.
YIKES
FART!
Vrr vrr vrr vrr
MEIKO INOUE

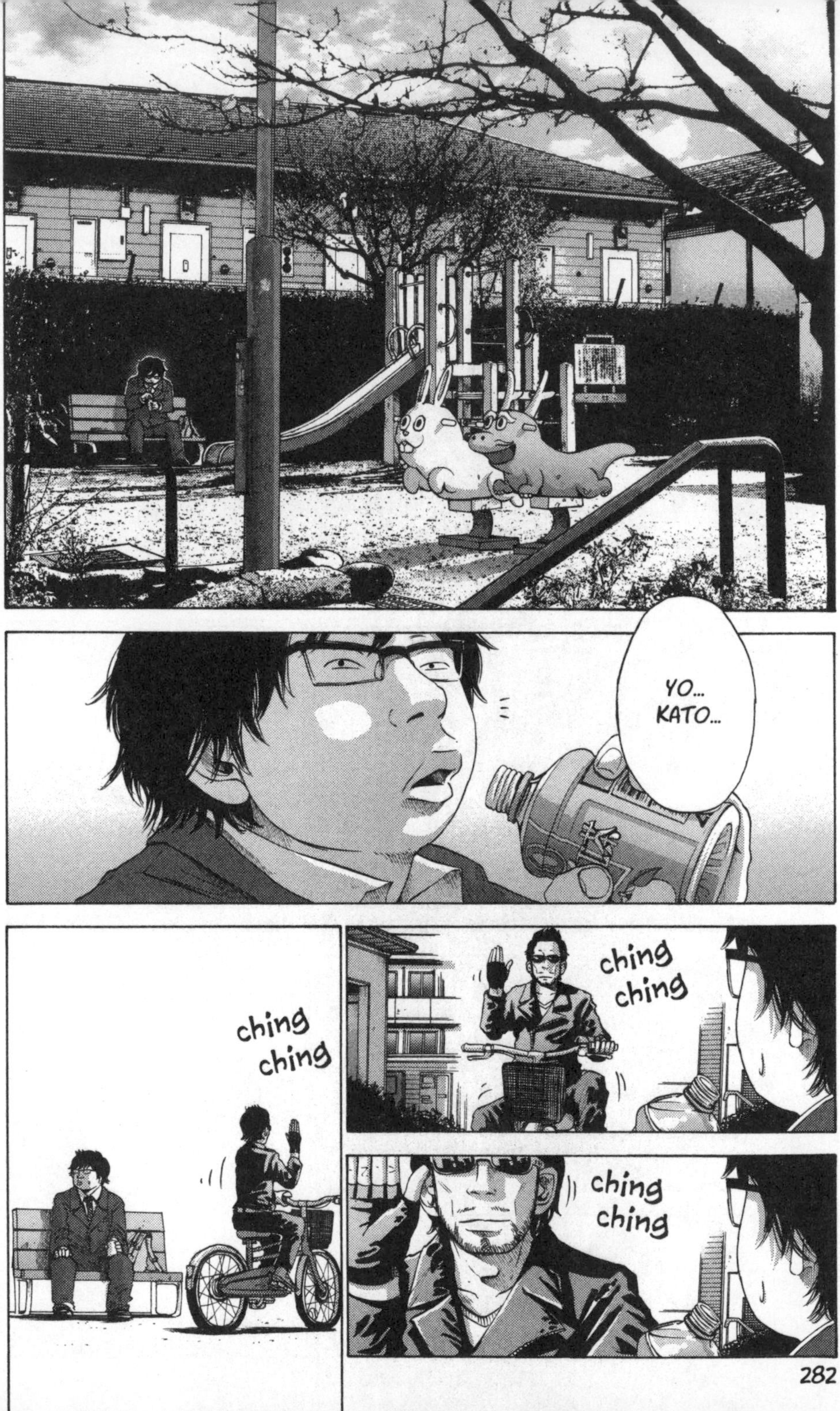
YO...
KATO...
ching
ching
ching
ching
ching
ching

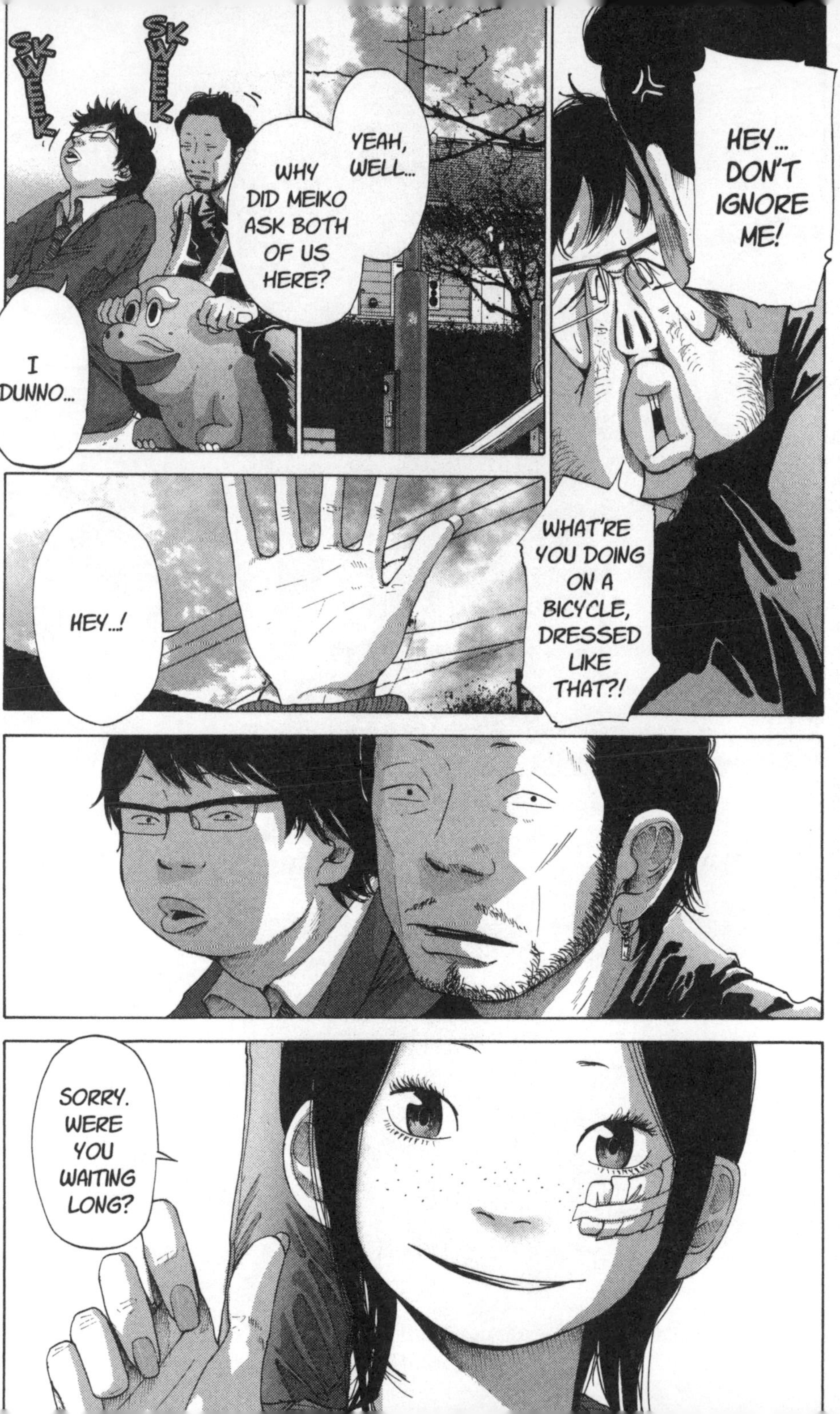
HEY... DON'T IGNORE ME!
WHAT'RE YOU DOING ON A BICYCLE, DRESSED LIKE THAT?!
SKWEEK
SKWEEK
YEAH, WELL...
WHY DID MEIKO ASK BOTH OF US HERE?
I DUNNO...
HEY...!
SORRY. WERE YOU WAITING LONG?

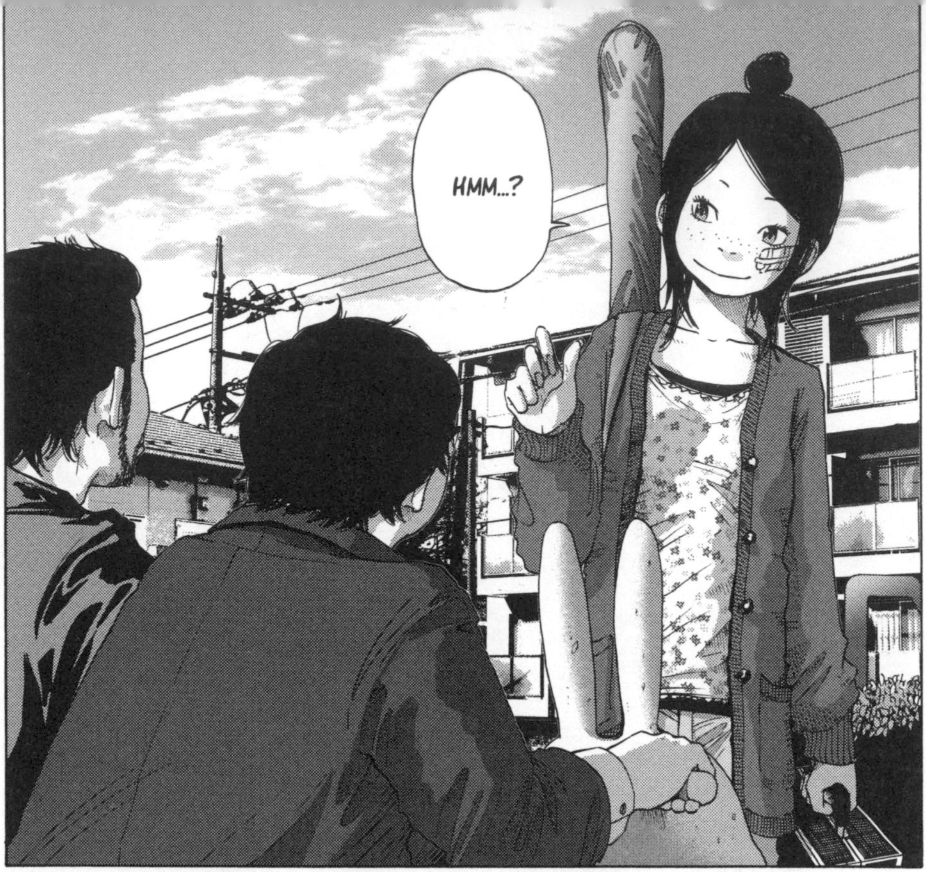
HMM...?
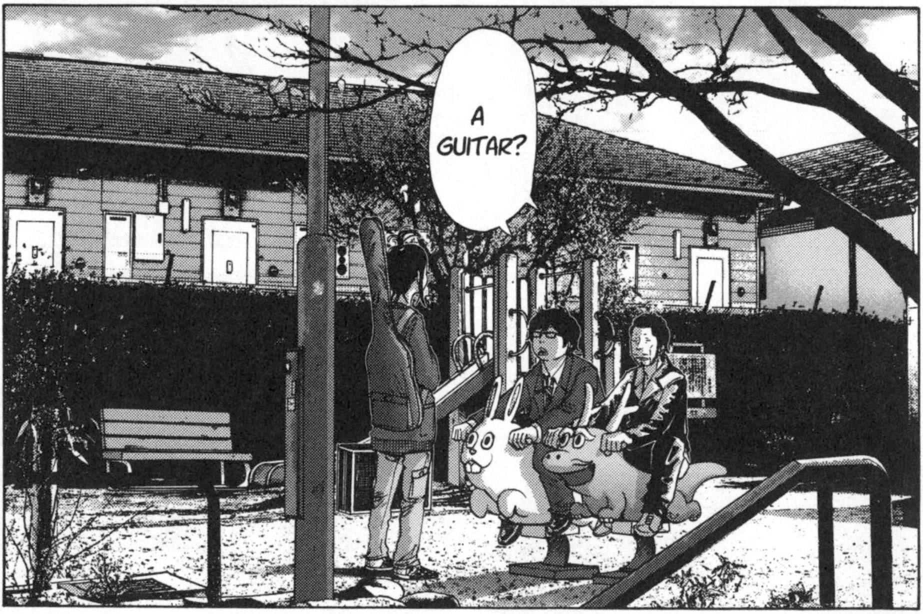
A GUITAR?

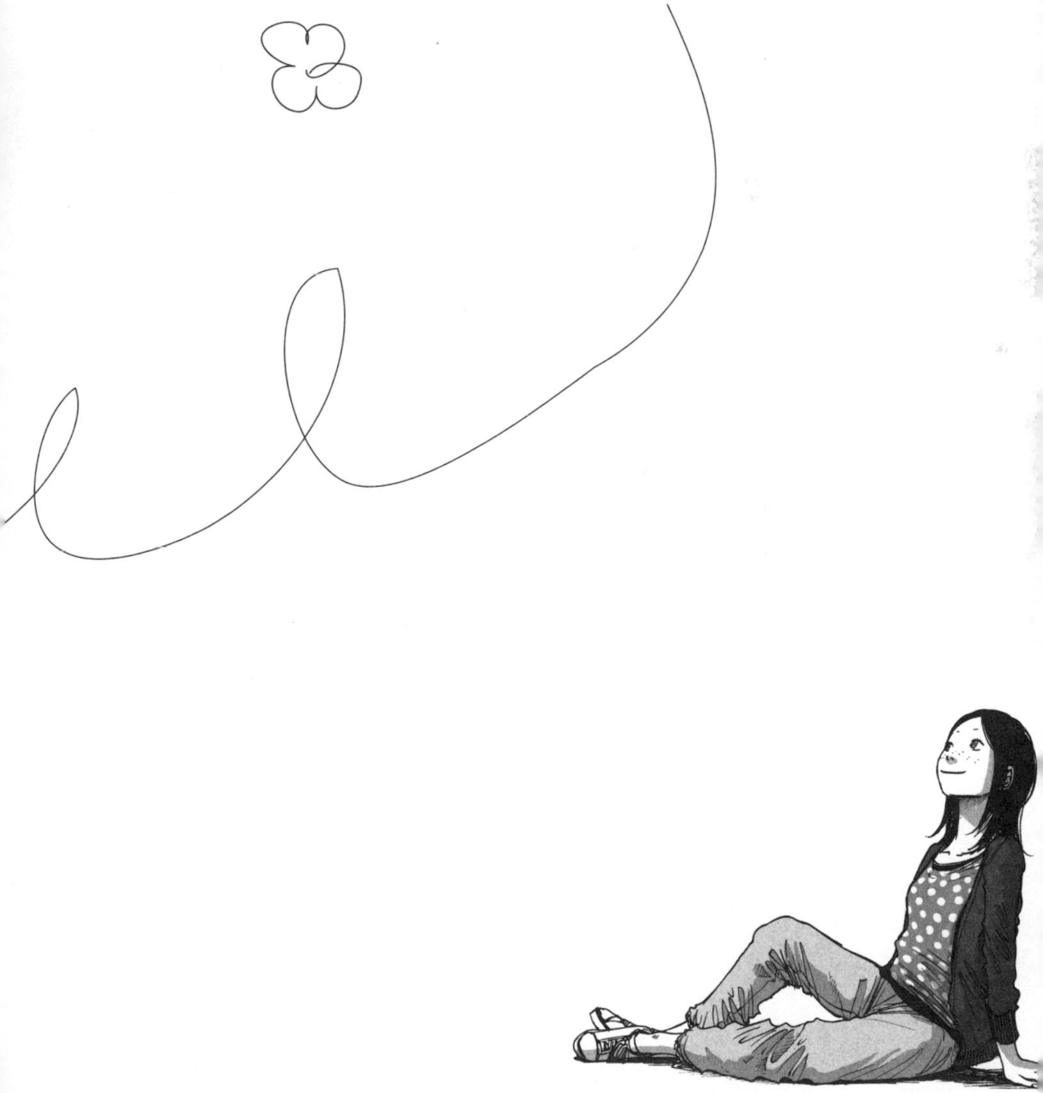

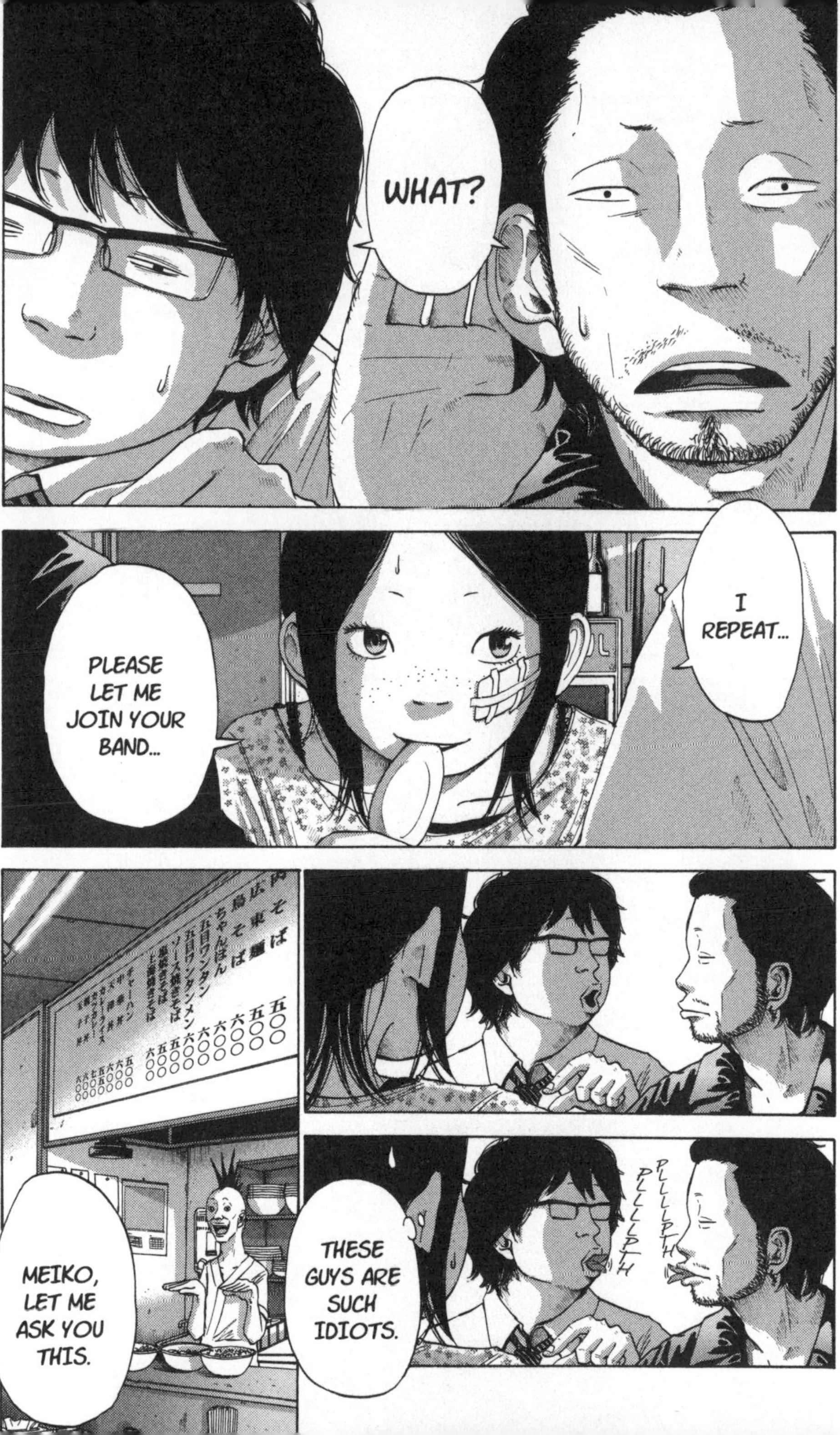
WHAT?
I REPEAT...
PLEASE LET ME JOIN YOUR BAND...
PLLLLPTH
PLLLLPTH
THESE GUYS ARE SUCH IDIOTS.
MEIKO, LET ME ASK YOU THIS.

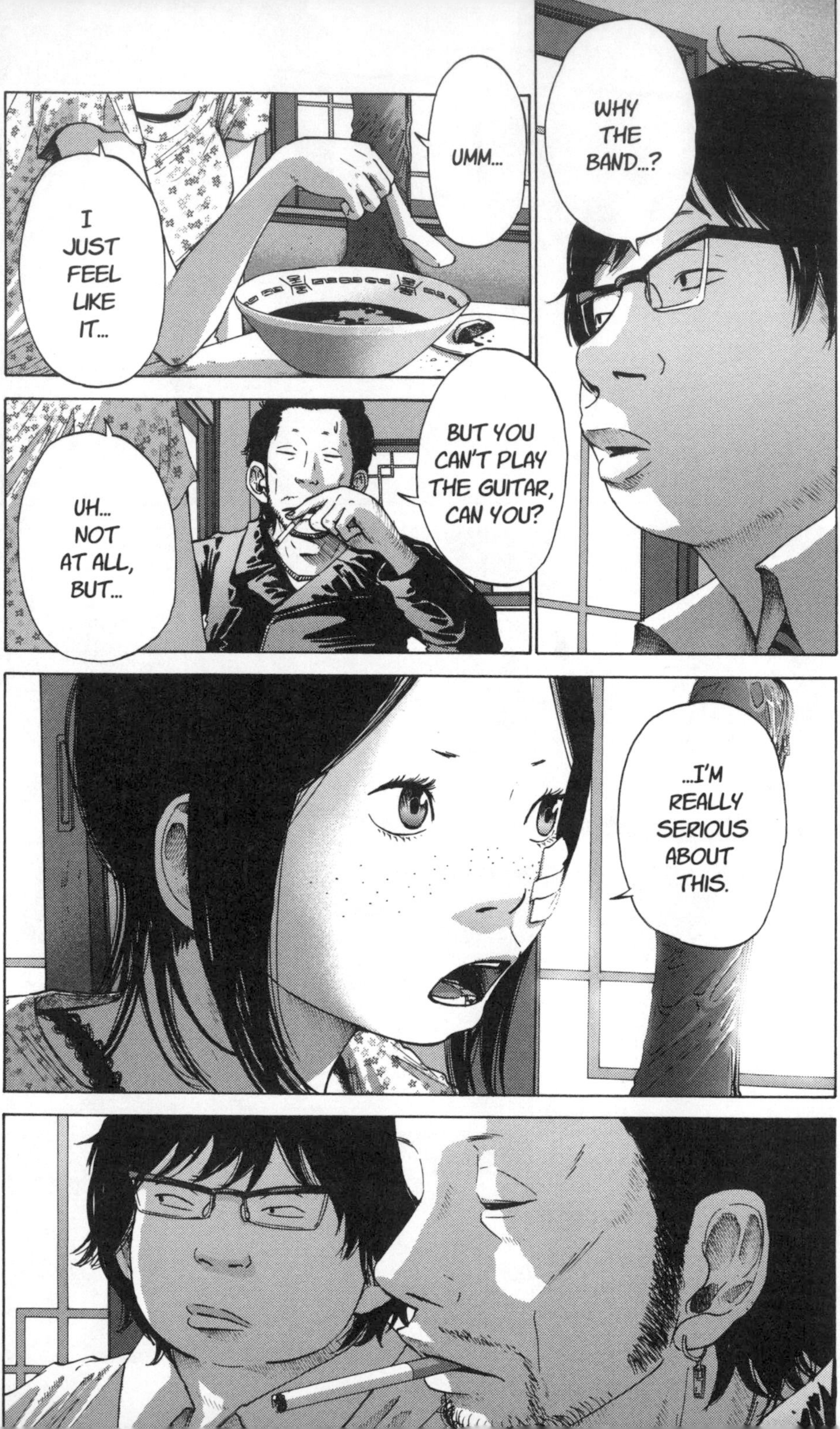
WHY THE BAND...?
UMM...
I JUST FEEL LIKE IT...
BUT YOU CAN'T PLAY THE GUITAR, CAN YOU?
UH... NOT AT ALL, BUT...
...I'M REALLY SERIOUS ABOUT THIS.

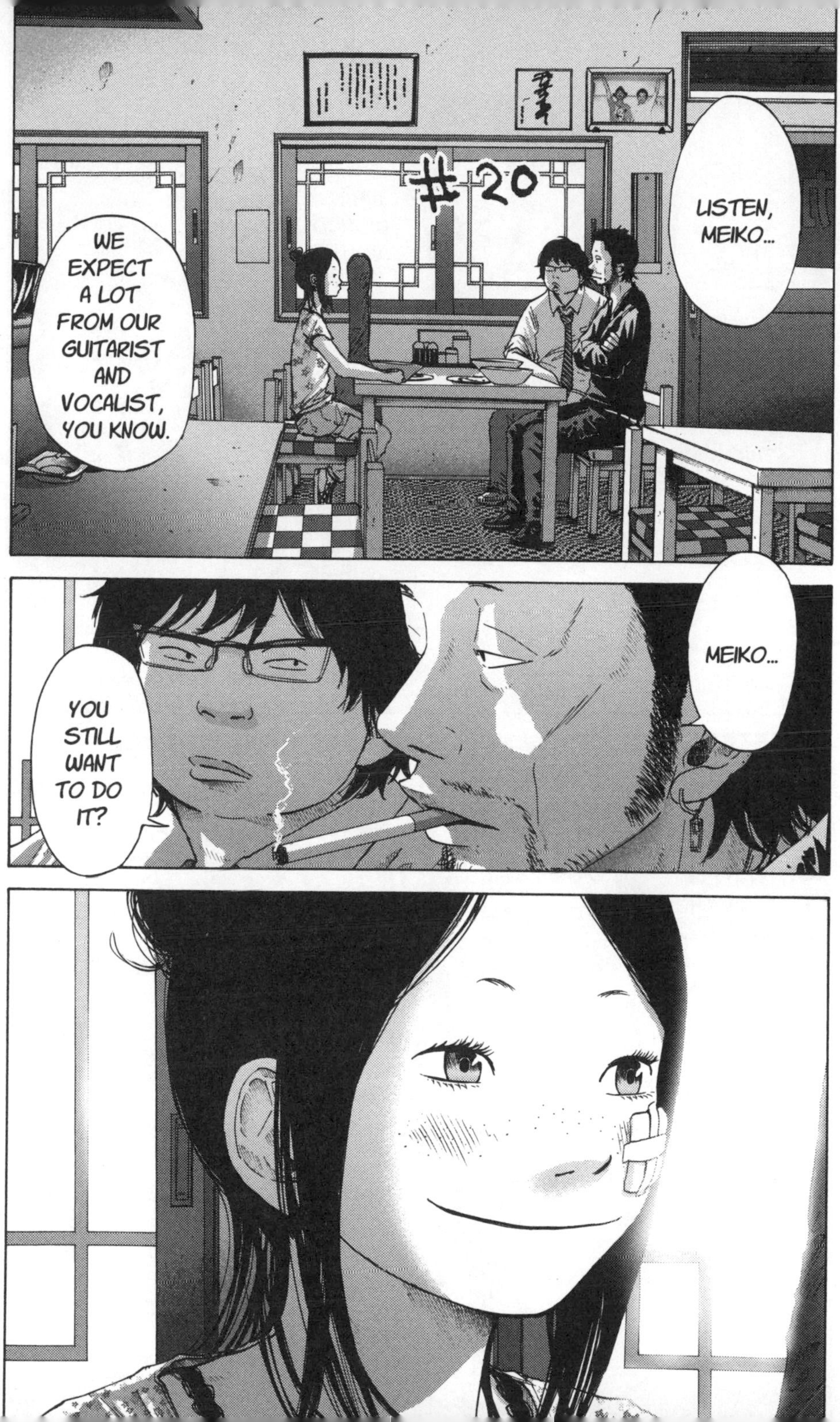
#20
LISTEN, MEIKO...
WE EXPECT A LOT FROM OUR GUITARIST AND VOCALIST, YOU KNOW.
MEIKO...
YOU STILL WANT TO DO IT?

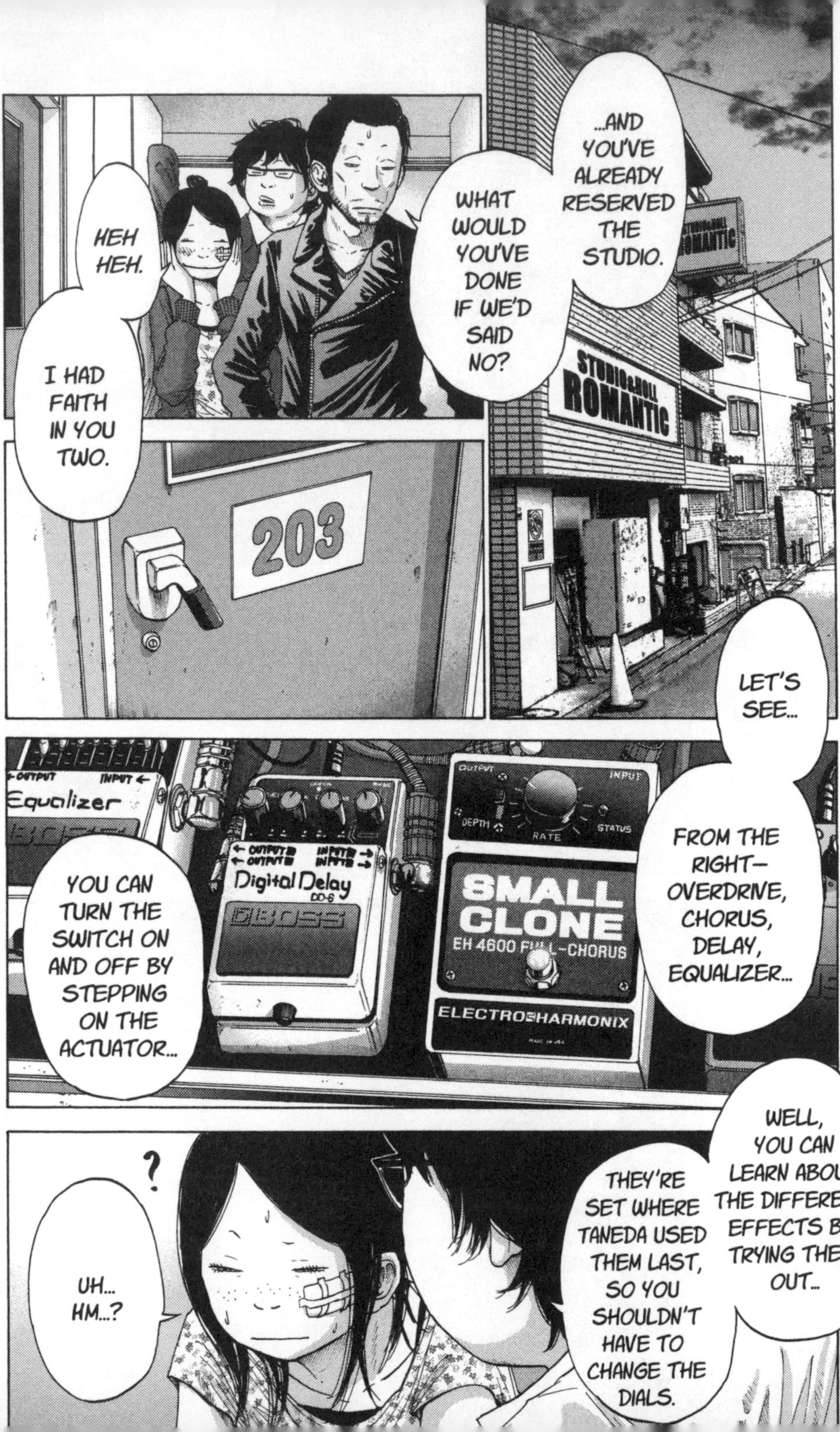
...AND YOU'VE ALREADY RESERVED THE STUDIO.
STUDIO&ROLL ROMANTIC
STUDIO&ROLL ROMANTIC
WHAT WOULD YOU'VE DONE IF WE'D SAID NO?
HEH HEH.
I HAD FAITH IN YOU TWO.
203
LET'S SEE...
FROM THE RIGHT— OVERDRIVE, CHORUS, DELAY, EQUALIZER...
OUTPUT
INPUT
DEPTH
RATE
STATUS
SMALL CLONE
EH 4600 FULL-CHORUS
ELECTRO-HARMONIX
Digital Delay
DD-6
BOSS
Equalizer
YOU CAN TURN THE SWITCH ON AND OFF BY STEPPING ON THE ACTUATOR...
WELL, YOU CAN LEARN ABOUT THE DIFFERENT EFFECTS BY TRYING THEM OUT...
THEY'RE SET WHERE TANEDA USED THEM LAST, SO YOU SHOULDN'T HAVE TO CHANGE THE DIALS.
?
UH... HM...?

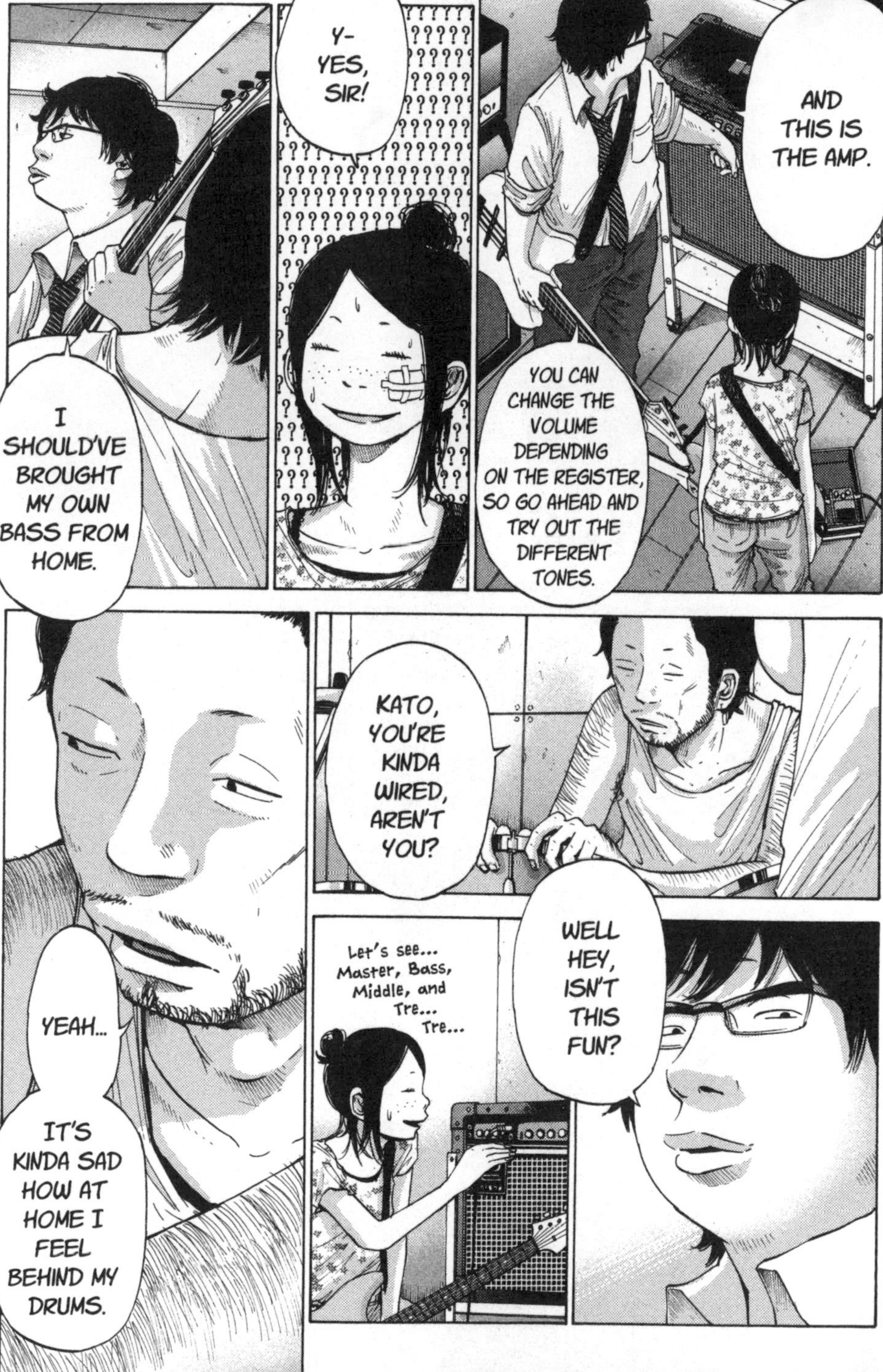
AND THIS IS THE AMP.
YOU CAN CHANGE THE VOLUME DEPENDING ON THE REGISTER, SO GO AHEAD AND TRY OUT THE DIFFERENT TONES.
Y- YES, SIR!
I SHOULD'VE BROUGHT MY OWN BASS FROM HOME.
KATO, YOU'RE KINDA WIRED, AREN'T YOU?
WELL HEY, ISN'T THIS FUN?
Let's see... Master, Bass, Middle, and Tre... Tre...
YEAH...
IT'S KINDA SAD HOW AT HOME I FEEL BEHIND MY DRUMS.

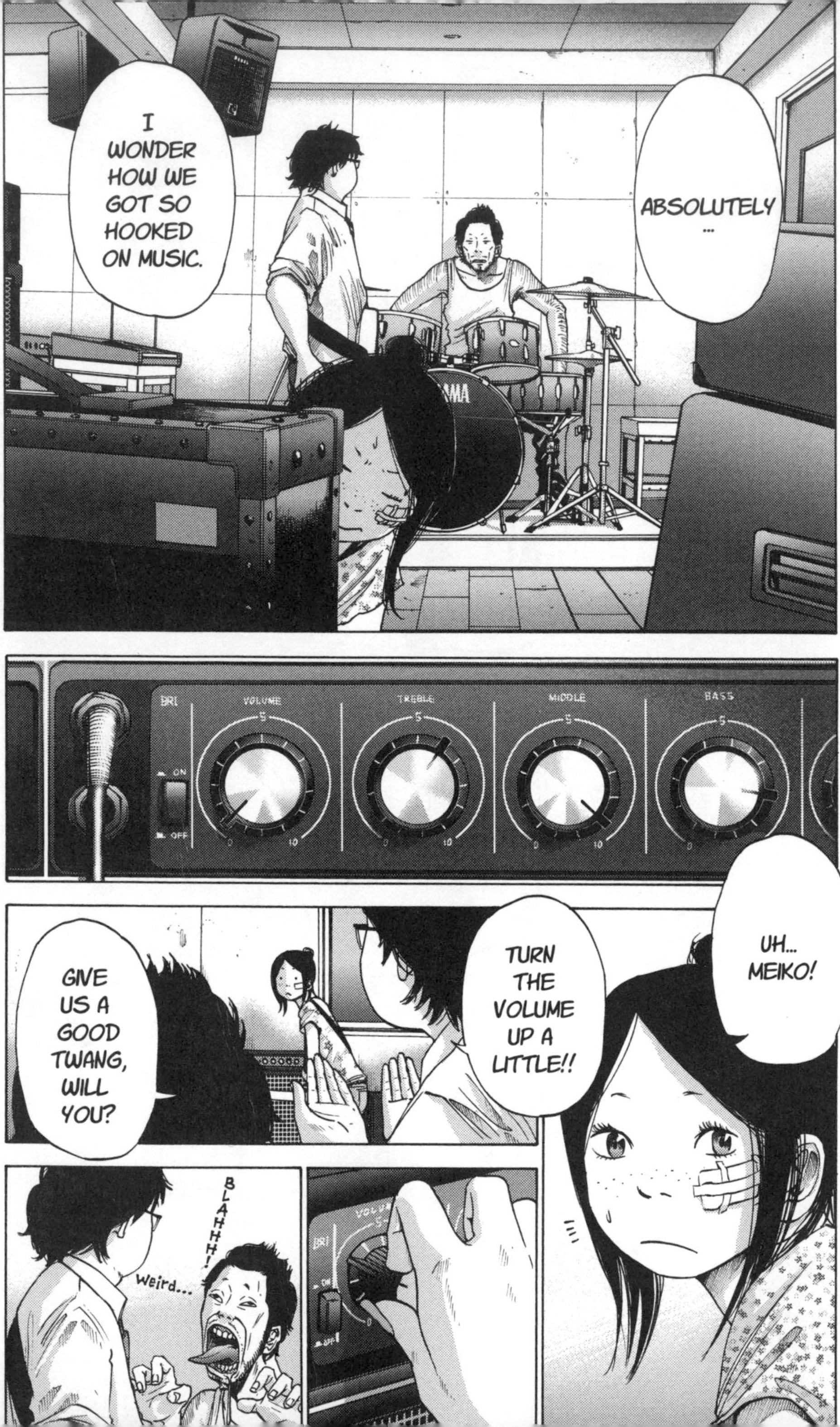
ABSOLUTELY ...
I WONDER HOW WE GOT SO HOOKED ON MUSIC.
BRI
VOLUME
TREBLE
MIDDLE
BASS
ON
OFF
UH... MEIKO!
TURN THE VOLUME UP A LITTLE!!
GIVE US A GOOD TWANG, WILL YOU?
BLAHHH!
Weird...

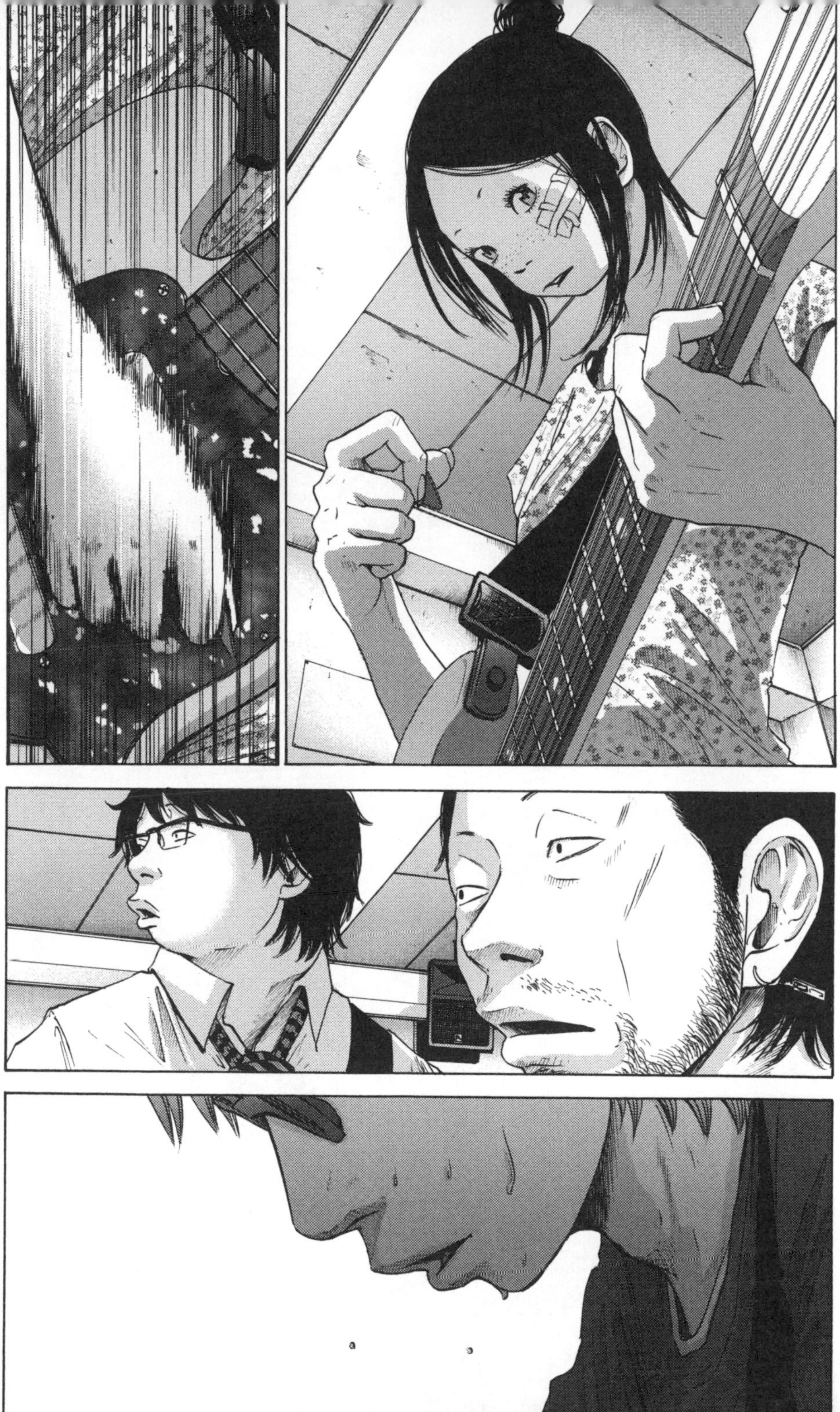

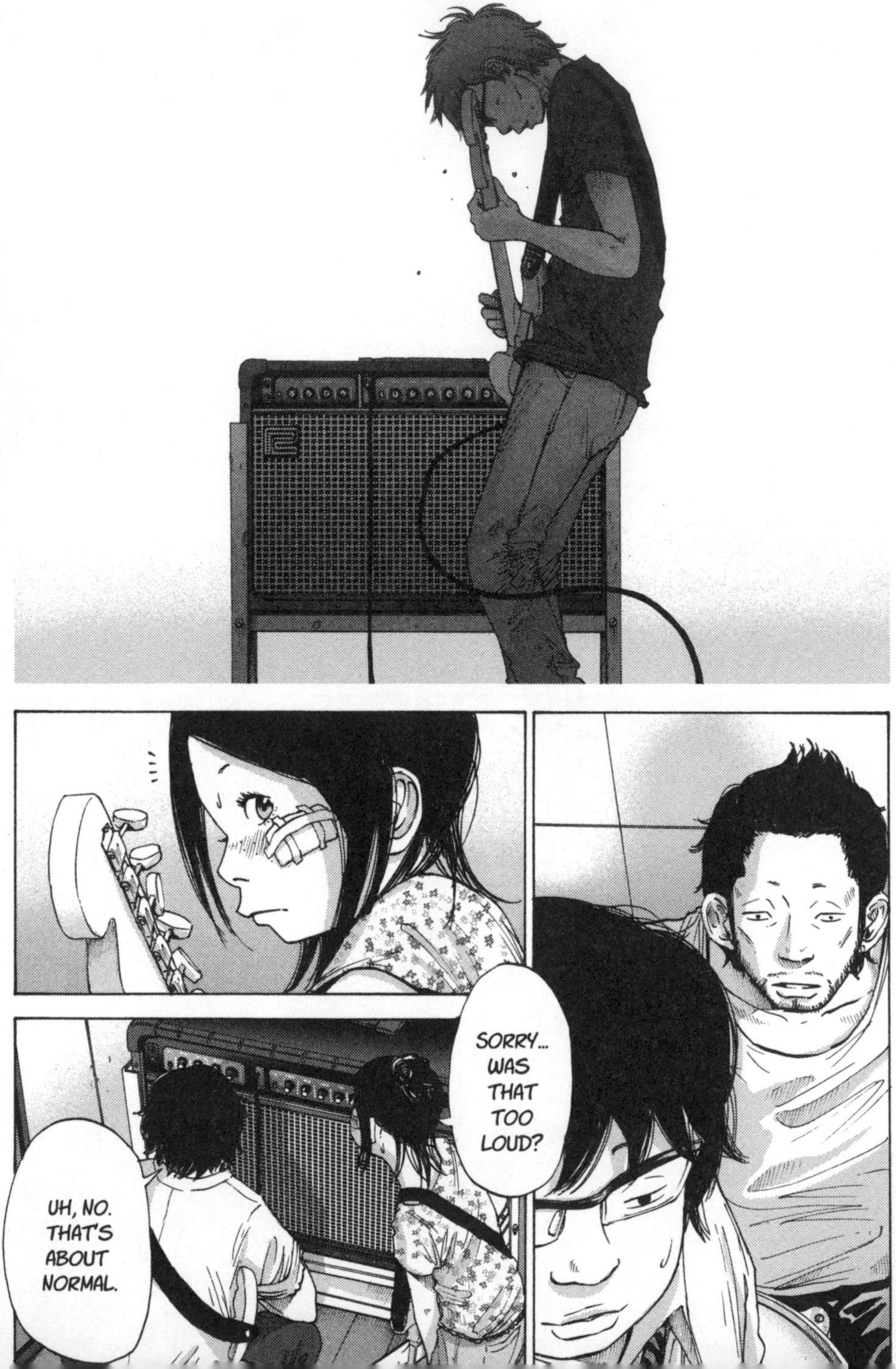

SORRY... WAS THAT TOO LOUD?
UH, NO. THAT'S ABOUT NORMAL.

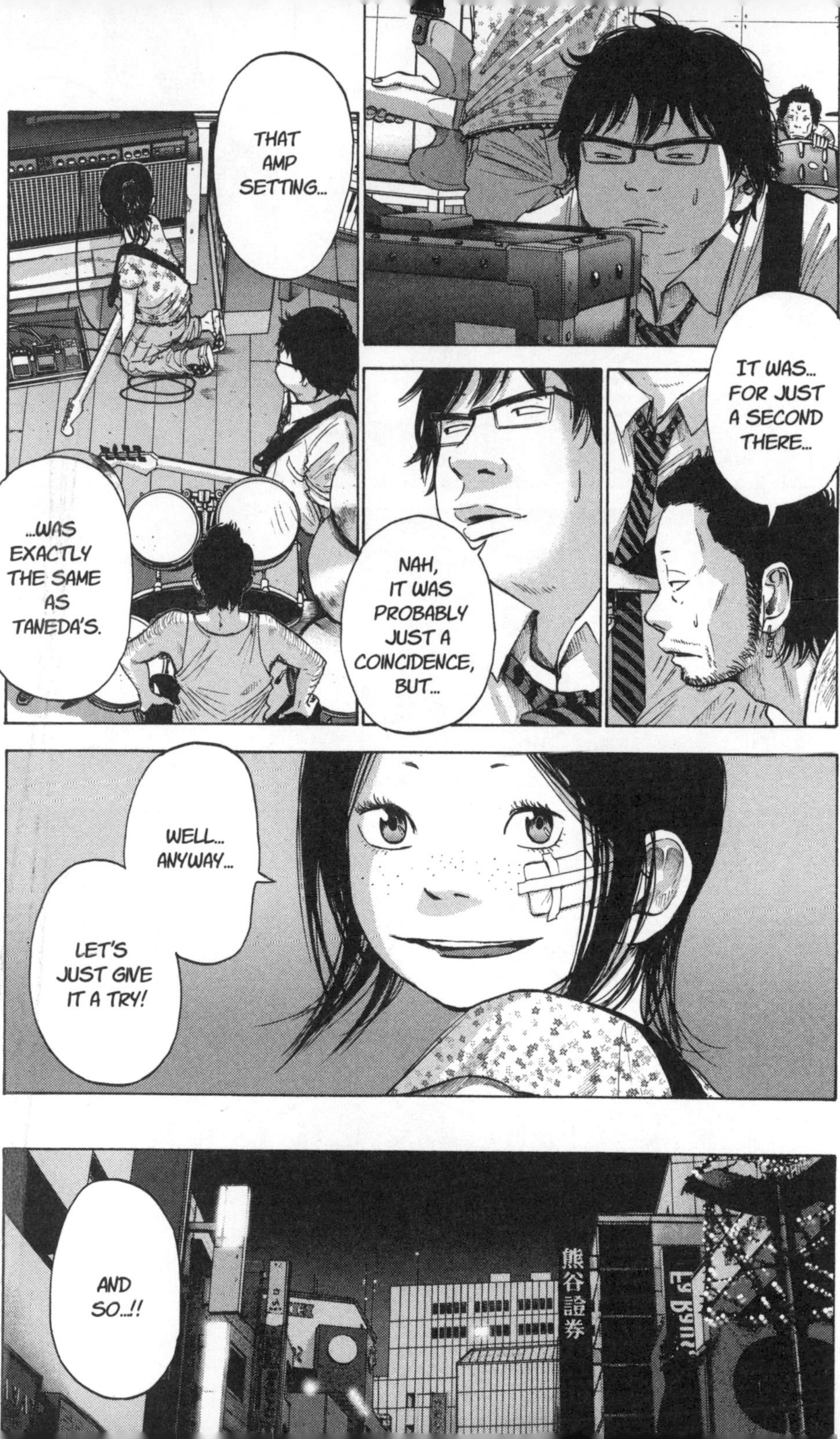
IT WAS... FOR JUST A SECOND THERE...
NAH, IT WAS PROBABLY JUST A COINCIDENCE, BUT...
THAT AMP SETTING...
...WAS EXACTLY THE SAME AS TANEDA'S.
WELL... ANYWAY...
LET'S JUST GIVE IT A TRY!
AND SO...!!
熊谷證券

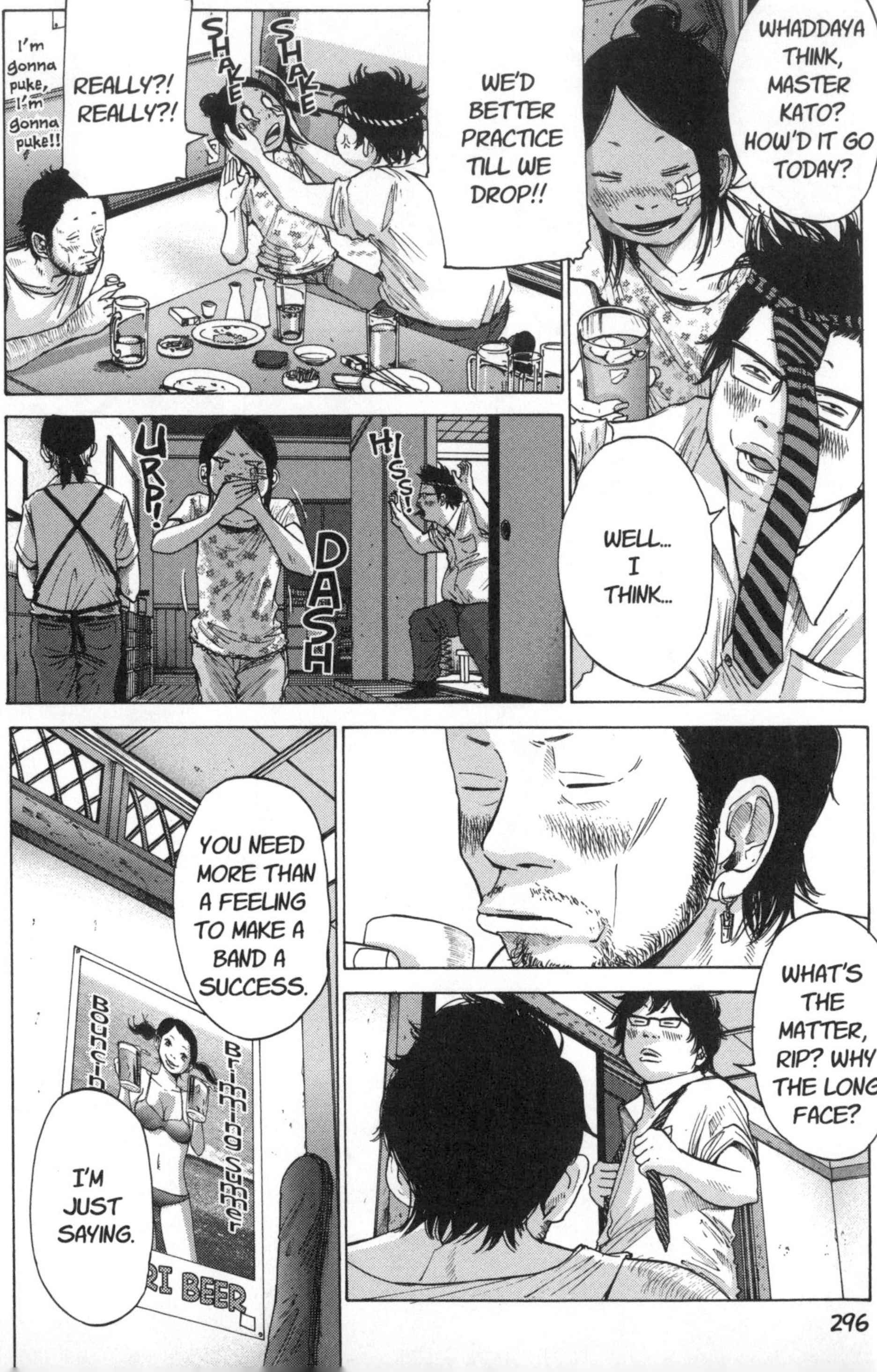
WHADDAYA THINK, MASTER KATO? HOW'D IT GO TODAY?
WELL... I THINK...
WE'D BETTER PRACTICE TILL WE DROP!!
REALLY?! REALLY?!
SHAKE
SHAKE
I'm gonna puke, I'm gonna puke!!
HISS!
DASH
URP!
WHAT'S THE MATTER, RIP? WHY THE LONG FACE?
YOU NEED MORE THAN A FEELING TO MAKE A BAND A SUCCESS.
Brimming Summer
I'M JUST SAYING.

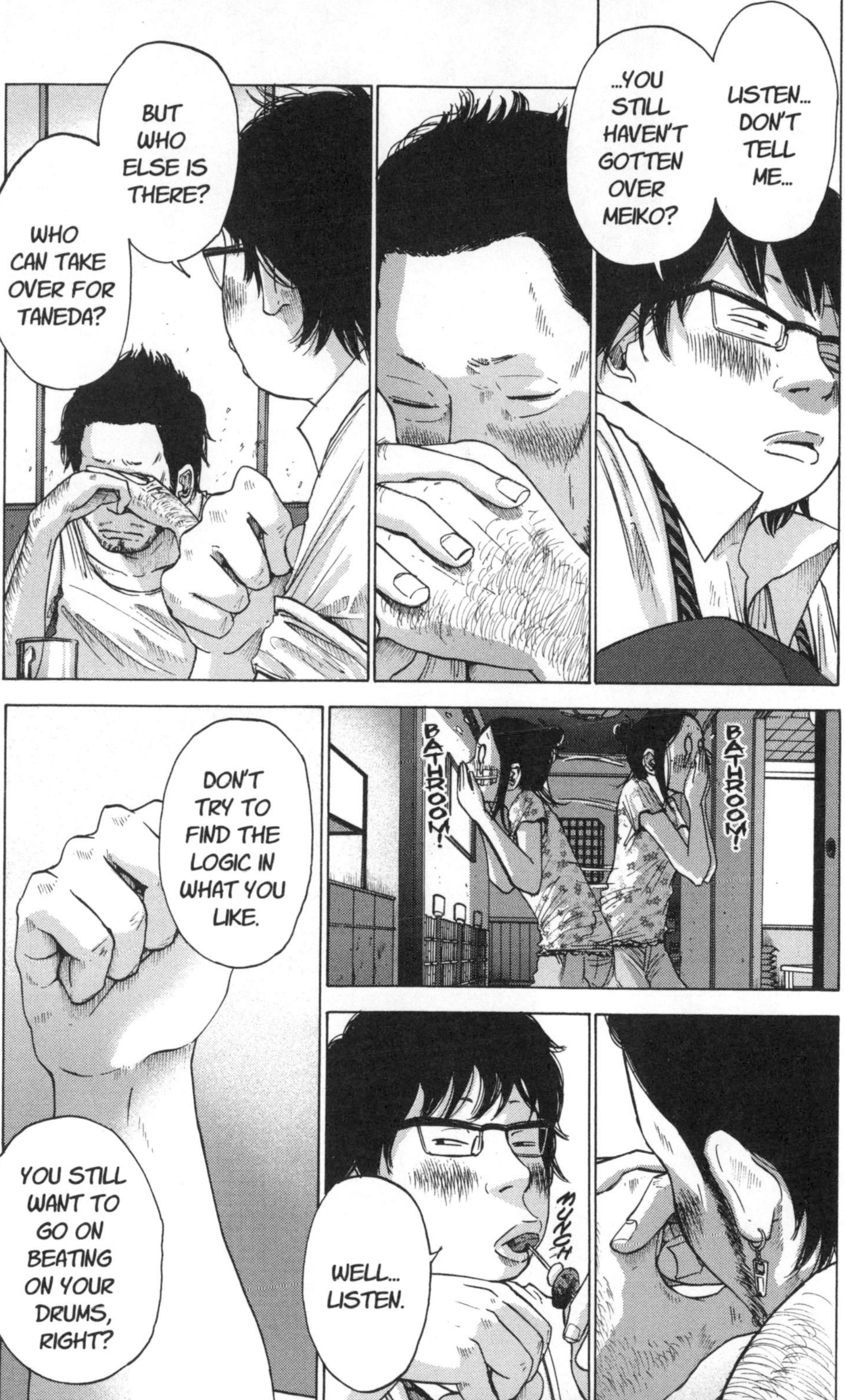
LISTEN... DON'T TELL ME...
...YOU STILL HAVEN'T GOTTEN OVER MEIKO?
BUT WHO ELSE IS THERE?
WHO CAN TAKE OVER FOR TANEDA?
BATHROOM!
BATHROOM!
MUNCH
WELL... LISTEN.
DON'T TRY TO FIND THE LOGIC IN WHAT YOU LIKE.
YOU STILL WANT TO GO ON BEATING ON YOUR DRUMS, RIGHT?

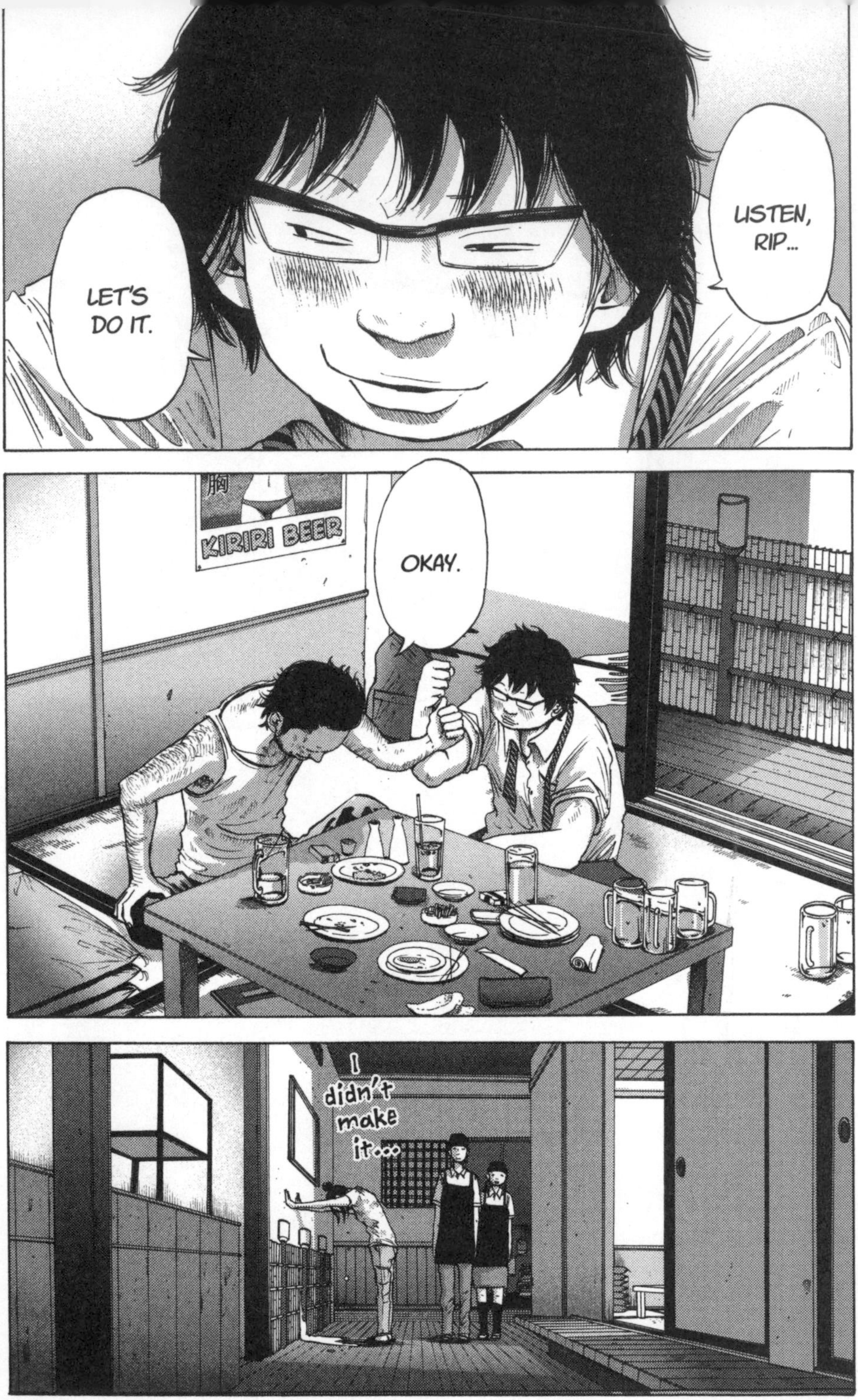
LISTEN, RIP...
LET'S DO IT.
KIRIRI BEER
OKAY.
I didn't make it...

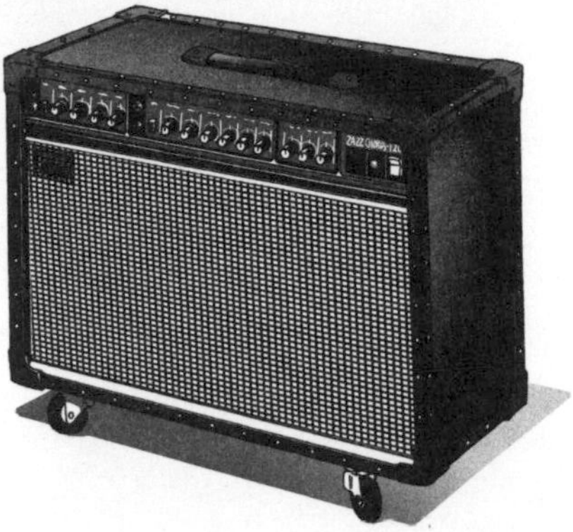

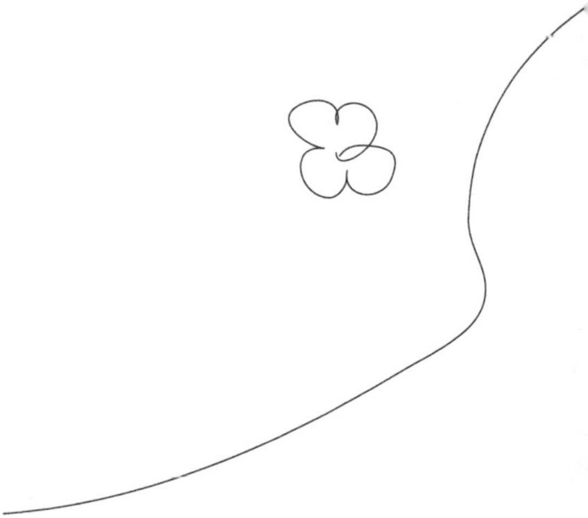

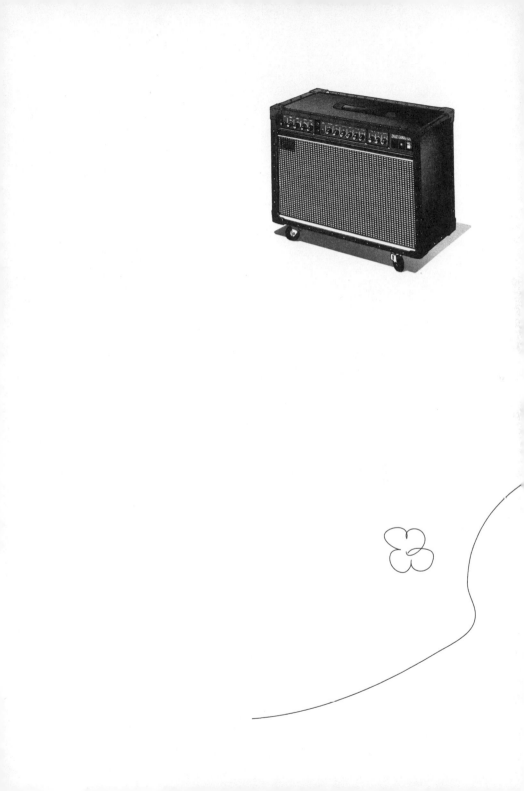

DIARY
DIARY

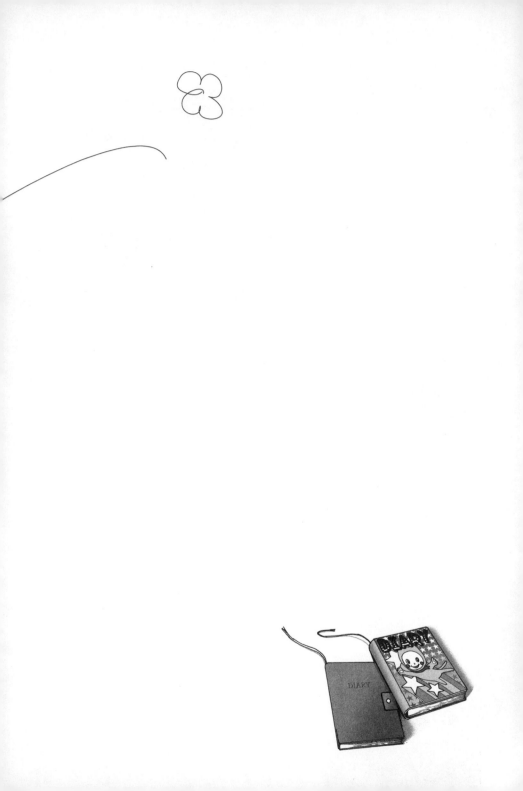

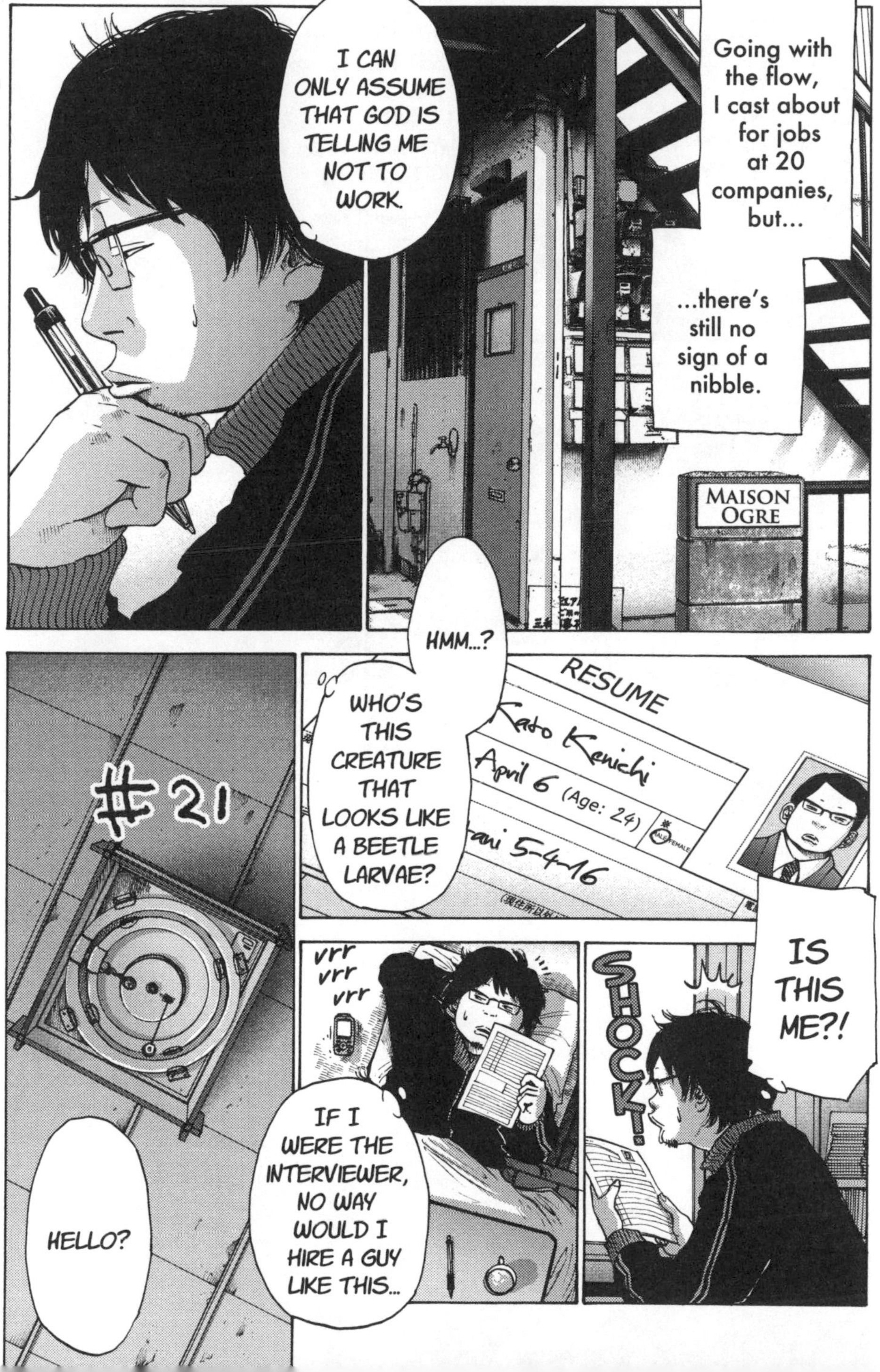
Going with the flow, I cast about for jobs at 20 companies, but...
...there's still no sign of a nibble.
MAISON OGRE
I CAN ONLY ASSUME THAT GOD IS TELLING ME NOT TO WORK.
HMM...?
WHO'S THIS CREATURE THAT LOOKS LIKE A BEETLE LARVAE?
RESUME
Kato Kenichi
April 6 (Age: 24)
SHOCK!
IS THIS ME?!
vrr vrr vrr
IF I WERE THE INTERVIEWER, NO WAY WOULD I HIRE A GUY LIKE THIS...
#21
HELLO?

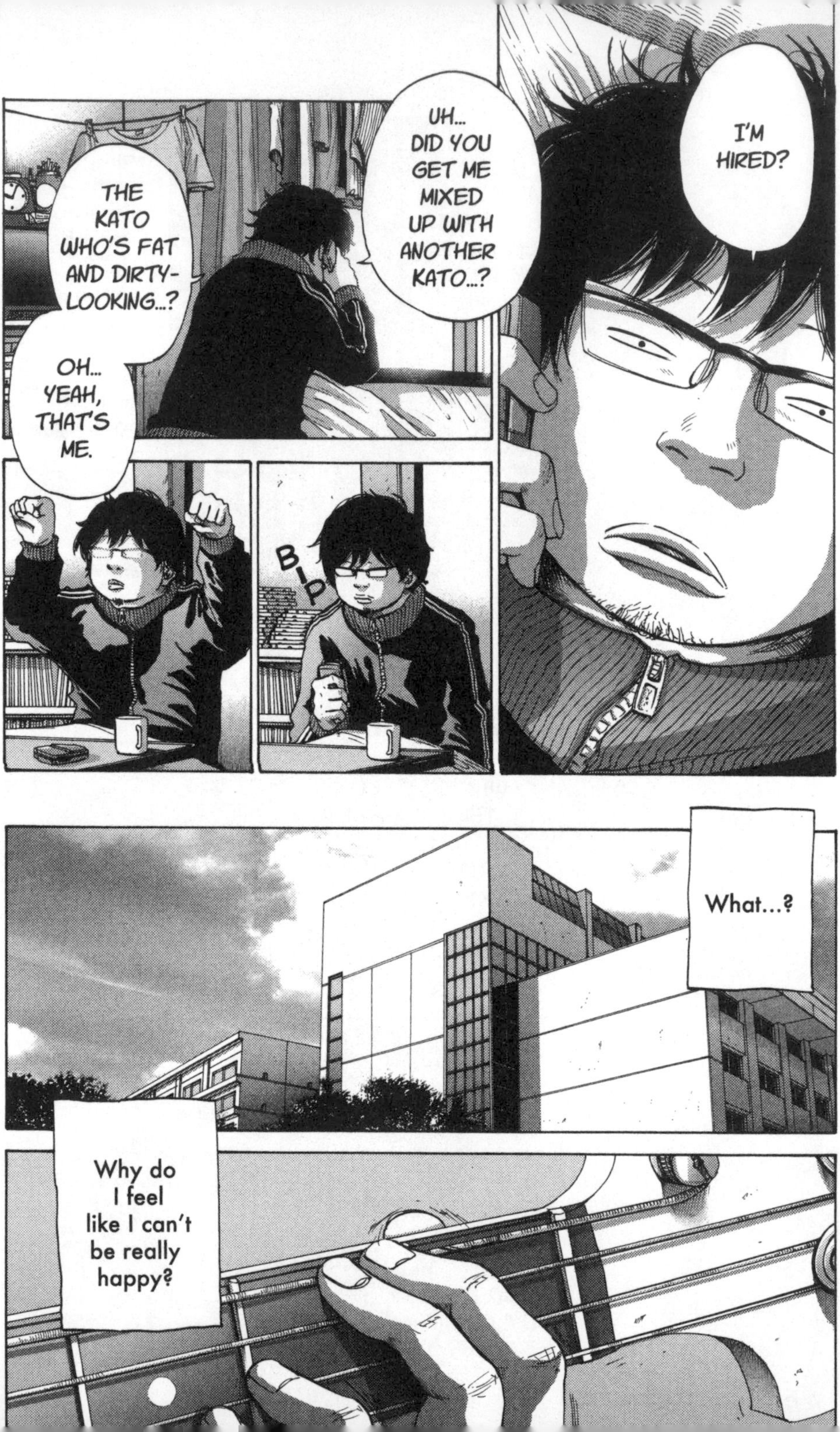
I'M HIRED?
UH... DID YOU GET ME MIXED UP WITH ANOTHER KATO...?
THE KATO WHO'S FAT AND DIRTY-LOOKING...?
OH... YEAH, THAT'S ME.
BIP
What...?
Why do I feel like I can't be really happy?

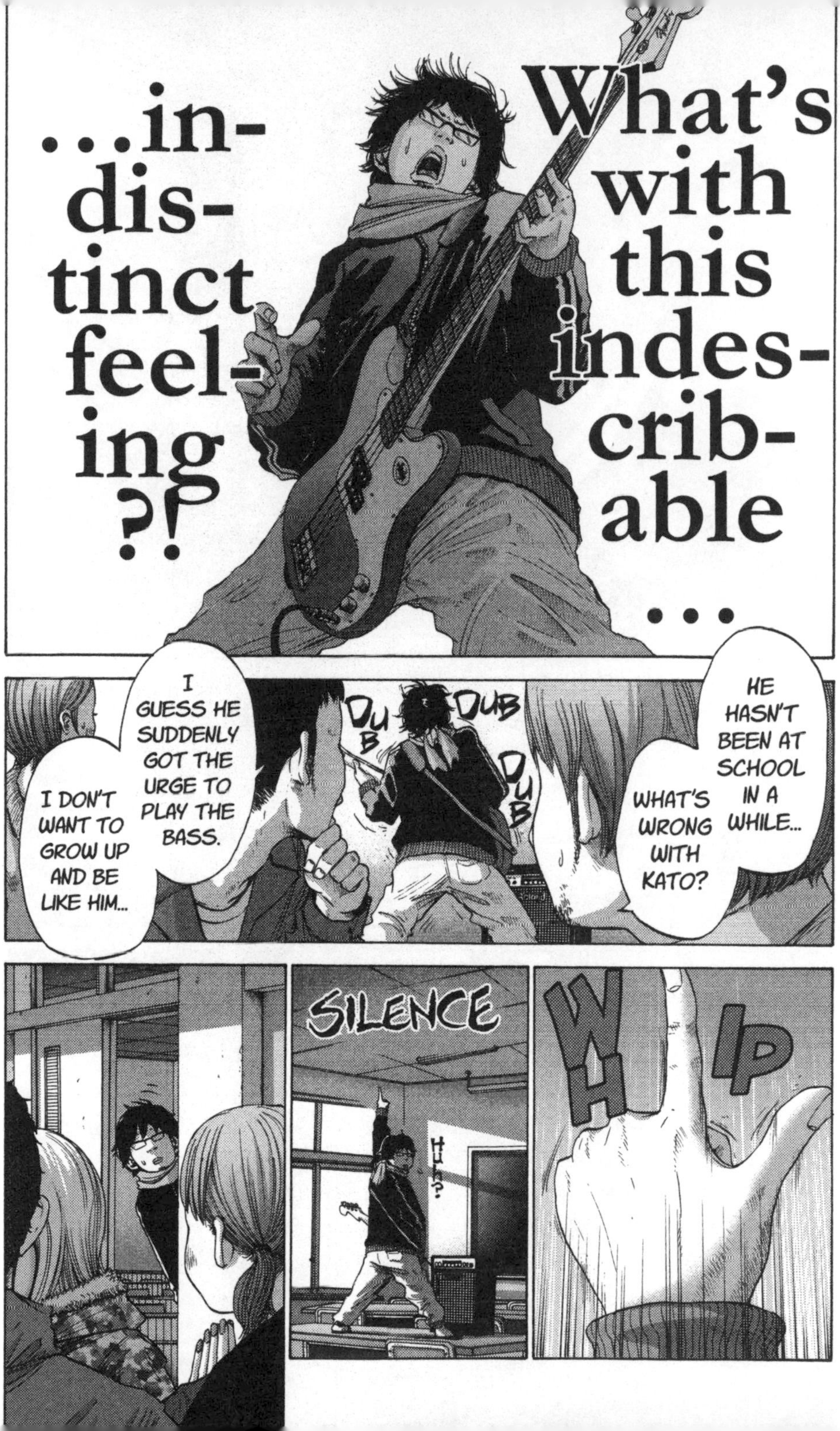
What's with this indes-crib-able...
...in-dis-tinct feel-ing?!
HE HASN'T BEEN AT SCHOOL IN A WHILE...
WHAT'S WRONG WITH KATO?
DUB DUB DUB
I GUESS HE SUDDENLY GOT THE URGE TO PLAY THE BASS.
I DON'T WANT TO GROW UP AND BE LIKE HIM...
WHIP
SILENCE
Huh?

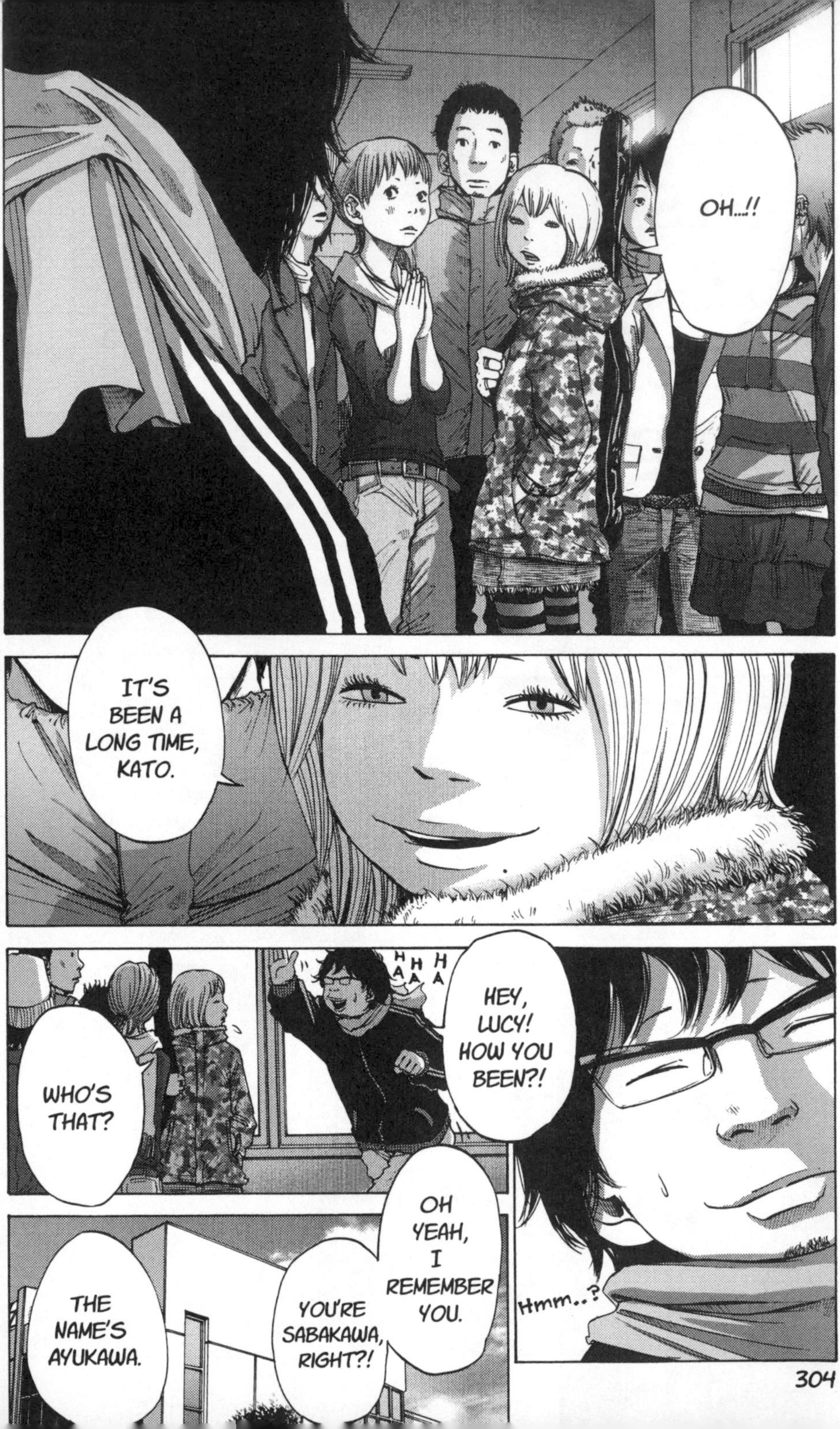
OH...!!
IT'S BEEN A LONG TIME, KATO.
HA HA HA
HEY, LUCY! HOW YOU BEEN?!
Hmm..?
WHO'S THAT?
OH YEAH, I REMEMBER YOU.
YOU'RE SABAKAWA, RIGHT?!
THE NAME'S AYUKAWA.

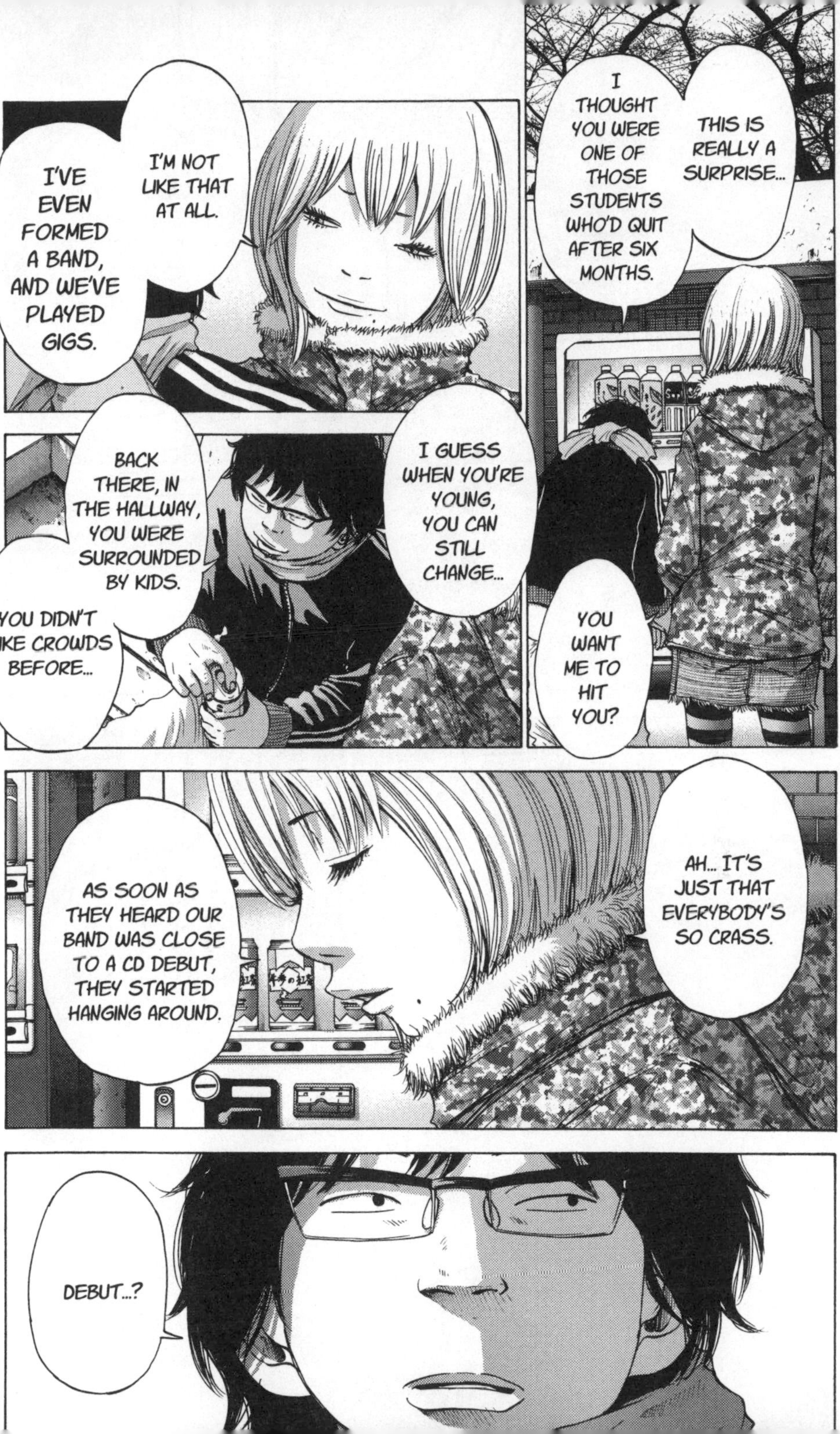
THIS IS REALLY A SURPRISE...
I THOUGHT YOU WERE ONE OF THOSE STUDENTS WHO'D QUIT AFTER SIX MONTHS.
YOU WANT ME TO HIT YOU?
I'M NOT LIKE THAT AT ALL.
I'VE EVEN FORMED A BAND, AND WE'VE PLAYED GIGS.
I GUESS WHEN YOU'RE YOUNG, YOU CAN STILL CHANGE...
BACK THERE, IN THE HALLWAY, YOU WERE SURROUNDED BY KIDS.
YOU DIDN'T LIKE CROWDS BEFORE...
AH... IT'S JUST THAT EVERYBODY'S SO CRASS.
AS SOON AS THEY HEARD OUR BAND WAS CLOSE TO A CD DEBUT, THEY STARTED HANGING AROUND.
DEBUT...?

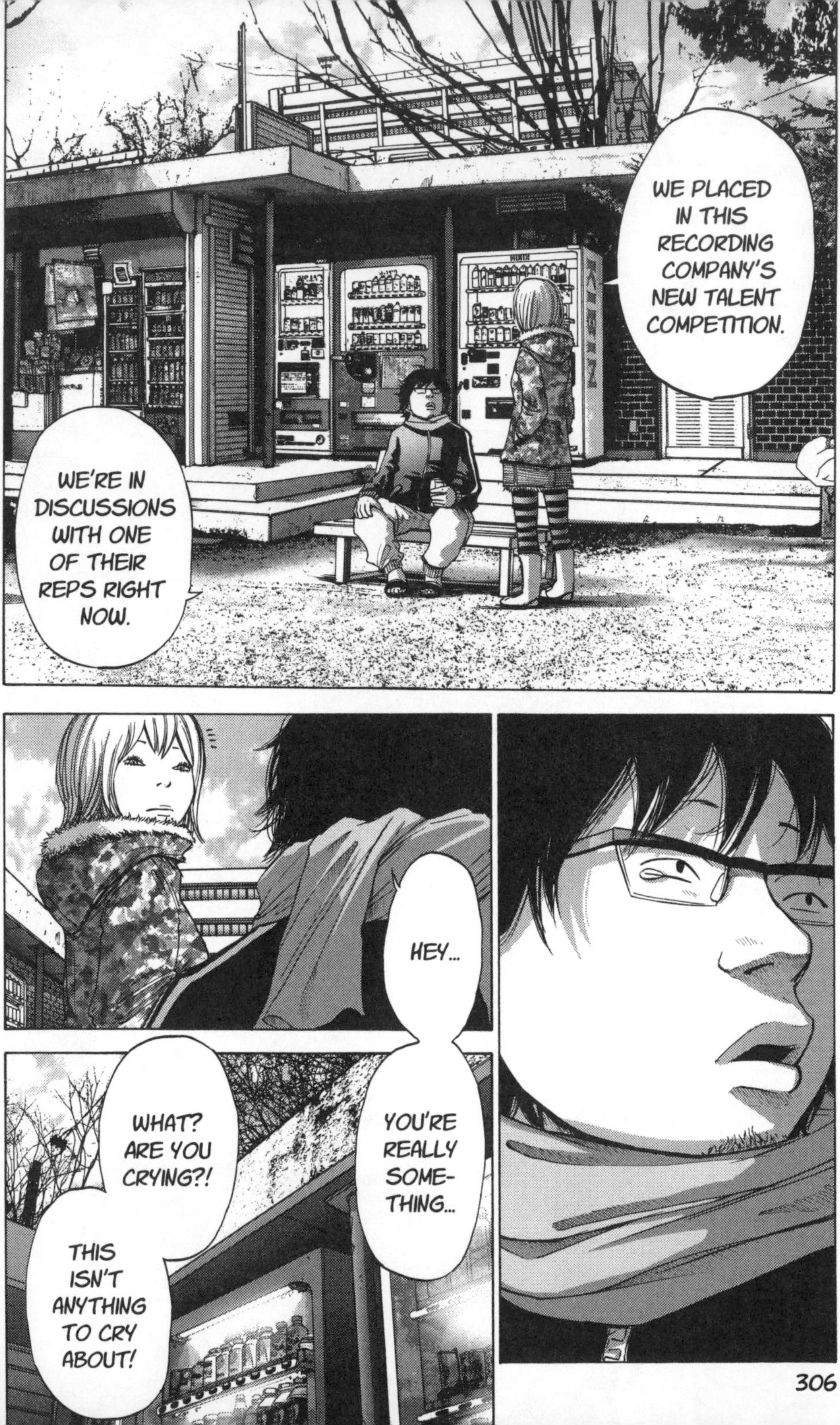
WE PLACED IN THIS RECORDING COMPANY'S NEW TALENT COMPETITION.
WE'RE IN DISCUSSIONS WITH ONE OF THEIR REPS RIGHT NOW.
HEY...
YOU'RE REALLY SOME-THING...
WHAT? ARE YOU CRYING?!
THIS ISN'T ANYTHING TO CRY ABOUT!

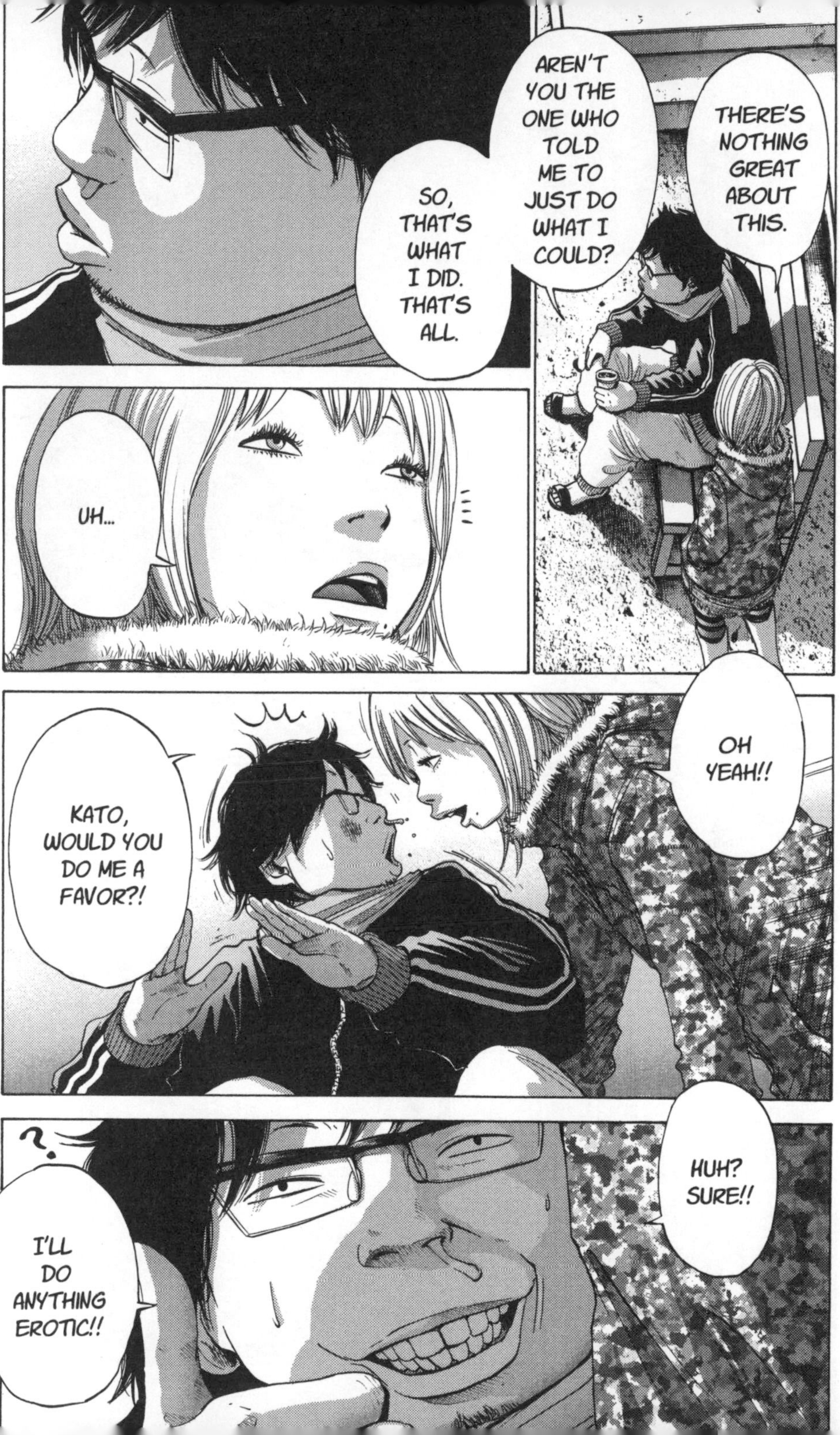
THERE'S NOTHING GREAT ABOUT THIS.
AREN'T YOU THE ONE WHO TOLD ME TO JUST DO WHAT I COULD?
SO, THAT'S WHAT I DID. THAT'S ALL.
UH...
OH YEAH!!
KATO, WOULD YOU DO ME A FAVOR?!
HUH? SURE!!
I'LL DO ANYTHING EROTIC!!

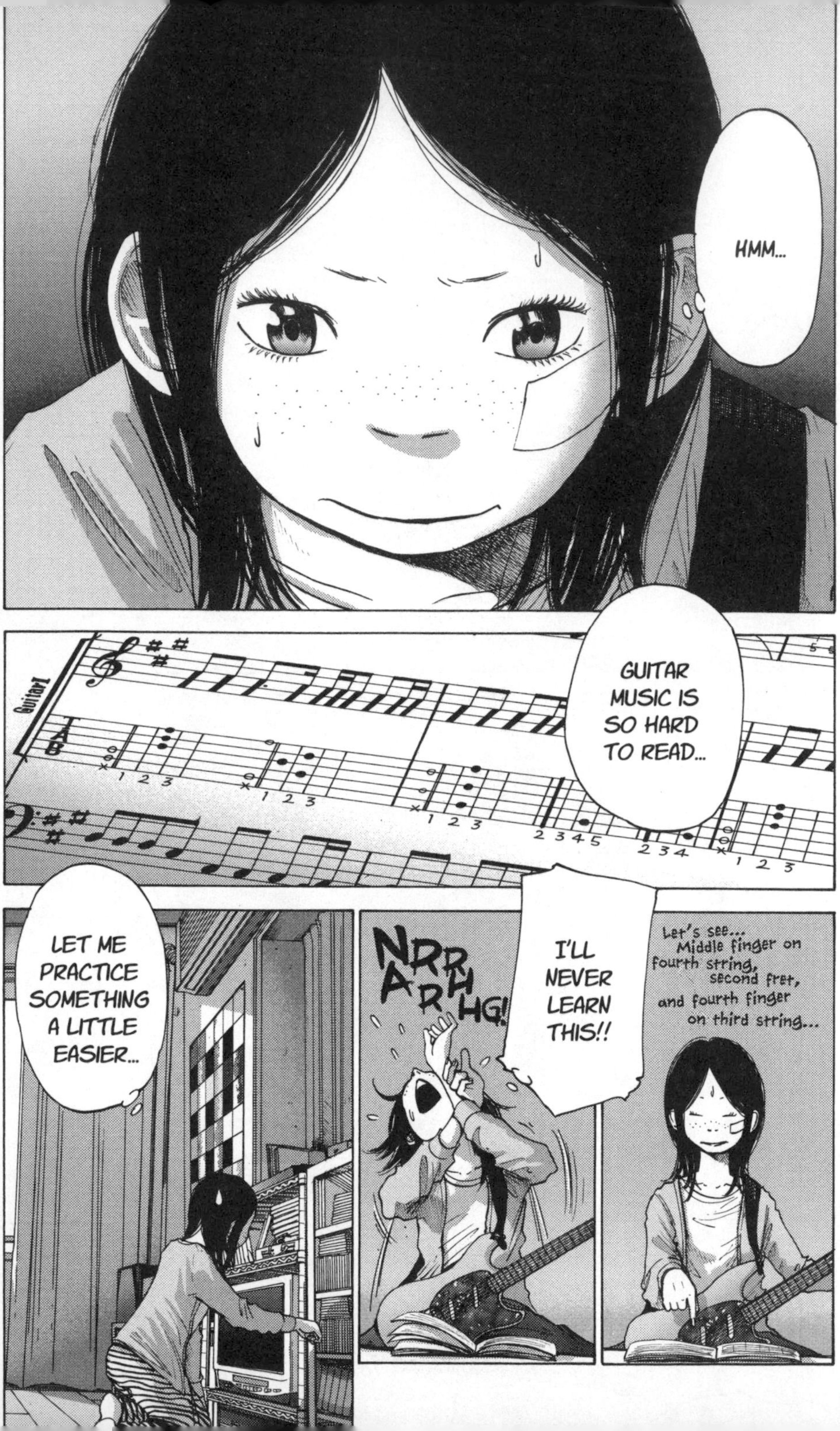
HMM...
GUITAR MUSIC IS SO HARD TO READ...
Guitar1
Let's see... Middle finger on fourth string, second fret, and fourth finger on third string...
I'LL NEVER LEARN THIS!!
NRRARHHG!
LET ME PRACTICE SOMETHING A LITTLE EASIER...

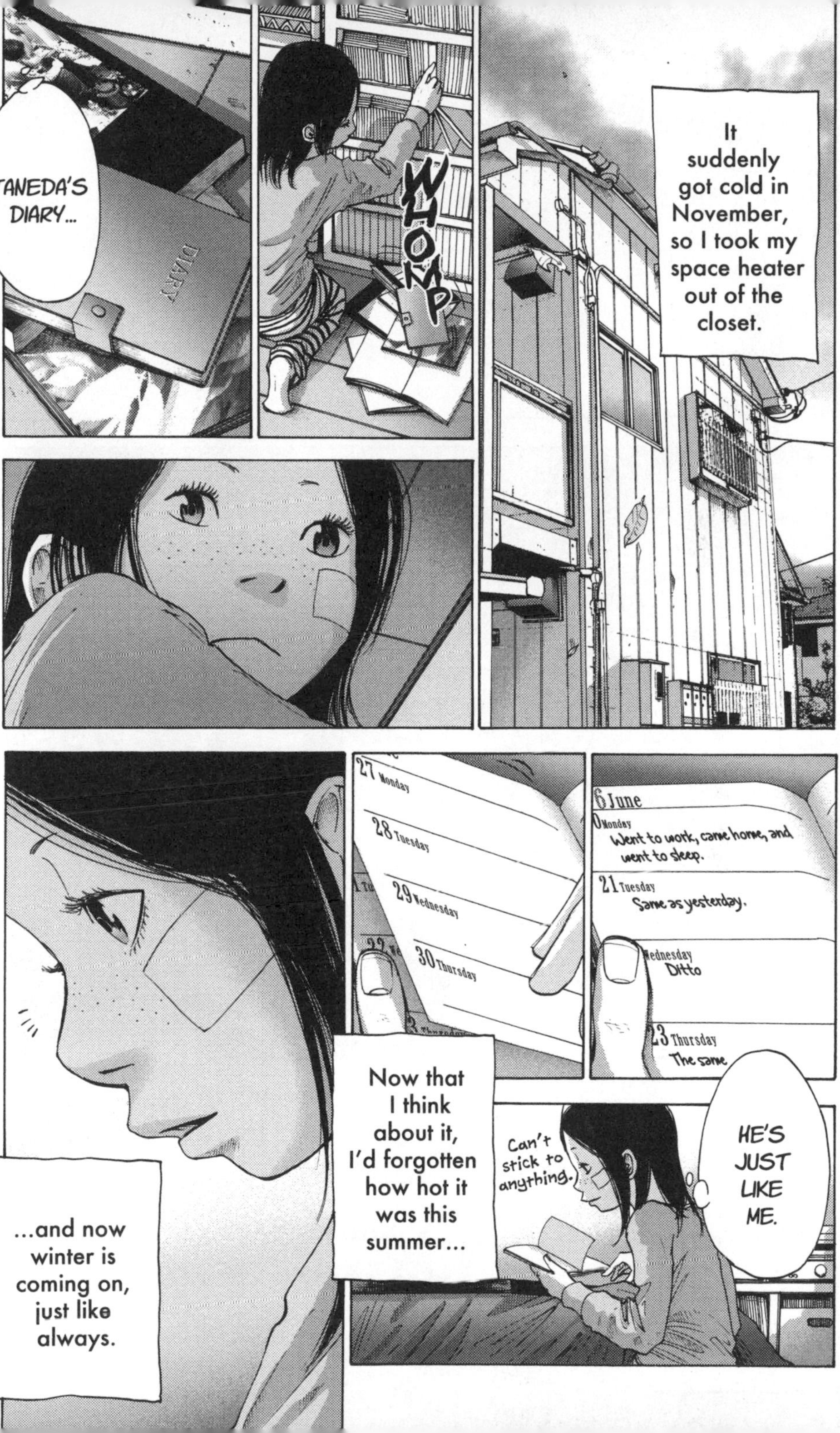
It suddenly got cold in November, so I took my space heater out of the closet.
WHOMP
TANEDA'S DIARY...
DIARY
June
Monday
Went to work, came home, and went to sleep.
21 Tuesday
Same as yesterday.
Wednesday
Ditto
23 Thursday
The same
27 Monday
28 Tuesday
29 Wednesday
30 Thursday
Now that I think about it, I'd forgotten how hot it was this summer...
HE'S JUST LIKE ME.
Can't stick to anything.
...and now winter is coming on, just like always.

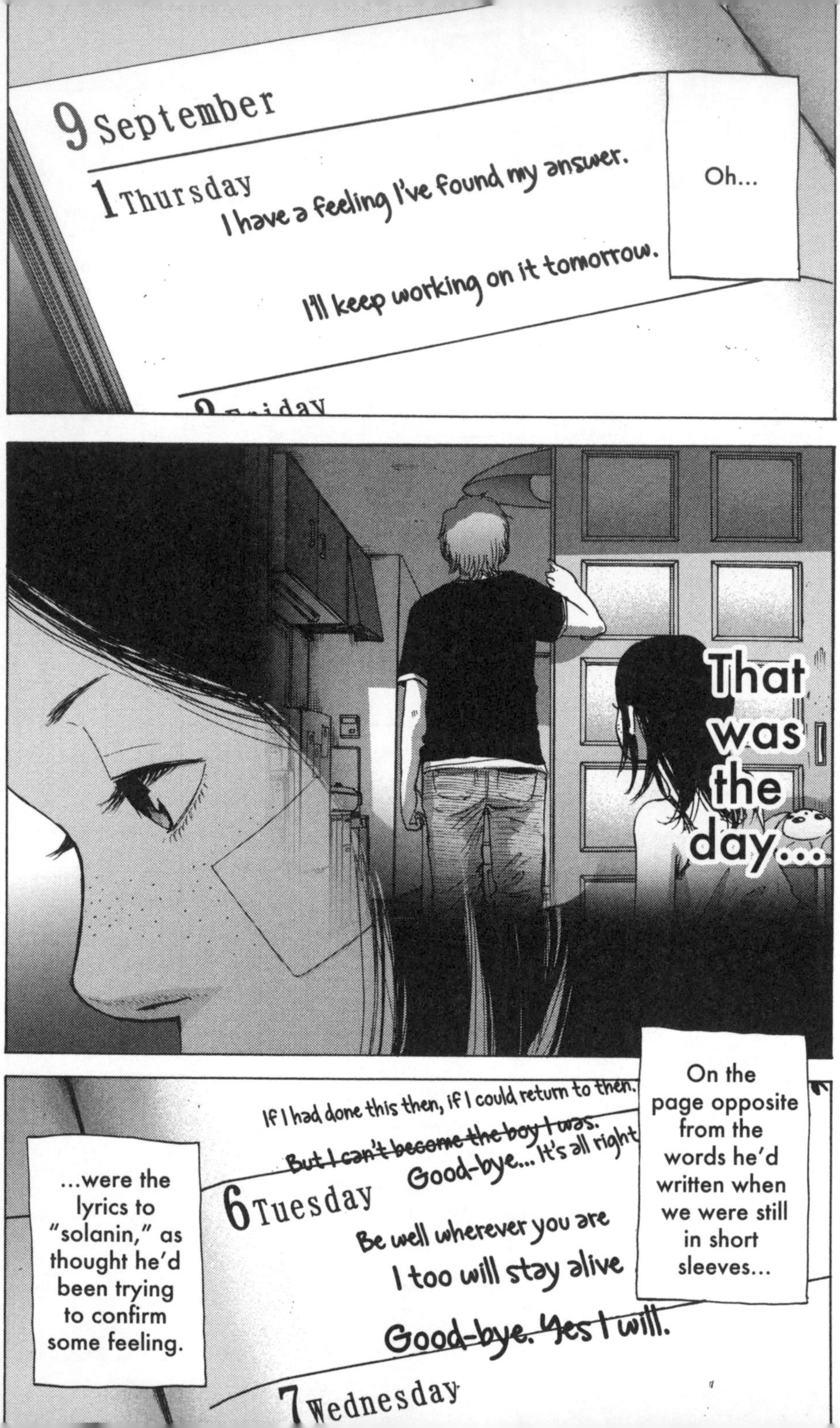
9 September
1 Thursday
I have a feeling I've found my answer.
I'll keep working on it tomorrow.
Oh...
That was the day...
On the page opposite from the words he'd written when we were still in short sleeves...
If I had done this then, if I could return to then.
But I can't become the boy I was.
Good-bye... It's all right
6 Tuesday
Be well wherever you are
I too will stay alive
Good-bye. Yes I will.
7 Wednesday
...were the lyrics to "solanin," as thought he'd been trying to confirm some feeling.

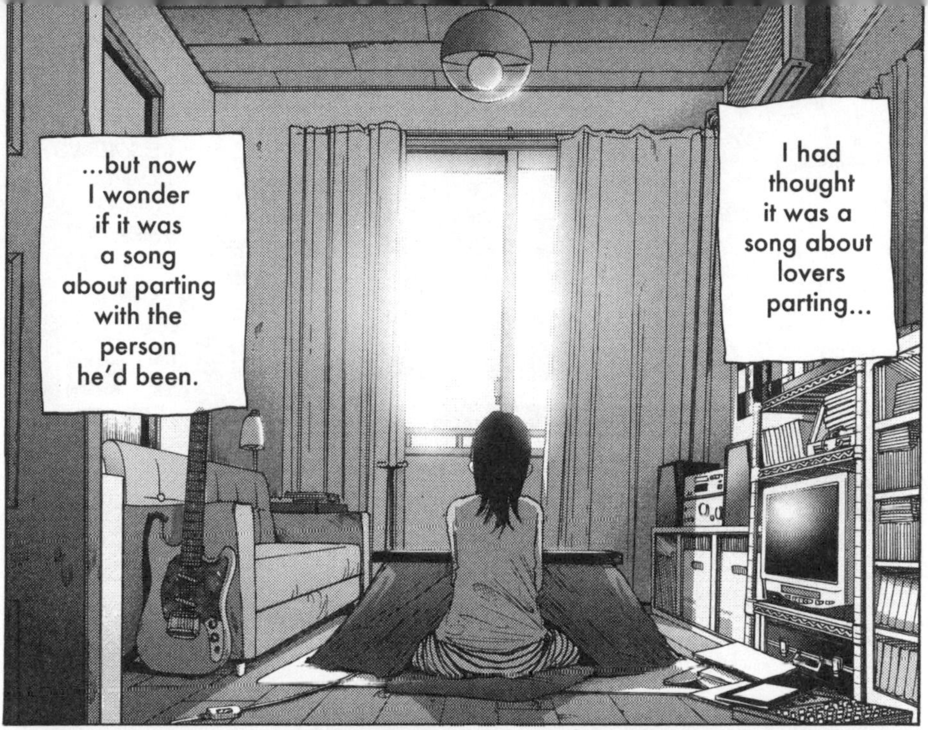
I had thought it was a song about lovers parting...
...but now I wonder if it was a song about parting with the person he'd been.

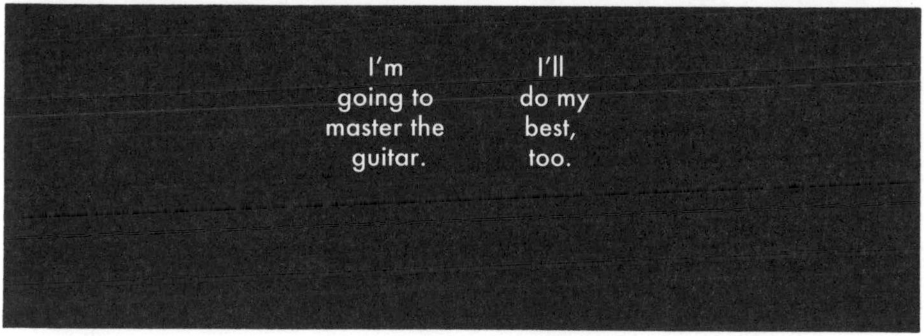
I'll do my best, too.
I'm going to master the guitar.

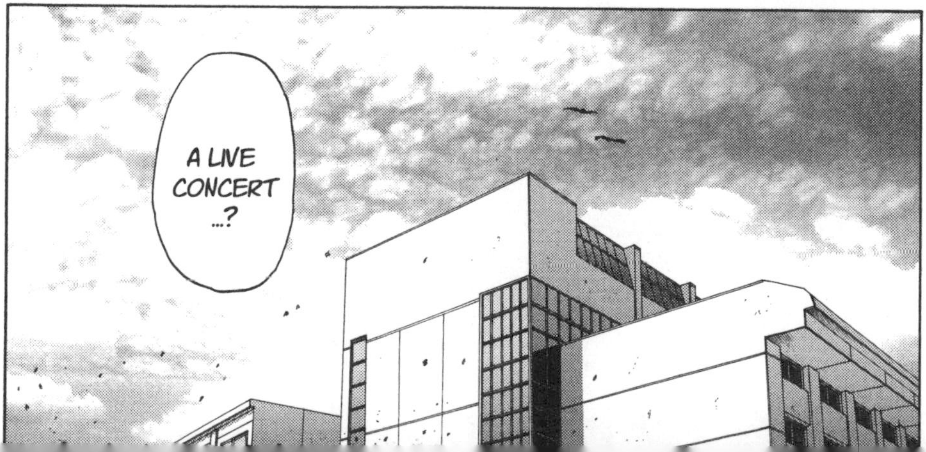
A LIVE CONCERT ...?

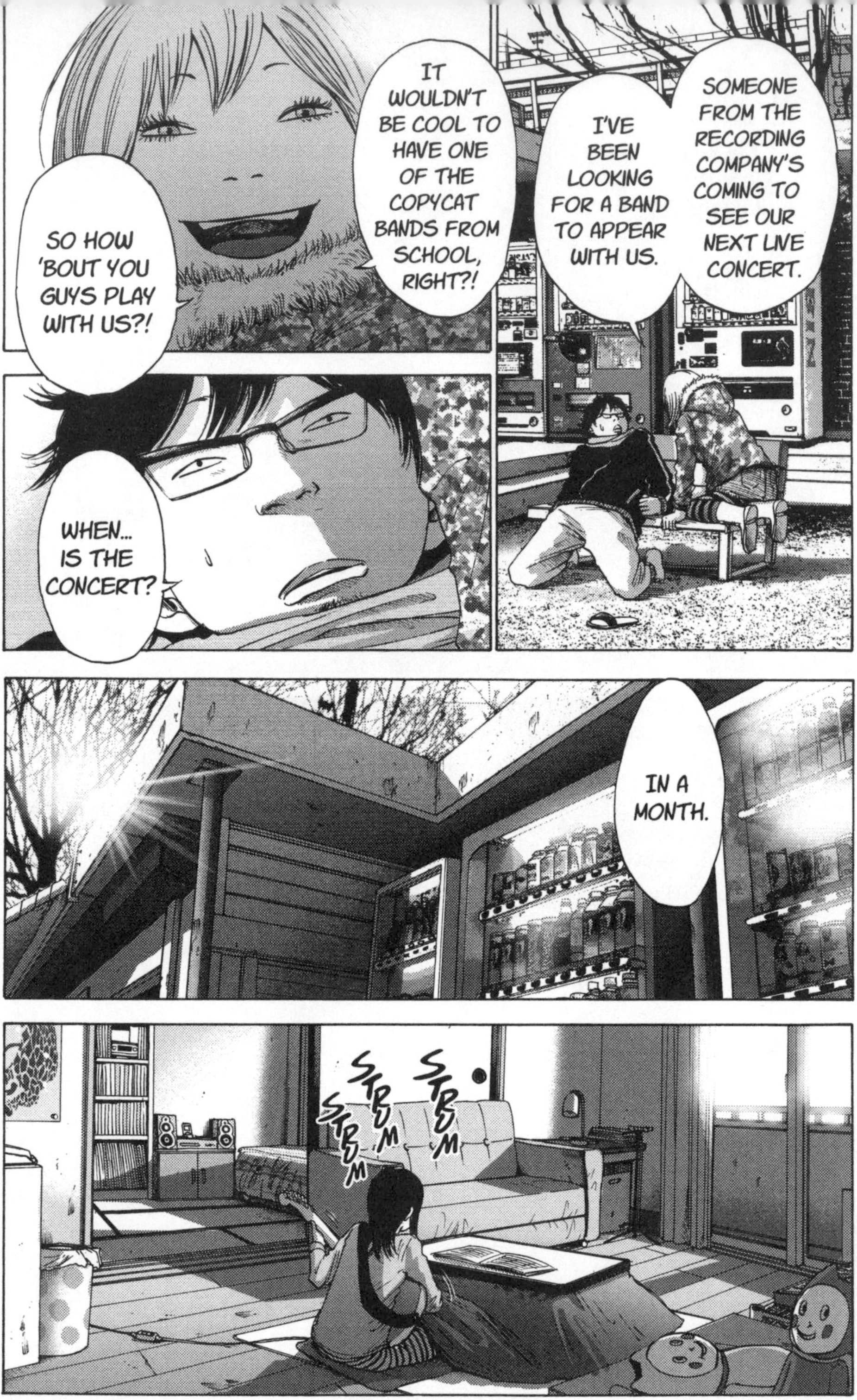
SOMEONE FROM THE RECORDING COMPANY'S COMING TO SEE OUR NEXT LIVE CONCERT.
I'VE BEEN LOOKING FOR A BAND TO APPEAR WITH US.
IT WOULDN'T BE COOL TO HAVE ONE OF THE COPYCAT BANDS FROM SCHOOL, RIGHT?!
SO HOW 'BOUT YOU GUYS PLAY WITH US?!
WHEN... IS THE CONCERT?
IN A MONTH.
STRUM
STRUM
STRUM

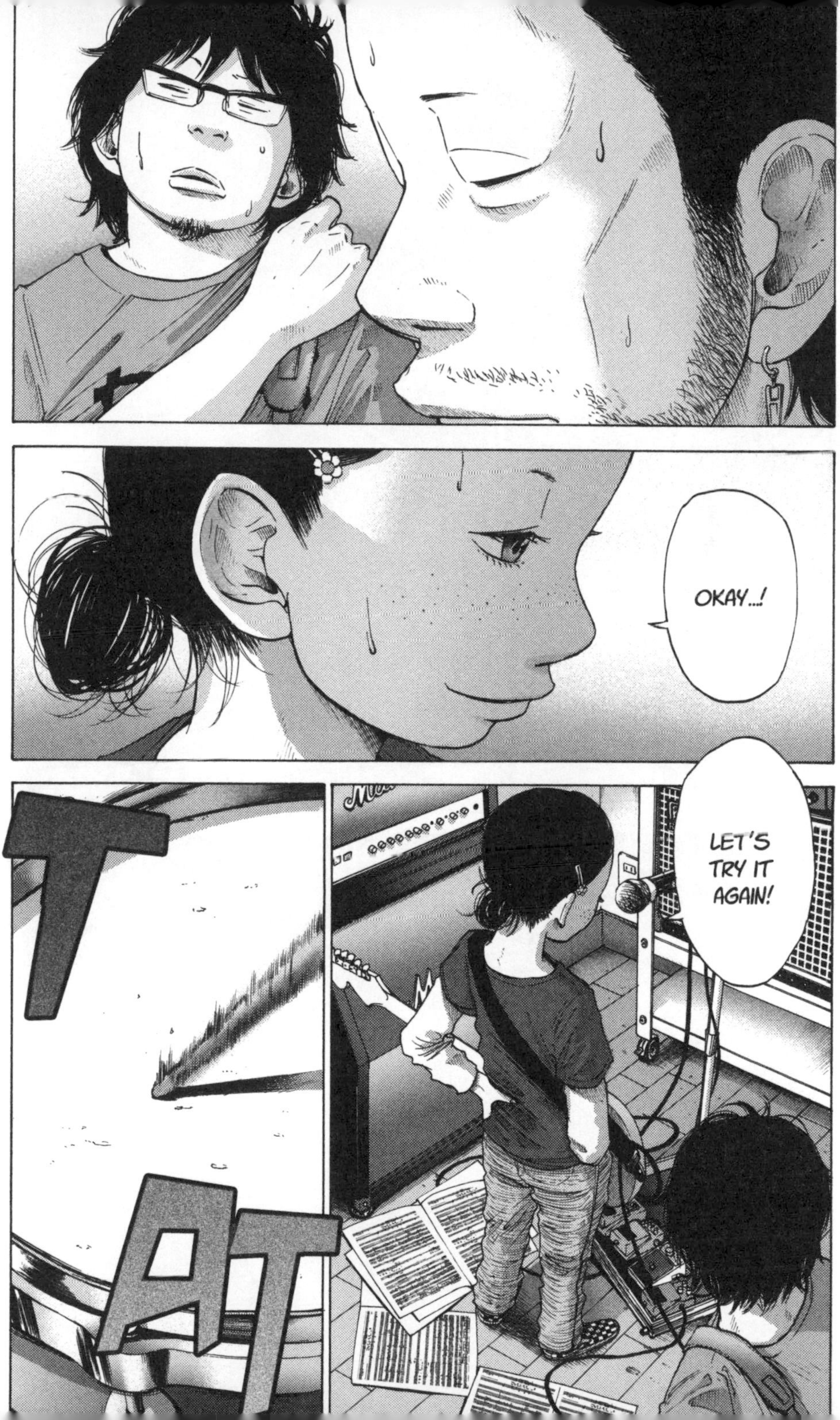
OKAY...!
LET'S TRY IT AGAIN!
TAT

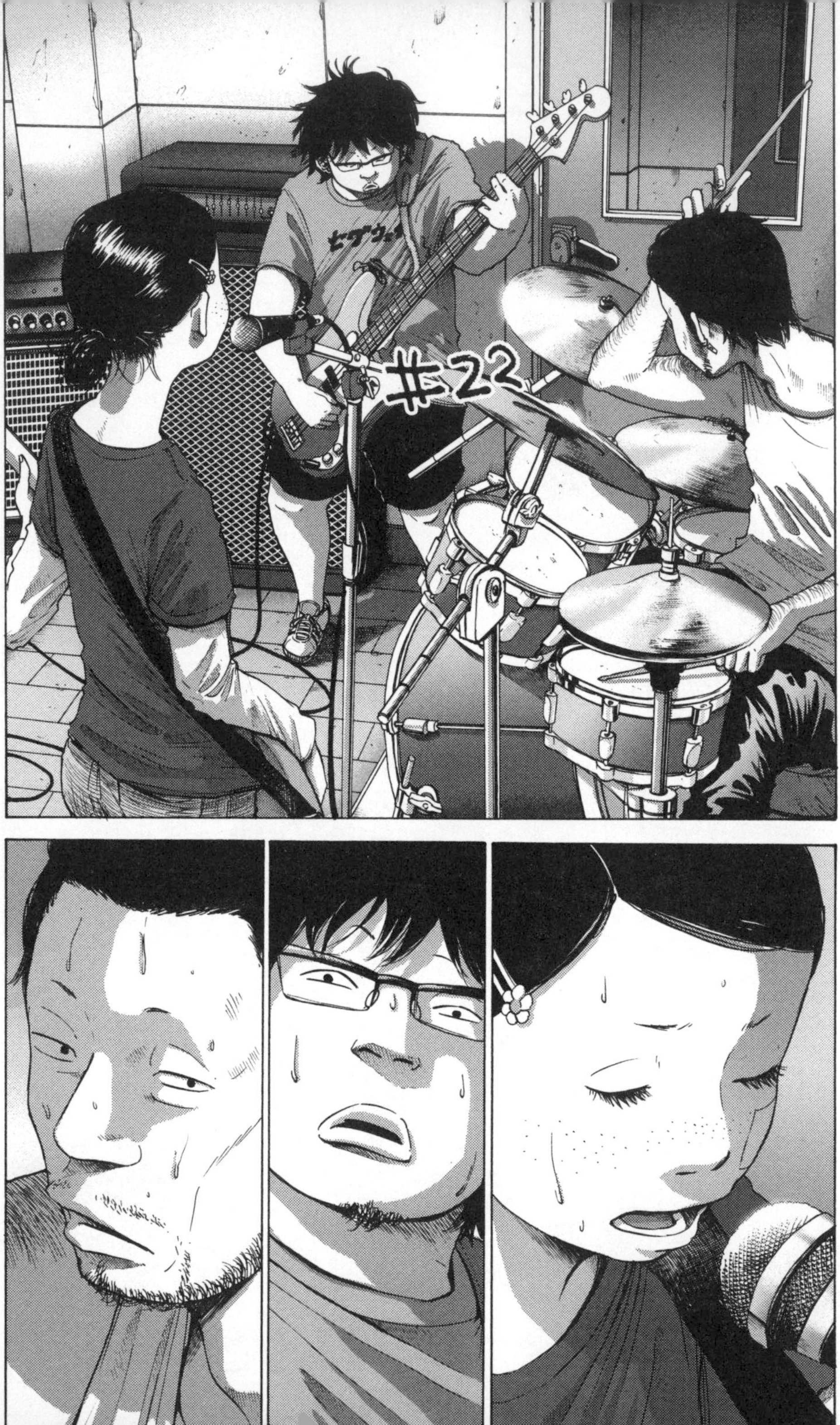
#22

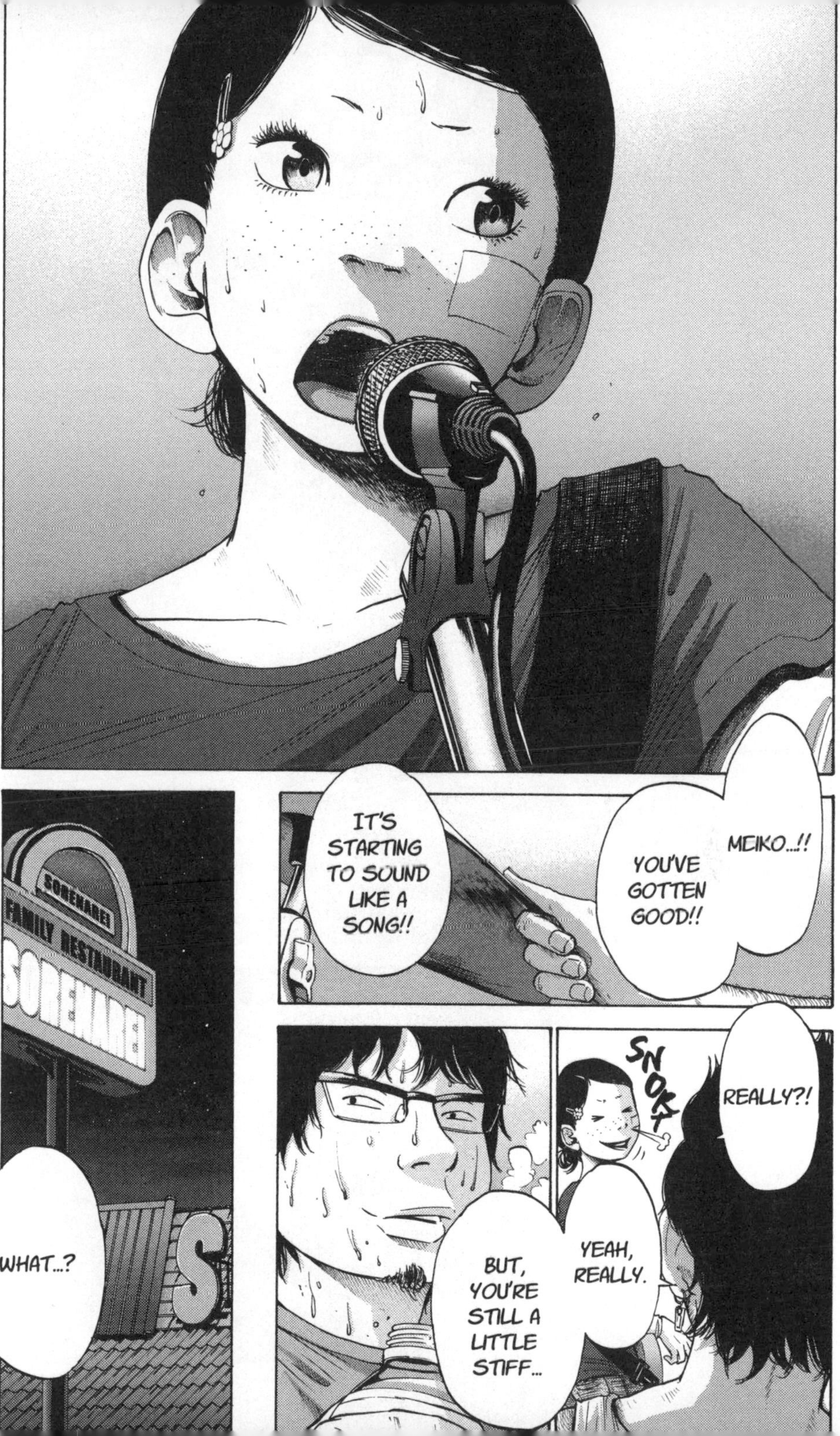
MEIKO...!!
YOU'VE GOTTEN GOOD!!
IT'S STARTING TO SOUND LIKE A SONG!!
SNORT
REALLY?!
YEAH, REALLY.
BUT, YOU'RE STILL A LITTLE STIFF...
SORENARE!
FAMILY RESTAURANT
SORENARE!
WHAT...?

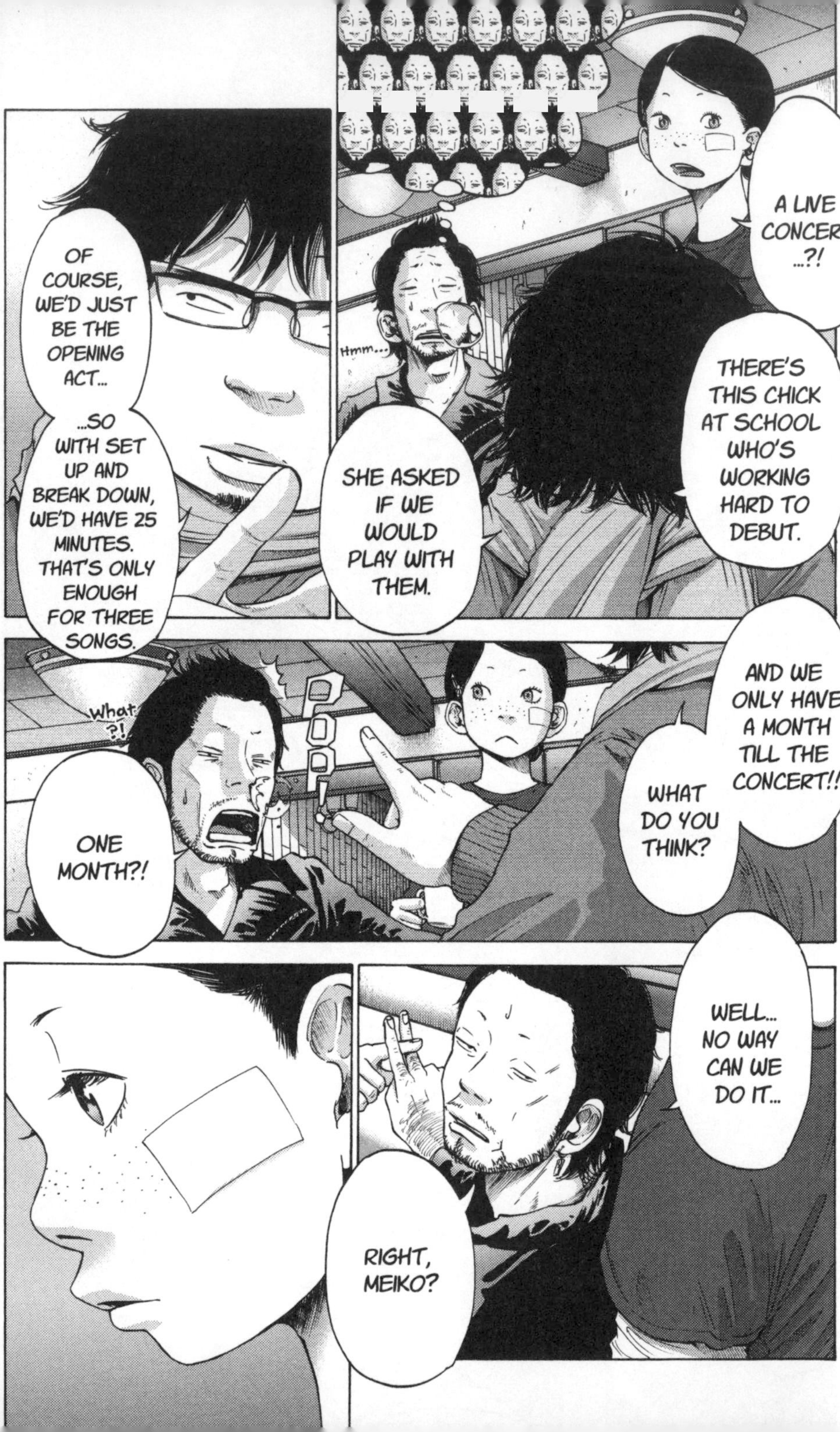
A LIVE CONCERT ...?!
THERE'S THIS CHICK AT SCHOOL WHO'S WORKING HARD TO DEBUT.
Hmm...
SHE ASKED IF WE WOULD PLAY WITH THEM.
OF COURSE, WE'D JUST BE THE OPENING ACT...
...SO WITH SET UP AND BREAK DOWN, WE'D HAVE 25 MINUTES. THAT'S ONLY ENOUGH FOR THREE SONGS.
AND WE ONLY HAVE A MONTH TILL THE CONCERT!!
WHAT DO YOU THINK?
POP!
What ?!
ONE MONTH?!
WELL... NO WAY CAN WE DO IT...
RIGHT, MEIKO?

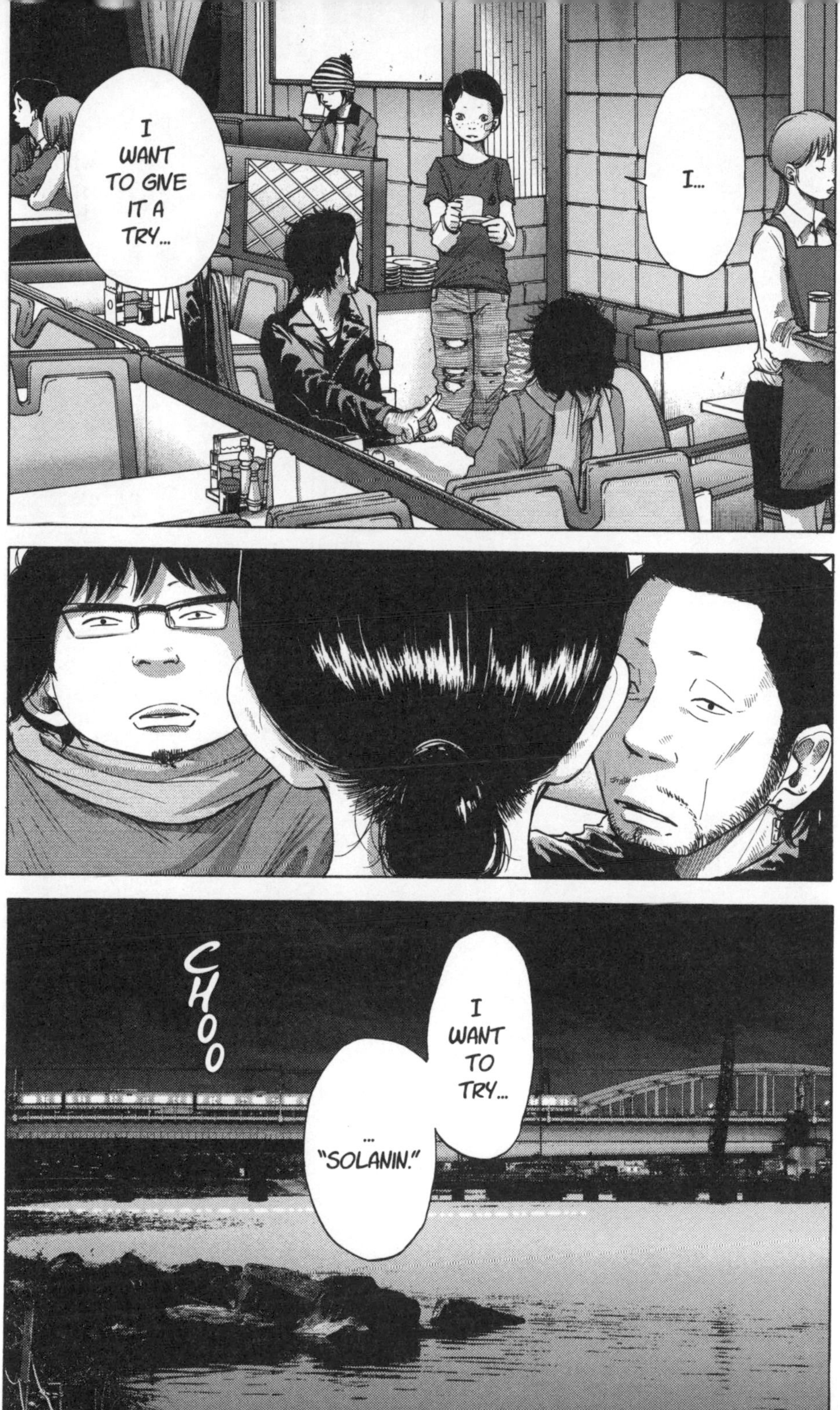
I...
I WANT TO GIVE IT A TRY...
I WANT TO TRY...
... "SOLANIN."
CHOO

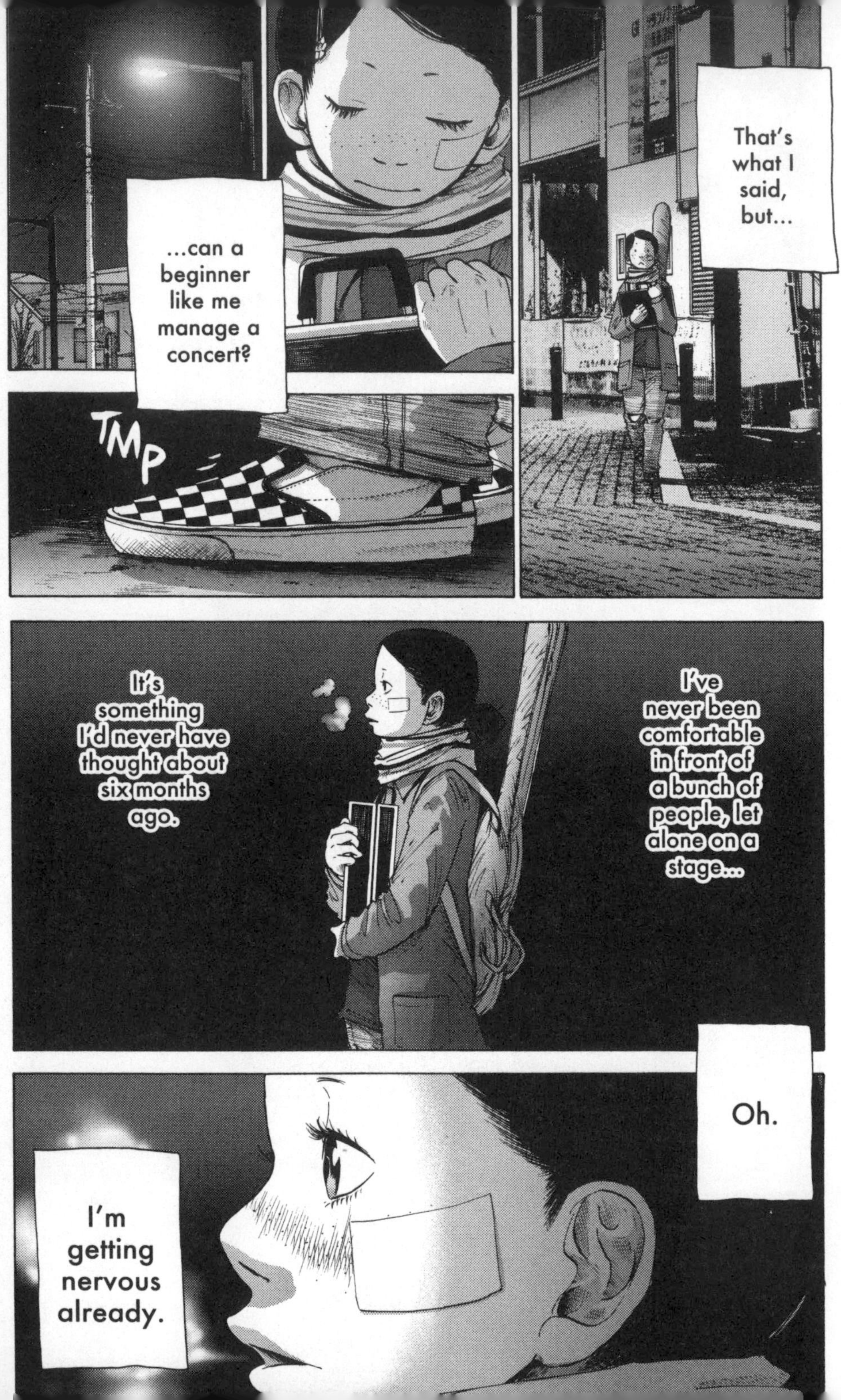
That's what I said, but...
...can a beginner like me manage a concert?
TMP
I've never been comfortable in front of a bunch of people, let alone on a stage...
It's something I'd never have thought about six months ago.
Oh.
I'm getting nervous already.

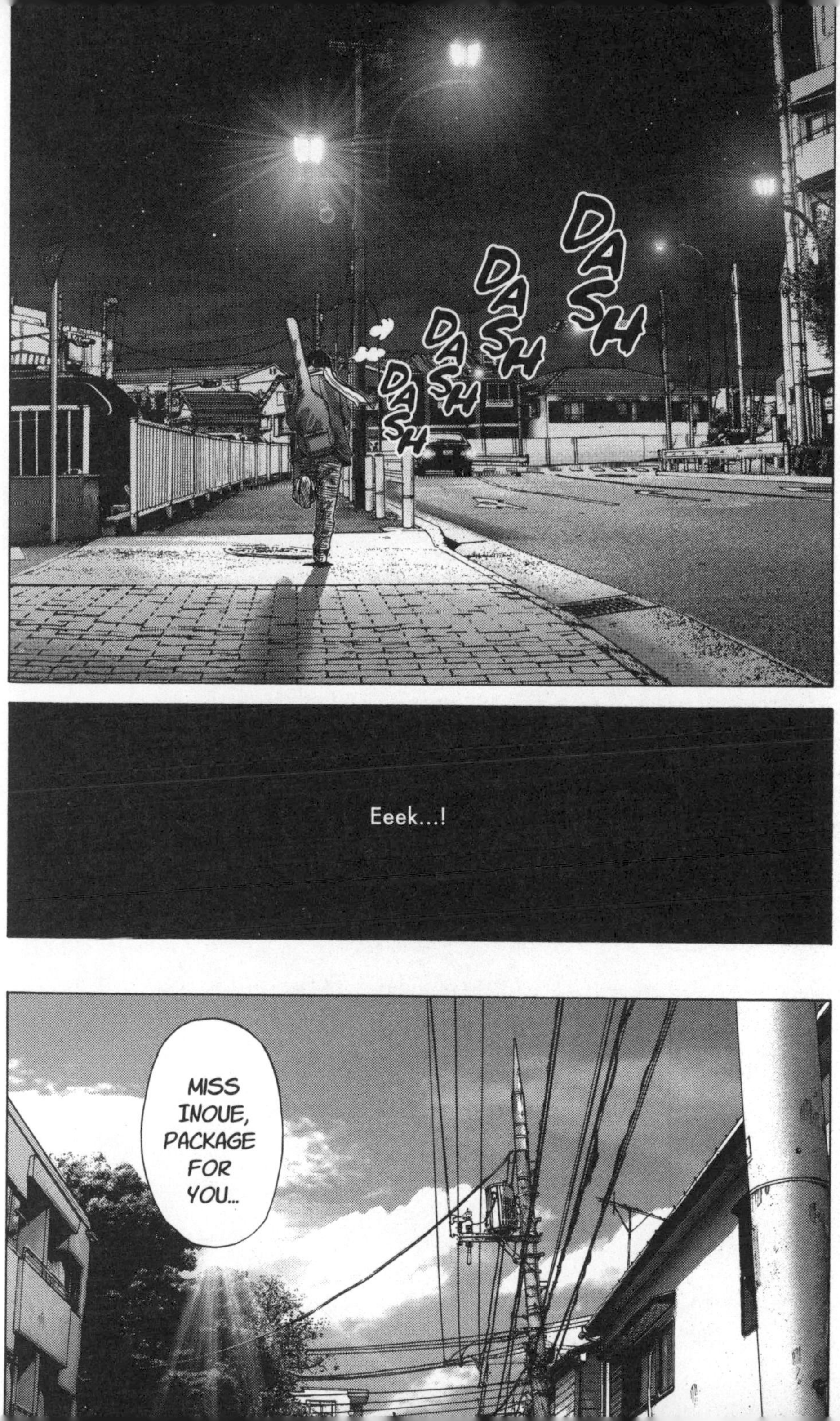
DASH
DASH
DASH
DASH
Eeek...!
MISS INOUE, PACKAGE FOR YOU...

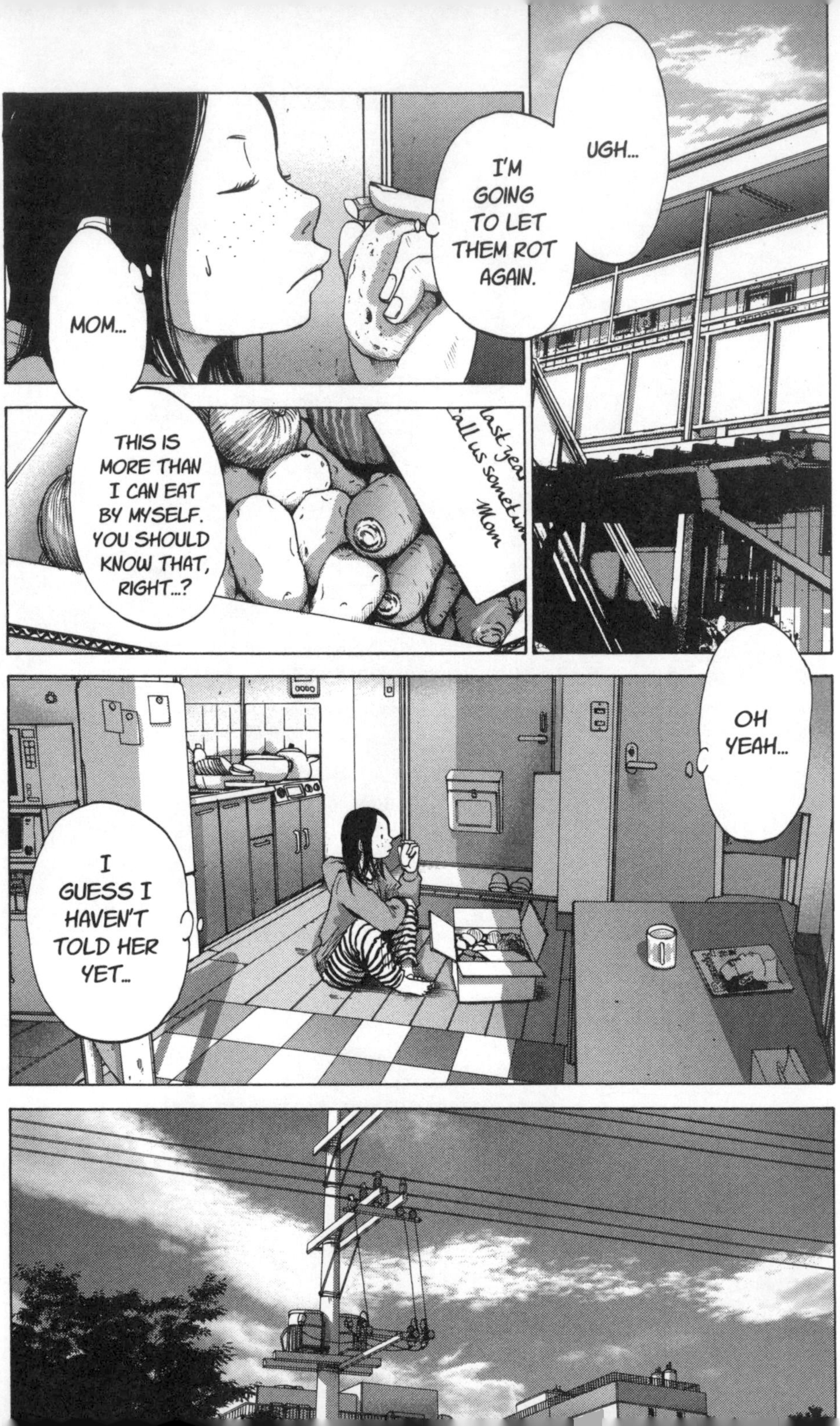
UGH...
I'M GOING TO LET THEM ROT AGAIN.
MOM...
THIS IS MORE THAN I CAN EAT BY MYSELF. YOU SHOULD KNOW THAT, RIGHT...?
Mom
OH YEAH...
I GUESS I HAVEN'T TOLD HER YET...

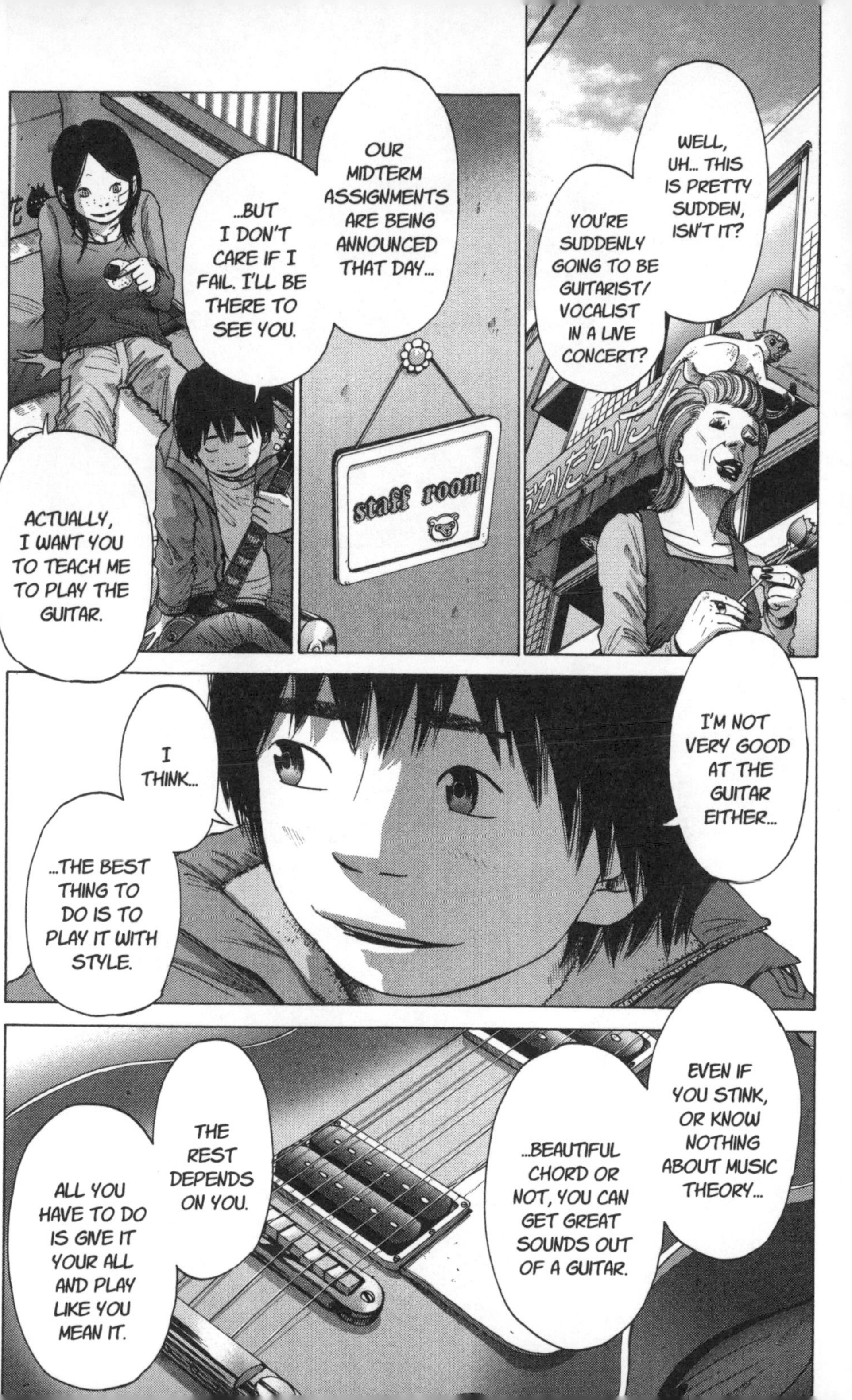
WELL, UH... THIS IS PRETTY SUDDEN, ISN'T IT?
YOU'RE SUDDENLY GOING TO BE GUITARIST/ VOCALIST IN A LIVE CONCERT?
OUR MIDTERM ASSIGNMENTS ARE BEING ANNOUNCED THAT DAY...
...BUT I DON'T CARE IF I FAIL. I'LL BE THERE TO SEE YOU.
staff room
ACTUALLY, I WANT YOU TO TEACH ME TO PLAY THE GUITAR.
I'M NOT VERY GOOD AT THE GUITAR EITHER...
I THINK...
...THE BEST THING TO DO IS TO PLAY IT WITH STYLE.
EVEN IF YOU STINK, OR KNOW NOTHING ABOUT MUSIC THEORY...
...BEAUTIFUL CHORD OR NOT, YOU CAN GET GREAT SOUNDS OUT OF A GUITAR.
THE REST DEPENDS ON YOU.
ALL YOU HAVE TO DO IS GIVE IT YOUR ALL AND PLAY LIKE YOU MEAN IT.

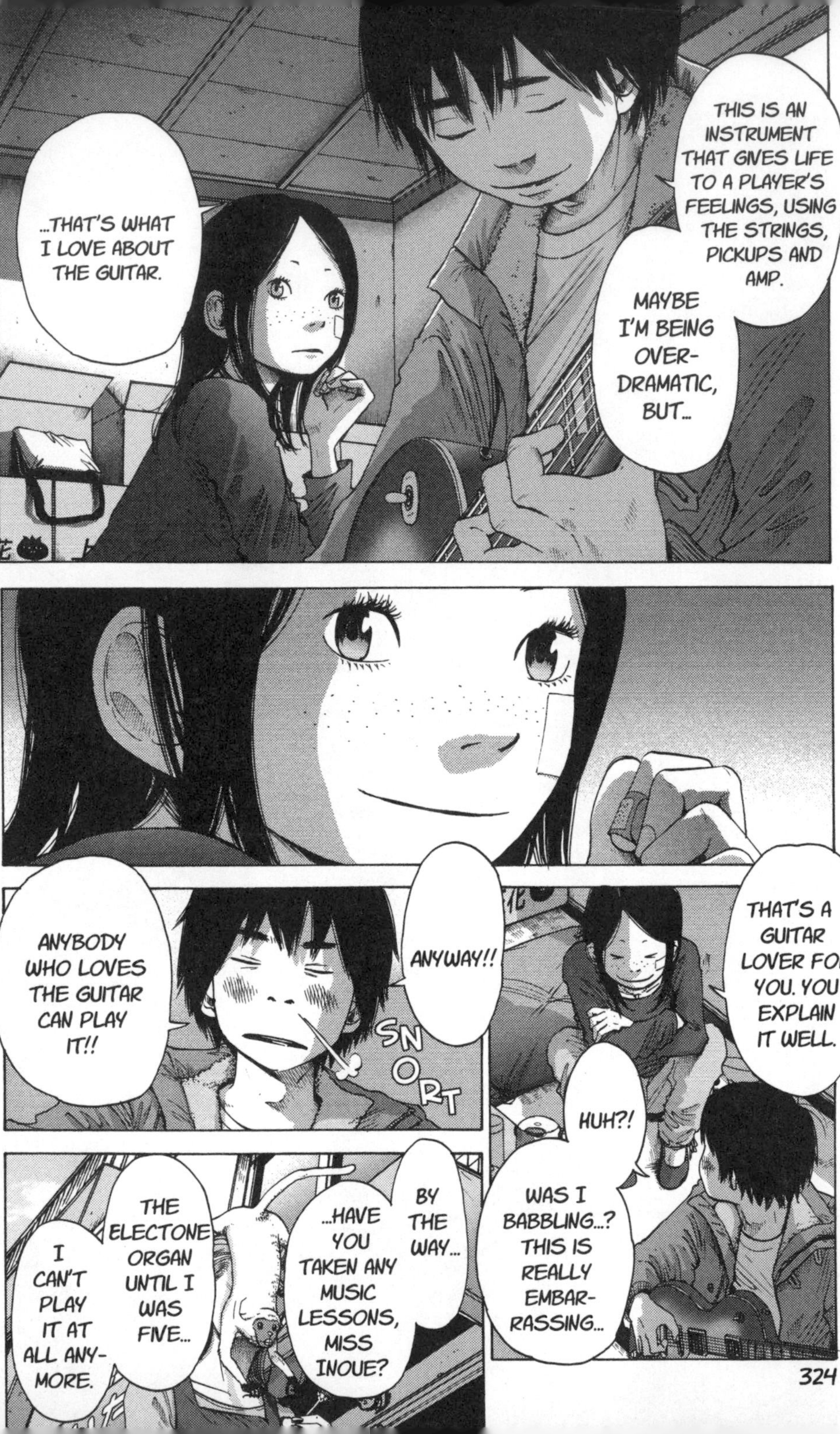
THIS IS AN INSTRUMENT THAT GIVES LIFE TO A PLAYER'S FEELINGS, USING THE STRINGS, PICKUPS AND AMP.
MAYBE I'M BEING OVER-DRAMATIC, BUT...
...THAT'S WHAT I LOVE ABOUT THE GUITAR.
THAT'S A GUITAR LOVER FOR YOU. YOU EXPLAIN IT WELL.
HUH?!
WAS I BABBLING...? THIS IS REALLY EMBARRASSING...
ANYWAY!!
ANYBODY WHO LOVES THE GUITAR CAN PLAY IT!!
SNORT
BY THE WAY...
...HAVE YOU TAKEN ANY MUSIC LESSONS, MISS INOUE?
THE ELECTONE ORGAN UNTIL I WAS FIVE...
I CAN'T PLAY IT AT ALL ANYMORE.

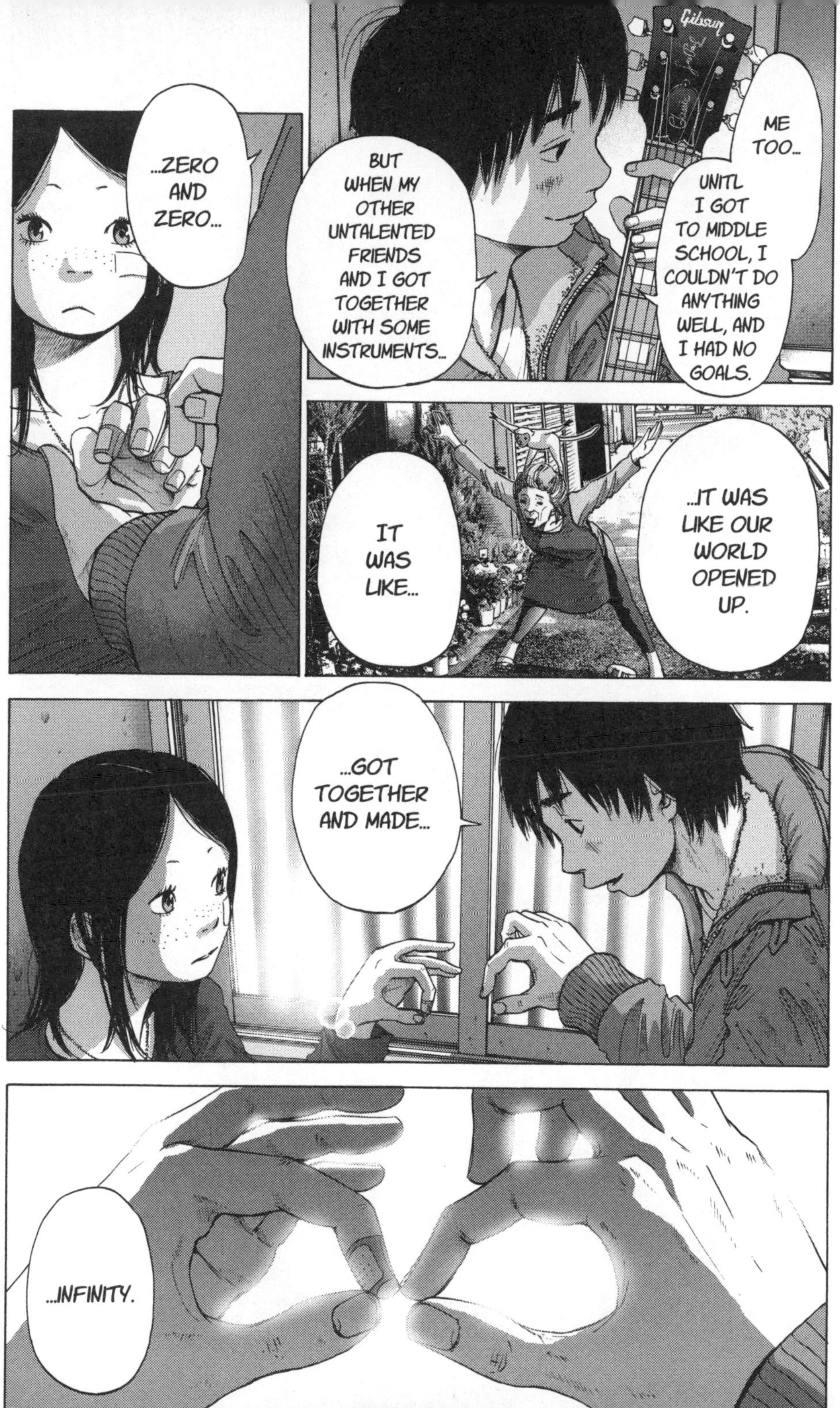
Gibson
ME TOO...
UNITL I GOT TO MIDDLE SCHOOL, I COULDN'T DO ANYTHING WELL, AND I HAD NO GOALS.
BUT WHEN MY OTHER UNTALENTED FRIENDS AND I GOT TOGETHER WITH SOME INSTRUMENTS...
...IT WAS LIKE OUR WORLD OPENED UP.
IT WAS LIKE...
...ZERO AND ZERO...
...GOT TOGETHER AND MADE...
...INFINITY.

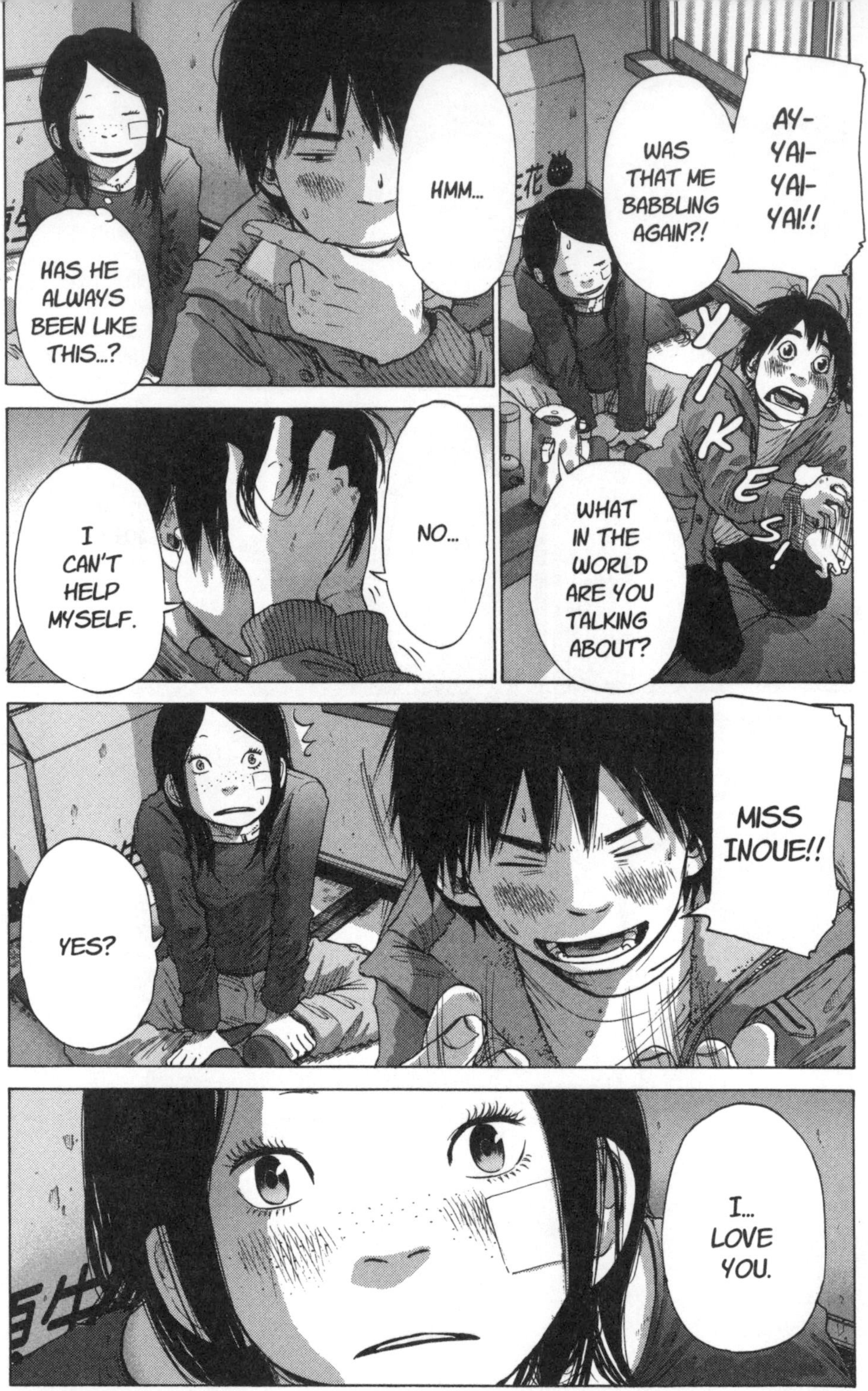
AY-YAI-YAI-YAI!!
WAS THAT ME BABBLING AGAIN?!
YIKES!
WHAT IN THE WORLD ARE YOU TALKING ABOUT?
HMM...
HAS HE ALWAYS BEEN LIKE THIS...?
NO...
I CAN'T HELP MYSELF.
MISS INOUE!!
YES?
I... LOVE YOU.

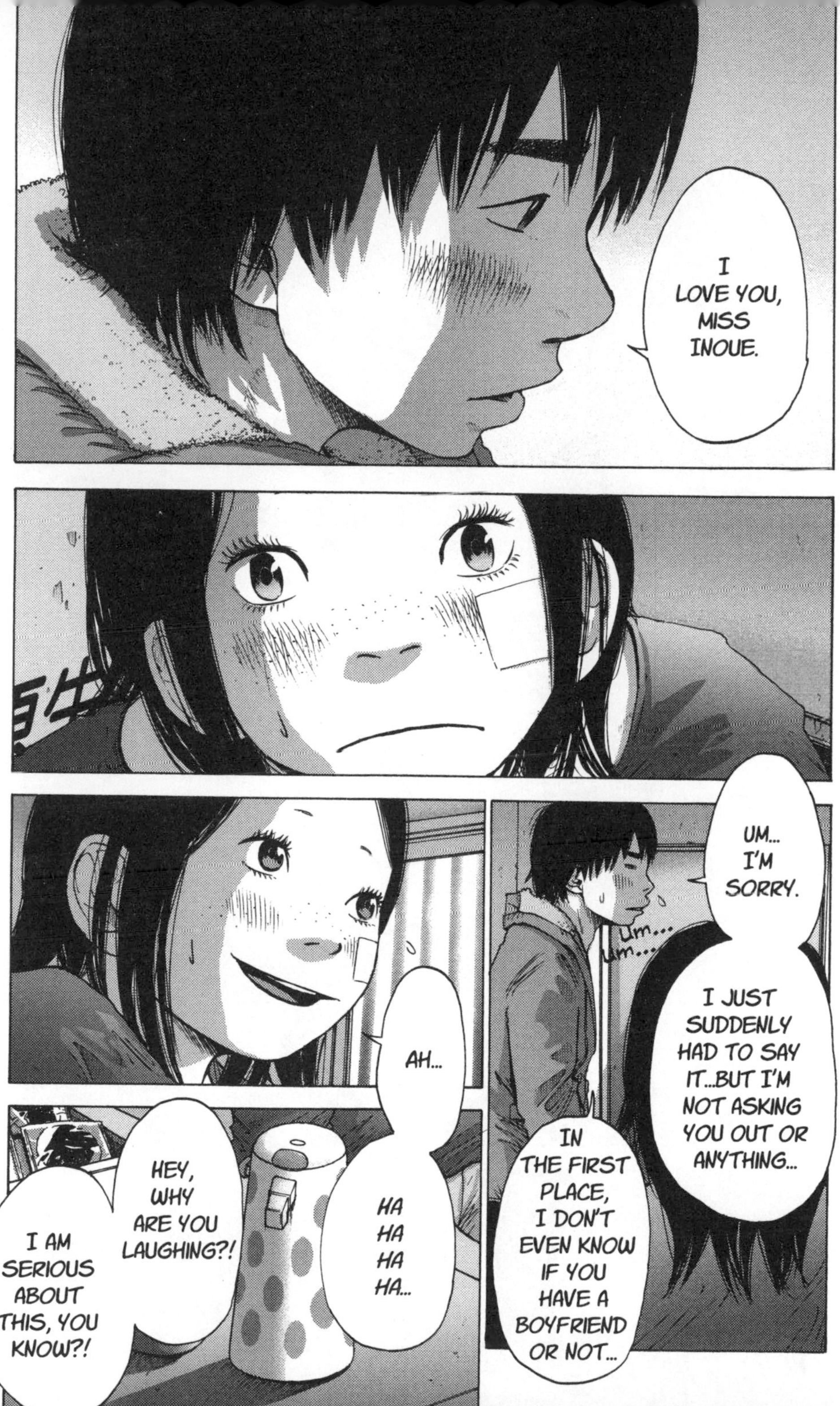
I LOVE YOU, MISS INOUE.
UM... I'M SORRY.
Um... Um...
I JUST SUDDENLY HAD TO SAY IT...BUT I'M NOT ASKING YOU OUT OR ANYTHING...
IN THE FIRST PLACE, I DON'T EVEN KNOW IF YOU HAVE A BOYFRIEND OR NOT...
AH...
HA HA HA HA...
HEY, WHY ARE YOU LAUGHING?!
I AM SERIOUS ABOUT THIS, YOU KNOW?!

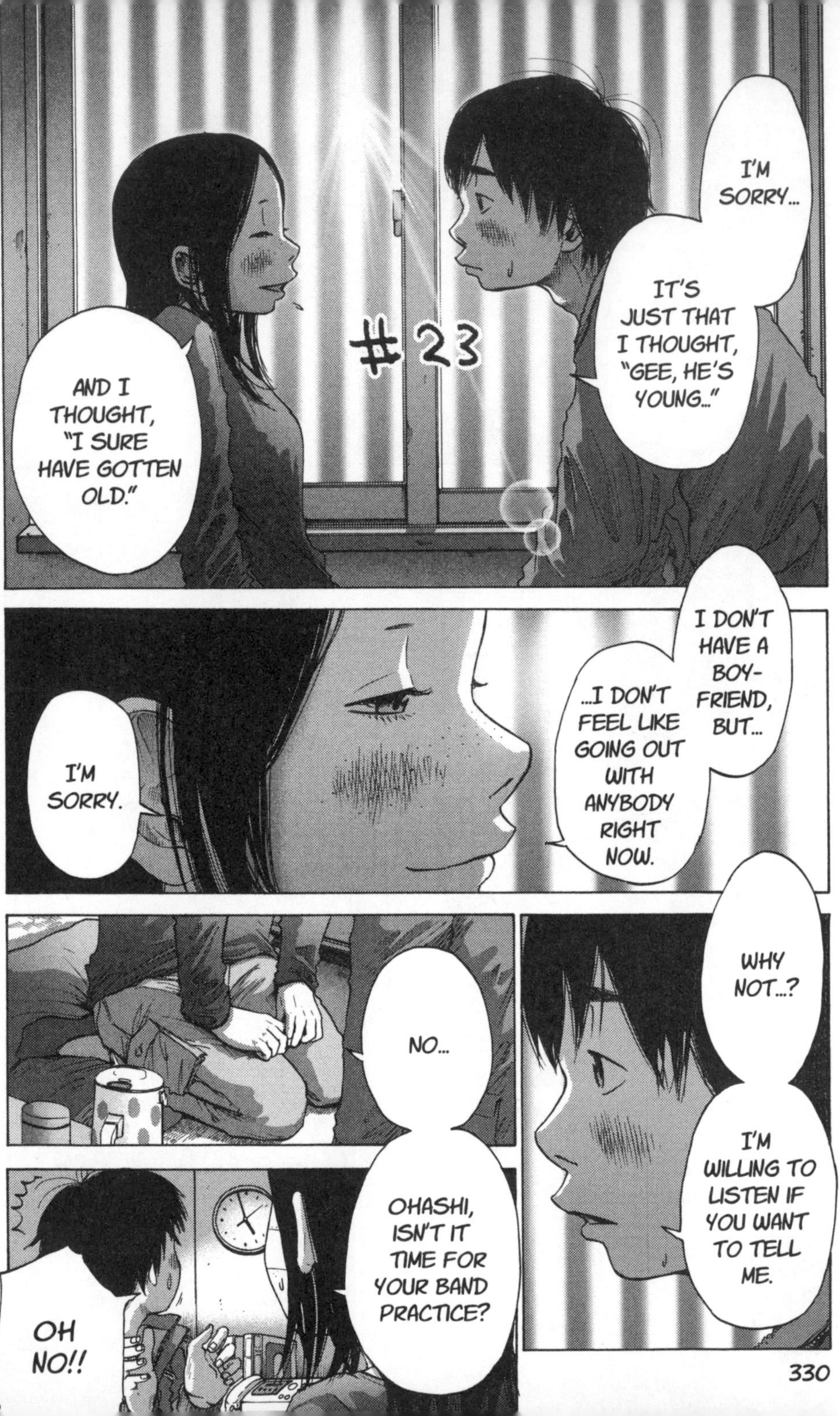
I'M SORRY...
IT'S JUST THAT I THOUGHT, "GEE, HE'S YOUNG..."
#23
AND I THOUGHT, "I SURE HAVE GOTTEN OLD."
I DON'T HAVE A BOY-FRIEND, BUT...
...I DON'T FEEL LIKE GOING OUT WITH ANYBODY RIGHT NOW.
I'M SORRY.
WHY NOT...?
I'M WILLING TO LISTEN IF YOU WANT TO TELL ME.
NO...
OHASHI, ISN'T IT TIME FOR YOUR BAND PRACTICE?
OH NO!!

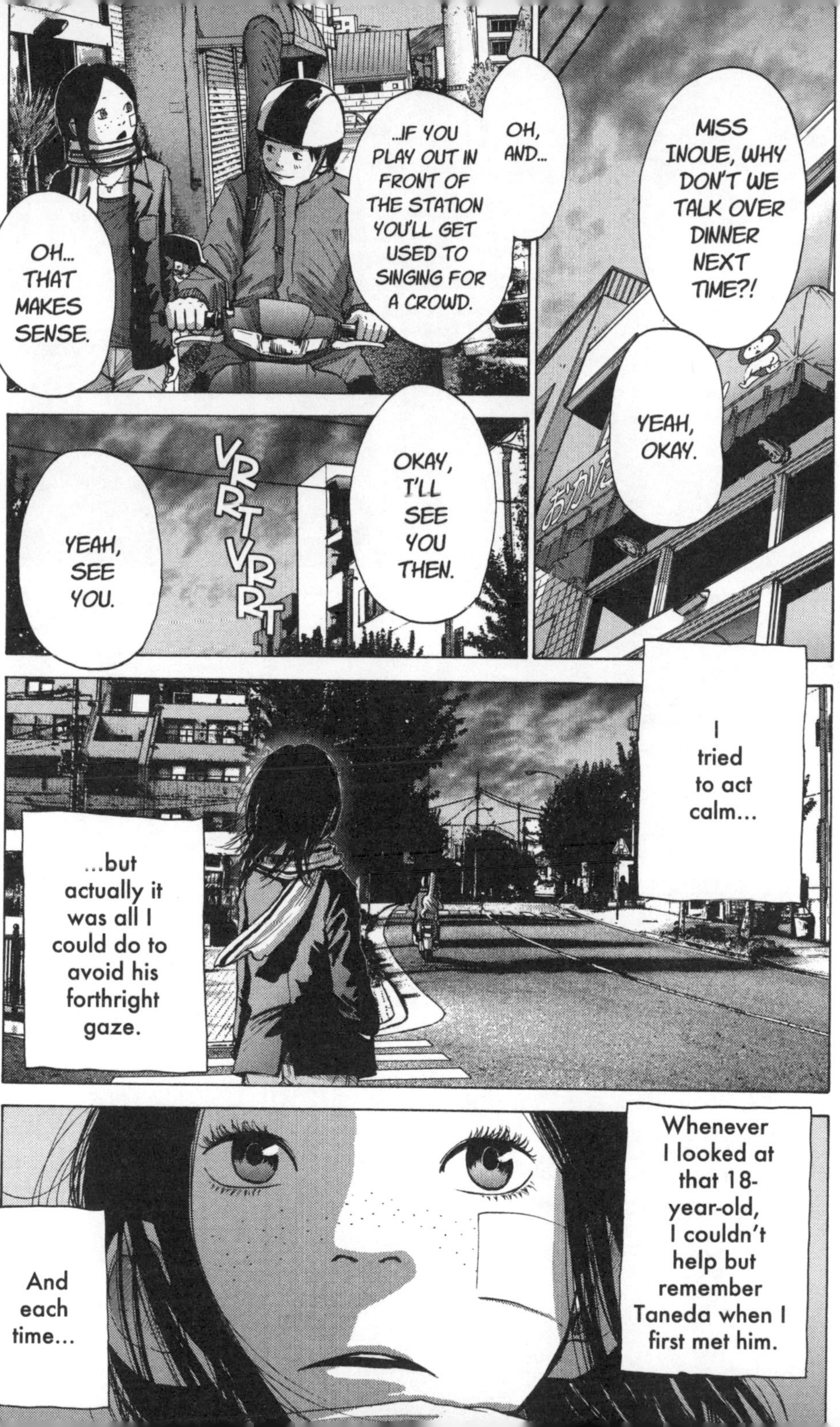
MISS INOUE, WHY DON'T WE TALK OVER DINNER NEXT TIME?!
YEAH, OKAY.
OH, AND...
...IF YOU PLAY OUT IN FRONT OF THE STATION YOU'LL GET USED TO SINGING FOR A CROWD.
OH... THAT MAKES SENSE.
OKAY, I'LL SEE YOU THEN.
VRRT VRRT
YEAH, SEE YOU.
I tried to act calm...
...but actually it was all I could do to avoid his forthright gaze.
Whenever I looked at that 18-year-old, I couldn't help but remember Taneda when I first met him.
And each time...

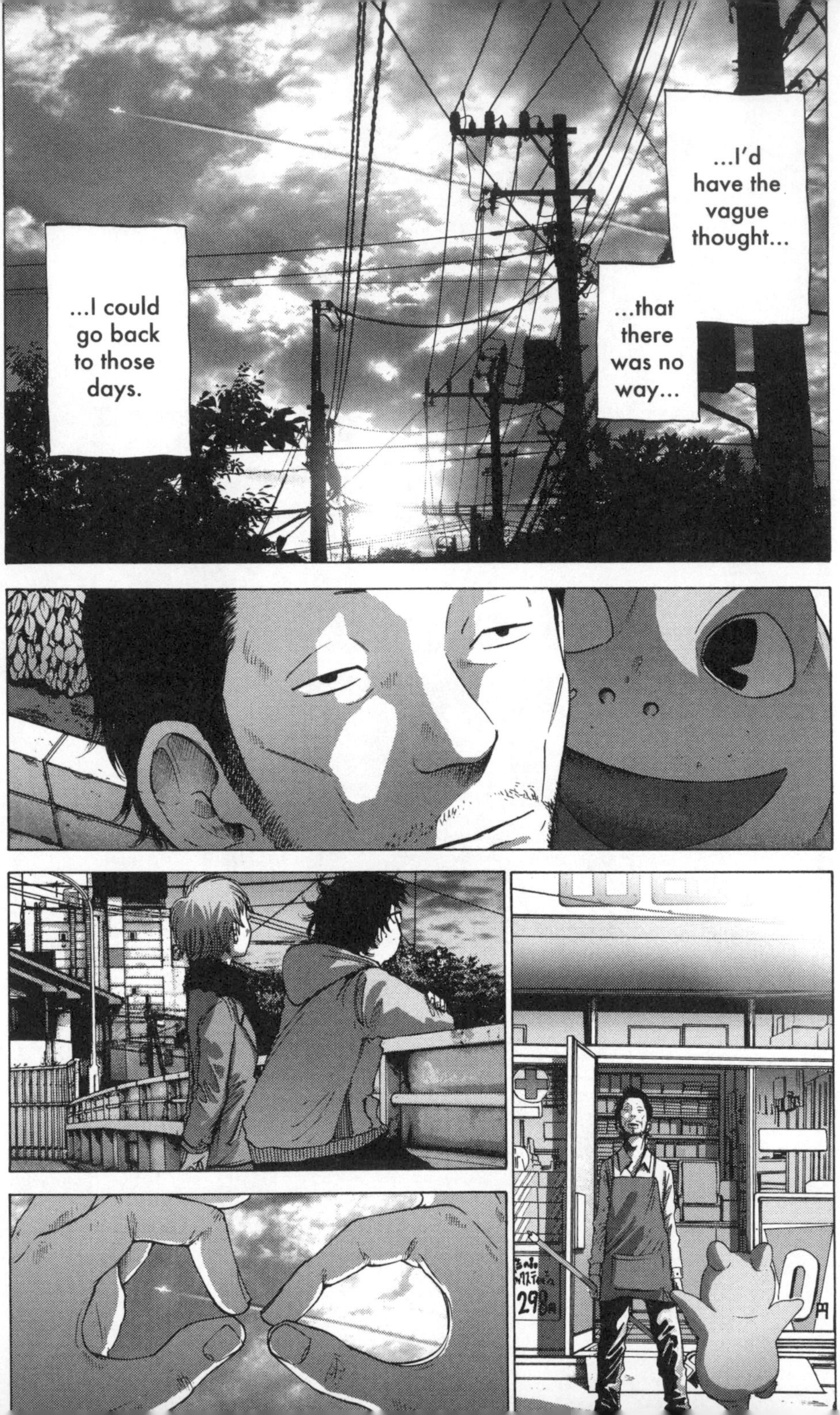
...I'd have the vague thought...
...that there was no way...
...I could go back to those days.

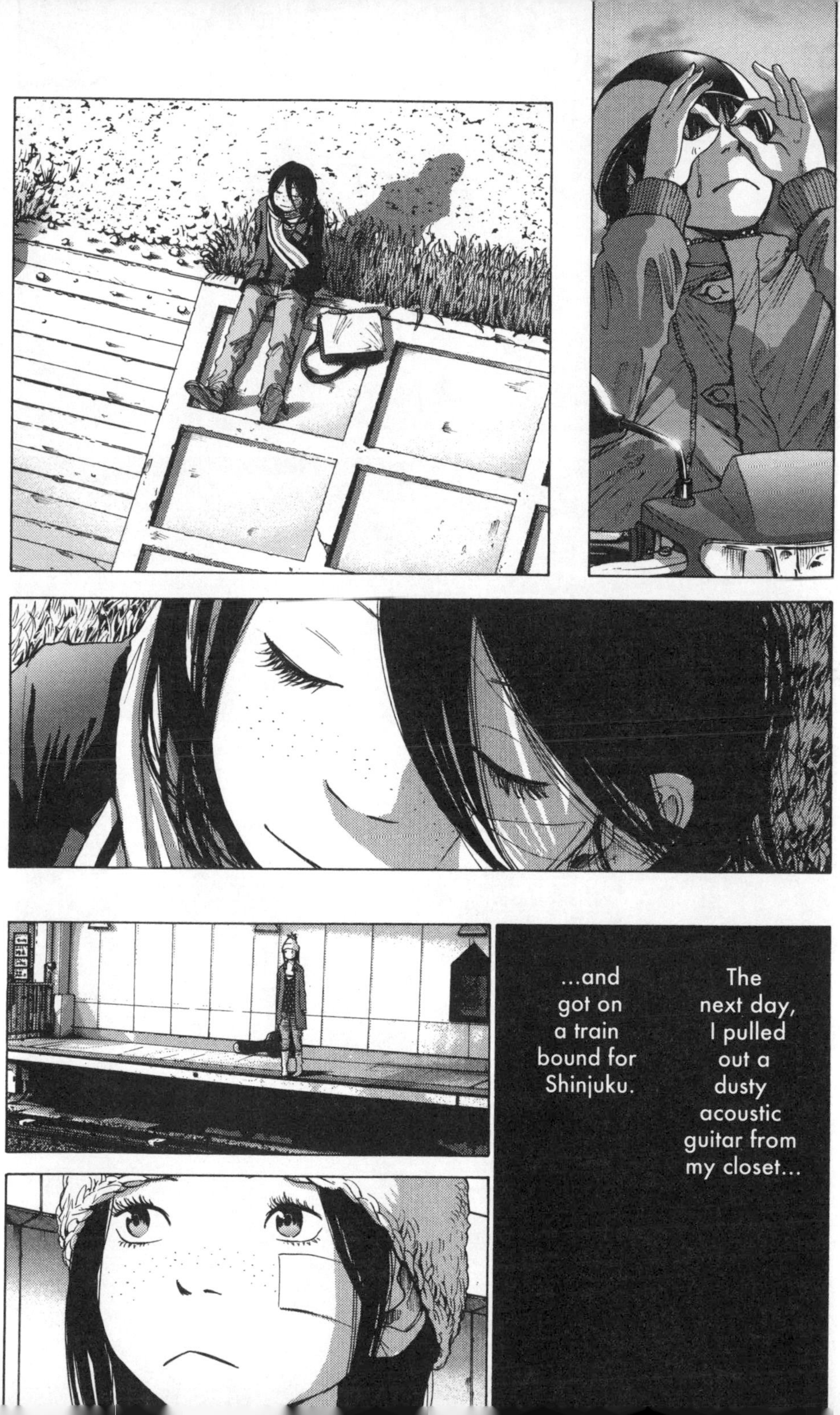
The next day, I pulled out a dusty acoustic guitar from my closet...
...and got on a train bound for Shinjuku.

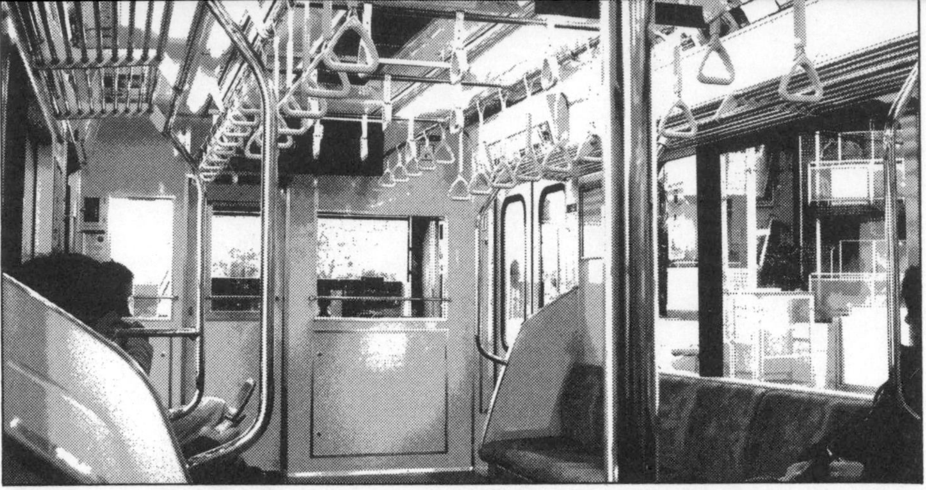

The midday train was empty...

...but it slowly got filled as we drew closer to the city.

Outside the station...

...I was struck once again by the masses of people, things, and information...

...and I stood frozen for minute.

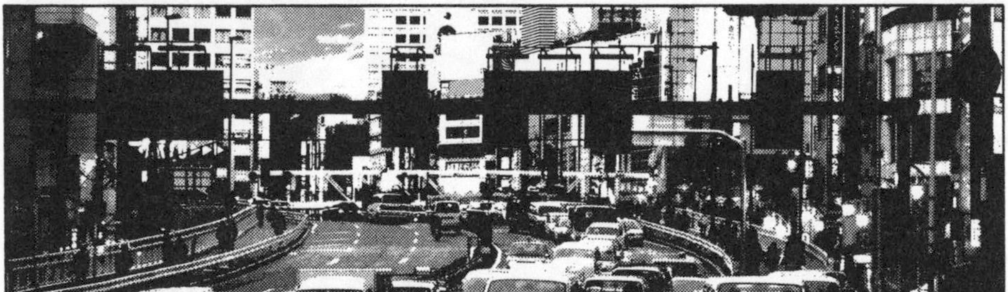

There were buildings...

...and streets...

...and cars rushing...

...and people.

Happy things and sad things.

Everything seemed to exist in a miraculous balance.

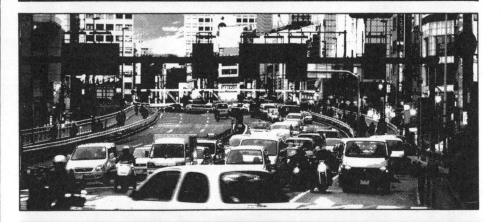

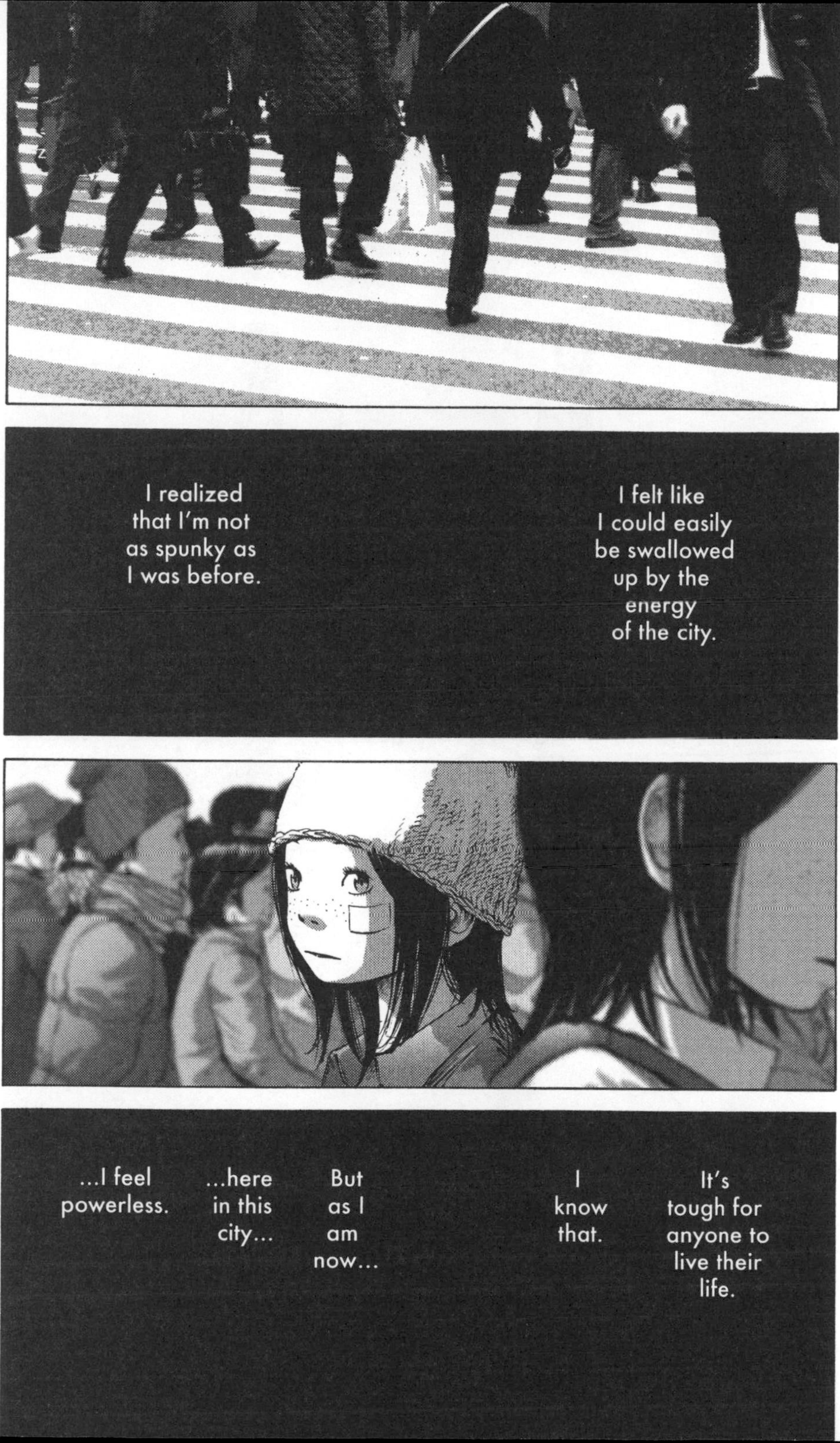
I felt like I could easily be swallowed up by the energy of the city.
I realized that I'm not as spunky as I was before.
It's tough for anyone to live their life.
I know that.
But as I am now...
...here in this city...
...I feel powerless.

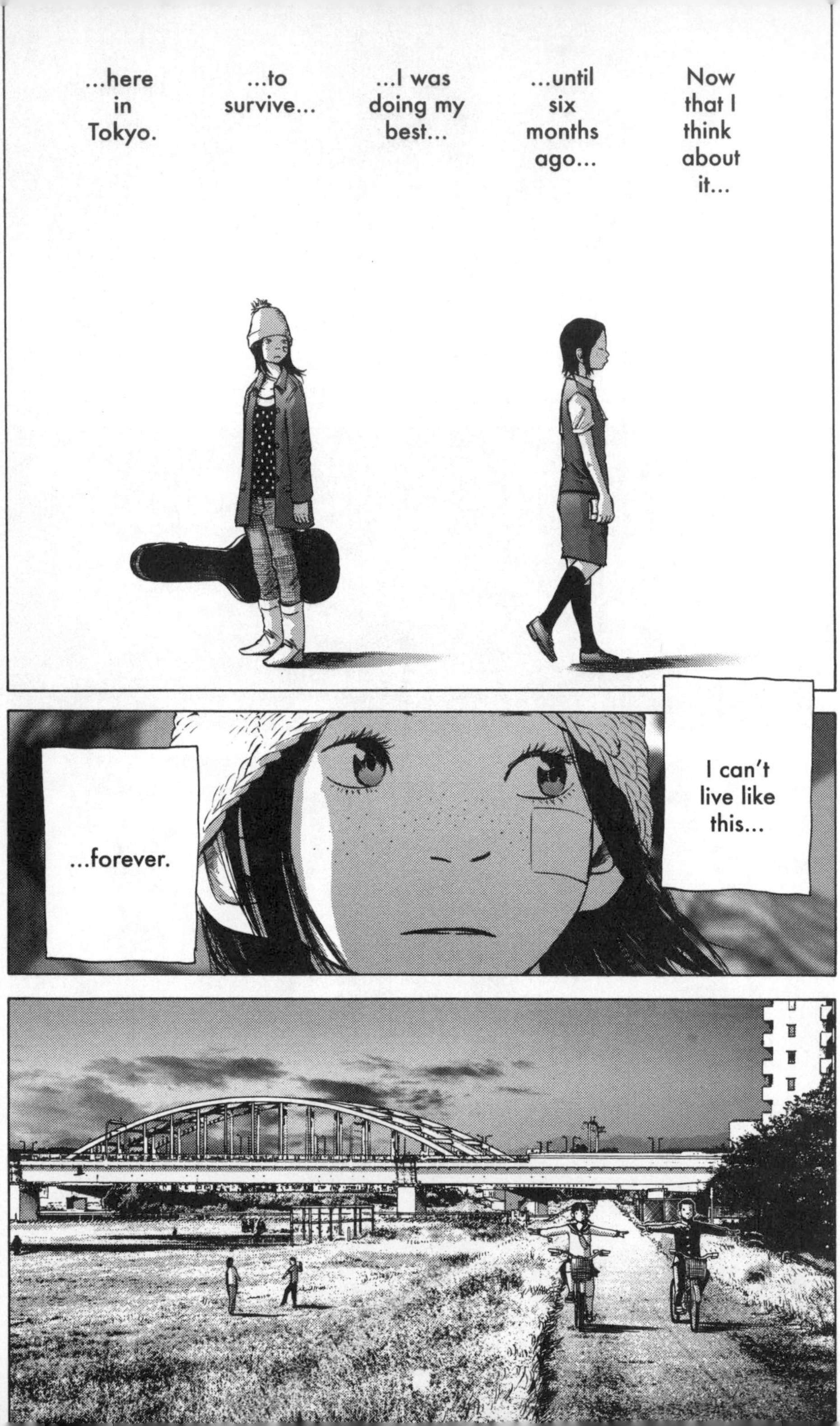
Now that I think about it...
...until six months ago...
...I was doing my best...
...to survive...
...here in Tokyo.
I can't live like this...
...forever.

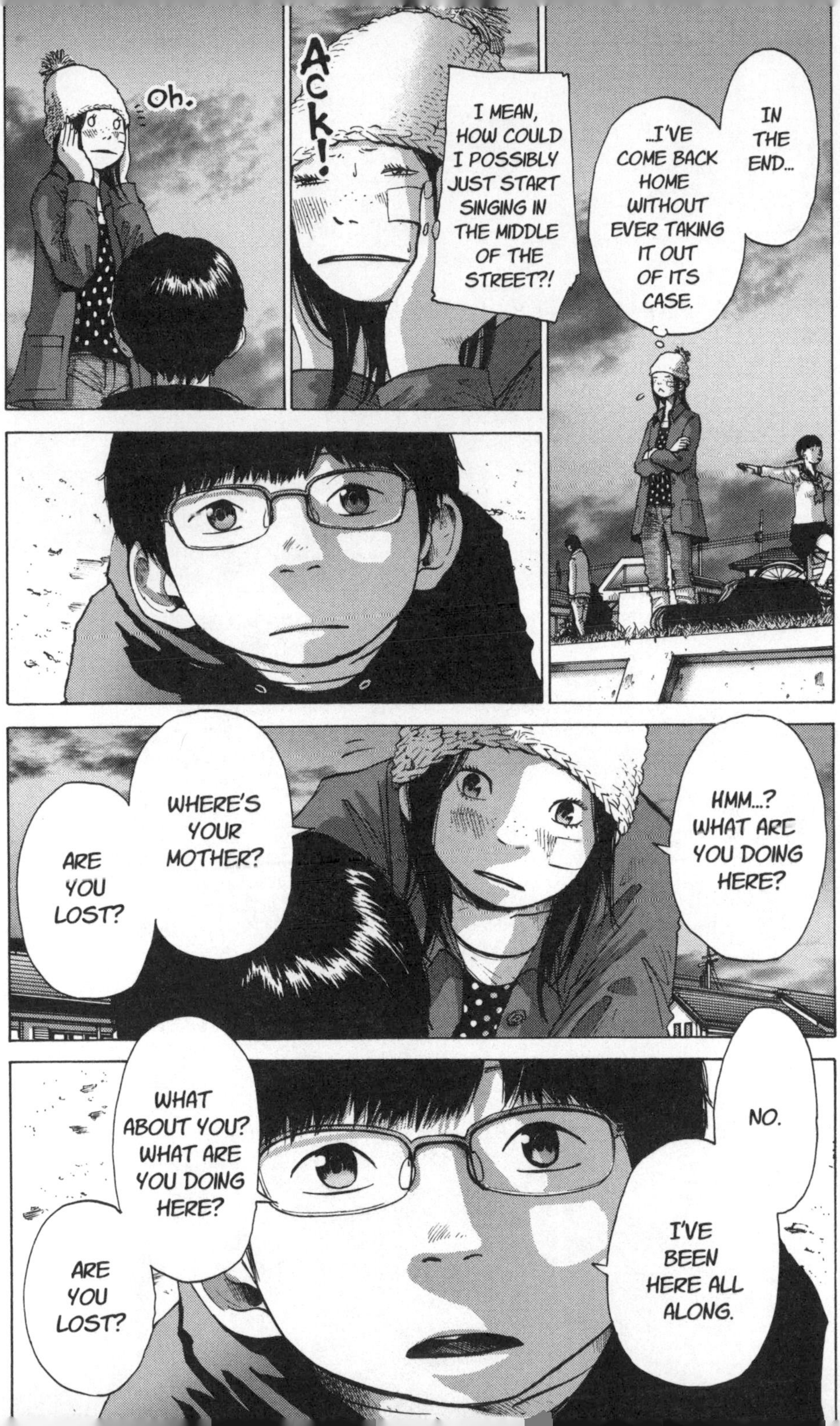
IN THE END...
...I'VE COME BACK HOME WITHOUT EVER TAKING IT OUT OF ITS CASE.
Ack!
I MEAN, HOW COULD I POSSIBLY JUST START SINGING IN THE MIDDLE OF THE STREET?!
Oh.
HMM...? WHAT ARE YOU DOING HERE?
WHERE'S YOUR MOTHER?
ARE YOU LOST?
NO.
I'VE BEEN HERE ALL ALONG.
WHAT ABOUT YOU? WHAT ARE YOU DOING HERE?
ARE YOU LOST?

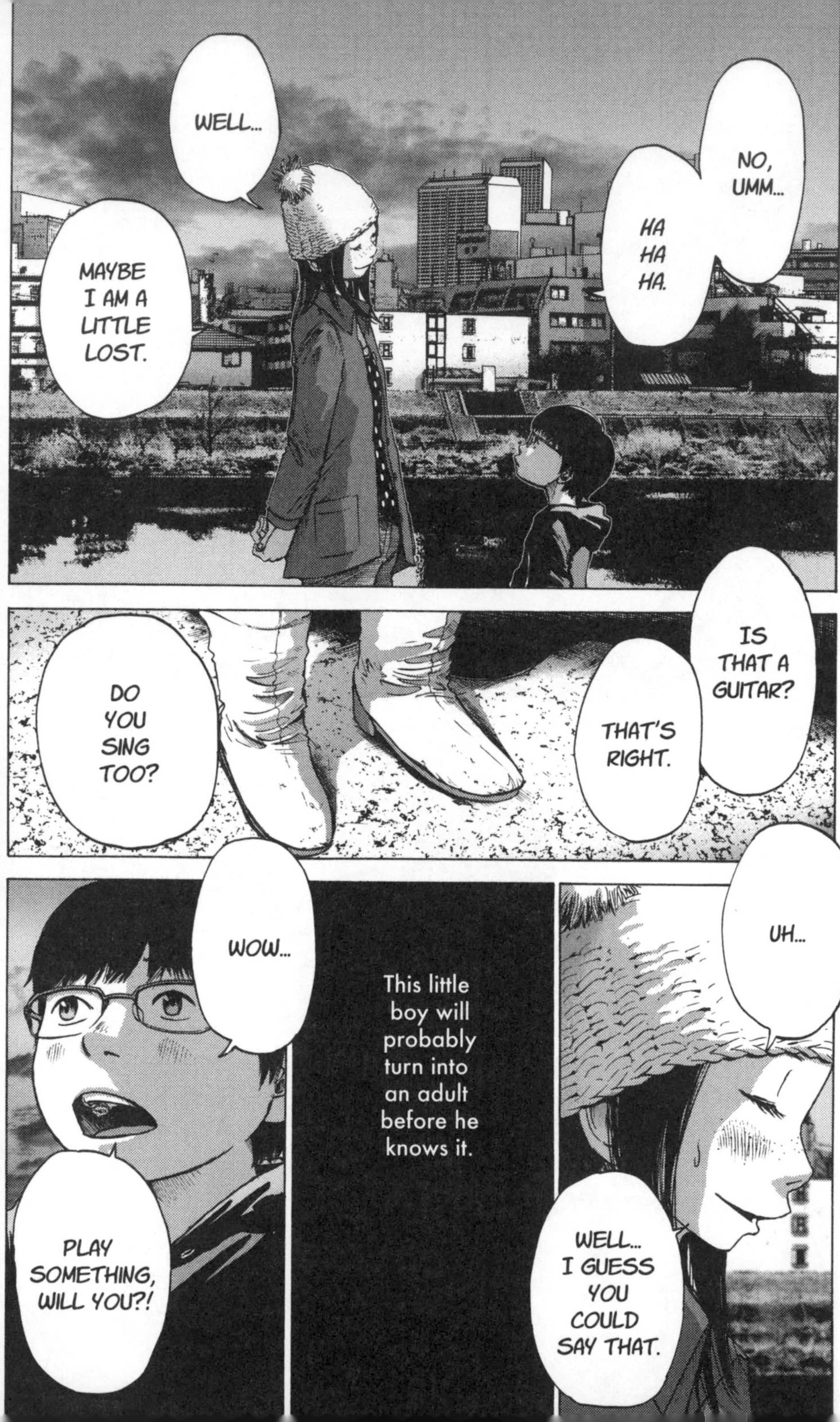
NO, UMM...
HA HA HA.
WELL...
MAYBE I AM A LITTLE LOST.
IS THAT A GUITAR?
THAT'S RIGHT.
DO YOU SING TOO?
UH...
WELL... I GUESS YOU COULD SAY THAT.
This little boy will probably turn into an adult before he knows it.
WOW...
PLAY SOMETHING, WILL YOU?!

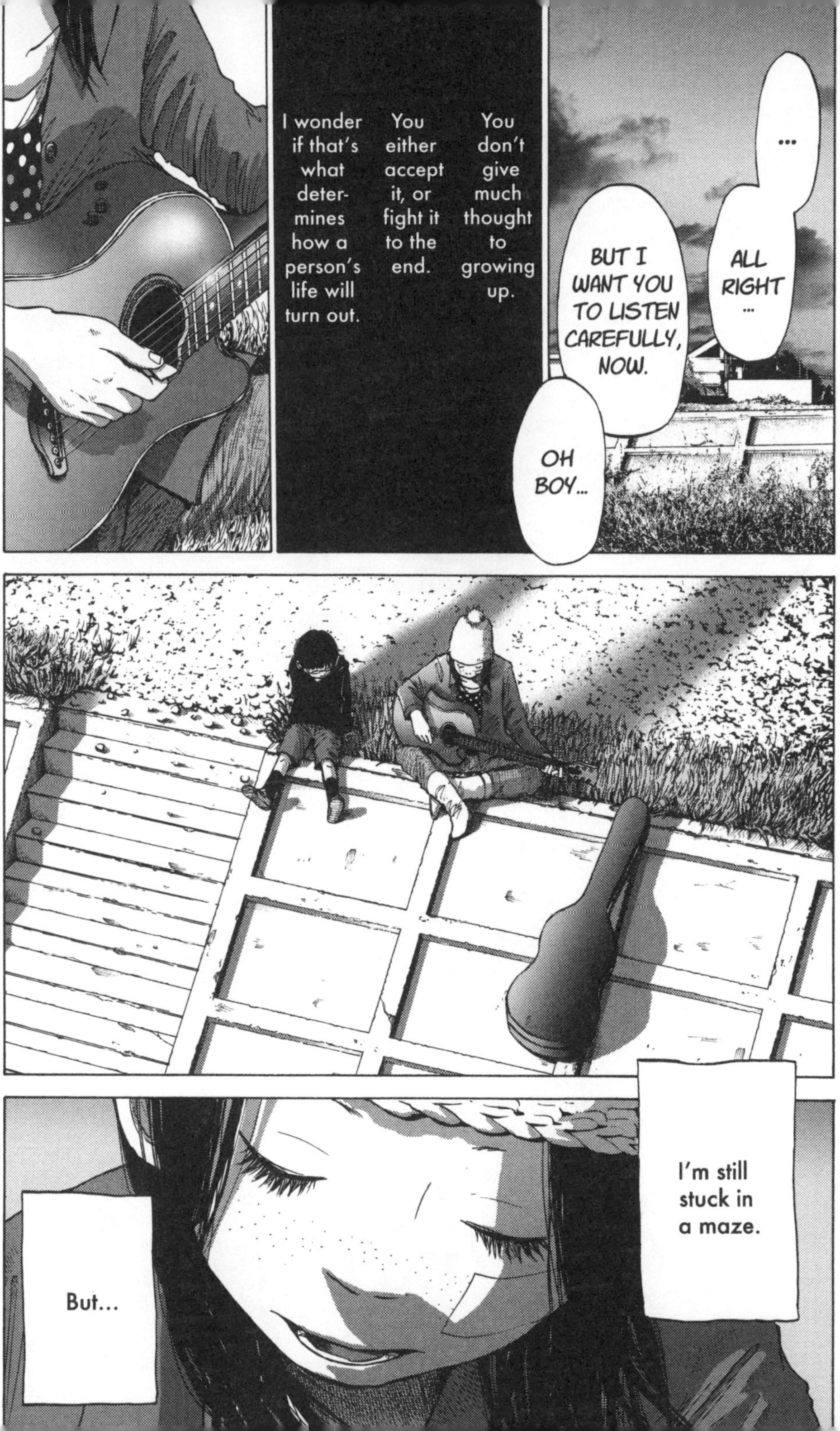
...
ALL RIGHT...
BUT I WANT YOU TO LISTEN CAREFULLY, NOW.
OH BOY...
You don't give much thought to growing up.
You either accept it, or fight it to the end.
I wonder if that's what determines how a person's life will turn out.
I'm still stuck in a maze.
But...

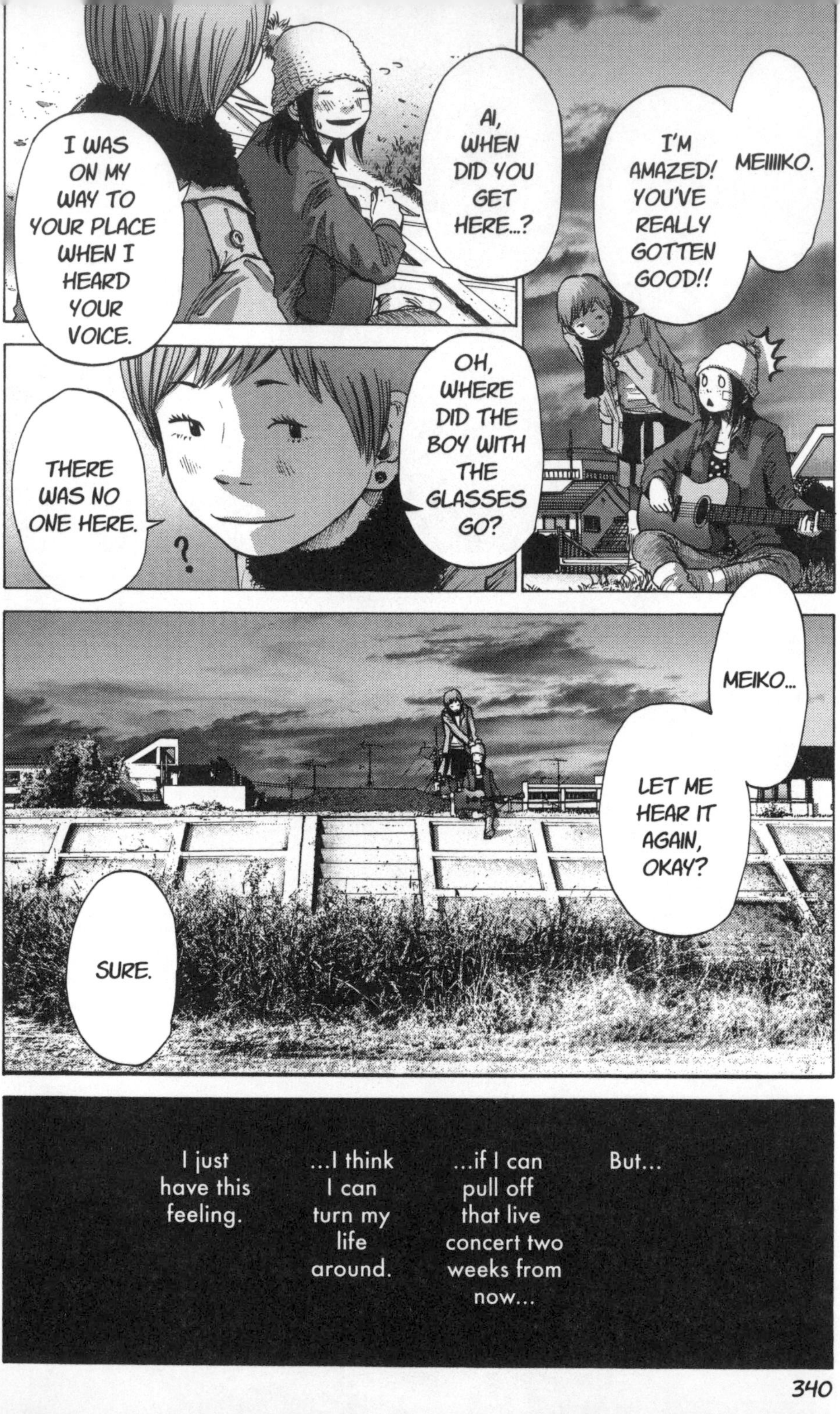

MEIIIIKO.
I'M AMAZED! YOU'VE REALLY GOTTEN GOOD!!
AI, WHEN DID YOU GET HERE...?
I WAS ON MY WAY TO YOUR PLACE WHEN I HEARD YOUR VOICE.
OH, WHERE DID THE BOY WITH THE GLASSES GO?
THERE WAS NO ONE HERE.
?
MEIKO...
LET ME HEAR IT AGAIN, OKAY?
SURE.
But...
...if I can pull off that live concert two weeks from now...
...I think I can turn my life around.
I just have this feeling.

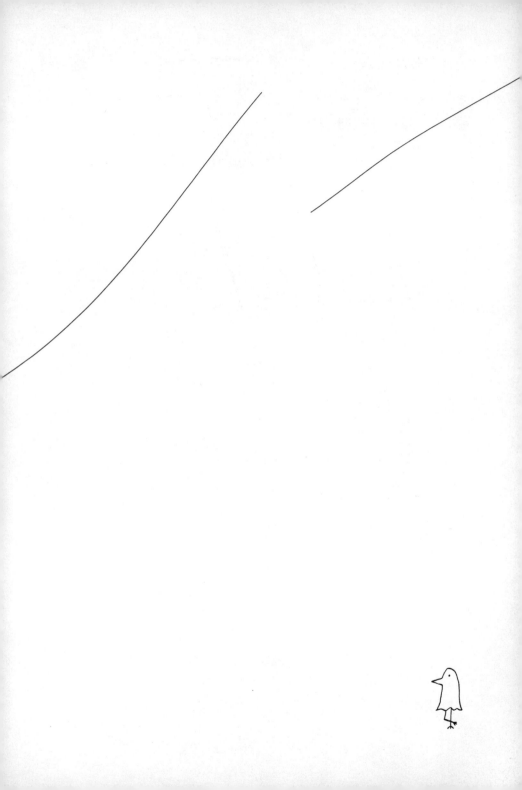

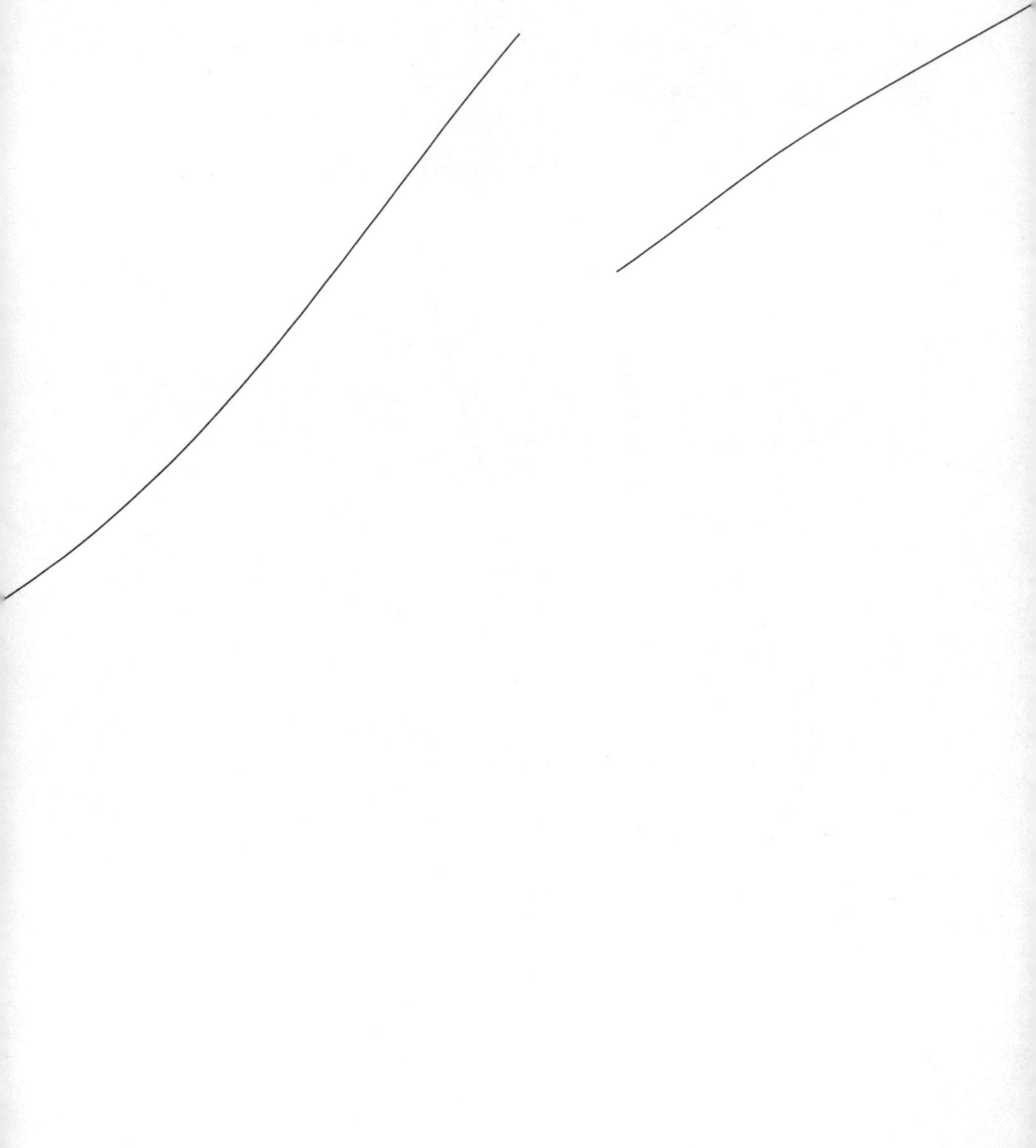

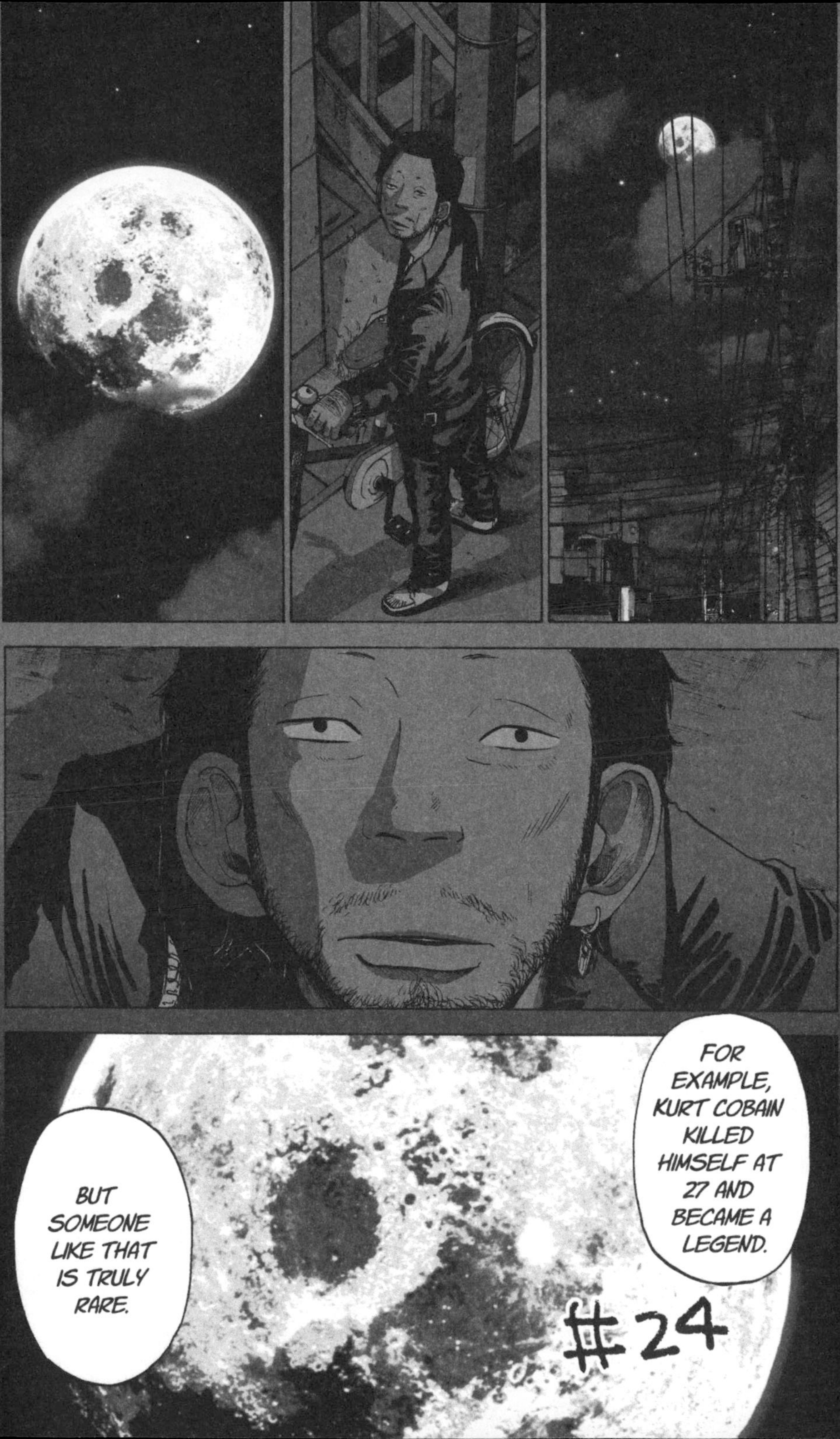
FOR EXAMPLE, KURT COBAIN KILLED HIMSELF AT 27 AND BECAME A LEGEND.
BUT SOMEONE LIKE THAT IS TRULY RARE.
#24

I WAS JUST AN AVERAGE GUY...
...WHO KEPT WORRYING AND SUFFERING, BUT ALWAYS LAUGHING.
PEOPLE ALL DIE ONE DAY AND VANISH AS IF THEY'D NEVER EXISTED...
...BUT THAT'S ONLY NATURAL.
I ALWAYS THOUGHT I WASN'T AFRAID TO DIE.
NO... NO ONE IS AFRAID OF DEATH ITSELF.
YOUR PAIN AND SUFFERING IS OVER IN AN INSTANT.
WHAT REALLY MAKES ME SUFFER...

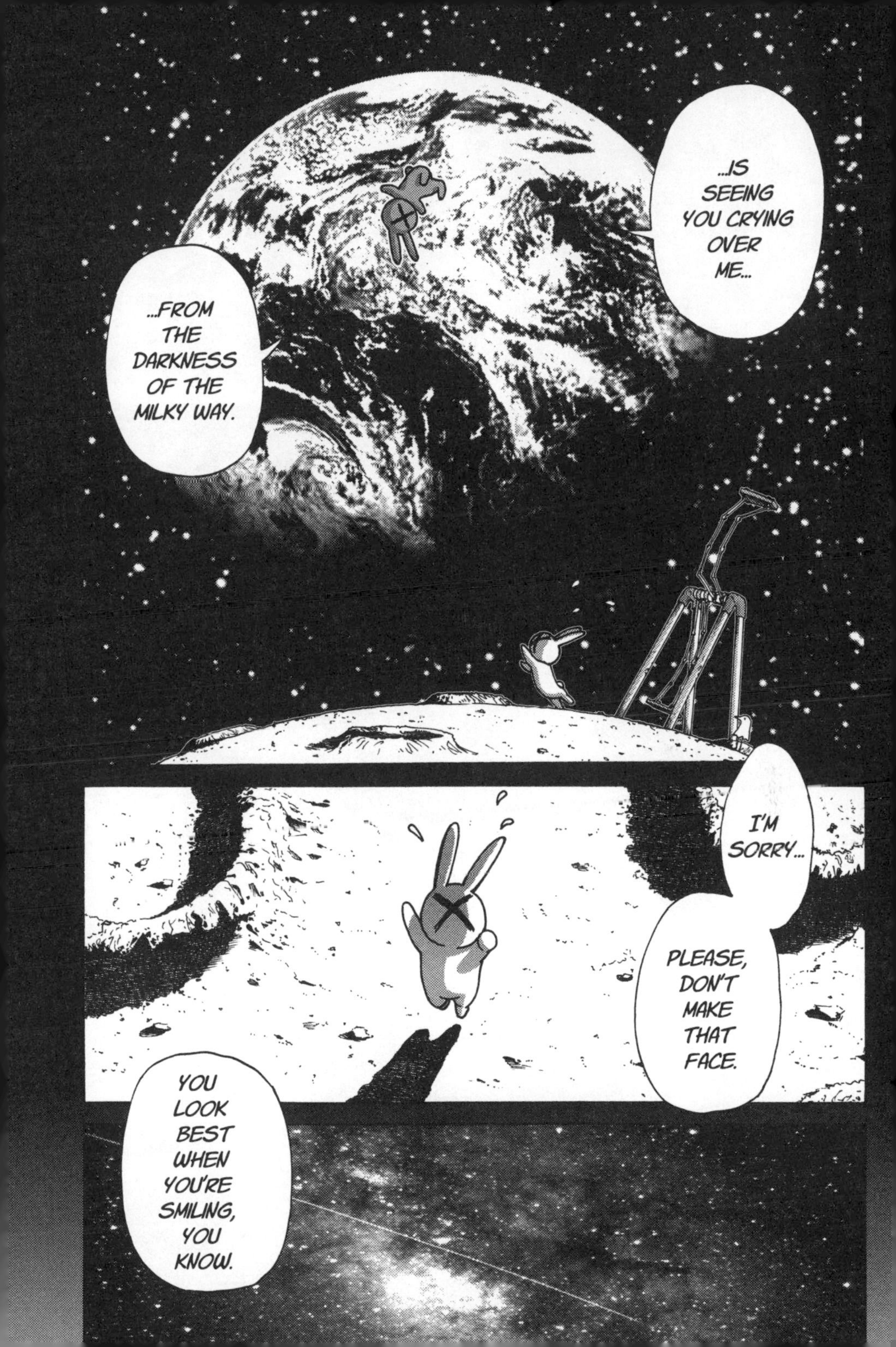
...IS SEEING YOU CRYING OVER ME...
...FROM THE DARKNESS OF THE MILKY WAY.
I'M SORRY...
PLEASE, DON'T MAKE THAT FACE.
YOU LOOK BEST WHEN YOU'RE SMILING, YOU KNOW.

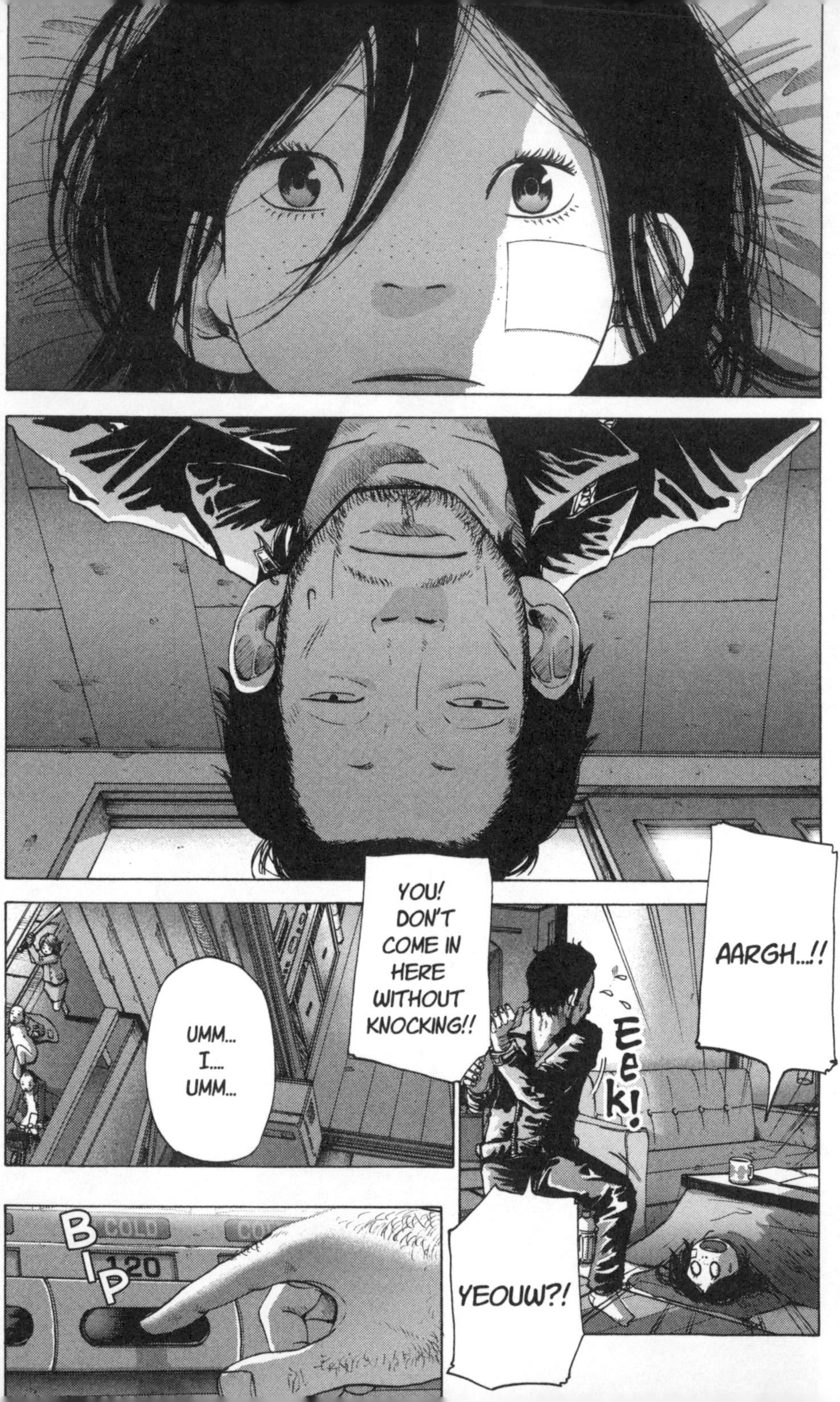
AARGH...!!
YOU! DON'T COME IN HERE WITHOUT KNOCKING!!
Eek!
YEOUW?!
UMM... I... UMM...
BIP
COLD
120

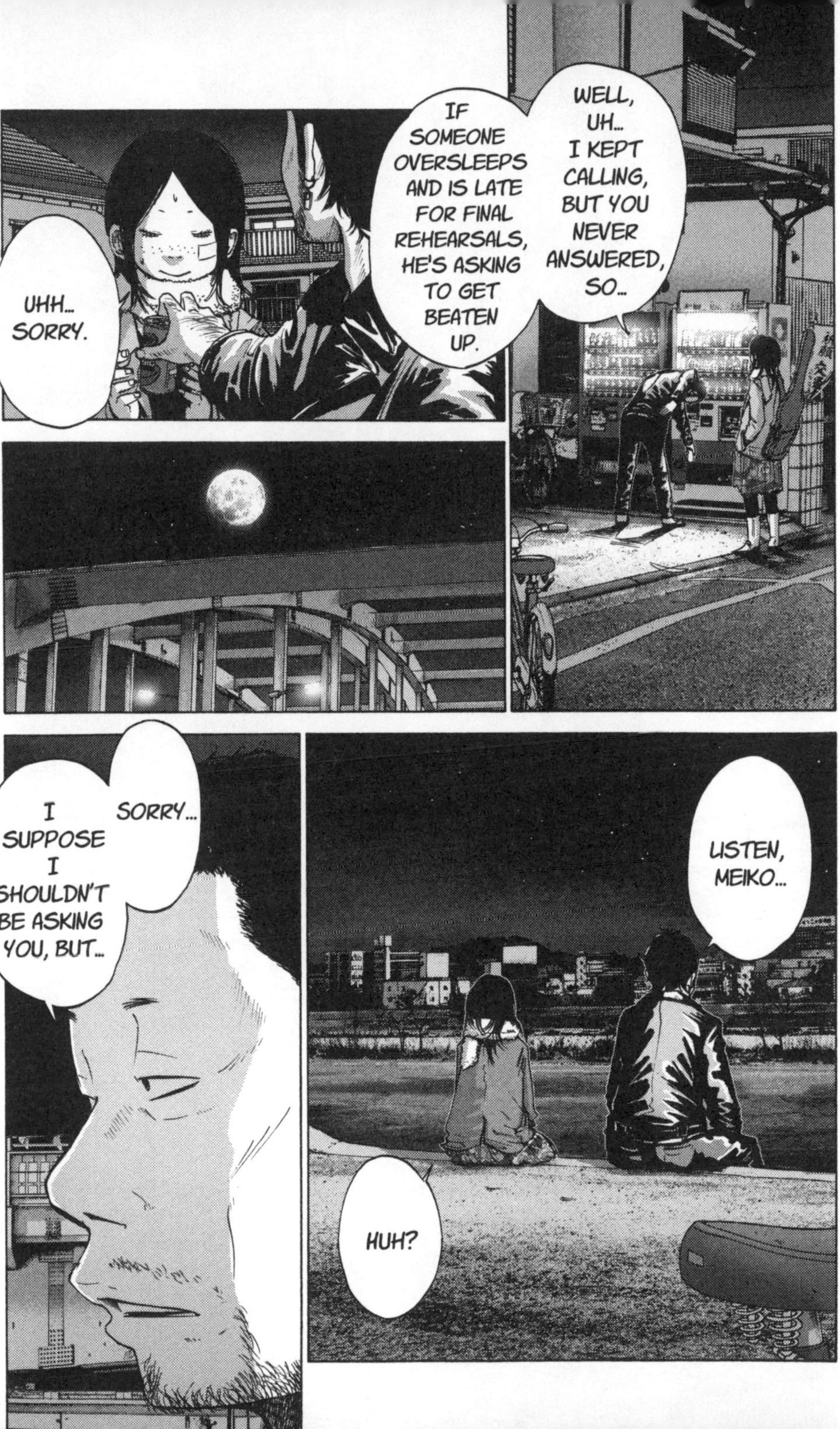
WELL, UH... I KEPT CALLING, BUT YOU NEVER ANSWERED, SO...
IF SOMEONE OVERSLEEPS AND IS LATE FOR FINAL REHEARSALS, HE'S ASKING TO GET BEATEN UP.
UHH... SORRY.
LISTEN, MEIKO...
HUH?
SORRY...
I SUPPOSE I SHOULDN'T BE ASKING YOU, BUT...

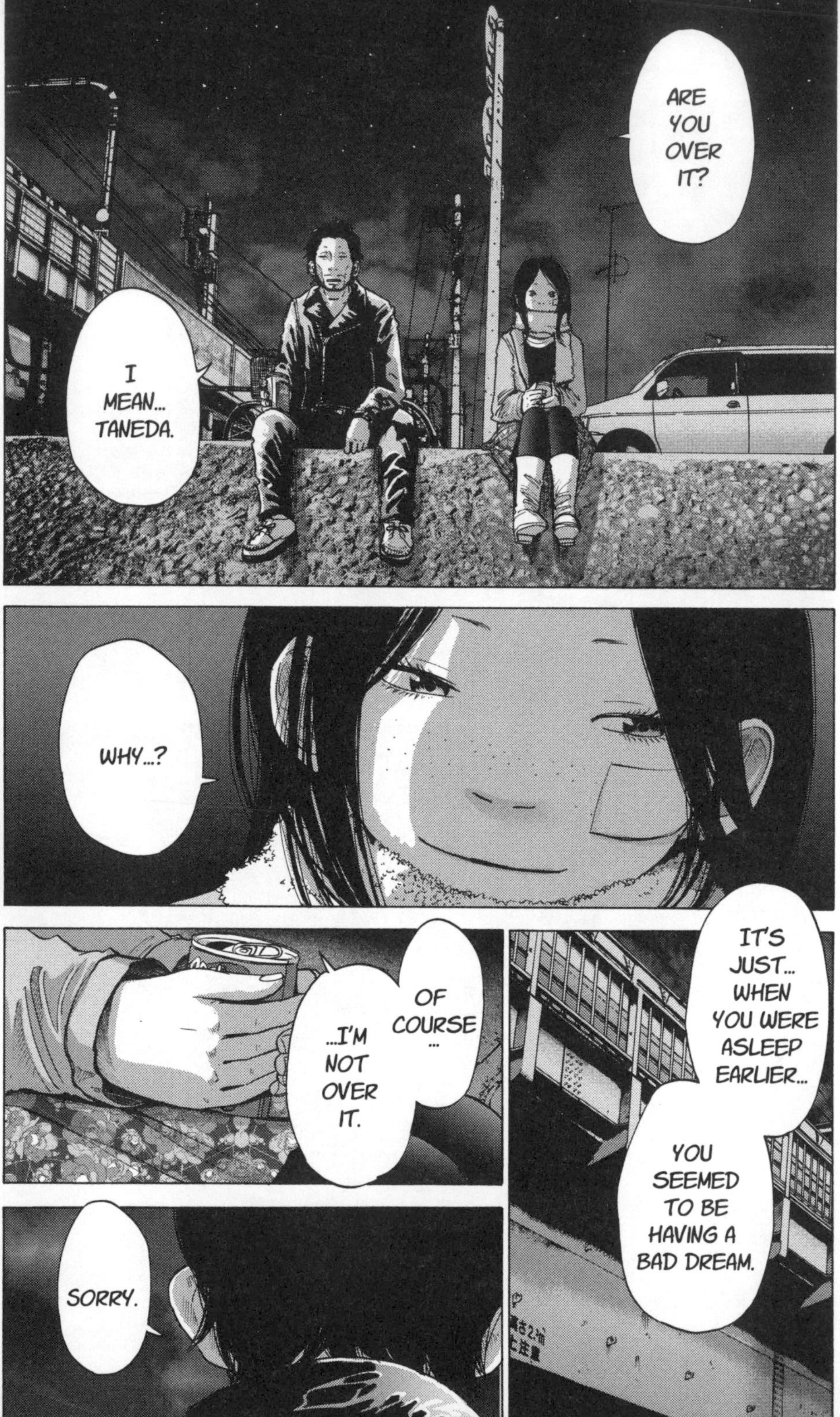
ARE YOU OVER IT?
I MEAN... TANEDA.
WHY...?
IT'S JUST... WHEN YOU WERE ASLEEP EARLIER...
YOU SEEMED TO BE HAVING A BAD DREAM.
OF COURSE...
...I'M NOT OVER IT.
SORRY.

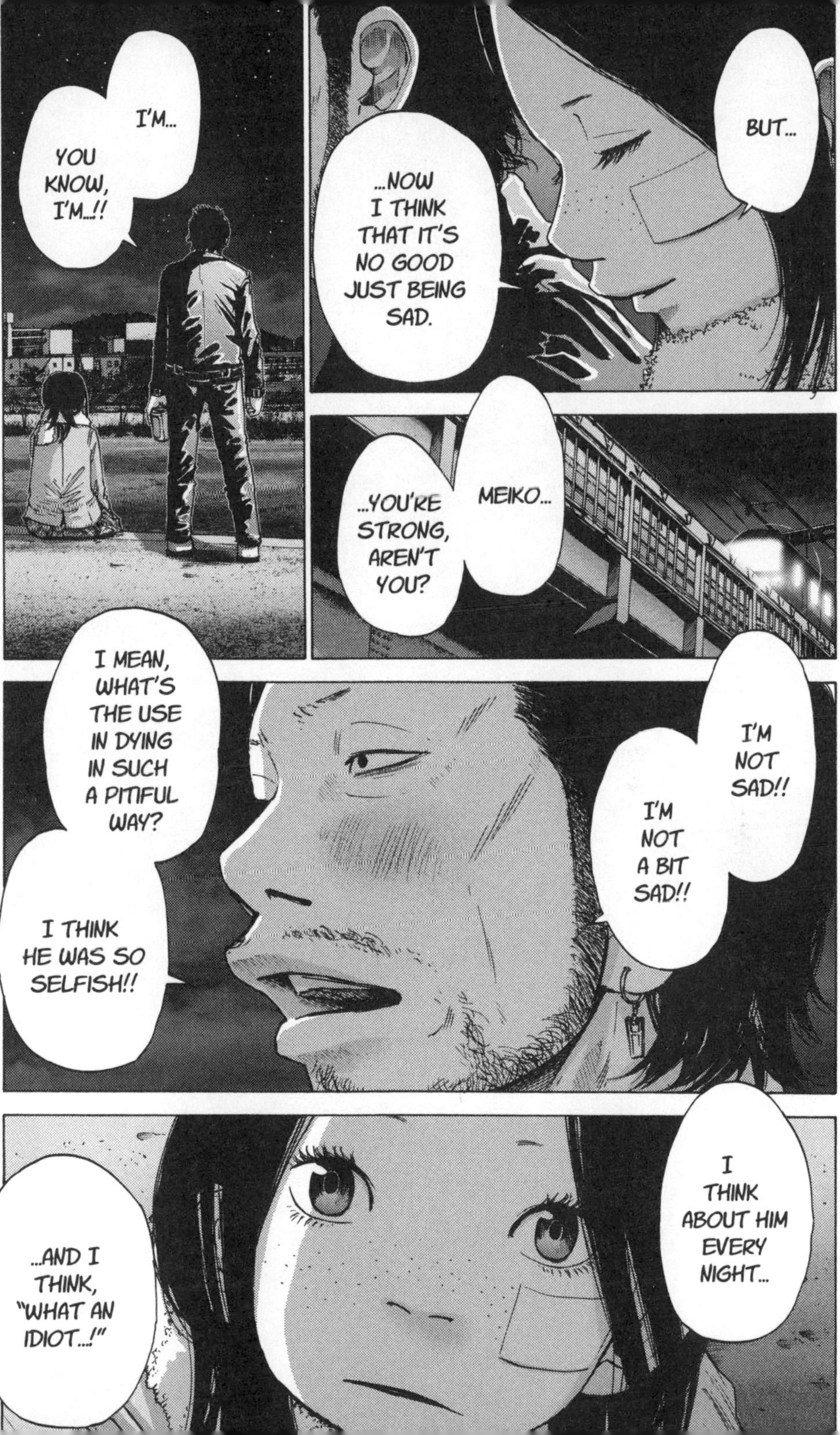
BUT...
...NOW I THINK THAT IT'S NO GOOD JUST BEING SAD.
MEIKO...
...YOU'RE STRONG, AREN'T YOU?
I'M...
YOU KNOW, I'M...!!
I'M NOT SAD!!
I'M NOT A BIT SAD!!
I MEAN, WHAT'S THE USE IN DYING IN SUCH A PITIFUL WAY?
I THINK HE WAS SO SELFISH!!
I THINK ABOUT HIM EVERY NIGHT...
...AND I THINK, "WHAT AN IDIOT...!"

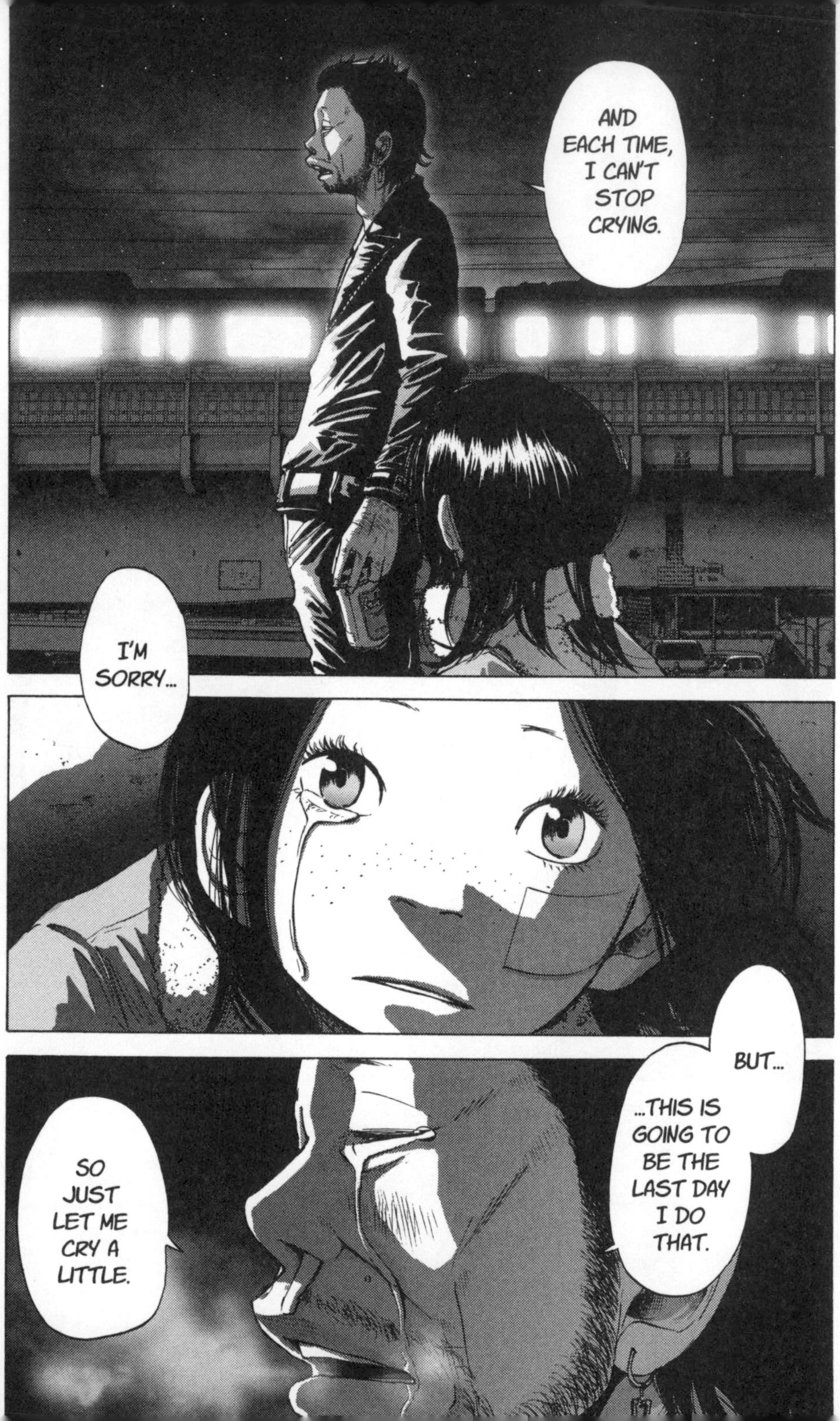
AND EACH TIME, I CAN'T STOP CRYING.
I'M SORRY...
BUT...
...THIS IS GOING TO BE THE LAST DAY I DO THAT.
SO JUST LET ME CRY A LITTLE.

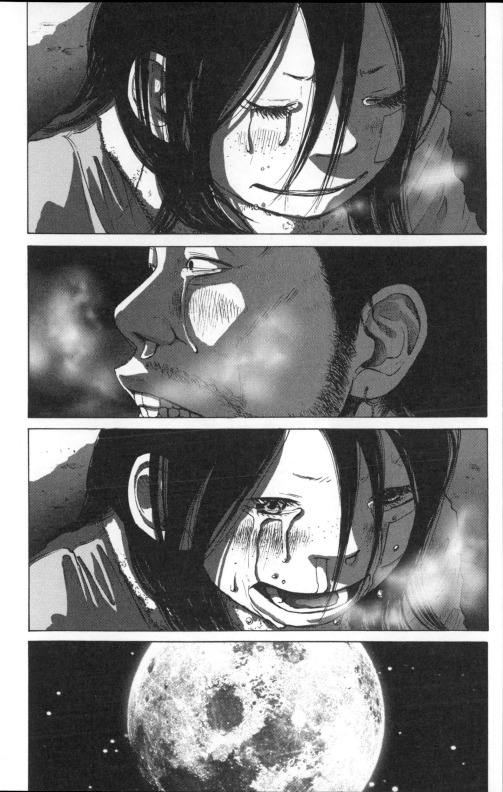

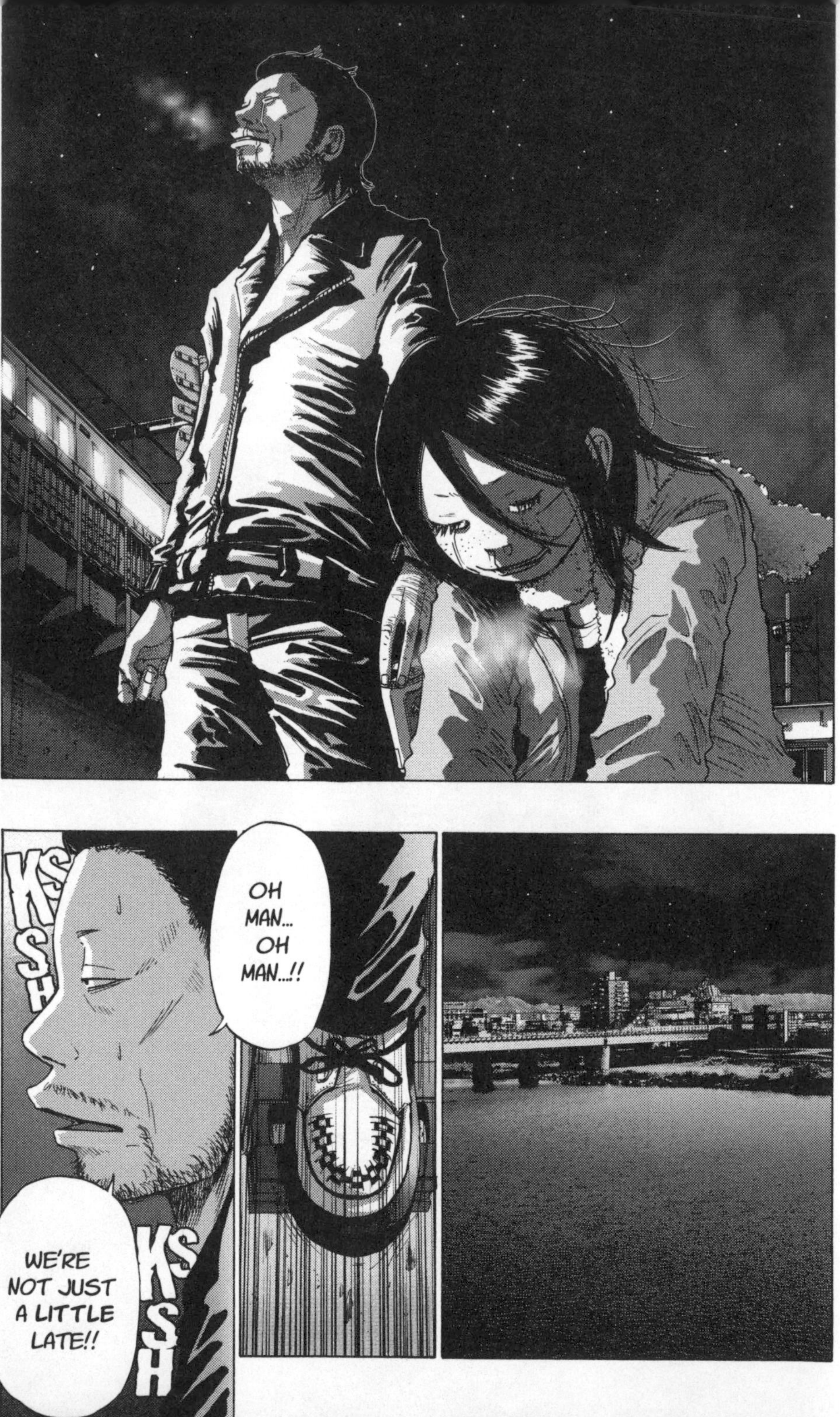
OH MAN... OH MAN...!!
KSSH
WE'RE NOT JUST A LITTLE LATE!!
KSSH

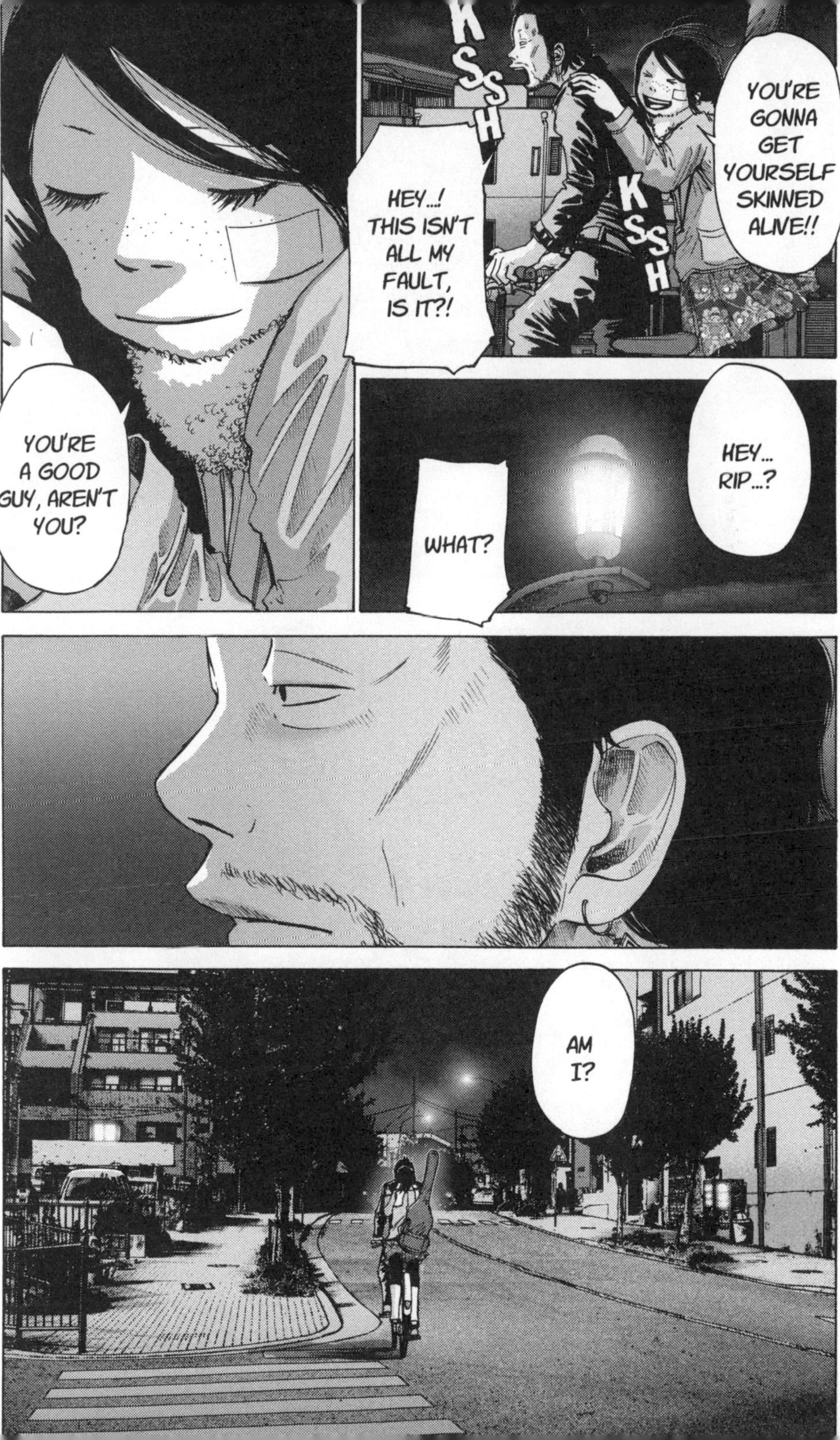
YOU'RE GONNA GET YOURSELF SKINNED ALIVE!!
KSSH
KSSH
HEY...! THIS ISN'T ALL MY FAULT, IS IT?!
HEY... RIP...?
WHAT?
YOU'RE A GOOD GUY, AREN'T YOU?
AM I?

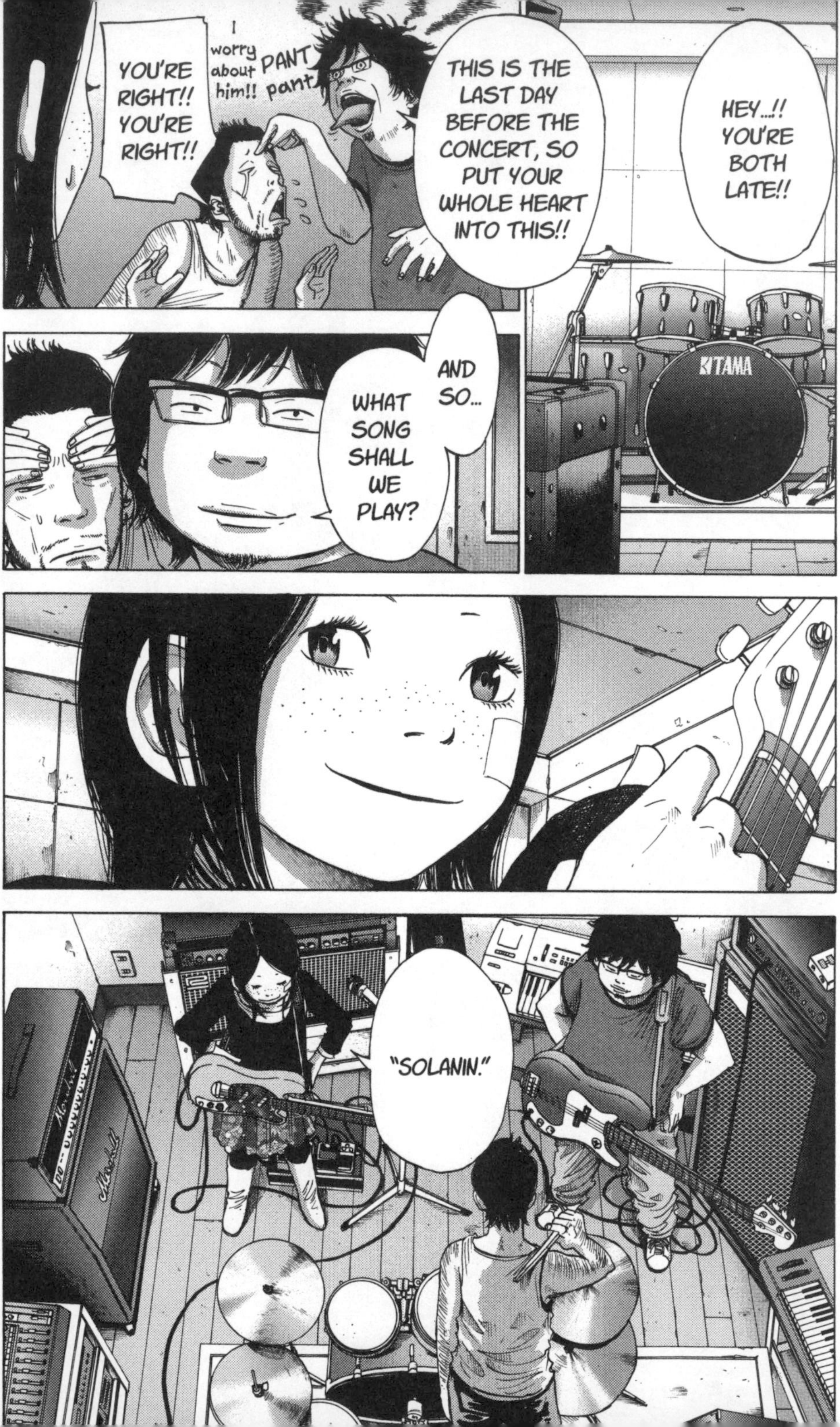
HEY...!! YOU'RE BOTH LATE!!
THIS IS THE LAST DAY BEFORE THE CONCERT, SO PUT YOUR WHOLE HEART INTO THIS!!
PANT pant
I worry about him!!
YOU'RE RIGHT!! YOU'RE RIGHT!!
AND SO... WHAT SONG SHALL WE PLAY?
"SOLANIN."

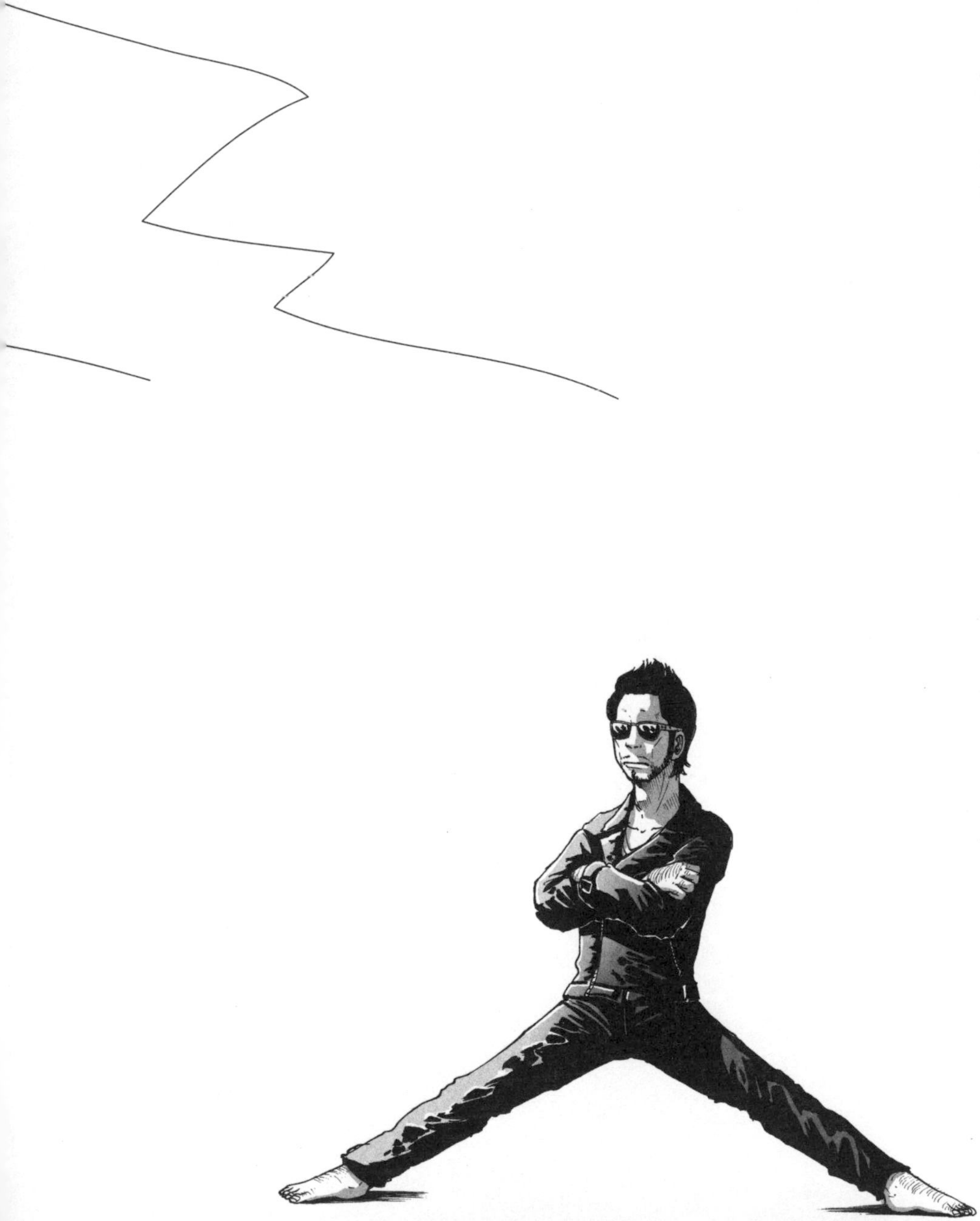

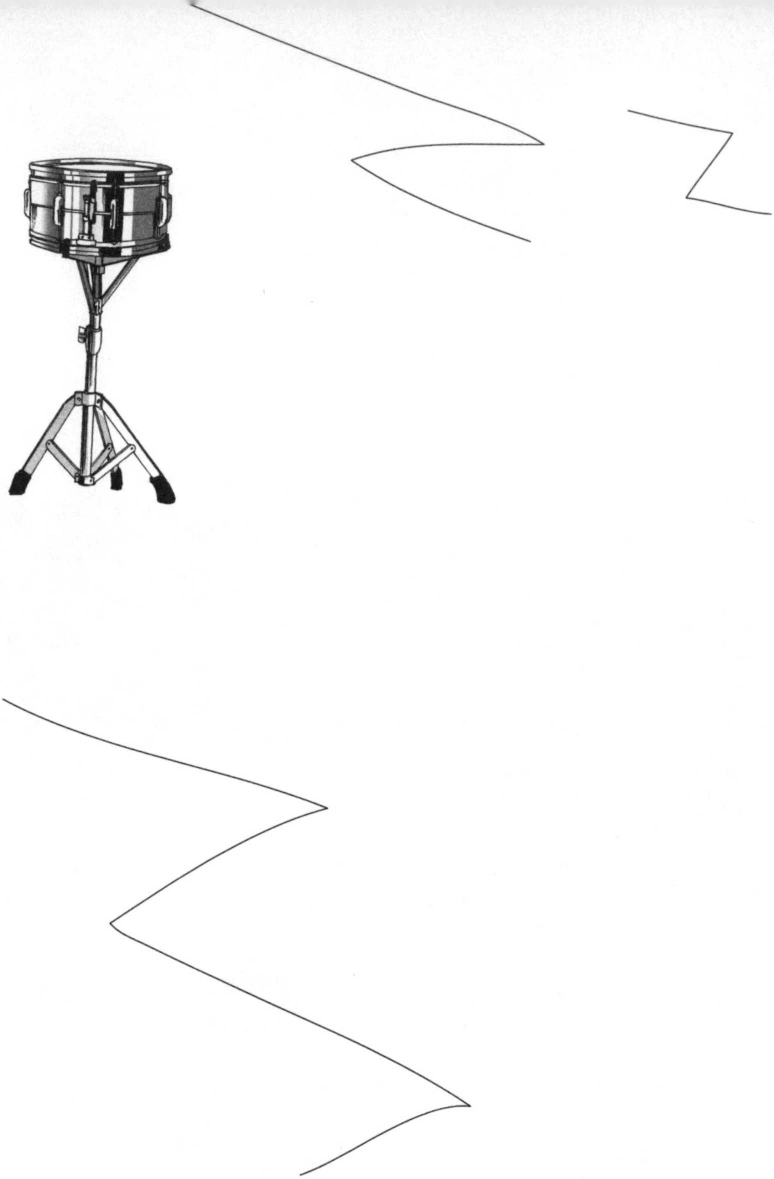

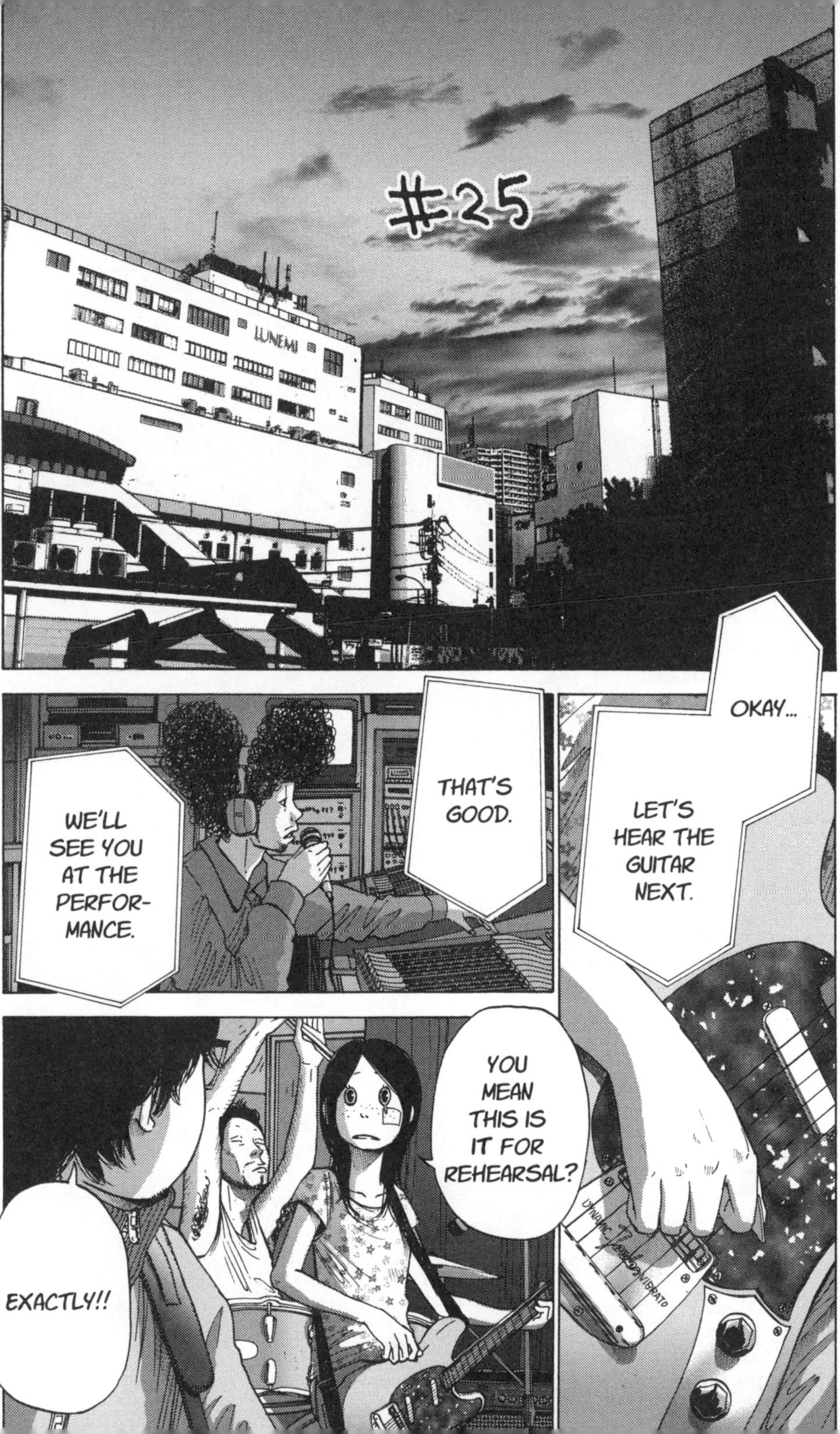
#25
LUNEMI
OKAY...
LET'S HEAR THE GUITAR NEXT.
THAT'S GOOD.
WE'LL SEE YOU AT THE PERFOR-MANCE.
YOU MEAN THIS IS IT FOR REHEARSAL?
EXACTLY!!

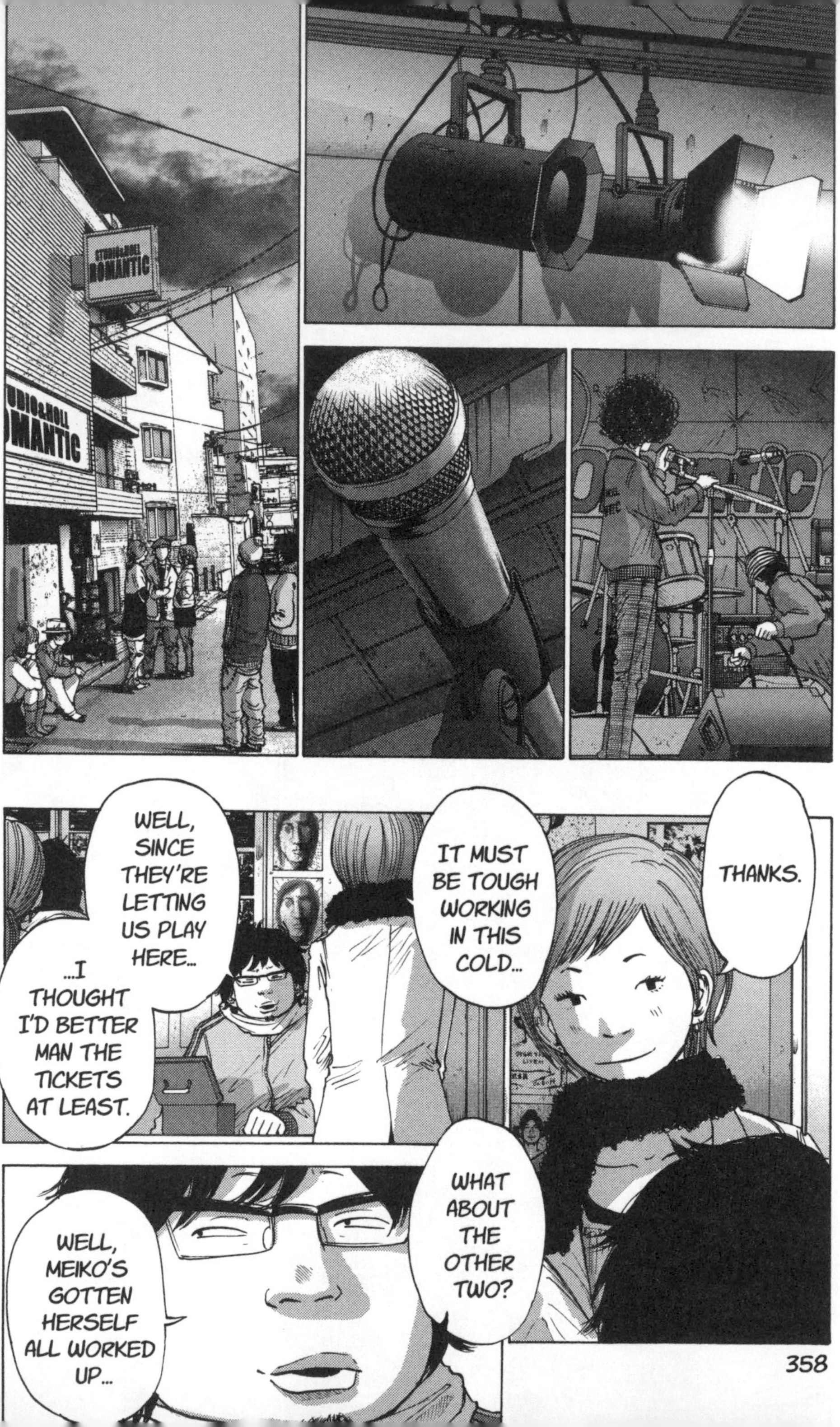
STUDIO&HOLL ROMANTIC
THANKS.
IT MUST BE TOUGH WORKING IN THIS COLD...
WELL, SINCE THEY'RE LETTING US PLAY HERE...
...I THOUGHT I'D BETTER MAN THE TICKETS AT LEAST.
WHAT ABOUT THE OTHER TWO?
WELL, MEIKO'S GOTTEN HERSELF ALL WORKED UP...

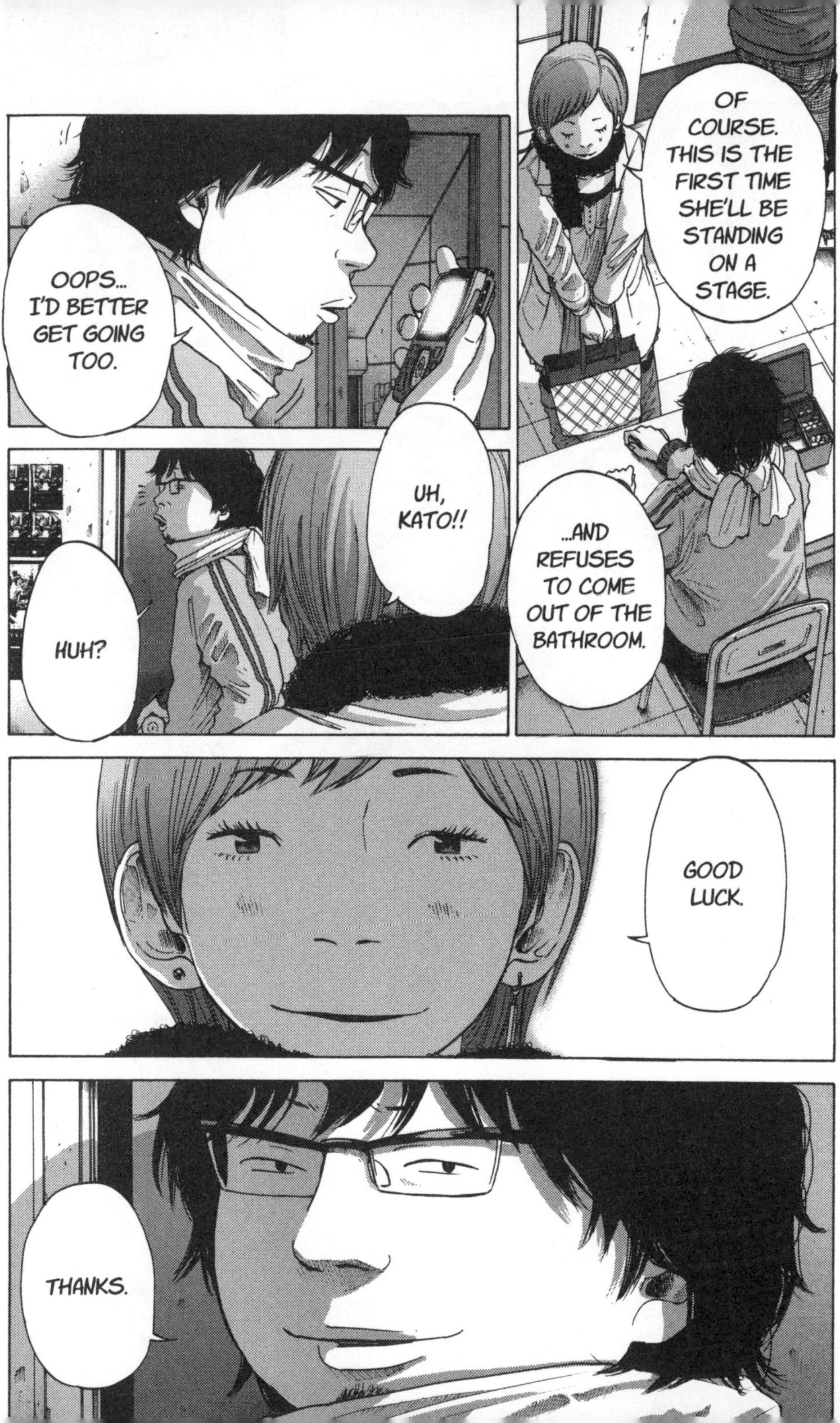
OF COURSE. THIS IS THE FIRST TIME SHE'LL BE STANDING ON A STAGE.
...AND REFUSES TO COME OUT OF THE BATHROOM.
OOPS... I'D BETTER GET GOING TOO.
UH, KATO!!
HUH?
GOOD LUCK.
THANKS.

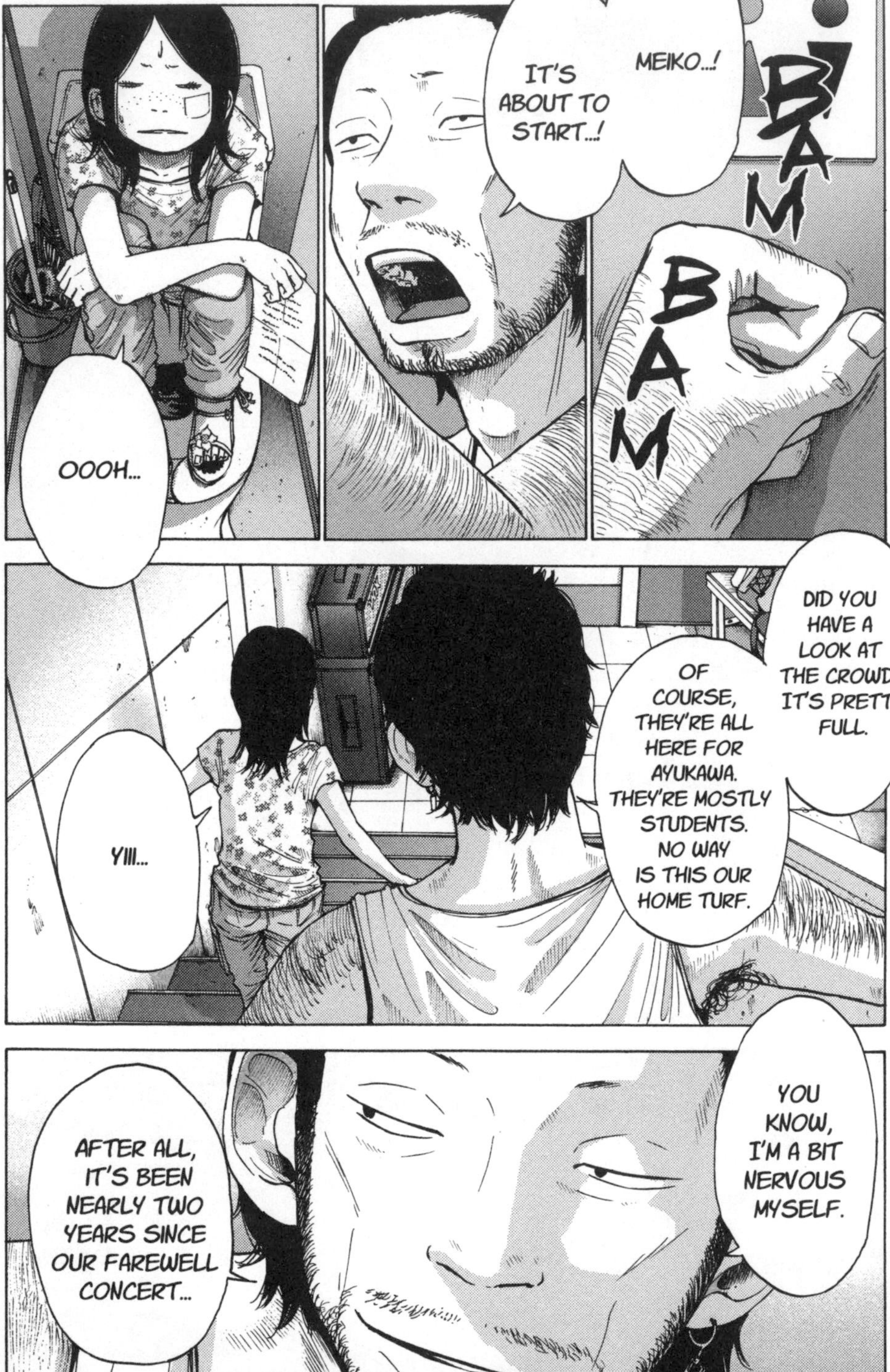
BAM
BAM
MEIKO...!
IT'S ABOUT TO START...!
OOOH...
DID YOU HAVE A LOOK AT THE CROWD? IT'S PRETTY FULL.
OF COURSE, THEY'RE ALL HERE FOR AYUKAWA. THEY'RE MOSTLY STUDENTS. NO WAY IS THIS OUR HOME TURF.
YIII...
YOU KNOW, I'M A BIT NERVOUS MYSELF.
AFTER ALL, IT'S BEEN NEARLY TWO YEARS SINCE OUR FAREWELL CONCERT...

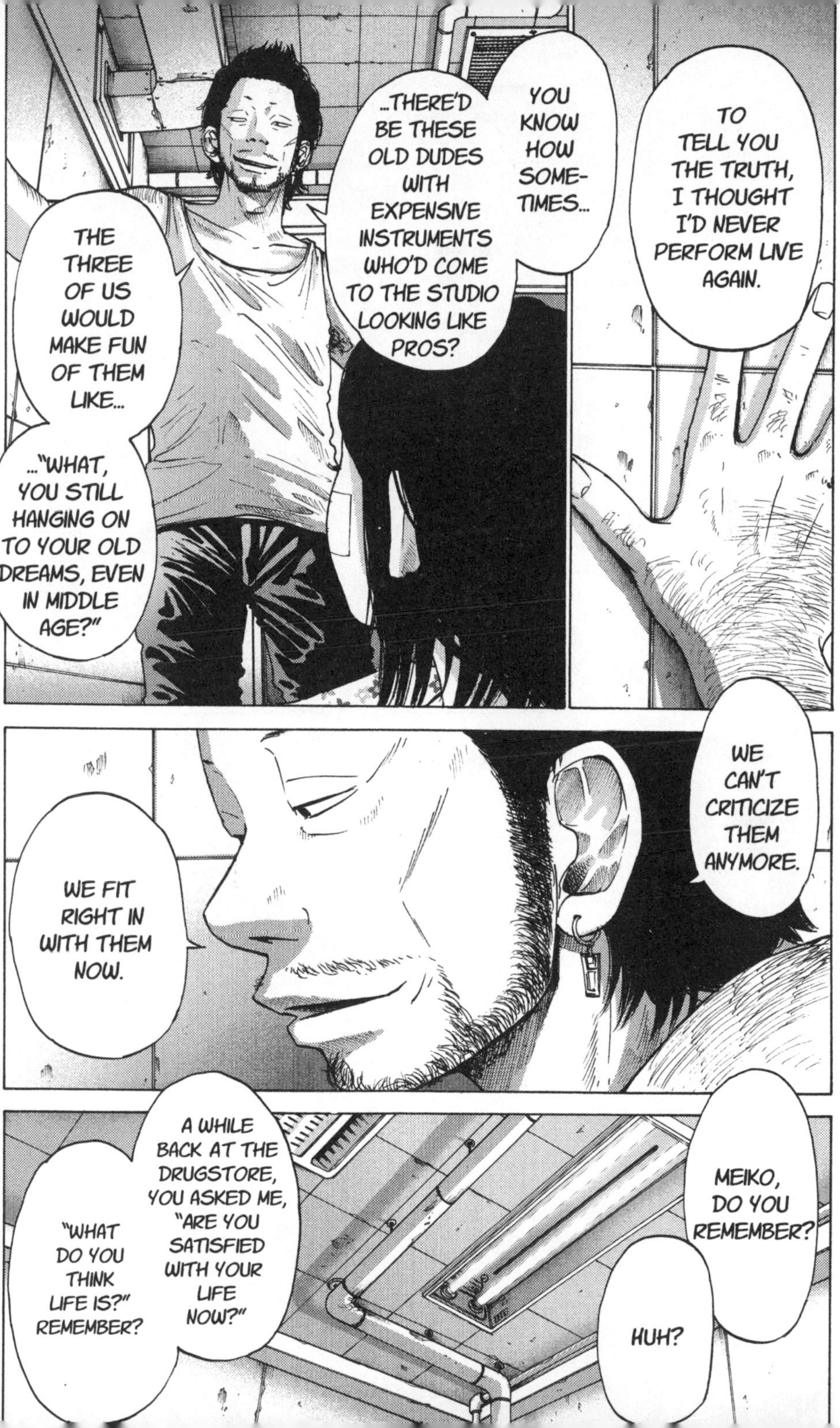
TO TELL YOU THE TRUTH, I THOUGHT I'D NEVER PERFORM LIVE AGAIN.
YOU KNOW HOW SOME-TIMES...
...THERE'D BE THESE OLD DUDES WITH EXPENSIVE INSTRUMENTS WHO'D COME TO THE STUDIO LOOKING LIKE PROS?
THE THREE OF US WOULD MAKE FUN OF THEM LIKE...
..."WHAT, YOU STILL HANGING ON TO YOUR OLD DREAMS, EVEN IN MIDDLE AGE?"
WE CAN'T CRITICIZE THEM ANYMORE.
WE FIT RIGHT IN WITH THEM NOW.
MEIKO, DO YOU REMEMBER?
HUH?
A WHILE BACK AT THE DRUGSTORE, YOU ASKED ME, "ARE YOU SATISFIED WITH YOUR LIFE NOW?"
"WHAT DO YOU THINK LIFE IS?" REMEMBER?

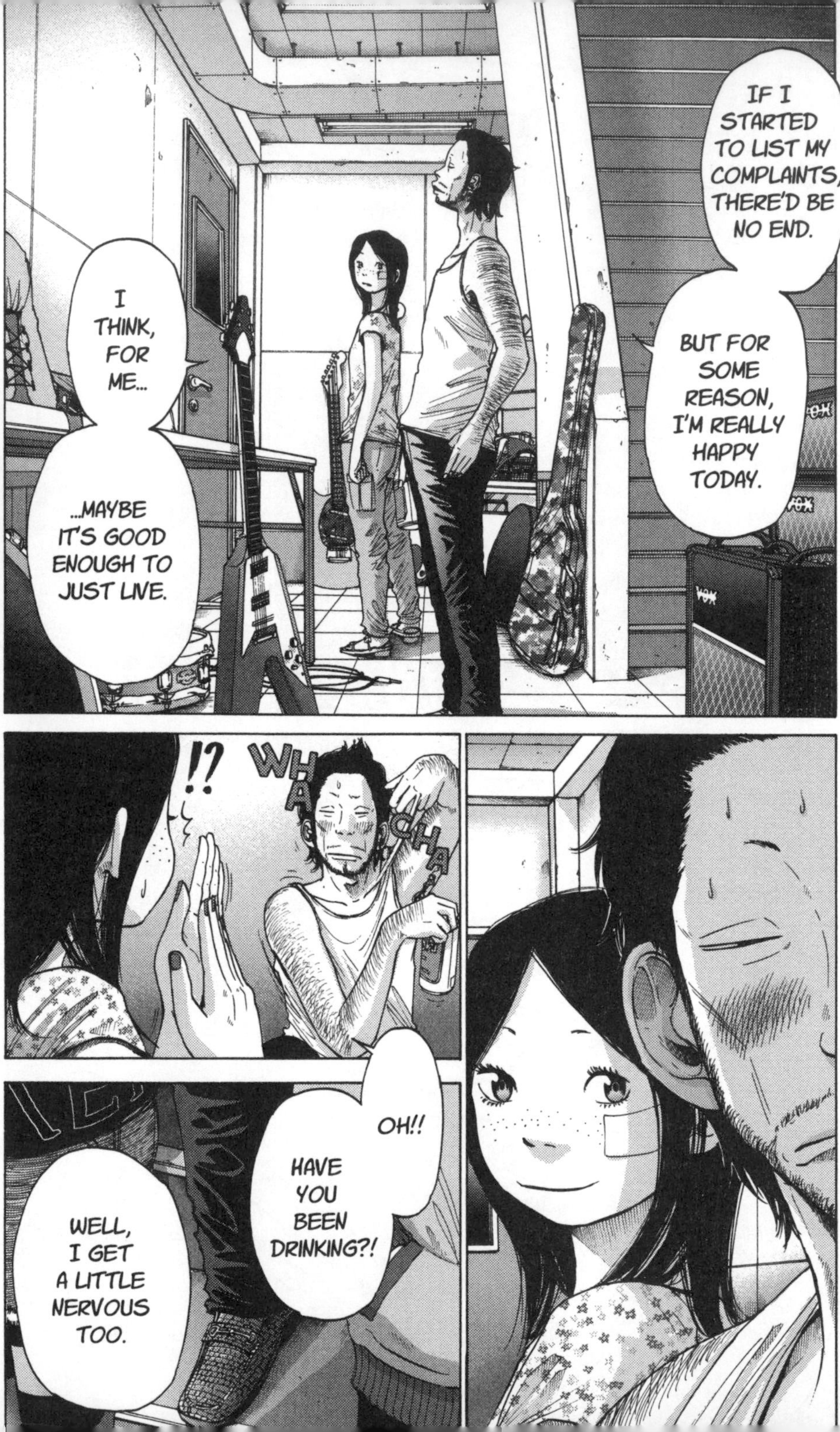
IF I STARTED TO LIST MY COMPLAINTS, THERE'D BE NO END.
BUT FOR SOME REASON, I'M REALLY HAPPY TODAY.
I THINK, FOR ME...
...MAYBE IT'S GOOD ENOUGH TO JUST LIVE.
!?
WHACHA
OH!!
HAVE YOU BEEN DRINKING?!
WELL, I GET A LITTLE NERVOUS TOO.

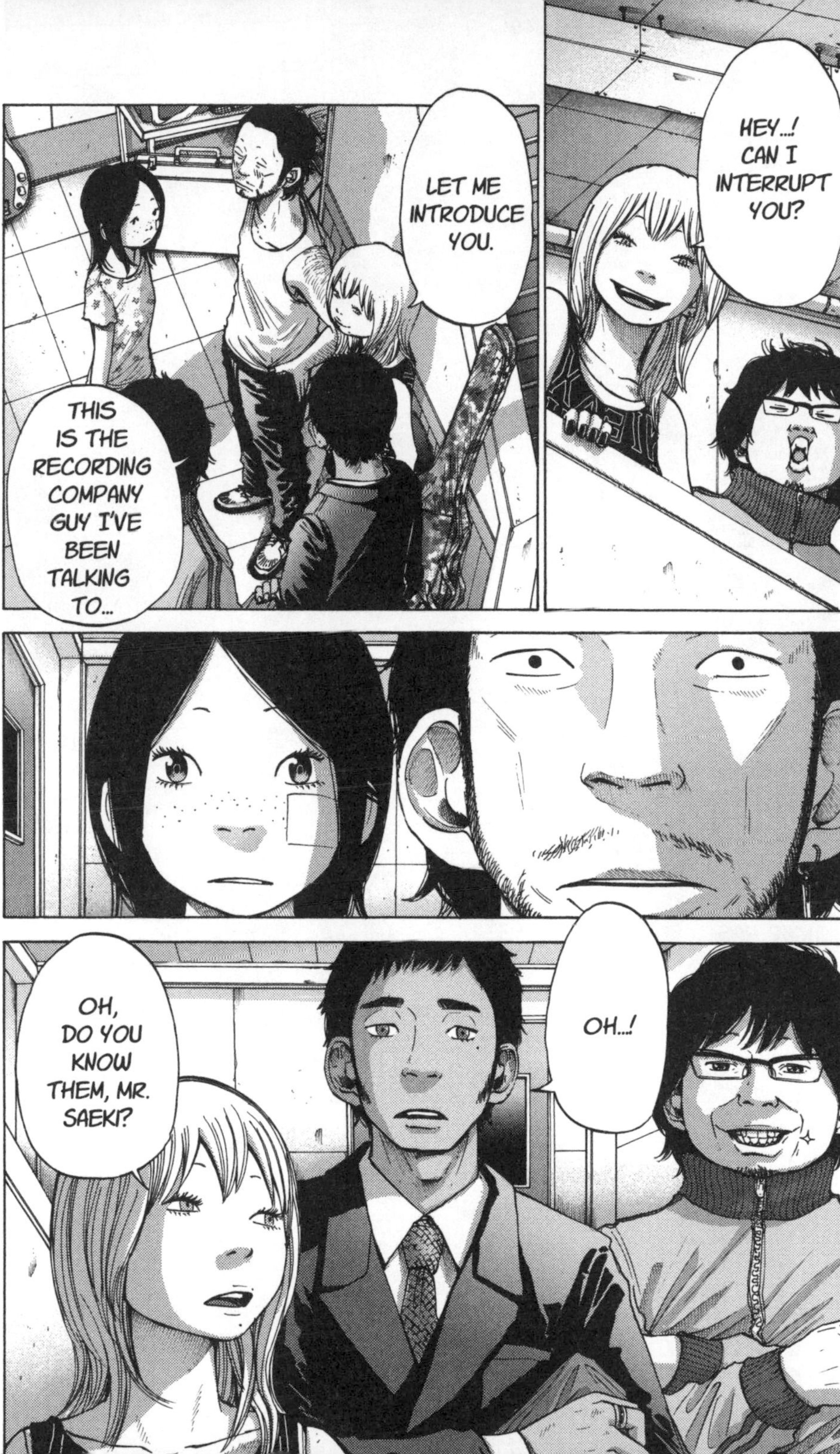
HEY...! CAN I INTERRUPT YOU?
LET ME INTRODUCE YOU.
THIS IS THE RECORDING COMPANY GUY I'VE BEEN TALKING TO...
OH...!
OH, DO YOU KNOW THEM, MR. SAEKI?

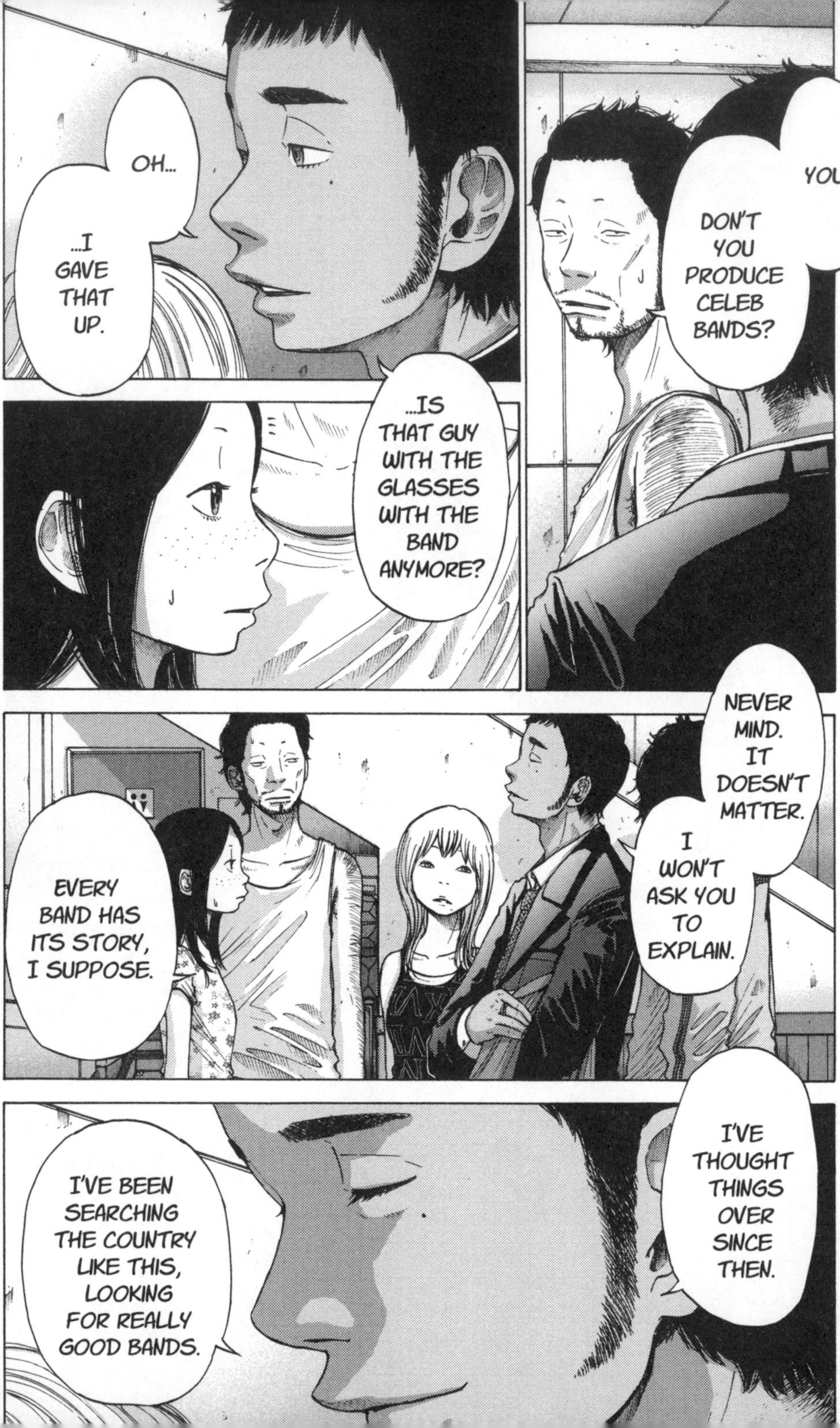
YOU...
DON'T YOU PRODUCE CELEB BANDS?
OH...
...I GAVE THAT UP.
...IS THAT GUY WITH THE GLASSES WITH THE BAND ANYMORE?
NEVER MIND. IT DOESN'T MATTER.
I WON'T ASK YOU TO EXPLAIN.
EVERY BAND HAS ITS STORY, I SUPPOSE.
I'VE THOUGHT THINGS OVER SINCE THEN.
I'VE BEEN SEARCHING THE COUNTRY LIKE THIS, LOOKING FOR REALLY GOOD BANDS.

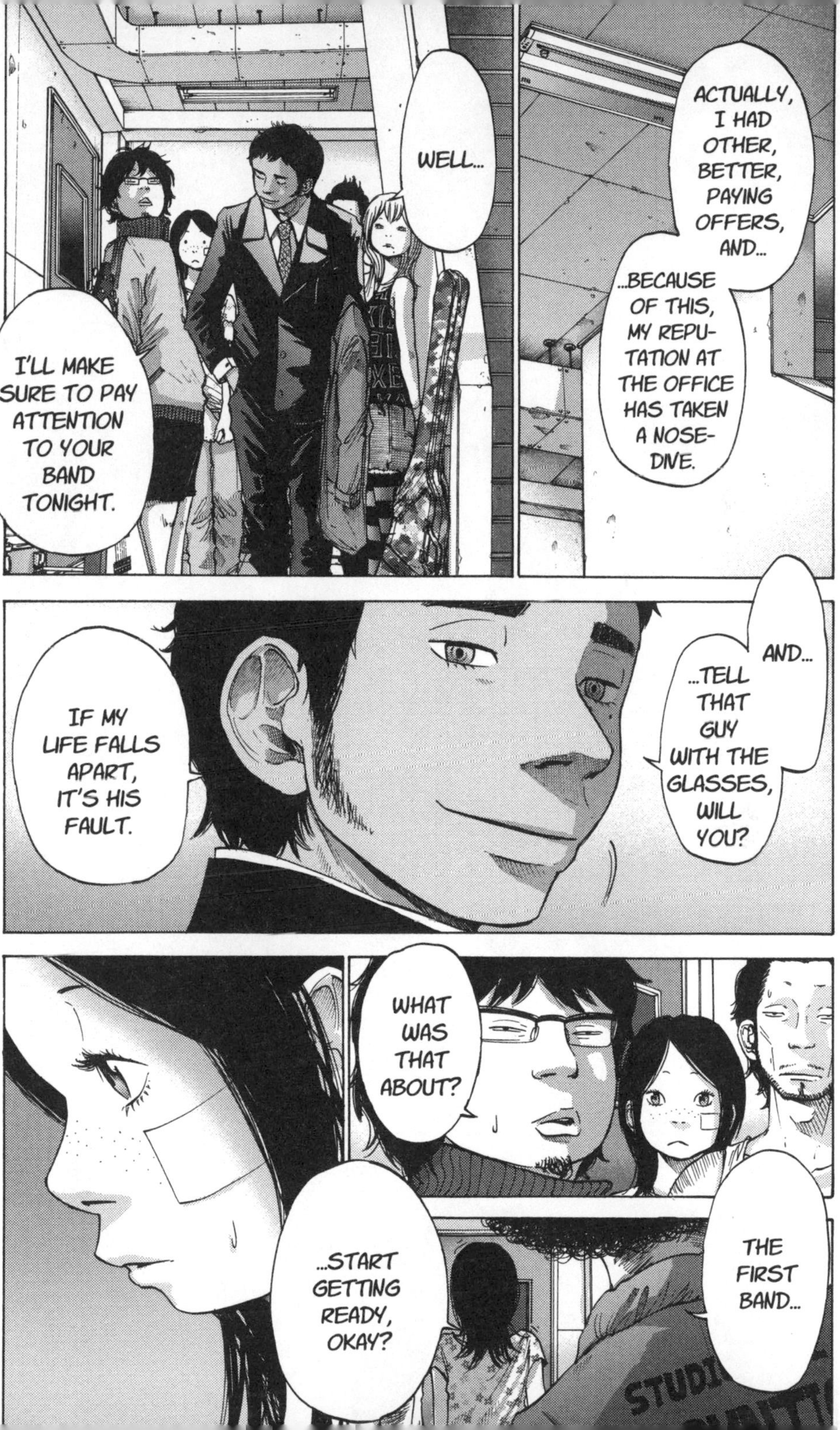
ACTUALLY, I HAD OTHER, BETTER, PAYING OFFERS, AND...
...BECAUSE OF THIS, MY REPUTATION AT THE OFFICE HAS TAKEN A NOSEDIVE.
WELL...
I'LL MAKE SURE TO PAY ATTENTION TO YOUR BAND TONIGHT.
AND...
...TELL THAT GUY WITH THE GLASSES, WILL YOU?
IF MY LIFE FALLS APART, IT'S HIS FAULT.
WHAT WAS THAT ABOUT?
THE FIRST BAND...
...START GETTING READY, OKAY?

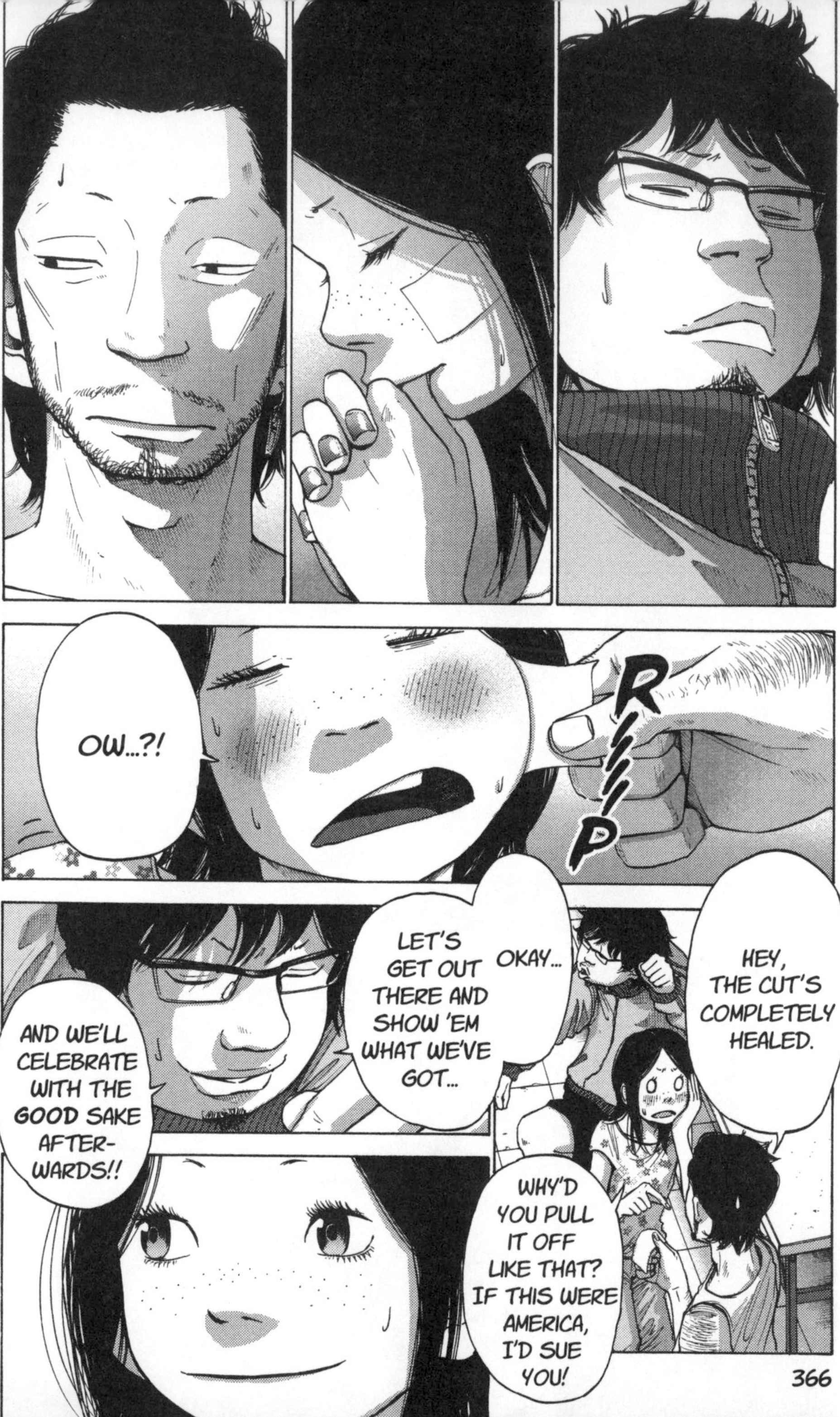
OW...?!
RIIIIP
HEY, THE CUT'S COMPLETELY HEALED.
OKAY...
WHY'D YOU PULL IT OFF LIKE THAT? IF THIS WERE AMERICA, I'D SUE YOU!
LET'S GET OUT THERE AND SHOW 'EM WHAT WE'VE GOT...
AND WE'LL CELEBRATE WITH THE GOOD SAKE AFTER-WARDS!!

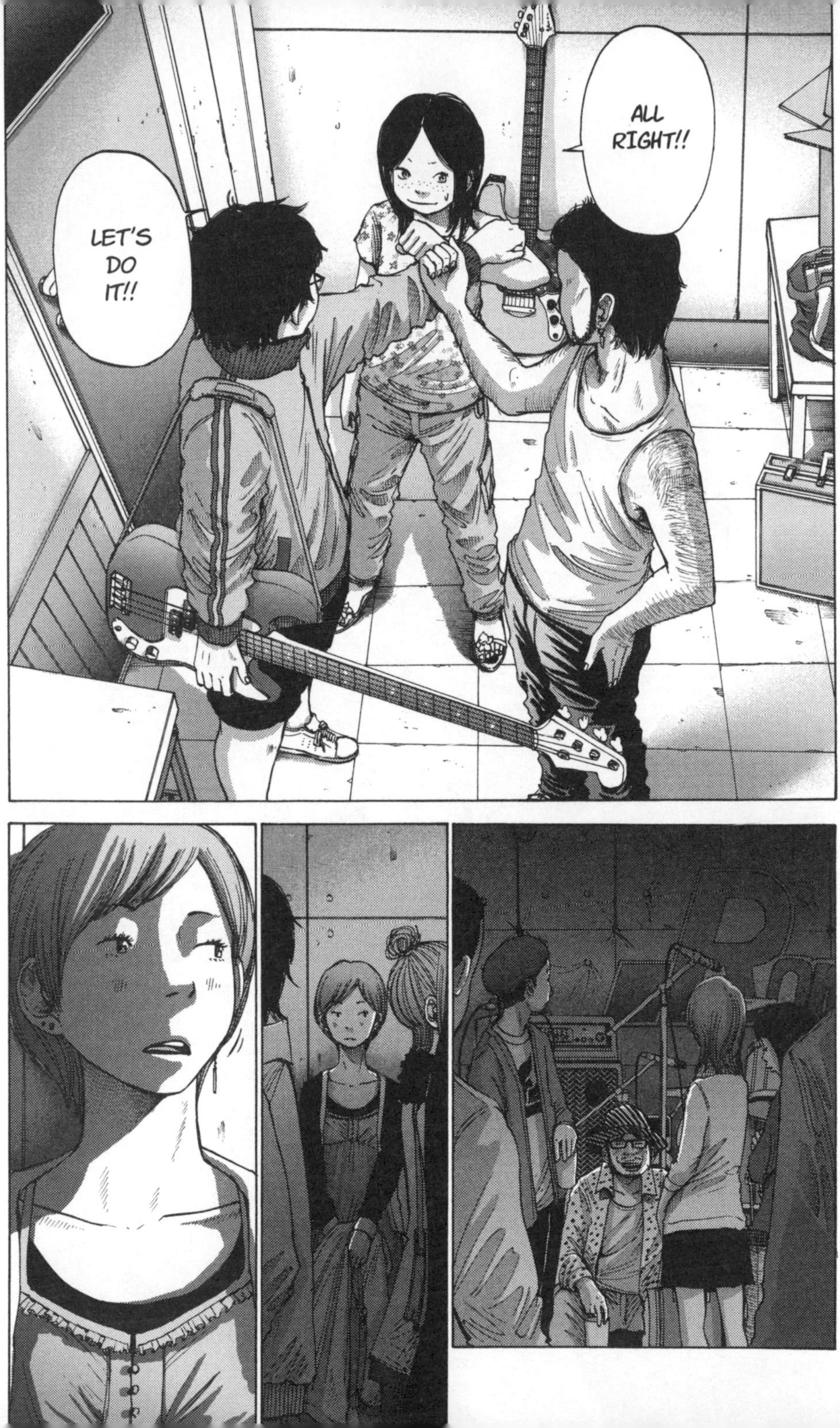
ALL RIGHT!!
LET'S DO IT!!

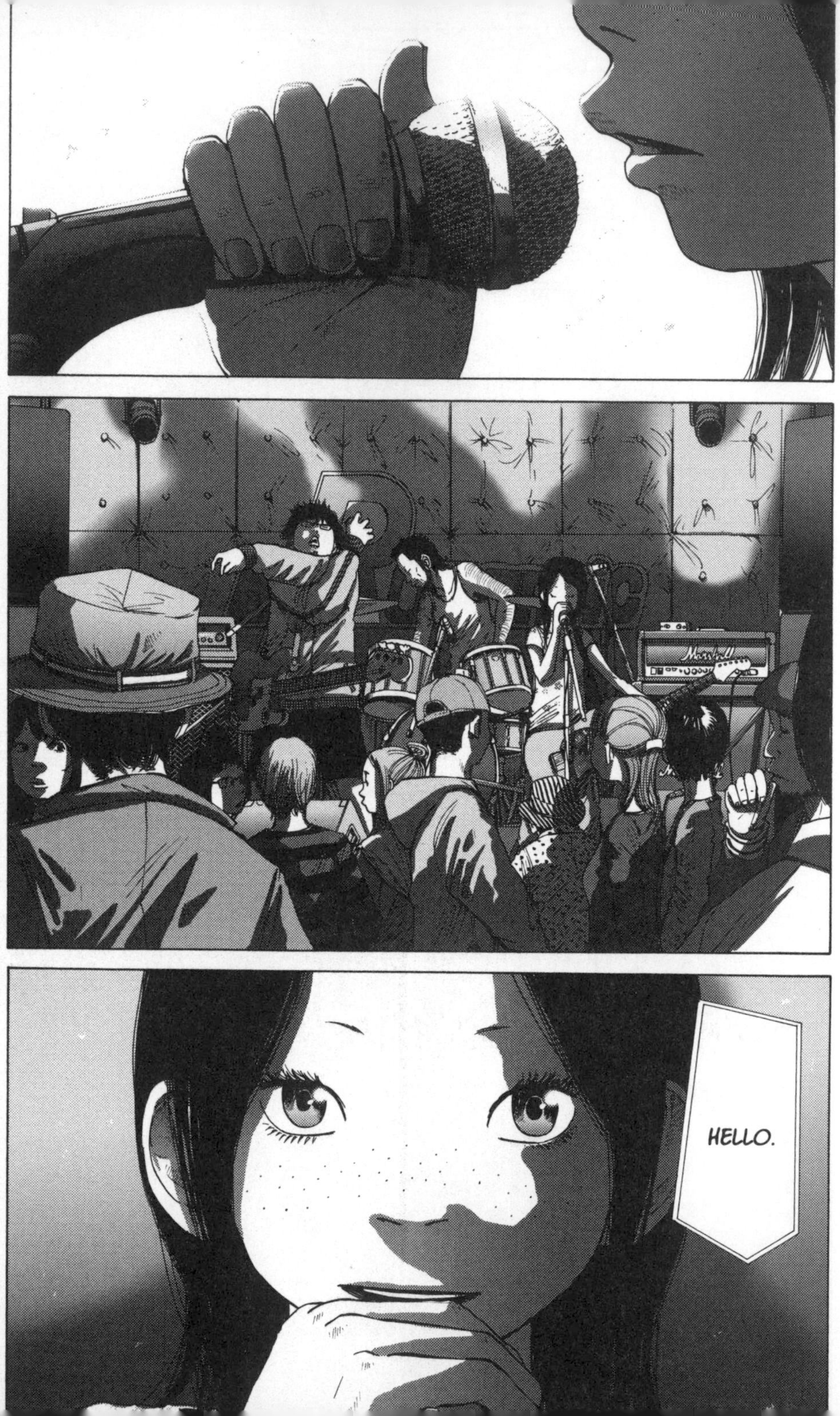
HELLO.

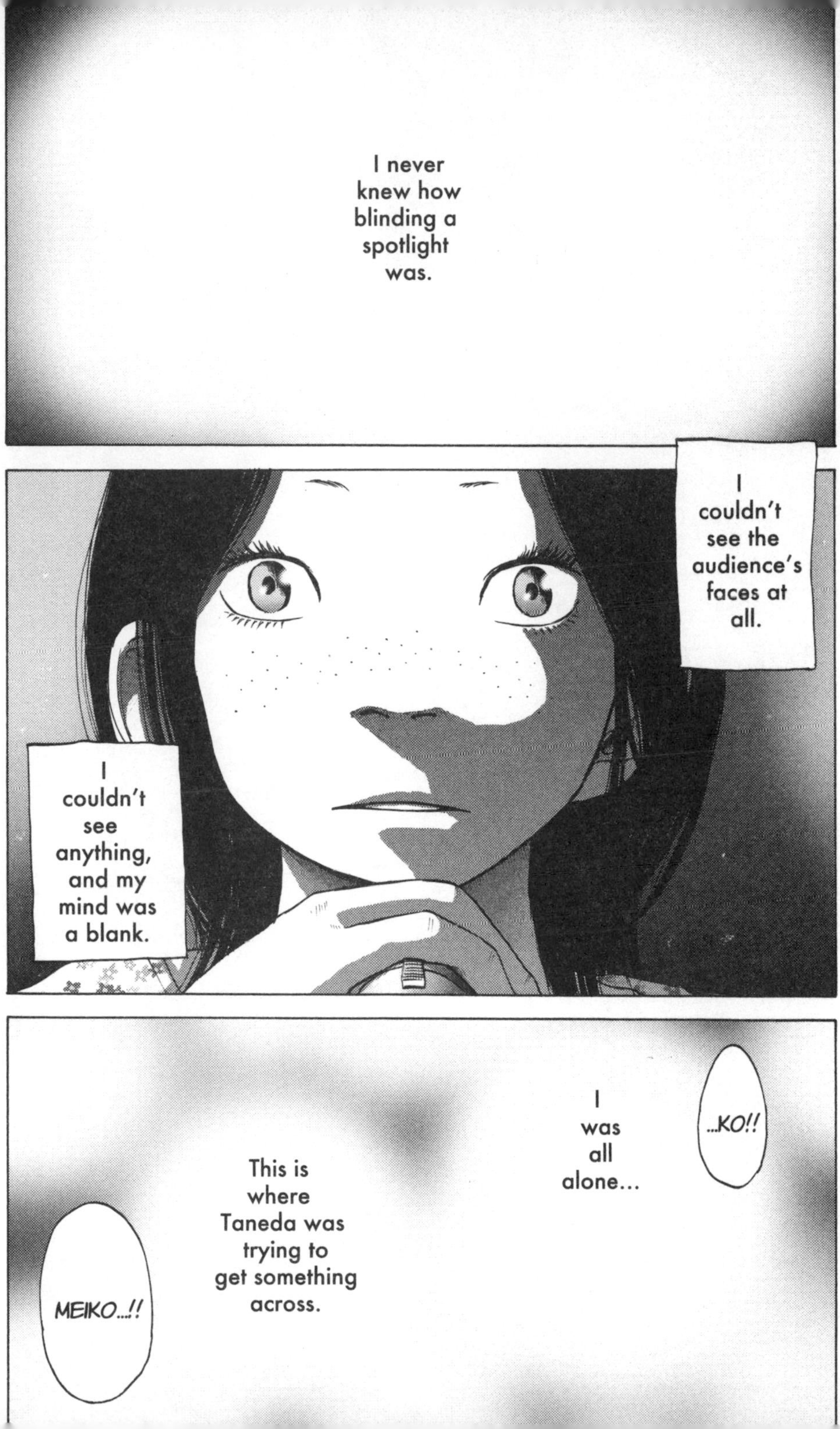
I never knew how blinding a spotlight was.
I couldn't see the audience's faces at all.
I couldn't see anything, and my mind was a blank.
...KO!!
I was all alone...
This is where Taneda was trying to get something across.
MEIKO...!!

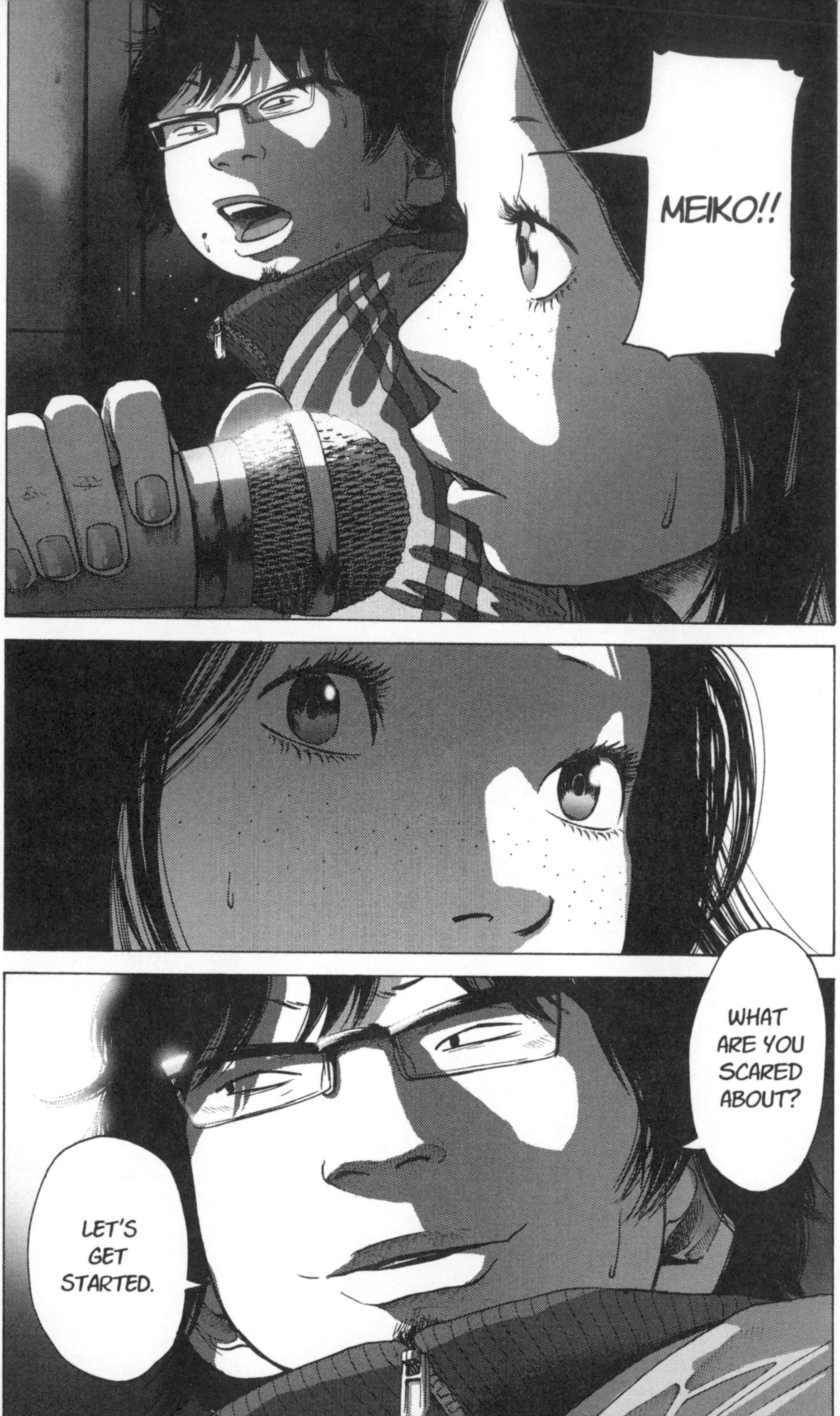
MEIKO!!
WHAT ARE YOU SCARED ABOUT?
LET'S GET STARTED.

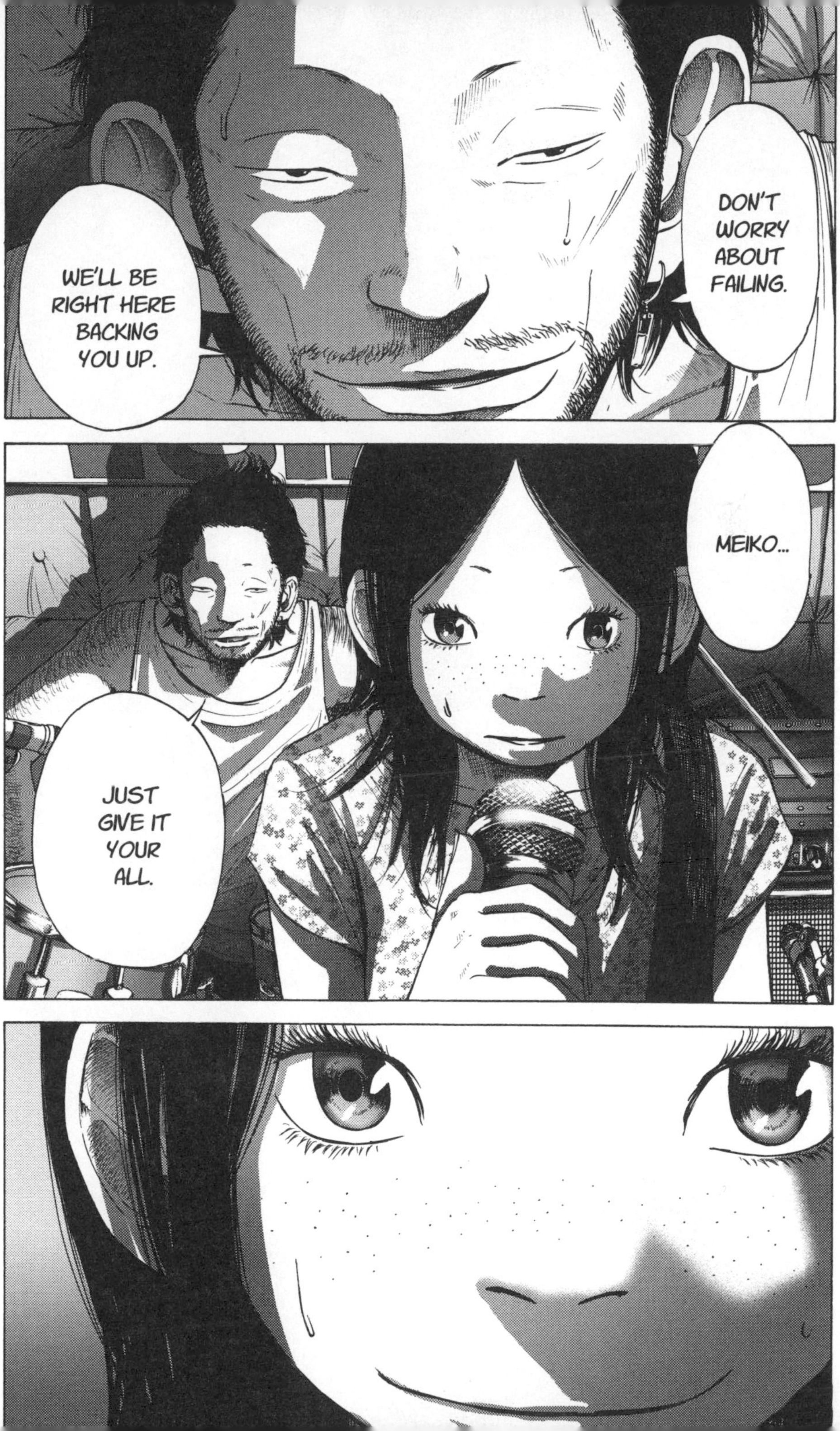
DON'T WORRY ABOUT FAILING.
WE'LL BE RIGHT HERE BACKING YOU UP.
MEIKO...
JUST GIVE IT YOUR ALL.

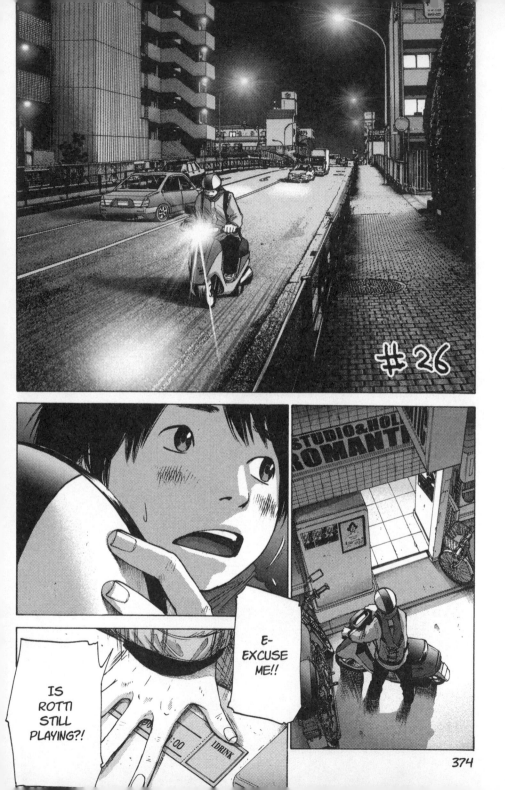

#26

E-
EXCUSE
ME!!

IS
ROTTI
STILL
PLAYING?!

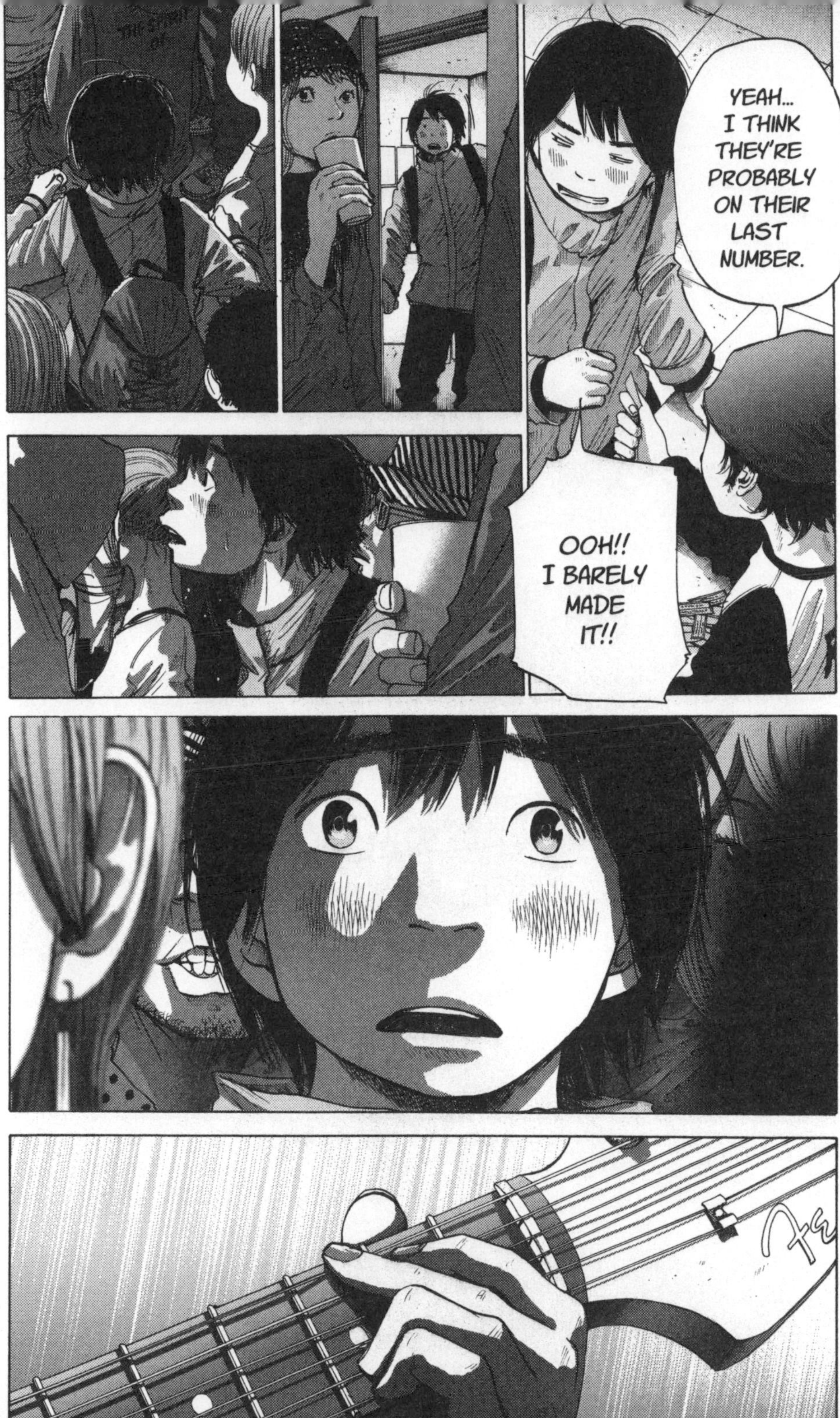
YEAH... I THINK THEY'RE PROBABLY ON THEIR LAST NUMBER.
OOH!! I BARELY MADE IT!!

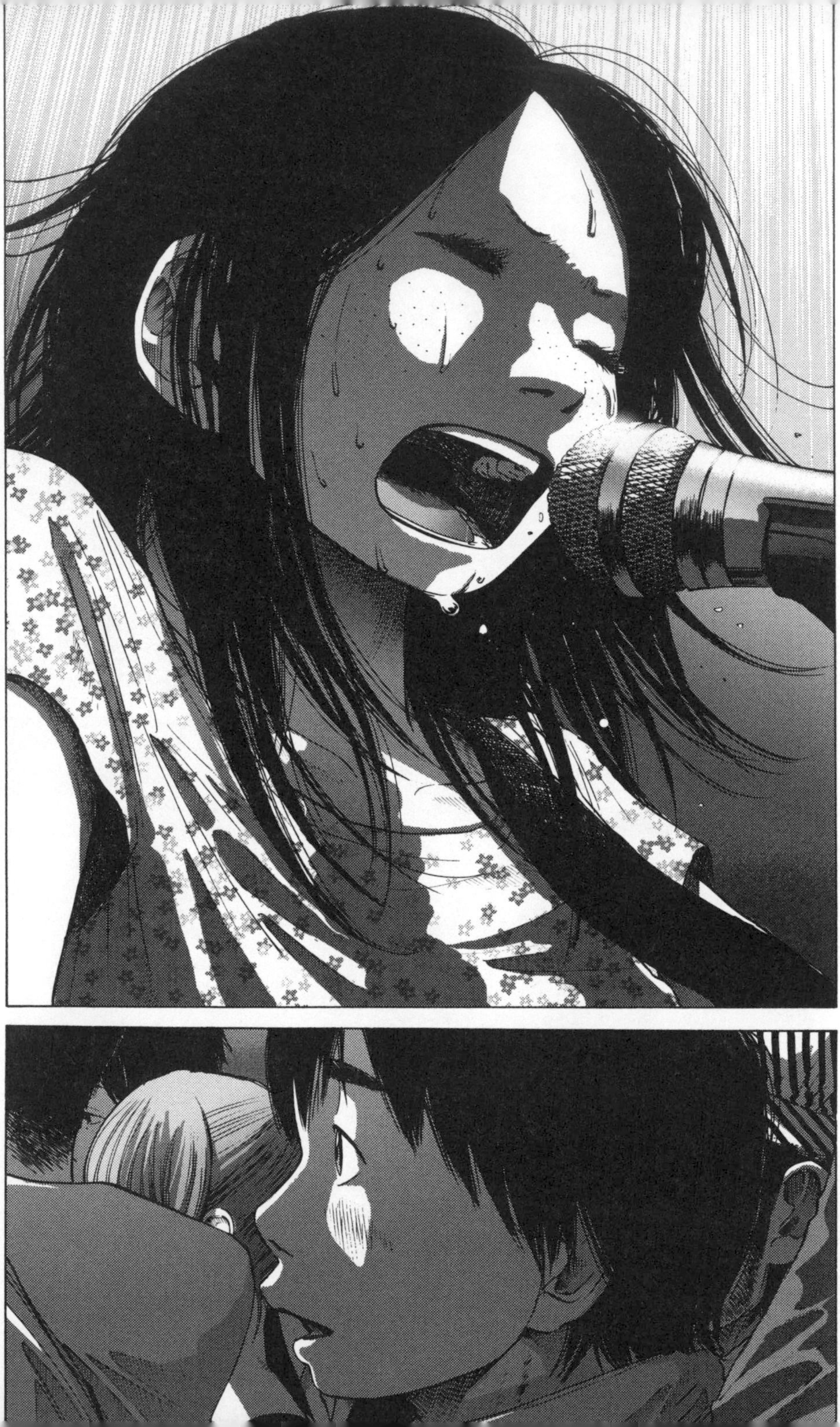

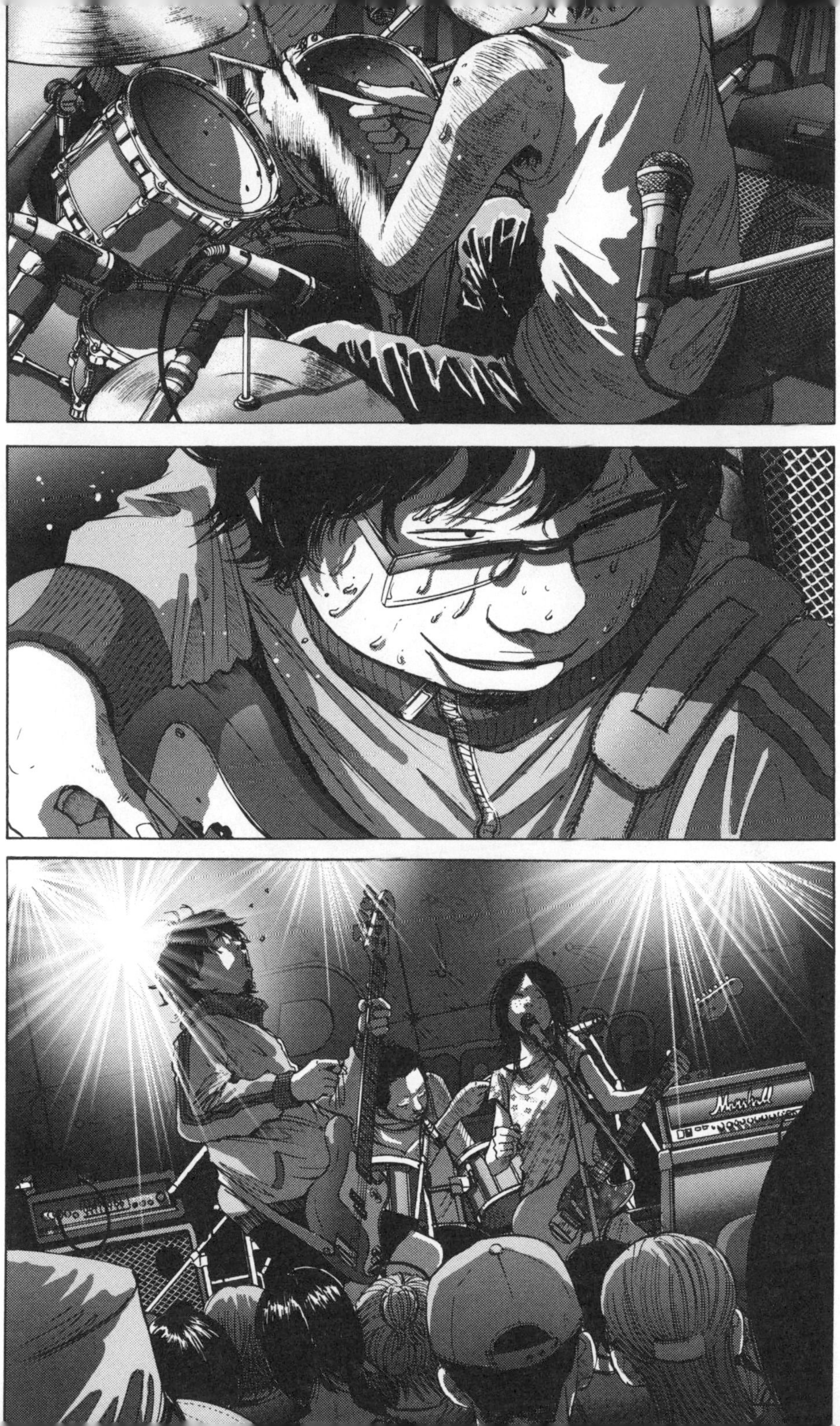
Marshall

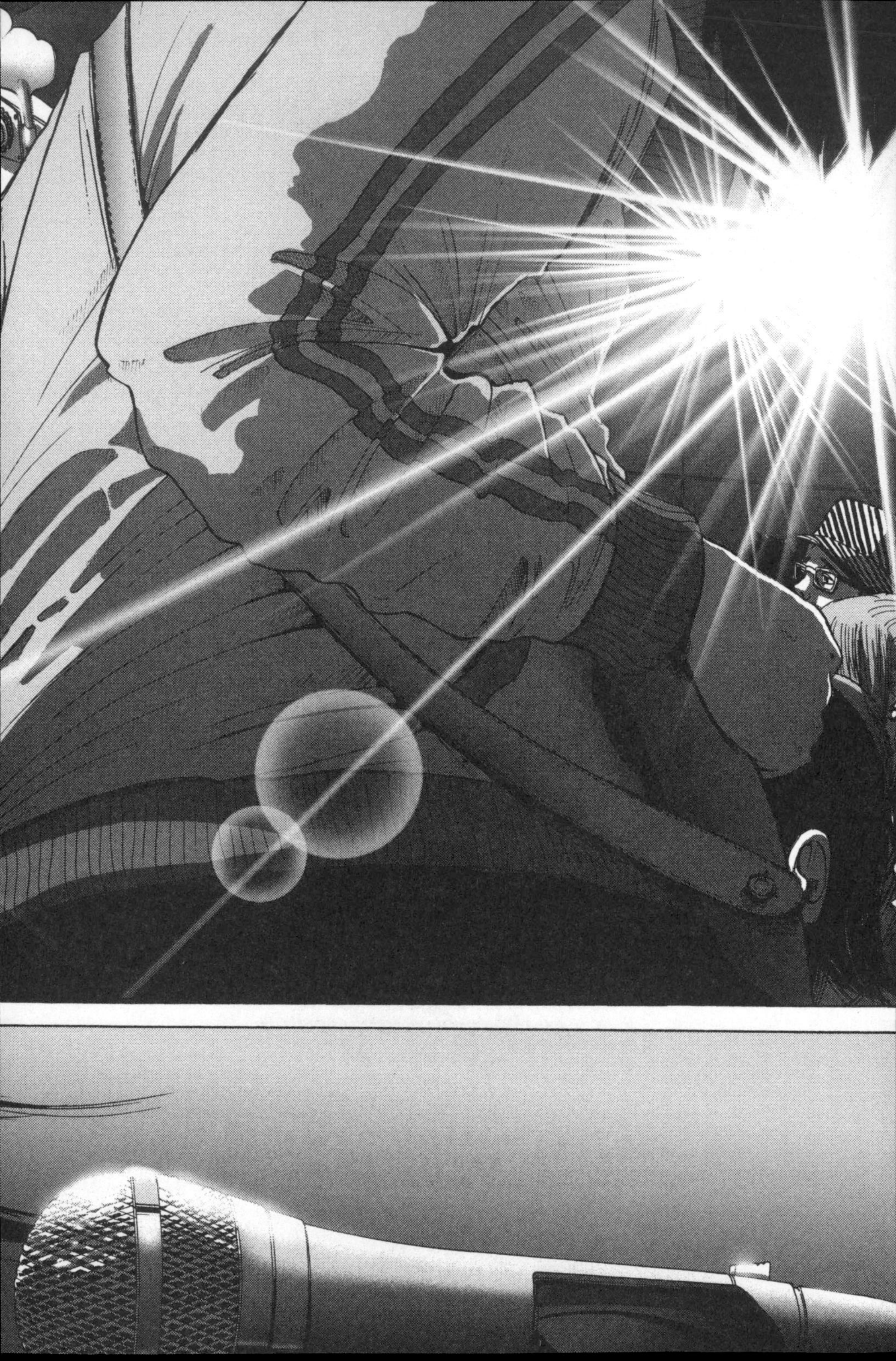

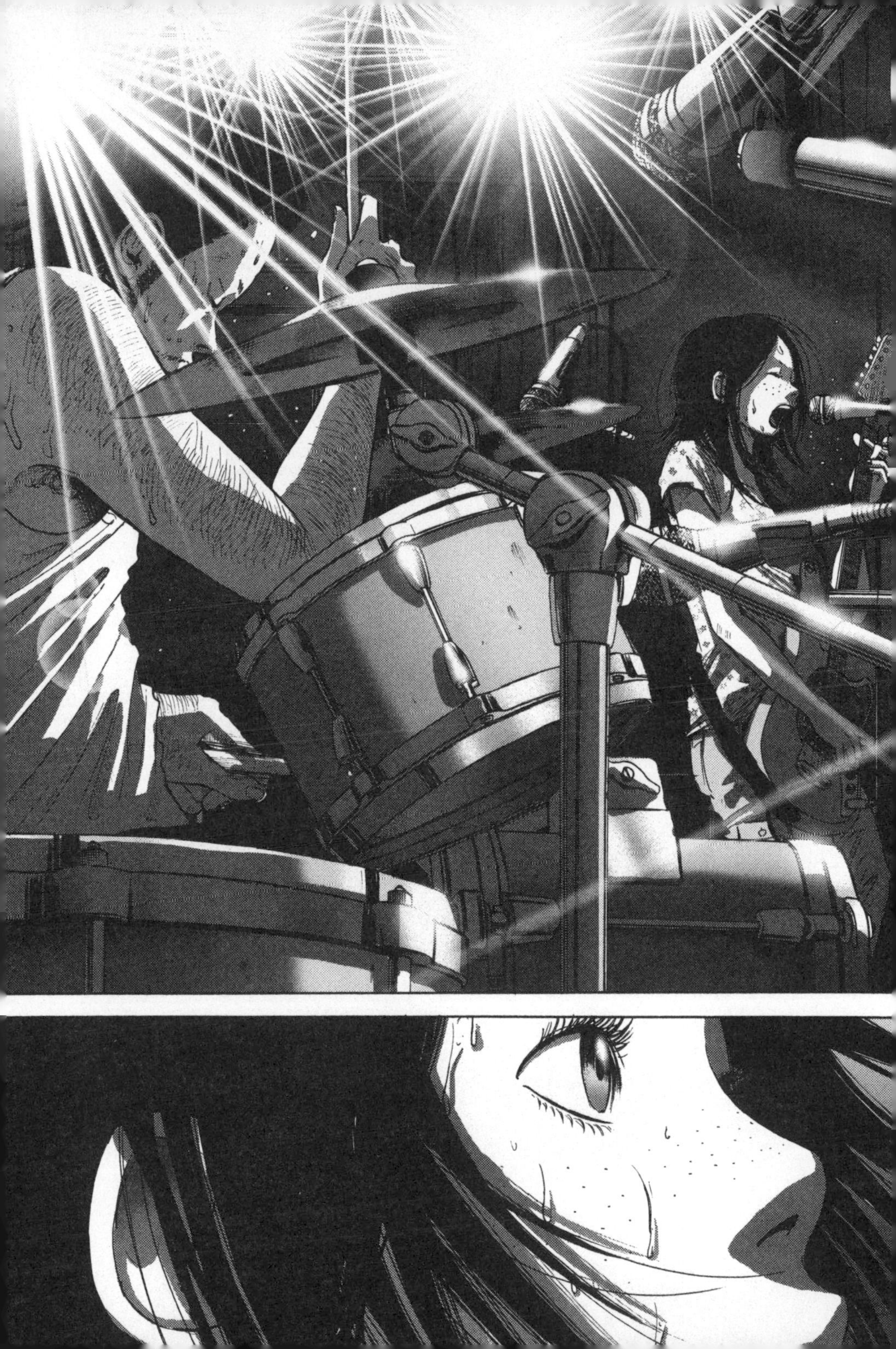

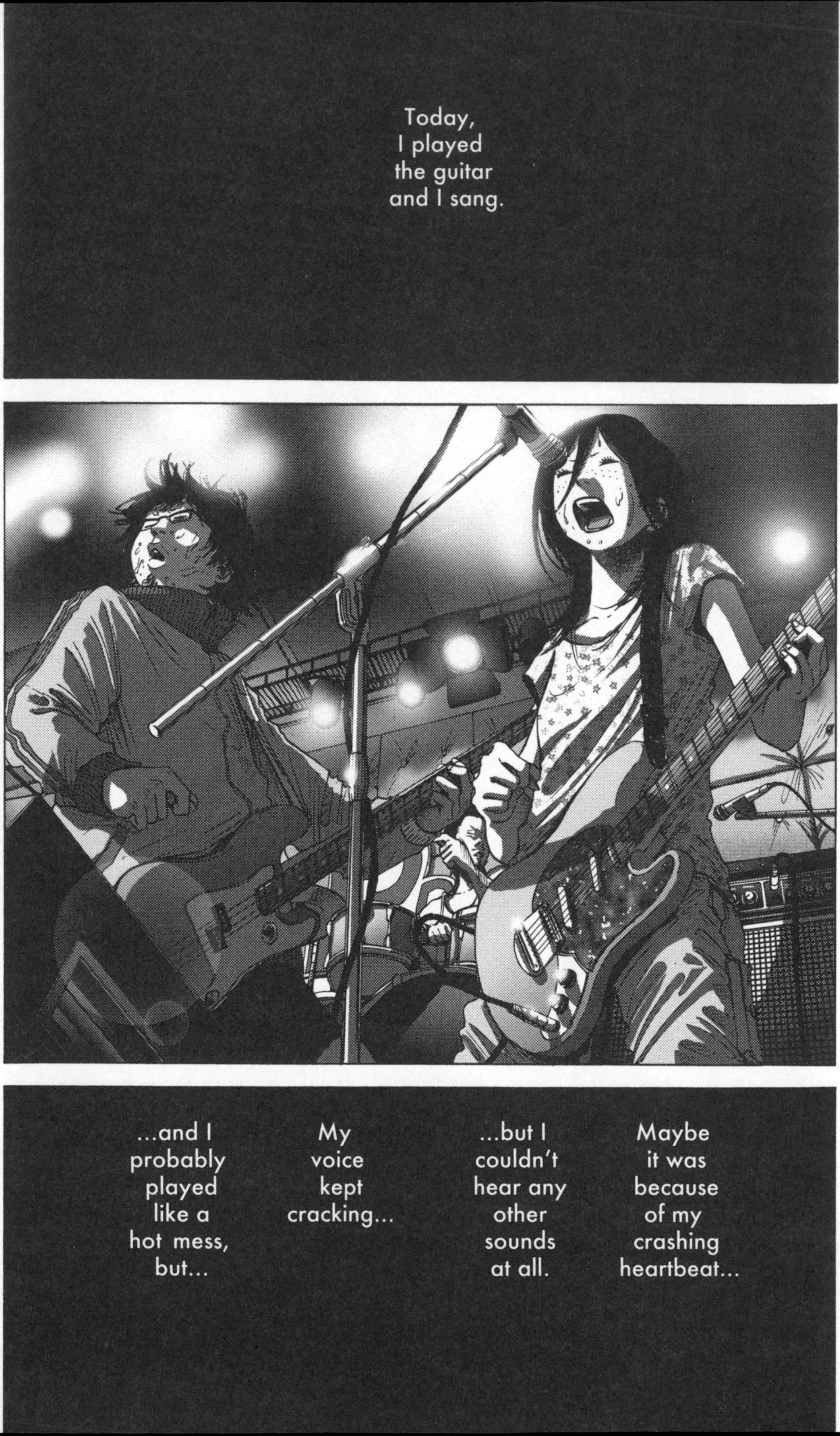
Today, I played the guitar and I sang.
Maybe it was because of my crashing heartbeat...
...but I couldn't hear any other sounds at all.
My voice kept cracking...
...and I probably played like a hot mess, but...

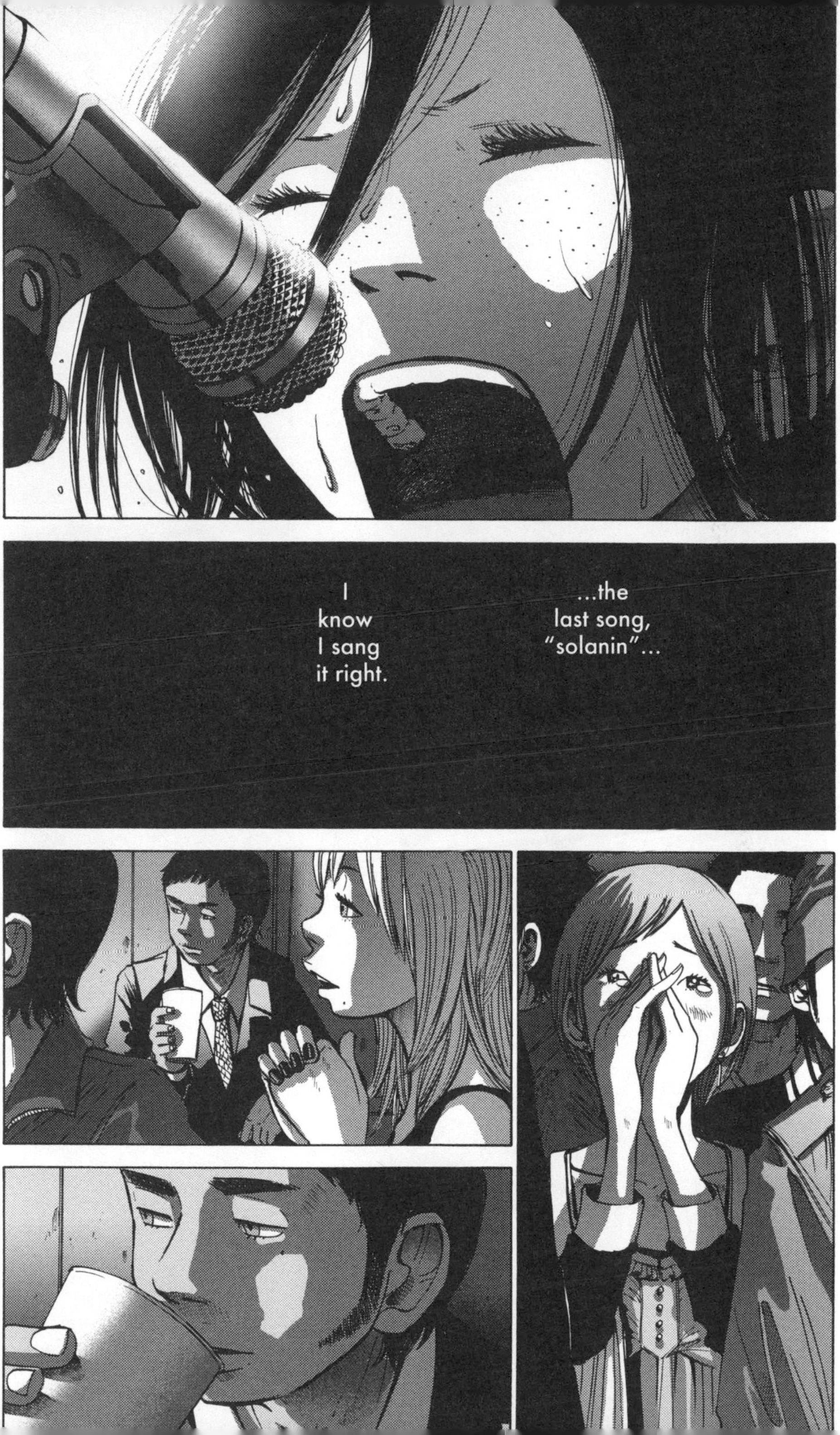
...the last song, "solanin"...
I know I sang it right.

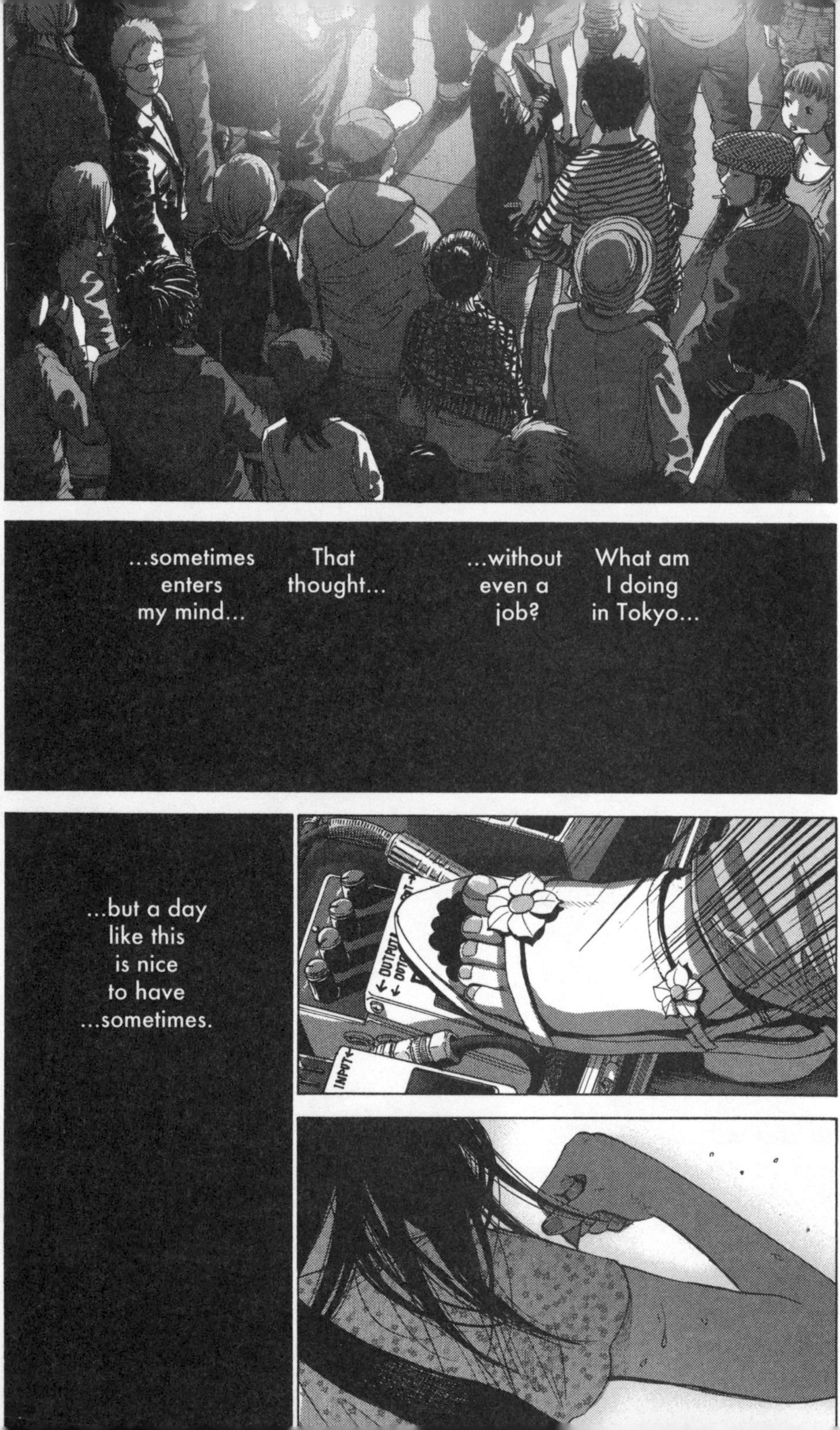
What am I doing in Tokyo...
...without even a job?
That thought...
...sometimes enters my mind...
...but a day like this is nice to have ...sometimes.

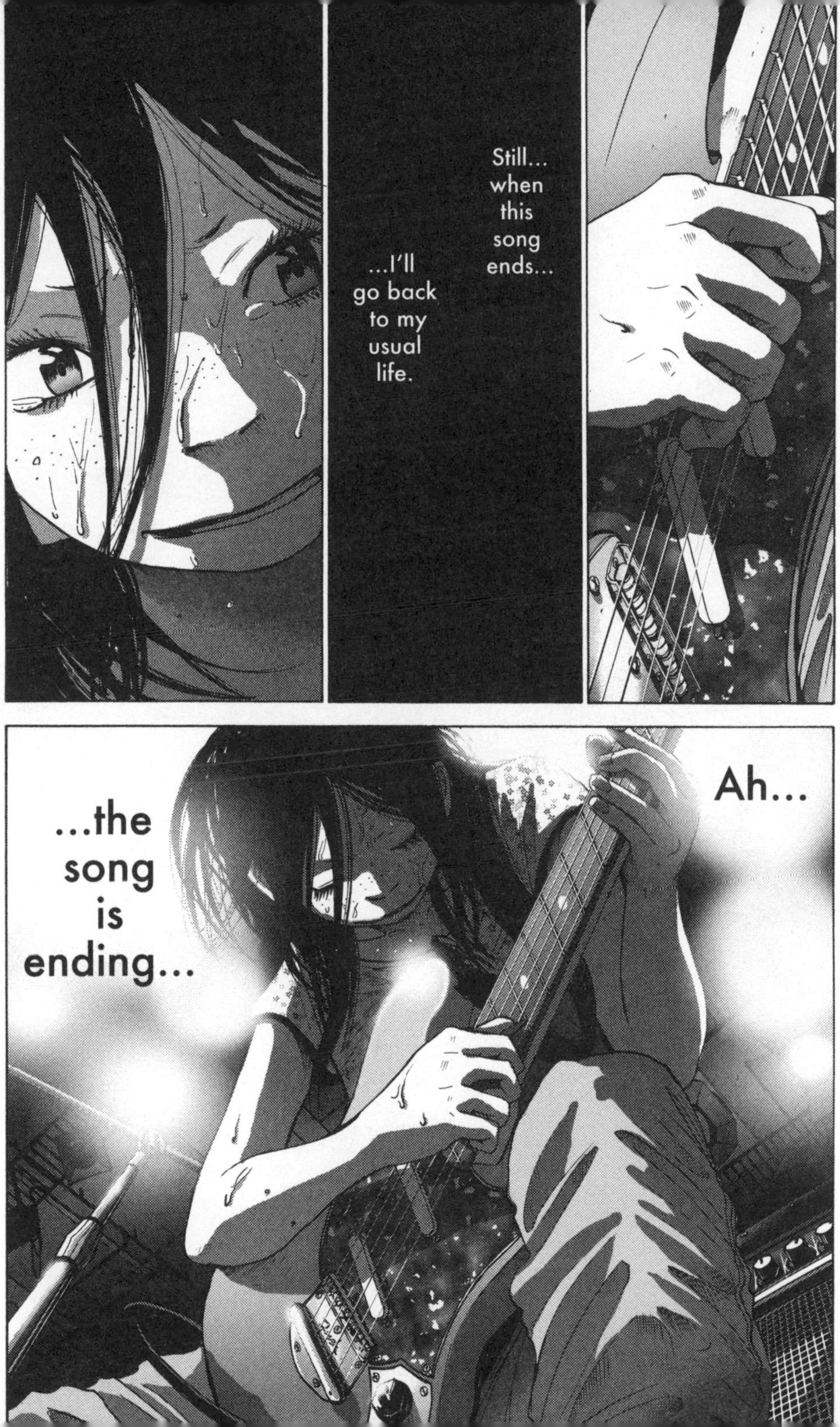
Still... when this song ends...
...I'll go back to my usual life.
Ah...
...the song is ending...

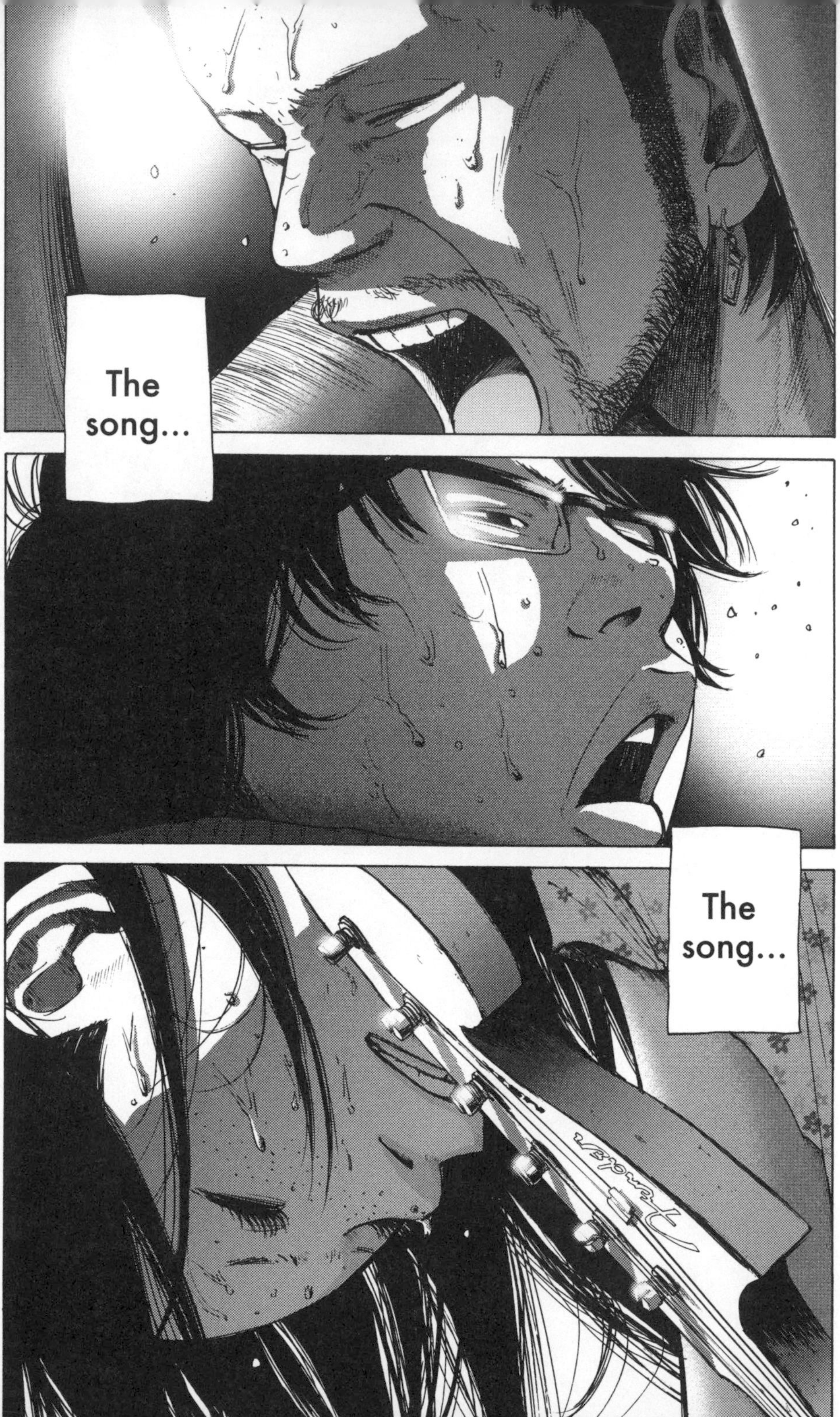
The song...
The song...

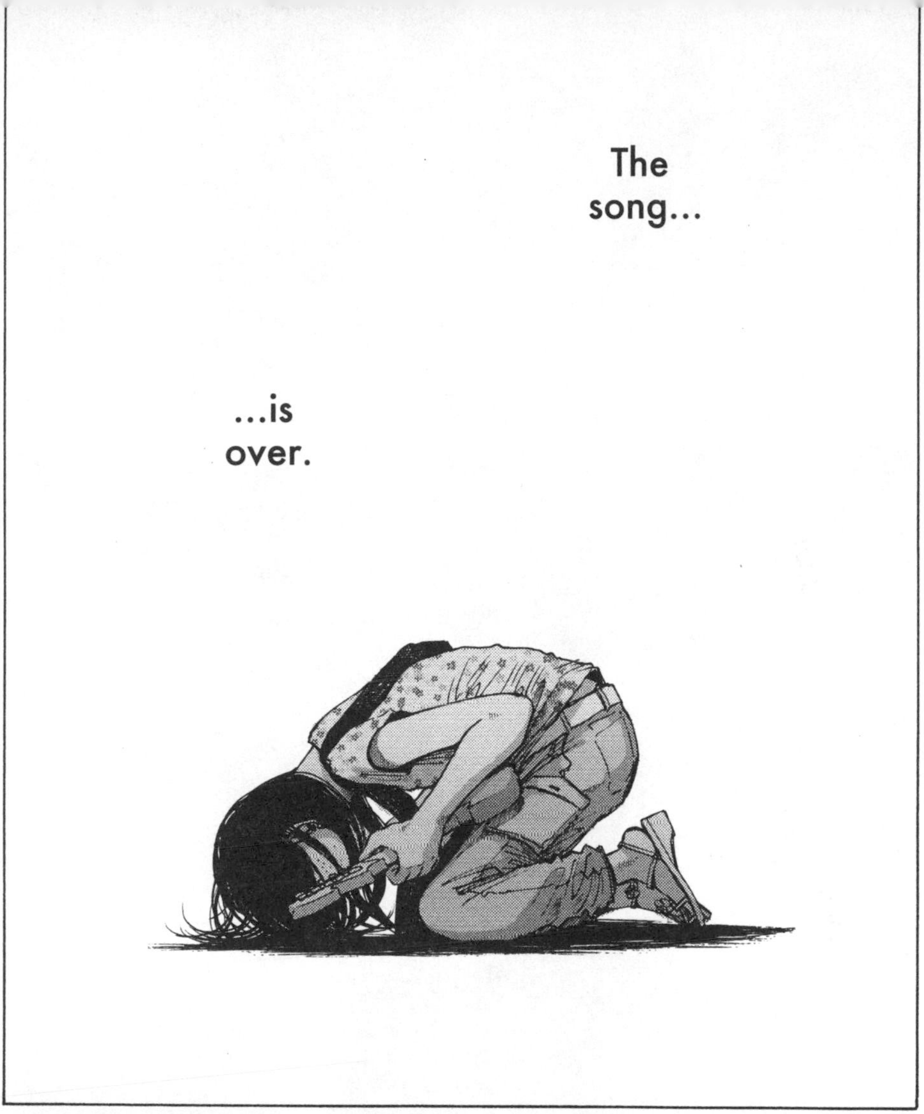
The song...
...is over.
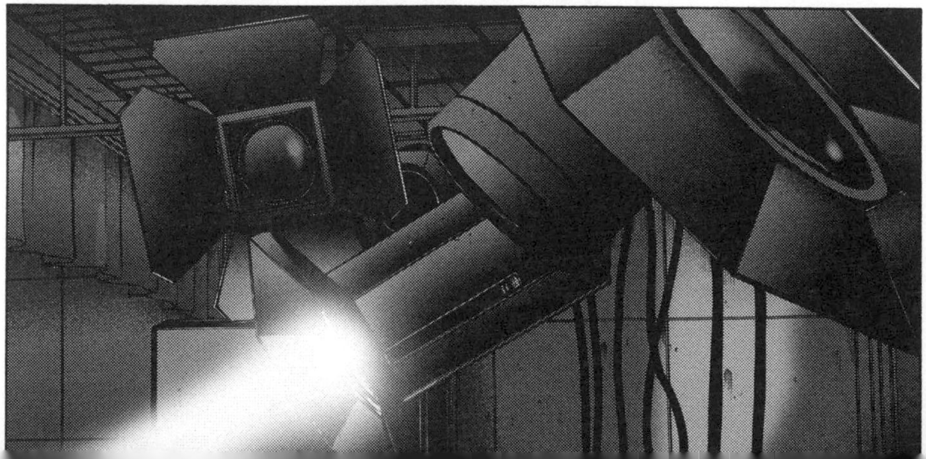

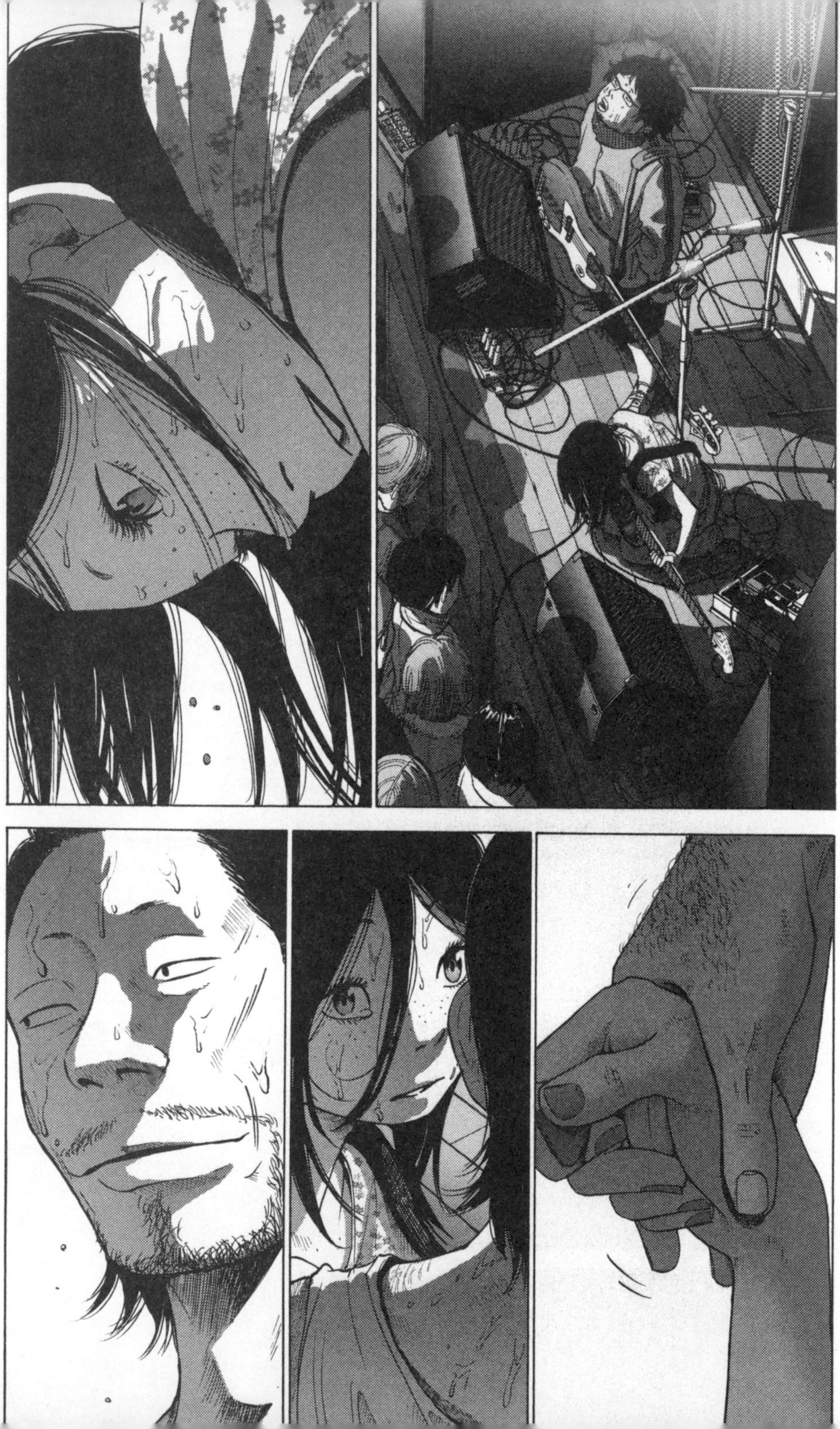

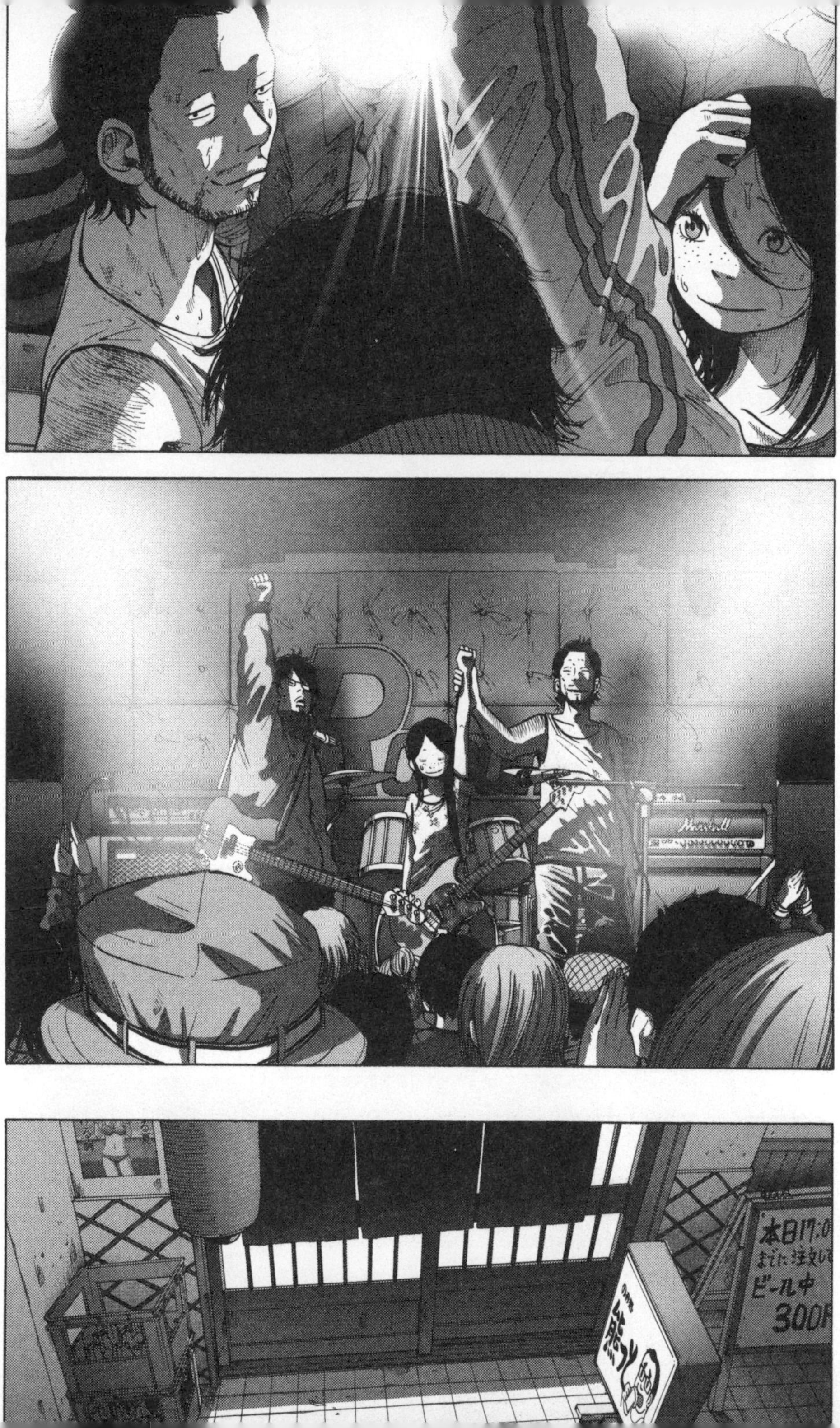
ビール中

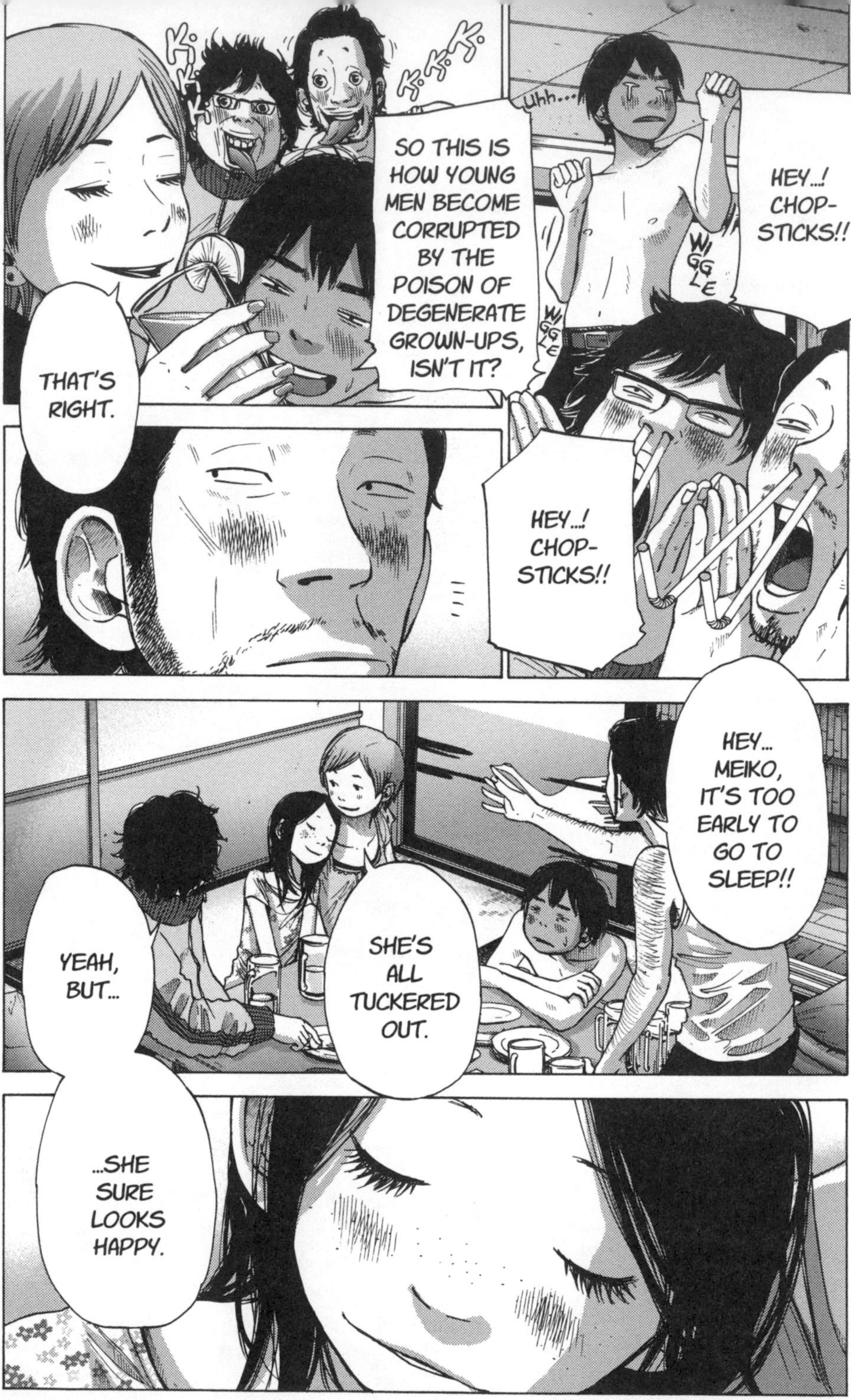
Uhh...
HEY...! CHOP-STICKS!!
WIGGLE
WIGGLE
SO THIS IS HOW YOUNG MEN BECOME CORRUPTED BY THE POISON OF DEGENERATE GROWN-UPS, ISN'T IT?
THAT'S RIGHT.
HEY...! CHOP-STICKS!!
HEY... MEIKO, IT'S TOO EARLY TO GO TO SLEEP!!
SHE'S ALL TUCKERED OUT.
YEAH, BUT...
...SHE SURE LOOKS HAPPY.

熊谷證券

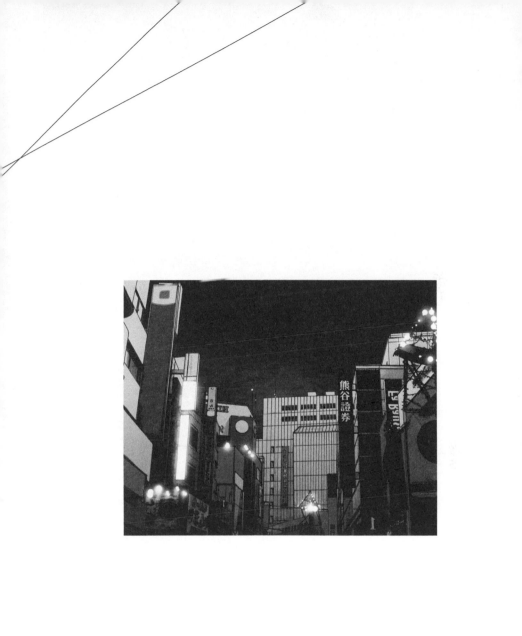

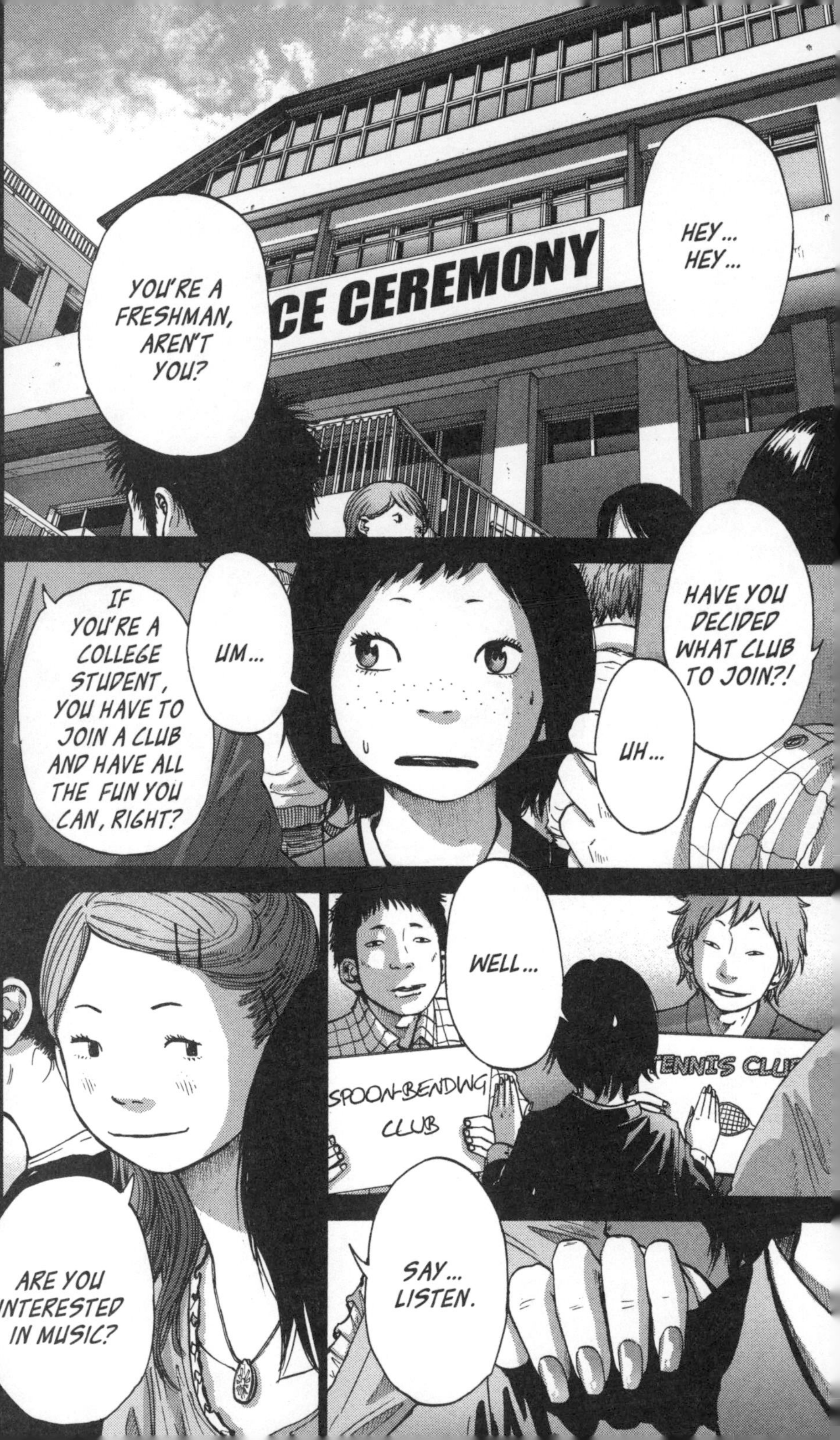
CE CEREMONY
HEY... HEY...
YOU'RE A FRESHMAN, AREN'T YOU?
HAVE YOU DECIDED WHAT CLUB TO JOIN?!
UH...
UM...
IF YOU'RE A COLLEGE STUDENT, YOU HAVE TO JOIN A CLUB AND HAVE ALL THE FUN YOU CAN, RIGHT?
WELL...
TENNIS CLUB
SPOON-BENDWG CLUB
SAY... LISTEN.
ARE YOU INTERESTED IN MUSIC?

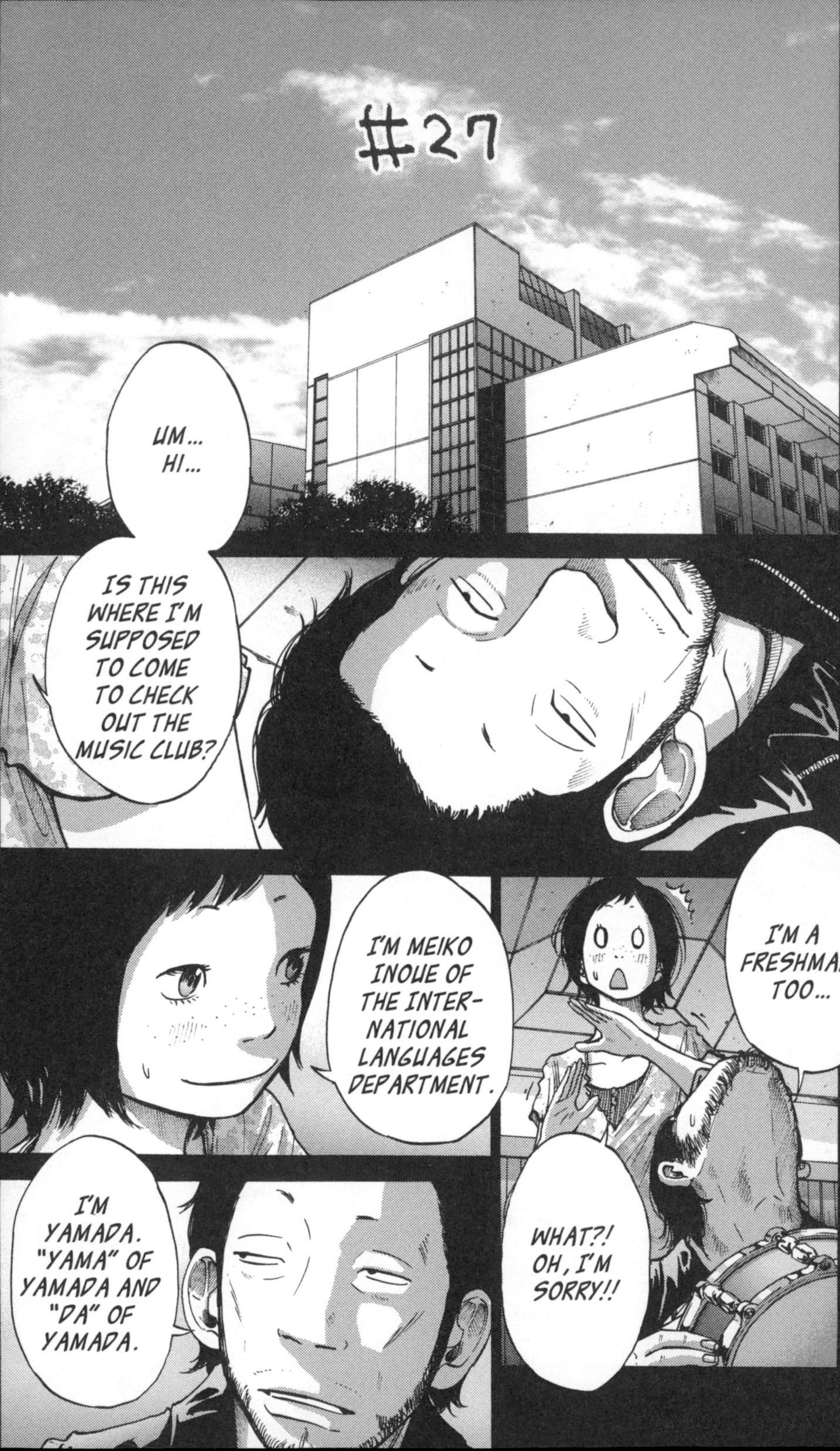
#27
UM... HI...
IS THIS WHERE I'M SUPPOSED TO COME TO CHECK OUT THE MUSIC CLUB?
I'M A FRESHMAN TOO...
WHAT?! OH, I'M SORRY!!
I'M MEIKO INOUE OF THE INTER-NATIONAL LANGUAGES DEPARTMENT.
I'M YAMADA. "YAMA" OF YAMADA AND "DA" OF YAMADA.

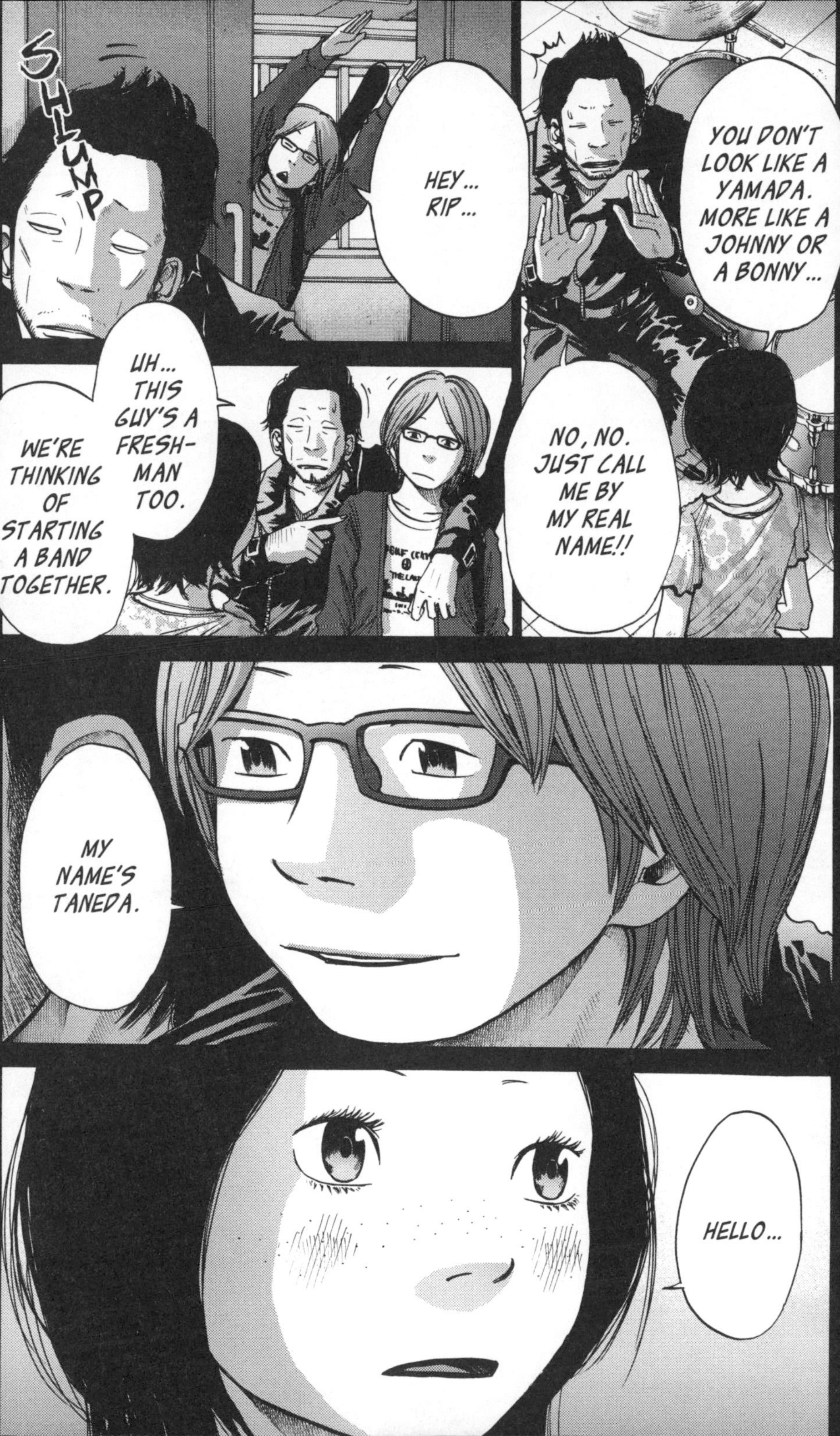
YOU DON'T LOOK LIKE A YAMADA. MORE LIKE A JOHNNY OR A BONNY...
NO, NO. JUST CALL ME BY MY REAL NAME!!
HEY... RIP...
SHLUMP
UH... THIS GUY'S A FRESHMAN TOO.
WE'RE THINKING OF STARTING A BAND TOGETHER.
MY NAME'S TANEDA.
HELLO...

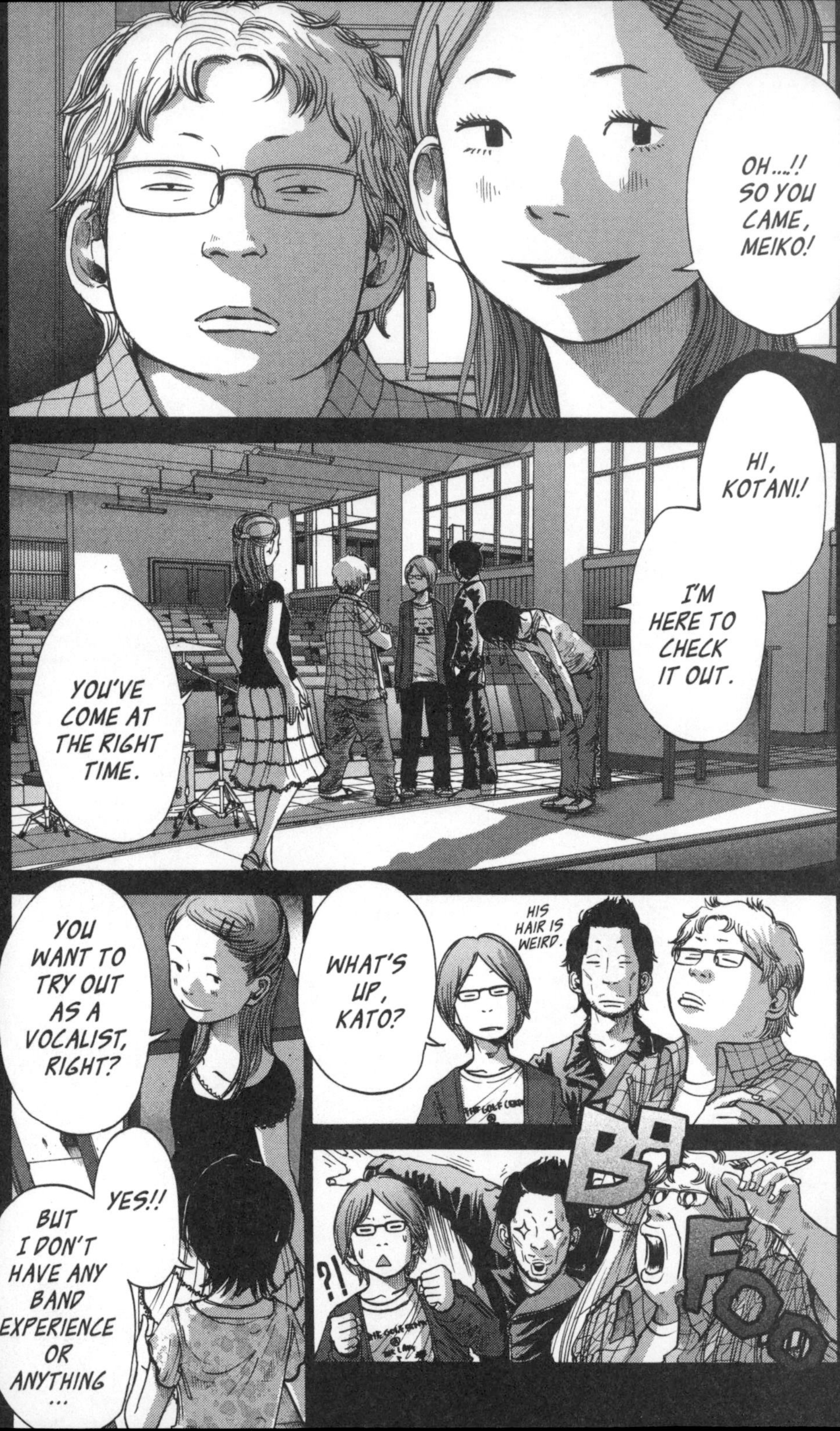
OH...!! SO YOU CAME, MEIKO!
HI, KOTANI!
I'M HERE TO CHECK IT OUT.
YOU'VE COME AT THE RIGHT TIME.
HIS HAIR IS WEIRD.
WHAT'S UP, KATO?
BAFOOO
?!
YOU WANT TO TRY OUT AS A VOCALIST, RIGHT?
YES!!
BUT I DON'T HAVE ANY BAND EXPERIENCE OR ANYTHING...

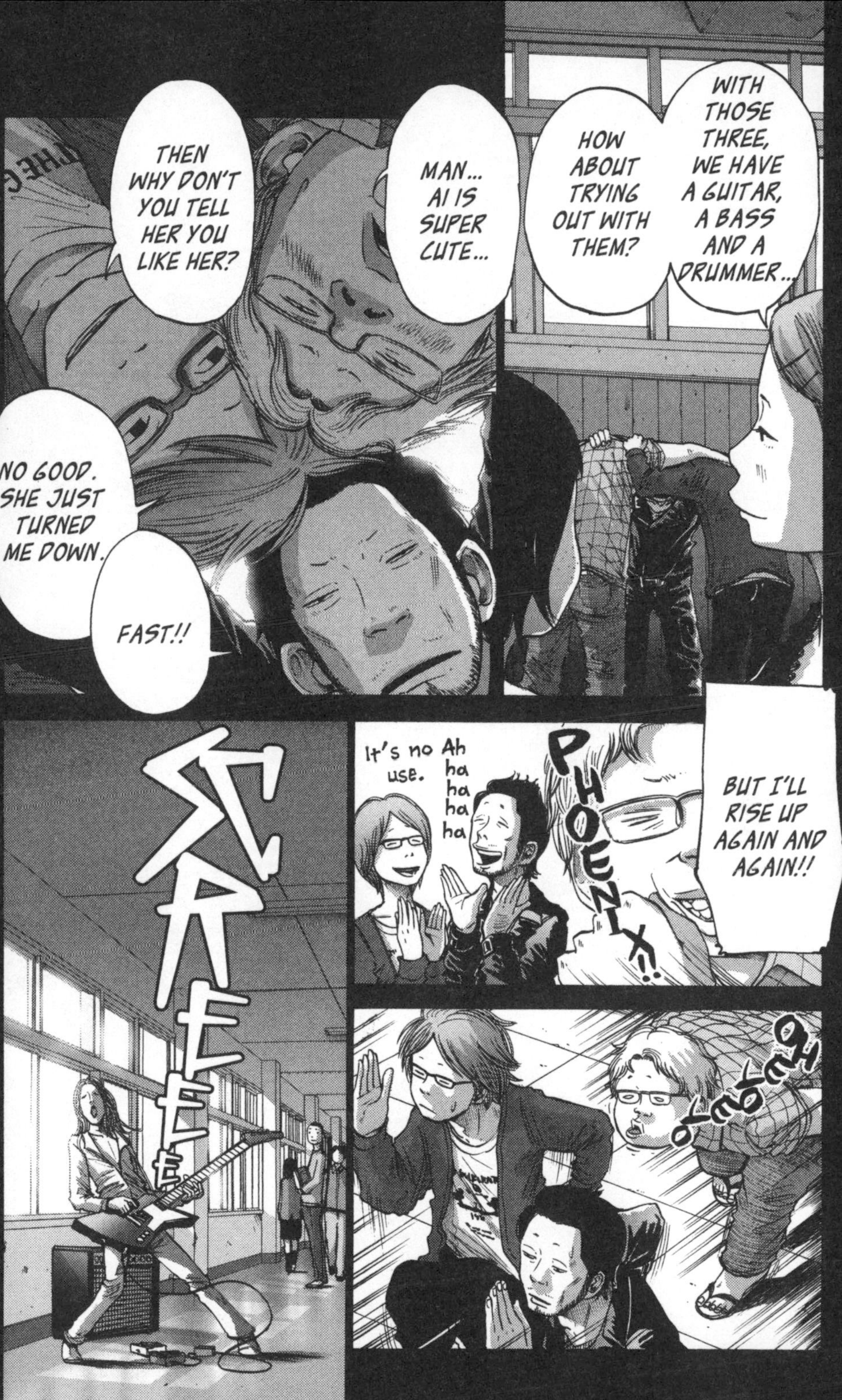

WITH THOSE THREE, WE HAVE A GUITAR, A BASS AND A DRUMMER...
HOW ABOUT TRYING OUT WITH THEM?
MAN... AI IS SUPER CUTE...
THEN WHY DON'T YOU TELL HER YOU LIKE HER?
NO GOOD. SHE JUST TURNED ME DOWN.
FAST!!
BUT I'LL RISE UP AGAIN AND AGAIN!!
PHOENIX!!
Ah ha ha ha ha
It's no use.
SCREEEE

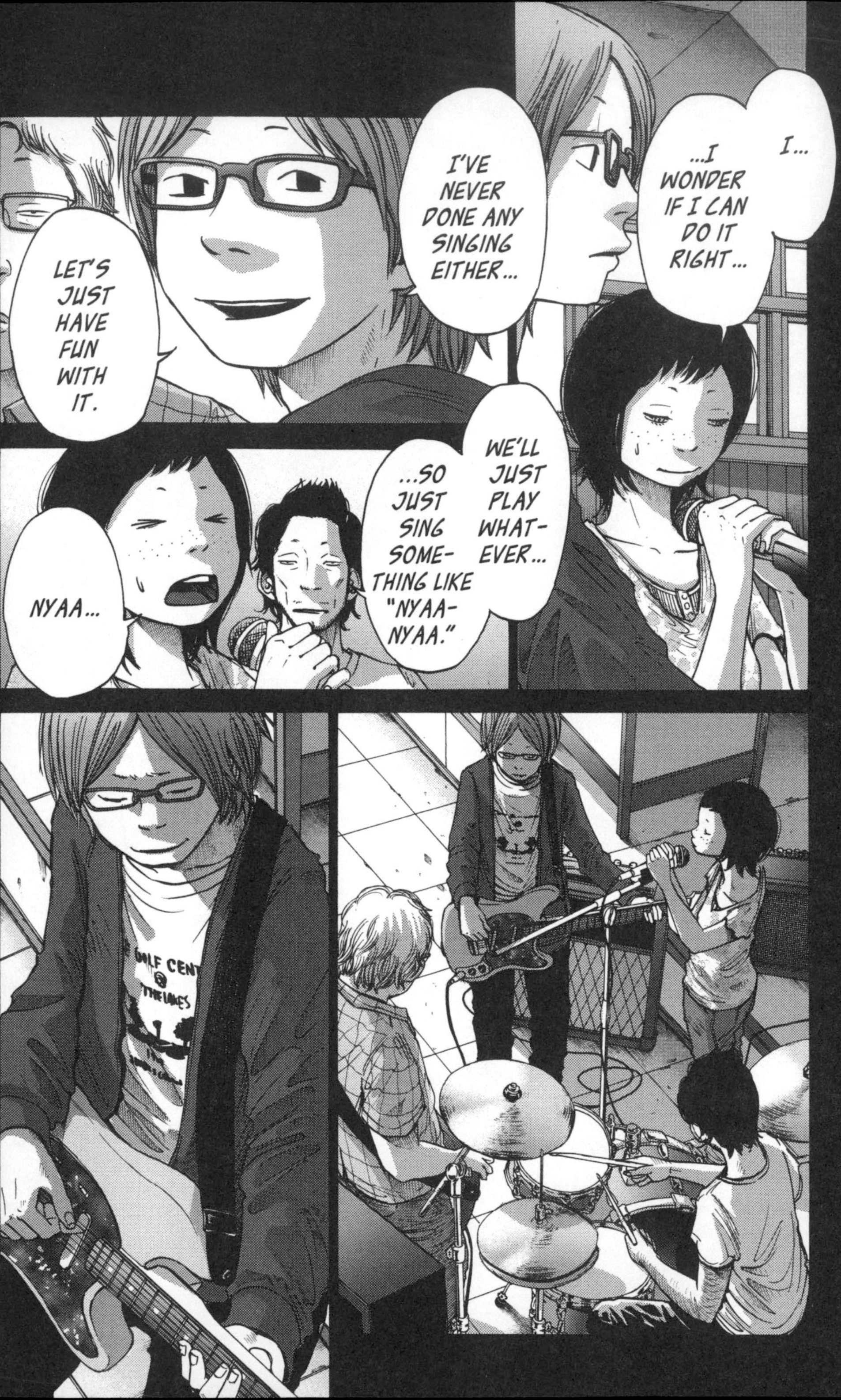
I...
...I WONDER IF I CAN DO IT RIGHT...
I'VE NEVER DONE ANY SINGING EITHER...
LET'S JUST HAVE FUN WITH IT.
WE'LL JUST PLAY WHATEVER...
...SO JUST SING SOMETHING LIKE "NYAA-NYAA."
NYAA...

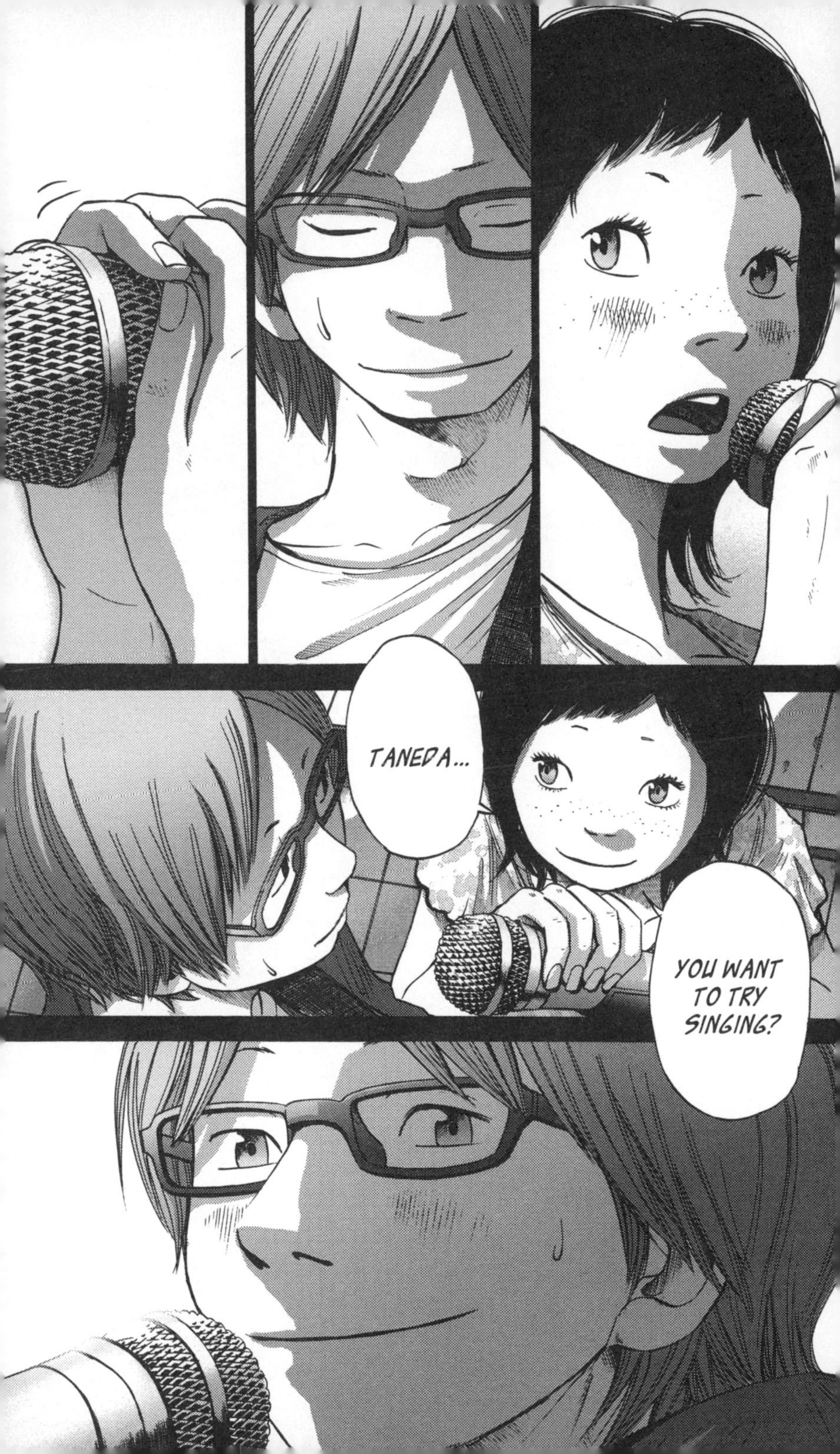
TANEDA...
YOU WANT TO TRY SINGING?

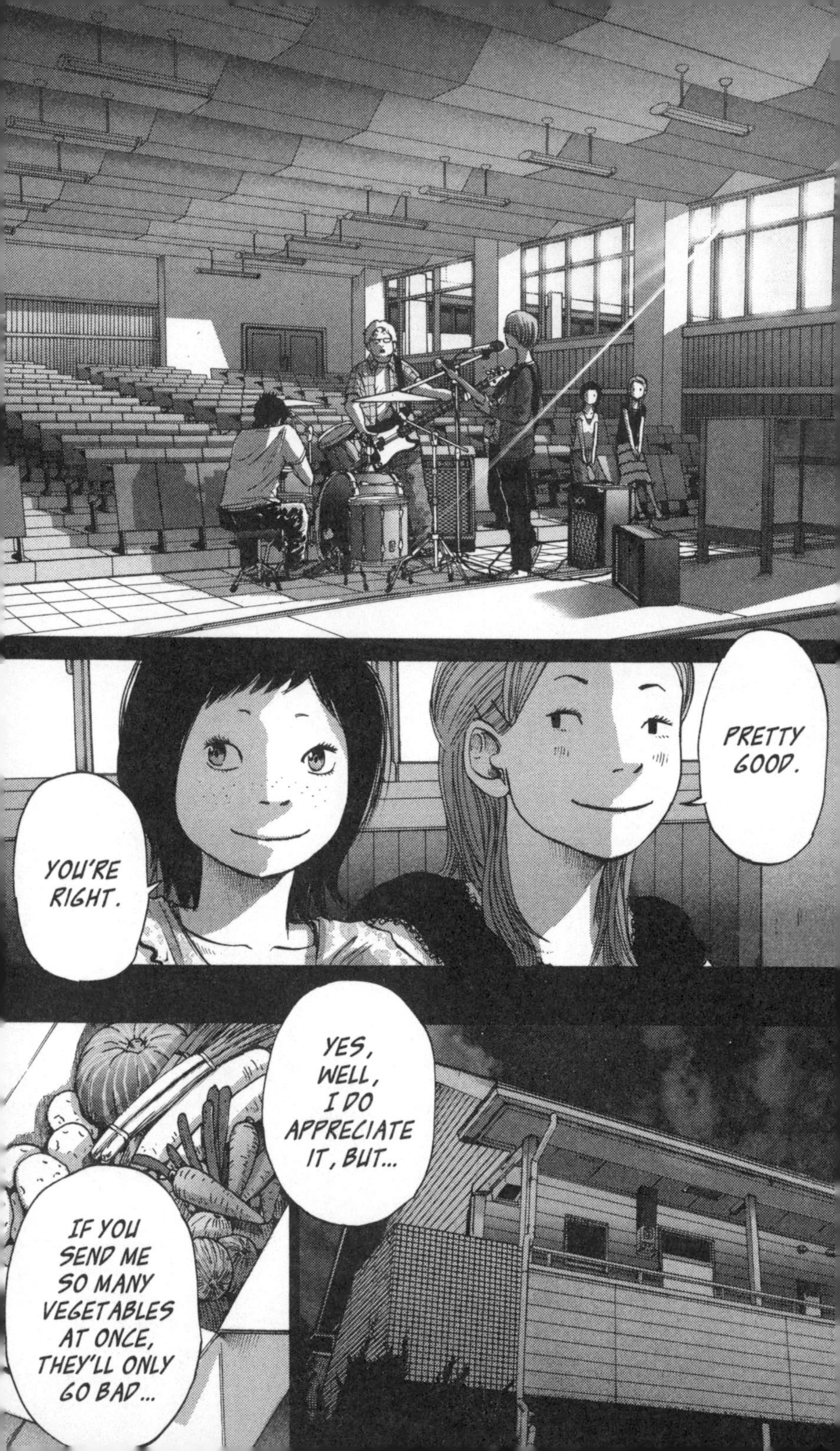
PRETTY GOOD.
YOU'RE RIGHT.
YES, WELL, I DO APPRECIATE IT, BUT...
IF YOU SEND ME SO MANY VEGETABLES AT ONCE, THEY'LL ONLY GO BAD...

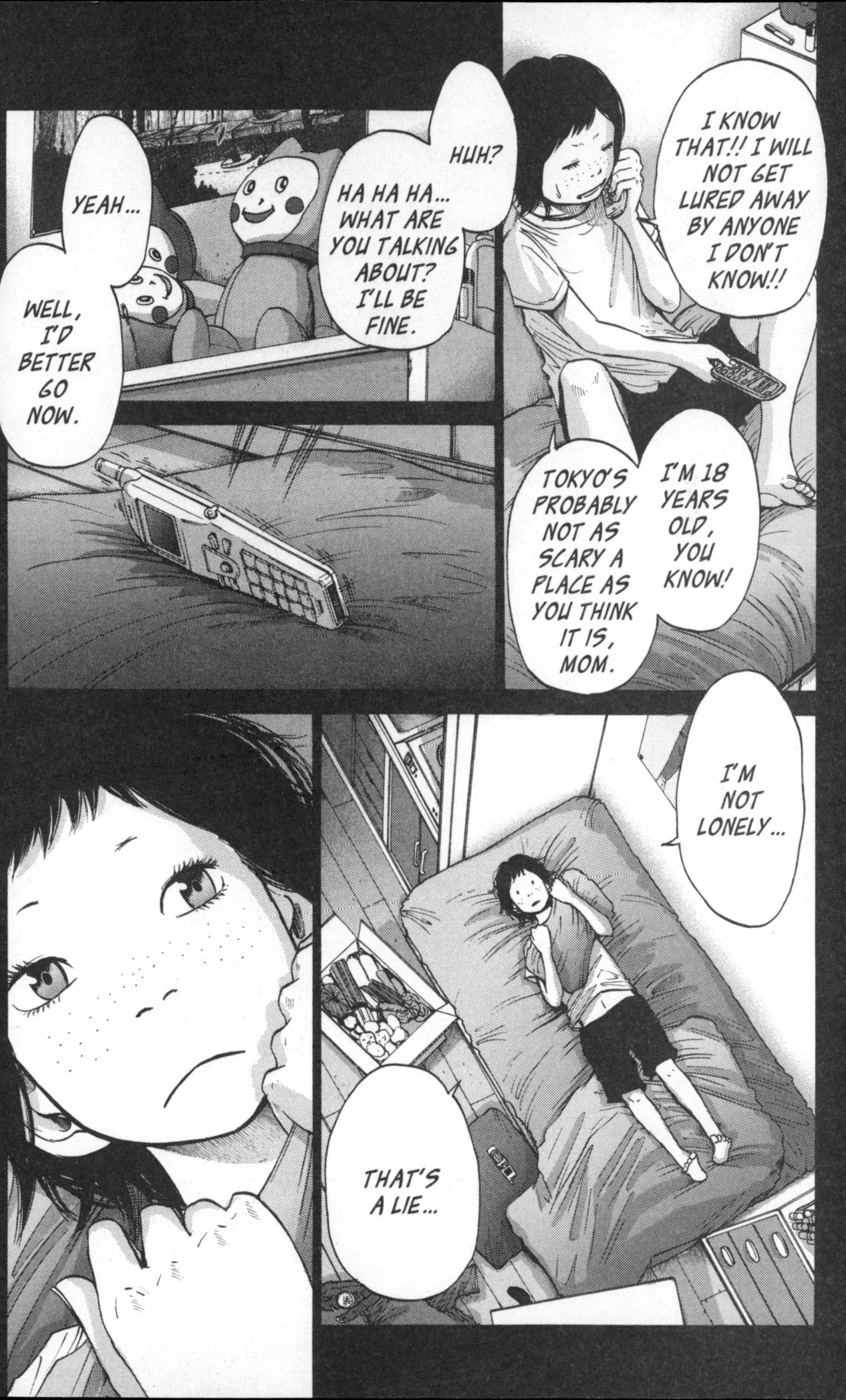
I KNOW THAT!! I WILL NOT GET LURED AWAY BY ANYONE I DON'T KNOW!!
I'M 18 YEARS OLD, YOU KNOW!
TOKYO'S PROBABLY NOT AS SCARY A PLACE AS YOU THINK IT IS, MOM.
HUH?
HA HA HA... WHAT ARE YOU TALKING ABOUT? I'LL BE FINE.
YEAH...
WELL, I'D BETTER GO NOW.
I'M NOT LONELY...
THAT'S A LIE...

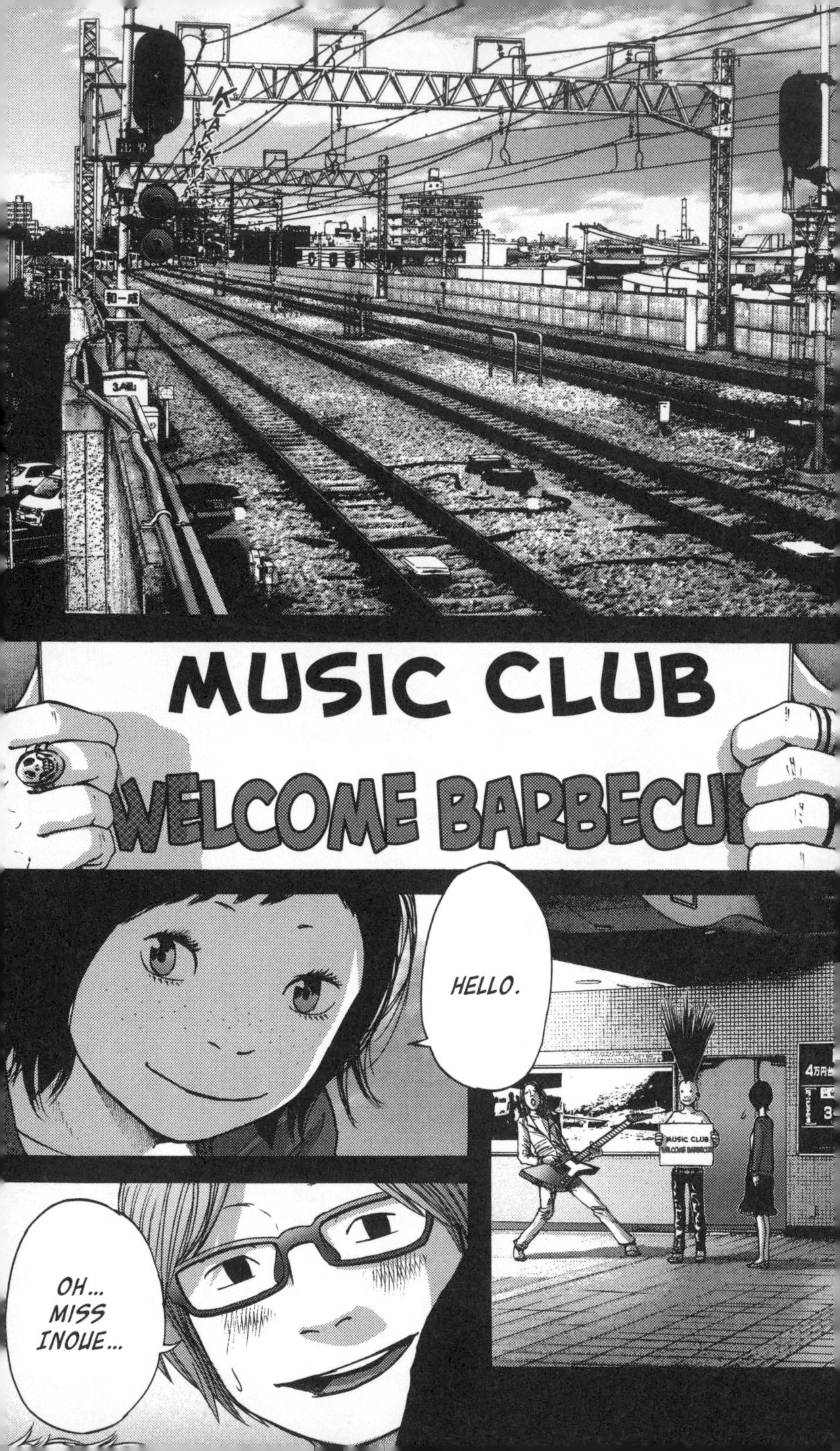
KLAK KLAK
MUSIC CLUB
WELCOME BARBECU
HELLO.
MUSIC CLUB
WELCOME BARBECUE
OH... MISS INOUE...

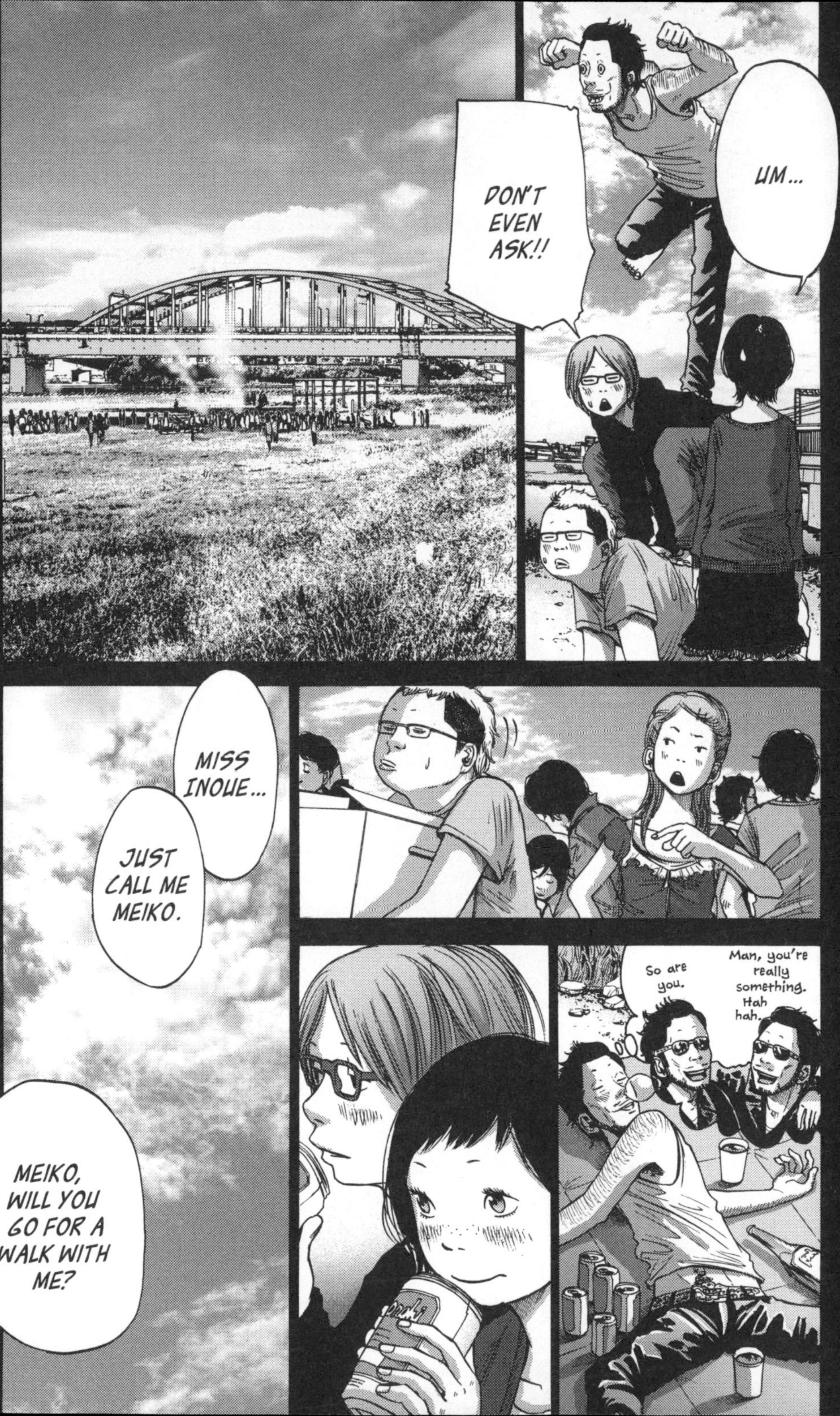
UM...
DON'T EVEN ASK!!
MISS INOUE...
JUST CALL ME MEIKO.
Man, you're really something. Hah hah.
So are you.
MEIKO, WILL YOU GO FOR A WALK WITH ME?

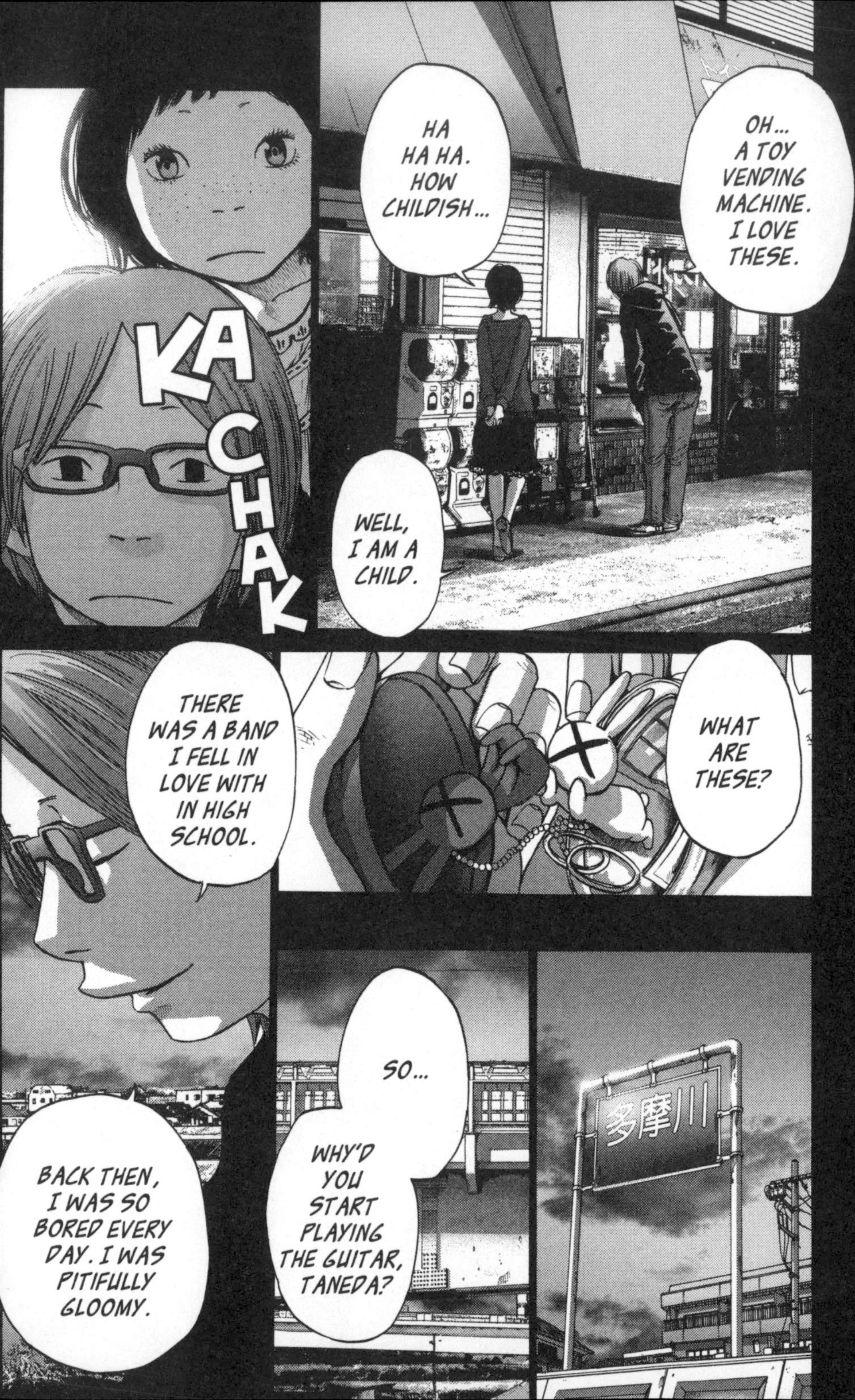
OH... A TOY VENDING MACHINE. I LOVE THESE.
HA HA HA. HOW CHILDISH...
WELL, I AM A CHILD.
KACHAK
WHAT ARE THESE?
多摩川
SO...
WHY'D YOU START PLAYING THE GUITAR, TANEDA?
THERE WAS A BAND I FELL IN LOVE WITH IN HIGH SCHOOL.
BACK THEN, I WAS SO BORED EVERY DAY. I WAS PITIFULLY GLOOMY.

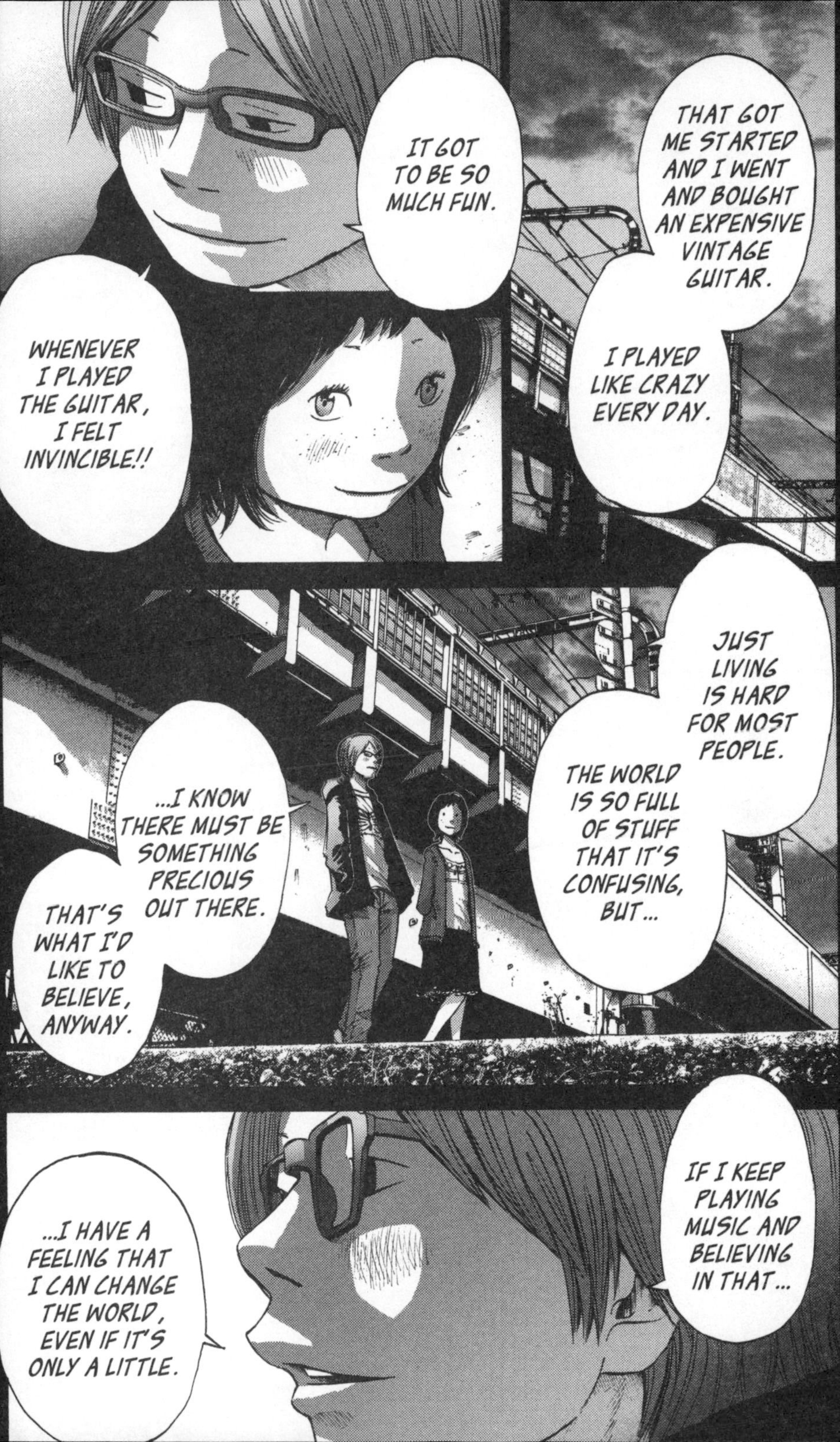
THAT GOT ME STARTED AND I WENT AND BOUGHT AN EXPENSIVE VINTAGE GUITAR.
I PLAYED LIKE CRAZY EVERY DAY.
IT GOT TO BE SO MUCH FUN.
WHENEVER I PLAYED THE GUITAR, I FELT INVINCIBLE!!
JUST LIVING IS HARD FOR MOST PEOPLE.
THE WORLD IS SO FULL OF STUFF THAT IT'S CONFUSING, BUT...
...I KNOW THERE MUST BE SOMETHING PRECIOUS OUT THERE.
THAT'S WHAT I'D LIKE TO BELIEVE, ANYWAY.
IF I KEEP PLAYING MUSIC AND BELIEVING IN THAT...
...I HAVE A FEELING THAT I CAN CHANGE THE WORLD, EVEN IF IT'S ONLY A LITTLE.

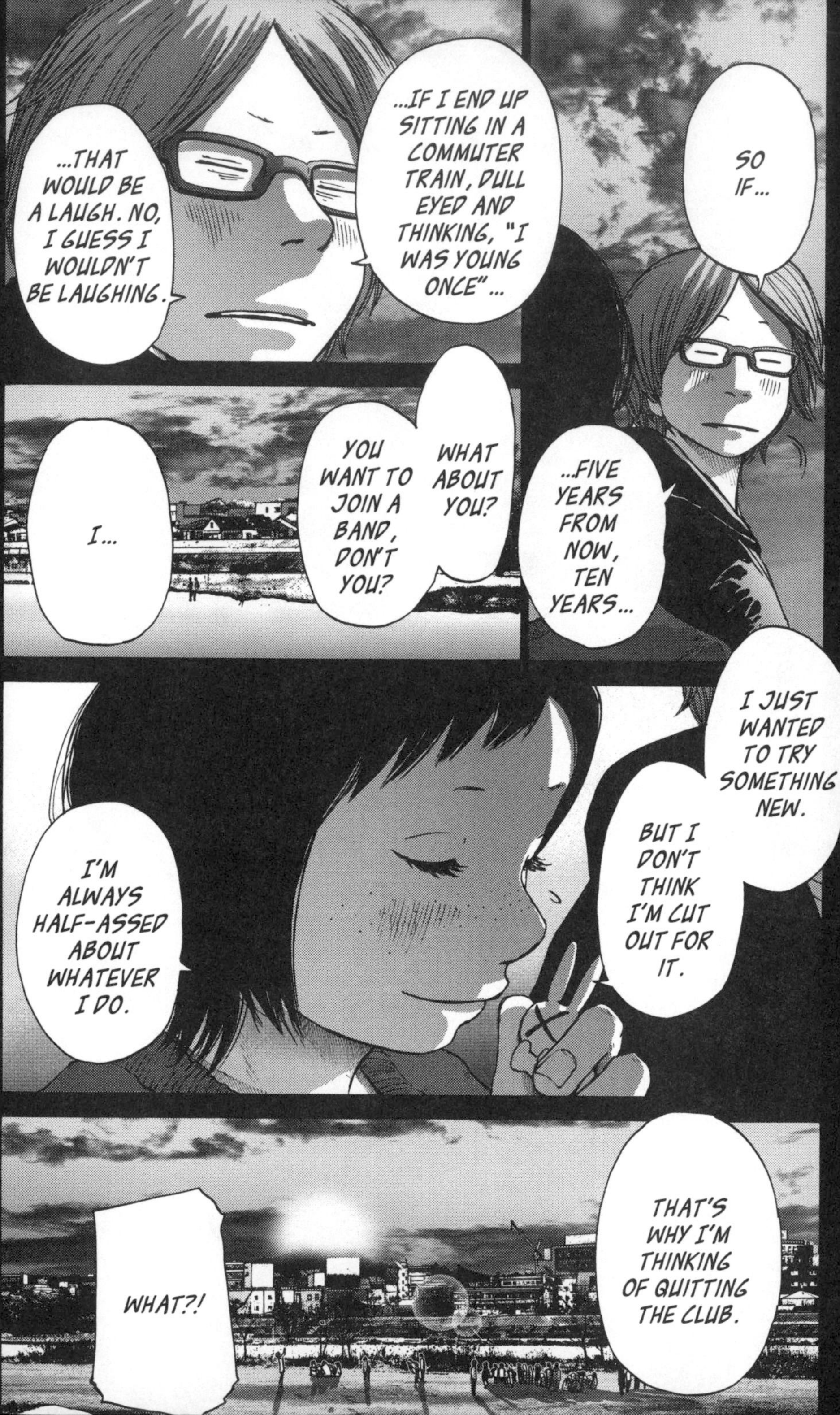
SO IF...
...FIVE YEARS FROM NOW, TEN YEARS...
...IF I END UP SITTING IN A COMMUTER TRAIN, DULL EYED AND THINKING, "I WAS YOUNG ONCE"...
...THAT WOULD BE A LAUGH. NO, I GUESS I WOULDN'T BE LAUGHING.
WHAT ABOUT YOU?
YOU WANT TO JOIN A BAND, DON'T YOU?
I...
I JUST WANTED TO TRY SOMETHING NEW.
BUT I DON'T THINK I'M CUT OUT FOR IT.
I'M ALWAYS HALF-ASSED ABOUT WHATEVER I DO.
THAT'S WHY I'M THINKING OF QUITTING THE CLUB.
WHAT?!

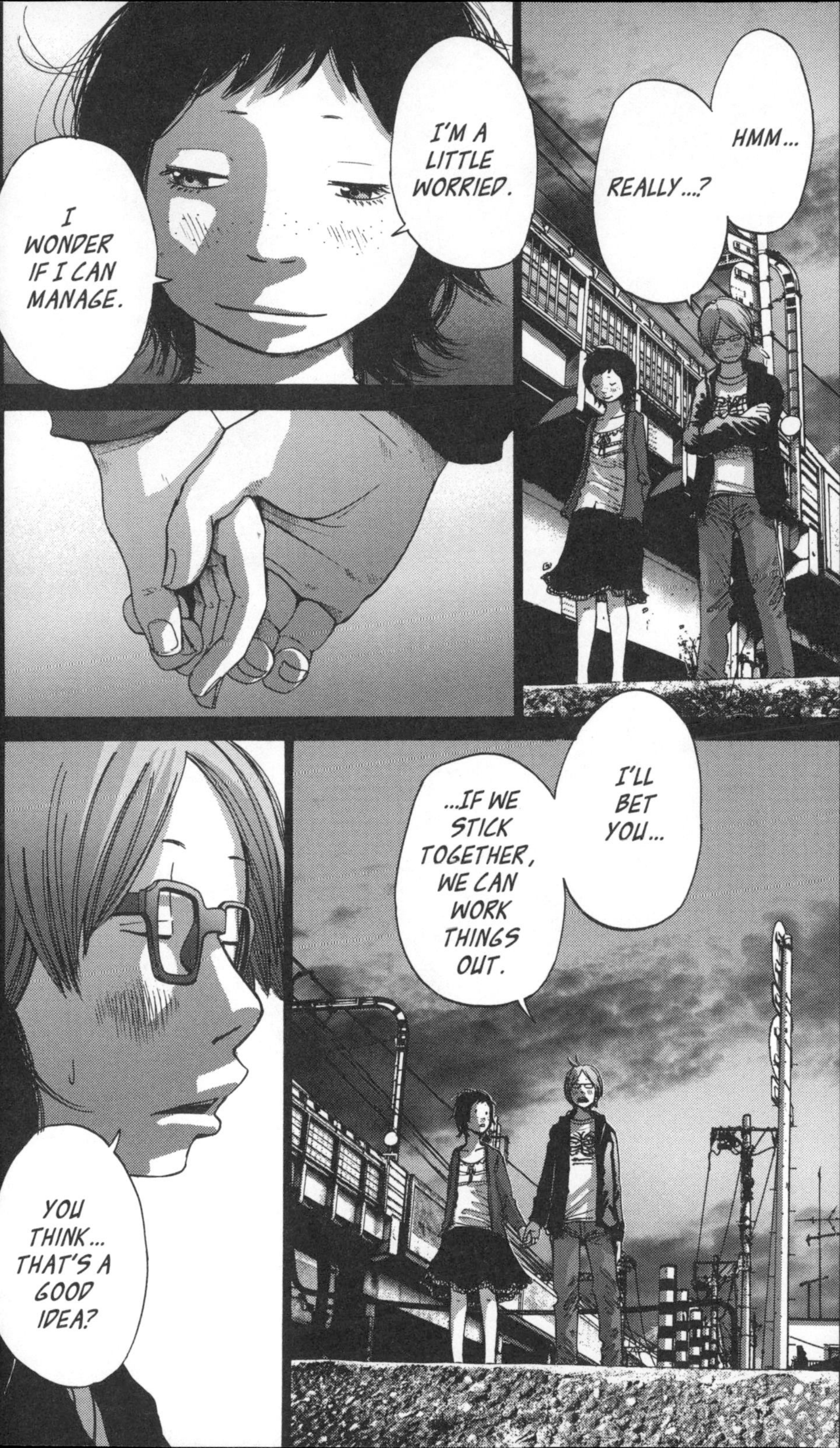
HMM... REALLY...?
I'M A LITTLE WORRIED.
I WONDER IF I CAN MANAGE.
I'LL BET YOU...
...IF WE STICK TOGETHER, WE CAN WORK THINGS OUT.
YOU THINK... THAT'S A GOOD IDEA?

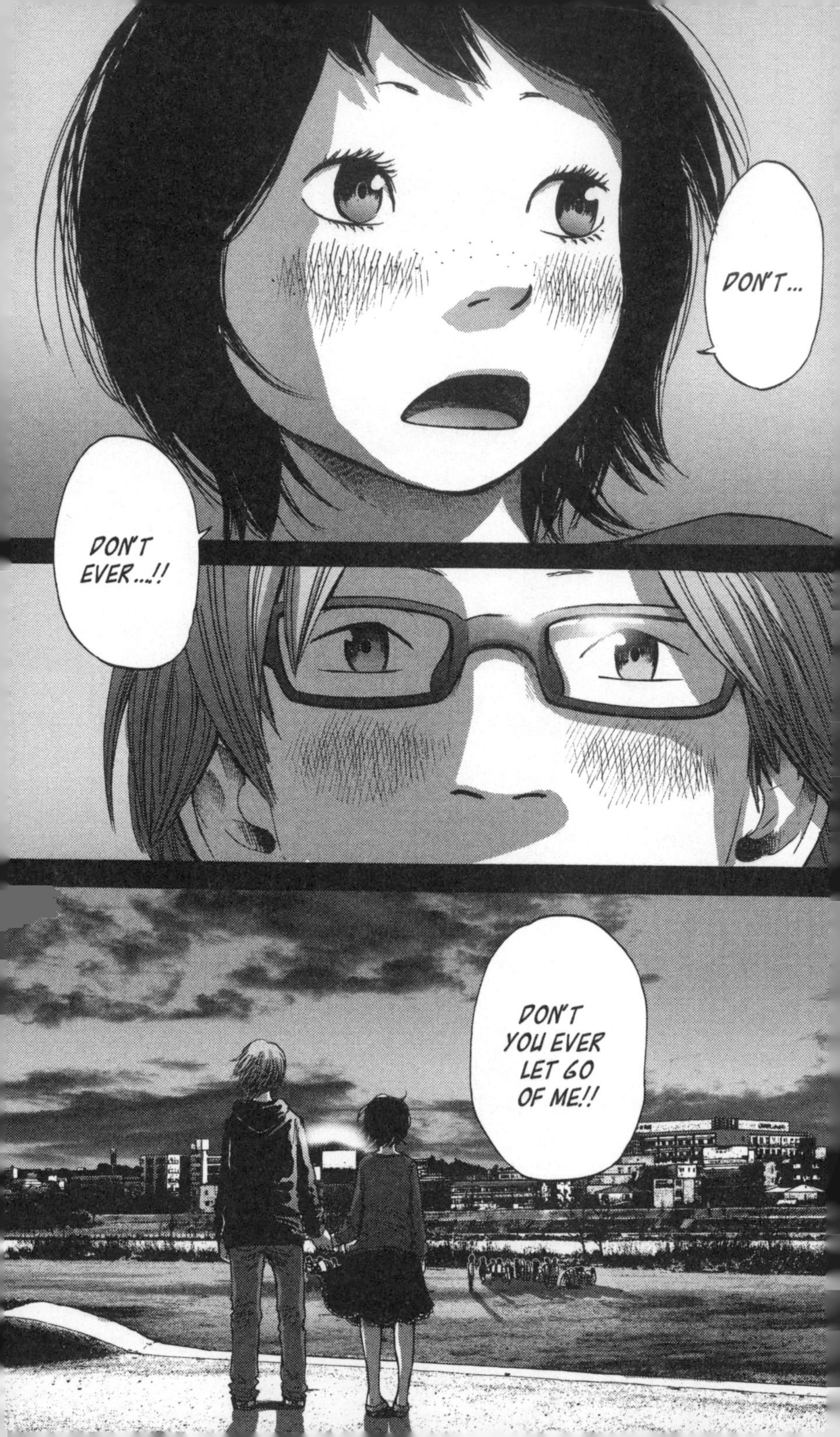
DON'T...
DON'T EVER...!!
DON'T YOU EVER LET GO OF ME!!

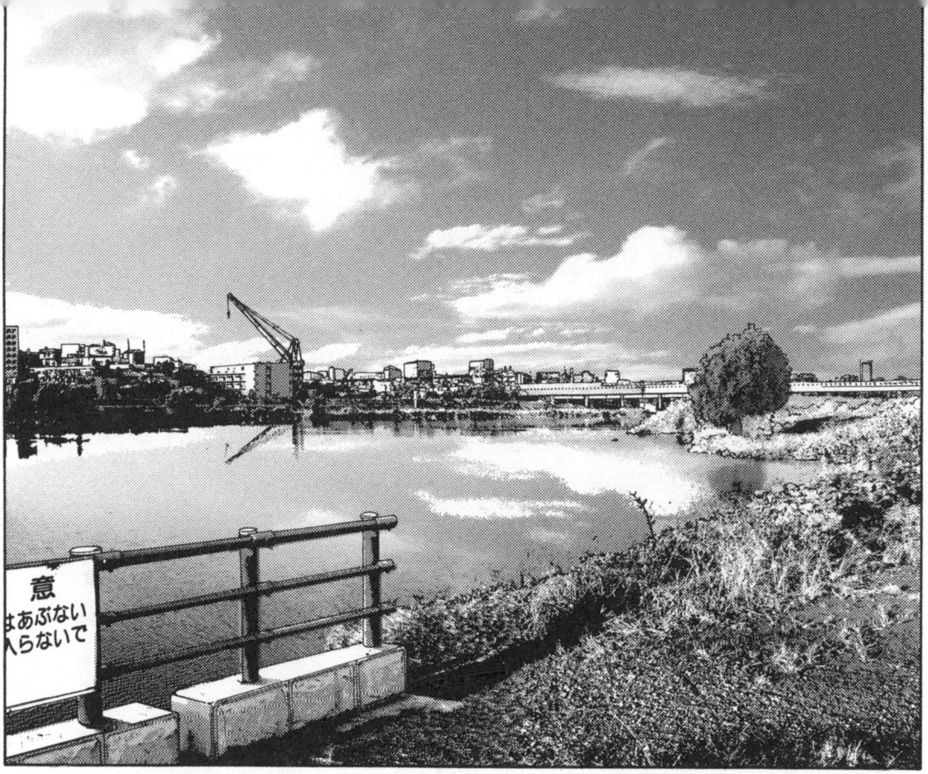
意
はあぶない
入らないで
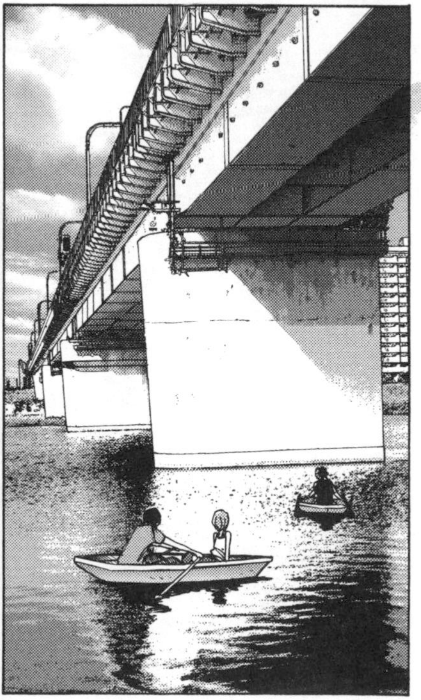
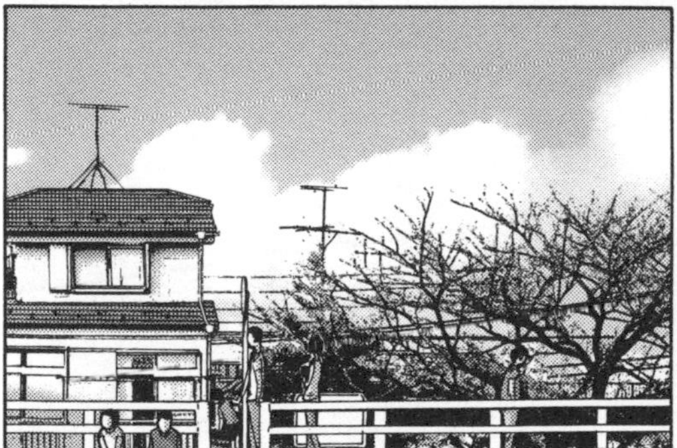
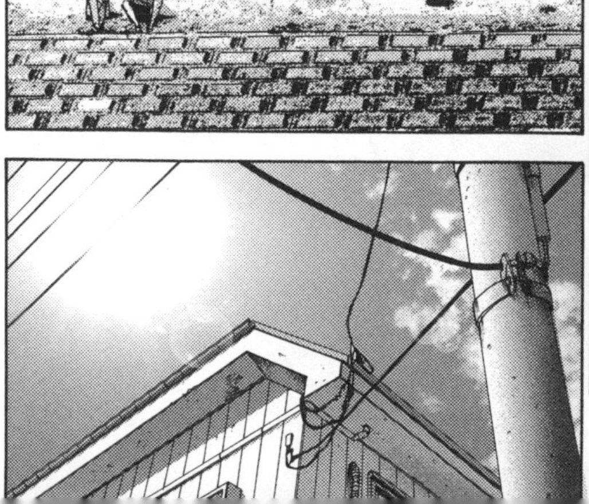

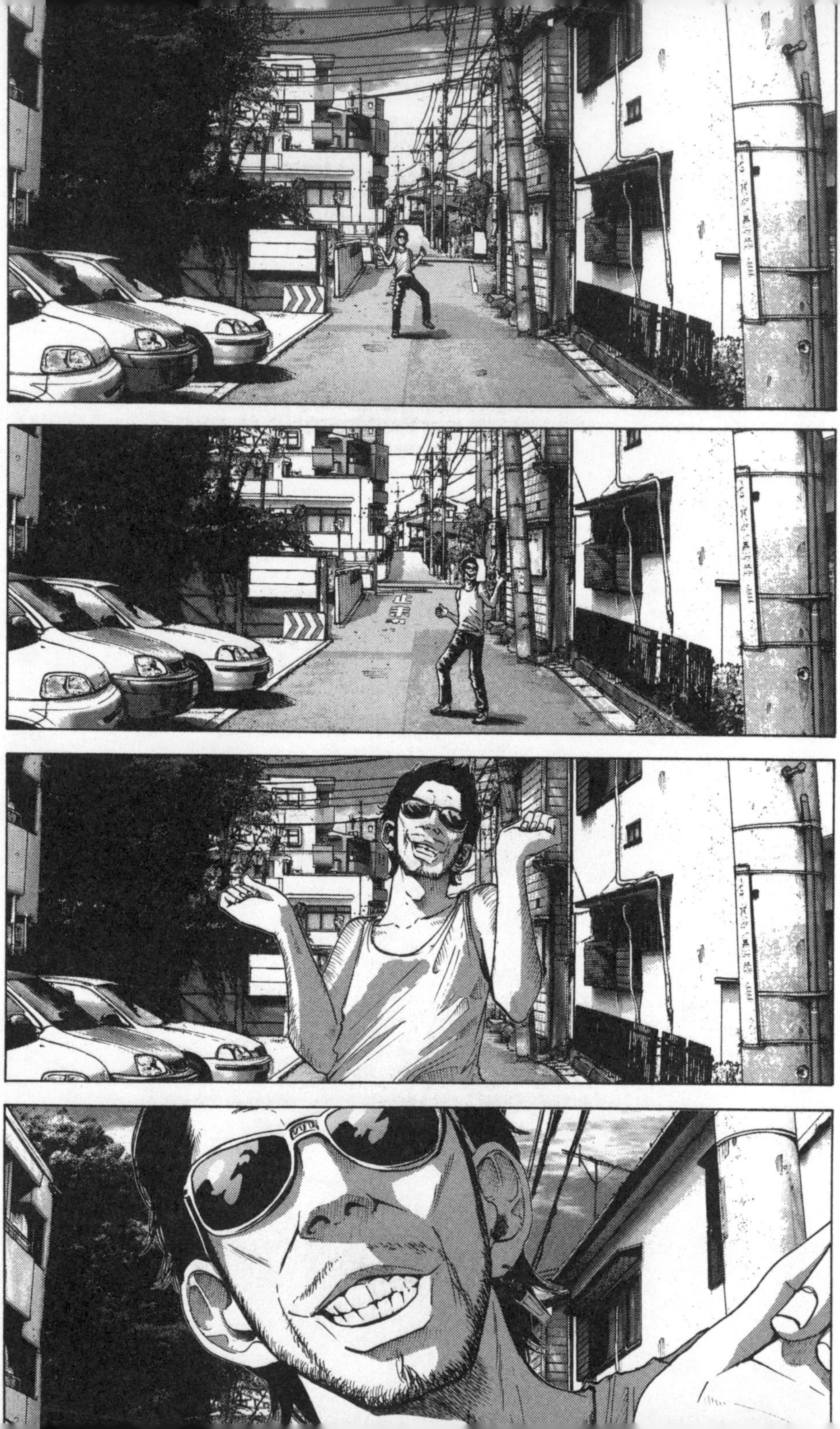

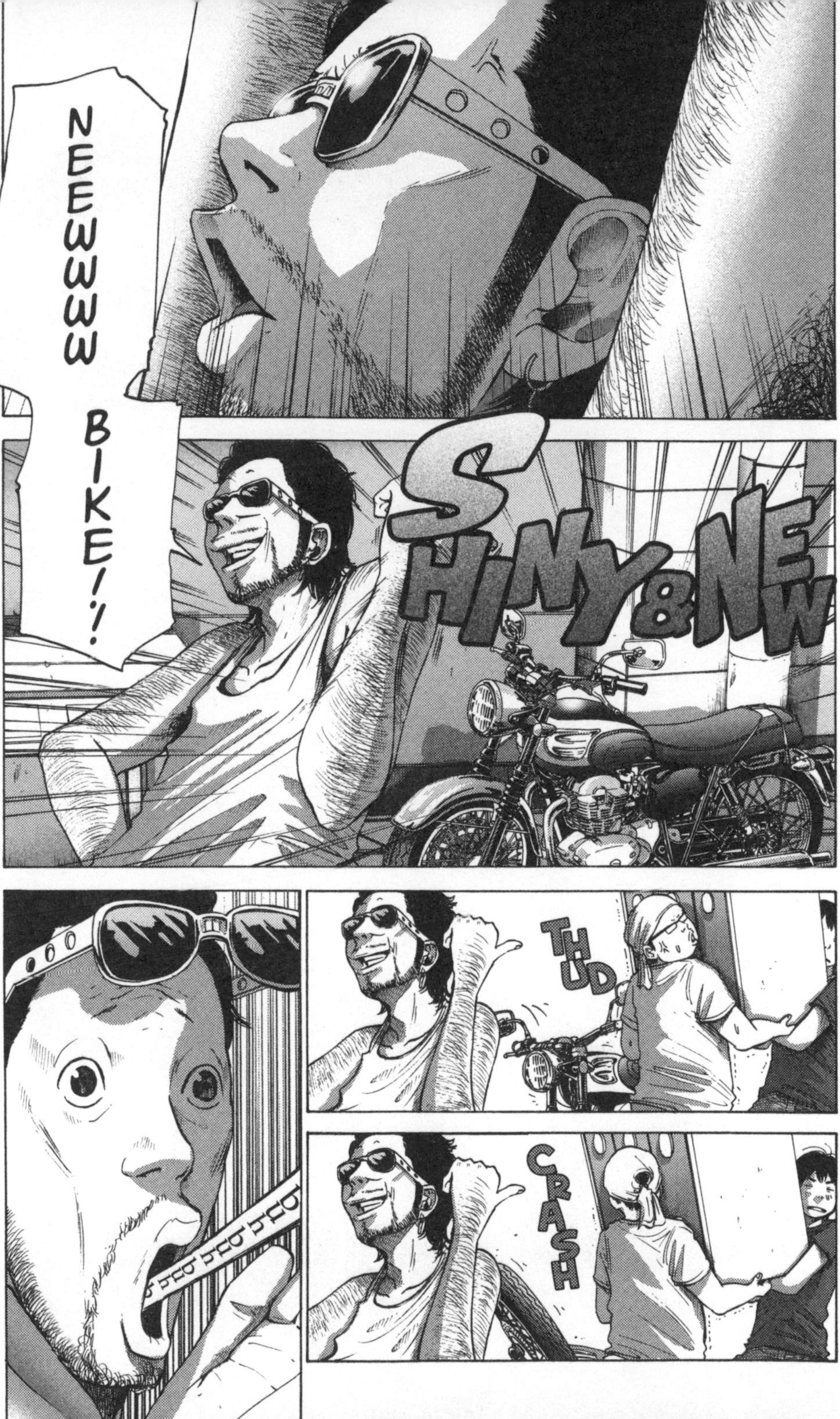
NEEWWWW BIKE!!
SHINY & NEW
THUD
CRASH
buh buh buh

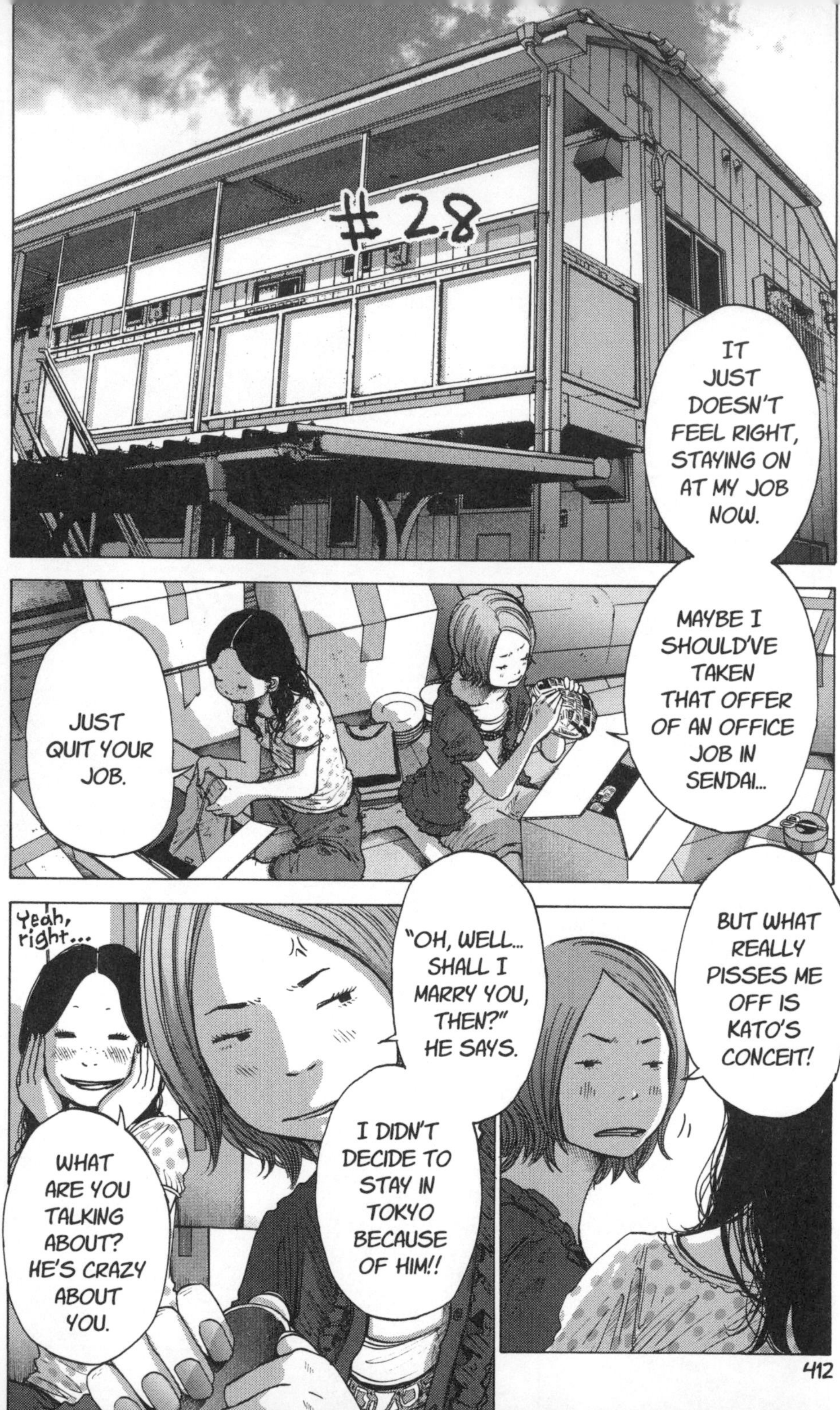
#28
IT JUST DOESN'T FEEL RIGHT, STAYING ON AT MY JOB NOW.
MAYBE I SHOULD'VE TAKEN THAT OFFER OF AN OFFICE JOB IN SENDAI...
JUST QUIT YOUR JOB.
BUT WHAT REALLY PISSES ME OFF IS KATO'S CONCEIT!
"OH, WELL... SHALL I MARRY YOU, THEN?" HE SAYS.
Yeah, right...
WHAT ARE YOU TALKING ABOUT? HE'S CRAZY ABOUT YOU.
I DIDN'T DECIDE TO STAY IN TOKYO BECAUSE OF HIM!!

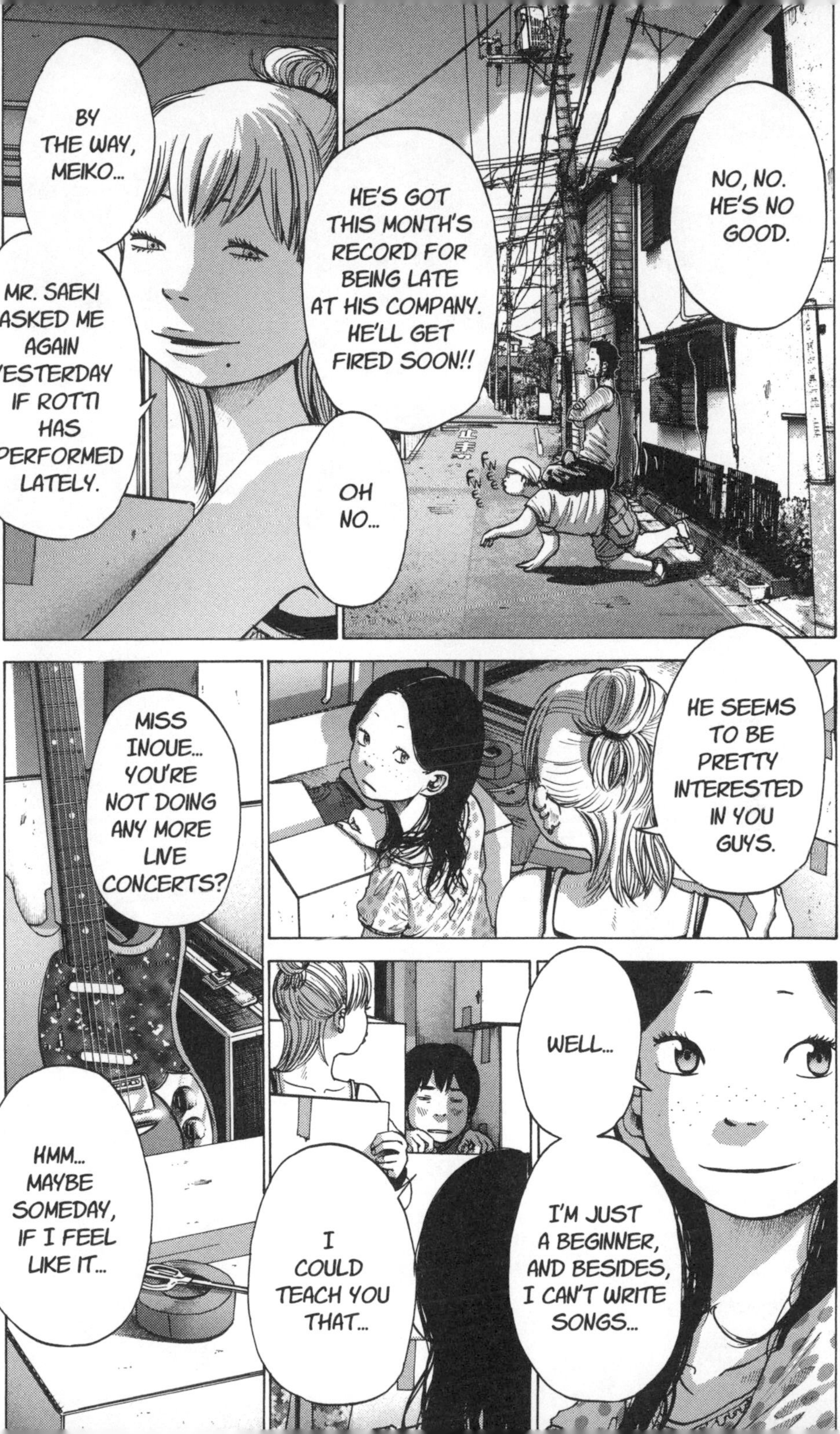
BY THE WAY, MEIKO...
MR. SAEKI ASKED ME AGAIN YESTERDAY IF ROTTI HAS PERFORMED LATELY.
HE'S GOT THIS MONTH'S RECORD FOR BEING LATE AT HIS COMPANY. HE'LL GET FIRED SOON!!
OH NO...
NO, NO. HE'S NO GOOD.
MISS INOUE... YOU'RE NOT DOING ANY MORE LIVE CONCERTS?
HMM... MAYBE SOMEDAY, IF I FEEL LIKE IT...
HE SEEMS TO BE PRETTY INTERESTED IN YOU GUYS.
WELL...
I'M JUST A BEGINNER, AND BESIDES, I CAN'T WRITE SONGS...
I COULD TEACH YOU THAT...

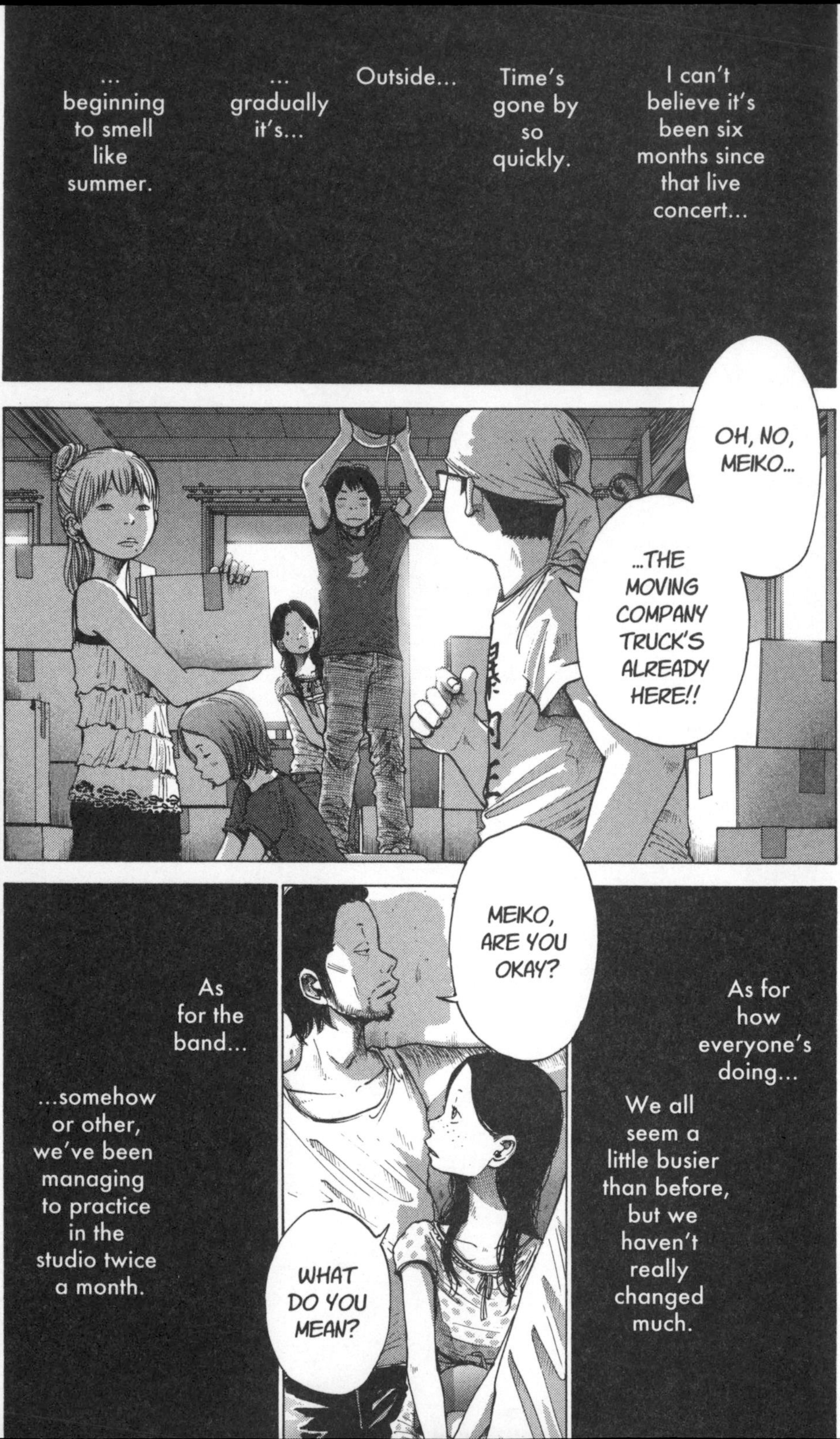
I can't believe it's been six months since that live concert...
Time's gone by so quickly.
Outside...
... gradually it's...
... beginning to smell like summer.
OH, NO, MEIKO...
...THE MOVING COMPANY TRUCK'S ALREADY HERE!!
As for how everyone's doing...
We all seem a little busier than before, but we haven't really changed much.
MEIKO, ARE YOU OKAY?
WHAT DO YOU MEAN?
As for the band...
...somehow or other, we've been managing to practice in the studio twice a month.

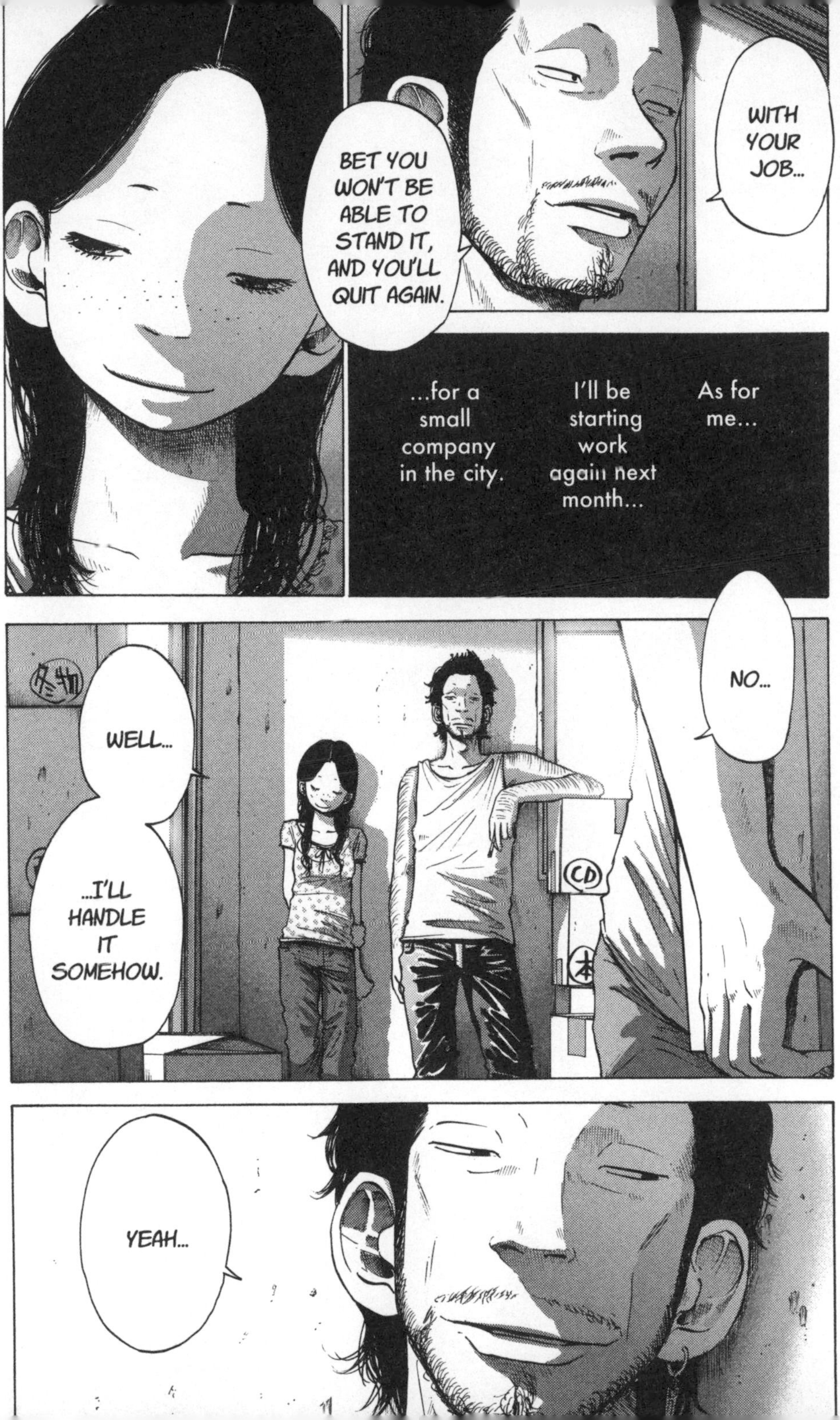
WITH YOUR JOB...
BET YOU WON'T BE ABLE TO STAND IT, AND YOU'LL QUIT AGAIN.
As for me...
I'll be starting work again next month...
...for a small company in the city.
NO...
WELL...
...I'LL HANDLE IT SOMEHOW.
YEAH...

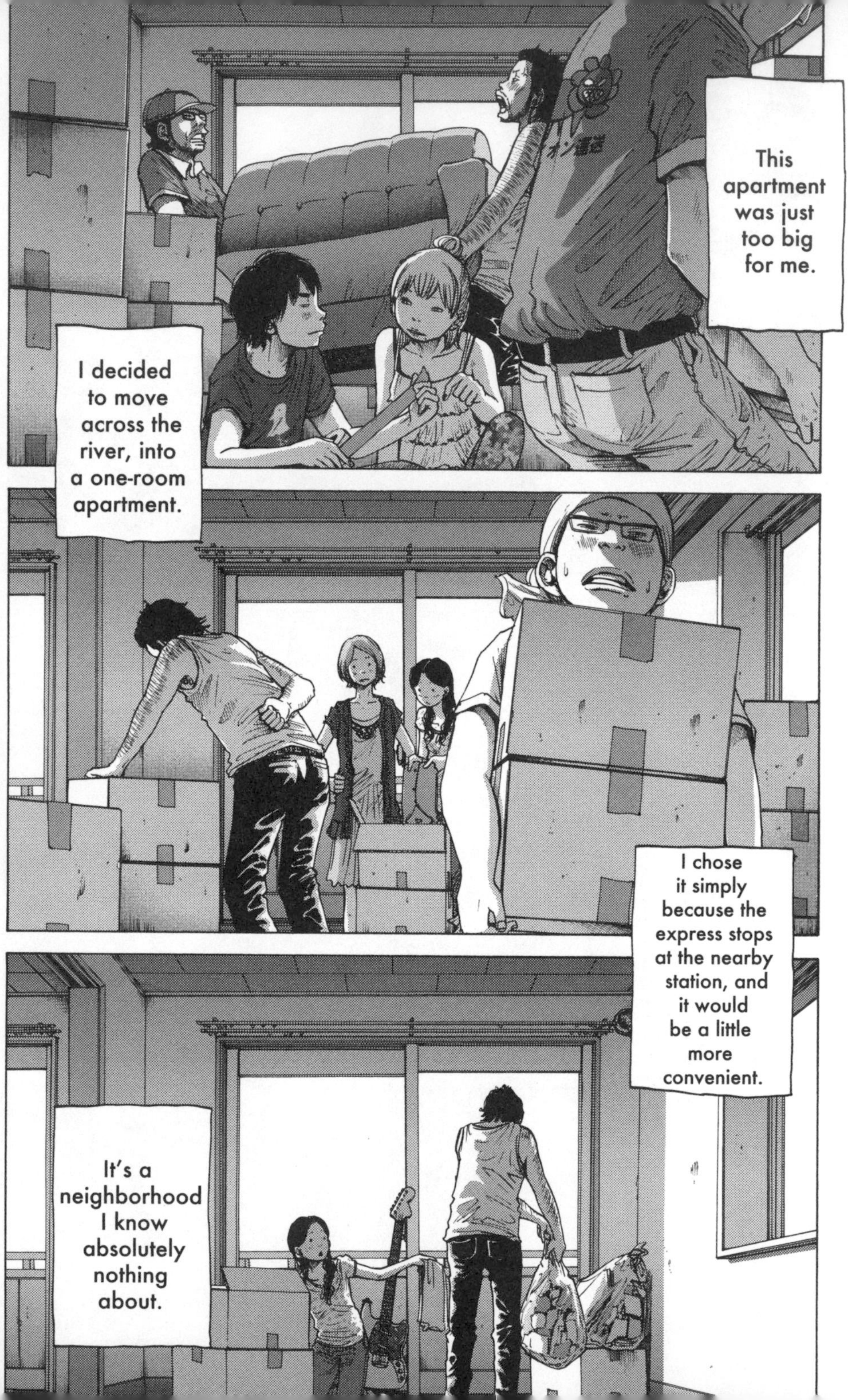
This apartment was just too big for me.
I decided to move across the river, into a one-room apartment.
I chose it simply because the express stops at the nearby station, and it would be a little more convenient.
It's a neighborhood I know absolutely nothing about.

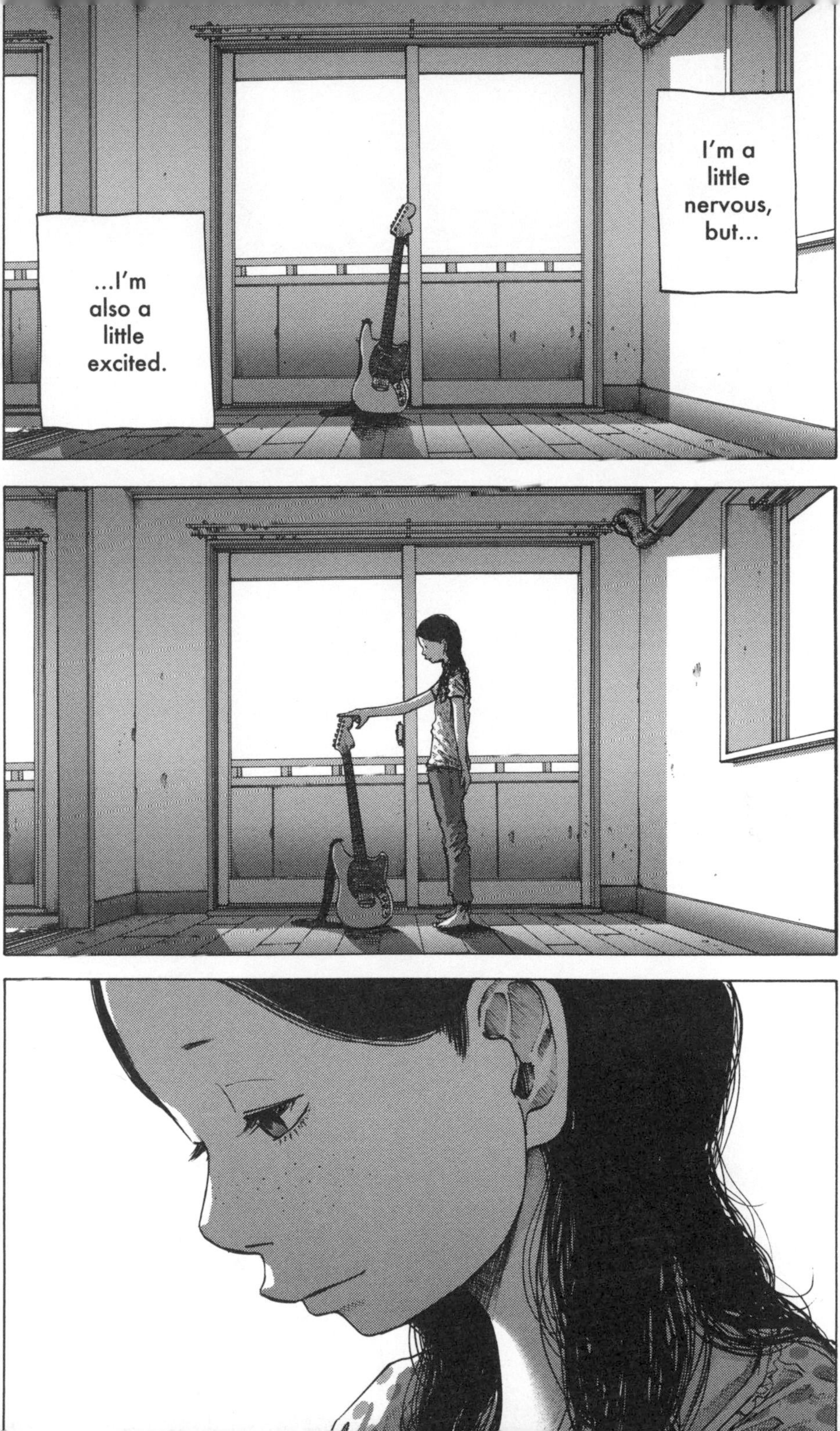
I'm a little nervous, but...
...I'm also a little excited.

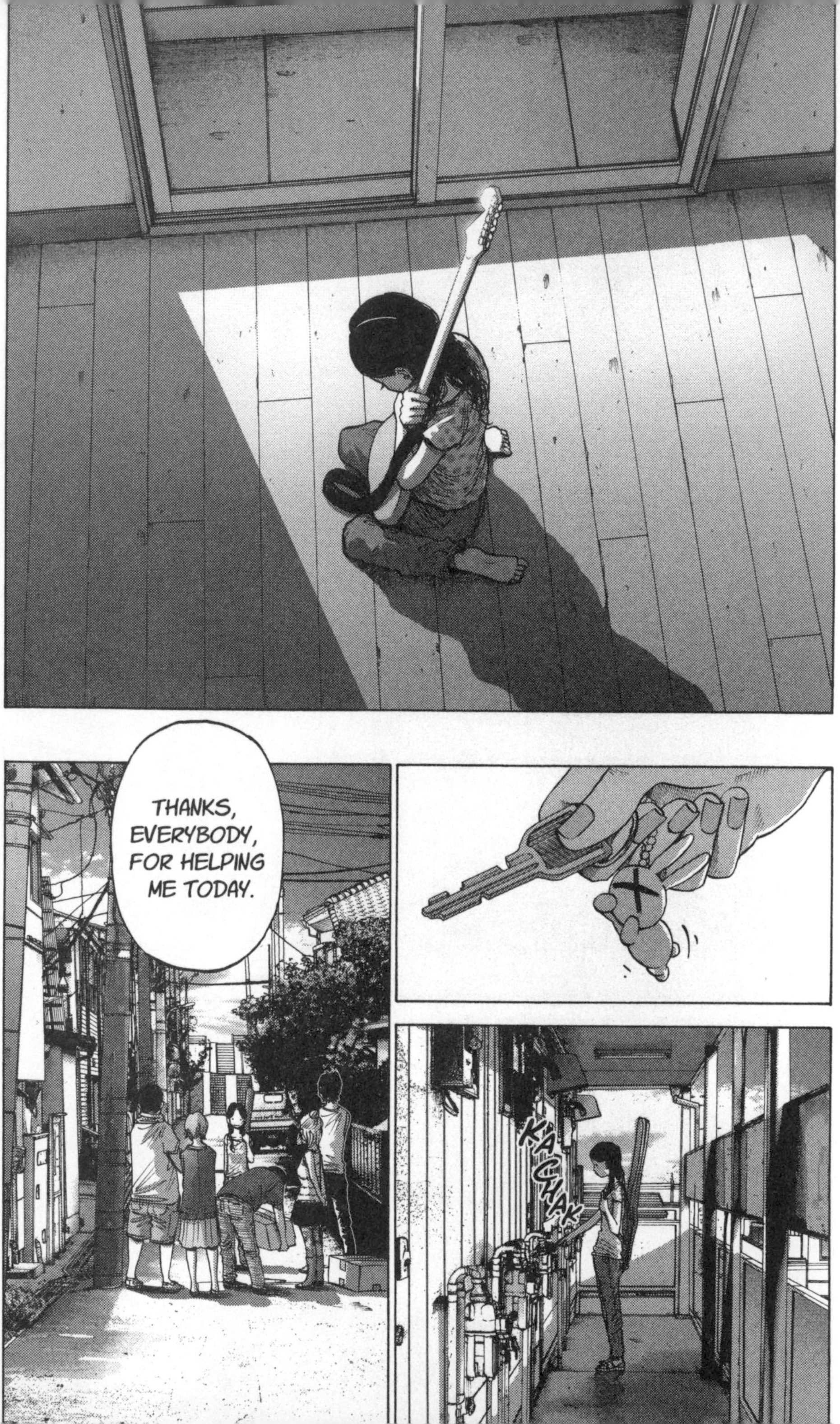
KA CHAK
THANKS, EVERYBODY, FOR HELPING ME TODAY.

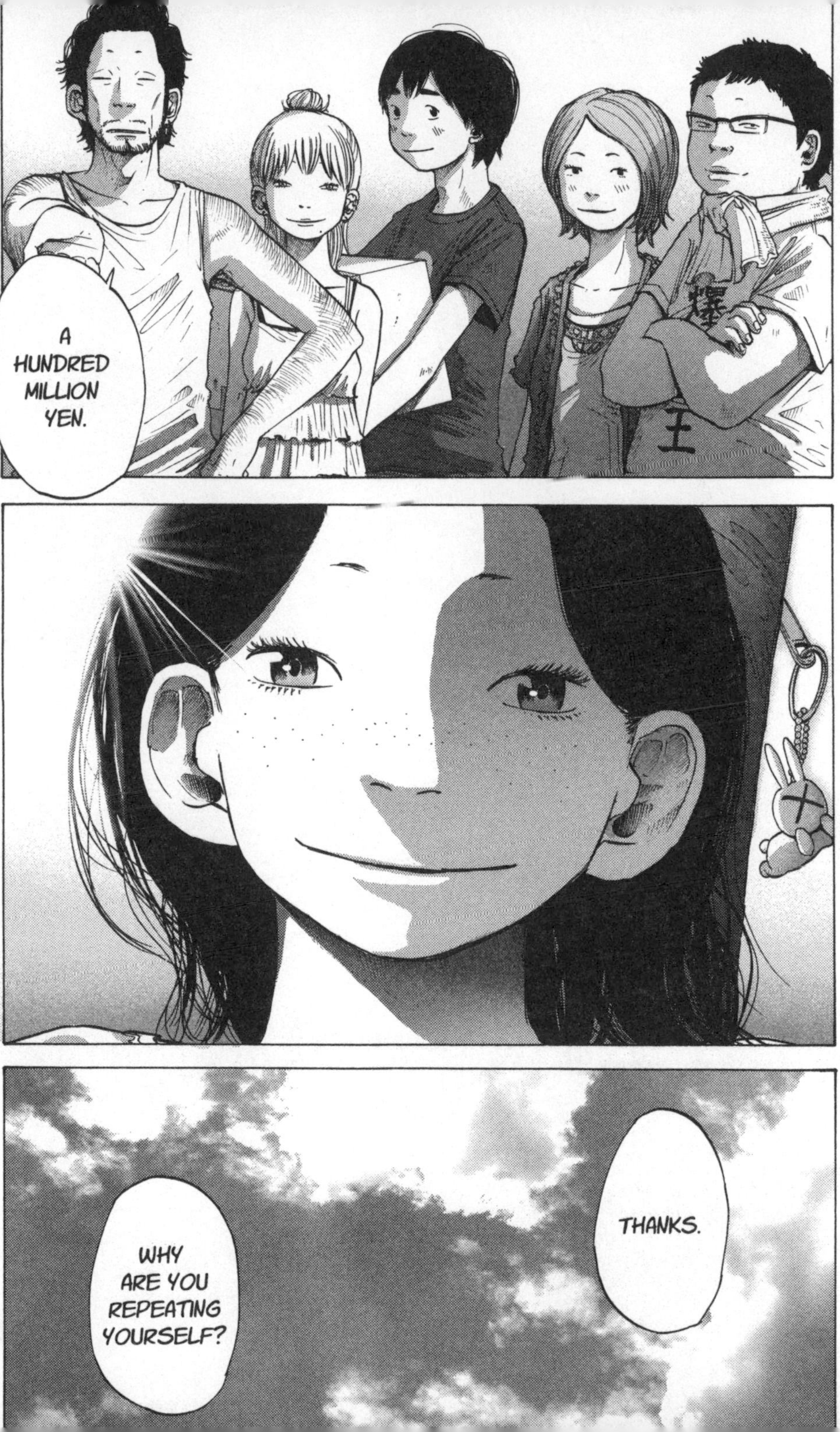
A HUNDRED MILLION YEN.
THANKS.
WHY ARE YOU REPEATING YOURSELF?

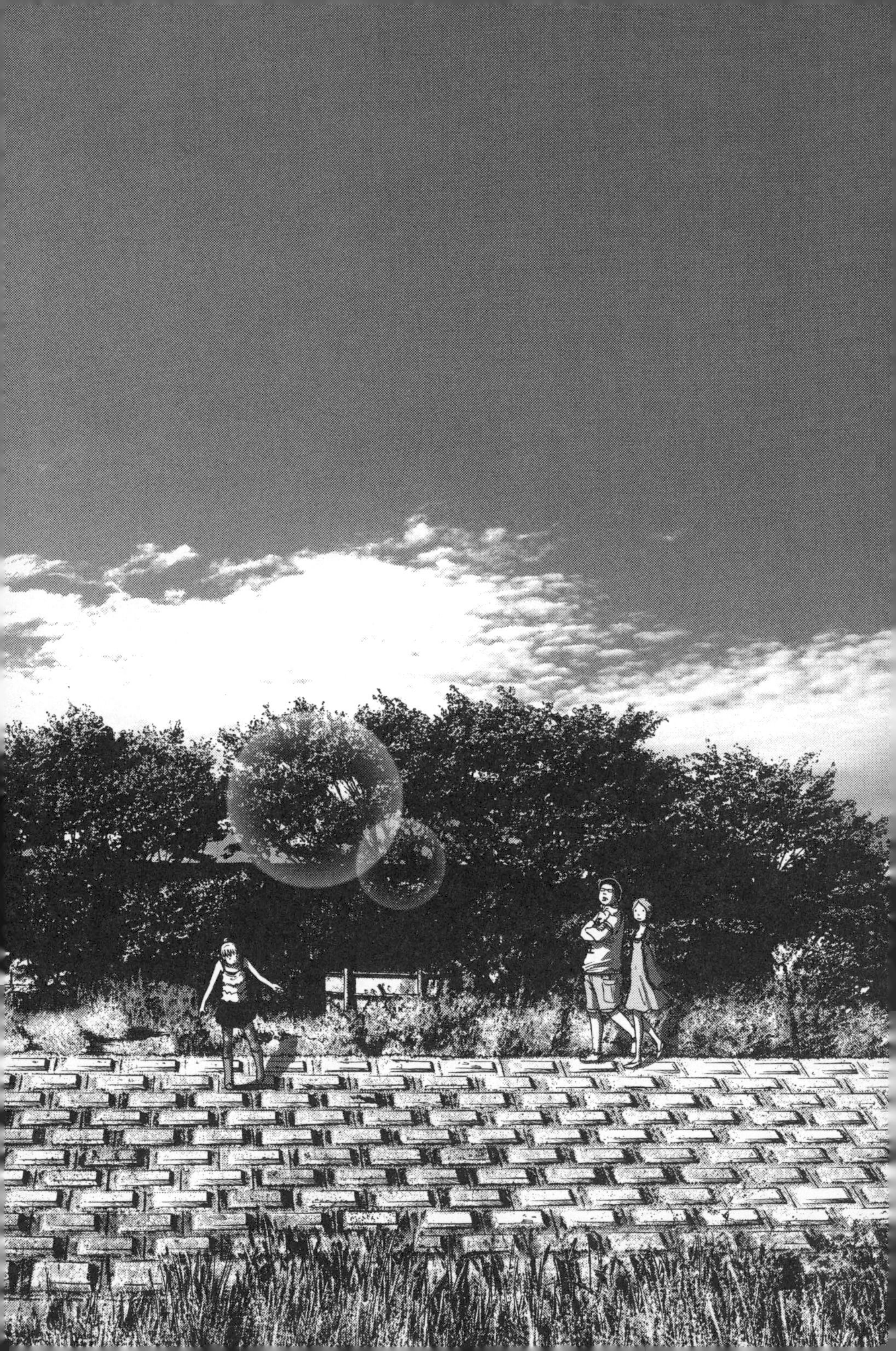

The weather was pretty nice today...

...and the Odakyu line was running as usual...

...and there were lovers paddling boats on the Tama River.

There's a war being fought somewhere today.

Many people are being killed.

But it's hard to believe that kind of thing is happening when you look at this peaceful scene.

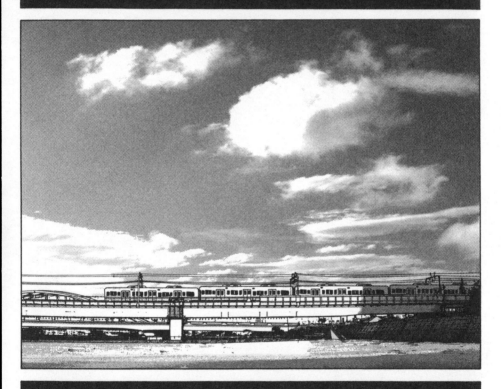

I thought it would be nice if it went on forever...

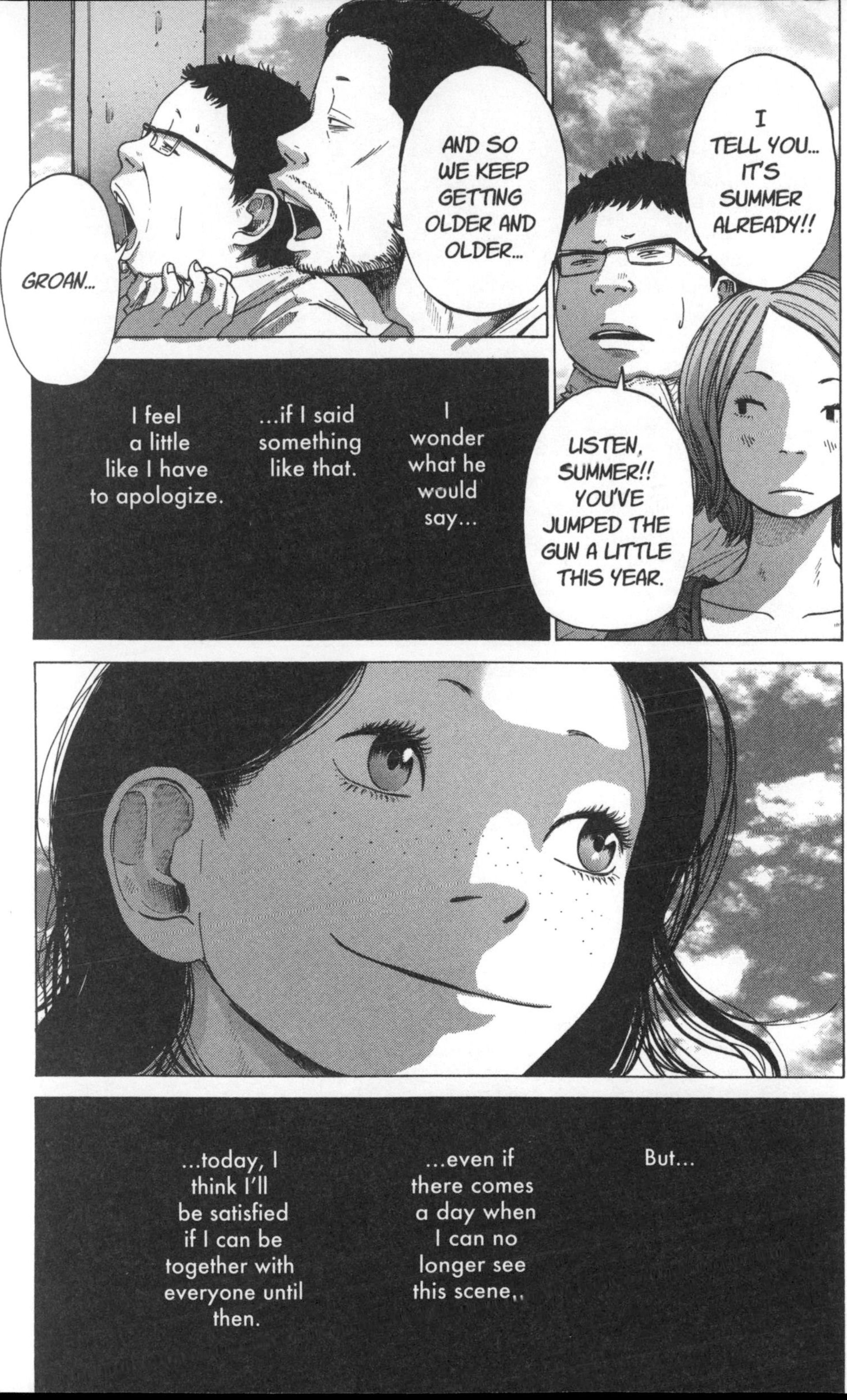
I TELL YOU... IT'S SUMMER ALREADY!!
LISTEN, SUMMER!! YOU'VE JUMPED THE GUN A LITTLE THIS YEAR.
AND SO WE KEEP GETTING OLDER AND OLDER...
GROAN...
I wonder what he would say...
...if I said something like that.
I feel a little like I have to apologize.
But...
...even if there comes a day when I can no longer see this scene,.
...today, I think I'll be satisfied if I can be together with everyone until then.

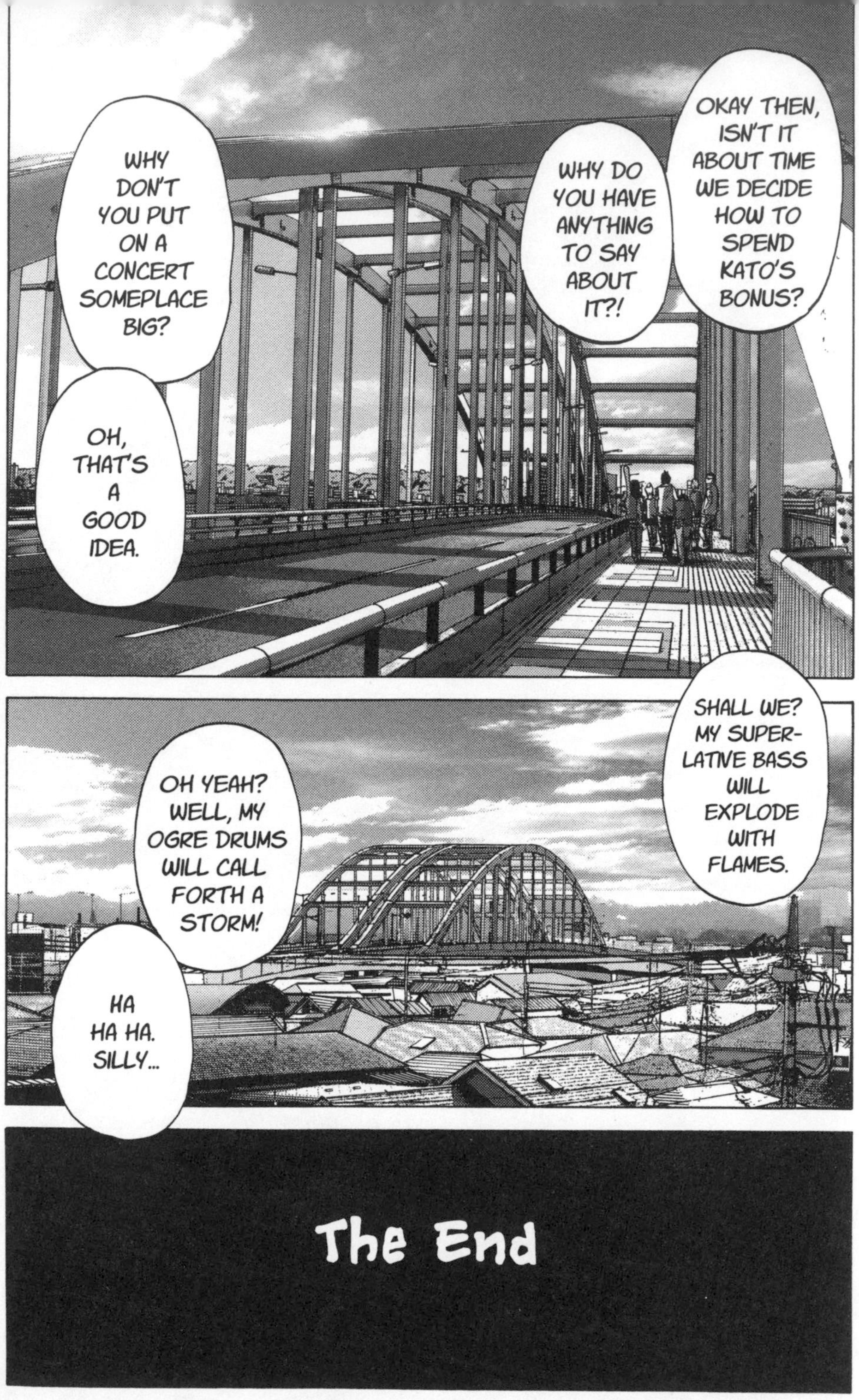
OKAY THEN, ISN'T IT ABOUT TIME WE DECIDE HOW TO SPEND KATO'S BONUS?
WHY DO YOU HAVE ANYTHING TO SAY ABOUT IT?!
WHY DON'T YOU PUT ON A CONCERT SOMEPLACE BIG?
OH, THAT'S A GOOD IDEA.
SHALL WE? MY SUPER-LATIVE BASS WILL EXPLODE WITH FLAMES.
OH YEAH? WELL, MY OGRE DRUMS WILL CALL FORTH A STORM!
HA HA HA. SILLY...
The End

solanin

Inio Asano

Drawing Assistants	Yuichi Watanabe Takashi Kondo
Gofer	Satoshi Yamada
Special Thanks	Kumatto, Shigeru, Mr. and Mrs. Inoue, Hisashi, Iwama, Junichi, Nonsan, Becky, Charlie

AFTERWORD

I drew *solanin* when I was about 24 years old. I had just graduated from college and was feeling a bit insecure about my ability to succeed as a manga artist and whether I would be able to continue to draw manga that were true to myself. In my anxiety and impatience, I felt that all I could do in my manga was try to get a true depiction of the times as experienced by my generation.

Lovers, friends, money, jobs, a society with an unclear future, one's own pride... Writhing in these multiple, entangling factors, perhaps they are unable to draw any conclusions. Perhaps this instant—now—is just a small part of their futile daily lives. The only thing that's certain is that they can never return to the days gone by.

There's nothing cool about these characters. They're just your average 20-somethings who blend into the backdrop of the city. But the most important messages in our lives don't come from musicians on stage or stars on television. They come from the average people all around you, the ones who are just feet from where you stand. That's what I believe.

-Inio Asano, 2008

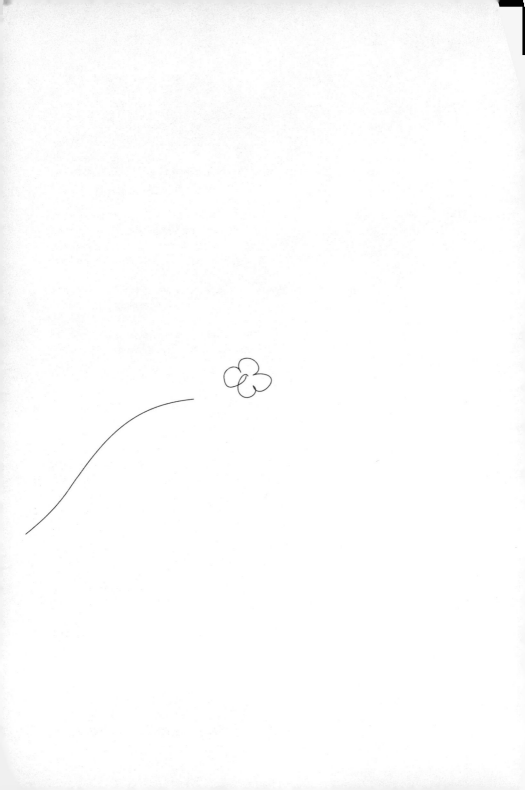

solanin

STORY AND ART BY INIO ASANO

Original Japanese edition "SOLANIN" published by SHOGAKUKAN Inc.

Translation/JN Productions
Touch-up Art & Lettering/Annaliese Christman
Design/Amy Martin
Editor/Pancha Diaz

Printed in the U.S.A.

Published by VIZ Media, LLC
P.O. Box 77010
San Francisco, CA 94107

VIZ Signature Edition
10 9 8 7 6 5
First printing, October 2008
Fifth printing, March 2016

VIZ SIGNATURE

VIZ MEDIA
www.viz.com

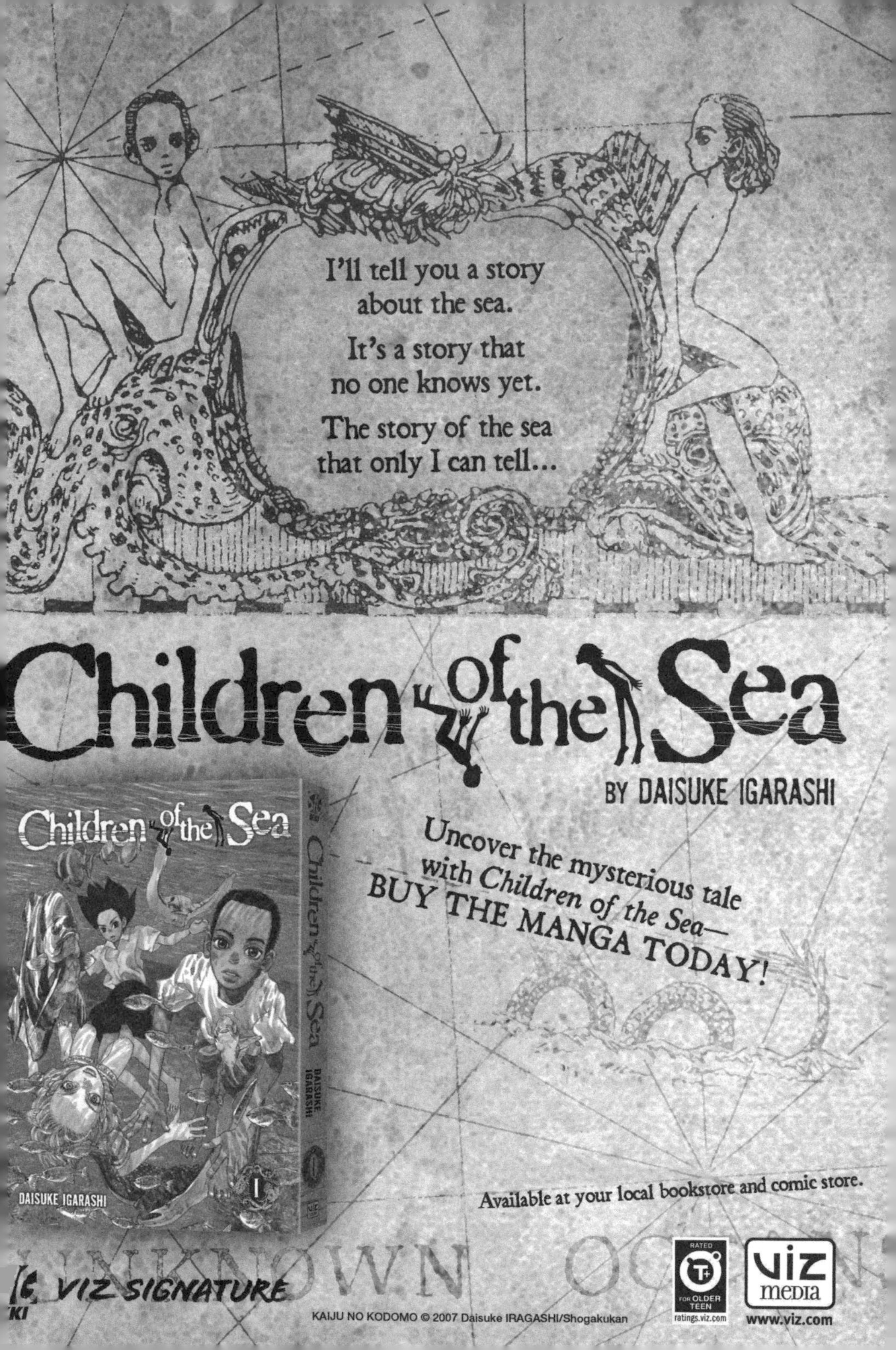
I'll tell you a story about the sea.
It's a story that no one knows yet.
The story of the sea that only I can tell...
Children of the Sea
BY DAISUKE IGARASHI
Children of the Sea
DAISUKE IGARASHI
1
Uncover the mysterious tale with Children of the Sea—
BUY THE MANGA TODAY!
Available at your local bookstore and comic store.
UNKNOWN OCEAN
VIZ SIGNATURE
KAIJU NO KODOMO © 2007 Daisuke IRAGASHI/Shogakukan
RATED T+ FOR OLDER TEEN
ratings.viz.com
viz media
www.viz.com